INFORMATION AT YOUR FINGERTIPS

*Up-to-date and comprehensive, Pitman Dictionaries
are indispensable reference books, providing clear,
crisp explanation of specialist terminology
in an easy-to-use format*

*A Concise Dictionary of Accounting and Finance
Accounting Terms Dictionary
A Dictionary of Economics and Commerce
A Dictionary of Management Terms
A Pocket Dictionary of Business Terms
Business Studies Dictionary
Dictionary of Banking
Dictionary of Banking and Finance
Dictionary of Law
Information Technology Dictionary
Office Practice Dictionary
Dictionary of Advertising*

DICTIONARY OF BANKING

THIRD EDITION

F E PERRY LLB, FIB

Revised by
G KLEIN FCIB, Cert Ed

Pitman

Pitman Publishing
128 Long Acre, London WC2E 9AN

A Division of Longman Group UK Limited

© Macdonald & Evans Ltd 1979, 1983,
Longman Group UK Ltd 1988

First published in Great Britain 1977
2nd edition 1983
Reprinted 1987
3rd edition 1988
Reprinted 1989, 1991

British Library Cataloguing in Publication Data
Perry, F.E.
    A dictionary of banking.—3rd ed.—
    (M & E professional dictionaries).
    1. Banks and banking—Dictionaries
    I. Title   II. Klein, G.
    332.1′03′21   HG151

ISBN 0-273-02961-4

Typeset by Poole Typesetting (Wessex Ltd),
printed and bound in Singapore

PREFACE TO THE THIRD EDITION

I can quite understand why Fred Perry opened the Preface to his second edition with the phrase '. . . any new work probably takes three editions to settle down and for its aims and ambitions to consolidate'. It seems that since 1983, when the second edition was published, a lot has happened in British banking. We have had, amongst other things, the Financial Services Act, the Insolvency Act, Big Bang, Black Monday, etc. So when I was approached to revise the Dictionary my first thoughts were, to whom is it of interest and what exactly *is* banking?

The initial problem was deciding what to insert and what to leave out. My first action was to take out the various foreign phrases that have little relevance to modern UK banking and those words and phrases that are used specifically by one or another bank. The major banks in this country are not simply banks, but financial conglomerates or financial supermarkets controlling estate agents, travel agents, car hire companies, credit card companies, stockbrokers, etc. So where does banking end and where do other financial services commence? I decided to include only those words and phrases that are used every day between bankers and with the public, whether at branch, area office or department level.

Obviously some words and phrases are not strictly banking terms, but originate from such areas as accounting or economics. Still, these are included as they have become everyday language between bank personnel. Many terms taken from current legislation have not, in a strictly legal sense, been fully defined, but as far as possible, I have given reasonable definitions covering the relevance of the law to bankers which, I trust, will not conflict with future legislation.

In any work of this nature there will be words or phrases that have not been included. The error of omission is entirely mine.

I would like to thank Mrs J Jackson for allowing me to revise this dictionary and David Thompson of Canterbury College of Technology for his very helpful review of the manuscript for the book. Thanks are also due to the staff of Pitman Publishing for their encouragement and to my wife, Anne, for her quiet patience and for keeping me going during the winter evenings.

G Klein, 1988

Gerald Klein, the revisor, is Vice President of the Association of Banking Teachers. He is also Principal Lecturer in Banking at Hammersmith and West London College, and Visiting Lecturer at the Royal Holloway and Bedford New College (University of London).

AUTHOR'S PREFACE

Any new work takes three editions to settle down and for its aims and ambitions to consolidate. In the case of a dictionary this is even more true. The aim of this work remains as it was in the beginning – it is principally directed towards bankers in any position and this includes a quite staggering range of activities.

It is clear that with the proliferation of bank branches, subsidiaries and representatives abroad, more and more staff from British banks will be required to serve overseas during the course of their careers, and not only in Europe. As the big clearing banks have now all established an important presence in North America it has become increasingly obvious that the dictionary should provide definitions of some American banking terms. In the American definitions the American style of spelling has been preserved, e.g. program, check, depository, etc.

Thanks are due to the following people who have helped to maintain the accuracy of the dictionary and to keep it up to date: P Marsland; D W Fiddes; A J W Watson; S Valentine; W F Stokes.

Permission to reproduce definitions of *money supply* from *Bank Briefing,* published by the Bank of England is gratefully acknowledged.

F E Perry, 1983

F E Perry was a former Principal of the London Training Centre of one of the UK's largest banks, and studied banking procedures all over the world. He was also the author of a large number of books and articles on banking and the law relating to banking.

A

absolute title. The best type of title which can be granted under the registered land system. It gives the holder an indefeasible title against all the world. In the case of freehold land, the grant of an absolute title indicates an undisputed chain of title culminating in the present holder. An absolute title can be given to an owner of leasehold land only if the relative freehold title is already indicated as registered, thus proving the lessor's right to grant the head lease, or after ten years during which the proprietor, or successive proprietors, have been in possession.

absorption. The result of the amalgamation of a small company with a large one, as a result of which the smaller company is incorporated into an existing business structure in such a way as to leave little of its original identity traceable.

absorption costing. A costing principle whereby fixed and variable costs are included in the costs of production. *See also* MARGINAL COSTING.

abstract of title. A summary showing the chain of title from the good root title of property – at least 15 years old – until point of sale by a vendor.

ABT. *See* Association of Banking Teachers.

acceptance. The signification by the drawee of a bill of exchange of his or her assent to the order of the drawer. The acceptance must be written on the bill, usually on the face of it, and must be signed by the drawee. This signature alone is sufficient, but usually the word 'accepted' is seen. If the bill is payable after sight, the drawee must add the date of sighting to his or her acceptance. The word is also used to describe the bill after it has been accepted. In the case of sale of goods, the buyer is deemed to have accepted the goods when he or she intimates to the seller that they have been accepted; or when the goods have been delivered, and the buyer does any act in relation to them which is inconsistent with the ownership of the seller; or when, after the lapse of a reasonable time, the buyer retains the goods without intimating to the seller that he or she has rejected them. *See also* GENERAL ACCEPTANCE; QUALIFIED ACCEPTANCE.

acceptance credit. The term is used to describe two separate functions. 1. An acceptance line, which is a clean credit facility used for the funding of trade collections or accommodation finance. This describes the drawing of a bill on a bank under an agreed facility, whereby the bank on whom the bill is drawn will accept it, after which it can be discounted by any bank and so turned into cash. If the bill is in sterling the quality of the accepting bank is significant for if it is an eligible bank, the accepted bill will be suitable for rediscount at the finest rate by the Bank of England through the discount houses. If the bill is in a foreign currency, the concept of eligibility is unimportant, for eligibility refers only to a sterling liability. 2. A documentary acceptance credit which is a documentary credit having bills drawn under it at a term other than sight. *See* DOCUMENTARY CREDIT.

acceptance for honour. Where a bill of exchange has been protested for dishonour for non-acceptance or for better security and is not overdue, any person not already a party to the bill may, with the consent of the holder, intervene and accept the bill *supra protest,* for the honour of any party liable thereon, or for the honour of the person for whose account the bill is drawn. A bill may be accepted for honour for part only of the sum for which it is drawn. An acceptance for honour *supra protest* in order to be valid must: 1. be written on the bill and indicate that it is an acceptance for honour; 2. be signed by the acceptor for honour. Where an acceptance for honour does not expressly state for whose honour it is made, it is deemed to be an acceptance for the honour of the drawer. Where a bill payable after sight is accepted for honour, its maturity is calculated from the date of the protesting for non-acceptance, and not from the date of acceptance for honour.

acceptance house. A financial institution, usually a merchant bank that specialises in accepting bills for customers. It lends its name to an international transaction. By their acceptance of the bill and their recognition as an eligible bank, the bills may be discounted at a finer rate.

ACCESS. The name given to a credit card company jointly owned by three clearing banks, namely, Lloyds, Midland and National Westminster. *See* CREDIT CARD.

accommodation bill. A bill of exchange that is accepted by a drawee who merely lends his or her name to the bill and has not received any consideration. When the bill falls due the drawee looks to the drawer to provide funds to make payment.

account. The recording in the ledger of the financial transactions that have taken place: the account will show the receipts, the expenditure and the outstanding balance. In commerce, a statement showing the amount owing for goods, services, etc; on the Stock Exchange, the time elapsing between one Settlement Day and the next; in banking, the current, deposit account either in sterling or currency maintained by the bank for a customer. A *current account* is one running from day to day on which cheques are paid and into which credits are paid. No interest

is usually paid, except in special circumstances. Overdrafts may be taken by arrangement. *Deposit accounts* are usually in credit. The balance or part of the balance is repayable after notice of seven days or other agreed times, or at the end of the fixed time for which the deposit has been made.

accountancy. The methodical recording of financial transactions of a business in ledger accounts and, from there, the production of final accounts and balance sheets at regular intervals.

accountant. A professionally qualified person who is able to record financial transactions of a business. A member of either the Institute of Chartered Accountants (ICA) or the Chartered Association of Certified Accountants (ACCA) may act as auditors for companies. The title of *Accountant* is often given to a senior bank official in a branch who is responsible for the flow of work within that branch and its daily agreement.

accounting bases. The methods developed for applying fundamental accounting concepts to financial transactions for the purpose of financial accounts.

accounting concepts or principles. Basic assumptions underlying the financial accounts of an organisation.

accounting policies. The specific accounting bases selected by management as being most appropriate to the circumstances of enterprise.

account payee. The insertion of these words in the crossing of a cheque has no legal recognition but it is an instruction to the collecting banker to ensure that the account of the payee is credited with the amount on the cheque. A bank will collect a cheque with these words for a customer who is not the payee, providing he or she is of undoubted integrity.

account sales. An account sent by a trader to the consignor of goods, showing details of the goods and the net prices obtained after deduction of all the expenses of sale; an account sent to a principal by an agent who has sold goods at public auction on the principal's behalf.

account stated. An account between two parties which consists of items which have been expressly or impliedly agreed between the parties as entries which have properly appeared on the account. Any balance showing is likewise agreed as correct.

accruals concept. Revenue and costs recognised as they are earned or incurred, not as money is received or paid.

act of bankruptcy. Under the Insolvency Act, 1986 the act of bankruptcy is merely a petition presented on the basis of the debtor being unable or unwilling to pay an unsecured debt of £750 or more owed to a creditor(s).

act of God. The operation of uncontrollable natural forces in causing an event, e.g. tempests, earthquakes, lightning, which causes exceptional and unforeseeable damage. No individual or insurance company is liable for such damage.

actuary. An officer of a mercantile or insurance company skilled in statistics, especially on the expectancy of life and the average proportion of losses by time and other accidents. Generally, an actuary is a member of the Institute of Actuaries.

ademption. A taking away; the revocation of a grant or bequest; the destruction of something subject to a specific bequest between the time the will is executed and the death of the testator.

adjudication order. An order made by the court declaring a debtor bankrupt. The effect is to vest the estate of the debtor in a trustee who will wind it up for the benefit of the creditors.

administration order. An application to a court either by the directors of a company or an unsecured creditor of a company to appoint an administrator to either continue the company as a going concern – if advantageous – or make proposals which would be beneficial to the creditors.

administrator. The appointment of a person or persons by the court, to wind up the affairs of an individual who has died intestate. Before a bank will allow a person to take over the assets of a deceased customer, letters of administration must be exhibited. Under the Insolvency Act, 1986 an administrator can be appointed by the court to take over the affairs of a company. The administrator has the power, if thought fit, to continue the business and restore it to a solvent position rather than sell the assets for the benefit of the creditors. To justify the appointment of an administrator the court must be satisfied that one of the following objectives will be reached: (a) the survival of the company as a going concern; (b) the approval of a voluntary arrangement; (c) a compromise agreement between the company and its creditors per s. 425 Companies Act, 1985; (d) a more advantageous realisation of the company's assets if winding up is effected.

ad valorum. According to value. VAT is an example of an *ad valorum* tax.

advance. A loan by one person, corporate or not, to another, corporate or not. A prepayment for services or work undertaken, e.g. an advance on salary. A general word indicating that a loan or overdraft has been given.

advice of fate. Where a bank or its customer requires notification of final payment of a cheque or bill of exchange, it is usual to make a special presentation of the instrument with a request by the presenting banker that *fate* should be notified to him or her. Frequently the presenting banker would telephone the paying banker to obtain the result of the presentation. When an enquiry is made as to the possibility of a cheque being paid on presentation, the paying bank would normally answer in terms such as 'If in our hands now and in order it will be paid'.

advice note. A letter informing the person to whom it is addressed that a transaction is being or has been completed, e.g. delivery of goods.

affidavit. A written statement to a person, such as a solicitor or notary, given under oath. It may be used as evidence in a court of law.

after acquired property. Property coming to the bankrupt after the date of the adjudication order. This property should be reported to the trustee.

age admitted. An endorsement on a life policy or a note attached to indicate that the assurance company is satisfied that the assured's age was correctly stated on the form of application for the policy, or that it has been since rectified. The assurance company calculates the premium from the statement of age given by the assured, and does not check the age until it is asked to pay over the policy monies. A birth certificate must then be produced and if the age is incorrect a deduction may be made from the proceeds. To avoid this, the banker who is holding a life policy as security prefers to make sure that the company has admitted that the age has been correctly stated.

agency. The relationship that exists between two persons, called the principal and the agent, which empowers the agent to act on behalf of the principal for the purpose of binding the principal in law. In banking, the principal is usually the customer while the agent is the bank.

agent. One entrusted with the business of another, one who is employed to represent his or her principal and to make contracts on the principal's behalf. Responsibility for such contracts will fall to the principal as long as the agent keeps within the powers conferred on him or her by the principal. *See also* DEL CREDERE AGENT; ESTATE AGENT; EXPORT AGENT; FORWARDING AGENT; GENERAL AGENT; IMPORT AGENT; INSURANCE AGENT; MERCANTILE AGENT; SPECIAL AGENT; TRANSFER AGENT; TRAVEL AGENT.

aggregate. To collect together, to bring into a mass or whole a sum or assemblage of particulars; to total; composed of individuals forming an association.

aggregate monetary demand. Total demand for consumer and capital goods backed by money.

agio. The difference in value between one kind of currency and another; money-changing; the charge for changing notes for cash, or one kind of money for another; the difference in value between metallic money and its paper equivalent; the difference, usually expressed as a percentage, between nominal or par value, and a higher price.

A.G.M. *See* ANNUAL GENERAL MEETING.

agricultural charge. A fixed charge upon the farming stock and other agricultural assets belonging to a farmer, whether a tenant or an owner, at the date of the charge, or a floating charge upon the farming stock and other agricultural assets belonging to the farmer, or both. Such a charge would form a security for a banker providing agricultural short-term credit, but it is invalid if the farmer, being insolvent at the time of creation, goes into liquidation within three months. Agricultural charges have to be registered within seven days with the Agricultural Credits Superintendent at the Land Registry, and this publicity can result in a restriction of the farmer's credit. Very few are now registered each year.

Agricultural Credit Corporation. (ACC). A corporation which was formed in 1965 to provide guarantees to banks providing finance for farmers. The ACC is a government sponsored body that enters into a relationship with a bank that loans to approved applicants who require finance for either working capital or fixed capital.

Agricultural Mortgage Corporation. This corporation was formed in 1928 to provide facilities whereby farmers could obtain long-term loans at reasonably favourable rates, secured by first mortgages on their farms, for the purpose of buying their farms, carrying out capital improvements, repaying money borrowed from other sources, or providing working capital. Loans are available for periods of up to forty years and the loan must not exceed two thirds value of the mortgaged property as certified at the time when the loan is made. Loans may be at a fixed or a variable rate of interest, usually at the borrower's option. Various methods of repayment may be selected: *(a)* by equal instalments of capital plus interest half-yearly on the reducing balance; *(b)* by the annuity method of half-yearly payments comprising interest plus an instalment of capital; *(c)* by the endowment assurance method, comprising half-yearly payment of interest only, plus endowment assurance premiums; or *(d)* for long-term borrowers only, the option of taking half under *(a)* and the other half under *(b)* or *(c)*.

air bill all risks. An insurance document issued where goods are being sent by air. It provides an extensive cover but this does not extend to special risks such as war, strikes, civil commotion or the perishing of goods.

air consignment note. *See below.*

air waybill. Made out by the consignor of goods to be transported by air. Often called *air consignment note.*

all-moneys debenture. A mortgage debenture containing both fixed and floating charges securing any sums owing to the bank by the company at any time on any account.

allonge. An attachment to a bill of exchange, when the back of the bill is full of endorsements and further written space has to be provided. The allonge is an integral part of the bill.

allotment. The issue of shares to persons who have applied for the purchase. The amount allotted may be in full, but if the issue is oversubscribed, only part of the number may be allotted.

allotment letter. A letter sent to an applicant for an issue of shares, stock or bonds on offer to the public, informing the applicant of the amount or number allotted to him or her and specifying the instalments of the balance of payment, together with the dates on which these should be made. The letter also contains a form which allows the shareholder to renounce the allocation by signing the form and to sell his or her rights *via* a stockbroker.

alpha. A listing of the most actively traded equities on the Stock Exchange – each transaction must be reported by dealers within five minutes. There is a continuous updating of the day's volume of shares trades and the prices of the latest bargains.

alteration of bill. Where a bill or acceptance is materially altered without the assent of all parties on the bill, the bill is avoided except as against a party who has personally authorised or assented to the alteration, and subsequent indorsers. If a bill has been materially altered, but the alteration is not apparent, and the bill is in the hands of a holder in due course, such holder may avail him or herself of the bill as if it had not been altered, and may enforce payment of it according to its original tenor. The following are *material alterations* – any alteration of the date; the sum payable; the time of payment; the place of payment; and, where a bill has been accepted generally, the addition of a place of payment without the acceptor's assent.

alternative payee. A bill of exchange, including a cheque, may be made payable to two or more persons in the alternative.

American Express card. This plastic card issued by the American Express Company is often classified as a leisure card or debit card, but because there is usually no arrangement for long-term credit, it cannot be defined as a credit card. Through its various offices in the UK and extensive advertising the American Express Company has increased the number of users of its card. Holders of the card have no limit placed on the sum they can spend, but all outstanding debts must be settled by a given date.

American-type share certificate. Often called an *American deposit receipt*. A certificate which has many of the characteristics of a *bearer bond,* but which is not a negotiable instrument because it does not give to a new owner any better title than the previous owner had. The name of the registered holder appears on the face of the document and a blank form of transfer is printed on the back. Usually the registered holder signs the form of transfer and this allows the certificate to pass from hand to hand like a bearer bond, delivery transferring title. Unlike a bearer bond, however, there are no coupons and the dividend is sent to the registered holder, from whom the owner must claim it. The owner can be registered by completing the back of the form and will then receive dividends, notices, etc. sent direct, but the certificate will have lost its readily negotiable characteristic. *See also* MARKING NAMES.

amortisation. The act, or the right of alienating land in *mortmain,* that is, of transferring lands in perpetuity to a charitable body or to an ecclesiastical authority; the redemption of bonds or loans by annual payment from a sinking fund. Payments into the sinking fund must be such as to make possible regular paying off of all bonds due to be redeemed plus the payment of all the interest due on bonds still outstanding.

ancillary credit business. For the purposes of the Consumer Credit Act, 1974, any business, so far as it comprises or relates to credit brokerage, debt adjusting, debt counselling, debt collecting or the operation of a credit reference agency.

annual general meeting (AGM). A yearly meeting between the shareholders and the directors of a company at which general information about the past year's activities and future prospects are given. Acceptance of the proposed dividends are made, election of directors and appointments of auditors also take place.

annual percentage rate (APR). The total charge for credit in a consumer credit agreement, which, in accordance with the Consumer Credit Act, 1974, must show the annual compound rate of interest to be charged.

annual report and accounts. These are documents that are prepared annually by the directors of a company who report on the activities of that company. This will include a flow of funds statement and the future prospects of the company. The audited profit and loss account and balance sheet will also be presented.

annual return. Every company having a share capital shall, at least once a year, make a *return* containing details as to the address of the registered office of the company, the situation of the register of members and debenture holders, a summary of share capital and debentures, particulars of any indebtedness, a list of past and present members and particulars of directors and secretaries. This information, together with a copy of the company's latest balance sheet, is sent to the Registrar of Companies.

annuitant. A person in receipt of an annuity.

annuity. A sum of money paid either monthly, quarterly or half yearly, during the lifetime of a person. A person will purchase an annuity, usually from an insurance company, in order to receive a regular income.

answer on a cheque. When a cheque is returned unpaid it is a rule of the Committee of London and Scottish Clearing Banks that an answer should be written on the unpaid instrument. These answers fall into two groups: those where payment is refused for a technical reason; and those where dishonour is due to lack of funds. In the second case, there is some risk to the banker if he or she does not exercise every care in checking the correctness of the return and the appropriateness of the answer, which must be such as to safeguard as far as possible the reputation of the customer. The customary answer where funds have proved inadequate is *'refer to drawer'*, which has for many years been considered safe.

antedate. The placing of the date on a document prior to that on which it is signed. A bill of exchange is not invalid by reason of it being antedated.

antedated cheque. A banker receiving a cheque antedated by six months or more for payment would regard it as *stale*, and would return it unpaid unless confirmation could be obtained from the drawer to pay it. A cheque can also be *stale* for purposes of negotiation. No time has been set by statute for this, but it is thought that a period of ten to twelve days after the date of the cheque will be enough to make it stale. A holder taking a cheque in negotiation cannot claim to be a holder in due course if the cheque is stale but has to take the bill 'complete and regular on the face of it'. A cheque which is stale is not *regular*.

applicant. The person who makes an application. In international trade it is the person who requests a bank to open a documentary credit on his or her behalf in favour of a named beneficiary. The applicant is usually the importer.

appropriation. The act of setting apart for a purpose; anything thus set apart. The assignment of funds for a special purpose or use; the allocation of funds to be disbursed out of public money.

appropriation account. The account which shows how the annual profit of a company is divided up between dividend, reserves, etc.

appropriation of goods. An act identifying goods with a contract.

appropriation of payments. The act of a customer who, when paying in a credit to his or her account, specifies the debit against which it is to be set. If the customer does not so appropriate, the banker is free to do so, and may appropriate the credit in discharge or partial discharge of the customer's indebtedness to the bank. For appropriation under the rule in *Clayton's case, See* CLAYTON'S CASE.

APR. *See* ANNUAL PERCENTAGE RATE.

arbitrage. A term formerly used to describe the activities of dealers in foreign exchanges when cross-dealing in various currencies quoted at differing rates in differing financial centres, with a view to making a profit. Now often used to describe the activities of bank customers who are able to switch money between a bank and a secondary market profitably for themselves. *See also* COMPOUND ARBITRAGE; DIRECT ARBITRAGE; HARD ARBITRAGE; REVERSE ARBITRAGE; SOFT ARBITRAGE.

ARIEL. *See* AUTOMATED REAL TIME INVESTMENTS EXCHANGE LTD.

arithmetic mean. An average, calculated by the division of the total of items by the number of items.

arrangement fee. A fee frequently charged by a bank over and above the interest payable on any accommodation taken. It first made its appearance in connection with bridging loans, where the time of the facility, often up to four months, did not allow very much profit to the bank, when one took into account the time and cost involved in setting up the loan. Often banks leave the matter of an arrangement fee to the discretion of their branch manager and, on occasions, no charge is made at all.

arrangement with creditors or members. The directors of a company may make a proposal to the shareholders of the company and its creditors for a composition of its debts or a scheme of arrangements of its affairs. The implementation of the arrangement must be under the supervision of a nominee who must be an insolvency practitioner. It may also be made by an administrator when an administration order is in force, or if the company is being wound up, by the liquidator.

arrear. The state of being behindhand; that which is overdue, unpaid or unsatisfied.

arrestment. A seizure of property by legal authority; an attachment of goods through court process; (in Scottish law) the process by which a creditor detains the effects of his debtor, which are in the hands of third parties, until money owing is paid. *See also* ATTACHMENT.

articles of association. In a limited company, the document setting out the rules which will govern the internal conduct of the company, and dealing with such matters as the transmission and forfeiture of shares, the powers and duties of directors, proceedings at general meetings, the voting of members, etc. *Articles of association* may be altered by special resolution of the company.

articles of partnership. The clauses and conditions of the agreement between partners defining the rights and duties of the partners as between themselves, expressed in writing. There is no statutory requirement that such clauses and conditions should be recorded and they do not affect the liability of the partnership to third parties.

Asian dollar market. The Eurocurrency markets of Singapore, Hong Kong and Tokyo.

asked. The price demanded by the seller. *See* OFFER PRICE.

assent. 1. The agreement of the holder of stocks or bonds to some change in the conditions or terms of issue, in particular where the original obligations of a foreign government have not been honoured on a bond issue and the holder has been offered new and less favourable terms of payment. 2. A document executed by the personal representative of a deceased person, which vests the legal estate in the *devisee*. It must be in writing, must be signed by the personal representative, and must name the person in whose favour it is expressed to be. This person may be the personal representative, but an asset is still necessary to constitute him or her the beneficial owner. The only time when no assent is necessary is when the land is to be sold following the death of the previous owner. Then the personal representative may execute a conveyance direct to the purchaser.

assented bonds. Bonds for which a plan of financial reorganisation or of adjusted repayment has been approved by the bondholder.

assessment for tax. The official estimate of the tax which an individual has to pay; evaluations for the purpose of taxation. This assessment is made from the taxpayer's annual return, so covering the amount of income from every source. Under Sch. A assessment will cover income from property rents, under Sch. B from woodlands, under Sch. D from interest not taxed at source and from trades, businesses and professions; and under Sch. E from earnings and pensions. A *provisional assessment* is one made on incomplete knowledge, such as where the annual return has not been made; this is usually based on the figures of the previous year. An *additional assessment* is one made to correct a previous assessment.

asset. An item of property or value. In accounting terms it is any item – real or fictitious – that can be given a monetary value.

asset liability management. The control of a bank's deposit and lending policies to ensure safety, liquidity and profitability.

asset stripping. The buying of a company for the purpose of making a profit by selling its assets due to under valuation. Such an opportunity will arise when a company is trading at a loss, or making poor profits although its *asset values* are high.

asset value. What the assets will actually realise when they are sold. *See* BOOK VALUE; BREAK-UP VALUE.

assignation. An assignment, writ or subpoena; an authority to pay to order similar to a bill of exchange, where the title is passed by endorsement; a contract by which a debtor or a holder is authorised to remit to an *assignee*, for the account of the assignor, a sum of money or document of title, etc., which the assignor has authority to collect in his or her own name; a deed of conveyance in favour of an assignee.

assignee. The person to whom *assignment* of any right or personal property is made.

assignment. The act of assigning allotment, legal transfer of a right or property; the instrument by which such transfer is effected; the right of property transferred. The writing of a cheque is not, except in Scotland, an assignment of funds. There, however, a credit balance on a current account which is insufficient to meet a cheque drawn on that account must be put on a *suspense account* towards the eventual payment of the debt.

assignment of debts. The transfer of a right to receive payment under an existing obligation from the original

beneficiary (the *assignor*) to a third party (the *assignee*). Future debts can be assigned only in equity. If made for valuable consideration, such equitable assignments are equivalent to contracts to assign and will be enforced by the court. Existing debts may be assigned at law or equity. A legal assignment is one which is absolute and in writing under the hand of the assignor; notice of the assignment must be given to the debtor. The lending banker will insist on a legal assignment of an existing debt. The assignment must be absolute and may take the form either of an irrevocable order or letter addressed to the debtor, or a mortgage assigning the debt absolutely, subject to a right of redemption. Notice must be given to the debtor at once and the debtor should be asked to confirm the amount, to state whether any counter-claims exist (to which the assignment would be postponed) and to confirm that there is no prior charge. The debtor should acknowledge the receipt of notice and undertake to remit the payment to the bank. The assignment should be of the debt only, for a document which purports to transfer the property in goods as well as to assign their proceeds is a *bill of sale* and must be registered as such. If the assignment is executed by a limited company it should be registered at Companies House within twenty-one days of the date of its execution.

assignment of life policy. The transfer of a right to receive the financial benefit under a policy of life assurance from the assured *(the assignor)* to a third party *(the assignee)*. The proceeds of the life policy may be assigned at law or in equity. A legal assignment is one made in writing, usually by a separate instrument, but possibly also by endorsement on the policy itself. Written notice of the assignment must be given to the assurance company, and the date of receipt of the notice by the company regulates the priority of the claim. The assurance company receiving notice must acknowledge its receipt in writing.

assignor. The person making an *assignment* of any right or personal property to another.

assigns. Persons to whom an *assignment* of any right or personal property is made – the plural form of *assignee*.

associate. A partner or colleague; a member of an association or institution. For the purposes of the Consumer Credit Act, 1974 *associate* shall be construed in accordance with s. 184 of the Act. The Insolvency Act, 1986, s. 435 gives a wide interpretation of the meaning of *associate*. Broadly, any person related to another, or a person in partnership with another and the husband/wife, a trustee with a trust, an employee, or a company that has control of another company and a director of a company is an associate of that company.

associated companies. An alternative to an amalgamation or setting up of a holding company. *Associated companies* usually have an interlocking directorate so that some influence can be brought to bear to ensure that the companies pursue similar policies. However, it is not essential to have directors in common, but the investing company will of course frequently be represented on the board of its associated company (who must not be a subsidiary). Participation should take the form of: *(a)* a partnership in a joint venture or consortium; or *(b)* a long-term substantial interest (about 20 per cent of the equity) on the part of the investing company, so that, taking into account the disposition of the other shareholdings, it is able to exert a significant interest.

Association of Banking Teachers (ABT). An organisation formed in 1978 to bring together fulltime and parttime teachers in banking subjects

as set forth in the syllabus of the Chartered Institute of Bankers. Its aims and objects are: *(a)* to foster and promote the study and development of banking and related subjects; *(b)* to guide and aid the professional development of both fulltime and parttime teachers of banking subjects; *(c)* to act as a consultative body on the tuition needs of bankers in cooperation with the Chartered Institute of Bankers and any other bodies concerned with banking education; *(d)* to cooperate with universities, colleges and other teaching institutions in furtherance of banking education; *(e)* to foster and promote cooperation with banks and bankers and with their educational and professional organisations. The Association provides a wide range of courses and conferences throughout each year and regular *Bulletins* containing informative and up-to-date articles, reports, letters, etc. An effective relationship between the Association and the Chartered Institute of Bankers has created a most efficient link between the administrators of banking education and the practitioners.

Association of British Factors (ABF). An association that was established in 1977 consisting of eight members representing those companies which provide full factoring services as their main business as opposed to those only interested in invoice discounting *(q.v.).* See FACTORING.

Association of Corporate Treasurers. A professional association composed of persons whose work is concerned with treasureship in companies and financial institutions. Membership is obtainable by examination and through being engaged in the industry for at least two years. Fellows are appointed from members who must have positions of management, engaged in the industry for at least five years, or who are involved in teaching treasurership.

association clause. The clause in the *memorandum of association* by which the original members agree to take up the number of shares written against their names.

Association of Investment Trust Companies (AITC). Formed in 1932, the AITC is the collective voice for UK trust companies. The main purpose of the Association is the protection, promotion and advancement of the common interests of its members and their shareholders.

assurance. *See* INSURANCE.

at a discount. *See* DISCOUNT.

at a premium. *See* PREMIUM.

at call. A phrase indicating the condition of repayment on which money is lent by a banker, namely that it is to be repaid immediately upon demand (especially in connection with bank loans to the discount houses in the City of London).

at par. In the case of stocks or shares, a quotation at a time when the nominal and market values are identical. In the foreign exchange markets, where the forward value is equal to the spot value.

at short notice. A phrase indicating the condition of repayment on which money is lent by a banker, namely, that it is to be repaid seven or fourteen days after demand (especially in connection with bank loans to the discount houses in the City of London).

at sight. *See* SIGHT BILL.

attachment. The seizure of persons or money or goods to secure a debt or demand. The first is usually the arrest of a person for failing to comply with a court order of some kind, and is usually dealt with under contempt of court procedure. The second is where sums are deducted from salaries or wages under the Attachment of Earning Act, 1971, e.g. for maintenance orders. The third is a remedy for creditors who have secured a judgment order against a defaulting creditor. *See also* GARNISHEE ORDER; GARNISHEE SUMMONS.

attest. To testify, especially in a formal manner; to vouch for; to bear witness; to put a person on oath.

attestation. A formal witnessing, especially of a signature. *See also* WILL; WITNESS.

attested copy. A true copy of an original document, certified as such by a witness by a declaration to that effect written on the copy and signed by the witness.

attorn. To assign or transfer; to recognise a new owner.

attorney. A lawyer; a solicitor; one legally authorised by another to transact business; an agent; a deputy. *See also* POWER OF ATTORNEY.

attornment. The recognition and acknowledgment of a legal relationship, such as landlord and tenant or principal and agent, e.g. as where, under the terms of a bank mortgage, the mortgagor *attorns* (acknowledges him or herself) tenant of the mortgagee at a rent, or where, in a produce advance, a bank sends a delivery order, signed by the customer and attached to the existing warehousekeeper's receipt, to the warehousekeeper who will thereupon send a new receipt to the bank by which he or she *attorns* to the bank (acknowledges that he or she now holds the goods on the bank's behalf).

auction. A public sale by a person licensed for that purpose, whereby the object to be sold is secured by the maker of the highest offer or bid; to sell by auction. Auctions are governed by conditions printed in the catalogues of sale binding both seller and purchaser. Where goods are put up for sale by auction in lots, each lot is *prima facie* deemed to be the subject of a separate contract of sale. A sale by auction is complete when the auctioneer announces its completion by the fall of the hammer, or in other customary manner. *See also* DUTCH AUCTION; SALE BY CANDLE; GILT AUCTION.

audit. An examination by a specially

appointed qualified person, of the books, vouchers and accounts of a business, public office or undertaking to prevent or discover fraud or inaccuracy on the part of the persons keeping them; to make such an examination. The audit should take place at regular intervals.

auditor. One who *audits* books and accounts. The auditors of a company are primarily responsible for making an independent investigation into the affairs of the company and for reporting to the shareholders. They must be members of a body of established and qualified accountants. At the conclusion of the audit, the auditors must append to the company's profit and loss account and balance sheet a statement to the effect that they have received all the information they required and that in their opinion the figures they have seen represent a true and fair view of the company's affairs. If they find that they cannot do this they must qualify their report accordingly.

auditors' report. Any report written by an auditor on a matter on which an opinion has been sought and within the scope and terms of the auditor's appointment. To comply with the Companies Act, 1985, s. 236 a report on the financial statements of a company must be made.

authorised banks. With the repeal of the Exchange Control Act, 1947, in 1987, this term ceases to have any relevance.

authorised capital. The sum mentioned in the *memorandum of association* of a limited company as being the amount which the company is authorised to raise.

authorised depositary. With the repeal of the Exchange Control Act, 1947, in 1987, this term ceases to have any relevance.

authorised institutions. Those institutions now recognised by the Bank of England under the Banking Act, 1987 to act as banks and accept deposits.

authorised investments. Investments which the trustees of a fund may make because they are sanctioned either by a statute or by the instrument setting up the trust.

Automated Real-time Investments Exchange Ltd (ARIEL). A system introduced in 1974 to enable the members of the *Accepting Houses Committee* to bypass the Stock Exchange procedures and to match large deals, thereby saving costs. Since the Big Bang, and the introduction of *Stock Exchange automated quotations system* (SEAQ), this company no longer exists.

automated teller machine. Commonly known as ATM. This machine permits the holder of the appropriate magnetic encoded card to obtain funds anytime of the day or night. Additionally the balance of the account may be obtained and cheque books and statements may be ordered. The machines are often called cash dispensers, although each bank has its own name for this service. UK banks now have the facility to permit customers to use encoded cards to obtain cash while in some European countries with the possibility of this service being extended.

automatic data processing. *See* DATA PROCESSING.

aval. The guarantee that a bill of exchange will be paid on presentation. Usually given by bankers at the request of their customers. The *avalisation* of the bill is by endorsement on the back of the bill. The *aval* is not recognised in English law and banks do not endorse bills in this manner unless they are asked to do so by customers of the highest integrity and with a suitable indemnity.

AVCO. *See* AVERAGE COST.

average. A number or quantity intermediate to several different numbers or quantities; a mean; the rate, proportion, degree, quantity or number generally prevailing; ordinary; normal; the apportionment of loss arising from damage to ship or cargo at sea as between the parties interested. *See also* GENERAL AVERAGE; PARTICULAR AVERAGE.

average adjuster. One who calculates the proportions which are to be borne by the owner of a ship and by the owners of the cargo respectively of any losses which result from sacrifices which have been made to preserve the safety of the ship or cargo.

average balance. The figure resulting from a mathematical calculation whereby the balance of an account is recorded daily for a given period and then totalled and divided by the number of days in the period.

average bond. A bond obtained by the master of a ship which has incurred a general average loss from the consignee of the cargo before delivery is made to them, under which they agree to pay their proportion of the *general average* as soon as it has been ascertained.

average clause. A clause in a marine insurance policy stipulating that certain articles shall be free from average, unless general, and that others shall be free from average, unless general, under a certain percentage. The clause is also being used in fire policies.

average cleared credit balance. The average balance on a credit account, adjusted for uncleared effects, used as the basis of an allowance made against the cost of keeping a current account before the commission charge is ascertained.

average cost. The total cost of production incurred by a company or firm in a given time, divided by the number of units of output.

average life. Maturity of a total borrowing after taking into account purchases by the borrower's sinking fund.

averaging. A system on a Stock Exchange whereby a speculator increases his or her purchases or sales as a result of a price movement of the stocks or shares, in order to average out the purchase or sale prices. Thus a *bull* averages by purchasing more stock if the price falls, a *bear* selling more stock if the price rises. *See also* BEAR; BULL.

B

back bond. A deed by which a party holding a title acknowledges that he holds it in trust for a certain purpose.

back freight. The charge for the return of goods not accepted at the port of delivery.

back to back credit. This is a description of the procedure where a customer of the bank, acting as a middleman, has had a documentary credit opened in his favour by the foreign importer of his goods. On the strength and security of this credit the customer's bank agrees to open a credit for the benefit of the original supplier of the goods. The two credits are put 'back to back', the one being issued on the security of the other. It is necessary to ensure that the documents called for under the second credit will satisfy the requirements of the first credit. The middleman's invoices are substituted for those of the seller and the ultimate buyer must not find out the identity of the seller. If he or she did it would then be possible to deal direct with the seller on subsequent occasions.

back to back loan. Accommodation devised to avoid exchange risks, sometimes arranged within a multi-national enterprise by way of 'netting' procedures, which can give rise on occasions to tax benefits, e.g. a Dutch company might need sterling for an outward investment in UK; a British company might need guilders for a similar operation in Holland. Each company funds the other's enterprise in its own country. While tax and exchange control problems can usually be surmounted, an interest rate differential often poses difficult questions.

backwardation. A consideration paid by a seller of stock, often a 'bear', on the Stock Exchange for the right to postpone delivery for a time. On the *London Metal Exchange,* the amount by which the price of cash metal exceeds that for a forward delivery.

BACS. *See* BANKERS AUTOMATED CLEARING SERVICES.

bad and doubtful debt. Debts which are bad and those which are not recoverable. Accordingly they are written off as losses. *Doubtful debts* are those of which the recovery, in full or in part, is uncertain. These are provided for by sums being set aside out of profits. Balance sheets will show an amount credited to Provision for Bad and Doubtful Debts as a deduction from the Debtors.

bail bond. 1. A bond given to the court in order to secure the release of a vessel under arrest. The warrant, nailed to the vessel's mast, is usually issued to obtain redress for damage to port facilities by a vessel. The bond is released after money is paid. 2. A bond given by a person who is being bailed and his surety.

bailee. One to whom goods are entrusted for safe keeping or for a specific purpose. A banker as a bailee, has no lien on the property kept in safe custody for his or her customer.

bailment. The delivery of goods to a person in trust on the terms that the goods will be returned when the purpose for which they were bailed has been effected; a contract whereby one person leaves property in the custody of another, the bailee, on the terms that he is to have it back when he wants it, and in the meantime the bailee is responsible for its safe keeping.

bailor. The person who leaves his property with another for safe keeping.

balance. The difference between the total credit entries and the total debit entries made in an account since it was last balanced. When the credit entries are larger than the debits there is a *'credit balance'*. When the debits are larger than the credits there is a *'debit balance'*. A debit balance in the current account of a customer of a bank is often called an 'overdraft'.

balance certificate. A document received by a shareholder when he has sold only a portion of shares represented by a share certificate.

balance of payments. The total of transactions with foreign countries in trade, services or capital, contained in the balance of revenue and balance of capital of a country.

balance of trade. The difference between the cost of the visible imports and exports of a country.

balance sheet. A statement showing, at a certain date, the capital, assets and liabilities of a business organisation.

balance sheet ratios. The various ratios that enable a banker and others, to interpret the balance sheet of the business. Basically the ratios are divided into three groups *(a)* profitability; *(b)* liquidity; *(c)* capital/solvency.

bank. A body corporate or not, that has been recognised by the Bank of England under the Banking Act, 1987, to accept deposits as defined by that Act. Other than this recognition, there is no statutory definition of a bank. As a verb, *to bank,* this term indicates that a customer has paid in for the credit of his or her account a sum of money, cheques or other financial documents. *See also* BANKER.

bank account. An account held by a bank or banker recording the deposits and withdrawals of a customer from that account. The account may be either a current or deposit account. A statement is sent by the bank to its customer at agreed or regular intervals.

bank balance. The balance of a customer's account as advised by the bank, either in a statement, by tele-

phone or as indicated via an Automated Teller Machine (ATM).

bank bill. A bill of exchange drawn by a bank or accepted by a bank.

bank charge. A charge made by a bank to a customer. This may be directly relevant for service of keeping the account, plus the interest if any, on accommodation enjoyed by the customer, but could cover a charge for any other specific service e.g. transmission of funds.

bank credit. The amount of new credit or money created by the action of banks in granting loans or overdrafts to their customers.

banker. A person conducting a banking business. The term is commonly thought to imply that the person is an individual rather than an incorporated company for which the term 'bank' is used. The term banker is used in statutes e.g. Bills of Exchange Act, but for the general public, the term 'bank' or 'banker' are synonymous.

bankers automated clearing services. BACS is the common name for the Bankers Automated Clearing Services, now known as BACS Ltd. A system whereby a bank may remit direct debits and standing orders through a computerised system to any customer of any bank or building society that has a link with BACS. Similarly, a customer who wishes to remit direct debits or funds in settlement of trade debts, salaries, wages, etc can do so, by linking into the BACS system or by sending his or her own magnetic or other tapes to BACS for processing. As well as the major clearing banks using these services, so do Citibank, Standard Chartered Bank, Halifax Building Society and Abbey National Building Society. As other banks and building societies obtain the necessary criteria, the number of participating members is likely to grow.

bankers' draft. A draft drawn by a

branch of a bank on its Head Office or main office. As this is usually paid on presentation, it is acceptable as the equivalent to cash. Such a draft does not satisfy the definition of a bill of exchange because it is not 'drawn by one person on another'. However, there is statutory protection for the paying banker under the Cheques Act, 1957 and the Bills of Exchange Act, 1882.

banker's lien. A general lien enjoyed by the banker over any borrowing customer's property that comes into his or her hands in the ordinary course of business as a banker. It is an exceptional lien in that it has a right of sale after reasonable notice to the customer. A banker's lien has been described as an implied pledge. Both the type of property and the reason it was handed to the banker are critical factors. The usual sort of property over which a banker has a lien consists of negotiable securities such as bills of exchange, promissory notes, or coupons. Cheques paid in for collection are very common types of valuable paper which may become subject to a lien. Where the property is handed to the banker for a particular purpose, however, he or she has no lien. Thus the banker has none over security handed over for the purpose of selling it through a stockbroker, or property handed over for safe custody.

banker's opinions. *See* STATUS ENQUIRY.

banker's order. A written order from customer to banker authorising the banker to make a series of periodic payments on the customer's behalf.

banker's payment. Any order or draft drawn upon any bank in the UK by a branch of that bank in favour of another bank and used for the purpose of settling some account between the two banks, e.g. a special presentation.

banker's references. *See* STATUS ENQUIRY.

Bank for International Settlements (BIS). A bank established at Basle in 1930 to implement the reparation payments to be made by Germany following the First World War. All the European central banks contributed to its establishment and were represented on its board. When reparation payments lapsed it maintained itself in existence by doing a small amount of commercial business. Its importance increased in 1950 when it became banker to the European Payments Union, in 1954 when it became banker to the European Coal and Steel Community, and in the 1960s when it became the centre for central bank cooperation.

bank giro. The name given in UK banks to the system of credit transfers, standing orders and direct debiting when the National Giro was established in 1968; on the Continent, any system between banks which allows for the settlement of mutual debts, without the use of cash, but by means of balance payments or set-offs administered by a central authority or clearing house.

bank holiday. a day on which banks are closed for business by Statute or Proclamation.

Banking Act. An Act of Parliament passed in 1979 which gives authority to the Bank of England to give a licence to deposit taking institutions to become either recognised banks or licensed deposit takers. It also gives the Bank of England *supervisory powers* over these financial institutions. No institution is permitted to accept deposits (deposits as defined by the Act) without the authority of the Bank of England. The 1979 Act which was strengthened by the Banking Act 1987 received the Royal Assent in May 1987 and had the following essential features: *(a)* it has strengthened the statutory basis of bank supervision; *(b)* it replaced the two tier system (banks and licensed deposit takers) into one single group of licensed institutions; (c) it invoked certain criteria before authorisation of institutions which briefly are: (i) every manager, director or controller shall be a fit and proper person to hold office (ii) the business of the institution will be conducted in a prudent manner (iii) the paid up capital and reserves shall not be less than £1,000,000; (d) The exemptions to Bank of England authorisation included Building societies authorised under the Building Societies Act, 1986, municipal and school banks, other central banks and international development and economic institutions.

banking education service. A service financed by the major banks and available to all educational establishments, particularly schools and colleges of further education, to provide information about the services of banks and the careers available in banks. This service provides books, notes, wallcharts, floppy disks, to cover a wide variety of banking operations. If required, speakers are available, usually free of charge.

banking information service. A service set up by the major banks to provide information to the public on all matters regarding the activities of the major banks.

banking ombudsman. The first appointment to this office was Mr Ian Edwards-Jones QC, in January 1986. The function of the Ombudsman is to resolve any complaints from personal customers, after the normal channels for dealing with such complaints have been exhausted. This is a free service which covers all personal banking services, but finance houses, travel agents and estate agent subsidiaries of banks are excluded, as are decisions regarding lending. The Ombudsman has the power to make an award of up to £50,000, but the customer has the

option to retain the right to take legal action.

bank interest. The interest allowed on money deposited with a bank; the interest charged on an overdraft, loan or accommodation.

bank interest certificate. A certificate issued by a bank to a borrowing customer stating the amount of interest paid by him on his bank loan, so that such information may be included in his tax return.

bank notes. Promissory notes issued by a bank of issue, payable to bearer on demand.

Bank of England. The central bank in the UK. Established in 1694 by Royal Charter, it had a capital of £1,200,000. This charter was renewed periodically and over the course of time, the bank very gradually moved from being a commercial to being a central bank. Under the 1844 Bank Charter Act the Bank of England was divided into departments – the *Banking Department* and the *Issue Department*. Both these departments had to issue a balance sheet each week and still do. The fiduciary issue was raised to £14,000,000 and the Bank of England acquired the note issuing monopoly in England and Wales. Its present functions are (a) banker to the Government; (b) bankers bank; (c) manages the Exchange Equalisation Account; (d) handles the issue of Treasury bills; (e) supervises the banking institutions in the UK; (f) maintains the sterling accounts of other central banks and international organisations; (g) lender of last resort (h) the note issuing authority in England and Wales.

bank rate. This term originally indicated the minimum rate that the Bank of England would be prepared to discount an eligible bill. This was superseded by the minimum lending rate which was suspended in August 1981, when it was decided to influence the market by ensuring adequate liquidity in the banking sector and open market operations. The Bank of England now keeps short term interest rates within various bands which are not published.

bank return. The weekly statement issued by the Bank of England in accordance with the provisions of the Bank Charter Act, 1844, disclosing its financial position for the information of the public.

bankrupt. An insolvent person who has been adjudicated bankrupt by the court. The bankrupt is then deprived of nearly all legal powers, his or her estate passing into the hands of a trustee in bankruptcy. A debtor can only be made bankrupt if *(a)* domiciled in England and Wales; *(b)* personally present on the day on which the petition is presented; *or (c)* at any time in the period of three years ending with that day he or she (i) has been ordinarily resident, or has had a place of residence, in England and Wales *or* (ii) has carried on business in England and Wales. This includes a firm or partnership of which the individual is a member and carrying on a business by an agent or manager for that individual or for that firm or partnership. Section 265 Insolvency Act, 1986.

bankruptcy debt. Section 382 Insolvency Act, 1986. *(a)* Any debt or liability to which the bankrupt is subject at the commencement of the bankruptcy; *(b)* any debt or liability to which he or she may become subject after the commencement of the bankruptcy by reason of any obligation incurred before the commencement of the bankruptcy; *(c)* any amount specified in pursuance of s. 39(3)(c) of the Powers of Criminal Courts Act, 1973 in any criminal bankruptcy order made against him or her before the commencement of the bankruptcy.

bankruptcy level. The amount for which a person can be made bankrupt is £750; but the Secretary of State may by order in a *statutory instrument* substi-

tute any amount specified in the order for that amount or for the amount which by virtue of such an order is for the time being the amount of the bankruptcy level, s. 267(4) Insolvency Act, 1986.

bankruptcy order. An order adjudging an individual bankrupt. Insolvency Act, 1986, s. 381(2).

bank reconciliation statement. A statement drawn up showing why a balance in the Cash Book is different from that shown on the Bank Statement.

bank statement. A mechanised or computerised statement supplied by banks to their customers, showing details of the customer's debit and credit transactions, and the balance.

bank sweep arrangement. A standing arrangement with a bank to move funds from current account to a deposit account, or vice versa, when appropriate, without specific instructions from the customer.

Barclaycard. A credit card introduced in 1966 by Barclays Bank. There is no entrance fee for new cardholders, but a credit limit for each individual is imposed. The cardholder receives a monthly statement. If the amount outstanding is paid by the date stated on the statement, there is no interest charge. If credit is taken, a minimum of 5 per cent or £5 whichever is the greater is required. The charge on the outstanding debt is a stated percentage per month. Barclaycard also acts as a cheque card. Cash advances, which attract interest from the day they are taken until the date of repayment are available. Barclaycard is now part of VISA.

bargain. An agreement between two persons concerning a sale; an advantageous purchase; the thing bought or sold; a transaction in stocks and shares.

barring the entail. The conversion of an estate tail by a tenant-in-tail into a fee simple by a deed called a disentailing assurance, with the consequence that the tenant may then freely dispose of the estate if he so wishes, thus defeating the rights of his issue and of the persons whose estates are to take effect after the determination of the entailed interest or defeasance of it.

barter. The exchange of goods for goods; to give (anything but money) in exchange for some other commodity. It is a characteristic of a primitive community, but today barter is accepted on an international scale to facilitate trading with countries of the Eastern bloc and others which are short of hard, convertible currencies. Barter is also called *compensation trading* or *counter-purchase*.

base drift. A phenomenon found in connection with the control of money supply by the central bank. All the main industrial countries now set formal targets for monetary growth. In the UK the experience has been that the central bank from time to time overshoots the target; that is, the monetary growth is in excess of what it is supposed to be. This poses the problem of what the base should be for the following year – the base has drifted away from the hoped-for figure. The Government has a number of choices. One is politically unacceptable, that is, to admit that control has been less than successful, and to start again for the following year. Another is to scale down the percentage increase allowed in the next year so that the growth over the two years will not exceed the sum of the intended growth in each of the two years. This gives the illusion that the central bank is still in charge of inflation.

base fee. An estate in fee simple into which an estate tail is converted, where the issue in tail are barred, but persons claiming estates by way of remainder or otherwise are not barred.

base rate. The basic lending rate of a bank or financial institution, on which its lending rates and deposit rates are founded. Each bank is free to fix its own base rate as it thinks best but, in practice, there is often no variation. From a bank's point of view, *base rate* represents the marginal cost of borrowing funds.

base year. A year chosen as a base for a series of index numbers such as, for example, the General Index of Retail Prices. The selected year is usually given an index number of 100, so that subsequent indices may be readily represented as percentage rises or falls.

basis price. In a 'futures' market, there will be an agreement to buy or sell a named commodity and the price agreed at the time between the parties is the 'basis' or 'striking price'.

basis of assessment. The period in which various financial transactions take place and are taken into account for the purpose of assessing the tax liability in that period.

B.E. The abbreviation for Bill of Exchange or Bank of England.

bear. A speculator on the Stock Exchange who anticipates a fall in the value of a certain security and therefore sells stocks which he or she does not possess in the hope of buying them back more cheaply at a later date (frequently in the same account period), thus making a profit.

bearer. The person in possession of a bill or note which is payable to bearer. A bill is payable to bearer which is expressed to be so payable, or one on which the only or last indorsement is an indorsement in blank. *See* INDORSEMENT IN BLANK. Title passes by simple delivery, coupled with an intention to transfer title.

bearer bill, bearer note. A bill of exchange, cheque or promissory note which is expressed to be payable to the bearer thereof, or a bill of exchange which is indorsed in blank.

bearer bond. A bond which is payable

to bearer and one in respect of which no register of owners is kept by the company concerned. It has attached to it a series of coupons, which are torn off at the right time and sent forward as evidence of the bondholder's right to receive the interest. A bearer bond is a negotiable instrument – that is, title passes by simple delivery coupled with an intention to transfer. The transferee must take in good faith and for value, and without notice of any defect in the title of the transferor.

bearer cheque. *See* BEARER BILL.

bearer note. *See* BEARER BILL.

bearer scrip. A temporary document issued as evidence of title by a government or company making a new issue until such time as all instalments have been paid, when the bearer scrip is exchanged for a bearer bond or for registered bonds or certificates. The bearer scrip is a negotiable instrument.

bed and breakfast. A term used in investment planning. It is a procedure whereby shares are sold on one business day and then re-purchased on the next, in order to establish a capital gain or loss for tax purposes. These transactions tend to occur towards the end of the financial year to reduce tax payable or to take advantage of capital gains exemptions (currently £5,000). *See* CAPITAL GAINS TAX.

below par. With regard to the purchase or sale of a security, it indicates that the current price is below the nominal value. For the purchase or sale of a currency, it indicates that the future value is below spot value.

beneficial owner. A person entitled absolutely to the benefit of any property, real or personal, of which the legal title is held by a trustee. Certain covenants for title are implied where the vendor conveys as beneficial owner (and in fact possesses that status) and the conveyance is for value. They are 1. that the vendor has a good right to

convey; 2. that the purchaser shall have quiet possession; 3. that the property is free from incumbrances; 4. that the vendor will do everything which is right and possible to perfect the title, should that prove necessary.

beneficiary. One that benefits from the act of another; a person named in a will as a legatee or devisee. A person named in a letter of credit who may draw drafts on the issuing/paying bank.

bequest. A gift or legacy of personal property under a will, especially to a public body or institute.

berth. The space at a wharf or quay allotted to a ship for loading or unloading.

B.E.S. *See* BUSINESS EXPANSION SCHEME.

beta. The name given to the second group of company securities that have a full listing on the Stock Exchange. Unlike the alpha group, these shares are unlikely to have the same volume of trading and consequently the prices will not change as frequently.

betterment. Improvement; enhanced value of property, as a result of local improvements; tax formerly levied by the Land Commission on the development value of land under the Land Commission Act, 1967. However, the levy is no longer charged and is replaced in appropriate cases by Development Land Tax.

bid. To offer a price; the offer of a price, especially at sales by auction. On the Stock Exchange the term means the price made either by the market to a member of the public or by an intending purchaser to the market at which he or she is prepared to buy shares. It is also used to describe the amount of money offered per share in the case of a take-over bid.

bid bond. *See* TENDER BOND.

bid price. A price quoted by a market maker on the Stock Exchange at which he or she will buy stocks or shares on offer. A price quoted by the management company of a unit trust at which they will buy sub-units of the trust.

Big Bang. This expression refers to the change in method of operations in the Stock Exchange from 27 October, 1986. Organisations on the Stock Exchange are now single capacity operators. Fixed commission agreements have been abandoned. Non-members are permitted to have a stake in member firms. With the advent of the international quotations of major companies, it was necessary to improve communications and information technology so from 27 October 1986 trading on the floor of the Stock Exchange for all practical purposes ceased, and deals were carried out through the medium of computers.

big five. This refers to the major clearing banks namely Barclays, Lloyds, Midland, National Westminster Banks and the TSB.

big ticket lease. The leasing of capital equipment for sums in excess of £1m. This form of leasing is often done by a consortium of leasing companies.

bill. This can refer to *(a)* legislation for discussion in Parliament; *(b)* a shortened expression for a Bill of Exchange; *(c)* paper money; *(d)* a negotiable security document.

bill broker. A merchant who buys and sells bills of exchange. Bill brokers are more commonly termed discount houses. Discount houses are an important part of the short term money market, one of their important functions being to provide a source of first class bills for bankers. They also tender for Treasury Bills and deal in short-dated Government Stocks.

bill for collection. A bill of exchange drawn by an exporter, usually at a term, on an importer overseas, and brought by the exporter to his or her bank with a request to collect the proceeds. The bank sends the bill to its agent in the foreign town where the importer lives and has the bill presented for acceptance and/or payment. It then brings back the proceeds, then credits the customers' account. If such a bill has documents attached it is called a documentary bill, if not it is a clean bill. Where documents are attached, the customer must instruct the bank whether the documents are to be released against acceptance by the importer (D/A) or only against payment (D/P). Bills for Collection are subject to *the uniform rules for collection. See* UNIFORM RULES FOR COLLECTION.

bill for negotiation. A bill of exchange drawn by an exporter at a term on an importer overseas, brought by the exporter to his bank with a request to negotiate it, that is, discount it. If the bank agrees to buy the bill it will pay the customer the face value of the bill less discount and other charges, with recourse. The bill will, in many cases, be drawn in a foreign currency. Once the bank has bought the bill, it is collecting the money for itself. *See* RECOURSE.

bill in a set. A foreign bill drawn in several copies, identical except that each is numbered and contains a reference to the other parts. They are sent for safety by separate mails. The drawee accepts only one copy of the bill.

bill mountain. The number of bills discounted and held by the Bank of England under the present monetary control arrangements. The value of such bills held, at the moment of writing, exceed £16 billion.

bill of exchange. An unconditional order in writing, addressed by one person to another, signed by the person giving it, requiring the person to whom it is addressed to pay on demand, or at a fixed or determinable future time, a sum certain in money to, or to the order of, a specified person or bearer. (Bills of Exchange Act,

1882). *See* ACCOMMODATION BILL; BANK BILL; BEARER BILL; CLEAN BILL; COMMERCIAL BILL; CORPORATION BILL; DOCUMENTARY BILL; ELIGIBLE BILL; FINE BANK BILL; FIRST CLASS BILL; INLAND BILL; LONG BILL; ORDER BILL; ORIGINAL BILL; PRE-FINANCE BILL; RE-FINANCE BILL; SHORT BILL; SIGHT BILL; SOLA BILL; TERM BILL; TRADE BILL; USANCE BILL.

bill of imprest. An order entitling the bearer to have money paid in advance.

bill of lading. Abbreviated to B/L. A receipt for goods received for carriage to a stated destination, signed by or on behalf of the master of a ship. The bill is also a negotiable document of title to the goods, transferable by indorsement, but is not a negotiable instrument in the true sense. It is furthermore evidence of the contract of carriage. Normally bills of lading are issued in sets of either two or three, while another copy is retained by the ship's master. *See also* CLEAN BILL OF LADING; DIRTY BILL OF LADING; FIRST OF EXCHANGE; ON BOARD BILL OF LADING; RECEIVED FOR SHIPMENT BILL OF LADING; SHIPPED BILL OF LADING; STRAIGHT BILL OF LADING; THROUGH BILL OF LADING.

bill of sale. A document given as security for a loan or debt whereby the debtor assigns personal chattels to the lender. It authorises seizure and sale in cases of non-payment, and must be registered at the Central Office of the Supreme Court within seven days of its execution. A bill of sale may be absolute (equivalent to an out-and-out transfer), or conditional by way of mortgage. Banks do not accept this type of security; possession remains with the borrower and there can be no control over the security. The assignment of a book debt is not a bill of sale, but a document which purports to transfer the property in goods as well as to assign their proceeds is a bill of sale and must be registered as such. *See* SHIP BILL OF SALE..

bill payable. A bill of exchange which is either payable at sight or has been accepted payable at some fixed or determinable future date. Often abbreviated to B/P. The acceptor of the bill has an outstanding liability.

bill rate. The discount rate on bills of exchange, varying according to the quality of the bill to be discounted.

bill receivable. In contrast to a bill payable, this is an asset in the hands of a true owner, or the bank who is an agent for collection. Abbreviated as B/R.

bills discounted. *See* DISCOUNT. *See also* TAP BILLS; TENDER BILLS.

Bills of Exchange Act, 1882. This act of codification, sets out the definition of a bill of exchange; its form, the responsibilities of the parties to the bill, the method of presentation and payment. The process in the event of non acceptance or non payment. It also deals with cheques; the crossings, definition, parties to a cheque, payment, etc. The final part of this act deals with the issue and payment of promissory notes.

b/l. *See* BILL OF LADING.

Black Monday. 19 October 1987 was so named as on that day the market value of all equities on the major international stock exchanges, fell sharply due to the US financial, economic and political situations.

blank cheque. A cheque signed by the drawer, but having no details filled in. *See* INCHOATE INSTRUMENT.

blanket policy. An insurance policy by the terms of which an underwriter accepts liability for a fixed figure for a certain time, adjustments of the premium paid being made when it is known exactly what the shipment was worth. This type of policy is used when similar goods are sent in consignments on a number of different voyages.

blank indorsement. *See* INDORSEMENT IN BLANK.

blank transfer. A transfer of stock or shares with the name of the transferee left blank, sometimes used when shares are mortgaged as security for a debt. If repayment is not forthcoming the lender may then fill in his or her own name as transferee, date the transfer, have it stamped, and send it to the company for registration of the shares in the lender's own name as owner. This procedure should not be used where a transfer has to be under seal, because such a transfer is a deed and takes effect from the date of its delivery. If on that day the deed is not complete, the blanks can only be filled in subsequently by the transferor, or by the transferor's authority which itself must be under seal. A further point is that stamping must be done within thirty days after execution; late stamping attracts a penalty.

block discounting. A variation of factoring, carried out by finance houses. Block discounting is the purchase by a finance house from retailers of blocks of existing instalment credit contracts, for an immediate cash sum.

blue button. A term used to describe an authorised clerk on the London Stock Exchange.

blue chip. Originally 'blue chip' was a gambling term, chips with the highest value being coloured blue. Over the years, however, the term has been accepted as denoting the ordinary shares of the highest class of company.

bona fide. In good faith. A term used in banking meaning to act in good faith and without negligence. An act can be in good faith yet there can be negligence.

bona vacantia. Unclaimed goods. When a person dies leaving no relatives in the category entitled to inherit the estate passes to the Crown.

bond. A legal engagement in writing to pay a certain sum of money or to fulfil certain conditions; a *certificate* of ownership of capital lent to a government, municipality, etc; a *surety* demanded by Customs authorities from persons holding dutiable goods,

on which duty still has to be paid. *See* ASSENTED BONDS; BAIL BOND; CONVERTIBLE BOND; DRAWN BOND; FLOATING RATE BOND; FOREIGN BOND; INCOME BOND; LOCAL AUTHORITY BONDS; MORTGAGE BOND; NON-ASSENTED BONDS; STRAIGHT BONDS.

bond creditor. A creditor secured by bond.

bonded. Placed in bond, mortgaged.

bonded goods. Goods stored, under care of Customs House Officers, in warehouses until duty is paid.

bonded warehouse. A Customs store for bonded goods.

bond holder. A person holding a bond granted by a private person, company or a government.

bond washing. Now illegal in the UK. A device of selling securities *cum div.* at a higher price, and re-purchasing them later *ex div.* at a lower price to avoid paying tax on the dividend.

bonus. Something over and above what is due; a *premium* given for a privilege, or in addition to interest for a loan; a *gratuity* over and above a fixed salary or wages.

bonus certificate. A statement received by an insurance policy holder from the insurance company on the occasion of a division of its profits, to inform the holder of the amount accruing to him or her, usually to be added to and payable with the sum assured under the policy.

bonus issue. An issue of stock or shares by a company to existing shareholders in proportion to their holding. It is a capitalisation of reserve, therefore, as no extra finance is raised. Even though a shareholder will have more shares, the value of the holding in theory remains the same, as does the percentage shareholding in the company. The usual reason for this issue is to improve marketability of highly-priced shares to make them more attractive to small investors. Often called a *scrip issue*.

book debts. The amount owing to a

trading concern for goods sold.

book entry. An accounting entry passed in a set of ledgers.

books of account. Documents and ledgers which must be prepared and kept by a business entity, including the profit and loss account and balance sheet.

book value. The value of a company assets as stated in the balance sheet.

borrowing powers. The legal ability of an entity to borrow money. A minor has no power to borrow and if allowed to do so cannot legally be compelled to repay. A limited company is an artificial person whose borrowing powers are defined in its Memorandum of Association. These powers may be exercised by the directors of the company or by the company in general meeting – information as to these matters, and as to any limits imposed will be found in the Articles of Association. Organisations not having a separate legal entity, such as an unincorporated association, have no power to borrow. Individuals acting in an official capacity such as trustees or personal representatives, have no power to borrow unless authority is contained in a trust instrument, a statute or a testamentary document. The borrowing powers of an agent must be strictly defined in the principal's mandate. The borrowing powers of building societies and local authorities are defined in statutes.

börse or bourse. A stock exchange.

bottomry bond. A document by which the master of a ship charges the keel or bottom of the ship (thus the ship in its entirety) as security for the repayment of a loan, such repayment being dependent upon the safe arrival of the ship at its destination. Such a bond may be effected where urgent repairs are necessary in the course of a ship's journey, or for refitting.

bought day book. A ledger containing a list of all items bought by a business.

bought note. The contract note supplied by stockbroker to client, detailing the particulars of a purchase made for the client.

bouncing. The common term used when a cheque is being dishonoured for lack of funds.

branch clearing. The operation within a large bank whereby the collection of cheques between the branches of the bank is organised through a department in the Head Office of the bank.

branch credit. A credit paid in by a customer for his account at a branch of the bank other than the one where he keeps his account.

breach of trust. The act of a trustee who does not observe the conditions laid down in the deed or will under which he or she is appointed, for example, by investing trust monies in an improper manner. More generally, the term signifies any failure by a person to observe certain expected standards of behaviour, for example where the person reposing the trust wrongly, supposed that such standards would be duly observed.

breach of warranty of authority. An agent contracting on behalf of his or her principal with a third party, by implication warrants that he or she has the necessary authority to make the contract. If this is not the case, the agent may be personally sued by the third party for breach of warranty of authority.

breakeven analysis. The name given to a device for presenting management with information which will show the effects of costs and income at various levels of output. This is best done in the form of a graph which will show the level of sales at which cost will be recovered.

breakeven chart. The chart which shows the fixed costs and the variable costs related to a product and the number of products needed to be sold in order to cover all costs and show neither a loss or profit.

breaking an account. The cessation of

operations on a running account leaving a balance outstanding. A fresh account may be opened for subsequent transactions. This is done to prevent the operation of the Rule in *Clayton's case*, as for example, upon the death of a guarantor, where the account of the principal debtor is overdrawn, and recourse against the deceased's estate is to be preserved.

breaking bulk. Opening a consignment for the purpose of selling part of it, or to take a sample.

break-up value. The value of a company's assets when it is viewed as a 'gone concern'; the value at current stock exchange prices of the holdings of an investment or unit trust.

Bretton Woods Conference. A meeting under the auspices of the United Nations at Bretton Woods, New Hampshire, U.S.A., in 1944, to set up some degree of cooperation in matters of international trade and payments and to devise a satisfactory international monetary system to be operated after the end of the Second World War. The particular objectives hoped to be achieved were stable exchange rates and free convertibility of currencies for the development of multilateral trade. Two important results of this conference were the establishment of the International Monetary Fund and the World Bank (International Bank for Reconstruction and Development).

bridging advance. A short term advance to a customer pending the customer's receipt of funds from another source. Very frequently this is in connection with a change of house. The customer is selling one house and buying another. The money for the house being bought is often required before the money comes in for the house being sold and the banker is asked to 'bridge' the gap. It is usual to obtain a solicitor's undertaking that the funds from the sale of the house will be remitted to the bank.

British Bankers' Association. An association formed in 1919, for the benefit of British banks whose principal business and head offices were in the UK, and British banks whose principal business was outside the UK and who were at that time members of the British Overseas Banks Association. The membership was widened in 1972 to include all recognised banks operating in the UK, whether British or foreign, including the discount houses. This step was inspired in part by the forthcoming British entry into the European Economic Community and the need to facilitate liaison with the banking industries of other member states, whose representative associations were organised on a similar basis. The Association is the British member of the European Banking Federation. At home, it has formed a series of committees which keep all aspects of money-market activity under review. To enable it effectively to take account of varying views within the Association in the regulation of the market, the Bank of England participates in many of these committees.

British Export Houses Association (BEHA). An organisation to advance the interests of its members, who consist of factors engaged in the business of the export trade, advancing money against debts owing from abroad and themselves undertaking the collection of such debts; confirming houses; and finance houses interested in export finance.

british overseas banks. British banks originally set up in the nineteenth century to provide banking facilities for settlers and traders in the colonies, but having their headquarters in London. In some countries their branches have been subjected to restriction in the course of the countries' development and in others they have been taken over and considerable adaptation has been necessary, particularly in adjusting to new opportunities in the business world and the emergence of major international companies. They have expanded in Europe and North America. They built up foreign currency deposits and participated in the money markets operations.

British Overseas and Commonwealth Banks' Association. An association formed in 1917 as the British Overseas Banks' Association. In 1964 the name was changed to the above as it included all the UK overseas banks and the London Offices of the Commonwealth banks. They are an affiliate of the British Bankers Association.

broker. An agent, a factor, a middleman, a person employed in the negotiation of commercial transactions between other parties in the interests of one of them. *See also* BILL BROKER; DEPOSIT BROKER; FOREIGN EXCHANGE BROKER; GOVERNMENT BROKER; INSURANCE BROKER; PRODUCE BROKER; STOCK BROKER.

brokerage. The commission charged by a broker for carrying out the instructions of a client, e.g. to buy or sell shares.

bronze coins. Coins of the lower denominations are of bronze; the alloy consists of ninety five parts of pure copper, four parts of tin, and one part of zinc. The bronze coins of the UK consists of one penny and two penny pieces. These are legal tender up to 20 pence.

bucket shop. Originally an office for gambling in grain or stocks for small amounts; the place of business of an *outside broker* who does not belong to any recognised stock exchange and who carries on risky and highly speculative business with questionable integrity. These days it often refers to travel agents who sell airline tickets at prices below the normal cost.

budget. The annual statement made by the Chancellor of the Exchequer in which the expected revenues and expenditure of the forthcoming year are estimated; a plan for systematic spending; a financial programme for an ensuing fiscal year. Its purpose is to provide an orderly administration of the financial affairs of an establishment to ensure their proper correlation and to achieve the most desirable results. It involves an examination of the past, taking stock of the present and setting priorities for future action. It is thus a report, an estimate and a proposal compounded into one. The Budget is presented to Parliament each year as a Finance Bill; when passed it becomes an Act.

budget account. A scheme to allow a customer to even out the regular payments which he or she has to make. The customer gives the details of usual outgoings to a bank which totals the annual cost, opens a budget account for the customer and issues him or her with a special budget account cheque book. Thereafter the bank will debit the customer's ordinary current account and credit the budget account with a monthly sum representing one-twelfth of the annual cost. The service costs a few pounds per year. Also a system of *credit-trading* operated by some big department stores by which the customer pays an agreed sum each month and in return obtains credit for a multiple of the sum. A service charge is built into the scheme.

budgetary control. The determination in advance of the financial requirement of a business in respect of expenditure anticipated and income necessary to meet the expenditure, and a subsequent comparison of the budgeted figures with actual costs and performances. Once a business target has been set, the next thing to do is to compare performance figures with target figures. This measure of performance will help management to find out the variances and the reasons for them. A continuous monitoring will help to determine how realistic or unrealistic the forecast is, and the adequacy or inadequacy of the machinery for carrying out the plan. *See also* STANDARD COSTING.

building agreement. A contract between a builder and the owner of a piece of land whereby the builder undertakes to build houses or flats on the land to meet certain specified standards, and the owner undertakes to grant a lease to each purchaser of a completed house, etc.

building lease. A lease by the freeholder for a term of years, usually 99 years, but sometimes 999 years, to a builder at a fixed ground rent. The builder undertakes to build houses upon this land and, when this has been done, to sell the houses to purchasers and sub-lease the individual plots to the individual buyers at a price, together with an increased ground rent. The right to receive the improved ground rents for the term of the lease may subsequently be sold to a finance company.

building societies. Societies existing to provide long-term loans for the acquisition of homes on the security of the houses and land so bought. In this capacity they are non-profit making bodies and their interest rates are loosely linked with money rates. To gather the funds which they need the societies must offer a rate sufficient to bring them in. If money is difficult to get, interest rates offered will have to be raised and this in turn will mean that mortgage rates will also have to go up. The present building societies maintain a variety of different accounts. Each building society gives the accounts offered by them an attractive name, but in broad detail they are basically, share accounts, deposit accounts and subscription accounts. All building societies are registered as friendly societies with the Registrar of Building Societies and the vast majority are members of the Building Societies Association. They are regulated by the Building Societies Act of 1986 which has expanded the role and activities of building societies in as much as they can now offer unsecured loans up to £5,000, offer standing orders, direct debits, ATMs, cash cards, cheque books, etc. They are also able to offer estate agency services, insurance, conveyancing, etc. They are now able to raise deposits on the wholesale money markets. While the services of building societies are growing, the number of societies offering these services is diminishing due to mergers.

bull. A speculator on the Stock Exchange who anticipates a rise in the value of a certain security and therefore buys such stocks, not intending to pay for the purchase, but hoping to sell them later, at a profit, before the settlement date.

'bulldog' bonds. Sterling issues by foreign borrowers in the British domestic market. Issues are usually priced to yield $\frac{1}{2}$-1 per cent more than the nearest equivalent gilt-edged security.

bullet. A straight debt issue without a sinking fund.

bullion. Gold or silver in bars or in specie. The term is also used to describe quantities of gold, silver or copper coins when measured by weight.

buoyancy. In an inflationary period, a tendency for stocks and shares to increase in price; revenue from taxation which is increasing as the result of rising prices and wages.

bureau de change. An office or place where currencies can be exchanged. Occasionally, banks which have a great deal of business in exchanging foreign currency will designate that counter or department with this name. In tourist areas of large towns, bureaux des change offer their services.

business development loan. A type of loan designed to meet the needs of smaller business for extended credit with planned and agreed repayments, which include interest charges. It is available for expenditure on property purchase, improvement or extension, the purchase of plant, machinery or vehicles, or the purchase of a business or professional practice, or by way of additional working capital for a new or existing business, or any other approved project. A term of from one to five years is usual, or, in exceptional cases, up to fifteen years. The term is phased on the appraisal of the profit flow and the expected life of any assets purchased with the proceeds of the loan. Interest is added to the initial amount of the loan and the total amount repaid in equal monthly instalments.

Business Expansion Scheme. With governmental encouragement, this scheme was started in 1981 to encourage investment in small unquoted trading companies. In order to encourage risk capital in these ventures, tax relief is available for invested amounts up to £40,000 per annum at the highest marginal rate if held for five years. The first year's disposal is exempt from CGT. The scheme does not apply to quoted companies or those on the USM, nor can employees, directors of the company, or the investor own more than 30 per cent of the capital.

business liability. Under the Unfair Contract Terms Act, 1977, this refers to a liability for breach of obligations or duties arising from anything done or to be done by any person in the course of business activity.

business names. Where in a business partners or a company trade under a name different from their own, they are using a business name. In the case of a company the name used may apply to some separate or distinct activity of the company and a banking account may be opened in a name which differs from that registered by the company. In the case of partners a descriptive title may be used to indicate the nature of the business, or originally true surnames may be retained for the sake of goodwill although partners may die and new partners may enter the business. A sole trader also may be trading under a name which is not his or her surname.

business start-up scheme. *See* BUSINESS EXPANSION SCHEME.

buyer. A person who buys, or agrees to buy goods, especially one who buys stock for a mercantile house.

buyer credit. An arrangement whereby an exporter negotiates a contract with an overseas buyer on a cash basis, the latter finding up to 20 per cent of the contract price and negotiating a separate loan from a UK bank for the balance owing to the exporter. The UK bank obtains an unconditional guarantee from the Export Credits Guarantee Department in respect of the principal and interest due from the buyer. These facilities are usually found for larger contracts (over £2 million), for which the repayment period is normally five years but can be as long as ten years. The buyer has the advantage of long-term credit, while the seller is virtually in the position of having cash payment, providing cover from ECGD has been obtained and they have approved the buyer credit finance.

buyer's market. A condition of markets in which goods are plentiful and there is little demand for them, so that the buyer can make his or her own terms.

buying in. If a seller of securities on the Stock Exchange has not delivered them to the purchaser by the proper time, they may be 'bought in' by an official of the Stock Exchange for delivery to the purchaser and any loss, charge, or expense must be borne by the seller.

buy-out. A scheme where a company is bought by its former management group, who have found the necessary capital, partly from their own resources, and partly from outside sources. Banks and other financial institutions are normally quite interested in putting up finance for good, viable businesses which are run by experienced managers who have an incentive to do well. Such a scheme nearly always occurs where the company has gone into liquidation. Management buy-outs have been seen in America for some years, often under the name 'leveraged buy-outs', reflecting the high proportion of loan finance to equity. Normally the amount of ordinary shares carrying voting rights is small, most of them are bought by the managers. The rest of the shareholding is often in non-voting preference stock, carrying a right of conversion into ordinary shares. The preference shares are very often unredeemable for the first five years with a redemption period spread over the following ten or twelve years.

C

CA. The abbreviation for the Companies Act. The designation for a member of the Institute of Chartered Accountants. The abbreviation for Court of Appeal.

cabinet bid. On the Stock Exchange Options Market 'Cabinet Bids' have been designed to aid the investor in his fight to stave off unnecessary taxation. Instead of allowing an 'out-of-the-money' option to expire (*See* TRADED OPTIONS), the cabinet bid system allows the holder to sell off his contract at 1p so that he may gain a contract note which will assist him *vis-à-vis* the Inland Revenue.

cable transfer. *See* TELEGRAPHIC TRANSFER.

C & F. *See* COST AND FREIGHT.

CAD. *See* CASH AGAINST DOCUMENTS.

CIF. *See* COST INSURANCE FREIGHT.

call. A demand by a company to shareholders for payment of an instalment, or the balance due on shares. This may refer to a period of flotation of a company, when the shareholders are usually asked to pay a certain portion of the capital on allotment and the remainder on call, or to any other time when a company, in need of more capital, calls up some or all of the uncalled capital on nil paid or partly paid shares. *See* OPTION.

callable fixture. Money at call or short notice forms the principal source of funds for the discount houses, whose representatives call at the various Head Offices of banks once each day to borrow or to arrange for repayment if the money is 'called'. It is an arrangement which suits both parties, the banks because this form of lending has reserve asset status, is undoubted, is invariably secured and can be recovered at very short notice; the discount houses because they can employ the funds in the financing of a 'book' of bills and short bonds, assets which they can use as security for their borrowing. The system of call money provides the banks with a means of balancing day-to-day shortages or surpluses, and is an integral part of the Bank of England's control over the amount of money in the banking system as a whole. An extension of this form of lending in recent years has been the so-called 'callable fixture'. This is money which is lent for a specified period of a few days to three months at a fixed rate of interest, but which may be called back at any time if the bank needs the funds.

call money. Money lent to bill brokers by bankers and others at interest on the terms that it is repayable 'at call' or on demand. The bankers are very happy to lend in this way to members of the discount market any surplus funds which they may have because such advances are fully secured and are practically certain to be repaid.

call option. *See* OPTION.

cancellable agreement. A regulated agreement which may be cancelled by the debtor or hirer in certain circumstances, such as where the debtor or hirer signs the agreement on premises which are not those of the creditor. Consumer Credit Act, 1974.

cancellation. A crossing out or an obliteration. A cheque is cancelled by the writing of the initials of the cancelling clerk in the paying bank across the signature of the drawer, or by perforation of the date on which payment is made, or by a stamp. A bill of exchange other than a cheque is cancelled by the cancellation of the acceptor's signature. Where a bill is intentionally cancelled by the holder or his agent, and the cancellation is apparent thereon, the bill is discharged. A bond or similar document is cancelled by writing across it the word 'cancelled' or by defacing it. A will is cancelled by revocation by the testator. *See also* REVOCATION OF WILL.

canvassing. Soliciting support, votes, contributions; for the purposes of the Consumer Credit Act, 1974, the soliciting of another person, the consumer, into a regulated agreement as debtor or hirer, or by oral persuasion, during a visit by the canvasser to a place which is not the business premises of the creditor, without having been asked to do so. (Sections 48 and 153.)

capacity. Power of containing or receiving, power to absorb; ability, scope; relative position, character or office; legal qualification. Capacity to incur liability as a party to a bill is coextensive with capacity to contract.

capital. Money used to run a business, often raised by an issue of shares; sums of invested money; the amount of money used or available to carry on a concern. *See also* AUTHORISED CAPITAL; CIRCULATING CAPITAL; FIXED CAPITAL; FLOATING CAPITAL; FREE CAPITAL; ISSUED CAPITAL; LIQUID CAPITAL; PAID UP CAPITAL; SHARE CAPITAL; SUBSCRIBED CAPITAL; VENTURE CAPITAL; WORKING CAPITAL.

capital account. In the accounts of a sole trader or partnership, it is the account that records the amount given by the owner/s to the business and used in the business, plus any profits that have been retained in the business. Any losses incurred in any financial period would be deducted from the balance.

capital allowances. Deductions allowed in a tax assessment for sums expended on certain capital equipment used in a business or profession. The allowances have to be specifically claimed.

capital asset. A term often used to denote the value of a fixed asset.

capital base. The Bank of England measures the capital of banks and deposit taking institutions under its control. The capital base is defined as paid-up capital, including ordinary and non-redeemable preference shares; subordinated loan capital, which incorporates no restrictive covenants, up to a maximum of one-third of the total capital base, and with the additional restriction that loan capital with less than five years to maturity is 'written down' to nothing on a straight-line basis; minority interests in subsidiary companies consolidated in the parent's accounts are included subject to scrutiny on an individual basis; so are general reserves, including inner reserves.

capital clause. This is a clause in the memorandum of association of a limited company which sets out the details of the authorised capital.

capital expenditure. The funds used to acquire fixed assets or to improve the efficiency or extend the life of an existing fixed asset.

capital gains tax (CGT). Introduced by the Finance Act 1965 to tax gains made on disposal of assets. Currently, in 1988/9, the first £5,000 of capital gains is free of tax and the remainder is subject to the same rate as the investor's marginal rate of income tax. *Not* subject to CGT include National Savings Certificates, the Yearly Plan, Friendly Society Bonds, insurance policies (subject to certain conditions), personal equity plans, gilt-edged stock and the first disposal of the Business Expansion Scheme. All gains made before 31 March 1982 are also exempt. After that date gains can be reduced in line with inflation.

capitalisation. Using a given rate of interest, the theoretical estimation of the capital amount representing the total sum lent or the periodic revenue; the stock exchange value of a company obtained by multiplying the share quotation by the number of issued shares.

capitalisation of profits. The conversion of retained profits into paid-up capital by a bonus share issue.

capitalised value. The value of an asset calculated by reference to its current annual earnings at the prevailing rate of interest.

capitalism. The economic system of employing capital to produce wealth; a form of economic, social and industrial organisation of society involving ownership, control and direction of production by privately owned business organisations.

capital redemption reserve fund. A reserve fund to be established by a company limited by shares which issues redeemable preference shares. In cases where such shares are redeemed otherwise than out of the proceeds of a fresh issue, there shall out of profits which would otherwise have been available for dividend, be transferred to a reserve fund (to be called the *capital redemption reserve fund*) a sum equal to the nominal amount of the shares redeemed, this fund to be regarded as equivalent to paid-up share capital of the company.

capital redemption yield. The profit made by holding a dated stock until redemption; the difference between the purchase price paid and the proceeds received on a redemption at par. It is usually expressed as a rate per cent, arrived at by dividing this figure by the number of years to redemption.

capital transfer tax (CTT). Since 1985 this has been replaced by inheritance tax. *See* INHERITANCE TAX.

captive insurance company. A subsidiary company set up by a large corporation to handle the group's insurance risks. Substantial savings can be made through retaining the profit element of the insurance contracts (although the larger risks would be laid off in the insurance market), particularly if the captive insurance company is established in a low-tax area, such as an offshore island, where the subsidiary can accumulate untaxed reserves for the benefit of the group generally.

cargo. Goods carried or taken on a ship or other vessel.

carnet. A book, a notebook. In the UK the term is used to describe the document by which exemption is obtained from the immediate payment of Customs dues.

carriage. Carrying, transporting, conveyance, especially of merchandise; the cost of conveying; the manner of carrying.

carriage forward. (of goods) to be paid on arrival.

carriage inward. The expense incurred in bringing goods purchased to the purchaser's premises.

carriage outward. The expense incurred in transporting the goods sold.

carry over. On the Stock Exchange, to continue a bargain from another account, to postpone the settlement of an account from one settling day to another.

cartel. An agreement among manufacturers to keep the price of their products at an artificially high level; an industrial combination for the purpose of regulating price and the amount of product.

case law. The law built up by judges from their case decisions.

case in need. The person whose name may be included in a bill of exchange by a drawer or by any indorser, so that such person may act as a 'referee in case of need' – that is, he can be contacted by the holder if the bill is dishonoured by non-acceptance or non-payment. When referring to *documentary collections,* the case in need, named by the remitter (exporter) will only have such authority to deal with the documents and/or goods as stated on the collection order.

cash. Generally considered to be made up by banknotes and coin plus deposits at the banks but a wider use of the word may include not only cash but those things which can readily be turned into cash, such as any readily negotiable instrument.

cash account. An account recording the payments in and out of cash and cheques, and showing the balance on the account as cash in hand.

cash against document (CAD). The delivery by the presenting bank to the importer of commercial documents against immediate payment.

cash at bank. The amount of money that a business will have on deposit with a bank or authorised institution. Amounts on current account can be withdrawn on demand, while amounts in a deposit account may be made available after due notice has been given.

cash basis. The delivery of goods against immediate payment.

cash bonus. A sum in cash given over and above any fixed amount of salary or wages; a *share of the profits* of a life assurance company paid to the assured in cash, in place of being used to increase the amount ultimately payable, or to reduce the amount of the premium.

cash book. A book containing a record of all transactions going through the cash and bank accounts. Three column cash books will contain one column for recording discounts received and discounts given.

cash card. Cards issued to customers of banks to enable them to obtain cash at any time of the day or night from a machine called either a cash dispenser or *automated teller machine* (ATM). The card is made of plastic and by introducing the card into the slot provided and by pressing the keys to give the *personal identification number* (PIN), funds up to agreed amount can be obtained, plus balances. The ordering of cheque books and statements can also be done by ATM.

cash discount. Discount allowed on a bill not yet due, in consideration of immediate payment or payment

before a stated date; a deduction from the invoice amount may be taken.

cash dispenser. A machine (ATM) situated either in the outwall of a bank or available inside the banking hall to enable persons with cash cards to withdraw funds as and when required. Many banks have their own names for these machines, e.g. Servicetill, Autobank, etc. *See* AUTOMATED TELLER MACHINE: CASH CARD.

cash float. An amount of money a bank cashier will keep to enable him to either give change to customers or cash their cheques. *Retailers* will also maintain a cash float, so that cash in small denominations is available when giving change to customers.

cash flow. The pattern of the flow of cash within a business over a period of time. This will be ascertained by calculating the profit of the business, adding the depreciation on assets, plus the receipt of any capital funds, less the outflow of either a capital or revenue nature.

cashier's check. American terminology for a banker's draft. *See* BANKER'S DRAFT.

cash in hand. The amount of money held in the form of notes and coin by a person or business as opposed to 'cash at bank'.

cash limit. The amount of cash that can be spent by a business for a given purpose in a given period. It also refers to the amount that can be drawn by a customer from an *ATM* or the amount given on an *overdraft* or loan.

cash management. A bank service introduced in the UK in 1982 to provide corporate treasurers with a means by which they can speedily obtain from a single source the details of their company's bank accounts in the UK and world-wide. The service consists of computer-based modules, available through the customer's own terminal, linked by telephone to the world wide time sharing network of Automatic Data Processing Network

Services. The balance-reporting module collects, consolidates and reports the data of the customer's bank account in any location or currency. Transaction reporting can show either the total of debits and credits, or details of all transactions passing through the account. Balance history reports are also available to give a trend of the account activity.

cash on delivery (COD). A service provided by the Post Office where the purchaser of mail order goods pays the postman.

cash ratio. The amount of cash held in a bank's tills or as a balance at the Bank of England, expressed as a percentage of the total of customers' balances held on current or deposit account. The Bank of England may insist on a certain cash ratio being retained by banks.

cast/casting. The act of adding or totalling figures; addition of figures.

catchment area. By analogy with the area in which water collects to form a river, the physical area of the country which contains the new staff which a bank needs to recruit; or the area from which a branch bank will draw its business. The establishment of a new branch, for example, must take into consideration the factors which will bring customers in, such as position of the branch, the local shopping facilities, the population figure, housing, industry and commerce and competitors.

caution. In registered land, a way of protecting certain interests of a lender or interested party by lodging a notice at the Land Registry; the name of the notice so lodged. Thus a pending action affecting the land would be subject of a caution. In Scotland the word means a *guarantee* by a third person to the court that a trustee in bankruptcy who has just been so nominated by the creditors, will faithfully perform his duties.

caveat. A warning, a caution; a *legal process* to stop procedure.

caveat emptor. 'Let the buyer beware'. The seller is not obliged to volunteer information about the property being sold, although he must answer relevant questions truthfully.

cedel. A clearing system for the Euro-currency market, based in Luxembourg and owned by several European banks. It is used by several European banks. It is used for the settlement of security transactions, especially of Eurobond business.

ceiling. The upper limit of production, wages, prices, etc; a *borrowing limit* for a customer maintained at Head Office or regional or area office of a bank, being somewhat above that recorded at the branch and agreed with the customer.

central bank. The bank in any country which is authorised by the government of the country to control the amount of credit in the country, to supervise the operations of the commercial banks, to carry out the business of the government and to maintain its accounts, to control the note issue and the country's reserves, and to preserve the value of the country's currency on the foreign exchanges. Such a bank may be working under a finance ministry, as in the UK, or enjoying a greater degree of independence from governmental control, as in West Germany or the USA.

central processing unit (CPU). That part of a computer installation which performs actual calculations and regulates the performance of its peripherals. Micro-circuitry and silicon chip technology have vastly reduced the size of the CPUs and equally enhanced their speed and power. 'Desk top' computers may well house a CPU, an operator's keyboard, visual display units (VDUs) and/or a printer all in one case. Nevertheless, these latter 'peripherals' and the CPU are still separate units, and in the large installations, as used by British clearing banks are separately housed machines.

certificate. A written testimony to the truth of a fact.

certificate of bonds. A certificate issued to a holder of registered bonds particularising the bonds which are registered in his name.

certificate of charge. A sealed certificate issued by the Land Registry when a lender registers a charge on registered land. It has the original charge, signed by the borrower, stitched inside it. As evidence of title it takes the place of the land certificate, which is withdrawn during the currency of the charge.

certificate of deposit. Evidence of a deposit with a bank repayable on a fixed date. It is a fully negotiable bearer document transferable by delivery. To ensure the marketability of the certificate there needs to be what is called a 'secondary' market, that is, somewhere where the holder of the certificate can sell it if he or she so wishes. The *secondary market* is provided by the discount houses and the banks in the inter-bank market. See Finance Act, 1968, s. 55. These can be issued either in sterling or US Dollars. *See also* STERLING CERTIFICATE OF DEPOSIT; DOLLAR CERTIFICATE OF DEPOSIT.

certificate of existence (life certificate). A certificate issued by a banker or solicitor to the effect that a customer or client was communicated with on a certain day and that a reply was obtained, or that he/she was visited and seen on that day. Such certificates are often required by companies paying annuities, as proof that the beneficiary is still alive.

certificate of fair rent. A certificate issued by a rent officer to a person who wishes to build, let, or convert premises which, when let, will be subject to the provisions of the Rent Acts. The certificate is not a final estimate of the rent which will be obtainable, but is intended to be an indication of the economic return to be expected.

certificate of incorporation. A certificate granted by the *Registrar of Companies* to a company just formed, after completion of certain formalities, stating that the company has been duly registered and is now incorporated under the Companies Acts. Before the granting of this certificate the company has no legal power to conduct business or to maintain a banking account. The banker should inspect this certificate and note the particulars in the bank's records.

certificate of insurance. A certificate issued by an insurance broker as evidence that a marine insurance has been effected. Such a certificate is not acceptable to a buyer under a CIF contract because the right of the insured cannot be transferred by indorsement and delivery of a certificate, but only of the policy of insurance, unless the certificate is one issued by Lloyds.

certificate of misfortune. *See* CERTIFIED BANKRUPT.

certificate of mortgage or sale of ship. A document issued by the registrar of the port at which a ship is registered to a registered owner who wishes to mortgage or sell the ship (or any share of it) to any person in any country other than the one in which the port of registry is situate, in order to enable this to be done.

certificate of origin. A certificate issued and signed by *Chambers of Commerce* confirming the place of growth, production or manufacture of goods.

certificate of posting. A certificate issued by a post office for a small charge to evidence the posting of a letter or packet.

certificate of protest. The official document given by a notary public, solicitor or householder evidencing the dishonour by non-acceptance or non-payment of a bill of exchange. Such a certificate is accepted as proof of dishonour in a court of law. A protest must contain a copy of the bill, and must be signed by the notary making it and must specify 1. the *person* at whose request the bill is protested; 2. the *place* and date of protest, the cause or reason for protesting the bill, the demand made, and the answer given, if any, or the fact that the drawee or acceptor could not be found. *See also* HOUSE-HOLDER'S PROTEST.

certificate of registration. A document issued by the *Registrar of Companies* evidencing conclusively that any mortgage or charge given by a limited company, and requiring registration under the provisions of the Companies Act, 1985 has been so registered.

certificate of search. A document issued by the *Registrar of a Charges or Land Register* giving the result of a search made in the register in respect of certain properties or names at the request of a lender against such property, or other interested party. Such a certificate is also issued in respect of certain local land charges by *local authorities*.

certificate of survey. A document issued by a Port Surveying Officer in respect of the outward appearance and condition of goods discharged from a vessel.

certificate of tax. *See* TAX CERTIFICATE.

certificate to commence business. A document issued by the *Registrar of Companies* to a public company in evidence that all the necessary formalities have been completed and that the public company now has official permission to commence trading. A private company requires no such certificate.

certified accountant. A member of the Chartered Association of Certified Accountants (ACCA).

certified bankrupt. A person who has been made bankrupt but who subsequently obtains his discharge from the court, together with a certificate to the effect that his bankruptcy was caused by misfortune without any misconduct on his behalf. *See also* CERTIFICATE OF MISFORTUNE.

certified check. Probably as secure as a UK bankers' draft, a certified check in the US is a customer's cheque which has been authenticated and guaranteed by a bank *See* MARKED CHEQUE. The certification guarantees that sufficient funds have been made available to meet the check upon presentation; in practical terms, the bank is responsible for paying the check.

certified interlocutor. In Scotland, the decree of the court. *See* JUDGMENT. It is this which empowers the pursuer *(q.v.)* in whose favour it is pronounced to give practical effect to the findings of the court.

certified transfer. A stock or share transfer form which has been marked in the margin with the words 'certificate lodged' by the Registrar of a company as evidence that the certificate for the stock or shares dealt with has been delivered to the Registrar's office. The certificate may be by rubber stamp, usually initialled or signed by an authorised company officer. The device is commonly used where part only of a holding has been sold and therefore, the certificate has to be split.

certiorari. An order at the discretion of the court which, if granted, operates to bring before the High Court for review any case decided or pending in an inferior court.

cestui que trust. The person on whose behalf land is held.

chain of representation. The mere naming of a man as executor in a will does not bind him to accept the duty, but usually (where the executor is a private person) the relationship is one based on friendship and trust. Because of this if *B,* an executor, dies before winding up of *A*'s estate, and *B* has name his executor as *C, C* will deal with *B*'s estate and will also finish the administration of *A*'s estate. Although perhaps *A* did not know *C,* he knew and trusted *B,* and *B* knew and trusted *C.* This is a 'chain' of executorship or representation.

chain of title. In the proof of title to land, the sequence of deeds and documents from the good root of title to the holding deed.

chairman's statement. A report by the chairman of a company which is published in the annual report and accounts of that company, setting out the opinions of that person regarding the past years trading and his or her views on the future prospects of the company.

chamber. A place where a legislative assembly meets; *the assembly* itself; a *hall of justice;* an *association* of persons for the promotion of some common object.

chamber of commerce. An association of businessmen formed to protect their commercial and trading interests in one particular area.

character. A term in data processing used to signify a term, fact, input or output.

charge. An office, duty or care; to debit; ask a price for; to take a pledge, mortgage or assignment of security belonging to a borrowing customer. In Scots law, a formal demand on a debtor for payment.

chargeable assets. Assets which are not exempt from capital gains tax.

chargeable gain. In accordance with the Capital Gains Act, 1979, it is the surplus between the receipt of the proceeds of a sale of an asset and the cost of its purchase, which unless it is exempt under the above act is chargeable for tax purposes.

charge account. An account held by a customer with a retail organisation where the purchases of the customer

are recorded and periodically (monthly) a statement is sent to the customer showing the amounts charged to the account and the balance due.

charges. In banking, the total cost of keeping the customer's account, traditionally divided into commission and interest on overdraft, and debited to the account quarterly or half-yearly; a bundle of cheques presented for payment by one bank, being a member of the Clearing House, to another through the medium of the House; mortgages, pledges or assignments over property given by customers to banks as security against accommodation; for tax purposes, reductions in income of taxpayers which operate to reduce the amount of tax payable. Charges on income for tax purposes must be legal charges such as annual payment by the taxpayer which he is committed to making by his signature on a legal document e.g. an annual payment under a deed of covenant.

charge card. A card issued by a large retail organisation to a person (cardholder) who may use the card for the purpose of buying goods – up to the credit limit available – and settling the account on presentation of a statement.

charges register. *See* LAND CERTIFICATE.

charging order. An order obtained from the court by a judgment creditor 1. charging property of the debtor with the amount of the debt. The effect of the order is to stop all transactions in respect of the property so charged for six months. If by that time the debtor has not paid, the creditor can get an order for sale from the court and take the benefit of the property; 2. charging securities belonging to a debtor with the amount of the debt; 3. charging money paid into court by the debtor; 4. placing a stop order on funds in court.

charitable company. A company

formed for the purpose of promoting art, science, religion, charity or any other like object, not involving the acquisition of gain by the company or by its individual members.

charitable trust. A trust for the relief of poverty, for the advancement of education or religion, or for the benefit of the community in some other way.

charity. As respects England and Wales, a charity which is registered under the Charities Act, 1960, or any exempt charity within the meaning of that Act; as respects Scotland and Northern Ireland, an institution or other organisation established for charitable purposes only.

charter. An instrument in writing granted by Parliament or by the Sovereign, incorporating a certain company or institution, or conferring certain rights or privileges; a formal document confirming privileges, titles or rights; the hiring of a vessel; to hire as a ship.

chartered accountant. One qualified under the regulations of the Institute of Chartered Accountants in England and Wales, Scotland or Ireland.

chartered company. A company deriving its authority to carry on business, not from the Companies Acts, but from a special charter granted by the Crown.

Chartered Association of Certified Accountants. A professional body of accountants who practise their profession either as accountants in public practice or who are engaged as accountants in public or private companies in industry or commerce.

Chartered Institute of Bankers (CIoB). 10 Lombard Street London EC3V 9AS and an office in Canterbury. The Chartered Institute of Bankers, founded in 1879, and granted Royal Charter in 1987, is one of the oldest professional bodies and certainly one of the biggest, with about 120,000 members engaged in banking and finance all over the world. The aims of the Institute are two-fold; to provide the educational foundation on which any man or woman can build a banking/financial career; and to keep its members in touch with the latest developments in banking and business generally. Like other professional bodies, the Institute maintains educational standards through qualifications which are awarded to those who are successful in the examinations. The Institute's members are men and women engaged in banking and finance at all levels. They range from full time students, trainees who have just left school or university to chief executives and directors. Membership is individual. Banks as banks are not members. The whole emphasis is on personal development. Associates of the Chartered Institute of Bankers (ACIB) are elected exclusively from those who have passed their Associateship examinations. For those members who wish to only reach a supervisory grade in their careers, are able to obtain by examination a Banking Certificate. Graduates of relevant degrees and associate members who wish to further their knowledge of banking may study and obtain the Financial Studies Diploma (FSD). Fellows (FCIB) are elected by the Council from Associates who have achieved senior professional status. Their function is to give a lead in Institute affairs at both national and local level. Policy is decided by an elected Council, and the central administration is in London. However the membership is so large and so widespread that many of these activities are organised by a network of local centres. These local centres – in the UK and abroad – are organised by the local members, who run seminars debates, group discussions, lectures and industrial visits, all of which make their contribution to professional education. The centres also help bankers to play their role in their local communities by bringing them into social and professional contact with other organisations in the area. The Institute publishes text books, study guides and other books on banking. The Institute's library in London contains an outstanding collection of financial commercial books and periodicals, and also provides information service facilities for the use of Institute members. At national level, the Institute runs seminars, management courses and study tours. Internationally, the annual International Banking Summer School attracts senior bankers from more than fifty countries to discuss topics of professional importance. This was started in 1948 and is now held all over the world, returning periodically to the United Kingdom. Further information about the Institute and details about its examinations are obtainable from its London headquarters.

Chartered Institute of Public Finance and Accountancy (CIPFA). An association of treasurers and financial officers of British public and local authorities. An important section of its work, which is to promote the best interests of its members and to maintain a high standard, is carried on by its Loans' Bureau which channels funds from commercial, industrial and private lenders to those local authorities desiring to borrow, and also direct funds from local authorities having cash surpluses to those looking for a loan. The Bureau keeps in close touch with the rates and trends in the interbank market and in other sterling markets.

charter party. A contract between the owners of a ship and the charterer, whereby the vessel is hired to, or placed at the disposal of, the charterer for a certain voyage or for a certain time for the conveyance of goods.

charter party bill of lading. A bill of lading which is subject to the terms and conditions of the charter party.

chattels. All property other than freehold land.

chattels personal. Goods, furniture and other articles capable of complete transfer by delivery, and, when separately assigned, fixtures and growing crops as soon as severed from the land.

chattels real. Leasehold property.

cheap money. Money which can be borrowed at a low rate of interest.

checking account. The American term for a bank current account. This term is being used with greater frequency in the UK.

cheque. A bill of exchange payable on demand, drawn on a banker (Bills of Exchange Act, 1882). *See also* ANTE-DATED CHEQUE; BEARER BILL; BLANK CHEQUE; CROSSED CHEQUE; MARKED CHEQUE; OPEN CHEQUE; ORDER CHEQUE; PAYMENT OF CHEQUES; STOPPED CHEQUE; TRAVEL CHEQUES.

cheque as an assignment of funds. In England a cheque does not operate as an assignment of funds, but in Scotland, where the drawee of a bill has in his or her hands funds available for the payment of it, the bill operates as an assignment of the sum for which it is drawn in favour of the holder, from the time when the bill is presented to the drawee. Thus, if the balance of an account is not sufficient to pay a bill or cheque, nevertheless the presentation of the instrument operates to assign the available funds. When the instrument is returned unpaid, the balance must on the same day be transferred to an *attached funds* account.

cheque book. A book of cheque forms, usually containing twenty five or thirty cheque forms. For the corporate customer, cheque books containing five hundred or more cheques are available. The cheque will normally be of a design of the drawee bank, but with the approval of the bank and providing the paper and details conform to the criteria laid down by the Committee of London and Scottish Clearing Banks, customers can arrange to have their own cheque books printed.

cheque book register. A record, usually kept on the computer of the bank, of cheque books issued to customers.

cheque card. A piece of plastic about 85mm by 54mm, bearing (in the UK) an amount of £50, the name of the bank, the name and signature of the customer, the sorting code number of the branch maintaining his account, the card number and the expiry date. It is normally renewed annually. The issuing bank undertakes that any cheque not exceeding £50 will be honoured as long as the cheque has been signed in the presence of the payee, is drawn on a bank cheque form whose code number agrees with the code number on the card, and is authenticated by a signature which agrees with the specimen signature on the card. The cheque must be drawn before the expiry date of the card, and the card number must also be written on the reverse of the cheque by the payee. *See also* EUROCHEQUE SCHEME.

cheque rate. The cost in one country of the purchase of a cheque or sight draft drawn in the currency of another country.

Cheques Act, 1957. This very important Act protects the paying banker when paying cheques without an endorsement (s. 1). It protects the collecting banker when collecting cheques for a customer who has not endorsed the cheque. Section 4 of the Act protects the banker who in good faith and without negligence collects a cheque either for himself or herself or a customer.

chief rent. A perpetual rent charge to which freehold land may be subject. In default of payment the owner of the chief rent has a right of re-entry upon the land.

Chief Registrar of Friendly Societies. Under the Building Societies Act 1962 the Chief Registrar obtains powers to register friendly societies, to receive annual returns and if necessary appoint inspectors to investigate the affairs of any society. The Chief Registrar has powers of responsibility over the conduct of Building Societies, *inter alia* to investigate a society, approve or withhold approval of any society, etc.

chinese wall. A type of organisational structure met with where bankers have to combine their business of banking with that of investment advice or investment management. In such cases there might be a danger of sensitive information passing from one department to another, to the advantage of the bank or some person connected with, or working for, the bank, unless proper safeguards are in force. The 'chinese wall' ensures that the business of the separate divisions of the banking organisation – investment advice, investment management, banking, corporate financial services – are kept rigidly apart, so that no improper information can pass from one to the other. An example would be the division of duties and responsibilities between the managers of a bank unit trust, and the trustee company which is another subsidiary of the same bank, where the principle that the management company and the trustee must be quite independent of each other is scrupulously observed. The importance of the 'Chinese Wall' type of organisation has been much increased by the provisions on insider dealing contained in the 1980 Companies Act and the 1985 Companies Act.

chose in action. A right enforceable in a court of law.

chose in possession. A sum of money or a good in the actual possession of the owner.

CIF. *See* COST; INSURANCE; FREIGHT.

circulating capital. Property bought with the intention that it shall be resold over a short period at a profit. Such property is completely changed in form or used up in the preparation of a new product. Thus, in a manufacturing company, cash is converted into new materials, which are made up into finished goods, which are sold for cash or to debtors who will in a short time pay cash.

CIoB. *See* CHARTERED INSTITUTE OF BANKERS.

circulating medium. Money such as banknotes or any other form used as a means of exchange.

cite. To quote, to allege as an authority; to quote as an instance; to refer to; to summons to appear in court.

cital. A summons, a citation.

city. A collective description of the financial institutions of the City of London.

city code on taker-overs and mergers. The published rules setting out the rules to be observed during any merger or take over by all parties concerned.

claim. A real or supposed right; a title; in taxation, a claim for an allowance, normally made by inserting the appropriate particulars in the annual tax return, or for a refund of tax, as where dividends form part of the income and the total of the personal allowances exceeds earnings plus any other untaxed income. Part or all of the tax deducted from interest will then be repayable on the claim.

claim form. An inter-branch form used when one branch of a bank claims upon another for a sum due as a result of some customer transaction e.g. for an unpaid cheque.

claused bill of lading. A bill of lading that has a clause or notation either in writing, typed, or stamped, stating that either the goods or packaging is in a defective condition.

claw back. A term used originally to describe a refund of tax due to the taxpayer; more recently a recovery by the Inland Revenue of tax relief formerly granted, notably in the case of certain family allowances and in

some cases of early surrender or conversion of life policies. Claw back is also instanced in connection with stock relief, where deferred tax becomes payable. The phrase is also used in more general commercial terms for obtaining a recovery of funds paid to a third party.

Clayton's case: *Devaynes* v. *Noble* **(1916).** This important old case has left two lessons: 1. where a debtor keeps two or more accounts with a creditor, and pays such creditor a sum of money in reduction, the debtor has the right to allocate or appropriate his payment to such account as he may choose. If the debtor does not exercise this right of appropriation, the creditor is free to do so. 2. the Rule in *Clayton's case* is of great importance to bankers, and its operation is frequently guarded against in bank forms of charge. The rule is as follows: *'In a running account payments in are presumed to be appropriated to payments out in the order in which the items occur'*. In a credit account, therefore, credits are paid in before debits are paid, and the money paid into the bank is regarded as being available to meet the debits in date order. In an overdrawn account the credits paid in are similarly allocated towards repayment of the debits and therefore in reduction of the overdraft. This reduction is often concealed by the payment of fresh debits. To avoid the operation of the Rule an overdrawn account must be ruled off on notice of certain events (notice of a second mortgage, notice of death of a partner, expiry of notice of termination of a guarantee) to protect the bank's position. A new account must be opened to continue the customer's business and will normally be maintained in credit. The overdrawn balance of the old account is left as it stands and must not be taken into account in the working of the new account. If the overdrawn account is not broken in this way (and if any form of charge does not guard against the risk), as the running account continues to operate, credits as they are paid in are deemed to repay the old overdraft (which was secured, or in respect of which there was a claim against a guarantor or his estate, or a deceased partner's private estate), while fresh debits as they are paid gradually build up a new overdraft which is not secured, or in respect of which there is no claim against a person or his estate.

clean bill. A bill of exchange or any other negotiable instrument which has no commercial documents attached.

clean bill of lading. A bill of lading which has no superimposed clauses which indicate that either the goods or packaging are in any way defective or damaged.

clean credit. A credit opened by a banker which provides for payment by the banker of bills drawn upon him, but such bills having no commercial documents attached.

clean rate. A dealer's term for a rate on a deposit where no certificate of deposit has been issued.

clearance. Completion of the formalities and procedure before a ship or an aircraft may leave; of a *bill or cheque,* the obtaining of money in place of the bill or cheque; *of goods,* the performance of duties and formalities which are necessary before goods can be dispatched or allowed to enter e.g. customs duties.

clear days. Days reckoned exclusively of those on which a notice is given and those on which some event, in respect of which the notice was issued, takes place.

clearing. Presenting a cheque, draft or other negotiable instrument, through the banking procedure, that is the presentation for its ultimate payment through the Clearing House by the drawee bank. *See also* IN CLEARING; OUT CLEARING.

clearing bank. Any bank which is a member of any of the subsidiary companies of the *Association of Payment Clearing Services* (APACS). The clearing companies and their member clearing banks are as follows. Cheque and Credit Clearing Co. Ltd: *Bank of England; Barclays Bank; Bank of Scotland; Co-operative Bank; Lloyds Bank; Midland Bank; Girobank; National Westminster Bank; the Royal Bank of Scotland; TSB England and Wales.*

Chaps and Town Clearing Ltd: *Bank of England; Bank of Scotland; Barclays Bank; Citibank; Clydesdale Bank; Co-operative Bank; Coutts & Co; Lloyds Bank; Midland Bank; Girobank; National Westminster Bank; the Royal Bank of Scotland; Standard Chartered Bank; TSB England and Wales.*

Bankers' Automated Clearing Services Ltd: *Bank of England; Bank of Scotland; Barclays Bank; Clydesdale Bank; Co-operative Bank; Coutts & Co; Lloyds Bank; Midland Bank; Girobank; National Westminster Bank; the Royal Bank of Scotland; TSB England and Wales; Yorkshire Bank.* The Abbey National and Halifax Building Societies are also members of this clearing company.

clearing house. The Clearing House of the Committee of London and Scottish Clearing Banks is situated in 10 Lombard Street, where it has been since its origin in the 1770s. Representatives of each of the clearing banks attend there each business day to exchange bills of exchange and cheques, etc drawn upon each other, and to settle for them.

Clearing House Automated Payments System (CHAPS). This is the automated part of the Chaps and Town Clearing Co. Ltd. The participating banks are able, through the terminals in each of their town branches, to transmit and receive large payments. The banks/branches using this system are known as settlement banks and the system can be used as follows: 1. urgent payments received from abroad; 2. telephonic requests from branches outside the town area to make urgent payments to branches of other banks outside the town area. The recipient bank will on receipt of funds advise the beneficiary branch by the quickest possible means; 3. non-settlement banks wishing to pay same-day value funds to another bank; 4. large corporate customers who wish to pay funds to another. The system will give same day value and has a built in series of checks and audits and should a discrepancy occur remedial action can be taken immediately.

Clearing House Interbank Payments System (CHIPS). CHIPS is a system for paying and receiving funds through the use of electronic terminals situated at banks who are members or associates of the CHIPS system. Banks within the system include the twelve New York Clearing House Association members and other banking institutions which participate by either affiliation or association. Associate members, which include many foreign banks operating in the US must select a correspondent, one of the twelve member banks, through which daily CHIPS transactions will be settled. Once the system has closed on any business day, the clearing house notifies each designated clearing bank of the net credit or debit positions of each customer associate member. A 'due to CHIPS' balance of an associate member bank is cleared by drawing down on its balances or credit line established at the correspondent or clearing house member bank. A 'due from CHIPS' is cleared by credits made to the associate member's account with its correspondent bank. Correspondent banks, which are all members of the Federal Reserve System, settle their own and their associate members' net positions with each other through balances maintained at the Federal Reserve Bank of New York. CHIPS is essentially a New York City System; nationwide transfers in the US are carried out through the *Fed Wire,* which is a clearing house system used by members of the Federal Reserve System.

clients' accounts. Current or deposit accounts in the name of a solicitor at a bank, in the title of which account the word 'client' appears. Under the Solicitors' Act, 1974, money held for clients must be kept separate from the solicitor's personal or office accounts. They should not become overdrawn. There is no set-off between clients' accounts and the personal or office accounts. Clients' accounts must also be maintained for estate agents, dealers and investment managers and insurance brokers.

close company. A category of company whether public or private, which has been established by legislation for tax purposes. It is a company which is under the control of five or fewer persons being directors, however many directors there may in fact be; or a company in which a person is considered to hold control by possessing a major portion of the capital or voting rights; or a company in which such a person would, in the event of the company going into liquidation be entitled to more than 50 per cent of the assets. Excepted are companies not resident in the UK, companies controlled by the Crown, and registered industrial and provident societies.

closing entries. The entries which close off standing accounts at the times when the books are balanced.

closing prices. The final prices quoted on a market at the end of the trading for the day, especially those on a stock exchange.

closing rate. In the foreign exchange markets the rates for the purchase/sale of spot currency at the close of that day's business. For balance sheet purposes, a company will use the closing rate of exchange in order to produce balance sheet and profit and loss accounts, in order to calculate its various foreign currency accounts into the notional value of the home currency.

closing stock. The value of all raw materials, work in progress and finished goods at the end of the trading period.

club. *See* UNINCORPORATED ASSOCIATION.

COD. The abbreviation for 'cash on delivery'.

code number. An integral part of the PAYE system of tax deduction. The net allowances, less any untaxed interest, of any taxpayer are listed on a notice of coding and the net total is given a code number by reference to a list of allowances at various levels. An employer is thereby enabled to look up the appropriate code number for any employee in the tax tables issued to the employer and so to discover the correct amount of tax to be deducted weekly or monthly and subsequently handed over to the Collector of Taxes.

codicil. An additional document varying the terms of a will or revoking part of it. The codicil must be signed by the testator and witnessed in a similar fashion to the execution of a will.

codifying statute. An act which codifies the whole of case and statute law on a particular matter. One of the earliest of such statutes was the Bills of Exchange Act, 1882, with the recent Companies Act, 1985 having the same effect.

coin. A piece of metal stamped and current as money; money, especially coined money; to mint or stamp, as money; to acquire money rapidly, to invent, to fabricate, to make counterfeit money.

coinage. The act of coining; the pieces coined; the monetary system in use.

coin of the realm. The coins authorised for circulation in the UK are the penny (1p), two pence (2p), Ten pence (10p), Twenty pence (20p), fifty pence (50p) and the one pound (£1). Under the Coinage Act, 1971, coins have limited legal tender as follows: up to 20p (1p and 2p coins), up to £5 (5p and 10p coins), up to £10 (20p and 50p coins).

collateral. Subsidiary, concurrent, subordinate; additional security, security deposited by a third party, as opposed to primary security deposited by the borrower. In USA the word has the same meaning as our word 'security'.

collecting banker. The banker who collects for his or her customer's account the proceeds of bills, cheques and other instruments which have been paid in to the bank for that purpose. If the customer has a faulty title (as where it has been obtained by fraud) the collecting banker may be sued by the true owner for the tort of conversion. The collecting banker can look to statutory protection against this claim so long as he or she has collected the cheque(s) in question in good faith, without negligence and for a customer. (Cheques Act, 1954 s.4).

collection. The handling by banks of a *financial* document with or without *commercial* documents; or the handling of *commercial* documents with or without a financial document. Uniform *Rules for Collection* define the dealing with the presentation, acceptance, payment and other matters regarding all collections whether documentary or clean.

collection order. The written instructions from a customer (the principal) instructing the bank (the agent) on the presentation and ultimate payment of the specified documents. Instructions should also be received in the event of non-acceptance or non-payment of the draft/documents.

collector of taxes. An official of the Inland Revenue whose job it is to collect the taxes as notified by the Inspector of Taxes.

co-manager. Bank ranking next after the lead manager in the marketing of a new issue.

combine. A permanent or temporary

association of two or more firms or companies for business purposes; an association of persons formed to control the course of trade, especially in relation to prices; a cartel, a trust.

combined transport. The carriage of goods by at least two modes of transport.

combined transport bill of lading. A bill issued to cover goods transported in containers, etc. It covers both the sea journey and the journey overland to the final inland destination. Such bills are acceptable in cover of banking facilities and should show the goods as 'shipped on board m.v. at '.

comfort letter. *See* LETTER OF COMFORT.

commercial bank. A bank licensed under the Banking Act, 1987. This term is often used to refer to those banks involved in international trade and corporate banking.

commercial bill. A bill of exchange drawn against a commercial transaction. The expression is also used to cover all bills other than Treasury Bills.

commercial court. The court that hears actions arising from disputes between merchants, traders and others. It will also deal with the interpretation of mercantile and commercial documents, export and import, banking, insurance and other mercantile phraseology that has led to a legal action.

commercial documents. Amongst the most common documents are Invoices, Documents of Movement, Insurance Documents, Certificates of Origin, or any other documents that are likely to be given to a bank for the purpose of a collection.

commercial intelligence department. A department in a bank or large organisation which provides information for the bank/organisation, for customers or traders on the conditions of trade in various countries or provides reports on buyers at home or overseas.

commercial invoice. A commercial document which describes the goods, unit and/or total price, shipping terms, buyer's and seller's references, etc.

commercial paper. A US and UK term for unsecured promissory notes issued by, generally large US and UK corporations. Commercial paper represents a major source of short-term funds for a company although only financially strong, highly rated borrowers have access to the market. Most commercial paper carries an initial maturity of sixty days or less and to ensure payment at maturity, issuers often maintain back up lines of credit at banks. Investors in commercial paper tend to be large institutions such as insurance companies and bank trust departments; because of its relatively low risk and short maturity, commercial paper can be regarded as a close substitute for Treasury Bills, certificates of deposit and other money market instruments.

commission. An allowance made to a factor or agent; a percentage, a charge.

commission agent. A person who buys and sells goods for another, receiving a percentage for the contracts so arranged.

commissioner for oaths. A solicitor legally authorised to administer oaths.

commission on current account. A charge made by bankers keeping current accounts which do not maintain a sufficiently profitable cleared average balance.

Commissioners of Inland Revenue. Officers of the Inland Revenue appointed to hear appeals by the taypayer/s. The General Commissioners are lay persons and unpaid. Special Commissioners and full-time civil servants who are specialists in the law of taxation.

committee. A board elected or deputed to examine, consider and report on any business referred to them; the executive body of an unincorporated society.

committee of inspection. A committee appointed by resolution of creditors for the purpose of superintending the administration of a bankrupt's property by the trustee, or of a company's winding up by the liquidator.

Committee of London and Scottish Clearing Banks. (CLSB). A constituent body of the British Bankers Association, it was formed on 1st December 1985, to take over the functions of the Committee of London Clearing Banks. It constitutes a forum for discussion of matters of common interest, which acts as a medium for the circulation downwards to the clearing banks of governmental directives and instructions, and which also communicates upwards to the Treasury any requests, suggestions or recommendations which the committee members, as representatives of their banking organisations, may wish to make.

common carrier. A transport organisation obliged by law to carry any goods offered to them at a reasonable charge for delivery to any destination served by the carrier. The goods have to be delivered in an undamaged state; if they are damaged the negligence of the carrier is assumed.

common law. The unification, by the itinerant justices of Henry II, of the varying systems of law prevailing in different parts of the country into a single coherent and consistent body of rules. Common law is sometimes contrasted with Equity, a system of law developed in the Court of Chancery based on the principles of fairness and justice, or with statute law, which is law passed by Parliament.

common market. An association of European states formed for commercial and political reasons. Its aims are a common currency, the abolition of customs duties, the setting up of a common agricultural policy, and freedom for citizens of member states to travel without restriction within the Community. The UK joined the Common Market nations, known as the European Economic Community, in 1973. The Community consists of West Germany, France, Belgium, Italy, Netherlands, Luxembourg, Denmark, UK, Ireland, Greece and Spain. Some harmonisation of various matters has been achieved. The supervision of banks was dealt with in the Banking Act, 1979 and the 1987 Act, and the regulation and classification of companies in the Companies Act, 1980/1, now codified in the Companies Act, 1985. The European Currency Unit (ECU), is now being more widely used for commercial and trading purposes and accounts in this currency may now be opened in banks in the UK.

common ownership enterprise. An entity which is certified, having no capital but limited by guarantee and registered under the Industrial Provident Societies Act, 1965–75 as a co-operative society. This organisation is controlled by its workforce.

common stock. The term used in the USA which indicates the equity of a company. The equivalent term in the UK is ordinary shares.

company. A number of persons associated together by interest or for carrying on business, or a corporation. A limited company incorporated under the Companies Act, 1985 must have a Memorandum and Articles of Association. The Memorandum contains, in its objects, a list of the legal powers of the company. The Articles are a collection of rules for the internal conduct of the company. A certificate of incorporation, issued by the Registrar of Companies, is the legal birth certificate of the company. In the case of a public company, a trading certificate is also required. When a company wishes to borrow from its bankers, a resolution should be passed by the directors or by the company in general meeting, whichever is appropriate, authorising the advance and naming the security to be offered, and a copy of this resolution should be furnished to the banker. The company exists in law as a being in its own right. Limited companies are built around the principle of limited liability. A shareholder in a limited company can lose the value of his shares, but beyond that he has no liability for the debts of the company. An important series of legal changes affecting all types of limited companies was initiated by the Companies Act 1980, most of whose provisions were implemented by December 1980, namely those concerning insider dealings (see INSIDER), the requirements for directors to have regard to the interests of the company's employees as well as those of the shareholders, the definitions of public and private companies (q.v.) the definition of distributable profits (q.v.), the provisions restricting loans and the provisions protecting shareholders against unfair actions by companies. Companies can either be public companies in which case the letters PLC are added to the name or alternatively they could be private companies in which case the words Co. Ltd, is added after the name. See also CLOSE COMPANY; HOLDING COMPANY; LIMITED COMPANY; LISTED COMPANY; ONE-MAN COMPANY; PARENT COMPANY; PRIVATE COMPANY; PUBLIC COMPANY; STATUTORY COMPANY; SUBSIDIARY COMPANY; TRADING COMPANY; UNLIMITED COMPANY; UNREGISTERED COMPANY.

company accounts. Accounts prepared under the Companies Act, 1985. The balance sheet must show a true and fair view of the state of affairs of the company.

company limited by guarantee. A company in which the liability of the shareholders for the debts of the company is limited to the amount they guarantee to pay in the event of the company being wound up. In the past it was possible to have some share capital, but it is now no longer possible.

company insolvency. See INSOLVENCY.

company limited by shares. A company in which the liability of the shareholders for the debts is limited to the amount of their shareholding.

company meetings. See ANNUAL GENERAL MEETING; EXTRAORDINARY GENERAL MEETING; STATUTORY MEETING.

compensating balance. The practice of requesting compensating balances as part of the pricing of a loan is a typical feature of US banking where prime rate lending is involved; there is some similarity with set-off arrangements in the UK. The balances, which are held in the current or checking accounts in the US, provide a part of the 'compensation' for the credit and the amount to be maintained is often specified in a formal agreement. Where compensation balances are deficient under the agreed formula, a charge is often made.

compensating errors. An error in the book-keeping system whereby both sides agree, but an error or errors on one side, conceals the possibility or an error or errors on the other side, e.g. errors of £60 and £40 on the debit side, equal errors of £70 and £30 on the credit side.

compensation trading. Another name for Barter. See BARTER.

compensatory damages. Damages awarded to compensate a plaintiff for his loss.

competition and credit control (CCC). The name of a document produced in May 1971, by the Bank of England, setting out a new system of financial control which would allow freer competition between the banks, while at the same time allowing the authorities to exercise comprehensive control over the national credit. All banks were to be included in the scheme, the merchant and overseas banks along with the clearing banks. Some measure of competition was also to be introduced into the discount houses' bidding for Treasury Bills. The basic policy points were put into operation as from September 1971. These were 1. quantitative directives to the banks would end; 2. banks and discount houses would abandon their mutual agreements on various rates so as to allow for freer competition and their greater efficiency; 3. bank overdraft, loan and seven day deposit rates were no longer to be linked with Bank Rate (now replaced by minimum lending rate), but each bank would calculate them by reference to its own 'base' rate, which it would vary as it wished; 4. instead of keeping a liquidity of 28 per cent, banks would maintain day by day a uniform minimum reserve asset ratio of 12 per cent of its eligible liabilities; 5. reserve assets and special deposits would be calculated as percentage of eligible liabilities; 6. London Clearing Banks must keep about $1\frac{1}{2}$ per cent of their eligible liabilities in cash at the Bank of England. A similar scheme with a reserve asset ratio of 10 per cent was applied to deposit-taking finance houses. There can be no doubt that Competition and Credit Control brought great benefits to the clearing banks and, more indirectly, to the banking system as a whole. Expanded deposits and lending, and higher interest rates produced higher profit, the greater part of which, after taxation, was ploughed back to strengthen the banks' capital structures. However, it was less successful in the control of credit. Intended to put industry on its feet again and to lead a massive revival in productivity, in the event it proved to be of most benefit to the speculative operators in the property market and to personal borrowers, and cannot escape some of the blame for the rampant inflation which started in 1973 and led to many company failures with a corresponding increase in unemployment. Competition and Credit Control was abandoned in August 1981 and a new system was introduced in August 1981.

completion. The final stages in a contract. The delivery of land with a good title by one party and the payment of the agreed price and the acceptance of the title by the second party.

compliance cost. A phrase used to describe sums paid to the revenue on account of value added tax (*q.v.*).

composition. The adjustment of a debt, etc., by compensation mutually agreed upon by a debtor and creditor; the amount so accepted.

composition with creditors. A payment by debtor of some or all of the debts owing, by instalment or on deferred terms. Such an arrangement must be agreed to by the creditors. A liquidator may make a similar arrangement with company creditors.

composite rate of tax. A rate of tax charged on banks and building societies in respect of interest paid to depositors. It is normally lower than the basic rate of tax as it is calculated on the approximate average rate of tax payable by all depositors. The depositors who receive such interest on their deposits can regard that tax has been deducted at the basic rate. Higher rate taxpayers will have to pay an additional charge, while non tax payers cannot under this system claim a refund.

compound arbitrage. Dealing in foreign currencies involving more than one centre when a free market exists in foreign exchange.

compounded annual return (CAR). The net percentage available to an investor after adding the interim interest payable, less tax at the appropriate band rate.

compound interest. interest on the principal and also on the added interest as it falls due.

comprehensive policy. One covering all risks except Acts of God.

compulsory liquidation or winding up. Under the Insolvency Act, 1986, an order for the compulsory liquidation of a company rests in the hands of the Court. The grounds for winding up a company are (s.122) (a) the company has by special resolution resolved that the company be wound up by the court; (b) being a public company which was registered as such on its original incorporation, the company has not been issued with a certificate under s.117 of the Companies Act and more than a year has expired since it was so registered; (c) it is an old company, within the meaning of the Consequential Provisions Act; (d) the company does not commence its business within a year from its incorporation or suspends its business for a whole year; (e) the number of members is reduced below 2; (f) the company is unable to pay its debts; (g) the court is of the opinion that it is just and equitable that the company should be wound up. Under s.123, Insolvency Act, 1986, a company is deemed unable to pay its debts: (a) if a creditor to whom the company is indebted in a sum exceeding £750 then due has served on the company, by leaving it at the company's registered office, a written demand (in the prescribed form) requiring the company to pay the sum so due and the company has for 3 weeks thereafter neglected to pay the sum or to secure or compound for it to the reasonable satisfaction of the creditor, or, (b) if, in England and Wales, execution or other process issued on a judgment, decree or order of any court in favour of a creditor of

the company is returned unsatisfied in whole or in part, or, (c) if, in Scotland, the *induciae* of a charge for payment on an extract degree, or an extract registered bond, or an extract registered protest, have expired without payment being made, or (d) in Northern Ireland, a certificate of unenforceability has been granted in respect of a judgement against the company or (e) it is proved to the satisfaction of the court that the company is unable to pay its debts as they fall due. A company is also deemed unable to pay its debts if it is proved to the satisfaction of the court that the value of the company's assets is less than the amount of its liabilities, taking into account its contingent and prospective liabilities.

computer. An electronic device designed to store and process large volumes of data at high speed. Input is by paper tape, punched card, magnetic tape, disk or other means. Output is by high speed printer or visual display unit. Most accounts of bank customers are now kept in the memory stores of computers, and are updated daily. Each generation of computers is becoming smaller and yet more powerful. The growth of banking over the last decade has been such that the total volume of work now handled could not possibly be dealt with by any other system.

computer language. The language of a particular computer in which instructions are given to the processing unit.

computer program. A sequence of instructions to a computer to enable it to carry out a particular function or series of functions.

concert party. The law requires a shareholder holding 5 per cent or more of the share capital of a company to notify the company in writing (Companies Act, 1985). However, this legal requirement did not extend to a number of investors acting 'in concert' to acquire a stake of 5 per cent or over. The object has been to take over control of a publicly quoted company by stages, and secretly so that it is not necessary to make a general offer to all shareholders. This abuse, as it is seen to be, has been tackled by the Companies Act, 1985 where notification to the company is now required where persons acting together have built up a group interest in the target company. Failure to comply with the Act constitutes a criminal offence.

condition. A stipulation, an agreement, a term of the contract, that on which anything depends; in *land law*, the specification of some event which, if it takes place during the time for which an estate has already been limited to continue, will bring that estate to an end.

conditional acceptance. *See* QUALIFIED ACCEPTANCE..

conditional indorsement. An indorsement where the indorser has attached a condition to his indorsement. Such a condition may be disregarded by the paying banker. As between indorser and indorsee the condition is valid and if the indorsee received the proceeds of the bill without the condition being fulfilled, he or she would have no claim to the money, but would hold it as trustee for the indorser until the condition is fulfilled.

conditional order. A conditional order upon a banker to pay a certain sum of money on the fulfilment of a condition, very often that a receipt on the back of a draft shall be signed. Where this condition is clearly stated on the draft, and is addressed to the banker, the draft is not an 'unconditional order' and hence not a bill of exchange. Accordingly the banker loses any statutory protection applicable to a bill of exchange and will only consent to deal with such orders if the customer will give him an indemnity. There is protection for the paying banker under the Cheques Act, 1957 s.1, for crossed or open conditional orders or for crossed orders only under s.5 of the Cheques Act, 1957. For the collection banker s.4 of the act will apply.

condition precedent. A stipulation that some event must occur before a contract becomes fixed and binding.

conditions of sale. The terms and conditions upon which goods are to be sold at public auction.

condition subsequent. The making of a contract conditional upon the happening or the non happening of a specified event at a later date – e.g. the contract between banker and a new customer is made subject to a condition subsequent that a reference satisfactory to the banker shall be obtained; in land law, where a condition is annexed to a conveyance, providing that, in case a particular event does or does not happen, or if the grantor or the grantee does or does not do any particular act, the interest shall be defeated – e.g. a grant of land to X 'on condition that he never sells out of the family'.

confirmation dative. The Scots legal term for LETTERS OF ADMINISTRATION (*q.v.*).

confirmation nominative. The Scots legal term for PROBATE (*q.v.*).

confirmed credit. A credit which is open by a bank in the importer's country in favour of an exporter in another country is notified to the exporter through a bank in his own country. If this bank adds its confirmation to the notification, the exporter will enjoy the benefit of a confirmed credit. Not only has the issuing bank undertaken to pay the exporter against specified documents, but also a bank in his own country has given a definite undertaking, either that the provisions for payment and acceptance will be duly fulfilled, or in the case of a credit available by negotiation of drafts, that such drafts will be duly negotiated by the confirming bank without recourse to the drawer.

confirming house. An agent in one country for the buyer in another country. The agent's function is to assist in the trouble-free shipment of the goods purchased by the overseas buyer and pay for them promptly.

conglomerate. This term is used when describing a large group of companies. Frequently, the relationships between companies within the group are complex.

connected lender liability. A liability introduced by the Consumer Credit Act, 1974. The liability was stated in s.75 and laid down that where a lender provided credit for a debtor to purchase goods from a supplier, and the debtor subsequently has any claim against that supplier in respect of misrepresentation or breach of contract, then the debtor shall have a like claim against the creditor, who with the supplier, shall accordingly be jointly and severally liable to the debtor. The credit card companies are liable with the supplier for defective articles (or a cancelled service) and any damage which flows directly from the breach of contract.

connected persons. For the purposes of the Insolvency Act, 1986, a connected person is one who is connected with a company: if *(a)* he is a director or shadow director or; *(b)* he is an associate of the company (s.249). *See also* ASSOCIATE.

consideration. The price paid. The term has been defined in relation to the law of contract as 'some right, interest, profit or benefit accruing to one party, or some forbearance, detriment, loss or responsibility given, suffered or undertaken by the other.

consign. To give, transfer or deliver in a formal manner; to entrust goods to a carrier for transport by rail, air or sea.

consignee. The person to whom goods are consigned.

consignment. The act of consigning; the goods consigned.

consignment note. A form describing and particularising goods to be sent by rail, addressed by the consignor to the railway company, requesting and authorising it to deliver the goods to the named consignee at the address stated.

consignor. The person who consigns goods.

consolidate. To form into a compact and solid mass; to strengthen; to bring into close union; to combine a number of different debts of the customer (e.g. overdraft, hire-purchase commitments, money owing on a credit card) and to replace them by a single debt with a unified repayment programme.

Consolidated Annuities, Consols. British Government irredeemable securities, consolidated into a single stock in 1751, bearing interest at 3 per cent (now $2\frac{1}{2}$ per cent).

consolidated balance sheet. The balance sheet of a parent company, in which are found figures of the parent company itself plus all the reserves, balances on profit and loss accounts and fixed and floating assets and liabilities of all the subsidiaries, shown in total with no particulars and no breakdown. All unrealised profits on inter-group trading, and all inter-company balances, are eliminated before the figures are grossed up. The consolidated balance sheet will show details of minority interests, and these will also appear in the consolidated profit and loss account. If the cost of the shares acquired by the parent company exceeds the share of net assets acquired this will give rise to a figure of goodwill on acquisition; if the cost is less, to a capital reserve. *See also* GROUP ACCOUNTS.

Consolidated Fund. A national fund for the payment of certain public charges, first formed in 1786 by consolidating the aggregate, general and South Sea funds, to which the Irish Exchequer was added in 1818; now the fund of the National Exchequer into which is paid revenue from Customs and Excise, Income Tax, Inheritance Tax, etc.

consortium. An agreement between several countries or large organisations for mutual assistance and joint action, especially in financial matters; an association of large international banks for the purpose of financing major undertakings. Such consortia arrange, manage and underwrite international bond issues, assist with mergers and acquisitions involving companies in different countries, provide financial advice to multinational companies, and arrange syndicate term loans needed to finance major projects on a world wide basis.

constructive delivery. *See* SYMBOLIC DELIVERY.

constructive trust. A trust imposed by law independently of any person's intention.

consular invoice. An invoice issued in differing formats by different countries, to be legalised by the consul of the importing country and required by the Customs of that country to confirm such details as the origin of the goods.

consumer. The one who, or that which, consumes or uses up; the purchaser of an article; for the purpose of the Consumer Credit Act, 1974, any individual or unincorporated body to whom credit is extended under a regulated agreement.

consumer credit. Credit from banks, usually by way of personal loan, or hire-purchase finance. In the UK, comprehensive safeguards for the credit consumer were provided by the Consumer Credit Act, 1974. The Act is principally concerned with credit transactions up to £15,000, in the personal sector only. Bank lending comes within the scope of the Act, as well as hire purchase and credit sale agreements, credit cards, private loans and mortgages. The true cost of a facility must in all cases be disclosed, and written agreements will be required – this does not apply to overdrafts. Certainly many security forms have had to be re-written.

consumer credit agreement. A personal credit agreement by which the creditor provides the debtor with credit not exceeding £15,000. CCA s. 8.

consumer hire agreement. An agreement made by a person with an individual (the 'hirer') for the bailment of (or in Scotland the hiring of) goods to be hired, being an agreement which 1. is not a hire-purchase agreement, and 2. is capable of subsisting for more than three months, and 3. does not require the hirer to make payments exceeding £15,000.

consumer spending. The current expenditure of individuals including purchases of so-called 'consumer durable' articles such as television sets, washing machines and items used in the home.

container bill of lading. A bill of lading issued by a container operator; a document which in itself is not a bill of lading, e.g. a forwarder's receipt evidencing the dispatch of goods in one container in a groupage shipment.

contango. The charge made by a stockbroker on the Stock Exchange for allowing a bull or bear transaction to be carried over to the next settlement.

contango day. the first of the Stock Exchange settling days, and the day on which arrangements are made for the carrying over of transactions to the next account. Also known as *carrying over day, continuation day* or *making up day.*

contemnor. One who is held to be in contempt of court.

contemptuous damages. Damages of a trifling amount where a plaintiff's claim, though proved, has little merit; an expression of the court's opinion of the plaintiff's worth.

contingency plan. A plan to deal with a chance event, a possibility. Thus at branch level there should be a contingency plan to deal with a shortage of staff through sickness, if the staff department can provide no relief, by which the duties will be re-arranged among the available staff. At the corporate level the bank, or any company, should have plans to meet any contingencies which can be envisaged, but particularly one for financial emergencies. Companies should estimate ahead their working capital resources and cash flow levels, and should then provide for the possibility of unexpected shortfalls. Their contingency plans might in this case include a reduction in planned output with a corresponding reduction in staff, the use of uncommitted reserves, liquidation or perhaps sale and release of some assets, factoring of debts, etc.

contingent. Liable to happen, but not certain to do so.

contingent account. An account to provide for unforeseen or uncertain liabilities.

contingent annuity. An annuity which is payable only in the event of the happening of some uncertain event.

contingent interest. An interest in property which will become vested only upon the happening of an uncertain event, e.g. the interest of a minor who is left, under a will or settlement, a capital sum provided that he or she attains majority.

contingent liability. A liability which can exist definitely only upon the happening of some uncertain event, e.g. the liability of an indorser upon a bill of exchange, or of a guarantor upon the guarantee which he has given.

contingent remainder. A reversionary

interest where the passing of the benefit is made to depend upon the happening of an uncertain event, e.g. the attaining by the remainder of his or her twenty-fifth birthday. If death occurs before that day, the benefit passes to some other person.

continuation day. *See* CONTANGO DAY.

continuing security. A security taken to secure an account which fluctuates or changes from day to day, as for example, a current account. The security will then be good to secure the 'ultimate balance' on the account. A form of guarantee/indemnity, for example, will expressly state that it is a continuing security; if this were not done the guarantee would be good for the balance on the day the guarantee was taken, but would thereafter be subject to the operation of the Rule in Clayton's Case, to the detriment of the bank, as the current account continued to operate.

contra account. An account which is debited or credited against another account, e.g., an account holding funds as cash cover for a documentary credit will show entries passed to its debit/credit from the current account of a customer. In a trading organisation, a customer can be a supplier at the same time and consequently entries may be passed between the accounts.

contract. An agreement between bargaining parties, which is intended to be legally enforceable. The parties must be of full contractual capacity. Where a special formality is required by law (e.g. writing), that formality must be complied with. To be enforceable at law, a contract must be either supported by consideration, or be under seal. *See also* CONTRACT UNDER SEAL; EXECUTED CONTRACT; EXECUTORY CONTRACT; OPEN CONTRACT; SIMPLE CONTRACT; SPECIALITY CONTRACT; STANDARD CONTRACT; UNILATERAL CONTRACT.

contract note. When an order to buy or sell stock or shares on the Stock Exchange has been complied with, the broker sends a contract note to the client giving particulars of the transaction and its costs or proceeds.

contract of sale. A contract of sale includes an agreement to sell as well as a sale. An agreement for the sale of a house must be in writing if it is to be enforceable prior to the exchange of contracts. Such a written agreement or memorandum must be signed by the party to be charged or by some person lawfully authorised by him or her. It should contain the address of the property, the consideration to be paid, and the names of the buyer and seller.

contract guarantee. An agreement between parties whereby one person will guarantee the other that performance will take place, otherwise some form of compensation will be given. These guarantees are usually covered by such documents as tender bonds, performance bonds, etc.

contract under seal. A contract to which the maker's seal is attached and delivered as his or her 'deed'. Such contracts are made when there is no consideration, for example, the conveyancing of land.

contribution. A payment legally imposed on a person or payment to a loss where other persons will make their contribution. The difference between the sales value of a product and the variable costs.

contributory. A person who, as an existing or past member of a company, is liable in certain circumstances to contribute to the assets of the company if it is wound up.

contributory negligence. *See* NEGLIGENCE.

contributory negligence of plaintiff. Where a defendant is found negligent, the damages he will have to pay may be reduced if it is found that the plaintiff was also negligent, and that his negligence contributed in some part to the loss or damage complained of. This doctrine is well known in the case of collisions between vehicles or ships, but was not applied to banking until 1971, because prior to that the relevant statute – the Law Reform (Contributory Negligence) Act, 1945 – was thought to apply only to actions for negligence, whereas the banker is sued for conversion. In that year, however, this view was modified, and since then a customer may be partly liable, in cases where a banker is found to be negligent, if the customer has by his or her actions contributed to the loss – as for example, by recklessly issuing blank signed cheque forms, or by failing to exercise proper supervision over a clerk or agent. In 1977 a section of the Torts (Interference with Goods) Act of that year said: 'Contributory negligence is no defence in proceedings founded in conversion, or on intentional trespass to goods' (s.11[1]). It therefore appeared that from the date of the Act coming into force – 1 June 1978 – the case decision of 1971 referred to above was overruled. With this in mind, the banking lobby in the House of Commons was able to get a section inserted in the Banking Act, 1979 as follows: 'In any circumstances in which proof of absence of negligence on the part of a banker would be a defence in proceeding by reason of the Cheques Act, 1957, s.4, a defence of contributory negligence shall also be available to the banker notwithstanding the provisions of s.11(1) of the Torts (Interference with Goods) Act, 1977 (s.47).'

contributory pension. A pension paid to a worker on his retirement, towards which worker, and employer, have contributed during the employee's working life. The amount of the pension depends upon the number of contributions paid and upon the average salary over a number of years, or upon the final salary.

control. To regulate, to check, to

restrain; *authority* or power; any *test* or check, especially in an experiment, to provide a standard for future experiments; in a bank, a *system of listing* and detailing all debits and credits passing through an office in the course of a day's work, whether handwritten, machined or computerised.

control account. An account which hold the same total debits, credits and balances as the ledger/s it represents and to which the individual items have been posted. In effect the total of all the individual balances of a ledger should equal the balance of the control account.

controller. One who controls; a public functionary appointed to oversee the accounts of others. For the purposes of the Consumer Credit Act, 1974, 'controller', in relation to a body corporate, means a person 1. in accordance with whose directions or instructions the directors of the body corporate or of another body corporate which is its controller or any of them are accustomed to act, or 2. who, either alone or with any associate or associates, is entitled to exercise, or control the exercise of, one third or more of the voting power at any general meeting of the body corporate or of another body corporate which is its controller.

controlling interest. The interest held in a company by a person or by another firm or company who/which holds shares in it carrying at least 51 per cent of the voting rights.

control period. The period between two specified dates when comparisons are made between the budgeted amounts and the actual amounts.

control of the money supply. A system of control that was put into operation by the Bank of England in August 1981. The Bank controls the level of liquidity in the banking system and influences the interest rates almost exclusively by open market operations, rather than by lending to the discount houses. This involves buying

and selling eligible bills. To make the market in Treasury bills and commercial bills large enough to allow interest rates to be influenced rather than by operation of the *Minimum Lending Rate*. An eligible bill, is a bill which has been drawn or accepted by one of about 100 banks who have been given 'eligible' status by the Bank of England. All banks are requested to maintain a minimum of $2\frac{1}{2}$ per cent and an average of 5 per cent of their eligible liabilities in the form of bills with the London Discount Market Association. As an additional control, the Bank of England will keep the short term interest rates within an unpublished band which it will change as it thinks desirable. The old reserve asset rations imposed by *Competition and Credit Control* no longer apply, but liquidity of individual banks will be prescribed by the Bank of England. Banks have to maintain 0.45 per cent of eligible liabilities with the Bank of England as non-interest bearing non operational balances.

convention. A convention is an understanding between persons and parties who agree, from long practice, to a standard of practice or behaviour in conducting business. A tacit understanding of a conduct of behaviour and an absence of formal rules of conduct.

conversion. A tort committed when one person wrongfully interferes with the property of another in such a way as to show that he or she denies or is indifferent to the title of that other. It is no defence that the tort is committed innocently. Any banker who collects a cheque for a customer who has a defective title or no title to it commits conversion when the proceeds are credited to the customer's account, and the banker is rendered liable to an action in conversion by the true owner of the cheque. Against this risk the banker has the statutory protection contained in s. 4. of the Cheques Act, 1957, if he or she can comply with the conditions therein, to collect in good faith, for a customer and without negligence. The word is also used to indicate an *operation* whereby a government which has issued stock carrying a high rate of interest is able to repay it on maturity (if interest rates are then lower) by offering in its place a new stock carrying a lower rate of interest, possibly with the inducement of a bonus to the stockholder who exercises this option to convert his or her holding into the lower paid stock. Another meaning describes the *transfer* to a loan account of an overdraft which has grown out of the customer's immediate ability to deal with.

conversion stocks. Government stocks which have been offered to holders of other stocks, due for repayment as an alternative to receiving cash payments.

convertibility. A state of affairs where traders in goods and services between countries can make or receive payments in their own currencies at a rate of exchange fixed within given limits. Convertibility is associated with an absence of exchange restrictions and can be sustained only by countries with satisfactory balances of payments.

convertible. Exchangeable for another thing. When used of a currency, it indicates that the currency is freely exchangeable into another currency.

convertible bond. A bond which, on demand by the bearer, can be exchanged for a holding in shares.

convertible stocks or securities. 1. Securities which may readily be turned into cash; 2. securities having the right to transfer from one form of holding to another, e.g. fixed interest securities that are exchangeable at a later date into ordinary shares on predetermined terms. Most convertible stocks take the form of unsecured loan stocks; there are also a few convertible debentures and preference shares. Convertibles have to be considered both as fixed interest stocks and as potential equities. The expense of purchasing what is in effect an equity option has to be taken as the difference between the yield on the convertible stock and the yield on any investment which gives a fixed interest but has no option built in. Usually the holder of a convertible stock would do better in terms of yield to invest in a debenture or similar stock, but may think it worthwhile to pay the option cost, and a possible conversion premium at some later date, to keep the two-way 'hedge'.

conveyance. The act of conveying real property from one person to another; the *deed* by which it is tranferred.

conveyance on sale. Every instrument, and every decree or order of any court, or of any commissioners, whereby any property, or any estate or interest in any property, upon the sale thereof is transferred to or vested in a purchaser, or any other person on his or her behalf or by his or her direction.

conveyancing. The act or profession of drawing up deeds for the conveyance of real property.

cooling off period. Under CCA, 1974, a period during which a debtor may cancel a regulated agreement.

co-ownership. The ownership of property by more than one person. Such co-ownership may be co-parceners, tenants in common or joint tenants.

co-parceners. Co-heirs to whom land devolved where a tenant in a fee simple or a tenant in tail died intestate leaving only female heirs, whereupon the females succeeded jointly to the estate. This method of inheritance was abolished in 1925, and co-parcenary can now arise only in the case of entailed interests.

co-partnership. A system of management by which employees are entitled to a voice in the management of a concern and a share in any profits.

copyhold. A tenure of land where the tenant's right is evidenced by a copy of the rolls made by the steward of the lord's court; property held by such tenure. In the UK, copyhold was converted into freehold with effect from the beginning of 1926.

copyright. The exclusive right of the author of a literary or artistic production, or his or her heirs, to publish or sell copies of the author's works. This right endures for the term of the author's life and for fifty years thereafter.

corner. To buy up the whole existing stock of a commodity in order to raise or control the price of it; to establish a monopoly.

corporation. A united body; the authorities of a town or city; a legal, municipal, mercantile or professional association, authorised to act, plead or sue as a single person, governed by its own by-laws, and electing its office bearers from its own body; a company or association for commercial or other purposes, created by an Act of Parliament or by a charter granted by the Crown.

corporation aggregate. One consisting of many persons, as, for example, a corporation of a town.

corporation bills. Under the Local Government Act, 1972, which came into force on 1 April 1974, local authorities, subject to rate income and Treasury consent, may issue bills for periods not exceeding twelve months.

corporation sole. One consisting of a single individual and his or her successors, e.g. a bishop.

corporation tax. A tax payable by a company on its profits and capital gains.

corporeal hereditaments. Tangible, visible property, such as land itself and houses built on it, which may be passed on to one's heirs; hence, an interest in land possession, a right to enjoy the possession of land.

correspondent bank. A bank in one country which acts when so required for a bank in another country. The relationship is one of agency. The choice of the correspondent bank may depend on its position, or on the amount of business which has formerly taken place between the two banks.

corset. Introduced in December 1973, the supplementary Special Deposits scheme was known as the 'corset'. It restrained the growth of the main category of bank deposits – interest bearing eligible liabilities – so that bank lending, based on bank deposits, might be checked at one remove. Limits specified from time to time by the Bank of England on the growth of these liabilities were exceeded by the banks only under a penal obligation to place additional non-interest earning Special Deposits with the Bank, the rate of such Special Deposits rising progressively in relation to any excessive growth in interest-bearing eligible liabilities. To avoid these penalties the banks had to restrain the growth of their assets while remaining free (subject to the need to maintain the minimum reserve asset ration and to the general guidance on priority lending) to determine their composition. The 'corset regulations were terminated in June 1980. *See also* SPECIAL DEPOSITS.

cost. The price charged or paid for anything, expenditure of any kind; the evaluation in monetary terms of the resources, time and labour which have gone into a product. *See also* DISTRIBUTIVE COST; FACTOR COST; FIXED COST; MARGINAL COST; OPPORTUNITY COST; PRIME COSTS; REAL COST; RETAIL COST; VARIABLE COSTS; WHOLESALE COST.

cost accounting. A system of accounting in which the costs of all stages of production is calculated in order to show where useful economy is possible. It is also used as a basis for pricing. *See also* ABSORPTION COSTING; BREAK-EVEN ANALYSIS; STANDARD COSTING.

cost allocation. The assignment of costs to stages in the production sequence in the proportions in which they have attracted them.

cost centre. An area of activity in a business to which costs may be attributed. All costs are identified and a cost centre is allocated or apportioned to it.

cost and freight (C & F). A contractual term indicating that the price quoted to the buyer includes transit costs. The cost of insurance must be paid by the buyer.

cost, insurance, freight (CIF). A contractual term indicating that the price quoted to the buyer includes transit costs and insurance.

cost of sales. The total cost of either producing or purchasing the goods sold in a stated trading period. It is an important figure in the trading account in a business entity.

cost price. The wholesale, as opposed to the retail price.

cost push theory of inflation. The theory that rises in wages and in other manufacturing costs lead, after a time lag, to price rises, which in turn lead after a further time lag, to further rises in wages.

costs. The expenses of a law suit.

cost unit. The amount or quantity of goods upon which a cost assessment can conveniently be made.

counter. The opposite, the contrary; a *raised bench* across which goods are sold; the fixture in a bank which *divides* the office space from the public space across which customers pay in and draw out.

counter claim. A claim set up by the defendant in a suit to counter that of the plaintiff.

counterfeit. To coin, to imitate in base metal; *forged*, made in imitation with intent to be passed off as genuine.

counterfeit coin. Coin not authorised by the state. It may be detected by its appearance, its malleability, and its tone when thrown down, which will be dull. Silver or gold coins lend themselves to counterfeiting because of their intrinsic value, but modern cupro-nickel coins do not.

counterfeit note. A forged banknote.

counter-foil. A perforated slip attached to a cheque, receipt, dividend, interest warrant, share certificate, etc., retained by the issuer, on which to note particulars of the instrument issued. The word is used in a specialised sense in the case of dividend and interest payments.

counter-indemnity. An indemnity given by a customer to his or her banker when the latter has given an indemnity to a third party at the customer's request.

countermand. An order contrary to, or revoking a previous order.

countermand of payment. An order to a banker from a customer to stop payment of a cheque which the customer has issued. The customer may give this over the telephone but must subsequently confirm in writing. The bank must be told the number of the cheque, and preferably also the date, amount, and name of the payee. An order to stop the payment of a direct debit, the bank would wish to know the name of the creditor, the amount if known, and the date the debit is due to be received by the debtor's bank.

countermark. An additional mark for identification or certification, put upon goods or safe custody articles belonging to several persons that they may not be opened except in the presence of all; the mark of the *Goldsmith's Company* to attest the quality of the metal.

counterpart. A correspondent part, duplicate or copy, one or two corresponding copies of an instrument, especially the copy of a lease, signed by the lessee, received by the lessor.

counter purchase. Another term for barter *(q.v.)*.

countersign. To attest the correctness of a document by adding an additional signature to ratify, as where a company customer may instruct its bankers to honour its cheques if signed by a director and countersigned by the secretary.

coupon. A detachable certificate for the payment of interest on bonds. When the time for the payment of interest has arrived the appropriate coupon must be cut off and presented for payment to the bond-issuing authority. A banker is responsible for doing this on a customer's behalf where he or she is the depositary of the customer's bonds.

coupon sheet. A sheet of coupons issued with, and usually attached to, a bearer bond so that each coupon may be cut off and forwarded for payment of interest at the right time.

covenant. A mutual and solemn agreement, a contract, a compact, a written agreement; to agree to do a certain thing, e.g. to make periodic payments to a charity; any promise touching and concerning land that is contained in a tenancy agreement made otherwise than by deed. *See also* DEED OF COVENANT.

cover. To be enough to defray; *to protect,* by insurance; *sufficient to meet a liability* or insure against loss; *security deposited* by a customer at a bank against a borrowing; a *deposit* of cash or marketable securities by a client with a broker to protect him or her against loss.

cover for dividend. The profit available for distribution by way of dividend. If the profit is twice the sum actually paid out by way of dividend the dividend is said to be 'twice covered'. Both amounts are usually quoted after corporation tax, but the dividend is taken before deduction of income tax.

cover note. A document issued by an insurance company indemnifying the insured person against any damage or loss suffered in the interval between the acceptance of the proposal and the issue of the insurance policy.

crawling peg. A method of adjustment to the system of fixed international currency parities which were established following the Bretton Woods agreement of 1944. It was recognised that some countries might experience considerable strains by holding too long to a parity which was becoming untenable. The crawling peg would make for small and frequent adjustments which would seem less drastic and would upset the system to a lesser degree. The adjustments would be automatic, and would, it was claimed, prevent speculators jobbing against a currency. Finally it seemed more logical to let currencies find their own level.

credit. A reputation for solvency; the *time given* for payment of goods sold on trust; *trust* reposed with regard to property handed over on the promise of payment at a future time; *anything due* to any person; the *side of an account* in which payment is entered, opposed to debit; an *entry* on this side of a payment received. For the purposes of the Consumer Credit Act, 1974 'credit' includes a cash loan, and any other form of financial accommodation. Where credit is provided otherwise than in sterling it shall be treated for the purposes of the Act as provided in sterling of an equivalent amount.

credit advice. A notification from a bank to a customer advising the customer of the receipt of a payment which has been placed to the credit of his or her account.

credit broker. Under the Consumer Credit Act, 1974, it means a person carrying on business as a credit broker and who has a licence for this purpose.

credit brokerage. The effecting of introductions of 1. individuals desiring to obtain credit; or 2. individuals desiring to obtain credit to finance the acquisition or provision of dwellings occupied or to be occupied by themselves or their relatives, and prepared to offer the security of land; or 3. individuals desiring to obtain goods on hire, to businesses likely to be able to meet these requirements, or to other credit-brokers.

credit card. A piece of plastic about 85mm by 54mm, bearing the name and computer number of the holder and the period of availability. The holder must sign it. The best known cards in the UK are the VISA card and ACCESS; the American Express and Diners' Club are leisure or entertainment cards as no credit is permitted. With the credit card, goods can be bought in any retail outlet in the UK and many other parts of the world e.g. shop, petrol station, etc. The retailer pays in a copy of all credit card transactions to the credit of his or her account at a bank which will then transmit the vouchers to the appropriate credit card company. The credit card company will debit the retailer each month with a sum equal to between 2 and 5 per cent of the turnover. The customer on the other hand will receive a monthly statement which will specify the transactions and the outstanding balance. The person is obliged to pay either 5 per cent or £5 whichever is the greater. Any outstanding balance is charged at a rate of interest, which can vary, but is at the moment $1\frac{1}{2}$ per cent per month. Under s. 14(1) Consumer Credit Act, 1974 a credit card is defined as 'a card, check, voucher, coupon, stamp form, booklet or other document or thing given to an individual by a person carrying on a consumer credit business who undertakes – (a) that on production of it he or she will supply, cash, goods and services (or any of them) on credit, or (b) that where, on the production of it to a third party (whether or not any

other action is also required), the third party supplies cash, goods and services (or any of them), the consumer credit business will pay the third party for them in return for payment to the company by the individual.

credit cardholders. Any credit worthy mature person can be a credit card holder. They do not necessarily have to have an account with the bank whose subsidiary is the issuing credit card company. Before a card is issued, certain details are supplied and references given. On approval a credit card is given to the holder and the cardholder is at the same time notified of the maximum credit available to him/her. The credit card can be used at any retail outlet displaying the credit card company symbol. It is usual for settlement or partial settlement to be made by the credit cardholder within 25 days of receipt of the statement.

credit clearing. The credit clearing is now part of the Cheque and Credit Clearing Co. Ltd. It handles the clearing process of branch and other bank credits paid in over the branch counters. They are sorted and cleared in the same way as cheques and it takes three working days for a credit to be received on the account of the beneficiary.

credit insurance. A means of insuring the payment of commercial debts against the risk of non-payment by the buyer because of insolvency, or for some other reason.

credit limit. The figure to which a bank customer may borrow whether by way of overdraft, loan or any other account, or on a credit card such as Access. On the inter-bank market, the figure to which any one bank may borrow from any other bank, a limit assessed by the lending bank according to its opinion of the standing of the borrowing bank. For the purposes of the Consumer Credit Act, 1974, the maximum debit balance which, under the credit agreement, is allowed to stand on an account during a given period (disregarding any term of the agreement allowing that maximum to be exceeded merely temporarily).

credit note. A document sent to a person advising that his or her account is credited with a stated amount in respect of goods returned or when any discount or allowance is made, or when there has been an overpayment.

creditor. One to whom a debt is due. A banker is a creditor when a current account is overdrawn, the customer is the creditor when a current account is in credit. For the purposes of the CCA, 1974, 'creditor' means the person providing credit under a consumer credit agreement or the person to whom his or her rights and duties under the agreement have passed by assignment or operation of law, and in relation to a prospective consumer credit agreement, includes the prospective creditor.

credit rating. An opinion as to the credit-worthiness of a person, obtained by a party who is considering entering into a business contract with the person or supplying goods to him or her. It is usual to obtain the opinion through the banking system, or a trade reference may be given, or the use of a credit reference agency.

credit reference agency. For the purposes of the CCA, 1974, a person carrying on a business comprising the furnishing of persons with information relevant to the financial standing of individuals, being information collected by the agency for that purpose.

credit risk. In general, the risk that a lender will not be able to get the money loaned back from the bor-rower. To guard against this, the credit risk is assessed either by a lending manager at an interview, or by the submission of a specially prepared form which is designed to score the credit rating.

credit-sale agreement. An agreement to sell with a term which provides that payment shall be by instalments. The property in the goods passes at once to the buyer.

credit scoring. A method of assessing a potential borrower's credit-worthiness, or a potential employee's suitability, or an examinee's knowledge of a subject. The system is designed to handle large numbers, using comparatively unskilled labour. In the case of a bank considering the granting of a personal loan, for example, the applicant submits the answer to a series of questions on the bank form provided. These questions usually cover the age of the applicant, marital status, whether owner, tenant or living with parents, how long at present address, length of service in present employment, monthly net income, whether paid monthly or weekly, bank accounts held and the amount and purpose of the loan. A master scoring table is then matched up to the completed form, enabling the banker to run down the edge with a series of marks. These can be designed to give a good result or poor result according to the marks scored. The loan can be accepted, declined, or referred to a senior official.

credit slip (or paying-in slip). The form which is filled in to accompany the cash, bills of exchange and cheques which are paid in by a customer to the credit of his or her account. Each slip should show the name of the bank, the branch, the personalised details of the account holder, the computerised sorting code number and the account number. The person paying in the credit will enter the date, plus the details of the items/cash to be paid in and sign it. The duplicate or the counterfoil will be stamped with the bank/branch stamp, initialled by the cashier and returned to the customer. It is usual for customers to have a book of credit slips, or alternately, a single credit slip is available at branch counters.

credit squeeze. The name given to a period of credit restriction, when banks are directed to lend only to certain classes of borrowers (qualitative controls) and hire-purchase is made more difficult by the imposition of higher down payments and shorter periods of repayment. Banks may be subjected to special deposits.

credit token. For the purposes of the Consumer Credit Act, 1974, a credit token is a card, check, voucher, coupon, stamp, form, booklet or other document or thing given to an individual by a person carrying on a consumer credit business who undertakes 1. that on the production of it he or she will supply cash, goods and services (or any of them) on credit; or 2. that where, on production of it to a third party, the third party supplies cash, goods and services (or any of them) the credit business will pay the third party for them, in return for payment to the company by the individual.

credit token agreement. A regulated agreement for the provision of credit in connection with the use of a credit token.

credit transfer. A system by which any person is enabled to pay money in at any branch of any clearing bank for the credit of another person having an account at any other branch of any other clearing bank.

credit union. A system, popular in North America, by which people with a common bond – membership of the same club, church, tenants' association or trade union – can collaborate to put their savings into a joint fund. Members can then apply to borrow from the fund and make repayments at an annual rate of interest of 12 per cent. The Credit Union Act, 1979 included the following: 1. the Chief Registrar of Friendly Societies supervises all Credit Unions; 2. the mini-

mum membership shall be 21 and the maximum 5,000; 3. the maximum savings permitted per person to be £3,000; 4. the unions must be non profit making and the purpose is to provide a service to its members.

creditor's petition. A creditor's petition must be for a debt or debts owed to a creditor/s *(a)* equal to or exceeding the bankruptcy level – at the moment this is £750, but may be amended by the Secretary of State; *(b)* the debt is unsecured; *(c)* the debtor appears either to be unable to pay or to have no reasonable prospect of being able to pay; *(d)* there is no outstanding application to set aside a statutory demand served (under s.268 Insolvency Act, 1986) in respect of the debt or any other debts. Insolvency Act, 1986 s. 267.

cross border leasing. Leasing to a concern in another country not through a subsidiary in that country, but directly.

crossed cheque. A cheque bearing across its face two parallel transverse lines, with or without the words 'not negotiable'; or two parallel transverse lines, with the name of a banker. A crossed cheque must be collected through a banking account and cannot be cashed across a counter. The crossing therefore constitutes a protection for the drawer, who should always cross cheques which he or she is intending to send through the post, as a precaution against the cheque falling into the wrong hands. *See also* NOT NEGOTIABLE.

cross firing. Where one person draws a cheque in favour of another, or upon his or her own account at another bank and at the same time a similar cheque is drawn by the other person in favour of the first, or by the first on his or her other account, for the credit of the first account. If the banker mistakenly allows drawings against uncleared effects, the cross-firing will inevitably increase in the amount for which the cheques are drawn and will continue until one branch returns a cheque unpaid. At the time the other account will, because of the debiting of the returned cheque, show an overdraft, which will be difficult or impossible to recover. Sometimes the process involves more than two accounts.

cross guarantees. Security given for a loan to a parent company or to any subsidiary in a group, which takes the form of a guarantee from each of the other companies in the group. Cross guarantees are particularly appropriate where the banker is lending to more than one company. In the event of a liquidation, the banker will be able to prove against each company for the amount of its individual debt, plus the total of its guarantees on the account of all other companies.

cross rates. The rates of exchange arrived at by expressing the quotations for any two currencies in terms of a third.

crown. A coin of the value of 25p, formerly a five-shilling piece. Any of several foreign coins.

crownhold. A tenure of land established by the Leasehold reform Act, 1967 to denote land which has been compulsorily acquired by the Land Commission and regranted by the Crown on sale or by lease. If by lease, the buyer receives a Crownhold Lease, normally of 999 years, which may be subject to restrictions on future development. These restrictions are known as *Crownhold Covenants,* and have to be registered against the land in the Land Charges Registry, or if they concern registered land, in the Land Registry.

cum div. Together with the dividend about to be paid. The buyer of stock or shares sold *'cum div',* takes the benefit of the dividend about to be distributed.

cum drawing. When bonds are sold near the time when a periodical drawing is about to take place, there is always a chance that one or more of the bonds included in the sale will fall to be repaid, at par, or at a premium. When such bonds are sold *'cum* drawing', any advantages gained or profit made from such drawing accrues to the buyer.

cum rights. Shares sold *'cum rights'* pass to the buyer not only the shares but also any rights attaching to them, e.g. a right to take up further issues.

cumulative preference shares. Those where a deficiency one year is made up later if subsequent yearly profits permit.

cupro-nickel. An amalgam of three-quarters parts of copper to one-quarter part nickel. Post war currency has been cupro-nickel in place of the earlier silver currency, which has now become too expensive to maintain. The intrinsic value of a cupro-nickel coin is minimal.

currency. The time during which anything is current, the state of being in use; the circulating medium by which purchases and sales are made; money, gold, silver and copper; banknotes, bills of exchange, cheques. *See also* FOREIGN CURRENCY; HARD CURRENCY.

currency bills. Bills of Exchange which are drawn and payable in a foreign currency.

currency bonds. Bonds issued in a foreign country and repayable in the currency of that country.

currency of a bill of exchange. The period which a bill of exchange has to run before its maturity.

currency note. The banknote of a country in which it is the legal and acceptable medium of exchange, i.e. money.

current account. An account with a bank from which any part of the balance may be withdrawn on demand. Withdrawals may be in the form of cheques payable to the drawer or a third party, by direct debits, standing orders and via an Automated Teller Machine (ATM). Funds in the form of cash, cheques and other financial instruments may be credited to the account. In the UK these accounts may be overdrawn and where necessary charges may be made by the banker.

current assets. *See* LIQUID ASSETS.

current balance. The balance of visible and invisible items in international trade, but not including any movements of capital. In retail banking, this could refer to the balance on an account as at close of business of the previous working day.

current cost accounting. *See* INFLATION ACCOUNTING.

current liabilities. Debts arising in the normal course of a business which are due for payment within the next twelve months, such as debts due to trade and hire purchase creditors, amounts due to the bank, and taxation payable.

current ratio. The ratio between the current assets and the current liabilities. It indicates the liquidity of a business.

custodian trustee. A trustee who takes charge of the property of a trust and is responsible for its safe keeping. The duties of a custodian trustee are quite distinct from those of a managing trustee and the same person(s) or organisation(s) are not allowed to discharge both functions at the same time. There appears to be no method of retirement from the duties of custodian trustee except by application to the court. *See also* MANAGING TRUSTEE; UNIT TRUST.

custodier. A term in Scots law meaning one who has the custody or guardianship of anything. *See* BAILEE.

custom. Fashion, usage, habit, business patronage; long established practice or usage, which may have the force of law; a source of law; toll, tax or tribute.

custom duties. Taxes, levied chiefly on imported goods, but occasionally on some exports.

customer. As there is no statutory definition of a customer, reliance must be placed on case law definitions. They include; 1. 'to make a person a customer of a bank there must be either a current or deposit account, or some similar relation'; 2. 'the relationship of a banker and customer begins as soon as money or a cheque is paid in and the bank accepts it and is prepared to open an account'; 3. 'the word 'customer' signifies a relationship in which duration is not of the essence. A person whose money has been accepted by the banker on the footing that the banker undertakes to honour cheques up to the amount standing to the person's credit is a customer of the bank irrespective of whether the connection is of short or long duration'. The question of whether a person is a customer in a period between his or her first contact with the bank and the receipt of the final letter anthenticating the reference introduction is not free from doubt. If the reference is satisfactory the person is a customer and probably always has been; if it is not, and no satisfactory reference can be supplied, the banker will probably decide not to proceed. In this case the person is not a customer and never has been. If in this interval the banker has collected a cheque for the person, he or she may be at risk, for the banker cannot claim the statutory protection of s. 4. of the Cheques Act, 1957.

customs house. The office or place where payment is made of duties on imports and exports.

customs invoice. An invoice made out on a special form to comply with the requirements of the importing country.

cy-près doctrine. The principle that where the terms of a trust, as set out by a testator or a settlor, cannot be exactly adhered to for some reason, then the courts shall have power to order that these shall be carried out 'as nearly as possible'. The doctrine is particularly important in cases of bequests to charity, where the original charity has been changed, taken over, or amalgamated with another, or where the state has made itself responsible for the ends formerly served by the charity.

D

D/A. *See* DOCUMENTS AGAINST ACCEPTANCE.

damages. Legal compensation in money paid to an injured party on the basis that, as far as money can do it, the injured party shall be placed in the same position he or she was in before the act complained of occurred. Damages are a common law remedy. They are claimed by an injured party as of right.

data. Information of any kind, not necessarily in any particular form, but for business purposes; information needed by bankers is often found in the final accounts and balance sheet of the trading entity.

data processing. The handling of accounting and other information by a computer.

Data Protection Act, 1984. This Act gives the individual the right to know any personal details that are kept on computer files. Not only that, a copy of such information can be obtained and, if incorrect, application can be made to the Data Protection Registrar or the courts to have such incorrect information corrected or erased, or, if the courts see fit, to obtain compensation if such incorrect information has caused damage to that individual. All entities that use, process or control information about individuals on a computer must by law register. No matter how small or unimportant this information is, failure to register will break the law. However, there are four areas of exemptions to registration: (*a*) calculating pay and pensions; (*b*) keeping accounts or records of purchases or sales; (*c*) distributing articles or information (mailing lists); (*d*) preparing the text of documents.

date. The period or time of an event; the time when a writing was executed, especially a deed. A deed must be 'signed, sealed and delivered', and thus takes effect from the date of its delivery, whatever may be the date of its execution, or indeed if no date is stated. A bill of exchange is not invalid by reason that it is not dated. Any holder may insert the true date of issue or acceptance and the bill shall be payable accordingly. Any holder may insert the true date of the issue on a cheque. This right lasts for a reasonable time only. The date on a bill or cheque is a material part of it, and any alteration to it requires the concurrence of all parties liable on it, otherwise the bill is void except as against anyone who made the alteration or agreed to it, and indorsers subsequent to him or her. *See also* ANTEDATE; INTERNATIONAL DATE LINE; POSTDATE.

dated stock. Gilt-edged stock issued by the government having a date by which it will be repaid. Where there are two dates, as in the case of $6\frac{1}{4}$ per cent Treasury 1995–98, the stock may be redeemed at any time between the dates stated.

days of grace. No longer applicable to bills of exchange. Often a time given for a person to accept or reject a simple contract. Nowadays this may refer to the renewal of an insurance policy, whereby the insurer will allow a period of time (say 30 days) after the expiry of the insurance contract, to allow the insured to pay the premium for the renewal of the policy. Should payment not be made by the expiry of the days of grace, the policy is then considered void.

day to day money. Sums of money lent by banks to the discount houses and stockbrokers overnight. Such loans may be renewed from one day to another if both parties are agreeable.

dead money. Money which can only be

borrowed at a high rate of interest.

dead stock. Unsaleable goods left on hand.

dead weight. The weight of a ship's cargo which brings the ship down to the Plimsoll mark, at which point the ship is fully laden.

dealer. A trader, a merchant; a dealer in foreign exchange; on the Stock Exchange, or any other money or commodity market.

death of a customer. The duty and authority of a banker to pay a cheque drawn on the bank by a customer are determined by notice of the customer's death The account must be stopped on receipt of notice and cheques drawn and issued before death but presented after notice received should normally be returned unpaid with the answer 'Drawer deceased'. However, if it is possible for the personal representative to be ascertained, and his or her permission for payment obtained, the cheque may be honoured. Notice of death may come from a notice in a newspaper, or from a letter from the deceased's solicitor, or from a member of the family. All mandates such as standing orders, and all delegated powers, are revoked by death. However, a contract in course of execution, such as an order for the purchase of stock, may be completed and the account debited. Cheques drawn against a cheque card may also be paid, on the grounds that the payee was induced to accept payment by cheque by the guarantee of the card, and that it would be inequitable therefore to dishonour such an inducement. If the account is overdrawn, the personal representative must be advised of the liability – if it is in credit, they alone can give a valid discharge after probate or letters of administration have been taken out. In due course a death certificate should be exhibited and noted. A small estates procedure where the deceased has left no will and the value of the estate does

not exceed £5,000 permits the bank to hand over the balance to the next of kin against a simple receipt and a counter indemnity.

debenture. An acknowledgment of indebtedness, usually given by an incorporated company often under seal, and frequently including a charge on the assets of the company. It may be a registered debenture or one payable to bearer. A debenture holder has a right to a fixed rate of interest regardless of the profits made in the trading period and, in the case of redeemable debentures, the right of repayment of the principal at the agreed date. *See also* ALL MONEYS DEBENTURE; FIXED DEBENTURE; FLOATING DEBENTURE; INCOME DEBENTURE; IRREDEEMABLE DEBENTURE; MORTGAGE DEBENTURE; NAKED DEBENTURE; REDEEMABLE DEBENTURE; SANDWICH DEBENTURE; SECURED DEBENTURE; SIMPLE DEBENTURE.

debenture holder. The holder of a debenture, whether registered or payable to bearer.

debenture stock. A debenture which is expressed as part of a total debt. Certificates of debenture stock may be for any amount.

debit. An entry in the accounting records of an entity. By convention, it is an entry on the left hand side of the account and represents an increase in the value of the asset represented. A debit entry in the account of a liability will reduce the value of that liability. In the accounts of a bank, the payment of a customer's cheque will be debited to the account, i.e. if the balance is a credit one, it will reduce the amount due to the customer. If the balance is overdrawn, it will increase the amount due to the bank.

debit note. A commercial document advising a person or firm that a debit entry has been made in his or her account in the books of the sender. This will arise if an underpayment has been made, or an incorrect price given.

debt. Something owed to another, a liability, an obligation. A chose in action which is capable of being assigned by the creditor to some other person. The assignment must be in writing and must apply to the whole of the debt. The debtor must be notified.

debt adjusting. For the purposes of the Consumer Credit Act, 1974, negotiating with the creditor or owner, on behalf of the debtor, or hirer, terms for the discharge of a debt, or taking over, in return for payments by the debtor or hirer, the obligation to discharge a debt.

debt capital. *See* LOAN CAPITAL.

debt collecting. For the purposes of the Consumer Credit Act, 1974, the taking of steps to procure payment of debts due under consumer credit agreements or consumer hire agreements.

debt counselling. For the purposes of the Consumer Credit Act, 1974, the giving of advice to debtors or hirers about the liquidation of any debt due under consumer credit or consumer hire agreements.

debt/equity ratio. The ratio of the shareholders' equity to total liabilities, sometimes taken as shareholders' equity to long-term debts.

debtor. One who owes money, or is under some obligation, to another. For the purposes of the Consumer Credit Act, 1974, 'debtor' means the individual receiving credit under a consumer credit agreement or the person to whom his or her rights and duties under the agreement have passed by assignment or operation of law. In relation to a prospective consumer credit agreement the form includes the prospective debtor. Often abbreviated as *Dr*.

debtor-creditor agreement. A regulated consumer credit agreement being: 1. a restricted-use credit agreement which falls within s. 11(1)(*b*) of the Consumer Credit Act, 1974 but is not made by the creditor under pre-existing arrangements, or in the contemplation of future arrangements, between the creditor and the supplier; or 2. a restricted-use credit agreement which falls within s. 11(1)(*c*) of the Act; or 3. an unrestricted-use credit agreement which is not made by the creditor under pre-existing arrangements between himself/herself and a person (the 'supplier') other than the debtor, in the knowledge that the credit is to be used to finance a transaction between the debtor and the supplier.

debtor-creditor-supplier agreement. A regulated consumer credit agreement being: 1. a restricted-use credit agreement which falls within s. 11(1)(*a*) of the Consumer Credit Act, 1974; or 2. a restricted-use credit agreement which falls within s. 11(1)(*b*) of the Act and is made by the creditor under pre-existing arrangements, or in contemplation of future arrangements, between the creditor and the supplier; or 3. an unrestricted-use credit agreement which is made by the creditor under pre-existing arrangements between himself/herself and a person (the supplier) other than the debtor in the knowledge that the credit is to be used to finance a transaction between the debtor and the supplier. *See* CONNECTED LENDER LIABILITY .

debtor days ratio. The average time taken by the debtors to pay the debt due. The formula normally adopted to ascertain this ratio is:

$$\frac{\text{average debtors in the period}}{\text{average value of the credit sales}}$$

debtor's petition. Under the Insolvency Act, 1986 s. 2 that 1. a debtor's petition may be presented to the court only on the grounds that the debtor is unable to pay his or her debts; 2. the petition shall be accompanied by a statement of the debtor's affairs containing: (*a*) such particulars of the debtor's creditors, of the debts and other liabilities and of his or her assets as may be prescribed and (*b*) such other information as may be prescribed.

deceased partner. Subject to any agreement between the partners, the death of one of them dissolves the partnership. The surviving partner(s) must wind up the firm; usually, however, the partnership deed will provide that, notwithstanding the death of a partner, the business will be carried on. The share of the deceased partner must be ascertained and paid over to the deceased's personal representatives. If the firm's bank account is overdrawn it should be ruled off on notification of the death, to retain the liability of the deceased partner's estate for the debt.

deceit. The tort of fraudulent misrepresentation (*q.v.*).

declaration of dividend. The publication by a company of the decision of its board of directors that a dividend of a stated amount will be paid.

declining balance method. *See* REDUCING BALANCE METHOD OF DEPRECIATION.

decree. (*Sc Law*). The judgment of the court having been given, and no appeal having been notified, the decree of the court is extracted, i.e. an authenticated copy of the judgment is handed to the successful claimant. *See* JUDGMENT CREDITOR.

deed. A written document under seal, evidencing a legal transaction; an instrument containing the terms of a contract, and sealed as a formality. A deed must be signed, sealed and delivered by the parties to it. The date of delivery is the effective date of the deed.

deed of arrangement. Under the Insolvency Act, 1986 s. 260(3) this no longer applies to an approved voluntary arrangement. A voluntary arrangement as summoned under .258,

will allow the meeting of creditors to propose certain arrangements, but the debtor must consent to each and every proposal and modification.

deed of covenant An agreement under seal by a contributor to a charitable, etc., association that he will subscribe a fixed sum annually for a specified number of years. Such associations, if approved by the Inland Revenue, are then enabled to reclaim the tax paid by the contributor on these subscriptions.

deed of gift. A document under seal effecting the conveyance of property by way of gift.

deed of partnership. The agreement between partners recorded under seal. The deed will record the terms and conditions of the partnership, the ratios in which profits are to be shared, whether the business is to continue after the death, bankruptcy, etc., of a partner and so on.

deed of postponement. Where a bank is asked to lend money to a company and finds on examination of the balance sheet that a director has made a loan to the company it may feel that, if the director's loan is repaid by the company during the currency of the bank advance, then the company will be, by that amount, less able to repay the bank. The bank may therefore make it a condition of granting the loan that a deed of postponement be executed, by which the director undertakes not to accept repayment before the bank has been repaid, and the company similarly undertakes not to make repayment to the director. A clause may be inserted that in the event of the liquidation of the company the director will claim as an unsecured creditor, but hand any dividend received to the bank.

deed of priorities. A document which may arise when a company has given a floating charge to a bank as security, and the bank has stipulated that the company will not create any subsequent specific charge on an asset which would rank *pari passu* or ahead of the bank's charge. If the company later wishes to borrow from another source by means of a fixed charge over a particular asset, which would normally fall under the bank's floating charge, the company will have to request the bank's permission for this step. If this is granted, the document which the bank will then seal, together with the other lender, and the company customer, is called a Deed of Priorities.

deed of settlement. A deed made in consideration of marriage, for the benefit of the wife and/or any issue of the marriage; a deed, or will, or other instrument under which any land or other property stands for the time being limited in some way, e.g. in trust for any person by way of succession, or limited to, or in trust for, a married woman. *See also* SETTLED LAND.

deep discount. A large discount on the issue of a redeemable security.

de facto. In fact, actually.

defalcation. The misappropriation of any property by a person to whom the property was entrusted.

defamation. The publication of a statement which tends to lower a person in the estimation of right-thinking members of the community generally. Spoken defamation is slander, written defamation is libel. There are three special defences to an action for defamation – privilege, justification and fair comment. In certain cases an offer of amends, coupled with an apology, will entitle the defendant to some relief.

default. Fault, neglect, defect, failure to appear in a law-court when summoned. Failure to account for money held in trust, failure to repay a loan or an overdraft as promised. A person may be convicted or a default order made against him or her if found to contravene; 1. ss. 24 and 713 Companies Act, 1985; 2. ss. 41 and 170 Insolvency Act, 1986. *See also* JUDGMENT BY DEFAULT.

default notice. For the purposes of the Consumer Credit Act, 1974, a notice in a prescribed form, to be served on a debtor or hirer before a creditor or owner can become entitled, by reason of any breach by the debtor or hirer of a regulated agreement, to terminate the agreement, or to enforce any security, or to recover possession of goods or land, etc.

default order. An order by a court requesting an officer of a company to remedy a default in filing the accounts and returns of that company. Companies Act, 1985, s. 297.

defeasance. A condition relating to a deed and incorporated in it, which being performed renders the deed void; the act of annulling a contract.

deferred. Put off, postponed.

deferred annuity. An annuity which does not begin to operate until after a certain period.

deferred charges. Prepaid items for a period greater than the current accounting period, so that there is a balance of value to be carried forward to the subsequent accounting period, e.g. where rates are paid in advance, or a railway season ticket purchased for a year instead of for three months.

deferred expenditure *See* DEFERRED CHARGES.

deferred shares. Shares postponed to ordinary shares; they receive a dividend only if the dividend on the ordinary shares reaches a certain level. These are sometimes called *Management* or *Founder's shares*, and are created to renumerate the founders or promoters of a company. When the company profits are good the return from deferred shares may be very considerable.

deferred taxation. Tax which is payable in the year after which the profit was earned. Reference to this is in SSAP 15.

deficit. The excess of expenditure over

income. Frequently used in the accounts of non-profit organisations, whose aim is to match income and expenditure. An amount of money lost or missing.

defunct company. A company which has ceased to do business, and which has had its name struck off the register of companies.

del credere agent. An agent who guarantees to his or her principal that third parties with whom the agent contracts on the principal's behalf will always meet their obligations to the principal; if they do not, the *del credere* agent will make good the deficiency.

delegated authority. The agent to whom authority has been delegated by his principal may not further delegate. He or she must personally do the work. There are some common law exceptions to this rule. An agent may delegate if an express or implied agreement to that effect exists; where delegation is necessary for the proper performance of the work; where there is a trade usage to sanction the delegation; or if there is a sudden emergency necessitating delegation. Executors may delegate amongst themselves, i.e. one alone may sign cheques for the executors, but all trustees must sign. A trustee may, however, by statutory authority employ an agent, whether a solicitor, banker, stockbroker or other person to transact any business or to do any act required to be done in the execution of the trust, or may, by power of attorney, delegate for not longer than twelve months the execution of duties and powers vested in the trustee to any person except his or her only other co-trustee (unless a trust corporation). A trustee may delegate duties if so empowered by the instrument creating the trust.

delegation. The act of assigning work, a duty, or a completion of an order, to another. The ability to delegate is an essential requisite of successful management.

delivered at frontier. Terms indicating that the goods will be transported and all expenses paid up to the frontier of the buyer or the frontier of the country named in the contract, further expenses, including import duty should be paid by the buyer.

delivery. The act of delivering, transfer; the act of putting another in formal possession of property; the handing over of a deed to a grantee. Every contract on a bill, whether it be the drawer's, the acceptor's, or an indorser's, is incomplete and revocable until delivery of the instrument in order to give effect thereto

delivery note. A document accompanying the delivery of goods, particularising the items delivered, so that the consignee may check them.

delivery of bill or cheque. Transfer of possession, actual, or constructive, from one person to another. Ownership of a cheque or bill payable to 'bearer' is tranferred on delivery; of one payable to 'order', by indorsement and delivery.

delivery of deed. A deed must be signed sealed and delivered and until it is delivered, it is ineffective.

delivery order. An order by the owner or the holder of title to goods, addressed to a warehouse keeper, to the superintendent of a dock or wharf, or to a railway company holding the goods, authorising and requesting the superintendent to deliver the goods, whether in whole or in part, to the bearer of the order, or to the party thereon named by indorsement. The beneficiary should at once take delivery of the goods, or obtain a receipt or warrant, or have his or her title registered, whichever is appropriate; if this is not done, he or she runs the risk that a later delivery order will be issued and acted upon.

delivery terms. Indications as to whether consignor or consignee are to pay the delivery charges on goods consigned, e.g. carriage forward, carriage paid, CIF, FOB, etc.

demand. An authoritative claim or request; the desire to purchase or possess; a legal claim; the quantity of a product which will be bought at a particular price. *In demand.* Much sought after. *On demand.* At call, whenever requested.

demand and supply. A phrase used to denote the relation between consumption and production; if demand exceeds the supply the price rises, and *vice versa.*

demand deposit. An account with a bank or other financial institution e.g. a building society, where any or all of the money is repayable on demand, e.g. cheque account, current account, etc. In general, no interest is paid on this type of bank account, but accounts with certain minimum balances or cheque accounts with building societies and others do attract interest.

demand draft. A bill of exchange payable on demand; a cheque; a draft drawn by a bank on itself, its head office, or on a correspondent bank and payable on demand.

demand pull inflation. Demand for goods and services exceeds the supply, causing buyers to bid up the prices for such goods and services.

demise. To transfer or convey by lease or will; a transfer or conveyance by lease or will for a term of years or in fee simple; the granting of a lease.

demise charter. A charter party where the charterer of the ship makes all the arrangements for working it, hires the crew, etc., so that for the time being the charterer is effectively the owner.

demonetize. To deprive of its character as money; to withdraw (a metal) from currency; to diminish or deprive of monetary value.

demurrage. The undue detention of a ship; compensation paid by freighters if goods cause delays to barges, ships or wagons for such delay, or by port authorities if there is unreasonable

delay in berthing. There is usually a free period before the charge starts to operate.

deposit. To entrust, to lodge with anyone for safety or as a pledge; an earnest, a first instalment, a trust, a security. For the purposes of the Consumer Credit Act, 1974, 'deposit' means any sum payable by a debtor or hirer by way of deposit or down-payment, or credited or to be credited to him or her on account of any deposit or down-payment, whether the sum is to be or has been paid to the creditor or owner or any other person, or is to be or has been discharged by a payment of money or a transfer or delivery of goods or by any other means. For the purposes of the Banking Act, 1987 this refers to funds placed with a bank to be placed on either a deposit or current account and repayable, with or without interest, either on demand or at a time agreed between the parties. It can also refer to a payment made for the sale of land so as to bind a bargain.

deposit account. A bank account on which a rate of interest is payable. Such interest will be paid net of tax if the account holder is neither an overseas resident or a corporate customer. Funds are normally repayable at seven or fourteen days' notice. A statement is normally issued to a customer periodically.

deposit broker. Intermediaries who arrange for deposits to be placed with one bank or financial institution by another.

deposit insurance. In the UK the payment by banks of a sort of premium to a central fund whose resources will be used to repay depositors if they are in danger of losing their money on the failure of a bank. The Banking Act, 1987 gave protection to bank depositors by the formation of a deposit protection fund which is managed by the Bank of England. All recognised banks must contribute a total sum of not less than

£5m. The maximum contribution, applicable to the big clearers, is £300,000, but for small banks and deposit taking institutions any contribution is related to the deposit base, with a minimum of £5,000. The fund will be used to pay a depositor an amount equal to three-quarters of the deposit held if the institution which received this deposit becomes insolvent. This protection will apply for sums up to £20,000 for any depositor.

deposition. A written declaration (signed before a magistrate) by a witness who must later appear to testify in court.

deposit rate. The rate of interest paid by a bank on money on a deposit account.

deposit receipt. A receipt issued by bankers and others when money is lodged in a deposit account and no statement is issued.

deposit taking business. A business whose main function is to accept deposits. Under the Banking Act, 1987, no person, corporate or not, may accept a deposit unless authorised by the Bank of England. The minimum criteria required for a deposit taking business is stated in the Act.

depreciation. Of assets, a loss in value by fair wear and tear, obsolescence, etc., or normal deterioration in value which takes place during the life of an asset. This loss in value is recognised by a depreciation figure which may be calculated in a number of ways, of which two of the most common are the *Straight Line Method* and the *Reducing Balance Method.*

depreciation of a currency. Where exchange rates are floating, the value of the national currency will be determined by the demand for, and the supply of, that currency. If the demand is small because the country is exporting less than it is importing, or because investors in that country are losing confidence in the stability of its currency, or both, the exchange rate will fall and the currency will depreciate.

depression. A period of heavy unemployment, reduced business activity, and loss of confidence generally.

determination. Termination, conclusion, bringing to an end; settlement by a judicial decision. A debt due to a bank may be determined by a call on a guarantor, and the appointment of a receiver under a debenture, or notice of the death, bankruptcy or liquidation of the customer, etc.

devaluation. The reduction of the official par value of the legal unit of currency in terms of the currencies of other countries. Devaluations become necessary when one country's costs are rising faster than those of other countries, so that it becomes increasingly difficult to keep its exports competitive. The strain on the currency is often made worse by the activities of international money dealers who transfer their holdings of the weak currency into stronger currency, to avoid being caught with it after a devaluation, and thus intensify the weakness. Devaluations do not deal with the central problem, which is the country's lack of competitiveness, but only with the symptom or effect of the problem.

development land tax. Tax on the realised development value accruing to a seller on the disposal of an interest in land in the UK. Exempt from tax are individual's only or main residence (Development Land Tax, 1976) and, as from the Finance Act, 1980, charities. Since the latter date it is now possible for a developer to have the DLT liability on an intended project assessed up to two years before construction commences.

devise. The act of bequeathing landed property by will.

devisee. One to whom real property is left by will.

devolution. Transference or delegation of authority (as by Parliament to one of its committees); passage from one person to another; descent by inheritance; descent in natural succession.

diarising. The noting of points which need attention in the future. A banker will need to know the dates on which various instalments on an allotment letter are to be paid, the date on which a customer's life policy falls due for repayment, the days by which various returns must be made to Head Office, and many other matters. All these details can be listed under the relevant date on sheets of paper and sorted away in a filing system under months and days. Alternatively, a computer system may be used. Each morning a clerk will distribute around the office to the people who are going to attend to them the diary notes for the day. Diary notes should be made out for a few days before the actual or last possible dates.

dictum. An observation made by a judge on matters arising while hearing a case. *See also* OBITER DICTUM.

difference. Disagreement, the amount by which one total fails to agree with another; on the stock exchange, payment or receipt by a speculator on settlement day of the difference between the price at which his or her bargain was recorded on the day of its transaction and the price on settlement day.

differential duties. Variable duties imposed on the same commodity coming from different countries.

diligence *(Sc. Law).* A legal method by which an unsatisfied creditor may proceed to seize his or her debtor's property in satisfaction of the debt, or to prevent dissipation of the property by the debtor *(see* MAREVA INJUNCTION) either personally or by his or her agent *(see* INTROMISSION); the warrant issued by a court to enforce the attendance of witnesses, or the production of documents. Summary Diligence *(q.v.)* refers to certain cases where the creditor can use any of the

appropriate forms of diligence without having to establish the claims by an action in court.

Diners' Club. A credit card company originating in the USA in which National Westminster Bank has an interest. Since there is no specified limit, these cards are sometimes referred to as leisure cards.

direct. Straightforward, immediate, in a straight line.

direct access. The ability to obtain access to a location in a computer system directly without going via another location.

direct arbitrage. Dealings in foreign exchange which are confined to one centre.

direct cost. The cost of production in monetary terms. A cost that can be directly attributed to one or more products.

direct debit. A direct claim made by a creditor on a customer's account, to be paid by the bank on each occasion. The customer must approve this arrangement before any transfers are made and must authorise his or her banker to meet the claims. A single signed form will be enough to authorise the regular payments until further notice. The system, which is particularly suitable in the case of large creditors such as local authorities, gas and electricity boards, and insurance companies, permits variations in the periodic claims, such as may be expected in the case of, for instance, index-linked assurance policies.

direct expense. All items of cost in the manufacture of a product which are essentially linked with any stage of the production process, as opposed to overhead costs which continue irrespective of production.

directive. Tending to guide or advise; general orders from a supreme authority outlining procedure to be followed in the implementation of a new plan or policy; an instruction from the Bank of England to the lending banks imposing qualitative or quantitative limitations.

direct security. Security given directly by a borrower to a lender in consideration of the loan or advance being granted.

direct selling. Sales by the producer, manufacturer, or the supplier of a service directly to the consumer bypassing wholesaler, distributor and retailer.

direct tax. A tax levied on the taxpayer, e.g. income tax, as distinct from a tax levied on goods or services.

director. A member of a board of managers in a large commercial business. In a limited company a director is a member of the company appointed by his or her fellow members to administer the company's affairs. *See* SHADOW DIRECTOR; LOANS TO DIRECTORS.

director of savings. An officer appointed under Part 5 of the Post Office Act, 1969, under whose control the national savings facilities known as the National Savings Bank, the National Savings Stock Register, National Savings Certificates, Savings Bank Annuities and Insurances, and Premium Savings Bonds would be continued.

directors – duty of care. Directors have a duty of care to the company, its members and the employees. They are not liable for mere errors of judgment.

Director-General of Fair Trading. The Fair Trading Act, 1973 was concerned with both competition and consumer protection, and created new machinery for the control of unfair business practices, and consolidated the old law on monopolies, mergers and restrictive trade practices. The Act provided for the appointment of the Director-General and charged him or her with the tasks of 1. keeping under review commercial activities relating to the supply of goods and services to consumers; 2. collecting information about activities which may adversely affect the economic interests of the consumer; 3. reviewing commercial activities in monopoly conditions; 4. making appropriate recommendations on these matters to the Secretary of State for Trade. The Director-General is also obliged to take action with respect to courses of action detrimental to the interests of consumers. The Consumer Credit Act, 1974 placed on him or her the duties of 1. administering the licensing system set up by the Act; 2. exercising the adjudicating functions conferred on him in relation to the issue, renewal, variation, suspension and revocation of licences; 3. generally superintending the working and enforcement of the Act, and regulations made under it; and 4. where necessary personally taking steps to enforce the Act and the regulations made under it. The Director-General must keep these matters under review and from time to time advise the Secretary of State of social and commercial developments in the United Kingdom and elsewhere relating to the provision of credit or bailment or (in Scotland) hiring of goods to individuals and related activities, and about the working and enforcement of the Act and regulations and orders made under it.

directors' interests. Under the Company Act, 1985, a company must keep a register recording information of shares and debentures held by directors. Contracts with directors must be disclosed in the accounts.

directors' report. The report that must be attached to the annual final accounts and balance sheet of a company and circulated to the members of the company. The report must give a fair review of the development of the business of the company and its subsidiaries during the financial year of the balance sheet; the recommendations of the directors as to the application of profits; the principal activities of the company and its subsidiaries; and details of any major changes that have occurred and any likely future developments. Companies Act, 1985 s.235 and Sch.7.

dirty bill of lading. A bill of lading marked or claused to show that the goods or packing were received in a damaged condition.

dirty float. The essence of a floating currency is that the central bank shall not intervene either by buying or selling its own currency on the foreign exchange markets. However, the generally stated intention is to regard a floating rate of exchange as a temporary measure only, and to return to fixed parities when the currency has stabilised itself. A central bank may therefore look ahead to this time and push its currency to a level which it would like to see established, by quiet intervention in the currency markets.

discharge. To unload (from ship, vehicle, etc); to get rid of; to dismiss from employment; to set free from a binding obligation; to pay off, to settle, to perform, to pay a debt; to release from a duty by the issue of a suitable document, e.g. an executor's discharge; an entry in a bank's books to show that an item of security or safe custody has been released to a customer or to a third party; the signature of a customer in a Boxes and Parcels Book or in a Night Safe Wallet Record Book.

discharged bankrupt. A bankrupt is discharged from bankruptcy when the court is satisfied that all conditions of the court have been satisfied. The person concerned may consider his or her debts as settled and can therefore make a fresh start subject to the conditions imposed by the Insolvency Act, 1986 s.281.

discharged bill. A bill of exchange is discharged when payment is made in due course by or on behalf of the drawee or acceptor; where the acceptor of a bill becomes the holder of it at or after its maturity; where the holder of a bill at or after its maturity; unconditionally renounces his or her rights against the acceptor; or where a bill is intentionally cancelled by the holder or by the holder's agent. *See also* CANCELLATION.

disclaimer. A renunciation, disavowel or repudiation. Thus a beneficiary under a will may disclaim the gift, or a trustee in a bankruptcy may disclaim any asset in the bankrupt's estate which is burdened with onerous clauses. Insolvency Act, 1986, s. 315.

disclosure. *See* SECRECY.

discount. To deduct a certain sum or rate per cent from an account or price; the deduction of a sum for payment in advance; the act of discounting; the rate of discount; the depreciation in value of an investment. The amount of deduction at an agreed rate per cent per annum, which is calculated when the holder of a term bill which has still a period to run before its maturity wishes to cash it immediately. There must be two good names on the bill, which must be in respect of a genuine trade transaction. Discount is usually worked at overdraft rate and represents a charge on the amount of the bill for the number of days to its maturity. *See also* RECOURSE. In the foreign exchange market, the forward margin applied to a currency which is cheaper forward than it is spot in terms of another currency. It is added to the spot rate. *See also* CASH DISCOUNT; TRADE DISCOUNT. *At a discount.* Goods offered or bought at a reduction made as an inducement to an immediate sale; the market prices of bonds, shares or stock which are below the nominal value, so described.

discount broker. *See* BILL BROKER.

discounted cash flow. A way of comparing alternative capital projects by assessment of the present values of expected cash flows during the existence of each capital project.

discount house. *See* BILL BROKER.

discount market. The members of the

London Discount Market Association together with those money brokers and traders who are recognised and approved by the Bank of England. The discount houses make their profits by absorbing surplus funds from the banking system and investing them, mainly short-term, in a mixture of commercial and government paper. The market is at the centre of short-term money dealings. The principal functions of the discount houses may be summarised thus; 1. they provide a source of short-term funds for commerce and industry by discounting bills of exchange which have been accepted by the accepting houses and other financial institutions; 2. they provide a source of reserve assets for the banking system repayable AT CALL (*q.v.*) or short notice, thus making it possible for the banking system to work to minimum cash ratios; 3. they deal with the Treasury Bill issue, covering the whole of the tender; 4. they provide a secondary market in dollar and sterling certificates of deposit; 5. they help the Bank of England by dealing in short bonds and gilts which are nearing maturity and this assists in refinancing the National Debt.

discount rate. This is the rate at which the Federal Reserve bank will lend to its member banks on an overnight basis for the reserve purposes and can be regarded as the Central Bank Rate of the US. The discount rate is an important indicator of official government policy and the Federal Reserve has, on occasions, imposed a surcharge or premium on the discount rate to discourage unwarranted borrowing. In the UK the Bank of England discount rate is the rate at which it will discount first-class bills.

discount window. *See* WINDOW.

discretion. Prudence, discernment, liberty to act according to one's judgment.

discretionary income. That which re-

mains out of a person's income when all that person's basic needs and commitments have been met.

discretionary limits. *See* MANAGERS' DISCRETIONARY LIMITS.

discretionary trust. A trust calling for the exercise of discretion by the trustee(s), whether in the variation of the investments composing the trust, the timing of payments under the trust, the choice of beneficiaries of the trust, or the amount of a payment to be made. It is now the most convenient form of trust and the most widely used. There may also be some tax benefits.

disentail. To break the entail of (an estate), the act of disentailing. *See* BARRING THE ENTAIL.

disentailing assurance. *See* BARRING THE ENTAIL.

dishonour of a bill. A bill of exchange may be dishonoured either by non-acceptance or non-payment. It is dishonoured by non-acceptance when the drawee of a bill refuses to accept it. It is dishonoured by non-payment when the acceptor fails to pay it on the due date. A cheque is dishonoured when it is returned unpaid by the banker on whom it is drawn.

disinflation. The act or process of correcting an inflationary situation, but not to the extent of causing deflation. Disinflation is the concept of a target set by the authorities; deflation is one method which can be used to achieve that target.

disintermediation. A name given to the activities of the inter-company market. When money rates are high, it is often to the advantage of a company to borrow from another company rather than from a bank. These transactions were at their peak just before the secondary banking crisis.

disk. A circular container for the storage of computer data and programs. They have tracks which gives random accessibility for the speedy retrieval of information.

dispense. To divide out in parts; to

administer, as laws; to excuse from, to grant a dispensation from a duty or obligation.

dispensing notice. For the purposes of the Consumer Credit Act, 1974, an authority signed by a joint account holder waiving his/her right to receive separate current account bank statements.

disposable income. Income left after all direct taxes have been deducted.

disposition. The act of disposing, arrangement, guidance, conveyance of property.

disseize. To deprive of an estate in freehold wrongfully.

disseizin. Unlawful dispossession of freehold land.

dissenting creditor. Under the Insolvency Act, 1986, a general meeting of creditors (creditors committee) the actions of this committee being limited (s. 301/2). If any creditor (or bankrupt) is dissatisfied by any act, omission or decision of a trustee of the bankrupt's estate, he or she may apply to the court; and on such an application the court may confirm, reverse or modify any act or decision of the trustee, may give the trustee direction, or may make such other order as it thinks fit. Section 303.

dissolution. Disintegration, termination (of marriage, partnership, etc); dismissal of an assembly (as of Parliament before a general election).

dissolution of a company. The termination of a company and its business by winding-up and striking off the register of companies. *See* COMPULSORY LIQUIDATION OR WINDING-UP; VOLUNTARY LIQUIDATION.

dissolution of partnership. The ending of a partnership by expiration of an agreed term; or by notice by a partner; or by the death, bankruptcy or retirement of any partner; or by charge on a partner's share for a separate debt; or by the happening of an event which makes it unlawful to continue the partnership; or by an order of the

court on application of a partner; or by the insolvency of the partnership; or by the completion of the purpose for which the partnership was established.

distrain. To seize for debt, to take the personal chattels of, in order to satisfy a demand or enforce the performance of an act, to take possession of.

distraint. The act of seizing goods for a debt.

distress. The act of distraining, goods taken in distraint. *See also* DISTRINGAS.

distress borrowing. High interest rates are supposed to discourage people from borrowing money. In the UK, in recent years, this system has demonstrated that this is not always so. Companies see that the alternative to liquidation is to borrow more money, whatever the rate, just to keep going, just as the motorist or the heavy smoker will continue to pay heavier charges. Companies may even be forced to borrow to finance high interest payments – if they can. This is 'distress borrowing'.

distributable profits. The profits of a limited company that are available for distribution to members as a dividend. They must not contravene current law. For the purposes of the Companies Act, 1985 s.263(3), it is accumulated, realised profits, so far as not previously utilised by distribution or capitalisation, less its accumulated, realised losses, so far as not previously written off in a reduction or reorganisation of capital duly made. For a public company s. 264 of the Act states that a company is further restricted in that its net assets must not be less than the aggregate of its called-up share capital and undistributable reserves at the time of or after a distribution.

distribution. Apportionment, division; the apportionment of wealth among the various classes of the community; the allotment of goods by producers among consumers.

distribution expense. The cost of dispersion among consumers of a finished product; those expenses which are associated with the distribution of goods, e.g. warehousing facilities, carriage outwards, postage, packaging and containerisation.

distributive cost. The cost of getting the goods from the place where they are produced to the point of consumption.

District Land Registry. Following the decentralisation of the work of the Land Registry a number of district land registries were set up, each handling the registration of titles within its own district. A list of all counties, county boroughs and London boroughs, with the district land registries which serve them can be obtained from the Land Registry.

distringas. An old writ that was abolished in 1883. In its place is the *notice in lieu of distringas. See* NOTICE IN LIEU OF *DISTRINGAS.*

dividend. 1. A payment made out of the profits of a company to the shareholders or stockholders. The payment may be at a fixed rate, as with preference shares (always assuming that profits permit), or at a variable rate, reflecting trading success, to the ordinary or 'equity' shareholders. It may be omitted altogether if the company has made no profit, or insufficient profit, or is in trouble with its cash flow. 2. A distribution by a trustee in bankruptcy paid to creditors in respect of realisation of the bankrupt's assets, or by a liquidator in respect of the realised assets of a company which is being wound up. *See also* DIVIDEND IN BANKRUPTCY; EQUALISING THE DIVIDEND; FINAL DIVIDEND; INTERIM DIVIDEND; PASSING THE DIVIDEND.

dividend counterfoil. The top or side portion of a dividend warrant, containing the name and address of the shareholder, number of shares held, the gross amount, tax credit and the net amount payable. Where the dividend has been paid direct to a bank for

the credit of the shareholder's account, the dividend counterfoil will be used as a credit voucher and should be handed to the customer, with his or her statement, to be used as evidence of income received and tax deducted.

dividend cover. The money needed for a dividend payment divided into the profits (after tax) of the company available for the payment.

dividend in bankruptcy. Should a trustee in bankruptcy have sufficient funds, after dealing with preferential debts as stated in the Insolvency Act, 1986, s.386, the trustee may give notice to declare a dividend. In the trustee's calculation of the amount to be distributed, consideration must be given in his/her provisions to 1. bankruptcy debts due but not yet proven; 2. bankruptcy debts claimed, but not yet determined; 3. disputed claims and proofs – s.324. Section 330 states: '1. When the trustee has realised all the bankrupt's estate or so much of it as can, in the trustee's opinion, be realised without needlessly protracting the trusteeship, he/she shall give notice in the prescribed manner either *(a)* of the intention to declare a final dividend, or *(b)* that no dividend, or further dividend, will be declared.

dividend limitation. Restriction on any increase in dividend payments as a measure to check inflation.

dividend mandate. An authority from a shareholder to the company to send shareholding dividends direct to his or her bank for credit to his or her account.

dividend warrant. An order or warrant issued by a company and drawn on its bankers, authorising them to pay the dividend specified thereon to the stock or shareholder.

dividend yield. The gross dividend on a share divided by the share price.

docket. A summary or digest; a register of judgments; an alphabetical list of cases for trial; a similar summary of business to be dealt with by a committee or assembly; an indorsement of a letter or document summarising the contents; a warrant certifying payment of duty, issued by a customs house; a ticket or label showing the address of a package, etc. Used in a legal sense, to make an abstract, summary or digest of judgments and enter in a docket; to make an abstract or note of the contents of (a document) on the back.

dock warrant. A warrant issued by a dock company in respect of goods in their possession, specifying details of the goods, naming the ship in which they were imported, the consignee to whom they are addressed, and the date from which they were warehoused. If dock warrants are accepted by a banker as security, they should be indorsed by the customer and accompanied by a lien letter or a memorandum of deposit. A safer alternative is to have the goods transferred into the bank's name in the books of the dock company or, if the goods have been warehoused, the warehouse keeper.

document. A written or printed paper containing information for the establishment of facts; to furnish with documents necessary to establish any fact, to prove by means of documents. Documents include maps, plans, drawings and under the Civil Evidence Act, 1968 can include, photographs, discs, sound tracks tapes or any similar device.

documentary bill. A bill of exchange or promissory note which is accompanied by commercial paper, such as bills of lading, invoice, insurance documents, certificates of origin, etc.

documentary credit. A method of financing overseas trade whereby the contracting parties insert in the sales contract a provision that payment shall be made by a banker under the provisions of a documentary credit. Under this system, a banker under-

takes to pay the amount stated on the documentary credit or accept a bill of exchange, in return for the delivery to him or her by the exporter of the commercial and shipping documents provided they are in strict conformity with the terms and conditions of the documentary credit. The undertaking on the letter of credit may be irrevocable or revocable. All letters of credit are opened in accordance with the International Chamber of Commerce publication *Uniform Customs and Practice for Documentary Credits, 1984. See also* ACCEPTANCE CREDIT; BACK TO BACK CREDIT; CONFIRMED CREDIT; IRREVOCABLE CREDIT; NEGOTIATION CREDIT; PRE-FINANCE CREDIT; REFINANCE CREDIT; REIMBURSEMENT CREDIT; REVOCABLE CREDIT; REVOLVING CREDIT; RED CLAUSE; SIGHT CREDIT; TERM CREDIT; TRANSFERABLE CREDIT.

documentary evidence. The production of documents with the intention that they shall be made available for inspection, e.g. in a court of law.

document of title. A document which enables the possessor to deal with the property described in it as if he or she were the owner (as indeed may often be the case), e.g. a share certificate, a life insurance policy, a bill of lading.

documents against acceptance (D/A). *See* BILL FOR COLLECTION.

documents against payment (D/P). *See* BILL FOR COLLECTION.

dollar certificate of deposit. Certificates of deposit were introduced in the United States in1961, and were so successful that similar dollar certificates were issued by US banks on the London market five years later. A substantial market developed in these certificates. The certificates appeal to short term holders of dollars who would like to invest a sum of dollars which is not large enough to be of interest to the Eurodollar market, or who do not know for certain how long they will wish to hold them. By investing them in dollar certificates of deposit they are certain to get the dollars back when they need them and in the meantime enjoy a rate of interest. Certificates are issued in multiples of $1,000 with a minimum of $25,000, for maturities of 30, 60, 90, 120 days. Longer term certificates are also available.

domestic banking. The normal course of business between banker and customer as opposed to *wholesale* banking or *international banking*.

domestic credit expansion (DCE). Bank and overseas lending to the public sector plus bank lending in sterling to the private and overseas sector plus changes in the public's holdings of notes and coin. The importance of DCE is that when the domestic supply of money exceeds the domestic demand, the excess tends to flow abroad. Sterling is sold in exchange for foreign currency bought and reserves have to be used, or the rate drops, or both.

domicile. The place at which a bill of exchange is made payable; the place where a person has a permanent place of residence or home, the fact of residence in a particular country with the intention of remaining there.

domiciled bill. A bill whereupon the acceptor, at the time of accepting it, has specified a place, such as a bank, where the bill is payable.

donation. A sum of money given by one person to another. An asset given as a gift to another person. Donations given by businesses are not normally justifiable expenses.

dormant. Sleeping, undeveloped, inactive, inoperative, in abeyance.

dormant account. An account which has not been used by the customer for a long time, so that the balance has remained unchanged. Such balances are eventually transferred from a branch to a central account, but this is

for good administration only. The Statute of Limitations does not apply to dormant accounts, which may be claimed at any time.

dormant company. A company, under the Companies Act, 1985, which for any period has had no significant accounting transaction as defined by s.221 of the Act. If a private company is dormant then its members can resolve not to appoint auditors for the period in which it has been dormant.

dormant partner. One who has money invested in the firm, but takes no active part in it. The dormant partner shares in the profits and is also liable for the firm's debts.

double coincidence of wants. A term used in the study of monetary theory. Thus when speaking of barter (*q.v.*) it is usual to posit a primitive community where there is no money. But as primitive communities develop into more advanced societies people specialise in what they can do best, and barter becomes a clumsy method of exchange. The cobbler who wanted to advertise the shoes he made had not only to find a printer who was willing to print the hand-bills, but also a printer who happened to want a pair of shoes. This was called the 'double coincidence of wants'.

double entry. A system of book-keeping in which every transaction is entered twice, once on the credit side of the account that gives, and once on the debit side of the account that receives.

double taxation relief. Relief given to a taxpayer so that he or she is not taxed twice on the same income under two separate jurisdictions. For example, a UK citizen, residing in the UK, receives an income from abroad, then it is quite likely tax had been deducted at source. Providing there is a taxation treaty between the UK and the other country, the taxpayer will receive credit for the overseas tax paid when the UK tax liability on this income is determined.

Dow Jones Index. *See* INDICE DOW JONES.

down payment. A deposit of part of the purchase price as evidence of good faith, an earnest; a deposit in connection with a hire purchase transaction.

d/p. *See* DOCUMENTS AGAINST PAYMENT.

draft. The first outline of any scheme, writing or document; a rough sketch of work to be executed; a written order for the payment of money; a cheque or bill drawn, especially by a department or branch of a bank – usually on its head office, other branch or another bank. *See also* BANKERS' DRAFT; DEMAND DRAFT; FOREIGN DRAFT.

drain on the reserves. A run on the stocks of foreign currency held by a country which may become sufficiently serious to lead to a devaluation, or, in the case of a floating rate, an adverse movement which necessitates support by the central bank; an adverse influence on the liquid position of a company caused, e.g. by inflation.

draw. To picture or portray; to write a cheque, draft or order upon a banker.

drawback. Money paid back, especially excise or import duty remitted or refunded on goods exported; a deduction, a rebate.

draw down. To take up part or all of an agreed standby facility – not normally applied to retail banking in the form of overdrafts, but more often found in connection with standby facilities in the wholesale market of £100,000 and upwards.

drawee. The person on whom a bill is drawn. When this individual has accepted the bill he or she is known as the *acceptor*. The acceptor of a bill, by accepting it engages to accord to the tenor of his or her acceptance, and cannot deny to a holder in due course 1. the existence of the drawer, the genuineness of his or her signature, and capacity and authority to draw the bill; 2. in the case of a bill drawn to drawer's order, the then capacity of the drawer to indorse, but not the genuineness or validity of his or her indorsement; 3. in the case of a bill payable to the order of a third person, the existence of the payee and the payee's then capacity to indorse, but not the genuineness or validity of the payee's indorsement. The acceptor accepts a bill by signing his or her name across the face of it. *See also* ACCEPTANCE.

drawer. The person who writes out and signs a cheque or a bill of exchange. By drawing the bill the drawer engages that on presentation it will be accepted and paid according to its tenor, and if it is not he or she will compensate the holder or any indorser who is compelled to pay it, provided that the requisite proceedings on dishonour are taken. The drawer cannot deny to a holder in due course existence of the payee and his or her then capacity to indorse.

drawing account. A current account; an account used to record all sums drawn by a partner or business proprietor for amounts taken for his or her personal use.

drawing rights. *See* SPECIAL DRAWING RIGHTS.

drawn bond. A bond which has been drawn or selected for repayment upon a certain date.

drive-in bank. A branch office having a cashier so positioned that he/she may pay money to, or receive money from, a customer through the window of the customer's car.

droplock stock. An issue of stock by a borrower on the terms that interest will be paid at a certain figure which will float up and down with market rates, but if the rate falls to a certain minimum the loan will automatically convert into a period loan at a stated fixed interest rate. The idea has been used both in local authority financing and in commercial borrowing arrangements. For borrowers it is a means of securing long-term money when interest rates are either volatile or expected to rise. Investors gain some protection of their income together with a stable capital value. The 'trigger' for locking in the loan is known in advance, and may be at the borrower's option. Bank lending has used this principle for many years; for example a loan at 2 per cent above base rate, minimum 7 per cent.

dual capacity. Since October 1986, the functions of broker and jobber have merged, so that the market makers are now acting in dual capacity. *See* BIG BANG.

dual control. The principle that two bank officers, one preferably being a senior, must together take some act such as entering the bank's strongroom; the system of keyholding to ensure this; the appointment of not less than two trustees to administer a trust.

dual purpose trust. *See* SPLIT CAPITAL TRUST.

due date of bill. The date on which a bill of exchange is payable. This is on the last day of the time of payment as fixed by the bill, or, if that is a non-business day, on the succeeding business day. The time of payment as fixed by the bill is at a fixed and stated period after date or sight, or on or at a fixed period after the occurrence of a specified event which is certain to happen. A demand bill is payable on demand, or at sight, or on presentation. A cheque, unless post-dated is payable on demand. A post dated cheque is payable on or after its date.

dumping. Selling goods in overseas markets at a cheaper rate than in the home market.

Dun and Bradstreet. An organisation, known in banking and financial circles as one that provides information about public quoted companies. Useful to stock exchange investors.

duopoly. A situation where there are only two producers of a particular commodity.

duplicate. A copy of an original document having equal binding force; a copy made in lieu of a document lost or destroyed; the second copy of a bill drawn in two parts; Where a bill has been lost before it is overdue, the person who was the holder of it may apply to the drawer to give him or her a duplicate bill, giving the drawer an indemnity if required.

duration of bankruptcy. Insolvency Act, 1986 s.279(1): Subject as follows, a bankrupt is discharged from bankruptcy: *(a)* in the case of an individual who was adjudged bankrupt on a petition under s.264(1)*(d)* – i.e. under the powers of the Criminal Courts Act – or who had been an undischarged bankrupt at any time in the period of 15 years ending with the commencement of the bankruptcy, by an order of the court under the section next following and *(b)* in any other case, by the expiration of the relevant period under this section. 2. That period is as follows; *(a)* where a certificate for the summary administration of the bankrupt's estate has been issued and is not revoked before the bankrupt's discharge, the period of two years beginning with the commencement of the bankruptcy and *(b)* in any other case, the period of three years beginning with the commencement of the bankruptcy.

duress. Hardship, imprisonment or constraint actual or threatened violence. If, in an action on a bill, it is admitted or proved that the acceptance, issue or subsequent negotiation of the bill is affected with fraud, duress, force or fear, or illegality, the burden of proof is shifted, unless and until the holder proves that, subsequent to the alleged fraud or illegality, value has in good faith been given for the bill.

dutch auction. A sale in which property is offered above its value, and the price is gradually lowered until someone accepts an offer. *See also* AUCTION; SALE BY CANDLE.

duty. A legal or moral obligation to another; a tax on either imports or exports.

duty of care. Taking reasonable care to avoid acts or omissions which could injure a person e.g., a banker is under duty of care to ensure the safety of a customer's items on safe custody. As agent, a banker must deal promptly and diligently with his or her customer's instructions.

E

E&OE. *See* ERRORS AND OMISSIONS EXCEPTED.

earmark. Any distinctive mark or feature; to set a distinctive mark upon; to allocate for a particular purpose – used especially of the allocation of funds or of a balance on an account.

earned income. For tax purposes, income derived from paid employment, whether as an employee or as a self-employed person, as contrasted with *Unearned Income*.

earned income relief. A fundamental distinction has always been made in UK taxation between earned and unearned income, the latter being taxed at a higher rate. Especial relief was given to earned income because it was the direct result of the personal labour of the taxpayer. With the introduction of unified tax, the earned income relief was abolished, a compensatory increase in personal allowances being given in lieu.

earnest. A pledge, an assurance of something to come. Money given by a buyer to a seller to bind an oral agreement between them.

earning assets. Those assets of a bank which earn an income for the bank, i.e. money at call and short notice, bills discounted, investments and advances.

earnings. Money received from employment. The net profit of a business before deduction of tax.

earning yield. The profit of a limited company in relation to the total of the ordinary share capital, after all charges have been paid; that yield which would be obtained if all the company's profits were paid out as dividends and no amounts were retained.

easement. A liberty, right or privilege, without profit, which one proprietor has in or through the estate of another, e.g., a right of way, air, light etc. An easement may be legal or equitable.

ECGD Policy. A policy issued by the Export Credits Guarantee Department (*q.v.*), issued to exporters by the Department of Trade to give them cover against the insolvency or default of the overseas buyer and various other risks not ordinarily insurable. A charge on such a policy may be taken by a bank.

ECU. *See* EUROPEAN CURRENCY UNIT.

econometrics. The use of statistical and mathematical methods in the evaluation and testing of economic theories.

economic growth. The rate of expansion in the volume of production of goods and services of a country, the rate at which the gross national product increases from one year to another.

economic planning. The allocation of the factors of production of a country following a decision as to the amount and kind of goods and services which shall be produced in an ensuing period.

economics. The science which deals with the rules governing the production, distribution and consumption of the world's resources and the management of State income and expenditure in terms of money.

Edge Act Corporations. Edge Act Corporations are federally chartered institutions organised under s. 25(*a*) of the Federal Reserve Act and governed by the regulations of the Board of Governors of the Federal Reserve System. The name is derived from Senator Walter E. Edge, who engineered their existence in 1919. 'Edge Acts', as the offices are commonly referred to, can engage only in international or foreign banking operations. They have traditionally been used by US banks to conduct banking operations outside their home states although any deposits gathered by an Edge Act must be directly related to the financing of foreign trade. The International Banking Act, 1978 allowed foreign banks for the first time to form Edge Act corporations; until then these had to be owned by citizens of the US.

edict. A proclamation or decree issued by authority.

edictal, edictal citation. *(Sc. Law)* A citation, *see* CITE, by a proclamation when personal citation is impossible.

effective date. For the purpose of the provisions of utility services to a company, arrangement may be made by the office holder i.e. the administrator, administrative receiver, the supervisor of a voluntary arrangement or the liquidator, for the giving of gas, electricity, water, etc. The supply will depend on the date *(a)* the administration order was made *(b)* the appointment of the administrative receiver *(c)* the approval by the meetings of the voluntary arrangement *(d)* the liquidation of the company *(e)* the appointment of the provisional liquidator. Insolvency Act, 1986, s. 233 refers.

effects not cleared. *See* UNCLEARED EFFECTS.

elasticity. The ability of a bank to meet its credit and currency demands when necessary and reduce the availability of credit and currency during periods of over expansion and curtailment.

election. A choice. A legal doctrine where a person must choose between one of two courses, as where a plaintiff may elect to sue one or other of joint defendants, but cannot sue first one and then the other; or where a beneficiary under a will must choose one of two advantageous courses, but cannot take the benefit of both together.

electronic banking. Any banking service which is likely to involve the use of home banking facilities and plastic cards, i.e. for EFTPOS services, ATM, etc. It can also include the transmission of funds via SWIFT, CHAPS and BACS. There are pilot schemes in the use of computer terminals and plastic cards for customer records, interview notes, and the ability for customers to obtain advances, purchase/sell stocks and shares, etc by use of a card and a personal identification number (PIN).

Electronic Data Processing (EDP). The collection, storage, manipulation and retrieval of data by the use of computers. Most procedures in UK banking, consist of fairly simple but repetitive operations which take place millions of times each working day. It is these operations that are essential for the smooth operations in the banking system that allow customers to transmit funds wherever they wish either by cheque, standing order or direct debit; to draw out funds either at another branch or through any ATM, or request the bank to perform any one or more services on their behalf. Data processing is the means whereby the banks internal management and customers services are recorded, stored and processed.

electronic funds transfer at point of sale (EFTPOS). Generally this service is only at an experimental stage in 1987/8 in the UK, although it is in full use in Scandinavia and other countries. It is commonly known as EFTPOS or referred to as *The Smart Card.* It is a method of purchasing goods and services by the use of a plastic card which has in its metallic strip all the necessary information, then with the amount being tapped into the computer, the amount owed by the customer to the retailer is then transferred from the customer's account to the retailer's account, whether or not they use the same bank. In order to effect a transfer of funds, the customer hands over the card to the cashier who 'wipes' it through a card-reader where the information is read. The cardholder will then enter his or her Personal Identification Number (PIN) which is then checked and if the amount is within the agreed limit, there is no record that the card has been reported as lost or stolen, and the amount is acceptable, the transaction is authorised within thirty seconds. A receipt for the transaction is given to the customer and depending on the time of day the transaction took place the transfer of funds will take place within twenty-four to forty-eight hours.

electronic office. Often called a 'paperless office'. The computers being at an advanced stage, some of the larger banks are experimenting with branches that will have little or no paper and the needs of customers can be responded to by machines by the use of the 'plastic card'. The customer can, for example, order a statement, purchase/sell stocks and shares, transfer funds. The clerks in the branch, will store, retrieve and amend information via the computer.

eligibility. For a banker's acceptance to be 'eligible' for re-discount at the US Federal Reserve the acceptance must be for less than 180 days and created: 1. to finance the importation or exportation of goods; shipping documents conveying or securing title to the goods must be provided at the time of acceptance; 2. to cover the domestic shipment of goods within the US against a negotiable inland carrier bill of acceptance; 3. to cover the financing of goods in warehouse whether in the US or in a foreign country, provided that the accepting bank is secured throughout the life of the acceptance by a negotiable warehouse receipt or other such document conveying or securing title in their name covering 'readily marketable staples'. *See also* BANKERS' ACCEPTANCES.

eligible bill. A bank bill payable in the United Kingdom accepted by a British or Commonwealth bank whose name appears on a list published by the Bank of England, including the London and Scottish clearing banks, members of the Accepting Houses Committee, the larger British Overseas banks and those Commonwealth banks which have had branches in the City of London for many years, together with certain other banks and some Bank of England customers of long standing. These bills are eligible for re-discount at the Bank of England. A new system for control of the money supply was put into operation by the Bank of England in August 1981. Under the new monetary arrangements the Bank controls the level of liquidity in the banking system and influences interest rates entirely through open market operations, rather than by lending directly to the discount houses. This involves buying and selling eligible bills. To make the market in Treasury Bills and commercial bills large enough to allow interest rates to be influenced there rather than by announcements about minimum lending rate (*q.v.*) (which is now discontinued) and direct lending to the discount houses, the bank has widened the field of 'first-class names' by accepting a further 51 banks which are included for the first time in the privileged list of 'eligible names' into the group as described above. These new eligible names not only already had to have a substantial high-quality bill business in London, but to come from countries providing reciprocal facilities to British banks in their domestic markets. American, Japanese, Swiss, German and French banks have been selected among others. Banks receiving eligible status can then issue bills which are then eligible for re-discount at the Bank of England, through the intermediary of the discount market. This privilege makes bills particularly attractive as investments to the discount houses, which are consequently prepared to pay a premium for them. The one penalty for banks receiving eligible status is that they will be required as a *quid pro quo* (*q.v.*) for the benefits conferred to hold a minimum of 2½ per cent and an average of 5 per cent of their deposits with the discount houses. This recent widening of eligibility removed what was probably the last head of discrimination in London against EEC banks.

eligible liabilities. The sterling deposits of the banking system as a whole, excluding deposits having an original maturity of more than two years, plus any sterling resources gained by switching foreign currencies into sterling, and including promissory notes, bills and other negotiable paper, items in suspense and 60 per cent of credit items in transmission. Interbank transactions and sterling certificates of deposit (both held and issued) are taken into the calculation of individual banks' liabilities on a net basis, irrespective of term. *See also* CORSET; RESERVE ASSETS; SPECIAL DEPOSITS.

embargo. A prohibition by authority upon the departure of vessels from ports under its jurisdiction; a complete suspension of foreign commerce or of a particular branch of foreign trade; an order forbidding the despatch of a certain class of goods, usually munitions, to a foreign country; a prohibition of any travel in or out of a country, whether by land, sea or air, as a result of an attempted coup.

embassy documents. Consular and legalised invoices required by certain importing countries' authorities.

embezzlement. The fraudulent misappropriation by an employee to his or her own use of money or goods rightfully belonging to his or her employer.

emblement. The produce of land sown or planted; growing crops annually produced by the labour of the cultivator, which belong to the tenant, though the tenant's lease may terminate before harvest, and in the event of death fall to his or her executors; sometimes extended to the natural products of the soil.

emoluments. The total monetary payments for work done or services given. The amount of money so given whether it is for fees, salaries, wages, share of profits, etc is chargeable for tax.

Employment Protection Act, 1975. This Act was intended to improve the relationship between employer and employee and at the same time establish ACAS. The Act was amended in 1978 and consolidated the Redundancy Acts of 1965 and 1969, the Contracts of Employment Act, 1972 and the Trade Union and Labour Relations Acts of 1974 and 1976.

encoding. The imprinting of MICR (Magnetic Ink Character Recognition) characters on cheques, credits and other documents to permit them to be processed by computers.

encumbrance. *See* INCUMBRANCE.

endorsement. *See* INDORSEMENT.

endowment mortgage. A life assurance policy coupled with a mortgage contract. Thus a lender buying a house on mortgage can insure his or her life on the terms that upon death the outstanding debt on the mortgage will be paid off, thus leaving a widow or widower somewhere assured to live. As the years pass and the mortgage debt reduces, the time will come when the endowment element of the policy exceeds the mortgage debt and there will be something left over for the estate of the policyholder, should he or she then die, or for payment to the policyholder on age say sixty, should he or she survive that long. Endowment mortgages may be full with-profits or low-cost. With a low-cost endowment mortgage, a with-profits policy, with a sum assured of less than the actual mortgage loan, is taken out. If the policyholder should die, the mortgage is paid off as before: if the policyholder survives the eventual proceeds of the policy, plus bonuses, should be enough to cover the loan. At the same time, borrowers take out a term policy, to cover their houses. The main disadvantage of low-cost endowment mortgages is that in the early years annual payments are higher than those on an ordinary prepayment mortgage. Another disadvantage is that endowment mortgages are inflexible. When mortgage rates increase, borrowers cannot extend the term of their loan. The advantage is that the proceeds of the policy are almost certain to produce not only enough cash to clear the loan, but also a surplus for the borrower as well. The net cost of the mortgage should therefore eventually be smaller than that of a repayment mortgage.

endowment policy. A life assurance policy under the terms of which a fixed sum of money is payable at the end of a certain number of years if the insured has survived that long, e.g. payable at the age of sixty. Such policies may be with or without profits.

endowment profits. Profits made by banks from higher interest rates imposed as a matter of governmental policy, and not as a result of any particular action taken by them. The very high minimum lending rate (*q.v.*) obtaining throughout 1980 resulted in record bank profits and there is a body of opinion which thinks that anyone making money out of high interest rates should pay a special tax on profits made. A 'windfall' tax (*q.v.*) on bank profits was imposed in 1981.

enfranchisement. The conversion of a copyhold into freehold on commutation of services due to the lord of the manor. The granting of a vote to shares that were previously non-voting.

engage. To enter into employment, or to do something. To enter into a contract.

enquête par sondage. Sample survey.

enquiry (status or bankers). *See* STATUS ENQUIRY.

entailed interest. *See* ESTATE IN FEE TAIL..

enterprise zones. Zones of about 500 acres in inner city locations where conventional Government policies in the UK have not succeeded in generating economic activity. Originally the idea of Professor Hall, Head of Geography at Reading University, the concept was adopted by the Chancellor in his Budget speech in March 1980 and passed in the Finance Act of that year. The concessions for these areas include 1. no rates on commercial and industrial property; 2. no development land tax; 3. 100 per cent capital allowance for income and corporation tax purposes; 4. simplified planning rules; 5. faster customs facilities; 6. no training levies; 7. a reduction to the basic minimum of government requests for statistical information. The aim is to stimulate economic activity by removing the hand of government as far as possible. The important thing is that people should make money and generate new jobs. Consultations were held with local authorities responsible for the sites already short-listed by the government, and the first enterprise zone at Swansea opened in June 1981. It got off to a slow start and there were many complaints about unfair competition from businesses just outside the zone. Nevertheless, by July 1982 there were twelve enterprise zones.

entrepôt. A bonded warehouse; an intermediate warehouse for goods in transit. *See also* RE-EXPORT.

entrepreneur. A contractor, an organiser of trade or business, one who brings land, capital and labour together in pursuit of some defined commercial end.

entry. The act of inscribing in a book; an item so entered; a credit or debit amount passed to a customer's account; the act of *taking possession* by setting foot upon land or tenements; the *depositing* of a document in the proper-office; the formal placing on record. *See also* DOUBLE ENTRY; SINGLE ENTRY.

Equal Credit Opportunity Act. This Act, which became law on 28 October 1975, was originally introduced to ban discrimination in the grant of credit on the basis of sex or marital status. It was later amended in March 1976 to cover also discrimination based on race, colour, religion, national origin and age.

equal pay. Equal remuneration for both men and women for work of equal value; the removal of discrimination between men and women concerning pay and conditions of employment.

equalising the dividend. If necessary, supplementing a dividend payment from reserves, or reducing a possible dividend sum so as to permit a transfer to reserves, in order to maintain a dividend at a consistent and reliable level.

equipment bond. On the Continent, railway company bonds secured by a charge on rolling stock.

Equipment Leasing Association. The growth of the business of equipment leasing led to the formation in 1971 of the Equipment Leasing Association, whose aims are to represent to the authorities the view of its members on any proposed or actual legislation which may affect the leasing industry; to increase awareness of leasing and its role in helping the economic development of the country; and, because leasing in the UK is closely linked to the system of taxation, to keep taxation and monetary policy under special and continuous review. At May 1982 there were fifty-nine members in this association.

equitable assignment. An assignment is a transfer by a creditor to an assignee of the right to receive a benefit (usually money) from a debtor. The requirements for a legal assignment were stated in the Law of Property Act, 1925. The assignment must be absolute and not purporting to be by way of charge only; it must be in writing and notice of the assignment must be given to the debtor. If these conditions are satisfied the assignment passes, subject to prior equities, the legal right to the debt together with all legal remedies for non-payment. An assignment which does not satisfy all these statutory conditions is an equitable assignment. Bankers are concerned with assignment in three cases; bills of exchange, life policies, and book debts. In the case of bills of exchange, including cheques, the proceeds are assigned every time the bill, or cheque, is negotiated. In the cases of life policies and book debts, the banker is concerned because he commonly takes both these forms of security. *See also* ASSIGNMENT.

equitable charge. *See* EQUITABLE MORTGAGE.

equitable doctrine. A legal principle belief stemming from equity, which offers a more just alternative to a common law principle.

equitable estate. The estate enjoyed by a beneficiary to whom come all the income and advantages of the estate, as opposed to the *Legal Estate,* which may be held by trustees who must negotiate any matters relating to the legal ownership of the estate, which they hold for the benefit of the owner of the equitable estate. A person may be both the legal estate owner and at the same time the owner of the equitable estate, as a person who owns the unencumbered house in which he or she lives.

equitable interest. An interest which before 1873 would have been enforceable only in a court of equity. Since then common law and equity have been administered side by side in the same courts, and equitable interest is one dependent not on common law but upon principles of equity.

equitable lien. A lien which most generally arises when a seller has passed property to a buyer before payment has been made. He or she becomes entitled to an equitable lien for the amount of the unpaid purchase money which is enforceable by a sale under the direction of the court.

equitable mortgage. A mortgage in which both possession and ownership of the security remain with the borrower.

equitable waste. A tenant for life under a settlement is nearly always unaccountable either for voluntary or permissive waste, and may therefore at common law open new mines or fell timber and sell it as absolute owner. In equity, however, wanton or extravagant acts of destruction, e.g. felling ornamental trees, will be restrained by an injunction coupled with an order to rehabilitate the premises. These acts are described as equitable waste because before 1873 they could be restrained only in a court of equity. Now, however, a tenant for life is by statute declared to have no right to commit equitable waste unless such a right can be construed from the instrument of creation.

equity. Justice, fairness; a *body of legal principles* which slowly developed in England to remedy injustices due to a too rigorous application of the letter of the law, being administered until 1873 in the Chancery Divison of the courts, but now having its administration merged with that of the common law.

Equity Capital for Industry (ECI) (the Equity Bank). A fund raised in 1976 from various investing institutions (principally insurance companies and life offices, pension funds, and investment trusts) to be invested in fresh equity capital for quoted and unquoted small- to medium-sized industrial companies. The new institution met with mixed reactions from those who, it was hoped, would subscribe the capital, the main stumbling block being a doubt that there was a significant gap in the present lending system of finding capital for industry. Funds from banks and financial institutions were thought to be usually quite readily available to industry, although there have been criticisms of the major investing institutions for being too remote from manufacturing industry and too insensitive to its needs. Eventually the objects and advantages of ECI were stated to be that – it would assist those recipients who would normally be too small for major institutions, and who could not turn to other sources of cash for some reason or other, e.g., where a company is unable to make a rights issue because its shares are standing at or below par; or where a company needing equity capital cannot obtain it because it is highly geared. £40.9m capital has been raised for these purposes. ECI takes an active interest in the management of companies in which it invests.

equity of a company. *See* ORDINARY SHARES.

equity of redemption. The right allowed to a mortgagor to have a reasonable time within which to redeem his or her estate when mortgaged for a sum less than its worth; the right of a legal mortgagor of real or personal property to have this property re-transferred to him or her on repayment of the sum so secured.

ergonomics. The study of the relationship between a worker's abilities and the work done, with the objective of suiting the worker to the work.

escalation clause. A clause in a contract, usually one for a major project which can take a number of years to complete. As inflation makes it difficult to ascertain the costs throughout the construction period, an escalation clause is inserted which permits the overall price to be increased to allow for the additional labour and material costs.

error. A mistake in a calculation. A discrepancy in the value or condition of an item. An amount shown on a statement, invoice, commercial document or books of account which is not correct.

errors and omissions excepted. This is inserted on an invoice or statement so that if the document contains an error or there is some omission, then a revised invoice or statement could be issued.

escheat. The reverting of property to the lord of the fee, or to the Crown, or to the State, on the death of the owner intestate without heirs; property so reverting. This legal process was abolished in 1925, since when the same end has been achieved by the transfer to the Crown of the property as *bona vacantia*.

escrow. A deed, kept in the possession of a third person, which cannot be put into legal operation until the grantee has met certain conditions. When the conditions have been complied with, the document is then delivered to the grantee, and takes effect as a deed.

estate. Everything which a person possesses, the total of his or her goods, property and money; the length of time for which an interest in land will exist. *See also* EQUITABLE ESTATE; FREEHOLD ESTATE; LEASEHOLD ESTATE; LEGAL ESTATE.

estate agent. An agent who arranges for the sale and purchase of houses and properties. *See also* CLIENTS' ACCOUNTS.

estate contract. A contract by an estate owner to create a legal estate, including a contract conferring either expressly or by statutory implication a valid option of purchase, a right of preemption, or any other like right. This in practice means a contract for the sale of a legal fee simple, an agreement for the grant of a term of years absolute, or an option to acquire either of these interests, e.g., a tenant's option to renew a lease. Estate contracts are registrable as land charges in the sub-division C(IV); *see* LAND CHARGES; LAND CHARGES REGISTER.

Estate Duties Investment Trust Ltd (Edith). This company was founded in 1953 to help the small company in which the majority of shares are held by the founder and the founder's immediate family, where the payment of estate duty might mean that the company would have to be sold or at least control would be lost. Edith takes over a sufficiently large minority interest to assure the continuity of the business, at the same time providing the funds for the payment of the duty. It is a subsidiary of Finance for Industry (FFI) (*q.v.*).

estate duty. *See* INHERITANCE TAX.

estate for life. An estate where land is limited to a tenant for his or her own lifetime, or for the lifetime of another person (*pur autre vie*).

estate in fee simple. The word 'fee' meant that the estate would endure until the owner died intestate, leaving no heir. If the deceased left an heir the estate passed to him or her, and so on. 'Simple' meant that the estate would pass to any heir and that the descent was not restricted to any particular class of heir. The doctrine of heirship (except in the case of an entailed interest) was abolished in 1925, since when the land no longer passes to the nearest heir, but on the death of its owner intestate is held by administrators on a trust for sale. Either the land, or the money for which it has been sold, now passes to the nearest relations, so that the fee simple is still an estate which is inheritable even if it has been converted into money. The *fee simple absolute in possession* is the highest type of land holding and the nearest to absolute ownership that is is possible to get. It is capable of lasting indefinitely. 'Absolute' means 'not subject to conditions' and 'in possession' means in possession and enjoyment of the land itself or receiving the rents and profits from the land, or having the right to receive the same. A *determinable fee simple* is one which, according to the express terms of its limitation, may be brought to an end by some happening or event before the completion of the full period for which it may possibly continue.

estate in fee tail. An estate in land which continues to exist only so long as the original tenant, or any descendants of this tenant survive. Thus the right to interest is restricted to a class of heirs specially mentioned in the gift. (Also called *estate tail* or *entailed interest*). See also BASE FEE.

estate owner. A person or body of persons in whom an estate in land is vested. In the case of a fee simple absolute in possession the 'estate owner' may be a beneficial owner entitled in his or her own right, a personal representative, a mortgagor, a tenant for life or trustees for sale. *See also* SETTLED LAND.

estate tail. *See* ESTATE IN FEE TAIL.

estimate. An assessment by an individual, firm or company of how much a certain job will cost. An assessment is not binding and the actual cost may be more or less.

estoppel. Anything which prevents a person by his or her own acts or words from denying or confirming a fact, or the true validity of a document. Estoppel is given when a representation, overt or implied, which is meant to induce a certain course of conduct on the part of the person to whom the representation is made, is followed by an act or omission by that person as a result of the representation, such act or omission leading directly to loss or damage to such a person.

estovers. The right enjoyed by a tenant to take wood from an estate, either for repairs or for fuel; any *necessaries of life* allowed by law; *alimony*.

et al. *Et alii, aliae, alia:* and others.

Eurobonds. The Eurobond complements the market in Eurodollars (see EUROCURRENCY), out of which it developed, by making longer-term funds available. Most bonds are payable to bearer and all are paid without deduction of tax. They are generally issued by consortia of banks and issuing houses, and are designated in dollars, deutschmarks and some other European currencies, being placed with such investors as nationalised industries, governments, multinational corporations and municipal authorities. A secondary market in the bonds has developed in London and Luxembourg. This market is a supranational market and is not subject to the normal domestic regulation, but is affected by international events.

Eurocard. A cheque card available for use in the *Eurocheque Scheme. See* CHEQUE CARD.

Eurocheque scheme. A scheme whereby holders of special cheque books and Eurocheque encashment cards can cash their personal cheques abroad for travel expenditure only. The extension of the use of the cheque card abroad relates only to the encashment of individual cheques, normally up to £50 at any one time with a maximum of £100 per day at banks participating in the scheme (nearly all European banks) and does not cover payments to hotels, restaurants or shops. Cheques will be drawn in local currency and when received by a UK bank will be converted into sterling at the current rate of exchange and debited with a collection charge to the drawer's account.

Euroclear. International clearing system for the settlement of transactions in securities, essentially Eurobonds. It is based in Brussels and is provided under contract by Morgan Guaranty for over a hundred banks which own it.

Eurocurrency. A term used to describe deposits of currency, at first dollars, but also guilders, Swiss francs, sterling and deutschmarks and other currencies, which are held by people who do not live in the country whose currency it is, and who keep the deposits in a third country. For example, a bank in France which received dollars from Spain (or any other country except the US) would have some Eurodollars. These could be lent out at a good rate of interest to anyone wishing to borrow in that currency. The actual dollars would throughout remain in the US, but as the borrowers and lenders concluded their agreements various accounts in the US would be credited and debited with the sums in question. There is a ready market for Eurocurrencies. The demand comes from banks and continental industrial firms. The main market for Eurosterling is in Paris, and for other Eurocurrencies in London.

Eurodollars. *See* EUROCURRENCY.

European Coal and Steel Community. An institution which aimed to establish a common market in iron, coal and steel, established in 1953; its members were France, West Germany, Belgium, the Netherlands, Italy and Luxembourg. The success of the European Coal and Steel Community, achieved in spite of the fact that the economic boundaries of the raw materials were quite dissimilar from the political boundaries of the member states, was one of the factors leading to the foundation of the COMMON MARKET (*q.v.*). Control of the European Coal and Steel Community was transferred in 1967 to the European Economic Community.

European Composite Unit (EURCO). A weighted 'basket' of the currencies of all countries of the EEC.

European Currency Unit (ECU). One of the results of the establishment of the European Monetary System was

	Rate of exchange			
		to £	£	%
W German mark	0.719 @	3.64 =	.198	32.5
French franc	1.31	11.13	.118	19.3
British pound	0.0878	1	.088	14.5
Dutch florin	0.256	4.14	.062	10.2
Italian lira	140	2293	.061	10.0
Belgian franc	3.71	73.55	.050	8.2
Danish krone	0.219	13.06	.017	2.8
Greek drachma	1.15	154	.007	1.1
Irish pound	0.00871	1.17	.007	1.1
Luxembourg franc	0.14	73.55	.002	0.3
			.610	

the revival of the ECU, the value of which is arrived at by a somewhat complicated formula based on a fixed amount of each member country's currency, weighted in proportions reflecting its economic importance in the EEC. Sterling is included in the formula although the UK has not yet decided to join the system. The ECU serves as a means of settlement between central banks, banks, merchants, etc. Financial institutions have started to use the ECU for the granting of Euroloans, issue of bonds or deposit certificates and currency notes. Current accounts have also recently been introduced so that ECUs may be purchased either at a spot rate or a forward rate.

European Economic Community (EEC). *See* COMMON MARKET.

European Free Trade Association (EFTA). An economic association of countries formed in 1960 with the object of achieving an area of free trade by the reduction of tariff barriers between them. The original members were the UK, Denmark, Austria, Norway, Sweden, Switzerland and Portugal, later joined by Iceland and Finland. The abolition of all internal tariffs and trade quotas was achieved in a few years while the level of external tariffs remained as a matter for each individual country to determine. The intention was to compensate for a possible loss of trade with the then Common Market countries by an increase in trade between themselves. In 1972 the UK and Denmark left EFTA on joining the EEC.

European Investment Bank (EIB). The function of the EIB was defined under the Treaty of Rome (1957) (*q.v*).: 'The task of the EIB shall be to contribute, by having recourse to the capital market and utilising its own resources (capital subscribed by member countries), to the balanced and steady development of the common market in the interests of the Community. For this purpose the Bank shall, operating on a non profit-making basis, grant loans and give guarantees which facilitate the financing of projects in all sectors of the economy'. These projects include Regional Development projects, Common Interest projects, and Modernisation and Conversion projects. The bank was formed in 1958 and has headquarters at Luxembourg. It makes or guarantees loans which are normally for £1m-£20m for from seven to twenty years against acceptable security or the guarantee of a member country, particularly for projects which aim at improved communications, those which help to cut dependence on oil imports, those aimed at environmental protection or the development of European capacities in high technology fields, and those which seek to increase support for industrial co-operation between enterprises from different member countries. The EIB also supports applications from outside the Community coming under the general head of development finance in most of the countries surrounding the Mediterranean and in African, Caribbean and Pacific States which have negotiated co-operation agreements with the EEC. For smaller transactions the EIB allocates a block sum to credit institutions (as, for example, the Industrial and Commercial Finance Corporation (*q.v.*)) and delegates the disbursements to them. Since the beginning of 1978 under an experimental scheme small- and medium-sized companies in development areas have been able to borrow in sterling on a seven-year term at $7\frac{1}{2}$ per cent fixed for purchase of fixed assets, and in May 1981 it was announced that a £10m loan facility is to be operated in the UK through the Midland Bank network; loans will be made in the range of £15,000-£50,000.

European Monetary Agreement. An agreement on the settlement in gold of outstanding debits and credits of the former European Payments Union when sterling and other West European currencies became fully convertible in 1959. With convertibility came a free and effective foreign exchange market, well equipped to handle the business of settling inter-European debts, and rendering the EPU superfluous.

European Monetary System (EMS). The system first came into being in the early 1970s but in 1972 lay dormant until 1979. Its purpose is to reorganise Common Market currencies in order to reduce the fluctuations among them. The system was planned to commence operations on 1 January 1979 but actually started on 13 March, because the French government were not willing to allow it to come into operation until certain questions affecting agricultural prices in the Community had been resolved. There are three broad aims: 1. the establishment of an exchange rate regime with intervention points (*see* EUROPEAN CURRENCY UNIT); 2. the promotion of a progressive convergence of the performance of member countries' economies; and 3. the emergence of the European Currency Unit (*q.v.*) as a new monetary unit which would act as a reference point against which to measure exchange rates and which would be used by central banks to settle up with each other. It was hoped that this system would eventually result in an expansion of credit facilities, and lead to a European Monetary Fund controlling a common currency unit for members of the European Economic Community (*see* COMMON MARKET): the EMS is thus a development of former exchange rate agreements. The UK does not at the moment participate in the Exchange Rate Mechanism (ERM), but neither do Greece and Spain. The ERM consists of three components: (*a*) ECU (*see* EUROPEAN CURRENCY UNIT); (*b*) the Parity Grid – an agreement whereby each member agrees a central rate with the ECU. The realignment of all member currencies has been made 11 times, the last on 12 January 1987 when the rates were as follows: Belgian franc – 42.4582; Danish krone – 7.85212; German mark – 2.05853; French franc – 6.90403; Dutch guilder – 2.31943; Irish pound – 0.798411; and Italian lira – 1483.58. Participating nations agreed to keep their currencies within a 2.25 per cent margin either side of parity, while Italy has a six per cent tolerance; (*c*) the divergence indicator provides a warning to members to take corrective action when the exchange rate reaches the 2.25 band. The EMS which will shortly include Portugal and possibly Turkey is making slow but steady progress in coordinating policies and economic structures. When participating countries agree on these various issues the exchange rate fluctuation will be avoided.

European Payments Union (EPU). A scheme introduced in 1950 to encourage multilateral trade between the European countries, to work towards convertibility and to act as a clearing house for financial settlements within the group. Each country was allotted a quota, based on its share of world trade, of the initial reserves of $350 million, provided by the USA. Surpluses and deficits between the fifteen member countries were recorded as debits or credits and there was a monthly settlement of net debit or credit positions, made in gold or US dollars, or by entries to the members' credit balances. The scheme was handled by the Bank for International Settlements based in Basle. With the coming in 1959 of convertibility of sterling and other West European currencies the EPU ceased to function, and its place was taken by the European Monetary Agreement.

European Unit of Account (EUA). Dating from the mid-1970s, the EUA was similar to the Special Drawing Right in that it was calculated as a 'basket' of currencies, but by reference to the various currencies of the member states of the European Economic Community only. As it was based on floating rates it had itself a floating value. *See* SPECIAL DRAWING RIGHTS.

evidence. The production of facts and/or documents which clearly demonstrate the truth on the point in issue. Contracts are often unenforceable unless evidenced in writing e.g. Guarantees. Evidence can be: 1. conclusive – share certificate, certificate of incorporation; 2. circumstantial – facts that can be ascertained by the conduct of the person.

ex-. Former, out of or from, without.

examination of title. The checking of a person's claim to be the owner of a valuable asset, particularly in a bank, in connection with security. Whereas in some cases the mere production of the certificate or evidence of ownership is enough (as in the case of stock exchange security where an equitable charge is to be taken), in others a more searching check is made (as in the case of land). In this last case the examination of title is done by a solicitor, whether the land is unregistered or registered. Because the bank may need to sell the land, if the advance is not repaid, it must be sure that it has a good title to offer a possible purchaser, this in turn depends upon the title of its borrowing customer. *See* LAND CERTIFICATE (for registered land); *PRIMA FACIE* CHECK OF DEEDS.

exception accounting. A term which is today used specifically in relation to direct debiting. An originator of direct debits will know that, with the 'exception' of those few items which are returned unpaid, and of which advice will be received within the same time scale as returned cheques, the total amount of direct debits originated will be available to him or her to use as required. Exception accounting therefore relates to the calculations required to deduct from this available money the total of the direct debits returned unpaid, which are not so available.

excess depreciation. In addition to that for ordinary depreciation of currency. A diminution or lessening of the power of the monetary unit over the market, diminution being shown by a rise in prices.

excess liquidity. The maintenance by banks of a greater degree of liquidity than is normally prudentially desirable. Such high liquidity is unlikely to be voluntary: it usually arises from the reluctance of borrowers to come forward, either because of a lack of confidence or because of high interest rates.

excess profits tax. Originally a tax imposed in the UK during both world wars. The rate at its highest point was 100 per cent, the basis on which the excess was calculated being the rate of profit earned by the particular concern before the war. In 1946 the tax was reduced to 60 per cent in January and abolished altogether in December. More recently the concept was revived and applied in the UK to bank profits under the name of the windfall tax (*q.v.*).

exchange. To give or receive in return

for something else, to hand over for an equivalent in kind; exchanging of coins for their value in coins of the same or another country; the system by which goods or property are exchanged and debts settled, especially in different countries, without the transfer of money; the place where merchants, brokers, etc., meet to transact business. *See also* BILL OF EXCHANGE; FORWARD EXCHANGE; PARITIES.

exchange as per indorsement. A clause put on a bill of exchange by the drawer to ensure that the importer pays an amount in his or her own currency which, when calculated at the rate of exchange quoted in the indorsement, will be equivalent to the sterling amount of the bill. The rate is inserted by the negotiating banker and represents the banker's buying rate of exchange on the bill.

exchange broker. An agent operating on the foreign exchange market for principals who pay him or her commission.

exchange clause. A clause put on a bill of exchange drawn in sterling on a person abroad to establish the method of calculating the rate of exchange at which the bill is to be paid, so as to ensure that any exchange charges will be paid by the drawee, e.g. 'Payable at the current rate of exchange for sight drafts on London', 'Exchange as per indorsement', etc.

exchange commission. The charge made for exchanging sums in one currency for sums in another.

exchange control. A system of control by government operating through the central bank over scarce supplies of the currencies of other countries. The nationals of a country are allowed to obtain foreign currency only on application to the central bank and only for purposes approved by the government. In this way, imports may be restricted to goods and commodities considered essential for the country's welfare, and foreign travel may be restricted to that designed to increase the country's export trade, to the exclusion of holiday-makers and tourists. Powers to approve applications may be delegated to authorised banks, and limits may be set to the extent of such delegation so that requests of a particular type or for larger sums must be forwarded to the central bank. Bank accounts may be designated resident or non-resident, the balances on the latter being freely transferable abroad. The purchase of foreign stocks or foreign properties may be forbidden or restricted by a requirement that such funds may come only from the proceeds of foreign currency resulting from sales of similar stocks or properties by nationals. The inadequacy of such investment currency itself creates a premium which is no part of official exchange control policy. There is also usually restriction on foreign business investment. In the UK exchange control restrictions were, except for transactions with Rhodesia, completely relaxed from 24 October 1979. Transactions with Rhodesia were freed from control on 13 December 1979.

exchange equalisation account. An account managed by the Bank of England on behalf of the Treasury, for the purpose of maintaining reasonable stability in the value of the pound sterling on the foreign exchanges. For that purpose the whole of the country's reserves of gold and foreign currency have been transferred to the account for the use of the managers as required. Since the floating of the pound the managers have been mostly concerned to prevent the rate from falling too steeply. This is effected by buying in sterling on the exchanges so as to increase the demand for it and so tend to raise the rate.

exchange rate mechanism (ERM). Calculated in terms of a weighted average of all EMS currencies, including sterling.

exchange rates. *See* PARITIES.

exchequer. The State treasury, the government department dealing with the public revenue, finances or pecuniary resources.

exchequer and audit department. A department charged with the function of authorising issues from the Exchequer and auditing and reporting to the House of Commons on all government expenditure.

excise. A tax or duty on certain articles produced and consumed in a country; the branch of the Civil Service which collects and manages the excise duties, namely the Commissioners of Customs and Excise; a tax of any kind.

excise duties. Taxes on home-produced articles, as contrasted with customs duties, which are levied on imports.

excise licences. A tax on the enjoyment of certain services or facilities, e.g. television, motor vehicle, driving and dog licences.

exclusion clause. A clause which excludes or modifies a contract that would otherwise be part of that contract by the implication of law. Under the Unfair Contract Terms Act, 1977, liability for loss or damage cannot be excluded by reason that the goods or service fails to satisfy a test of reasonableness. Liability for loss or damage due to negligent manufacture cannot be excluded or restricted.

ex coupon. Bonds sold without the benefit of the next instalment of interest to be paid.

ex curia. Out of court.

ex div. Shares sold without the benefit of the current dividend shortly to be paid.

ex drawing. Bonds sold without any benefit there may be from a drawing for repayment due to be made.

execute. To carry into effect, to put into force; to perform what is required to give validity to any legal instrument, as by signing and sealing.

executed agreement. This means a

document, signed by or on behalf of the parties, embodying the terms of a regulated agreement, or such of them as have been reduced to writing.

executed contract. One in which at least one party has actually performed his or her duties under the contract.

executive. A body appointed to administer the affairs of a corporation, a company or a club; a high official of such a body; under the parliamentary system, members chosen from the legislature to carry into effect the laws of the country; one who is responsible for seeing that a certain part or aspect of the company's work is carried out.

executor. A person appointed by a testator to pay his or her debts and to carry out the provisions of the testator's will.

executor and trustee corporation. Specialised companies attached to banks and other financial organisations which offer to act as personal representative or trustee. They have the advantage that, not being mortal as is a person, they can carry out their duties without any break. They will see to the deceased's funeral, agree and pay the capital transfer tax, obtain probate of his or her will, pay legacies, and act in the best interests of the beneficiaries. A will should contain a charging clause, empowering the bank to pass its fees to the debit of the estate. The corporation usually charges an acceptance fee on a percentage basis on the value of the estate as ascertained for capital transfer tax purposes, an annual fee for administration, which may include the judicious investment of trust funds, and a vacating fee on termination. It will act alone or jointly with a named executor.

executor *de son tort*. A person who without authority intermeddles in the estate of a deceased person.

executor's year. The period normally thought sufficient for an executor to deal with the estate of the deceased,

pay capital transfer tax, debts and legacies, etc., and wind up the estate. More complicated estates, however, will require a longer time.

executory contract. One in which all the duties set out in the contract remain to be performed in the future.

exemplary damages. Damages based on the principle of punishing the defendant rather than compensating the plaintiff (also known as *punitive* or *vindictive damages*).

exemplification. An attested copy of any proceedings in a court of record.

exemplification of probate. A duplicate copy of probate, issued by the court in cases where the original has been lost.

exemplify. To illustrate by example, to manifest, to witness; to prove by an attested copy, to make an authenticated copy of.

exempt agreement. A consumer credit agreement where the creditor is a building society or a local authority which finances the purchase of land, or the provision of dwellings on land, against the security of a mortgage on the land; any debtor-creditor agreement secured by mortgage of land.

exempted dealers. Dealers, including banks, insurance companies and independent pension funds, who are authorised by the Department of Trade to buy and sell securities on their own behalf.

exemption clause. A clause in a contract which seeks to protect one party from being sued by the other for negligence, non-performance, damage or loss, etc. Bankers use them in documents of foreign trade, where the clause states that the bank accepts no liability for any loss, damage or delay, however caused, which is not directly due to the fault or negligence of its own employees, and in replies to status enquiries, which are stated to be given without responsibility on the part of the sender. Such a clause will be effective except where the information is given fraudulently, provided that it passes the test of reasonableness under the Unfair Contract Terms Act, 1979, s.11. Guidelines for the application of the test are set out in Sch. 2 to the Act as follows: 'The matters to which regard is to be had are any of the following which appear to be relevant – (*a*) the strength of the bargaining positions of the parties relative to each other . . . (*b*) whether the customer received an inducement to agree to the term . . . (*c*) whether the customer knew, or ought reasonably to have known, of the existence and extent of the term . . . (*d*) where the term excludes or restricts any relevant liability if some condition is not complied with, whether it was reasonable at the time of the contract to expect that compliance with that condition would be practicable; (*e*) whether the goods were manufactured, processed or adapted to the special order of the customer'.

ex facie. Manifestly, on the face of it.

ex facie absolute disposition. See STANDARD SECURITY.

ex gratia. As a favour (not as a legal right).

exigible Due for payment.

ex **New.** Shares sold without the benefit of new shares being issued to existing shareholders – that is, the seller reserves to himself or herself the right to receive the new shares.

ex officio. By virtue of office, official.

exoneration, *exonération d'impôts.* A term in the Law of Succession. It may be found, in administering a will, that although the estate is perfectly solvent, there are not sufficient resources to satisfy all the beneficiaries in full. In such a case in the UK, the beneficiaries lose their rights in an order set out in the Administration of Estates Act, 1925 so that all creditors may be satisfied. It is provided that this order of application of the available moneys may be varied by the will. If, then, the testator shows a clear indication that a

special fund shall be set up for the payment of debts 'in exoneration of' all other funds, the proceeds of this special fund will be taken first. Similarly, a testator may direct that a fund be set up 'in exoneration' of the legacies, which otherwise might be subject to Capital Transfer Tax in the usual way.

ex parte. On one side only, one-sided.

expectation of life. The statistical basis of an assurance company's assessment of risk. Although it is not possible to say how long a man will live, it is possible to say how long a group of men, or women, will live from a given moment in time. Actuarial tables showing the expectation of life from different ages are compiled and regularly revised, and these form the basis of life assurance premium assessment.

expenses. Outlay, cost, expenditure; the costs of an action. For tax purposes, deductions from income before tax is charged. Employed persons must satisfy the tax inspector that the expenses have been incurred wholly, exclusively, and necessarily in the performance of the duties of the employment. Self-employed persons must show that the expenses have been incurred wholly and exclusively for the purpose of the business.

export. To send goods or produce out of a country, the act of exporting. *See also* INVISIBLE EXPORTS; VISIBLE EXPORTS.

export agent. An agent who arranges a contract between his or her principal, an exporter of goods or services, and a foreign buyer.

Export Credits Guarantee Department (ECGD). A Government department which since 1919 has provided insurance cover for British exports abroad. The principal risks covered are the insolvency of the buyer, political restrictions delaying payment, the imposition of new import licensing restrictions in the buyer's country and war. Over the years the types of policy available have broadened and diversified and the department provided in certain circumstances guarantees to banks lending to exporter-customers. Such guarantees covered short-, medium- and long-term finance. The Department now provides cover against cost escalation (where the contract is for £2m or over, and the manufacturing period five years or more); cover for investment abroad against appropriation, war risks and restrictions on remittances; and guarantees to assist in obtaining performance bonds. In the past ECGD has refinanced a considerable amount of export credit by taking it over from the banks for cash. New additions to this refinancing ended in April 1980. *See also* BUYER CREDIT; SUPPLIER CREDIT.

Exporters' Yearbook. A source of information of documentary requirements for different countries.

export factoring. Export factoring provides for British short-term exporters all those services which are available in the domestic market, plus the ability to invoice their customers in their own currencies. The factor looks after the exchange risks and the collection from the customers overseas. The factor's client enjoys an immediate sterling equivalent, has no problems dealing with difficult payers in a foreign language, and is not concerned with fluctuating exchange values between the date of invoice and the date of payment. Customer collections are made by local staff in the factor's own office, or through correspondent factors. Where the factor has overseas offices it is possible for the client company to arrange for factoring services to be provided for its overseas sales subsidiaries by the overseas offices of the factor. The factor can account to his or her client, if so desired, in the currency of invoice, and can provide, if necessary, a financial facility in the currency of

invoice. This offers advantages to certain exporters. *See also* ASSOCIATION OF BRITISH FACTORS; BRITISH EXPORT HOUSES ASSOCIATION.

export finance companies. Specialists in providing and arranging finance on a non-recourse basis for capital and semi-capital goods. These companies can offer to arrange ECGD cover themselves or they can accept assignment of the exporter's policy and, with the larger contracts, can arrange and manage the finance on behalf of a syndicate of banks in Britain. Finance can be provided for single transactions, or for a series of orders, or as a 'package deal' for a large project, or through a credit line negotiated with a bank in the buyer's country. Their services are thus similar to, and extended beyond, those provided by merchant banks. The export finance companies can also usually arrange finance for non-sterling contracts raising a proportion of the required finance overseas.

export houses. Specialists in handling goods destined for practically every market in the world, serving all kinds of companies from the largest to the smallest and financing entrepôt trade. They may be involved at any stage of a transaction between a manufacturer and overseas buyer, and their activities range from the promotion of sales to the collection of debts. Among the many combinations of services, the main ones undertaken are to buy and sell on their own account as principals or to act as agent for the manufacturer or overseas buyer. Their financial services include paying the manufacturer immediately on shipment, making arrangements for credit facilities on behalf of their clients where these are required, or as factors assuming the full responsibility for the collection of the debts. In the case of overseas firms engaged in importing direct from Britain, they will also act as 'confirming houses', financing and confirming contracts on behalf of the buyer.

Export-Import Bank (Eximbank). The Export-Import Bank of the US was formed in 1934 as a banking corporation registered under the laws of Washington, D.C. Originally established to 'aid in financing and to facilitate exports and imports and the exchange of commodities between the United States and other nations or the agencies or nationals thereof', the Bank can grant direct loans, issue loans and guarantee loans to private and government buyers abroad for the purchase of US goods. Very similar to the Export Credits Guarantee Department (ECGD) in the UK, the insurance program of Eximbank is administered by the Foreign Credit Insurance Association (FCIA). Eximbank is managed by a board of directors consisting of five members appointed by the President and confirmed by the Senate.

exposure draft. A draft of a proposed measure, whether Parliamentary or not, prepared for reading and criticism by those who will be affected by it. In this way, the views of all interested parties will be taken into account before preparation of the Bill or instruction in its final form.

express trust. A trust which is expressly created by the person who imposes it.

ex **quay.** Goods to be taken under the control of the purchaser as soon as they have been landed.

ex **rights.** *See EX. NEW.*

ex **ship.** A price quoted for goods on arrival at the port, not including costs of unloading and delivery to the premises of the purchaser.

extended credit. The purchase of goods that become the property of the buyer as opposed to hire purchase when the goods do not belong to the buyer until final payment. The giving to a customer an additional amount that may be borrowed either by way of loan or overdraft or extending the final date of

repayment of the borrowing. The permitted amount that has been authorised by a credit card company.

extension. To prolong the life of a contract or financial instrument. For example, a documentary credit can be extended subject to the agreement of the parties. The agreement that a loan or overdraft can be paid off at an agreed later date. The extension of the maturity date on a negotiable instrument.

external account. Sterling accounts of non-resident customers maintained by banks in this country.

external convertibility. A currency with limited convertibility for the people of the issuing country, but freely convertible among foreign holders.

external debt. The amount of debt owed by one country to another.

external loan. A public loan raised from sources abroad.

extortionate credit transactions. Covered by the US Consumer Credit Protection Act, 1968, extortionate credit transactions are extensions of credit at rates of interest over 45 per cent annual interest, or under conditions where collection of the debt would be illegal. Title II of the Consumer Credit Protection Act makes the advancing of credit under such conditions a felony. The purpose of the Act is to prevent racketeering in the credit field, whether in local or in interstate commerce; it is also felonious to attempt to collect illegal loans by extortion or threats of violence, as is the financing of such activities.

extraordinary general meeting. A meeting of the shareholders of a company for discussion and transaction of special business. Such a meeting may be called by the directors, or by members who hold at least one-tenth of the paid-up capital of the company, provided such capital holding carries the right to vote at general meetings.

extraordinary resolution. One passed by a majority of not less than three-fourths of such members as vote in person or by proxy, at a general meeting of which notice specifying the intention to propose the resolution as an extraordinary resolution has been duly given.

ex **warehouse.** The price to be paid if the purchaser collects the goods personally from the warehouse in which they are stored.

ex **works.** The price to be paid if the purchaser collects the goods personally from the factory.

F

face value. Apparent worth; the nominal amount shown on coins, banknotes, etc; the nominal value of stocks or shares.

face washing. A term used where a subsidiary company is acquired by a parent company, to indicate that the financing costs of the acquisition, plus any further costs incurred by the subsequent injection of more capital for necessary changes, will be roughly matched over a period of time by the income generated by the subsidiary, which can thus be expected to 'wash its face'.

facility. Ease, aptitude, ease of access; in banking, an overdraft or loan limit or some other banking service which has been made available for a customer.

facility letter. A letter from a lending bank to a borrowing customer, confirming the terms on which a loan has been agreed. Such a letter specifies the total sum to be lent, the rate of interest to be charged, the terms of repayment, and the security to be charged. It will also lay down certain conditions or covenants which have to be observed – e.g. balance sheet ratios, security margins, total borrowing from all sources, etc. For the purposes of the Consumer Credit Act, 1974, it is a letter which sets out certain terms of an overdraft agreement in a prescribed manner.

facsimile. An exact copy of handwriting, printing, picture, etc. *See* FAX.

facsimile signature. A signature placed on a document by rubber stamp. Such facsimile signatures on cheques are not acceptable to banks unless a suitable indemnity is given, because there is no guarantee that they have been placed on the cheque with the authority of the signatory.

factage. The cost of postage on small parcels or packets.

factor. An agent, one who transacts business for another on commission; a mercantile agent having in the customary course of his or her business as such agent authority either to sell goods, or to consign goods for the purpose of sale, or to buy goods, or to raise money on the security of goods; a steward or agent of an estate. A factor holds the goods he or she sells in personal possession and deals in his or her own name, although buying or selling for a principal. *See also* MERCANTILE AGENT.

factorage. The commission paid to a factor by an employer.

factor cost. The price of goods paid by the consumer, less any tax or duty included in the price.

factoring. The factor operates by buying from a client, a trading company, their invoiced debts. The client has fulfilled an order, dispatched the goods, and now awaits payment. Some debtors are slow to pay up, some may never pay. Credit control in the trading company may be lax. The factor becomes responsible for all credit control sales, accounting and debt collection. Thus companies are able to sell their outstanding book debts for cash. The selling company receives payment for the debts purchased on a calculated *'Average Settlement Day'*. The company passes its invoices to the factor as soon as it has made them out. The full factoring service comprises maintenance of the company's sales ledger, credit control over the company's customers, full protection against bad debts and collection from debtors. The combination of these services is sometimes called *Maturity Factoring*. If, in addition, the company is being financed ahead of the maturity date (up to 80 per cent against the indebtedness showing in the sales ledger) then this is *Financed Factoring.* Factoring is *'Disclosed'* or *'Undisclosed'* according to whether the supplier has notified his customers that payment is to be made to the factor or not. At one time there was a feeling that factoring was not quite respectable (a feeling which did not survive the entry of the big banks into the business) and a supplier who did not wish customers to know that the services of a factor were being employed set up some kind of arrangement to disguise this fact. Disclosed factoring is now by far the most common arrangement. Factors are usually interested only in companies with a turnover of £50,000 p.a. or more, with a reasonable spread of customer accounts and an average invoice value of £100 plus. *See also* EXPORT FACTORING; INVOICE DISCOUNTING; RECOURSE FACTORING.

failure. Cessation, deficiency, omission, non-performance, non-occurrence, breaking-down; insolvency, suspension of payment, bankruptcy or liquidation.

fair comment. This is a defence for an action for defamation and providing the defendant could show that whatever words were used were stated honestly and without malice, then the alleged defamation could be considered as fair comment.

fair credit reporting. The Fair Credit Reporting Act embodies a Federal regulation which imposes strict limitations on the nature of information that a bank may disclose concerning credit experience with one of its customers. Such disclosures must be confined to factual, non-interpretive data and cannot include matters of opinion or subjective comment. *See also* STATUS ENQUIRY.

fair rent. Either the tenant or the landlord of a regulated tenancy may apply to a rent officer to decide what is a fair rent. If the parties after consultation with the rent officer cannot agree, the rent officer will determine a fair rent. There is an appeal to a rent assessment committee, whose decision is final. The fair rent, once determined, must be registered in a local public register. *See also* CERTIFICATE OF FAIR RENT.

fair trading. Under the Fair Trading Act, 1973, should a firm not give an assurance to the Director of Fair Trading that a practice that is unfair to consumers will cease, then proceedings can be made against the firm in the Restrictive Practices Court.

fair wear and tear. Normal depreciation of an asset over a period, not covered by insurance.

fait accompli. An accomplished fact.

false pretences. Wilful misrepresentation for an ulterior motive. Paying for goods with a cheque which the drawer knows is worthless, or the obtaining of money by the cashing of a cheque by pretending to be the payee, is obtaining goods or money by false pretences and may attract a prosecution. A customer who tricks a bank into lending money to him or her may be liable to penalties under the Theft Act, 1968, s. 16(1), which applies to any person who by any deception dishonestly obtains for himself or another any pecuniary advantages.

falsification of accounts. The destruction, alteration, mutilation or falsification of any book, writing, security or account by any officer, clerk or employed person acting wilfully and with intent to defraud. This is a criminal act and can attract a term of imprisonment.

family protection policy. A life assurance policy which offers a large sum at an early date if the life assured dies, dropping to quite a small one at maturity, by which time the children have grown up and are not in such need of assistance.

Fannie Mae. *See* FEDERAL NATIONAL

MORTGAGE ASSOCIATION.

farm development loan. A type of loan available to sound, practical farmers for such purposes as buying stock, machinery and plant, and farm improvements. The loans are available for amounts up to £20,000. Interest is charged on the full amount of the loan for its full term, loan and interest being repayable in equal monthly instalments up to a period of five to seven years. The borrowing term will be fixed to take account of the expected life of any machinery and plant purchased with the proceeds of the loan.

farmer. As defined in the Agricultural Credits Act a farmer is: 'A person (not being an unincorporated company or society) who, as tenant or owner of an agricultural holding, cultivates the holding for profit, and "agriculture" and cultivation shall be deemed to include horticulture, and the use of land for any purpose of husbandry, inclusive of the keeping or breeding of livestock, poultry, or bees and the growth of fruit, vegetables and the like.' A firm of partners is within the definition, but a limited company, incorporated under the Companies Acts, or a society is not.

Farmers Home Administration (FmHA). A section of the US Department of Agriculture, the FmHA is responsible for the direction of credit to farmers, rural residents and communities. The FmHA also guarantees loans made by banks to farmers as well as making loans directly itself.

FAS. *See* FREE ALONGSIDE SHIP.

fate of a cheque. Whether it is honoured or not.

faux pas. A tactless remark or action.

favourable variance. A variance where the discrepancy is to the advantage of the organisation.

fax. This is the popular abbreviation for facsimile transmission. Businesses often have fax telephone numbers as well as normal telephone numbers on their headed notepaper. Fax is used to transmit letters, plans, diagrams, instructions, etc., to a recipient. The procedure simply involves the dialling of the recipient's Fax number, then inserting the document into a machine, within seconds an exact replica is then received by the recipient.

feasibility study. An enquiry into whether a particular project is capable of being done, or is practical, or will be profitable. Such a study may be performed by a bank as a preliminary to seeking a new market, extending its branch structure, introducing a new service, embarking upon a new training system, etc.

Federal Deposit Insurance Corporation (FDIC). Federal Savings and Loan Insurance Corporation (FSLIC). The FDIC was established as a result of the Bank Act of 1933, against the background of the 1930s recession and the Wall Street Crash of 1929. It is a government corporation, managed by a Board of Directors and responsible for insuring the deposits of every national and state member bank, currently up to $100,000 for each account, and is responsible for supervising and regulating the insured state-chartered non-member banks. Foreign banks in the US which engage in retail banking are also obliged to carry such insurance. The Federal Savings and Loan Insurance Corporation (FSLIC) is a sister organisation, which performs the same functions as the FDIC, for the savings and loans industry in the US. Savings and Loan associations can be likened to UK Building Societies, accepting savings deposits and financing long-term mortgage loans. In the early 1980s, many of the larger institutions began to expand their services into areas more traditionally covered by the commercial banks, such as checking (current) accounts and credit cards.

federal discount window. The use of the 'Fed window' by which member banks borrow for reserve and liquidity purposes is governed by Regulation A of the Federal Reserve Board. Under this regulation, the 'Fed' can grant advances, usually at the discount rate, to member banks secured by eligible paper, up to ninety days. Interest rates on borrowings are adjusted from time to time and reflect underlying economic conditions and prevailing money market rates as well as the current monetary policy of the Federal Reserve Board.

Federal Funds. The term traditionally refers to the reserves of the member banks of the US Federal Reserve System, which are traded between these banks at the Federal Funds rate; this can and does often fluctuate widely on any given day. The term was also used to describe funds which were 'immediately available' as opposed to 'clearing house' funds which existed until 1 October 1981. Immediately available funds, which are traded for longer periods than overnights, are referred to colloquially as 'term Feds'. In this context, 're- serve assets' are non-interest bearing deposits with the Federal Reserve System (*q.v.*). *See also* INTER-BANK STERLING MARKET.

federal home loan banks. Created in 1932 under the Federal Home Loan Act, these twelve banks in the system provide credit for member savings and loan associations, building and loan associations, savings banks, insurance companies and other organisations involved in home financing. Members of the system must hold stock in their regional bank in an amount related to the size of their outstanding loans. Each of the twelve home loan banks has the authority to make loans to its members and advances for more than one year are secured by securities of the US Government or home mort- gages.

Federal Housing Administration (FHA). FHA is a division of the Department of Housing and Urban Development, whose function is the insurance of residential mortgage loans made by private lenders.

Federal National Mortgage Associa- tion (FNMA). The FNMA is a cor- poration sponsored by the US Government to provide additional funds for private mortgages. The Association was originally chartered in 1938 as a constituent agency of the Housing and Home Financing Agency. The FNMA provides assist- ance to the secondary market for home mortgages guaranteed or insured by the Federal Government; it partici- pates in special housing programs through the financing of certain types of residential mortgages, and is re- sponsible for the management and liquidation in an orderly manner of mortgages acquired.

Federal Open Market Committee (FOMC). This Committee, which meets in Washington every month, is responsible for the application of the monetary policy of the US. All seven governors and all twelve Reserve Bank Presidents attend each meeting which seeks to determine how much money and credit the economy needs in relation to current business con- ditions. The Committee reviews infor- mation received from its own economics staff at the Federal Reserve Board as well as local opinion from the Board of Directors of the twelve Reserve banks and the Reserve bank branches, before deciding upon a course of action which will influence money and credit conditions through the purchase and sale of government securities in the open market.

federal reserve banks. These banks operate under the 'Federal Reserve System', for whom the banks act as central bankers. There are twelve districts covering the USA and a federal reserve bank is situated in each of the following cities: Boston, New York, Philadelphia, Cleveland, Richmond, Atlanta, Chicago, St. Louis, Minneapolis, Kansas City, Dallas, San Francisco.

Federal Reserve System. The Federal Reserve System of the United States was established by the Federal Reserve Act, 1913, which set up a centralised banking system along the lines of those in other countries. As with most other central banks around the world, the Federal Reserve System has the following responsibilities: 1. To regulate the money supply in the United States; 2. to determine and hold the legal reserves of member banks; 3. to furnish currency and complete elasticity for the economic demands of the members of the Federal Reserve System, the US government and the general public; 4. to make payments throughout the US; 5. to facilitate the clearance of cheques for all banks; 6. to supervise member banks and obtain regular reports from them; 7. to collect and interpret economic reports; 8. to act as bankers to the government; 9. to enforce the various regulations that are applicable; 10. to establish various rates of interest from time to time.

Fédération Bancaire de la Communauté Européenne. Avenue de Tervueren 168-1150 Bruxelles, Belgium. An instrument of common action of the professional banking associations to assist in attaining, within the sphere of banking activity, the European aims laid down by the Treaty of Rome, without prejudicing the maintenance and development of relations of member associations with the banking establishments of third-party countries. To this end, the Banking Federation maintains close relations with the Commission of the EEC, the Economic and Social Committee, the European Parliament and the Council of Ministers of the Community. It seeks to contribute to community policy-making by putting forward the opinion of the banks on any question which directly or indir-

ectly affects their activities. The Banking Federation publishes an annual report on 31 March and, from time to time, studies relating to specific subjects: thus, in 1980, two studies were published, one dealing with the use of the ECU in banking transactions, the other relating to monetary policy and the banking system in the countries of the Community. *See also* BRITISH BANKERS' ASSOCIATION.

fed wire. An electronic payments system linking all Federal Reserve banks and branches throughout the United States. *See also* CLEARING HOUSE INTERBANK PAYMENT SYSTEM (CHIPS).

fee. Payment, wages, money, remuneration to a public officer or a professional for the execution of official functions or for the performance of a professional service. *See also* BASE FEE RETAINING FEE.

feedback. The return or output of information either on a VDU or on paper after an input of data to the computer.

fee farm rent. In some parts of the UK it is customary for a purchaser of a fee simple to enter into a covenant to pay a perpetual annual rentcharge, often called a fee farm rent or a chief rent, instead of paying a lump sum for the purchase. The vendor retains a right of re-entry in the case that the annual payment falls into arrears.

fee simple. *See* ESTATE IN FEE SIMPLE.

fee tail. *See* ESTATE IN FEE TAIL.

feme sole. An unmarried woman, a spinster, a widow, a wife economically independent of her husband.

fiat. A formal demand, an authoritative order; the order or warrant of a judge or other constituted authority sanctioning or allowing certain processes.

fiat money. Paper money made legal tender by governmental decree.

fiction. Something feigned, invented or imagined. *See also* LEGAL FICTION.

fictitious asset. An asset which has no present value, e.g. preliminary expenses when a company is being formed. The money has been spent and therefore has to appear somewhere, but it will be written out of the balance sheet as soon as possible.

fictitious payee. A non-existent payee, or an existing person named as payee who never had, and was never intended to have, any legal interest in the proceeds of a bill. In such a case the bill may be treated as payable to bearer. *See* PAYEE.

fidelity guarantee. A guarantee by a person or insurance society that an employee will remain honest.

fiduciary. Holding or held in trust.

fiduciary capacity. The capacity descriptive of a trustee.

fiduciary issue. An issue of notes by a bank without reserves of gold or silver behind them, but having their value sustained by a general public confidence. The fiduciary issue in the UK is backed by securities. An upward change in the amount, if persisting over two years, must receive the sanction of Parliament.

fiduciary loan. A loan made without security because of the confidence of the lender in the honour of the borrower.

fiduciary relationship. A relationship between two parties where in the nature of things one trusts and depends on the other, e.g. a ward and his/her guardian. In such a case the law demands a higher degree of care and responsibility from the dominant party.

fief. An estate formerly held on condition of military service.

field. A section of a computer record on which designated information is stored. It can also be a specific space on a document for encoding details, for example, on a cheque, an amount field is available for a computer operator to encode the amount of the cheque, before it proceeds through branch accountancy system and onward to the paying branch-bank.

fieri facias (fi.fa.). A writ which may be issued on behalf of a judgment creditor, whereby the sheriff is authorised to seize goods of the debtor in satisfaction of a debt.

file. 1. A term used in the Consumer Credit Act, 1974, to refer to information retained by a credit reference agency on an individual; 2. an organised method of storing documents; 3. a bundle of documents, letters, etc., recording the correspondence between the firm and its customer/supplier. A folder/binder, box used to keep information. A name given to a particular set of records. Personnel file, computer file, sales file, etc.

filing of accounts. The submission of the accounts of a company to the Registrar of Companies as required by the Companies Act 1985.

FIMBRA. *See* FINANCIAL INTERMEDIARIES', MANAGERS' AND BROKERS' ASSOCIATION.

final accounts. The calculations of the gross and net profits of a business for the year, and the distribution of the net profit, are dealt with in four different accounts, called the manufacturing account, the trading account, the profit and loss account, and the profit and loss appropriation account. Because these four accounts are made up only at the end of each trading period they are called the final accounts. A trading concern which buys goods for resale does not, of course, manufacture them and will not, therefore, keep a manufacturing account.

final dividend. The last dividend paid by a company to its shareholders in respect of its financial year.

finance. The science of controlling public revenue and expenditure; the management of money affairs; to raise money by negotiations; to subsidise. *See also* FRONT END FINANCE; PROJECT FINANCE.

finance bill. 1. A bill put before Parliament by the government of the day concerning the raising of finance, which after being passed becomes the Finance Act of the year. 2. *A bill* drawn by a firm or company for the purpose of arranging a short-term loan. The bill is by arrangement drawn on another firm or on a bank or accepting house. When the bill is accepted it is discounted.

Finance Corporation for Industry (FCI). FCI was formed in 1945 to provide for industrial concerns, to help them in redevelopment schemes to assist them to work up to maximum efficiency. This objective was to be achieved by supplementing the efforts of other lenders. The aim of the corporation was to act in the national interest during the post-war reconstruction by providing funds for industry when money could not be wholly raised from market sources. It has thus restricted its investments to a small number of large companies. It did not provide finance unless the funds required exceeded £200,000 and could not be reasonably borrowed elsewhere. The share capital of the corporation was provided by the Bank of England, the insurance companies, and investment trusts. These institutional investors were paid out in cash when FCI merged with the Industrial and Commercial Finance Corporation (*q.v.*) in 1973 to form Finance for Industry (*q.v.*). After the reorganisation FCI is willing to consider loans in the range £1 million to £35 million. The period envisaged for service and repayment of such loans is seven to fifteen years. Interest rates are either fixed at the outset or linked to interbank rates. In 1982 FCI suffered an organisational change of name for identity purposes and its work was carried on under the name of the holding company Finance for Industry (FFI).

Finance for Industry (FFI). FFI was formed in 1973 by the merger of Finance Corporation for Industry (*q.v.*) and the Industrial and Commer-

cial Finance Corporation (*q.v.*). The new group had potential resources of nearly £500 million, about £300 million of which were absorbed by the existing commitments of ICFC and FCI. The merger created a two-tier structure. FFI as a new holding company acquired all the shares in ICFC and FCI, which each remained intact. The new company is concerned in cases where substantial sums of money may be needed for investment before profits can be seen, or with heavy programmes of capital re-equipment which must be spread over a number of years unless additional sources of finance can be found. All loans are, however, made subject to strict criteria of commercial viability. FFI lends primarily on a fixed-interest long- and medium-term basis. Its share capital is provided by the principal English and Scottish banks and by the Bank of England. Since the merger FFI has raised a further £125 by a loan stock issue, giving private investors the opportunity to contribute directly to industrial development, and has had £100 million made available by its shareholders as stand-by facilities. In addition to providing finance itself FFI also acts as the UK link with certain European lending institutions. All the operating functions are undertaken by subsidiaries of the holding company. The major subsidiaries are Industrial and Commercial Finance Corporation (ICFC) (*q.v.*), Finance Corporation for Industry (FCI) (*q.v.*), Technical Development Capital Ltd (TDC) (*q.v.*), and Estate Duties Investment Trust (Edith) (*q.v.*).

finance house. *See* HIRE PURCHASE COMPANIES.

finance house base rate. In a period of rapidly rising interest rates, finance houses' lending rates can get out of line, with a consequent 'windfall' benefit for the customer. To avoid this, it has become prevalent practice to link interest rates on industrial and commercial contracts with the Finance House Base Rate. This is a wholly objective indicator of changes in the cost of three-month interbank money, and is calculated by noting the rate each day, calculating an average rate for each week on a Friday, and then on the last Friday in each month taking an average of the previous eight weekly averages. This figure is rounded up to the nearest $\frac{1}{2}$ per cent, which rate will apply for the following month. *See also* BASE RATE.

Finance Houses Association. An association of about forty of the larger and better-known firms in Britain engaged in financing hire purchase transactions. Together they represent over 90 per cent of all finance house business.

finance lease. A leasing contract providing for the lessee to pay the rental for a minimum non-cancellable period of time (the primary period) which suffices in total to amortise the lessor's capital outlay, incurred in the purchase of the asset which is to be leased. These rentals commonly include also an element of interest. The lessee always assumes the liability to maintain the equipment: a service agreement may be offered by the suppliers of the equipment. Where the asset is not fully amortised during the hire period, the lease is called an 'operating lease' or a 'rental contract'. Here the lessor aims to engage one customer, or a series of customers, for a sufficient number of consecutive rental periods to achieve the desired return. Also known as a 'full payout lease'. *See also* LEASING.

finances. The income of a state or person, resources, funds.

financial accounting. The recording of the financial transactions of a business for a stated period of time, and to produce information to show the effect these transactions had on the business. Such information will include the production of the final accounts.

financial futures. *See* LONDON INTER-NATIONAL FINANCIAL FUTURES EXCHANGE.

Financial Intermediaries, Managers' and Brokers' Association (FIMBRA). A self regulating organisation (SRO) under the Financial Services Act, 1986, set up with the purpose of monitoring the activities of its members, providing regulations and standards for its members, and providing adequate investor protection.

Financial Services Act, 1986. Until this Act was passed, financial services in the UK were regulated either by a number of government acts or by codes of practice set up by bodies such as the Stock Exchange. It became clear that current measures to protect investors needed reform and additionally, with 'Big Bang' and the internationalisation of markets, some restructuring was necessary. Professor Gower was commissioned to examine the protection that was available for investors. His paper was published in 1984 and from this the government produced a White Paper 'Financial Services in the United Kingdom; a New Framework for Investor Protection'. This paper recommended that a new body should be established to be responsible for overseeing the self regulating bodies and the investment business and markets in which they operate. After due discussion and amendments in Parliament, the Act was passed and phased in throughout 1987/8. The Act primarily dealt with the protection of the investor through the structure of self regulating bodies. Under the Act it is a criminal offence to conduct an investment business without proper authority and those who may deal in investments have to meet stated criteria before authority is granted. The rules of any self regulating body must include not only a compensation fund, and adequate protection for clients' money, but such matters as advertising, conflict of interest within a firm or company, 'cold calling' on persons etc. The Act also defines security instruments such as shares, debentures, stocks, option warrants, unit trusts, futures contracts and some long term insurance contracts. Negotiable instruments are not included, nor are building society accounts, property documents and non life insurance documents. It should be noted that the investment risk still is with the investor. Should the value of the shares of a company go down, that is the investor's risk. The Act has established the Securities and Investment Board (SIB) which will oversee the whole operation. Although accountable to the Secretary of State for Trade and Industry, it will be financed by the financial services industry itself. Self Regulating Organisations (SROs) will be set up to regulate the activities of its members and provide regulations and standards on dealing with the public. With the need to regulate business on the various exchanges, Recognised Investment Exchanges (RIEs) have been set up so that there is an orderly and regulated market, adequate procedures for recording transactions, clearing arrangements and adequate financial resources.

financial statement. Any statement by a business entity, whether it is a sole trader, partnership or company, listing the capital, assets and liabilities of the organisation. The larger and more comprehensive organisation will have to conform to current legislation as well as having the accounts certified by qualified accountants. The financial statement should show the 'net worth' of the business and is an historical statement.

Financial Times Actuaries Indices. Equity indices calculated daily and covering 30 sectors of the Stock Market, aggregated in the 500 Index and the All-share Index. There are also gilt and fixed-interest indices. Introduced in April 1987, the world index covers about 24 countries subdivided into geographical areas, with each quoted in sterling, US dollars and local currency. Of the 2,400 or so companies, most are in the USA, Japan and the UK.

Financial Times 30 Index (FT Index). An index of price changes measured hourly, of industrial ordinary shares on the London Stock Exchange, based on thirty publicly quoted companies chosen to represent a wide range of British industry, which in the aggregate form a significant proportion of total equity capitalisation. The index is based on a figure of 100, fixed on 1 July 1935, which acts as a reference point, and is no more than a calculation of the percentage deviation from that point in time.

Financial Times Stock Exchange 100 Index (FTSE). An index of the 100 largest companies' shares, updated every minute throughout the working day. It is an arithmetic average and is weighted according to market capitalisation – representing about 70 per cent of total. Base date is 3 January 1984 at 1,000. Commonly known as 'FOOTSIE'.

financial year. Any twelve-monthly period for which public, official or company accounts are made up. In Great Britain it is the year from 1 April to the following 31 March, but for fiscal purposes it is the twelve months from 6 April of one year to 5 April of the year following (the tax year). For legal purposes the position is governed by the Companies Act, 1976, s.1, which defines the financial year of a company as 'the accounting reference period of the company (whether it is a year or not)'. The same Act (s.2) provides for a company to give notice to the Registrar of Joint Stock Companies of the date of the end of the company's accounting reference period, but if it does not do so then the date is taken to be 31 March. However, this may be changed at the company's instance at any time in the two years following.

fine bank bill (or prime bank bill). A bill drawn on, and accepted by, an accepting house or British bank with an unquestioned financial standing.

fine rate. The most favourable rate of interest charged to an undoubted borrower; the most favourable rate of discount to the seller of a fine bank bill.

fire insurance. A contract of indemnity by which an insurance company undertakes to make good any damage or loss by fire to buildings or property during a specified time.

fire policy. A policy guaranteeing compensation up to a stated limit in case of damage by fire.

firm. A partnership or association of two or more persons for carrying on a business; the name, title or style under which a company transacts business; a commercial partnership.

firm offer. A definite offer to purchase specified property at a stated price.

first class bill. A good commercial bill which is self-liquidating on a short-term basis.

first cost. The cost of production in money terms.

first mortgage. A mortgage on a property which is not subject to any prior mortgage.

first of exchange. Three bills of exchange drawn in connection with foreign trade are described as first, second or third of exchange respectively. A set may be of any number, but three is the most usual. *See also* BILL IN A SET.

fiscal. Pertaining to the public treasury or revenue.

fiscal drag. As money incomes increase the proportion of income paid in tax rises, because personal allowances, etc., are fixed. In inflationary times the real value of the fixed allowances decreases, until such time as they are increased. 'fiscal drag' is the amount, measured in real values, by which the allowances fall behind increasing tax. As a result the State takes in taxes a steadily increasing portion of incomes.

fiscal policy. The use of taxation in the Budget as a weapon of monetary policy.

fiscal year. The tax year or years of assessment in the UK, ending on 5 April.

fishing expedition. A name sometimes given to the practice of making a status enquiry on a customer of a banker for varying amounts, with the object of ascertaining the extent of the customer's resources. A banker should not make an answer for more than one amount, which should be in connection with a genuine business transaction.

fixed. Made firm, made permanent, established, secure, determined.

fixed assets. Those assets which have been acquired for the purpose of carrying on the business of a company and which will not be resold, but will be kept in permanent use until they wear out.

fixed capital. Items of property, equipment and machinery bought out of the paid-up capital. Fixed-capital items are meant to be used in the business of the company and to be kept for the whole of their working life. Their value should be progressively written off or depreciated in the company's books during their working life.

fixed charge. A periodic charge which has no relation to the amount of business done, an overhead charge, e.g. rent or rates; a charge for services rendered or work done, which has been established at a certain figure by agreement; a charge appearing in a mortgage debenture covering a company's land and buildings. Such a charge may also cover machinery, equipment, goodwill and even book debts.

fixed cost. The cost of a business which does not vary with output.

fixed debenture. A debenture charged on the fixed assets of a company, such as land.

fixed deposit. A deposit repayable on a pre-determined future date. Such transactions may be for periods ranging from overnight to five years. The interest rate applicable is also 'fixed' for the full period of the transaction.

fixed future foreign exchange contract. A legal binding contract to purchase/sell a stated amount of currency at a fixed rate of exchange on a specific date.

fixed loan. A loan repayable on a pre-determined future date. Such transactions may be for periods ranging from overnight to five years. The interest rate applicable is also 'fixed' for the full period of the transaction.

fixed rate contract. *See* HIRE-PUR-CHASE AGREEMENT.

fixed-sum credit. For the purposes of the Consumer Credit Act, 1974, a facility which is not a running-account credit, but which enables the debtor to receive credit (e.g. a loan).

fixed trust. A unit trust whose trust deed provides for a set list of security holdings for spreading risk over a period of ten to twenty years, with severe restrictions on the ability of the management to vary the investments.

fixings. *See* LONDON GOLD MARKET.

fixtures. 1. Chattels which are so affixed to land or to a building as to become part of it, passing with the ownership of the land; furniture or fittings permanently fastened to the structure of a building. 2. In international trade, a loan made for a fixed period of time and not repayable until the maturity date. Seven days fixed, one, two, three, four or six months, one year or annually up to five years, are common periods for fixtures. Loans may be in sterling or any other marketable currency on such terms.

flat (or running) yield. The annual return derived from the interest or dividend on an investment, divided by the price and multiplied by 100.

flexible trust. A unit trust whose trust deed empowers the managers to vary or substitute the security holdings of the trust at their discretion, although usually restricting their choice to a given list.

float. To set going, as a business company; to put into circulation; a sum of money kept on one side to meet small expenses or to assist in balancing a cashier's till; the action of a country's currency when it is allowed to find its own level on the foreign exchanges through the action of the laws of supply and demand.

floater. First-class bearer securities deposited with lending banks against overnight or call money.

floating assets. The assets of a company which are continually changing, e.g., cash or stock.

floating capital. Money available for the carrying on of any business concern.

floating charge. A charge on the floating assets of a company, included in a debenture. The floating charge crystallises to affix itself to the assets on the day on which a receiver is appointed.

floating currency. *See* FLOATING RATE.

floating debenture. A debenture charged on the floating assets of a company, such as stock. Such a charge 'crystallises' on the day on which a liquidator is appointed, and will then attach to whatever stock, etc., is available on that date.

floating debt. That part of the National Debt which consists of Treasury Bills, short-term Exchequer bonds, etc., and fluctuates according to circumstances; short-term loans or debts repayable at short notice.

floating money. Money in the hands of bankers and others at a time of excessive liquidity, for which no profitable use can quickly be found.

floating mortgage. *See* FLOATING CHARGE.

floating policy. A marine policy covering goods which may be widely spread over a district or area, or in whatever ship they may be.

floating population. Shifting population whose movements are controlled by the fluctuating demand for labour, especially in sea-ports or industrial areas.

floating pound. The pound sterling left to find its own level on the foreign exchanges through the operation of the laws of supply and demand.

floating rate. A stable rate of exchange, defended by a country's central bank which buys its own currency unit when it is under pressure, can prove more costly to maintain than the country concerned is willing or able to afford. The home currency unit has to be paid for in foreign currencies which have been earned by exporting, and if the pressure is too great the out-drain will, if it is allowed to continue, seriously endanger the country's reserves. One remedy for this situation is devaluation (*q.v.*); another is to allow the currency to float, that is, to find its own level on the foreign exchanges through the operation of the forces of supply and demand. This involves abandoning the Smithsonian Agreement (*q.v.*), but many countries have been forced to take this step. Under this system, equilibrium on the foreign exchanges is achieved by frequent small changes, rather than by irregular and precipitate ones.

floating rate bond. A bond whose coupon is linked to prevailing market rates of interest. It remains relatively stable in price, not suffering capital gains or losses as interest rates rise or fall.

floating rate notes. These are securities issued in the Euromarket where the interest rate is *floating* rather than fixed. Usually the rate is set at about $\frac{1}{2}$ per cent above six months' LIBOR with a stipulated minimum interest, e.g. $5\frac{1}{2}$ per cent. The rate is adjusted at six-monthly intervals.

floor limit. The maximum amount that can be withdrawn out in cash from an Automatic Teller Machine. The

amount authorised in any financial transaction.

flotation. The act of launching a commercial enterprise, especially a limited liability company; the launching of a new capital issue.

flow chart. A visual representation, by means of a graph, chart or pictorial summary, of the steps in sequence through which a productive operation is progressing.

fluctuation. A rising and falling, a vacillation, irregular changes in degree; changes in the value of stocks and shares, or in the value of a country's unit of currency on the foreign exchanges; varying intensities of demand for a product.

FOB. *See* FREE ON BOARD.

folio. A page number in a book or ledger; the number of words (seventy-two or ninety) taken as a unit in computing the total number of words in a document; a page of manuscript.

FOOTSIE. *See* FINANCIAL TIMES STOCK EXCHANGE 100 INDEX.

for cash. A Stock Exchange phrase referring to transactions which must be paid for at the time they are made (also *For Money*).

forecast. A written or spoken prediction of future events. Financial budgets, production budgets, sales budgets, etc. are essential for all businesses and often required to accompany a borrowing proposition. These forecasts are based on the strengths and weaknesses of the business, costing and selling policies, and general economic conditions.

foreclose. To prevent, to exclude, to deprive of the right to redeem a mortgage.

foreclosure. The method by which the mortgagee acquires for himself or herself land mortgaged to him or her, freed from the mortgagor's equity of redemption. Taking possession of an estate mortgaged to a lender, where repayment has not been made, and after a foreclosure order has been obtained.

foreclosure order. If the time in the deed of mortgage for repayment has passed, and no repayment has been made, the lender may apply to the court for an order for foreclosure, so that the lender may appropriate the fee simple if the borrower still fails to pay. The court issues an order for foreclosure *nisi* which orders that the mortgagor shall lose the property unless he pays upon a certain date (usually six months later) specified. The order is then made absolute and this vests the fee simple absolute in the mortgagee and extinguishes his or her mortgage term and all subsequent mortgage terms.

foreign. Situated outside a place or country, alien, subject to the law of another country.

foreign banks. Banks of foreign countries maintaining an office or offices in London but with their headquarters in their own country.

foreign bill. A bill drawn in the United Kingdom and payable abroad, or a bill drawn abroad and payable in the United Kingdom.

foreign bill for collection. *See* BILL FOR COLLECTION.

foreign bill for negotiation. *See* BILL FOR NEGOTIATION.

foreign bond. A security issued by a borrower in the national capital market of another country.

foreign corporation. Defined in the US as a corporation established under the laws of a state other than the state in which it is doing business, and of course includes companies with their head offices in other countries outside the US. Certain states in the US, e.g. Delaware, make it attractive for companies to register within their borders in terms of either tax advantages or less onerous reporting requirements. Foreign banking institutions operating in the US are regulated by the International Banking Act of 1978,

although again individual states often have their own banking laws.

Foreign Credit Insurance Association (FCIA). The FCIA administers the insurance program of the Export-Import Bank of the US (*q.v.*).

foreign currency. The money of any foreign country.

foreign currency account. A customer account maintained in a bank which is in the currency of a foreign country. The accounts of a UK bank which they have abroad for the purpose of giving services to their customers. These are usually called '*Nostro Accounts*'.

foreign currency securities. Securities on which interest or dividends are payable in a foreign currency, and repayment of which will be made similarly.

foreign draft. A bill drawn in a foreign currency and payable abroad.

foreign exchange. The exchange of one country's currency for another; foreign currency generally.

foreign exchange broker. A broker operating on the foreign exchange market for a principal, whether a financial institution, a bank, or a government.

foreign items. Bills of Exchange, cheques, drafts, other negotiable instruments with or without commercial documents attached to be sent abroad for collection or payment.

foreign trade. Commerce carried on between merchants in different countries, resulting in demands for foreign currencies which affect the balance of trade of the countries concerned.

FOREX. The abbreviation for foreign exchange or foreign exchange market.

forfaiting. The purchase by a bank of medium and long term bills of exchange which have been accepted by the drawee, usually guaranteed by the drawee's bank without recourse to the seller/drawer.

forfeit. That which is lost through fault, crime, omission or neglect; a penalty, a fine, especially a stipulated sum to be paid in case of breach of contract.

forfeit of shares. The articles of association of a limited company may provide that where a call is made to the holder of a number of the company's partly-paid shares, and the shareholder fails to pay the call, the company may declare the shares forfeit.

forfeiture. Deprivation, confiscation; the loss of the remainder of a leasehold term (subject to the court's decision) by a lessee for non-payment of rent.

forged banknotes. Unauthorised copies of the banknotes of a country, illegally put into circulation; counterfeit money.

forged indorsement. A forged signature by way of indorsement does not invalidate the bill, but where it purports to be a signature forming part of the chain of title to the bill it is ineffective to pass any title to the person who acquires the bill from the forger. But if the forged signature is unnecessary to the transfer of the title (as, e.g., where it appears on a bearer bill) it may be ignored.

forged share transfer. Signatures of customers on stock transfer forms taken in connection with a mortgage of stocks or shares to the bank as security should be made at the bank to avoid the risk of forgery. A bank forwarding a certificate and a stock transfer form to a company for registration is deemed to guarantee the genuineness of the signature on the stock transfer form.

forged signature. Where a signature on a bill is placed thereon without the authority of the person whose signature it purports to be, the forged or unauthorised signature is wholly inoperative. A forged signature cannot subsequently be ratified, but an unauthorised signature may so be. A banker paying a cheque having a forged signature cannot debit his or her customer's account with the amount of the cheque, unless the drawer is precluded from setting up the forgery. It is not a bill of exchange, as it is not signed by the person giving it.

forgery. The act of counterfeiting a coin or document, or falsifying a document whether in a material particular or in the copying of another's signature, or illegally using another person's signature.

formal protest. A protest of a dishonoured bill of exchange, made by a notary public, as opposed to a householder's protest.

for the account. A Stock Exchange phrase referring to transactions which are to be settled or paid for on the next account day or settling day.

forward. Onward in time; to promote, to re-address, to send out or despatch (of goods). *See also* CARRIAGE FORWARD.

forward budget. An attempt by a firm or company to estimate the inflows and outgoings of their organisation for the year ahead. A cash budget is prepared to exercise control over cash flow. The budget is intended to ensure that adequate cash will be available to meet the company's needs as and when necessary. It is prepared by estimating the expected receipts for the period in question, here taken as a year, in the light of the trading conditions and prospects of the company, and then subtracting an estimated total in respect of expected payments. There should be a balance in hand to be carried forward to the next period. Receipts come from sales, so credit periods allowed and trade and cash discounts must be reckoned with here. Short-term loans may come from the bank on a seasonal basis, long-term funds would follow a debenture or share issue. Other income may come on a regular or occasional basis such as rents or proceeds of sale of capital asset. Payments are estimated in much the same way. Wages, salaries, overtime can be forecast on the basis of what has been paid out in the recent past, allowing for any increases in wage rates or any upsurge in the work to be done. The effects of inflation will be considered and written into the budget. The manager of the company, having these figures at his disposal, is better able to take decisions on a day-to-day basis. This process has come to be described as 'management accounting'. The bank manager must recognise that the average forward budget is no more than an intelligent guess at best, and a misleading factor at worst. While it is an excellent exercise for a sophisticated company of some size to undertake, it is more open to question in the cases of smaller companies or firms or one-man businesses. In such cases the branch manager will do better to rely on a personal judgment of the customer as a businessman or woman. Volumes of impressive documentation as to future plans are no guarantee of the customer's ability to carry them out. *See also* CASH FLOW.

forward combination. An amalgamation between a company or a firm and the business which markets the company's product.

forward exchange. Buying or selling foreign currency in advance through the forward exchange market; the purchase or sale of foreign currency for delivery at a future date. *See also* LONDON INTERNATIONAL FINANCIAL FUTURES EXCHANGE (LIFFE); OPTION FORWARD RATE: SWAP.

forwarding. Despatching merchandise sending goods forward.

forwarding agent. An agent who undertakes the collection, forwarding, documentation and delivery of goods.

forwarding note. A note giving the description of goods, etc., and the name and address of the consignee, which is transmitted with the goods.

forward rate. The rate at which foreign currency can be bought or sold for delivery at a future time. *See also* OPTION FORWARD RATE; SWAP.

founders' shares. *See* DEFERRED SHARES.

fractional banking. A banking system where it is customary to keep a definite fixed ratio between total deposits and cash, or where such a ratio is imposed by law.

franchise. A privilege conferred by a government; the district to which such a privilege extends; the right to vote in elections; a percentage of the insured value of goods which an underwriter requires the owner of the cargo to cover himself/herself; a sort of collaboration offered to small independent shops in which a manufacturing enterprise puts at the disposal of all the shops taking part in the scheme, for a remuneration (the franchise), a complete and uniform marketing programme, a system of 'tied' agreements between brewers and publicans whereby each publican sells only the products of a particular brewery. *See also* ENFRANCHISEMENT.

franco, franko. Free of expense, at no charge.

frank. To send or cause to be sent under an official privilege; the right to send letters through the post free of charge; the letter thus sent.

franked income. Revenue on which a tax has been paid and which therefore is free of liability to that tax in the hands of the recipient.

franking. A term given to a practice by an employer who is dealing with the preserved pension rights of an employee who has left his or her employment for a post elsewhere. This consists, in the case of pension schemes which have been contracted out of the state reserve part of the state pension fund, of the use by the employer of the employee's preserved benefits to pay for the inflation proofing which the employer is obliged by law to provide for the employee's guaranteed minimum pension.

franking machine. A machine which stamps or franks envelopes with a symbol indicating that the postage has been paid.

fraud. An act or course of deception deliberately practised to gain unlawful or unfair advantage; such deception directed to the detriment of another; a deception, a trick, trickery. In the UK the Theft Act, 1968 makes it an offence for a person by any deception dishonestly to obtain, for himself or any other, any pecuniary advantage. The cases in which a pecuniary advantage is to be regarded as obtained for a person are cases where 1. any debt or charge for which he makes himself liable, or is, or may become liable (including one not legally enforceable) is reduced or in whole or in part evaded or deferred; 2. the person is allowed to borrow by way of overdraft or to take out any policy of insurance or annuity contract, or obtains an improvement of the terms on which this is allowed.

fraudulent. Practising fraud, intended to deceive; in bankruptcy, having the intention to defeat or delay creditors.

fraudulent conveyance. A transfer of property by a debtor which has the effect of defeating or delaying creditors, even though made in good faith. A fraudulent conveyance is void and the transferee must return the property to the trustee in bankruptcy. A conveyance is not fraudulent if it has been made for valuable consideration in good faith. Evidence of a fraudulent intent might be the gratuitous character of the transfer or the receipt of a purely nominal consideration. *See also* ACT OF BANKRUPTCY.

fraudulent misrepresentation. The tort of deceit. It is committed when a person makes a false representation of fact, knowing it to be false, or without believing it to be true, or recklessly, careless whether it be true or false. There must be an intention on the part of the maker that it shall be acted upon by the person deceived, that person must in fact act upon it, and must as a result suffer some loss. The remedy for the injured party is a right to rescind the contract (if the fraud is discovered in time), and an action for damages on the tort. *See also* FRAUD.

fraudulent preference. Any conveyance or transfer of money or property or charge thereon made by a debtor when insolvent in favour of a creditor (or of any person in trust for any creditor) with a view to giving such creditor (or any surety or guarantor for the debt to such creditor) an advantage over other creditors; paying one creditor in full or in part when all other creditors are not paid in full or proportionately. A fraudulent preference must be established by the trustee or liquidator. It must be a voluntary act on the part of the debtor, made entirely without pressure from the creditor. There must also be an intention to prefer, that is, the payment by the debtor must be deliberate and not accidental. *See also* ACT OF BANKRUPTCY.

fraudulent settlement. 1. A settlement made before and in consideration of marriage where the settlor is not at the time of making the settlement able to pay all his or her debts without the aid of the property comprised in the settlement; or 2. any covenant or contract made in consideration of marriage for the future settlement on, or for, the settlor's wife or children of any money or property wherein he had not at the date of his marriage any estate or interest. If the settlor is adjudged bankrupt, or compounds or arranges with creditors, the court may refuse or suspend an order of discharge or refuse to approve a composition or arrangement, if it thinks the transaction was done in order to defeat creditors or was not justifiable, having regard to the state of the debtor's affairs, at the time when it was made.

fraudulent trading. Insolvency Act, 1986 s. 213. 1. If in the course of winding-up of a company it appears that any business of the company has been carried on with intent to defraud creditors of the company or creditors of any other person, or for any fraudulent purpose, the following has effect; 2. the court, on the application of the liquidator may declare that any persons who were knowingly parties to the carrying on of the business in the manner above mentioned are to be liable to make such contributions (if any) to the company's assets as the court thinks proper.

free. Not under restraint, not subject to restrictions, duties, etc.; gratuitous, liberal.

free alongside ship. Delivered free on the dock or wharf.

free capital. Capital held in the form of cash and therefore available for transportation into any form of real capital. It is also a term now frequently used in connection with banks in the context of prudential ratios. Used in this way, it is usually taken to include reserves and subordinated loan stock less money tied up in property, equipment and trade investments. Cash in tills is sometimes also included in the formula.

free docks. A price quotation for goods by an exporter which includes the cost of the goods themselves plus the cost of transporting them to the docks where they will be loaded on board.

freeholder. The possessor of a freehold estate.

freehold estate. An estate in land which is properly described as an estate in fee simple absolute in possession, signifying the highest type of land ownership which anyone can possess; the tenure of property in fee simple or fee tail. *See also* ESTATE IN FEE SIMPLE; FEE.

free market. A market where stall-holders pay no tax; on the Stock Exchange, a market in shares which can be bought or sold without difficulty.

free of all average. A clause in a marine insurance policy meaning that claims for general or particular average cannot be recovered.

free of particular average. A clause in a marine insurance policy meaning that claims for particular average cannot be recovered.

free of tax. *See* TAX FREE.

free on board (FOB). A contractual term indicating that the price quoted to the buyer is the price of the goods plus the cost of putting them on board the vessel which is to carry them. All freight charges and the cost of insurance must be paid by the buyer.

free on rail (FOR). A contractual term indicating that the price quoted to the buyer is the price of the goods plus the cost of transporting them to the railway station from which the goods are to be despatched.

free port. A port where ships of all nations may load or unload free of duty.

free ship. A neutral ship, free from liability to capture.

free trade. The policy of unrestricted international trade; the free interchange of commodities without protective tariffs.

freight. A charge made for the carriage of goods in a ship; the cargo itself; the sum paid for the hire of a ship or part of it.

freight car. A railway car used for goods.

freight collect/freight payable at destination. An annotation to a bill of lading inserted by a shipper or shipping company to evidence that freight has not been paid, commonly associated with FOB contracts where the buyer is responsible for payment of freight.

freight forward. The term to indicate

that freight on goods is payable at the port of destination.

freight indemnity. A guarantee to a shipping line that freight charges will be paid, with the intention of obtaining the delivery of a bill of lading. It is mostly used where big companies having numerous contracts with a shipping company prefer to pay any freight due on a monthly basis rather than on each individual contract as and when it goes through. Pending the monthly settlement the shipping company is happy to accept a banker's indemnity for the amount of unpaid freight on any particular contract.

freight note. A document issued by a shipping company particularising the freight charge for a cargo.

freight paid. A clause stamped or marked on a bill of lading to indicate that the freight payable on the goods to which the bill refers has been paid. In a CIF or CAF contract it is essential for this point to be checked, for otherwise the shipping company will refuse to release the goods and the importer will have to pay the freight to get them.

friendly society. A mutual insurance society in which the members subscribe for provident benefits, in particular, sickness, old age, endowment and death benefits, and provisions for widows and orphans. Although the National Health Service now meets most of the needs for which the original friendly societies were set up, they still continue to operate and have diversified to include industrial insurance, industrial, provident and building societies; trade unions; certified loan societies; and some superannuation and pension schemes. All are closely regulated by the Friendly Societies Acts, 1896-1974.

fringe benefit. A benefit given to an employee in addition to a wage or salary. This may include non contributory pensions, private health arrangements, subsidised meals, cars, etc.

front end finance. An international trade payment may be made by way of loan to the buyer by a UK bank in the case of large contracts, to assist the UK exporter, repayment being guaranteed by the Export Credits Guarantee Department, but such advances will seldom exceed 80 per cent of the contract price. 'Front End Finance' is a further loan from another source to help the buyer meet the direct cash payment that he must make, the commonest source of funds for this purpose being the Euro-dollar market.

front end loading. A term applied to any loan where the borrower pays the interest on the whole term in one sum at the beginning, e.g. a discounted bill, as opposed to an overdraft where the borrower pays interest quarterly or half-yearly in arrears.

front loading. A sliding scale charge, usually about 5 per cent, which is added on to the principal sum borrowed by some finance houses. It is sometimes described as a *composite fee* or *administration charge*. Such charges are cleared first out of the repayment instalments, so that it can be a considerable time before the repayments begin to bite into the actual sum borrowed. The term is also used to describe any loan arrangement (such as a discounted bill) where the whole of the interest is paid by the borrower at the outset of the contract, as opposed to a loan or overdraft, where the borrower pays interest in arrears. It is also descriptive of unit trust charges.

frozen assets, frozen balances, frozen credits. Assets, etc., temporarily blocked and impossible to realise for the time being, e.g. the bank balances of foreign banks in a country which is at war with the bank's country.

frustration of contract. The occurrence of events which have not been foreseen and which operate to make the continued observance of a contract, which is intended to last over a period of time, impossible. Such events are sickness, war, accident, the interference of third parties, or subsequent legislation which renders any further performance under the contract illegal.

fully-paid shares. Shares where no call can be made on the holder, because the full value of the shares has been paid up in full.

functional. Having a special purpose, pertaining to a duty or office.

fund. Permanent stock or capital; an invested sum, the income of which is used for a set purpose; a store, an ample supply.

fund flow statement. A statement showing the movement of liquid funds in a business in any stated financial period. *See* SOURCE AND APPLICATION OF FUNDS STATEMENT.

funded debenture interest. Debenture interest which has, by agreement with the debenture holders, been paid not in cash but by way of further debentures.

funded debt. Government stock having no date for repayment, stock whose principal the government need not repay until it wishes. Sometimes called undated stocks, such securities have only an income yield, but no redemption yield.

funding. The act of process of establishing a funded debt; an operation whereby a government takes advantage of a prevailing low interest rate to repay stocks at the earliest date possible, replacing them by new issues bearing a lower rate of interest; repayment of bank borrowing by a company out of the proceeds of an issue of debentures.

funds. Money, finances, pecuniary resources; money lent to a government and constituting a national debt; the stock of a national debt regarded as an investment; Consols and other government securities are referred to as 'the Funds'. *Advisory Funds.* Funds left with a bank by a customer for investment on his or her behalf, after consultation. Such funds are held in large amounts by Swiss banks, and their use for investment in Eurobonds assists the ability of the bank to place new issues. Also known as *discretionary* or *in-house* funds.

fungible. A legal term to indicate that any article, object, or CHOSE IN ACTION (*q.v.*) is of such a nature that it may be replaced by another thing of the same class, without significant effect. The plural fungibles means movable goods which may be valued by weight or measure.

future goods. Goods to be manufactured or acquired by the seller after the making of the contract of sale.

futures. Good for delivery at some future time. Contracts of purchase or sale are made in the produce markets at prices fixed at the contract dates, but for future receipt or delivery of the commodities dealt in, and therefore at prices appropriate to the agreed delivery dates.

G

gage. Something given as security against a loan. A pledge.

gamma stocks. Stocks quoted on the Stock Exchange which are considered to be traded in a very small capacity, therefore prices stated on SEAQ are more of a guide than a firm price.

garnishee. One who has received notice not to pay any money which he or she owes to a third person, who is indebted to the person giving the notice.

garnishee order. A remedy open to a judgment creditor. The order *nisi* attaches money belonging to the judgment debtor (the customer) in the hands of the third party (the banker). The order restrains the garnishee from parting with any money due or accruing due to the judgment debtor. The order is effective from the moment it is served. It attaches money in all accounts in the debtor's name, including deposits, but excepting savings account balances. A debit balance on one account must be set off against a credit balance on another (there is no set-off with a loan account) so as to arrive at the attachable sum. If the account is an overdrawn one, or there is a net overdrawn position, there is nothing to attach, and the judgment creditor's solicitor should be informed of this, so that arrangements may be made for the order to be withdrawn. Where a balance is attached the account must be stopped. The garnishee must appear in court (in the case of a bank, through the bank's solicitor) a few days after the service of the order to show cause why the money he or she holds should not be taken in satisfaction of the debt due to the judgment creditor. If the judgment debtor wishes to enter a defence he or she attends also. Failing such cause shown, or defence, the order is made absolute and thereupon the garnishee must pay over to the creditor the amount of the debt plus costs, or the balance of the account if this is less. Because of the inconvenience caused by attaching a large sum for a small debt the limited order has been devised. This is issued for the amount of the judgment debt plus an estimate for costs, so that this sum may be transferred by the garnishee banker to a suspense account, leaving the main account of the customer capable of continued normal operation. The Supreme Court Act, 1981 made building society accounts equally available to this remedy, as are banking accounts.

garnishee summons. The operation of a garnishee summons is the same as that of a garnishee order, except that the summons is issued by a county court, where it is returnable, and service is made by an officer of the court. The banker may settle the matter as far as the banker is concerned by paying the amount due, or the amount of the balance, if less, to the county court registrar within eight days of the service of the summons. A garnishee summons is invariably limited in its nature.

GATT. *See* GENERAL AGREEMENT ON TARIFFS AND TRADE.

gavelkind. An old custom prevalent in Kent and Wales whereby the lands of a person dying intestate descend to all the sons in equal shares or, in default of sons, to all the daughters equally. The custom was abolished in 1925.

gazette. An official publication issued twice weekly giving details of petitions, bankruptcies, liquidations, statutory declarations, dissolutions of partnerships, etc. It is issued in London, Edinburgh and Belfast. *See also* STUBBS' WEEKLY GAZETTE.

gazumping. On the agreement for the sale of a house, but prior to the exchange of contracts by the solicitors acting for the parties, there exists a good but unenforceable contract (unless a written agreement or memorandum has been taken – (see CONTRACT OF SALE). The parties are bound to each other by their word only, and persons of repute will honour their word. However, where the seller is indifferent to the promised word, and subsequently receives a higher offer for the property from another, it may be accepted, to the disadvantage of the original would-be buyer. 'Gazumping' is a term recently coined to describe this disreputable act.

gearing. A relationship between the various classes of capital in a company. If some of the capital comes from loans, then gearing is the relationship between the loan capital and the total capital. The higher the loan capital, the higher the proportion of trading income allotted to meet the loan interest charge. But however much this may be, it is a fixed sum, and therefore any increase in trading income has a more than proportionate effect on the surplus available for net profit. If the gearing is between preference shares and ordinary shares, then a relatively small increase in profits over the level required to pay the fixed preference dividend will result in a more than proportionate sum becoming available for the payment of the ordinary dividend. As a general rule, if the greater proportion of the company's capital is in fixed interest loans, the company is said to be 'high-geared', whereas if the greater proportion is in ordinary shares it is said to be 'low-geared'. Gearing has become a term associated with inflation accounting (q.v.). ED 24, published in April 1979 by the Inflation Accounting Steering Group, proposed that in addition to historic accounts presented in the traditional manner a separate statement should be given showing current cost adjustments made to the historic profit for depreciation, cost of sales, and gearing. This gearing adjustment stems from the fact that the assets of the business will be partly financed from sources other than shareholders' funds and originally arose from the so-called 'interim recommendation' of November 1977. However, the single 'gearing adjustment' of the interim recommendation has now been refined into two separate adjustments, the monetary working capital adjustment, representing the working capital locked up in debtors (less creditors); and the gearing adjustment representing the loan capital used in financing the business. The 'incremental gearing ratio' refers to the ratios between the debt and equity elements in the additional finance a company raises in any one year. *Capital gearing* is the ratio of debt to total trading assets at replacement value. *Income gearing* is the ratio of interest payments to after-tax profits. *Interest gearing* reflects the relationship between a company's own finance and outside finance and is an assessment of all the interest and other charges due to the loan finance from sources outside the company. An example here might be commitments for leasing – not usually apparent from the capital gearing figure. ED 24 slightly modified, has now become SSAP 16. *See also* INFLATION ACCOUNTING.

general acceptance. One which assents without qualification to the order of the drawer.

general agent. An agent employed to conduct a particular trade or business, having implied or ostensible authority to do whatever is incidental to that trade or business.

General Agreement on Tariffs and Trade (GATT). An agreement made in 1947 to which the UK was a signatory, designed to maximise the growth of world trade by the progressive reduction of tariffs, quota restrictions and import controls between the signing nations. On a number of occasions the countries concerned have reduced tariffs by a set percentage, the 'Kennedy Round' being a conspicuously successful example. GATT also seeks to put an end to 'most favoured nation' clauses and any kind of discrimination amongst the member countries. There are certain escape clauses for countries getting into acute difficulties which might, for example, lead to a devaluation. The liberalisation of world trade which was GATT's primary aim is taking longer to achieve than was hoped. In the nature of things free trade benefits most the strongest and most advanced countries in technology and industrialisation. The poorer countries are the ones who most need help, and they have not in many cases yet been able to see their way to forego the advantages which restrictions on imports confer on their domestic industries. The organisation has no real power and economic blocs such as the EEC are contrary to its aims.

general average. A loss incurred by intentional measures taken at sea to preserve the safety of the ship or the cargo generally, e.g. by cutting away part of the ship, or jettisoning a part of the cargo. This loss is apportioned amongst the shipowner and the owners of the cargo, the proportions being calculated by an average adjuster.

general clearing. *See* CLEARING HOUSE.

general crossing. *See* CROSSED CHEQUE.

general equitable charge. An equitable mortgage of unregistered land not protected by deposit of the title deeds with the lender. It should be registered at the Land Charges Department as a land charge class C(iii). *See* LAND CHARGES REGISTER.

General Index of Retail Prices. This is commonly known as the Retail Price Index or RPI and has its origins in a

cost of living index which commenced in 1914. At that time it concentrated on basic goods such as bread, potatoes, clothing, lamp oil and candles. Other items which in those days were considered as luxuries were not included. These days, it measures the extent that prices change, not what people actually spend on consumer goods, so that it is strictly not a 'cost of living' index. The index is constructed by the Retail Prices Index Advisory Committee, which has members from the CBI, TUC, experts from universities, economists and statisticians. Since 1946, when the committee was known as the Cost of Living Advisory Committee, they have submitted ten reports to the Secretary of State for Employment, the latest being in September 1986. The index measures 130,000 separate price quotations for 600 items and is collected each month by staff of the Department of Employment making personal visits to shops. The index relates to the prices of goods taken on a single day each month, usually a Tuesday in the middle of the month. The total weighting given is 1,000 and the 'basket' is divided into the following groups.

	Weighting
Food	167
Meals purchased outside home	46
Alcohol and tobacco	114
Housing costs fuel and light	218
Household goods	73
Household services	44
Clothing and footwear	74
Personal goods and services	38
Motoring and travel costs	149
Leisure goods and services	77
Total	1,000

The reference date is simply a convenient point to which a continuous series of index values can be related and the latest date is that of 13 January 1987, when the index point of 100 measured all future movements from that date. The index is frequently used as a means of calculating the 'standard of living' and in wage and salary negotiations.

general issue. An issue of certain articles on a large scale; a legal issue which denies the whole declarations or charge, equivalent to a plea of 'not guilty' in contradistinction to a special issue.

general ledger. A part of the organisation of the accountancy system, where the accounts of the entity, other than the creditors, debtors and *cash book* are kept. In some small businesses this may be called the *private ledger*.

general lien. The right to retain goods in the possession of a dealer, warehouse-keeper, etc., which extends not only over the particular goods which gave rise to the debt, but over all the goods of that owner in his or her possession.

general meetings. *See* ANNUAL GENERAL MEETING..

general partner. *See* PARTNER.

general policy. Where an exporter is continually dispatching goods which the exporter wishes to insure, it would be tedious and time-consuming to arrange for a separate insurance policy on each occasion. Under a general policy an exporter may declare the value of each shipment to the insurance company as and when it is made, up to a total figure previously agreed with the company. Certificates under the general policy, often prepared by the insured, are issued as evidence of the cover.

general register of sasines. *See* SASINE.

general reserve. The retention of profits of the company in an account so named, for the purposes of expansion or the financial strengthening of the balance sheet.

genus. A stock, a species, a kind.

gift *inter vivos.* A gift which takes effect in the lifetime of the donor, a gift between living persons. Such a gift might have attracted duty before 1975,

but in that year the Finance Act provided that gifts *inter vivos* are, in the UK, subject to capital transfer tax. A gift *inter vivos* is now described as 'a chargeable transfer of value which reduces the estate of the transferor and is intended to benefit someone else'.

gilt auction. A recent method of selling government stock whereby there is no set price but investments are accepted from the upper price downwards. This is a risky method of purchase for the small investor, who can apply for the 'non competitive bid price' which is calculated at the average price of all institutional bids.

gilts (gilt edged). A term used to describe British government stocks. Gilts are one of the main instruments used by the government for borrowing, the other being the issue of Treasury Bills. The borrowing is required to pay for the public sector borrowing requirement, which is an estimate by the government of the total sum of money which it is going to need over the next financial year to run those national services for which it is responsible: e.g. the Civil Service, nationalised industries, the health service, the police, the fire brigades and so on. Gilts are divided into short, medium and long. Short gilts are those repayable in five years or under; medium gilts have over five and up to fifteen years to maturity; long gilts are those with more than fifteen years to maturity. Some have no date at all for maturity, such as $2\frac{1}{2}$ per cent Consols and $3\frac{1}{2}$ per cent War Loan. These are described as undated stocks. The prevailing market price takes account of redemption time and value with the result that the interest yield of an undated stock is not very much different from the interest yield of a high-coupon stock. Gilts are also divided into single-dated and double-dated. Single-dated stocks may be redeemed anytime during the year nominated. In double-dated stocks there is a spread so that the government has a choice over a number of years when to redeem, and will exercise this choice according to the prevailing market rate of money at the time Some issues were index linked in 1981 but purchase was restricted to pension funds and life insurance companies. However a year later these bonds were thrown open to anyone who wishes to buy marketable stock with a guaranteed real rate of return. Both principal and interest are indexed to retail prices, but capital return is guaranteed only if the stock is held to maturity. As with any gilt-edged stock the income is taxable and gains since 1986 are free of tax. Index-linked gilts thus become the yardstick by which all other investment opportunities are judged.

Ginnie Mae. *See* GOVERNMENT NATIONAL MORTGAGE ASSOCIATION.

giro. *See* BANK GIRO; GIROBANK.

Girobank. Formerly known as National Girobank. A giro banking system opened in 1968, and now run as a separate plc. It was set up to modernise the remittance services of the Post Office and in recent years has become a clearing bank in BACS, CHAPS and Town Clearing and the Cheque and Credit Clearing. The giro system is particularly appropriate for the payment of rates, instalment bills, hire purchase, mail order remittances, and payments for the renting of consumer durables. All accounts are kept at the centre in Bootle. The 'branches' are the post offices of the country. Debts between account holders are settled by transfers from one account to another, or in the case of non account holders by giro cheques. Withdrawals, up to £50 at a time, may be made from either of two post offices nominated by the account holder. Standing orders and automatic debit transfers are available; personal loans and overdrafts are also granted.

godown. An eastern warehouse for the storage of goods.

go-go fund. A unit trust which aims at a greater-than-average appreciation in values; this implies an aggressive and risk-taking investment policy, as well as frequent changes in the composition of the portfolio in order to make important gains quickly.

going concern. A business which is in full working order. The only type of business to which a banker will willingly give accommodation. *See also* GONE CONCERN.

going naked. In connection with an options trading market, when operators take option money on stock which they do not own and cannot deliver in the hope that it can be bought back at a lower level.

going public. A stage in the progress of an expanding business, which may start as a one-man concern, progress into a partnership and then into a private company. Further progress is made by the conversion of the company into a public company with a listing on the Stock Exchange. The services of stockbrokers acting on behalf of the company will be essential in the business of obtaining a Stock Exchange quotation for the shares and fixed-interest securities, if any, issued by the company, because the Quotations Committee will not deal except through a stockbroker. 'Going public' is usually advised when a company has already exhausted the sources of finance available to smaller private companies, or perhaps because the existing owners desire to reduce their involvement in the company because of capital transfer tax considerations. Companies wishing to make this step must satisfy stringent conditions of the Quotations Committee of the Stock Exchange as to their standing and reliability.

gold. It is quite illogical that gold should be so highly regarded: it pays no interest and, after all, is only a metal like any other. Yet throughout history it has aroused man's deepest admiration and greatest cupidity. As a base for a currency system it did well in the days when everyone was on the gold standard. But in modern times things are different. So there arose, particularly in America, an anti-gold lobby. Efforts were made in 1977 to get gold phased out of the international monetary system for good, but these met with considerable resistance from European countries for economic, financial and political reasons. There was still a belief that the most effective way of achieving the global restoration of monetary law and order lay in organising a new world monetary system wherein gold, would be given a central part to play. The gold price is widely seen as an index of international opinion – the higher it goes the less the faith in national currencies, and vice versa. But of course those mundane factors, supply and demand, have got something to do with it as well. There was a time when the United States administration chose to ignore a decline in the exchange rate of the dollar against stronger currencies, as a means of putting pressure on the governments concerned to reduce their balance of payments surpluses. When it modified this attitude the dollar was on a slide which could hardly be checked. As gold prices are quoted in dollars, the gold price climbed and climbed, from $40 per fine ounce in 1971 to over $800 per fine ounce during January 1980. In a world menaced by recession and inflation the lure of gold is irresistible. Residents in the United Kingdom have a number of choices if they wish to enter the gold market. They can invest in Krugerrands, the value of which climbs as the price of gold climbs, or in speculative gold shares in mining, or in specialised unit trusts. Since the lifting of exchange control restrictions in October 1979, there are no limits on the holding of gold bullion

by residents. Since December 1979, at least one bank has entered the retail gold market by putting gold bars on offer to the general public through its branch offices. The bars are 24 carat and weigh 5, 10, 20, and 50 grams. At the then price for gold the bars cost from £40 to £400 each. Unfortunately they are subject to VAT at 15 per cent. Perhaps a more attractive course for the buyer of gold bars is to instruct a Swiss bank to act on one's behalf. The minimum purchase is usually 10 ounces, plus commission at $\frac{1}{4}$ per cent and a safe custody charge of $\frac{1}{8}$ per cent. But for those who do not want to deal through a Swiss bank, the most convenient way to acquire non-jewellery gold must be the Krugerrand. It is easily transportable and internationally accepted for what it is – a transferable hedge against currency depreciation. Profits on Krugerrands and gold bullion are subject to Capital Gains Tax.

gold bullion. Gold in the form of metal bars each weighing 400 ounces (11.3 kilograms), held by central banks and dealers in a gold market.

gold bullion standard. A monetary system under which the export and import of gold is freely permitted for the settlement of international obligations, but where the internal currency consists of token paper. The gold bullion standard is therefore a modified form of the gold standard. When it was in use in the UK between 1925 and 1931, convertibility of paper into gold was secured by the availability of gold bars of 400 ounces (11.3 kilograms) for exchange with notes to the value of the gold. In this way important economies were made in gold, while the currency was still kept convertible. Gold bullion is quoted in US dollars per fine ounce. The morning and afternoon fixing prices are also given in sterling.

gold clause. A clause in an offer to

lenders to the effect that repayment will be made at the rate of the gold equivalent of the loan currency at the time the loan was floated. This offers protection against a devaluation of the currency.

gold credit card. A credit card issued by the credit card companies on behalf of the banks which indicate a higher financial status and automatically gives the holder additional credit, additional insurance and various concessions that differ slightly from bank to bank.

golden handcuffs/hello. An inducement paid by a company to attract an executive to join or remain on its staff. At the same time in order to retain his services, certain conditions are laid down.

golden handshake. Compensation paid by a company or firm to a highly-placed executive for loss of office. Such pay-offs are tax free up to £30,000 but any additional amounts attract the full rate of income tax.

gold exchange standard. A form of gold standard where a country using it has neither a gold currency in circulation nor reserves held in gold for external purposes, but instead keeps its reserves mostly in the currency and securities of another country which is on the gold standard. In this way both sterling and dollars have been reserve currencies.

gold fixing. Setting the price of gold on the Gold Market in London or Zürich.

gold market. See LONDON GOLD MARKET.

gold points. See SPECIE POINTS.

gold premium. Where any commodity can be exchanged into gold, and it also has an intrinsic or face value of its own, it may happen that it will be more profitable to exchange the commodity for the gold equivalent and then sell the gold than it is to simply sell the commodity for cash. When this happens, gold is said to be 'at a premium' and the difference is the 'gold premium'.

gold reserves. The reserves of gold coin and bullion held by any central bank for its government; these are the gold reserves of the country. In the UK the gold reserves of the nation are held on the Exchange Equalisation Account by the Bank of England.

goldsmiths' notes. Receipts given by goldsmiths in the seventeenth century, which acknowledged the deposit of money put with them for safe keeping, and incorporated a promise to return it on demand. These receipts circulated for value among merchants and came to be described as goldsmiths' notes. The original function as a receipt came to be superseded by the importance of the function as a promissory note. These were the forerunners of our modern banknotes.

gold standard. A system of note-issue backed by gold, used in the UK from 1821-1914. The system has the advantage that it gives an automatic check on inflation, and the disadvantage that the total of world trade must always be limited by the total output of gold in the world. Three conditions must be satisfied for a gold standard to work: 1. there must be free mintage of gold into the standard legal coins; 2. gold must be free to be imported into or exported from the country without restraint; 3. the legal paper money of the country must be convertible by the central bank into gold on request.

gone concern. A departure from the normal assumption that a business will continue to operate indefinitely (*see* GOING CONCERN), the 'gone concern' concept attempts to measure what a business is currently worth at a break-up value in the hands of a liquidator. Where it seems to a banker asked for accommodation that a company customer may be in danger of liquidation, the banker will assess the company's resources as a gone concern. Each asset has to be valued on a forced-sale basis; the estimated proceeds may then be notionally apportioned among the various classes of creditors and a very rough rate of dividend calculated.

good. Right, proper, safe, adequate, honest; commodity.

good and marketable title. A desirable form of words which solicitors acting for the banks are often asked to use when reporting on the title of freehold or leasehold property passing to the bank by way of security for a loan.

good consideration. Consideration which is enough to support a simple contract, i.e. good in a court of law.

good delivery. On the Stock Exchange, good delivery is made when a security which has been sold is handed over, perfectly in order. If anything is not in order, e.g. where bearer bonds are delivered with one or more coupons missing, it is not good delivery.

good faith. A thing is done in good faith when it is in fact done honestly, whether it is done negligently or not. To take a bill in good faith is to take it without any notice or even suspicion of any flaw or defect in the title of the negotiator.

good for. Able to pay, as in a banker's enquiry 'whether good for £200 in one amount'.

good leasehold title. A title granted by the Land Registrar for leases with twenty-one years or more to run, if they are in order. A good leasehold title gives the proprietor the same rights as an absolute title except that it says nothing about the lessor's right to grant the lease. A good leasehold title may be converted into an absolute title after ten years if the proprietor, or successive proprietors, have been continuously in possession.

good marking names. *See* MARKING NAMES.

good merchantable condition. Goods up to standard, and having no defect which will in any way affect their sale.

good money. Derived from 'Greshams Law'. Coins that are not debased will be retained, while mutilated or debased currency will be circulated. Cleared funds on a current account. A draft drawn by a UK bank on itself.

good root of title. A document which will act as the starting point for checking a land title. The document chosen must be at least fifteen years old. It must cover all the essential facts about the land, describing it in terms sufficient to identify it clearly, stating who then had the legal interest in it, saying whether there were any equitable interests, and if so who had them, and generally leaving no doubts or ambiguities about the authenticity of the title at that time. Examples are an assent, a deed of conveyance or a deed of mortgage.

goods. Property; wares, commodities, merchandise, freight; all chattels personal other than things in action and money, and in Scotland all corporeal movables, except money. The term includes emblements, industrial growing crops, and things attached to or forming part of the land which are agreed to be severed before sale or under the contract of sale. *See also* FUTURE GOODS; WARRANT FOR GOODS.

goods and chattels. Goods, possessions and property; belongings.

goods shed. A shed for the storage of goods at a railway station or docks.

goodwill. The established popularity of a business, sold with the business itself; the expectation that the customer will return to the same place for further purchases.

Government National Mortgage Association (Ginnie Mae). A corporation owned and funded by the federal government to invest in relatively high-risk mortgages on property. Ginnie Mae is administered by the US Department of Housing and Urban Development.

Government National Mortgage Association mortgage-backed

securities. Issued primarily by mortgage bankers and guaranteed by GNMA, the holders of such securities are protected by the full faith and credit of the US Government. Mortgages insured by the Federal Housing Administration and the Veterans Administration provide the collateral for these securities.

government securities. Funded stocks and Treasury Bills.

government stock. *See* NATIONAL DEBT.

'Granny Bonds'. *See* NATIONAL SAVINGS CERTIFICATES.

Grant. To transfer the title to; to confer or bestow (privilege, charter, etc.); the act of granting, the thing granted, a gift, an assignment, a conveyance in writing, the thing conveyed.

grantee. The person to whom property, etc., is transferred.

grant-in-aid. A grant made by central government to a local authority to reduce pressure on the local rates; a sum granted towards the maintenance of a school or other institution.

grantor. The person who transfers property.

gratuity. A gift, present or tip given voluntarily in respect of some service; an amount payable under a pension scheme at the time of commencement of the pension payments.

green baize door. *See* CHINESE WALL.

green field project. A new venture into business which requires initial capital, but has no past history, no plant, buildings or land and possibly an untried managing director with nothing more than a good idea.

green paper. The report of a committee appointed by the Government, to be circulated for discussion and comment, possibly as a guide to later legislation. *See* EXPOSURE DRAFT; WHITE PAPER.

green pound. The accounting unit, in which farm import and export prices are calculated in the EEC for transactions between the UK and the EEC. It is a special rate of exchange which does not necessarily move in line with the normal exchange rate.

Gresham's Law. When coins have been debased, coins of the proper weight and value will circulate side by side with the 'light' coins. When this happens people will tend to hoard the good coins and pass on the bad ones. This tendency for debased coins to drive good coins out of circulation is called Gresham's Law, after Sir Thomas Gresham, Queen Elizabeth I's financial adviser, who was the first official to note the working of this tendency.

gross. Unrefined; total, not net; general, not specific; twelve dozen. *In Gross.* In bulk, wholesale.

gross cash flow. The sum of a company's net profit after tax and directors' remuneration, and provision for depreciation as shown in the accounts.

gross dividend. The net dividend amount paid to a shareholder plus the amount of the tax credit.

gross domestic product. The value in money at market prices of all goods and services produced within a country, but excluding net income from abroad, for a given period, usually one year.

gross earnings. *See* GROSS RECEIPTS.

grossed-up redemption yield. The net yield adjusted by adding back income tax and, where applicable, capital gains tax and any other tax to which the recipient is subject. *See also* GROSS YIELD.

gross income. A person's total income from all sources before deduction of tax.

grossing up. A term used in connection with income which is paid free of basic tax (e.g. building society interest received). The grossed-up amount is the measurement of such income for tax purposes, and is calculated by adding notional tax, of a percentage of the interest according to the taxing rates currently in force. The inflated interest is then known as the 'gross equivalent'. In the example given, that of building societies, investors receive their interest with income tax at the basic rate already paid. The societies therefore quote a net interest figure. Investors, however, must know the grossed-up equivalent figure – first, to enable them to make accurate comparisons with similar investments which quote gross rates, and second, so that higher-rate tax payers can work out the additional tax to be paid on the interest. Liability is calculated on the grossed-up figure by the tax authorities. Building society interest is the usual example quoted, but of course grossing-up applies to any interest received net of tax at standard rate – e.g. debenture interest and interest on government stocks.

gross interest. Interest received on an investment before payment of tax.

gross national product (GNP). The total output of an economy – the domestic product of the nation plus net income from abroad – for a given period, usually one year. No depreciation is deducted from the figure, the calculation for which is usually at market prices. If indirect taxes are deducted and any subsidies added the result is at factor cost. The majority of items are included at price (cost to buy), but a figure is estimated for the product of the self-employed, for which no statistics are available, and the public services are included at cost.

gross profit. Total profit before deduction of expenses and tax.

gross receipts. Total receipts before deduction for expenses.

gross rental. The rent of a property before outgoings such as rates, taxes and repairs are deducted.

gross value. The annual rental of a property to be expected on the basis that the landlord pays maintenance, repairs and insurance, and the tenant pays rates and taxes.

gross weight. The weight of the goods together with the package, case or container in which they are packed.

gross yield. A yield which takes no account of the taxes which will have to be paid on the yield by the recipient. *See also* REDEMPTION YIELD.

ground rent. A yearly rent payable to the freehold owner of land by a lessee in return for the lease of the land for a number of years. Such a lease is often so that the lessee may build upon the land, thereafter selling the houses off to individual buyers. As the value of each plot has been enhanced by the building of a house upon it, the builder is able to charge a higher ground rent. The difference between this and the ground rent which the builder is paying to the freeholder is termed the *Improved Ground Rent.*

ground rent receipt. Ground rents are reserved to the owner of a freehold estate and are payable by the person to whom the land has been leased. A ground rent is a yearly rent, payable usually by four quarterly instalments on the quarter days, and if the bank is lending against leasehold property security the borrowing customer must exhibit the receipts for the payment of ground rent to the banker as they are received. The reason for this is that if the rent is not paid the landlord may after notice re-enter upon the property and bring the lease to an end. This would mean that the bank's security would disappear.

group accounts. A system of linking companies engaged in similar business, or a holding company acting as parent to a number of subsidiary companies, is found where taxation advantages are to be expected, where the problems of control and management are more easily handled, or where it is desired to gain the advantages of large-scale production and distribution. The banker asked to lend, whether to a holding or subsidiary company, is confronted by specialised balance sheets. He or she may well find, on examining the balance sheet of a subsidiary company, that it includes in its assets money owing by another subsidiary, or money lent to the holding company; the balance sheet of the holding company will show shares in the various subsidiaries and perhaps loans to them. It is therefore primarily a question of disentangling various inter-linked items, which will cancel each other out, if properly married up, so as to arrive at the true position. The banker must settle down to a study of the group balance sheets and must be satisfied that he or she has identified and discounted the debts, investments and contra-entries within the group itself. What the banker is left with should be the true assets and liabilities of the group. *See also* CONSOLIDATED BALANCE SHEET.

groupage documents. Container documents covering more than one consignee's goods.

groupage shipment. Shipments from different exporters handled in one or more containers by one forwarding agent to save freight charges and handling costs. The goods have a common destination.

group of seven. The finance ministers of the largest industrial nations of the world, namely, USA, Canada, France, Great Britain, Italy, Japan and West Germany, meet annually to discuss economic and financial matters that affect them and other nations of the world, e.g. US$ budget deficit. Their objectives are to secure stability of their own currencies and give some lead and indication of their views of international financial and economic matters.

group insurance. Insurance or life assurance obtained by a person as a member of a group, such as a professional organisation, rather than as an individual, because in this way better terms can often be obtained. This is because there is an administrative saving for the company, and sometimes also because a particular group has a better life expectancy than people in general.

group of ten. As a step towards ensuring that the International Monetary Fund should have an adequate supply of the currencies most useful in its lending operations, arrangements were made in 1962 (known as general arrangements to borrow) for the Fund to get, direct from member countries, additional supplies of the main currencies. The countries participating were the United Kingdom, the United States, France, Italy, Japan, West Germany, Canada, Belgium, Sweden and the Netherlands. The countries became known as the 'Group of Ten'. The original agreement, valid for four years only, has been extended indefinitely. The group was responsible for the new currency parities agreed in 1971. In 1974 the Governors of the Group of Ten agreed that it was the duty of central banks to provide lender-of-last-resort facilities to their national banks to support their Eurocurrency operations. Accordingly there was established in the same year the Committee on Banking Regulations and Supervisory Practices, composed of representatives of the supervisory authorities and central banks of the Group of Ten Countries and Switzerland and Luxembourg. It is based on the Bank for International Settlements, which provides its secretariat. The twelve countries represented consist of those housing the principal international markets and providing the principal banks operating in them. The aims of the Committee are, to establish broad principles, with which all supervisory systems might conform in establishing their own detailed arrangements, to try to identify gaps in the supervisory coverage of international banking, and to provide an opportunity for those who attend its meetings to learn from each other.

group trading. A method adopted by wholesalers and independent retailers in an effort to compete on more equal terms with supermarkets, multiple shops and big stores. The retailers associated with a wholesaler agree to make bulk purchases of various commodities from time to time, at lower prices. The retailers can then reduce their prices slightly to the consumer. Farmers also form groups for buying their farming requirements in bulk, and therefore at cheaper rates, and selling the produce to the market in bulk. Certain credit facilities are available to members of a co-operative.

growth share. A company share which offers a long-term appreciation in value because of expansion of the company's production, goods market, and initiative, shrewdness and good management on the part of the executives of the company.

growth stock. A stock or share which can be expected to appreciate in capital value. A growth stock is associated with a rather higher purchase price on the Stock Exchange and with a rather low current rate of yield. It is a good proposition for long-term investment. *See also* GROWTH SHARE.

guarantee. An undertaking to be collaterally responsible for the debt, default or miscarriage of another. In a banking context it is an undertaking given by the guarantor to the banker accepting responsibility for the debt of the principal debtor, the customer, should he or she default. The guarantor may or may not be a customer. A guarantee must be in writing if it is to be enforceable at law. A bank guarantee should really be called an indemnity, for it invariably contains an indemnity clause which puts a direct responsibility on the guarantor in place of a

collateral one. A direct responsibility leaves the guarantor liable whatever may happen: collateral responsibility leaves him or her with the same degree of responsibility as has the principal debtor. If, therefore, the principal debtor is excused for any reason, then the guarantor must be excused also. *See also* COMPANY LIMITED BY GUARANTEE; CROSS GUARANTEES.

Guaranteed Minimum Pension (GMP). Under UK pensions legislation a State scheme provides a pension in two parts, the basic pension and an additional earnings-related pension. Employers with their own pension schemes can arrange with the Occupational Pensions Board to contract out of the additional State pension. Contracting-out is subject to a number of conditions, of which one is that the individual employee's pension must be at least as much as the pensioner would have got from the additional State pension, had the scheme not been contracted out. This guaranteed pension is called the guaranteed minimum pension.

guaranteed stock. Stock upon which the interest is guaranteed (sometimes the interest and the principal) by the company issuing the stock, by another company, or by a government.

guarantee fund. A fund built up with a society or other organisation to replace any defalcations of an employee.

guarantor. One who undertakes that the promises of another will be fulfilled, a surety, a warrantor. The guarantor has certain rights which must be carefully observed if the contract of guarantee is to remain binding. Before the guarantor signs the guarantee he or she should ask any relevant questions about the principal debtor's account and financial position which are thought necessary, and the bank manager must answer them truthfully. This will (since the coming into force of the Consumer Credit Act, 1974) include disclosing the amount of the principal debtor's overdrawn position. If the guarantor is also a customer of the same bank even greater care should be employed. In particular, emphasis must be placed on what will or might happen in the event that the guarantor is called upon. After the guarantee is signed the guarantor may at any time enquire how much he or she is contingently liable for and must be told if the amount is below the amount of the guarantee. Otherwise the guarantor should be told that the guarantee is fully relied upon. A guarantor who pays off the principal debtor's borrowing in full is entitled to claim from the banker any securities which have been deposited against the debt, not only by the principal debtor, but also by any other person or body. If the bank is obliged to sue the guarantor for payment of the debt guaranteed, the guarantor is entitled to the benefit of any counterclaim or set-off which the principal debtor may have against the bank. As against the principal debtor the guarantor usually acquires an immediate right of action as soon as any payment is made under the guarantee. Before any payment is made, however, the guarantor may call upon the principal debtor to pay the debt, thus relieving the debtor of obligation should this step be considered to be worth taking.

guardian. One who has the charge, care or custody of any person or thing; a protector – one who has the charge, custody and supervision of a person not legally capable of managing his own affairs.

guild. A society or corporation belonging to the same class, trade or pursuit, combined for mutual aid and protection of interests.

guinea. A gold coin formerly current in the UK, whose value was fixed at 21s (now 105p) in 1717; a sum of money equivalent to a guinea. It was applicable to professional fees and subscriptions.

gült. (*Sw.*) Registered or bearer securities giving title to a plot of land, a building site, or a residential property. The security gives recourse against the land only; the debtor therefore has no personal liability for the debt.

H

Hague rules. These rules were drawn up in 1924 relating to carriage of goods at sea. They cover all goods from time of loading to final discharge at the port of destination. It has also been agreed the bills of lading shall be conclusive evidence of ownership when transferred in good faith to a third party.

half a bar. A transaction for half a million pounds.

half commission man. A member of the Stock Exchange who is attached to a member firm of brokers and receives half the firm's commission on any deal which he or she has introduced, plus a retaining fee.

half sovereign. The sovereign is the standard unit of British coinage. It is a gold coin representing one pound. A half sovereign is a coin whose standard weight is 61.63723 grains troy and eleven-twelfths fine gold. They are rarely minted and are collected as a hedge against inflation or by numismaticians.

hallmark. The mark used to indicate the standard of tested gold and silver; to stamp with this mark.

hammered. The fate of a member of the Stock Exchange who is unable to meet debts. Prior to Big Bang, three blows with a mallet were struck on the rostrum of the 'House' by a waiter to attract the attention of the members, after which the name of the defaulter was announced, and the defaulter was expelled from the House. Any loss to that member's clients was then met from the compensation fund, which was guaranteed by all members.

harbour dues. Charges for mooring or accommodating a vessel in a harbour.

hard arbitrage. Borrowing from a bank under an existing overdraft limit and re-lending the money at a profit on the inter-bank market or on some other secondary market. This device is only possible for the company which can borrow at the finest rates – base rate plus 1 or 1½ per cent. The minimum sum invested is usually £1m. The company needs to have undoubted credit standing, and direct lines to banks and brokers. Hard arbitrage (also known as 'round tripping') creates no real wealth nor any jobs. It is inflationary in its effects and bad for the control of the money supply. One way to overcome it would be to relate the overdraft rates of these companies, not to base rate, but to London Inter-Bank Offered Rate (*q.v.*). The difficulty is that all banks would have to decide this together, otherwise the offending companies would merely move their accounts to those banks still offering base-related money. Other markets also offer opportunities for the big company treasurer when the time is right, such as the inter-company loans market (*q.v.*) or the sterling certificates of deposit market (*see under* STERLING CERTIFICATE OF DEPOSIT) or the local authority loans market. Or it is possible, when the interest rate is relatively low, for the company to draw a bill on itself for one, two or three months, pay a bank its fee for an acceptance commission, discount it and still be able to invest the proceeds on the inter-bank market at a profit – another practice frowned upon by the Bank of England.

hard currency. The currency of any foreign country for which there is a greater demand that there is for the currency of one's own country.

hard sell. A determined, vigorous and often an aggressive method of selling goods or a service.

hardware. When used in reference to computers, this is the collective term for all pieces of equipment which together make up a computer installation. Subdivision is into 'Central Processing Units' (CPUs) (q.v.) and 'Peripherals' (q.v.).

haulage. The act of pulling; the charge for hauling a boat; the carrying of goods, material, etc., by road; the charge for this.

head lease. The original document executed by a freeholder in favour of the leaseholder on the occasion of the first granting of the lease.

head mortgage. Where a mortgagee of property offers the mortgage to a lender as security for a loan, a sub-mortgage is created. The original mortgage is then known as the head mortgage and the newly-created mortgage is a sub-mortgage.

health certificate. See ZOOLOGICAL CERTIFICATE.

hedge against inflation. An investment in land or shares which is expected to appreciate in value at a time of inflation, thus protecting the investor against loss due to the fall in money values.

hedging. The use of market machinery by a trader to gain protection against loss through fluctuation in the price of the commodity in which he or she is dealing; laying off a risk.

heir. One who by law succeeds or is entitled to succeed another in the possession of property or rank; one who succeeds to any gift, quality, etc. Originally the person entitled by law to the real property of a person deceased intestate. The heir was then the eldest son and his descendants, followed by any other sons in order, and their descendants. If there were no sons, but daughters only, they succeeded as co-parceners, i.e. equally. The doctrine of heirship was abolished in 1925.

heir apparent. The manifest heir, the one who will succeed on the death of the present possessor, in contra-distinction to the heir presumptive.

heirloom. A piece of property or chattel that has been in the family a very long

time. In some countries it is the custom that chattels follow the heirs and not the executors.

heir presumptive. An heir whose actual succession may be prevented by the birth of one nearer akin to the present holder of the title, estate, etc.

hereditament. A right capable of passing by way of descent to heirs; any real property which might upon intestacy before 1926 have passed to an heir. See also CORPOREL HEREDITAMENTS; INCORPOREAL HEREDITAMENTS.

heritable. Capable of being inherited, passing by inheritance, especially of lands and appurtenances, attached to the property or house as distinct from movable property.

heritable bond. In Scotland, a bond given by a debtor as security for the repayment of a loan, the security consisting of a conveyance of land in favour of the creditor, which can be implemented upon failure in repayment of capital or interest.

hidden reserve. A secret reserve not apparent from a scrutiny of the balance sheet, e.g. premises shown at less than their real value.

high coupon. Yielding a high rate of interest.

high-geared. See GEARING.

high street bank. The description of a bank that usually has branches in a large number of towns and cities.

hire. The price paid for labour or services or the use of things, the engagement of a person or thing for such a price; to procure at a certain price for temporary use; to employ a person for a stipulated payment; to grant the use or service of for a stipulated price.

hire purchase. A system by which a hired article becomes the property of the hirer after a stipulated number of payments.

hire-purchase agreement. An agreement, other than a conditional sale agreement, under which 1. goods are bailed (or in Scotland hired) in return for periodical payments by the person to whom they are bailed or hired, and 2. the property in the goods will pass to that person if the terms of the agreement are complied with and one or more of the following occurs; (a) the exercise of an option to purchase by that person (b) the doing of any other specified act by any party to the agreement, or (c) the happening of any other specified event. A 'fixed rate contract' signifies that the rate of interest to be paid by the hirer is fixed at the beginning of the agreement for the whole period. A 'variable rate contract' refers to agreements where the interest rate is based on the Finance House Base Rate (q.v.) and may vary in accordance with day-to-day fluctuations in that rate.

hire purchase companies. Finance houses engaged in the business of hire purchase, credit sale and leasing. They obtain their funds by way of discount, by advertising to the public, and by borrowing from banks and accepting houses. Periodical governmental directives control the amount of the deposit and the length of the repayment time, making hire purchase easier or more difficult according to the economic climate. About thirty of the larger and better known finance houses are members of the Finance Houses Association. Together they represent about 85 per cent of all hire purchase business. The Finance House Base Rate (q.v.) is an independently assessed rate which averages out the daily fluctuations of money market rates, and represents a guide to the rate of interest to be charged on hire purchase contracts.

hirer. The individual to whom goods are bailed (or in Scotland hired) under a consumer hire agreement, or the person to whom his or her rights and duties under the agreement have passed by assignment or operation of law. In relation to a prospective consumer hire agreement this includes the prospective hirer.

historical cost. The monetary amount at which the asset was originally purchased. Most assets are valued by this method, but during periods of high inflation, this cost can have very little meaning.

hive down. A description of an operation whereby a receiver buys an 'off-the-shelf' company, and sells the assets in his or her receivership company to the new company in exchange for shares: in this way the receiver 'drops' the liabilities. The receiver is a director of the new company and can continue trading. If and when a buyer appears the receiver sells the shares in the new company for a consideration, the cash for which falls in to the receivership. In some cases there are other tax and practical advantages in this device.

hive-off. Originally part of a swarm of bees separating fom the rest, now used in a business sense to denote the separation of functions within a firm or company, or the splitting off, especially on acquisition by a new owner, of complete subsidiary companies from a group operation, very often as part of a process of rationalisation.

holder. The payee or indorsee of a bill or note who is in possession of it, or the bearer thereof.

holder for value. A holder of a bill of exchange who has given value for it, or who is in possession of a bill for which value has at any time been given, is deemed to be a holder for value as regards the acceptor and all parties to the bill who became parties prior to such time. If the holder of the bill has a lien on it, whether the lien arises from a contract or by implication of law, he or she is deemed to be a holder for value to the extent of the sum for which the holder has a lien.

holder in due course. A holder of a bill

of exchange who has taken it, complete and regular on the fact of it, under the following conditions, namely 1. that he or she became the holder of it before it was overdue, and without notice that it had previously been dishonoured, if such was the fact; 2. that the bill was taken in good faith and for value, and that at the time the bill was negotiated the holder had no notice of any defect in the title of the person who negotiated it.

holding. That which is held, especially, land, property, stocks or shares.

holding company. A company which is a member of another company and either controls the composition of the board of directors of that other company, or holds more than half in nominal value of its equity share capital.

holding deed. The deed which transferred the ownership of land to the person now holding it.

holding out. Maintaining or representing oneself to be in a position in which one is not; by words or conduct encouraging an impression that a special relationship exists, i.e. that of an agent or a partner. Persons who are not partners may be treated as though they were when it is a question of being responsible for the debts of a firm, if they have held themselves out to be partners, so influencing another party to enter into a contract with the firm. In such cases the doctrine of estoppel may be applied.

holding over. Postponing until the next occasion, deferrring consideration until a subsequent hearing, as at a board meeting or in a court of law; in relation to land, remaining in possession of land without the consent of the landlord after a term has come to an end; on the Stock Exchange, deferring payment until the next settlement day.

holograph. Wholly in the handwriting of the author or signatory; a document, letter, etc., so written.

home banking. *See* TELETEXT.

home safe. Now a lapsed service. It was a function of banks to offer a savings box to young savers, who would from time to time take the box and its contents to the bank, who could credit the money to a home safe account. This type of account attracted a lower rate of interest than a deposit account. This type of account attracted a lower rate of interest than a deposit account. Withdrawals may be made on production of the passbook at any branch of the bank. Young persons who now wish to put their savings into a bank will open a deposit account, although a savings container – not necessarily a box – can still be obtained if required.

home state. Home state legislation applies to all foreign banks operating in the US and was introduced as part of the International Banking Act of 1978. Under these regulations, foreign banks with either a full service branch or subsidiary bank in the US were required to select a home state by 31 March 1981 or have a home state designated for them by the Federal Reserve Board. Once selected, the foreign bank is then precluded from expanding its deposit-taking operations outside of its designated home state. Since its inception the most popular choices for home state have proved to be New York and California.

homologate. In Scots law, to ratify a deed in itself informal or defective, by some subsequent act which expresses or implies assent to it. To adopt a deed by one who by personal conduct consents to be bound by it, although knowing it be defective.

honorarium. A fee or payment voluntarily made to a professional for his or her services.

honour. To pay on presentation, to meet a claim when due.

horizontal combination. An amalgamation or merger of two or more companies at a particular point or stage of manufacture in their common industry.

hotchpot. Bringing into account sums already received by a beneficiary under a will during the lifetime of the testator, so that his or her share of the total sum available shall not exceed that of other beneficiaries of equal title under the same will. Especially used in relation to a class of beneficiaries such as children of the testator. Also applicable to intestacy. In the case of wills, usually only applies if the gift is after the date of the will.

hot money. Speculative money which crosses frontiers rapidly to take advantage of changes in interest rates. As repatriation of such funds is not normally covered forward, any sign of falling rates of interest or exchange will cause it to flow out just as rapidly as it came in.

hot treasury bills. Treasury Bills allocated on the last day of the tender.

house. A noble family; a school boarding house; the audience at a place of entertainment; a general term in commerce to refer to a large or old-established firm or company, e.g. a discount house; the House of Commons or House of Lords; the Stock Exchange; the Bankers' Clearing House.

house bill. A bill drawn by a company or firm upon itself. *See also* PIG ON PORK.

house bill of lading. A bill of lading issued by forwarding agents.

householder's protest. A document in the form of a certificate given by any householder or man of some substance, attesting the dishonour of a bill of exchange. Such a certificate requires the signature of two witnesses and can only be issued in the case where a notary cannot be contacted at the place of dishonour. In such circumstances the householder's protest is equivalent in its effect to a formal protest.

housing association. An authority established by the Housing Act, 1964 and 1974, which is concerned in the assistance and promotion of registered housing associations and unregistered building societies.

housing trust. A corporation or body of persons whose object is to obtain funds for the provision of houses for those persons who are in need of accommodation.

human resources accounting. The measurement in monetary terms of the value of the persons employed by the business. Whereas historical cost accounting will only consider human beings from the point of view as costs for wages, salaries, insurance, training, it is often considered necessary to value the employees from the point of view of their contribution to present and future profits.

human relations. A general term covering the relationship between workers, who should be regarded as individuals rather than units of production, and management, together with such factors as affect the environment in which workers work, the facilities afforded to them (e.g. free medical attention during working hours), and conditions of remuneration and pension rights. The emergence of staff and personnel departments has paid witness to the increasing recognition of the importance of this subject, which should be based on the recognition of human dignity rather than on the mere expectancy of increased output. The relationship should work both ways; workers and staff who are well treated should feel that they wish to do a good day's work, and ought to feel a part of the organisation which employs them.

hypothec. A security in favour of a creditor over the property of his or her debtor, while the property continues in the debtor's possession.

hypothecation. A type of security where neither ownership nor possession passes to the lender. In maritime law, the term refers to the charging of a ship's cargo, or the ship herself, in certain circumstances; in banking, it means an agreement to give a charge over goods, or over the documents of title to goods, in circumstances which make it impossible to give the banker possession. If this were possible the banker would take a pledge. In recognition of this fact the agreement usually undertakes to give a pledge when the goods or documents become available.

I

idle money. Funds which are available, but uninvested.

illiquid assets. Those assets which are not easily convertible to cash. This could include premises, plant, machinery. There are grades of illiquidity depending on a variety of factors.

immediate annuity. One which takes effect at once.

immediately available funds. *See* VALUE DATE.

immediate parties. Those parties to a bill of exchange who are in a close relationship to each other, such as drawer/acceptor, drawer/payee, indorser/second indorser.

impersonal accounts. Accounts in book-keeping which deal with things rather than persons, e.g. interest, stamps in hand, premises.

impersonal payee. Drafts payable to 'Cash or order', 'Wages or order', etc. Such drafts are not cheques, not being payable to a specified person. They are usually paid to the drawer or his or her known agent only, against an indorsement.

implement. To instal; to put into use; a proposed service, system or procedure that is installed and actually working in a bank.

implied trust. A trust arising either from the presumed intention of the donor, or by the operation of the rules of law or equity.

import. To bring in goods or produce from abroad; the act of importing.

import agent. An agent who arranges a contract between his or her principal, an importer of goods or services, and a foreign seller.

import deposit. A restriction on imports by obliging importers to make a cash deposit to a central authority before permission to import can be given.

import duties. Taxes imposed on goods entering a country.

importer. One who has goods originating in another country consigned to him or her.

import licence. Where it is a feature of exchange control that certain types of goods imported have to be approved by the monetary authorities, a system of licensing may be instituted to restrict imports to those who have applied for permission to import certain goods and have received approval.

import quota. A means of restricting imports by the issue of licences to supplying countries, assigning to each a quota, after determination of the amount of any commodity which is to be imported during a period. The device works against free trade and the maximisation of international trade generally, but may be forced upon the government of a country by internal pressures from traders and workers suffering from competition which they cannot match.

import restrictions. A country with an adverse trade balance may desire to control the volume of goods coming into the country from other countries, and for that purpose may impose tariffs or import quotas, restrict the amount of foreign currency available to imports, institute import deposits, impose import surcharges or prohibit various categories of imports.

import specie point. *See* SPECIE POINTS.

import surcharge. A tax on imports, either general or particular, with a view to improving a balance of payments deficit.

impost. That which is imposed or levied as a tax, a tribute, a duty (especially on imported goods).

impressed stamps. Stamp duty on certain documents (such as a policy of life assurance) must be paid by impressing the right amount of duty on the document. This is done by a stamping office after the duty has been paid.

imprest. In book-keeping, the fixed sum of money available for petty expenses; a loan, an advance, especially for carrying on any of the public services.

imprest bill, bill of imprest. An order entitling the bearer to have money paid in advance.

imprinting. The procedure involved in for example the personalisation of cheques, credit slips and other documents. Frequently called encoding. This involves printing the customer's name, account number, cheque number, sorting code number, etc.

improved ground rent. See GROUND RENT.

improving lease. In Scots law, a lease granted for a longer period in order to encourage the tenant to make improvements to the property.

inability to pay debts. For the purposes of the Insolvency Act, 1986 s.123, a company is deemed unable to pay its debts (a) if the creditor is indebted for an amount exceeding £750, served a written notice on that company and that company has for three weeks neglected to pay the sum or settle the matter to the reasonable satisfaction of the creditor; (b) a judgment order in favour of a creditor of the company which is unsatisfied in whole or in part; (c) if in Scotland, the *induciae* of a charge for payment on an extract decree, or an extract registered bond have expired without payment being made; (d) if in Northern Ireland, a certificate of unenforceability has been granted in respect of a judgment against the company; (e) if it is proved to the satisfaction of the court that the company is unable to pay its debts as they fall due. Under s.268, 1. if a debtor appears to be unable to pay a debt immediately or (a) the creditor has served a demand on the debtor in the prescribed form requiring payment or satisfaction of the debt and three weeks have elapsed and the demand has neither been complied with or set aside in accordance with the rules; or (b) a judgment order in favour of one or more creditors has been served and the debt has been returned unsatisfied in whole or part: 2. the debtor appears to have no reasonable prospect of being able to pay the debt immediately or at least three weeks have elapsed since the demand was served and that demand has been neither complied with or set aside in accordance with the rules.

inactive account. See DORMANT ACCOUNT.

inactive stock. A security which has few transactions.

in arrears. Unpaid, unsatisfied, behind with instalments of repayment.

in bond. Goods on which customs duty has not yet been paid, pending which event they are kept in a Customs bonded warehouse.

in camera. In secret.

incapacity. The lack of legal power, ability or competence to enter into a legal contract. e.g. an infant, a bankrupt.

in case of need. See CASE IN NEED.

incentive shares. Shares issued by a company to its staff at preferential rates, sometimes convertible to ordinary shares at a later date, to encourage them to work hard and stay with the company.

inchoate instrument. An instrument incomplete in some respect, e.g. a cheque issued with no payee stated.

in clearing. See CLEARING HOUSE.

income. The amount of money (usually annual) accruing as payment, profit, interest, etc., from labour, business, professions or property. See also REAL

INCOME.

income and expenditure. The final account of a non profit-making organisation, e.g. a tennis club or amateur dramatics society, showing the surplus or deficit for a stated financial period.

income bond. A bond for a fixed period obtained in return for a single lump sum payment, where an element of life assurance cover is obtained together with the right to make regular withdrawals. Most income bonds are a combination of two types of life policy, and so high returns are dependent upon the extent to which tax relief is granted on the premiums of the related policies. Also issued by the Department of National Savings for deposits of not less than £2,000 on which income is payable monthly. The rate of interest will vary from time to time. This income is subject to income tax.

income debenture. A debenture which states that interest will be payable only out of the company profits.

income gearing. *See* GEARING.

income tax. A tax payable, subject however to various reliefs, by an individual who is resident in a country, on all sources of income, whether arising in that country or in another.

income yield. The interest paid to a holder of any stock over a period; of dated stocks, the proceeds received by way of interest as opposed to the capital redemption yield.

incoming partner. A new partner joining the firm. This new partner has no liability for any of the partnership debts contracted before the date of joining. If the firm's banking account is overdrawn it should be ruled off and a fresh one started, unless the incoming partner is prepared to sign a statement accepting liability for the overdraft. If there is any security, the incoming partner should add his or her signature to any completed forms of charge held by the bank.

inconvertible. Incapable of being exchanged for something else.

inconvertible paper currency. Paper money which cannot be exchanged for metal at the central bank on demand.

inconvertible stocks or securities. 1. Securities which cannot readily be turned into cash; 2. Securities having no right of transfer from one form of holding to another.

incorporated company. A company which has been registered in accordance with the requirements of the Companies Acts, and has received a certificate of incorporation.

incorporeal. Immaterial, intangible.

incorporeal hereditaments. Non-tangible interests attached to land, such as rent-charges or rights of way.

incoterms. The interpretation of the various shipping terms published by the International Chamber of Commerce and adopted by all trading nations. It not only defines the shipping terms, but sets out, in each case, the responsibilities of the buyer and those of the seller.

incumbrance. A burden, a hindrance to freedom of action or motion, a liability upon an estate, such as a mortgage.

in curia. In open court.

in demand. Much sought after.

indemnifier. One who guarantees to a lender that if any loss occurs, no matter how created, he or she will make it good. Thus the liability of an indemnifier is absolute, and does not depend on the position of a principal debtor.

indemnity. An agreement to render a person immune from a contingent liability; compensation for property annexed by the State or local authority in the public interest; an undertaking issued by a banker at the request of a customer in respect of missing bills of lading, lost share certificates, etc. *See also* COUNTER-INDEMNITY; GUARANTEE; STANDBY LETTER OF CREDIT;

SURETY BOND.

indent. To set in farther from the margin than the rest of the paragraph; to make an indent or order upon, as where a branch bank indents upon its stationery office for a supply of stationery; an order, placed through an agent, from an overseas buyer.

indenture. An agreement or contract under seal, especially one binding an apprentice to a master, so called because the two documents had thin edges cut or indented exactly alike so as to correspond with each other; a written agreement between two or more persons, each party originally receiving a copy of the deed, all copies being notched or indented so as to establish the authenticity of any copy of the document. Since 1925 a deed has the effect of an indenture although not requiring to be indented.

index. An alphabetical list; a directing sign; that which points out.

indexation. This is the adjustment of long-term contracts, such as insurance contracts, to take account of inflation; this means that debts would be expressed in real terms, wage settlements would incorporate cost-of-living clauses, and income tax thresholds would be automatically adjusted as prices rise. Indexation removes some of the distortions and injustices caused by continuing inflation. The arguments against include the view that the implied recognition that a permanent state of inflation exists tends to diminish the struggle to contain it, and that the link perpetuates a classic inflationary spiral. If one accepts the cost-push theory of inflation, then to build automatic adjustments into the system would tend to encourage the further progress of inflation.

index-linking. Index-linking of wages was introduced in Belgium for miners in 1920, and has been generally applied to both public and private sectors since shortly after the Second

World War. The sysem was introduced in France in 1937 and in Italy and Denmark in 1945. In Britian some SAYE contracts and savings certificates (the latter originally for pensioners only) were linked to the index in 1975. Index-linked house insurance and the first index-linked permanent life assurance contract appeared in the same year. The arguments in favour of linking wages with an index are that indexation contributes to monetary and labour stability, and obliges public authorities and companies to watch price rises very closely. The savings certificates referred to above were made available to all in 1981 irrespective of age or sex. For index-linking of government stock *see* GILTS (GILT-EDGED).

index number. A percentage figure, used in statistics, to show fluctuations over a period as compared with a fixed standard.

index of retail prices. *See* GENERAL INDEX OF RETAIL PRICES.

Indice. Index number, a number used for statistical comparisons of all kinds. A representative period is chosen as a base, then all other figures are related to and compared with it. *See also* GENERAL INDEX OF RETAIL PRICES.

indice **Dow Jones.** New York Stock Exchange index figure based on the mean prices of a selection of stocks and shares. It is calculated separately on industrial shares, railway shares and public utility shares. It serves in particular to indicate the tendencies of the market according to the theories of Dow. (Dow, Jones & Co. were owners of the *Wall Street Journal.*)

indirect. Oblique, circuitous, not resulting directly or immediately from a cause.

indirect arbitrage. *See* COMPOUND ARBITRAGE.

indirect evidence. Evidence deduced from collateral circumstances.

indirect exchange. Exchange operations between two countries carried out through the medium of a third.

indirect tax. A tax on a commodity which is collected from the manufacturer or supplier, but is ultimately paid by the consumer. e.g. value added tax.

indorse. Two write one's name, or a note of some kind, on the back of a document; to assign by indorsement; to ratify, confirm or approve. In the case of a bill of lading or a bill of exchange, to sign one's name on the back. *To Indorse Over*. To transfer one's rights (in a bill, etc.) to another person.

indorsee. The person to whom a bill of exchange, a bill of lading, a delivery order, or any such document of title is transferred by indorsement, thus enabling this person to deal with the instrument in his or her own right.

indorsement. A writing on the back of a document. In the case of a bill of exchange, the writing on the back by which the value of the instrument is transferred from one person to another. Indorsements may be blank, restrictive or special. The writing must be completed by the signature of the indorser. The simple signature of the indorser is sufficient to transfer the value (bearer instruments need no indorsement). Indorsement means indorsement completed by delivery. *See also* CONDITIONAL INDORSEMENT; QUALIFIED INDORSEMENT; RESTRICTIVE INDORSEMENT; SPECIAL INDORSEMENT.

indorsement in blank, blank indorsement. An indorsement which consists of the name only of the payee or indorsee of a bill of exchange, written on the back of the bill. Such an indorsement specifies no indorsee, and the bill becomes payable to bearer.

indorser. The person who signs on the back of a document of title in order to negotiate it to another person. In the case of a bill of exchange the payee wishing to negotiate the bill becomes the (first) indorser when he so signs, and when and if the bill is later negotiated to other persons each person may indorse it in turn and so become an indorser (second indorser, third indorser, etc.). Each indorser of a bill of exchange is liable upon it. By indorsing it the indorser 1. engages that on due presentment it shall be accepted and paid according to its tenor, and that if it be dishonoured he or she will compensate the holder, or a subsequent indorser who is compelled to pay it, provided that the requisite proceedings on dishonour are duly taken; 2. cannot deny to a holder in due course the genuineness and regularity in all respects of the drawer's signature and all previous indorsements; 3. cannot deny to an immediate or a subsequent indorse that the bill was, at the time of indorsement, a valid and subsisting bill, and that the indorser had a good title thereto.

induction course. Most banks are particularly anxious that new members of their staff understand the basic procedures and therefore arrange in house courses so that they may be introduced to the concepts of banking, on the job activities, conditions of service, etc. The general attitude is to assist the new employee to settle down as quickly as possible and become a member of the team.

Industrial and Commercial Finance Corporation (ICFC). From May 1985 this company is known as Investors in Industry or 3 i's. *See* INVESTORS IN INDUSTRY.

industrial and provident societies. A variety of institutions registered under the Industrial and Provident Societies Acts and other legislation which confer upon them a number of privileges, such as limited liability, and subject them to various obligations and limitations. They include wholesale and retail co-operative societies, building societies and trade unions. *See also* FRIENDLY SOCIETY.

industrial life policy. A policy of a life assurance where small premiums are collected weekly by door-to-door salesmen. The amount involved is small, and there is usually a prohibition against assignment, which will almost always, however, be removed on request by the banker.

ineligible bill. A bill payable in London and accepted by an agency bank or other bank, but which does not qualify for re-discount at the Bank of England. Ineligible bills may also be trade bills bearing a bank indorsement.

inertia selling. The delivery of goods which have not been ordered on the terms that they may be considered on approval for a specified term, on the expiry of which it is assumed that the receiver has decided to purchase them. An example of this was seen on the introduction of one of the major credit card companies in the UK.

infant. *See* MINOR.

infeft. To invest with heritable property, to place a person in possession of a fee simple.

inflation. A steady and progressive fall in the value of money, shown by price rises. The causes and effects of inflation are subjects of argument as much among economists as laymen. Suggested theories are those of demand-pull, where demand exceeds supply, thus causing buyers to bid up prices; cost-push, where rises in manufacturing costs, particularly wage costs, lead to price rises; and the excessive issue of paper money. It is clear that there is no one single cause of inflation. Also to be considered are external factors such as the world prices of raw materials affecting the balance of payments and the stability of the country's unit of currency. The sufferers in times of inflation are those on fixed incomes and those with little negotiating power.

inflation accounting. During the late 1960s and early 1970s it was clear that the historical accounting methods did nothing to take into consideration the inflation of those times. As a consequence, a Statement of Standard Accounting Practice (SSAP16) was introduced to reflect the changes in the purchasing power of money. It is now standard practice for companies to set out their final accounts to reflect the concept of current cost accounting.

information technology. Often referred as IT. Banks are regularly spending vast sums of money in the continuing pursuance of improved technology. The term applies to the gathering, transmitting, recording and updating of information. *See* DATA PROTECTION ACT.

ingot. A mass of cast metal, especially copper, steel, gold or silver; a bar of gold or silver for assaying.

in gross. In bulk, wholesale.

inherent vice. A particular quality of some product or element which renders it especially liable to cause damage or loss to itself or other goods, particularly during transport. In general, therefore, insurance companies exclude loss so caused from cover.

inherit. To receive by descent, or by will or intestacy, to fall heir to.

inheritance. That which is inherited – property, mental or moral quality, tradition, etc.

inheritance tax. An inheritance tax is payable when the value of the estate of the deceased exceeds an amount specified in the Annual Finance Act which changes from time to time.

inhibition. A writ to prevent a person from burdening heritable property to the prejudice of a creditor; in the law of registered land, a notification to the Land Registrar to protect a minor interest, such as a receiving order where land is affected.

in-house. Within an organisation. Thus if it is said that the credit provided is wholly in-house, it means that the bank has itself found all the funds necessary, without calling upon any other bank or banks to assist.

injunction. An order or command, an exhortation, a precept; an equitable remedy which takes the form of an order of the court commanding something to be done (a *'mandatory' injunction*) or forbidding something (a *'prohibitory' injunction*). An *interlocutory injunction* is one granted provisionally before the hearing of an action to prevent the defendant doing something before the case is tried. A *perpetual injunction* is one granted after the issue between the parties has been tried. All injunctions are at the discretion of the court.

inland. Carried on within a country, interior, domestic.

inland bill. A bill both drawn and payable in the United Kingdom.

inland revenue. National income derived from taxation, stamp duties, licences of various kinds, and duties levied on home trade, excluding *excise*. The collection of these taxes is supervised by the Commissioners of Inland Revenue, Somerset House, Strand, London WC2.

in locol parentis. In the position of a parent.

innocent misrepresentation. One made without intent to deceive. In the case of a contract so secured the injured party has a right to damages and/or rescission, the other party having the defence of proving, if possible, that he or she believed the representation was true.

in perpetuity, *in perpetuum.* For ever.

in personam. An action *'in personam'* is one against an individual, a person, who may have to pay damages or make restitution in some way.

input. Coded documents, tapes, punched cards, MICR numbers on cheques and credits, etc., are types of inputs. It is basically any medium which will accept data and transfer this to the computer for storage and retrieval.

in re. In the matter of.

in rem. An action *'in rem'* is one against property, usually land.

inscribe. To write, carve or engrave (in or upon a paper, stone, or other surface), to mark, to address, to enter in a book, list, etc., especially to register the name of a stockholder in the stock register of a company or corporation; to issue (loans) with the names of holders so registered.

inscribed stock. Stock where the name of a stockholder was inscribed in the books of the registering authority and a stock receipt issued. A stock receipt is no evidence of title, because it was never necessary to produce it on sale of the stock. It was a simple receipt, never withdrawn once issued. The system was discontinued for all British government securities in 1943, and all inscribed stock is now converted into registered stock.

insider. A person who holds information which it would be reasonable to expect a person in that position not to disclose except for the proper performance of his or her functions in relation to the company; an individual in possession of knowledge, by virtue of being connected with the company, which the insider knows is price-sensitive information in relation to the securities in question. Where such a person deals on privileged information for personal financial gain, the dealer is contravening the provisions of s. 68 or 69 of the Companies Act, 1985 and shall be liable on conviction on indictment to imprisonment for a term of up to two years, or a fine, or both; or on summary conviction to imprisonment for a term not exceeding six months, or a fine, or both.

in situ. In its original position.

insolvency. The state of being unable to pay one's debts as they arise. In Scotland the state of insolvency is divided into practical insolvency, which denotes a situation in which the debtor is unable to meet immediate obligations, although if the debtors total estate were realised it might be sufficient to meet all debts in full; and absolute insolvency, which means that the debtor cannot immediately, and could not in any event, pay all creditors in full.

insolvency practitioners. In relation to the winding up of a company, a person can either be a liquidator, provisional liquidator, administrator, an administrative receiver or a supervisor under a voluntary arrangement. So far as an individual is concerned, an insolvency practitioner can act either as 1. a trustee in bankruptcy or interim receiver; 2. as a trustee under a deed which is a deed of arrangement made for the benefit of creditors; 3. as supervisor of a voluntary arrangement; 4. in the case of a deceased individual, an administrator to the estate. A person who is not an individual cannot act as an insolvency practitioner. A person cannot act as an insolvency practitioner if (a) the person has been adjudged bankrupt and is not discharged (b) he or she is subject to an order under the Company Directors Disqualification Act (c) the person is a patient within the meaning of the Mental Health Act, 1983. A person must be a member of a professional body as recognised by the Secretary of State, which by its rules allows a person to act if (a) they are fit and proper persons to act (b) meet acceptable requirements as to education and practical training and experience.

inspect. To view narrowly and critically, to examine officially.

inspection. Careful survey, official examination; the examination of a branch bank by a party of inspectors appointed by the bank for that purpose, to confirm that the proper amount of cash is held and that the business of the branch is generally run in accordance with the bank's regulations. *See also* COMMITTEE OF INSPECTION.

inspection certificate. A certificate issued by a third party certifying that the goods are of a particular standard and/or agree that the goods conform to the contract details.

inspection of company's register. A company's register of members must be open to inspection by members free, and by other people on payment of a small charge, during business hours.

inspectorate. A body of inspectors generally; the inspection department of a large bank.

instalment. A part of a debt or sum due paid at successive periods; a part of anything supplied at different times.

instalment allotment. An allotment of stock, etc., where the purchase price is to be paid in a number of intalments.

instalment credit. Hire purchase finance.

instant access accounts. These are building society accounts where immediate withdrawal is permitted either on demand, by the issue of a cheque or by the use of an Automated Teller Machine, without the penalty or loss of any interest.

institute. To establish, to found, to appoint, to originate; a society or organisation established for the purpose of promoting some public object; the building in which such a society meets; the person who first takes estate or interest by deed of settlement of land on several people in succession.

Institute of Bankers. *See* CHARTERED INSTITUTE OF BANKERS.

Institute of Bankers in Ireland, The, Nassau House, Nassau Street, Dublin 2, Eire. The Institute is an association of those connected with the various branches of banking. Its objects are 1. to enable the members to acquire a knowledge of the theory and practice of banking and to promote the consideration and discussion of matters of interest to the profession; 2. to provide for the reading and discussion of approved papers, and for the delivery of lectures on banking and other professional subjects; 3. to maintain a library, consisting of works on banking, commerce, finance, political economy, etc.; 4. to afford facilities for the cultivation of social relations amongst its members.

Institute of Bankers in Scotland, The, 20 Rutland Square, Edinburgh EH1 2DE. The Institute was founded in 1875 'to improve the qualifications of those engaged in banking and to raise their status and influence'. This is done mainly through an educational scheme for young bankers and the conduct of examinations to assess candidates' performance. In addition short courses are run on specific topics, lectures and meetings are arranged through local centres and wider information is disseminated through *The Scottish Bankers Magazine,* published quarterly. Qualifications: FIB (Scot.), AIB (Scot.), Dip.IB (Scot.).

institutes. A book of precepts, principles or rules, a textbook on legal principles, e.g. *Justinian's Institutes.*

Institution. The act of instituting or establishing; an established law, custom or public occasion; the formal designation by one person of another to be his or her heir; an organised pattern of group behaviour established and generally accepted as a fundamental part of a culture.

institutional. Instituted by authority; educational; in advertising, having as an objective long-term goodwill and reputation, rather than quick sales.

institutional investors. Banks, pension funds, investment trusts, unit trusts and insurance companies.

instrument. A formal or written document such as a promissory note, bill, cheque, contract, grant, deed, etc.; a term sometimes used to describe a written order which is drawn on a banker, but does not satisfy the definition of a bill of exchange. Its meaning is not confined to this, however (e.g., a negotiable instrument includes a bill of exchange).

insufficent funds. A term sometimes used instead of 'refer to drawer', when a bank refuses to pay a cheque when the balance of the account is inadequate.

insurable interest. As a matter of public policy, the assured or insured person must have a pecuniary interest in the person or thing to be covered, to distinguish the transaction from one of a gambling nature. Insurable interests exist in these cases: 1. a man or woman may assure his or her own life; 2. a man may assure the life of his wife, or *vice versa;* 3. a creditor may assure the life of a debtor; 4. a litigant may assure the life of his or her judge; 5. a company may assure the life of its director; 6. an employer may assure the life of an employee, or *vice versa;* 7. a trustee may insure the life of a beneficiary; or 8. a donee may insure the life of his donor. An assignee need not have an insurable interest. The insurable interest need only exist at the time the policy is taken out.

insurance. A contract between two parties whereby the insurer agrees to indemnify the insured upon the happening of a stipulated contingency, in consideration of the payment of an agreed sum, whether periodical or fixed (the premium). Insurance falls into the main groups of life; property; marine, aviation and transport; motor vehicle; third-party liability; and personal accident and sickness. The term 'assurance' is generally limited to the first of these, because the event in respect of which the policy is taken out – namely the death of the person – is assured, or certain. Only the time of the death is uncertain. *See also* CREDIT INSURANCE; FIRE INSURANCE; GROUP INSURANCE; LIFE ASSURANCE; MARINE INSURANCE; MUTUAL INSURANCE; TITLE INSURANCE.

insurance agent. An agent who arranges a contract of insurance between the principal, an insurance company, and a beneficiary who will receive the sum covered when and if the risk insured against actually happens.

insurance broker. An agent arranging insurance on ships, cargo, etc. The Insurance Brokers (Registration) Act, 1977 provided for accounts and business requirement regulations to be made by statutory order. An order came into force with effect from 1 July 1979 requiring each practising insurance broker to maintain an account under the description 'insurance broking account' with an approved bank. The bank must, in writing, acknowledge that there is no entitlement to any right of charge, lien or set-off against such an account. No advances, whether by way of loan, overdraft or otherwise may in general be obtained by a broker for any purpose relating to the insurance broking account, but the regulations authorise the broker to borrow in order to purchase short-term assets, as long as the 'insurance transactions assets' of each of his or her businesses are not less than the 'insurance transactions liabilities' of that business. A bank asked to lend is absolved from the duty of enquiring whether the rules have been, or will be, complied with.

insurance certificate. A document issued to the insured certifying that insurance has been effected and that a policy has been issued. It is not transferable by indorsement and is therefore not usually acceptable under a documentary credit which stipulates for the insurance of goods. Such a certificate is not valid in a court of law without a policy, and is primarily used when goods are insured under the terms of a floating policy. It is widely used to save time and labour and is often prepared by the insured individual personally.

insurance policy. A document which is legal evidence of the agreement to insure, which may be issued at the time when the contract is made, or at a later date.

insurance premium. The payment of an agreed sum, whether in one amount of by instalments, to an insurance company by the person insured in return for the company's undertaking to indemnify the insured upon the happening of a stipulated contingency. *See also* POLICY UNDERWRITER.

intangible assets. Patents, trademarks or goodwill, which have a real value, sometimes a considerable one.

inter. Between, among.

inter-bank market 'bid' rate (LIBID). The rate of interest which first-class banks are prepared to pay for deposits for a specified period. Such 'bids' may be limited in amount.

inter-bank market 'offered' rate (IBOR). The rate of interest at which funds are offered on loan for a specified period in the inter-bank market to first class banks. Offers are subject to availability within dealing limits, and may be limited in amount. The London inter-bank offered rate (LIBOR) is a possible alternative to a bank's base rate from which the bank relates its interest charges on lending. LIBOR is always a true reflection of the cost of funds to the bank, and it is logical to use it as a true base rate, particularly in the case of medium-term lending where the inter-bank market is the only assured source of term funds.

interbankrate. Rate of interest for loans between banks on the Euromarket.

Inter-Bank Research Organisation, The, 32 City Road, London EC1Y 1AA. The Inter-Bank Research Organisation is the policy research and advisory unit of the London and Scottish Clearing Banks, set up by them in 1968 to study matters of common interest. Relatively little of IBRO's work involves 'research' in the academic sense of the term. It involves providing advice and assistance in whatever way may be appropriate on policy issues requiring collective decisions and actions by the banks. Over the years, IBRO has been involved to a greater or lesser extent in virtually every type of issue of joint concern to the banking industry in the money transmission systems and services field – including such matters as the economics of the money transmission business, the changing markets for the banks' services, technological changes, the legal environment, the rationalisation of existing transmission systems and the development of new automated systems. IBRO's output takes the form of management and research reports and also a wide range of shorter discussion papers and working papers for the banking committees it assists, as well as presentations to senior bankers. Part of its output consists of material which the banks incorporate in representations to government departments and other official bodies. IBRO's output also includes material of common interest to its sponsor banks, to be used by individual banks as they choose. Occasionally, work is undertaken for certain other *ad hoc* groupings of banks. IBRO does not normally undertake assignments for individual banks. IBRO is also responsible for the Inter-Bank Standards Unit, which develops and documents the technical standards that the banks observe in their data processing and money transmission activities, both domestically and internationally. Staff from the Unit represent the Clearing Banks in the development of relevant British and international standards. The IBRO library contains a comprehensive collection of reference books and journals relevant to the specialised work of the Organisation, and provides an information service for the consultant staff and for the sponsoring banks. Except in clearly prescribed circumstances, IBRO does not speak on behalf of the banks, and the views put forward by its staff do not necessarily reflect bank policy. IBRO thus enjoys a considerable degree of freedom to consider future developments in banking and engage in discussions with outside bodies without committing the banks to a particular policy or course of action. Overall control of the Organisation rests with the Director, and responsibility for overseeing its activies with a committee consisting of general managers from the sponsoring banks. Out of a total staff of twenty-eight, IBRO has a highly qualified consultant staff with backgrounds in such fields as economics, law, science and technology, market research, operational research and systems analysis, as well as in banking law and practice.

inter-bank sterling market. A market which has arisen to satisfy the placing and taking of sterling deposits between London banks. It acts as a way in which the banks can balance their books, or obtain the funds they need when lending would otherwise be limited by the amount of money deposited by the customers of the banks. (The terms 'wholesale' and 'retail' banking have been used to describe these two sources of funds.) All transactions on the market are unsecured, but each bank has its own limits on how much it will deposit with any one other bank. All agreements are arranged by telephone, usually through brokers. Most of the trade is for overnight money, although there are sometimes a few contracts for up to one year.

inter-company loans market. Loans for fixed sums made between larger commercial and industrial companies when bank accommodation is not forthcoming. The market originated in 1969 as a result of the qualitative and quantitative controls at that time exercised by the Bank of England over the lending banks.

interest. The profit per cent derived from money lent; payment for the use of borrowed money or on a debt; an advantage, an asset, a holding, a share in something. In land law there are five interests as set out in the Law of Property Act, 1925, s.1. They are 1. an easement (*q.v.*), a right or privilege in or over land for an interest equivalent to an estate in fee simple absolute in possession (*see* ESTATE IN FEE SIMPLE) or a term of years absolute (*q.v.*); 2. a rentcharge in possession (*q.v.*) issuing out of or charged on land being either perpetual or for a term of years absolute; 3. a charge by way of legal mortgage (*see under* LEGAL MORTGAGE); 4. land tax (*q.v.*), tithe rentcharge (*q.v.*), and any other similar charge on land which is not created by an instrument; 5. rights of entry exercisable over or in respect of a legal term of years absolute, or annexed, for any purpose, to a legal rentcharge. All other interests in or over land take effect as equitable interests. *See also* COMPOUND INTEREST; CONTINGENT INTEREST; GROSS INTEREST; SIMPLE INTEREST; VESTED INTEREST.

interest clause bill. A bill more commonly met in Eastern or Australian trading, which is drawn for a fixed amount plus interest at a stated rate per annum from the date of the bill or from the time of negotiation until the proceeds of the bill are received.

interest gearing. *See* GEARING.

interest in suspense. Interest calculated and passed to a suspense account because the borrowing customer is insolvent.

interest on deposit. The interest paid by banks to deposit account holders and by building societies to those depositing money with them.

interest on overdraft. *See* CHARGES.

interest warrant. An order or warrant issued by a government or a company and drawn on its bankers, authorising them to pay the interest specified thereon to the stockholder.

interim accounts. Financial information circulated by a company within a period of the financial year, e.g. quarterly or half yearly, showing in broad detail the turnover, profits and an abridged balance sheet. This information is usually unaudited, but will contain a brief report from the directors on the progress of the company.

interim budget. An additional budget, introduced part-way through the financial year, usually to increase taxation.

interim dividend. A dividend paid by a company during the course of the company's year, leaving a final dividend to be paid at the end of the year when the company's financial position at that time has become known.

interlocking directorate. The situation where a number of directors act on the boards of several companies, so that the policies of the companies may be unobtrusively harmonised or made complementary one to another.

interlocutory injunction. *See* INJUNCTION.

intermediary. One who acts as go-between or a mediator; a middleman, an agent, a broker.

internal debt. That part of a country's National Debt owed by a state to its own nationals.

internal loan. A public loan made within a country where the principal and interest are payable only in the same country.

Internal Revenue Service (IRS). Equivalent to the Inland Revenue of the UK, the IRS has overall responsibility for the collection of taxes in the US. The IRS also conducts audits of individual tax returns submitted by both individuals and corporations. Unlike in the UK, for example, most Americans are subject to both federal and local state income taxes and, in some case, e.g. New York, city taxes as well.

international. Pertaining to, subsisting

or carried on between, or mutually affecting, different nations.

International Bank for Reconstruction and Development (The World Bank). The bank was established, together with the International Monetary Fund, in 1945 after the Bretton Woods Conference of 1944. It was popularly known as the World Bank as this title described it jointly with the International Development Association (IDA). The purpose of IBRD was to help countries to reconstruct their economies after the damage inflicted by the war. By the early 1950s, it was switching its centre of interest to the underdeveloped countries and until the 1970s it lent sums to government agencies, or guaranteed private loans. Such loans were usually long term in the range of 15 to 20 years, and financed agricultural modernisation, hydroelectric schemes, port improvements and programmes of economic reconstruction in the hope that the benefits of economic growth in the modern industrial sector would percolate down to the whole population. Membership is essentially the same as the IMF and the capital contributions related to the wealth of the member state. The major source of funds for its lending came from borrowings from the world capital markets. Interest charged on loans was therefore related to market conditions. In addition to the provision of capital for various projects the bank will also provide technical assistance and organise cofinancing in conjunction with official aid or export credit agencies and private institutions. The headquarters of the bank is in Washington.

International Banking Act. This Act which was signed into law by the US President in September 1978 is considered to be the most significant piece of lawmaking in the history of banking legislation to affect foreign banks operating in the United States: before this date, there was no national policy concerning foreign banks, and in many respects they enjoyed certain competitive advantages over US domestic banks. The IBA was an attempt to establish the principle of parity of treatment between foreign and domestic banks in the US and to supplement individual state regulation and supervision within a national framework. The IBA strictly defines the types of offices which foreign banks may operate, such as a branch of foreign agency; it allows foreign banks to open Edge Act corporations (*q.v.*) and permits them also to establish federal branches or agencies in any state in which it is not operating a branch or agency pursuant to state law and where it is not specifically prohibited by state law. In the words of the Act: 'Except as otherwise provided in the Act or in rules, regulations or orders of the Comptroller of the Currency, operations of a foreign bank at a federal branch or agency shall be conducted with the same rights and privileges as a national bank at the same location and shall be subject to the duties, restrictions, penalties, liabilities, conditions and limitations that would apply under the National Bank Act to a national bank doing business at the same location.'

International Banking Facilities (IBFs). International banking facilities were first introduced in the US in December 1981. These offices enable banks to establish international banking free trade zones within the geographic confines of the United States and for regulatory purposes they are treated as though they were located abroad. Transactions of IBFs are considered as 'offshore' transactions and, as such, are free from reserve requirements and interest rate ceilings. Domestic US residents are not allowed to deal with IBFs and their business is strictly limited to the international sector. IBFs are permitted only to accept funds (deposits) from and to lend to, foreign-based individuals, corporations, governments and banks. Foreign subsidiaries of American and other multinationals, as well as other IBFs, can deal directly as long as the funds are not obtained from within the US or used for domestic (i.e. US) purposes. Transactions must be in minimum amounts of $100,000 and may be denominated in any currency. IBFs are not allowed to issue certificates of deposit (CDs) (q.v.) or other bearer instruments.

International Commodities Clearing House (ICCH). The ICCH clears and guarantees non-metal commodity futures trade on the London commodity markets, including gas oil, which make up the London Commodities Exchange (q.v.). It has interests in Australia, Hong Kong, Kuala Lumpur and France. It earns money through registration fees on contracts and interest on deposits and margin cover provided by commodity brokers, and is owned by the Big Five clearing banks. The company is expected to provide clearing guarantee services to the London Gold Futures Market and London International Financial Futures Exchange. *See also* INTERNATIONAL MONEY MARKET (IMM); LONDON INTERNATIONAL FINANCIAL FUTURES MARKET (LIFFE).

international credit clubs. Organisations devised to arrange medium-term credit for exporters, consisting of a number of European finance companies who have combined to facilitate instalment credit business as between one country and another.

International Date Line. The line on either side of which the date differs, running meridianally across the world from the poles and theoretically at 180° from Greenwich. When travelling westwards it is necessary to put one's watch back: this has the effect of lengthening the day or night for the westbound traveller. When travelling eastwards it is necessary to advance one's watch: this has the effect of shortening the day or night, for the eastbound traveller.

International Development Association (IDA). This association is administered by the International Bank for Reconstruction and Development (IBRD) and was established in 1960. The membership is open to all members of IBRD and its aims are the same as IBRD, but its purpose is to assist the poorest countries by longer term loans, i.e. up to 50 years with either no interest payable or at a very low rate of interest. As its lending is below market rates, it relies on subscriptions from members, special contributions and any funds that IBRD transfers.

International Finance Corporation. A corporation founded in 1956 to promote loans to under-developed countries where private enterprise has been unable to raise funds locally. The corporation is affiliated with the World Bank and is able to mobilise funds from other international banks as well as providing them from its own resources.

International Law. An accepted system of laws or jurisprudence regulating intercourse between nations.

International Monetary Fund (IMF). The fund was set up in 1946 as one result of the international monetary conference held two years earlier at Bretton Woods, USA. The intentions were to develop some method of economising in the use of gold and currency reserves, to establish free convertibility between the currencies of the participating nations, and to set up a scheme for giving temporary assistance to member countries in short or medium-term balance of payment difficulties. The IMF is therefore, in effect, a bank which smoothes out the fluctuations of the world trade cycle. The member countries have contributed gold and currencies to the fund based on the relative importance of the member's economy and its share of world trade. The quota determines: (a) members subscriptions to the Fund; (b) within given limits the voting rights of members; (c) their borrowing rights on the Fund; and (d) their share of allocations to Special Drawing Rights (SDRs). When a country finds itself in difficulties it can apply to the Fund for a loan to finance its deficit. At that time it must show that it is taking appropriate action to correct its deficit and restore and maintain the external value of its currency. However, with the move to floating exchange rates in the 1970s, it was expected that such moves would reduce the role of the IMF in international financing. In fact this led to the huge payment imbalances of the less developed countries and very large demands on the resources of the Fund. The expansion in lending and the support of the IMF to these countries indicated to the financial community some form of approval of the borrowing countries' economic policies, so that private sources of finance were then readily available, and foreign creditors agreed to negotiate either new loans or rescheduling old ones. Although the IMF has faced many difficulties in its relationship with LDCs., it has the expertise and experience to make some contribution to assist those countries to formulate correct economic policies, providing adequate funding is available from its members. While the role of the IMF is to support LDCs, it must also attempt to reduce the large payment deficits so that the provision of finance must in the long term be based on private capital and internal political and economic adjustments. Finally, its prime concern is the assistance it can render to members in the adjustment of their economies and the proper performance of the drawing of funds within the arrangements made.

International Money Market (IMM), Chicago Mercantile Exchange. The IMM, a division of the Chicago Mercantile Exchange, was opened for trading in May 1972, futures contracts being then on offer in seven currencies. The currencies are sterling, deutschmark, French franc, Mexican peso, Japanese yen, Canadian dollar, Swiss franc and Dutch guilder. The IMM is used by multinational companies, export and import traders, and others faced with the exchange risks caused by floating rates of exchange (see FLOATING CURRENCY). Later contracts were added in US silver coins and in gold bullion: in 1976 futures contracts in short-term interest rates were introduced. These took the form of thirteen-week US Treasury Bills. One-year bill contracts appeared in 1978, four-year bill contracts in 1979, and commercial bank certificates of deposit in 1981. These facilities have attracted a wide range of money managers who wish to guard against yield swings in their interest-bearing paper, and the resultant hedges have made these contracts among the fastest expanding in the futures industry. See also INTERNATIONAL COMMODITIES CLEARING HOUSE (ICCH); LONDON INTERNATIONAL FINANCIAL FUTURES MARKET (LIFFE).

international money order. A means of transferring comparatively small sums from one country to another through the agency of a bank.

international payment service. A service run by National Girobank but available to all members of the public at post offices. Money can be transferred, subject to a maximum figure of £50 per transaction, to any country in the world either by an International Payment, at a charge of £2.50, or by an International Rapid Payment, with a basic fee of £2.50 plus a charge of £3.00 to Europe or £3.50 elsewhere. Payment to the beneficiary is made either in cash, subject to satisfactory identification, or through a bank. The amount may be paid in foreign currency, in sterling for payment in currency, or in sterling for payment in sterling.

international securities. Securities which can be bought or sold on an international market, i.e. in several different countries, at more or less the same prices.

International Securities Regulatory Organisation (ISRO). A self regulating organisation that has been set up for the purpose of ensuring an orderly market in international investment business.

interplead. To take legal proceedings in order to discuss and determine an incidental issue.

interpleader. A suit by which the claims of two parties to money or property are determined, in order that a third party (such as a banker), on whom the claim is made, may know to which party payment or delivery is due.

inter se. Amongst themselves.

interventon rate. The rate at which the central authority will intervene on the foreign exchanges to buy its currency (if it is falling) or sell its currency (if is is rising). Since convertibility was established in 1958, central banks have normally had intervention points only in US dollars and have solely used that currency as a means of intervention. But *see* EUROPEAN CURRENCY UNIT (ECU) and EUROPEAN MONETARY SYSTEM (EMS).

interview. A meeting between two persons face to face; a discussion between a manager and a member of staff, or between a banker and a customer. An interview with a customer may be arranged by appointment or, less satisfactorily, requested by the customer when in the branch. As far as possible the manager should prepare for the interview by glancing at the customer's correspondence file, ledger balance, safe custodies and securities held, etc. At the interview the manager should ascertain as

quickly and thoroughly as possible what the customer wants, and decide how far he or she can go to satisfy him. The manager must be sure to elicit all the essential information and must remember that this is a public relations exercise on behalf of the bank. However, the interview may be at the request of the manager and may relate to the unsatisfactory conduct of the account, when the customer must be told the bank's views politely but firmly. A staff interview is at the branch with the manager, or at an area, regional, or head office with a staff or personnel manager. It may be at the request of the staff member, or by the direction of the staff manager. It may be an annual progress review, or it may be for the giving of advice of a disciplinary nature, or it may be a preliminary to promotion.

inter vivos. Among the living.

intestate. Not having made a valid will, not disposed of by will. In a case of intestacy an administrator will be appointed on the death to wind up the affairs of the deceased.

in the money. *See* TRADED OPTIONS.

intimation. The notice given to a debtor by the assignor of a debt or obligation. Such notice is not necessary in the case of negotiable instrument or securities.

in toto. Wholly.

in transitu. In the course of being transported from one place to another. *See also* STOPPAGE *IN TRANSITU.*

intra vires. Within the powers (usually of a company).

intrinsic value. Genuine or real value. When used of coin, it means that the metal in the coin is worth the face value of the coin.

introduction. The act of introducing or bringing into notice, the act of making persons formally acquainted with one another; a method by which a company can obtain a Stock Exchange quotation when it has reached such a size in terms of capitalisation and spread of shareholders as to meet the requirements of the Stock Exchange, or where its securites are already listed on another stock exchange. *See also* OFFER FOR SALE; PLACING.

intromission. *(Sc. Law)* The transactions of a subordinate or agent with the money belonging to his or her employer or principal; the action of intermeddling with the property of another, the assuming of the possession and management of the property of another.

in trust. Indicating that property is held by a trustee. In banking, documents are often held in trust by a customer, who having signed a trust receipt, holds the documents of title on behalf of the bank and has agreed that having sold the goods will deliver the proceeds to the bank. *See* TRUST LETTER; TRUST RECEIPT.

inventory. A detailed list or catalogue of goods and chattels, the articles enumerated on such a list. A list of the effects of a house, required for probate or insurance purposes.

inventory loans. Loans made to commercial companies for the purpose of accumulating and financing stock or inventories; the stocks are regarded as security or collateral for the loan. Inventory loans are very common where seasonal borrowing is concerned, particularly in the case of agricultural products, or to finance the accumulation of both raw materials and finished goods where their ultimate sale may be concentrated over a very short period of time, such as Christmas goods. The establishment of a lien on inventory by a bank is covered by various laws which can and do differ between the individual states. Such laws include the Uniform Warehouse Receipts Act, the Uniform Trust Receipt Act, the Factors Lien Law and the Chattel Mortgage Law. In most states, however, these have been replaced by the Uniform Commercial Code.

investment. The act of laying out money; the capital invested or lent to produce interest or profit; using money to buy something which it is hoped will bring in some return and will not lose its value. *See also* TRADE INVESTMENTS.

investment bank. A bank which provides long-term fixed capital for industry, in return taking over shares in the borrowing companies, so that some measure of influence or control can be exercised. Additionally it may exercise many merchant bank functions such as merger making, commodity trading, advising on investments, counselling in corporate finance, broking, etc.

investment club. A group of persons (up to twenty) who have formed an association with the object of making investments in stocks and shares with money provided from regular contributions by each of the members. Besides this, it also has a social purpose, so that the members meet regularly and discuss investment strategies.

investment grant. A grant given by central or local government to encourage the establishment of a new industry in areas of high unemployment.

investment portfolio. *See* PORTFOLIO.

investment trust. A public corporate body registered under the Companies Acts and formed for the purpose of holding investments, obtaining its capital from public issues. Investors in the trust can obtain holdings only by buying shares from existing holders. The investment trust enables small investors with limited capital resources to spread their risk over a wide range of securities under full-time specialist management. The net income earned on the investments in the trust's portfolio, which mainly comprises the shares of other companies, is passed on to the trust's shareholders as dividends, but capital gains made on the investments in the portfolio cannot be distributed as cash. The Companies Act, 1985 included investment trusts in those companies to be allowed to buy their own shares. *See also* UNIT TRUST.

investor protection. Protection for the investor has in the last decade expanded considerably. The spread does not lie in any one piece of legislation, but in a variety of areas: 1. Under the Banking Act, 1987, depositors are protected up to 75 per cent of their deposits up to £20,000; 2. The Building Societies Protection Scheme gives depositors protection of up to 90% of their deposits; 3. The Financial Service Act has established the Securities Investment Board, which through the various Self Regulating Organisations (SROs) offers protection to small investors by ensuring that only those authorised may advertise for investment business and prevents 'cold calling' on prospective clients. The SROs lay down stringent rules of conduct on its members and monitors their activities; 4. The Companies Act gives shareholders a measure of protection by the amount of disclosure that must be made in the report and accounts of public companies; 5. insider dealing is also covered by the Companies Act – *See* INSIDER; 6. brokers, solicitors and others must keep the funds of their clients separate from their own funds.

investors in industry (3is). Formerly ICFC. This company is better known as 3is. Its purpose is to provide medium and long term capital, expertise and advice for small and medium sized companies. The capital of this company is provided by the major banks.

invisible exports. The various services performed in one country for persons in another, for which payment has to be made, interest, profits and dividends on investments abroad, air transport receipts, profits on plays abroad and royalties, all cause a flow of currency into a country. In the case of Great Britain, whose banking, insurance and shipping facilities regularly earn large sums of foreign money, it is often the case that her invisible exports go far to offset or even reverse a deficit on the balance of visible imports and exports. After the proceeds of investment abroad and the services performed by the City, the money earned by tourism is the next most important factor. *See also* VISIBLE EXPORTS.

invoice. A list of goods dispatched, with particulars of quantity and price, sent to a consignee. *See also* CONSULAR INVOICE.

invoice discounting. A less comprehensive factoring service than Recourse Factoring where a company may sell its sales invoices at a discount in return for immediate payment. It provides no sales ledger accounting service or credit cover. Other names for this are Confidential Invoice Factoring and Receivables Financing. The purpose of invoice discounting is to enable a supplier to get the money owed earlier, so as to improve cash flow, or to use the money for obtaining discounts, or for any other reason useful in his or her business. Invoice discounting agreements are nearly always based upon the purchase by the discounter of the debts ('receivables') which are yet to be settled in much the same way as a factor would buy debts. There must be good status rating and regular orders on the part of the buyers. The discounter then appoints the client as agent to administer the sales ledger and collect the money. Strictly speaking, therefore, it is not a lending-borrowing arrangement at all, but rather a principal-agent relationship. The discount houses' approach to the prospective customer is a strictly banking one. At least three years' audited balance sheets are required for analysis and these must show acceptable ratios of borrowing to shareholders' funds. The maximum figure agreed for an advance is always smaller than the total of shareholders' funds. There is no credit control, and none of the other factoring services. The client pays a charge rather in excess of a bank overdraft rate. Invoice discounting is almost always undisclosed, the supplier's customers knowing nothing of the arrangement, but there are variations which involve disclosure.

invoice factoring. See INVOICE DISCOUNTING.

IOU. A written acknowledgment of a debt of a specified sum bearing these letters, addressed to the creditor, dated, and signed by the borrower, It is not evidence that money has been lent and it is not a negotiable instrument.

Irish Bank Federation. Nassau House, Nassau Street, Dublin 2, Eire. The Federation was formed in 1973 with the object 1. of providing facilities for the discussion of matters of common interest to Irish licensed banks, of protecting those interests, and, where appropriate, of making representations on their behalf; 2. of advising and assisting the authorities on all matters of material concern to Irish banking; 3. of representing Irish banking in matters relating to the European Economic Community. Membership is restricted to banks which are licensed under the Central Bank Act, 1971.

irredeemable debenture. A debenture with no date for repayment, intended to be a permanent debt.

irredeemable stocks. Government stocks which have no date of redemption.

irrevocable credit. Once this type of credit has been arranged, its terms cannot be varied or changed without the concurrence of all the parties to it. An exporter who is in a sufficiently strong bargaining position to do so should therefore always insist on payment by irrevocable credit. All credits are revocable unless it is specifically stated that they are irrevocable.

irrevocable power of attorney. See POWER OF ATTORNEY.

ISDA. INTERNATIONAL SWAP DEALERS ASSOCIATION.

ish. In Scots law, the expiry date of a lease.

ISRO. See INTERNATIONAL SECURITIES REGULATORY ORGANISATION.

issue. The act of sending out, the whole number sent out at one time to be put into circulation, as notes; a topic of discussion or controversy; publication, that which is published at a particular time; progeny, offspring; the specific point in an issue between two parties requiring to be determined; to come to a point in fact or law, on which the parties join, and rest the decision of the cause. See also GENERAL ISSUE; NEW ISSUE; PUBLIC ISSUE; RIGHTS ISSUE.

issued capital. That part of the authorised capital which is issued to shareholders and paid for by them, not necessarily fully paid up.

issue of bill. The first delivery of a bill, note or cheque, complete in form, to the person who takes it as a holder. There after the instrument is said to be 'negotiated'; only a drawer can 'issue' a bill, etc.

issue price. The price at which stock or shares are issued to the public; not necessarily the nominal price.

issuing bank. This is one of the parties to a documentary credit. On the instructions of the principal (the customer of a bank) that bank, the issuing bank, will issue a documentary credit in favour of a named beneficiary.

issuing house. A group of accepting houses, merchant banks and other institutions who act as intermediaries between those seeking capital and those who are able to supply it, sponsoring capital issues if they are satisfied that the amount required can be raised on conditions which are acceptable to investors. They make themselves responsible for taking up any of the issue which has not been taken up by others, although they may arrange for others to share the risk. (*See* UNDERWRITER.) The issuing house agrees the timing of the issue with the Bank of England, and where a quotation is to be granted it handles the negotiations with the Quotations Committee of the Stock Exchange. Issuing houses also give advice over a wide range of company problems.

Issuing Houses Association. An association formed in 1945 to represent the interest of the merchant banks and other institutions acting as issuing houses, to act as a consultant and advisory body and to be the spokesman for the views of its members on matters affecting their activities.

item. Any debit, credit or other documents used in banks for its accountancy, for transmission to the clearing house, or abroad, is in general terms described as an item. Amounts listed on sheets are often described as items. The only thing that does not normally carry this description is cash, either in coin or note form.

J

J Curve. A description of the state of the balance of trade of a country, graphically displayed, after a devaluation. This has the effect of making the country's exports cheaper, so they will increase, and the imports dearer, so they will fall. The initial effect, however, will be the other way, because many exports are made of imported raw materials. The immediate impact, therefore, is an increase in the cost of imports. The expansion in the volume and value of exports follows, but after an inevitable time lag. There is a short down turn, following the devaluation, followed by a long up turn. A graph of this would look like a letter J leaning backwards slightly. The effect can also apply to other types of remedial action, e.g. the delayed effect on unemployment of an increase in the level of production, because this first absorbs the surplus capacity and higher productivity sufficient to meet the requirements of the early stage.

job. A piece of work, especially one done for a stated price; habitual employment or profession; to act as a broker; to hire out for a specified time.

job analysis. The examination of industrial output with a view to eliminating waste of time or energy.

jobber. A middleman. A dealer in the professional inter-bank money markets. Since the 'Big Bang' there are no jobbers in the Stock Exchange. They are now market makers.

job card. A card to record time spent on any particular job; a card containing details of any particular task to be undertaken.

job evaluation. The calculation of the content of any particular job in an organisation, the qualifications required for it, and possibly the subsequent grading of staff accordingly.

joint account. A banking account maintained by two or more people. All must sign on any relevant documents unless the mandate provides otherwise. All are jointly liable for any overdraft unless the mandate establishes joint and several liability. On the death of one party to a joint account, any credit balance on the banking account normally becomes the property of the survivor(s). In some cases, however, particularly where a husband-and-wife joint account is in question, the appropriation of the balance of the survivor on the death of one may depend upon the intention of the party who opened the account in the first place. The banker should guard against any embarrassment arising from a claim on the bank by the personal representative of the deceased party by including in the mandate a specific clause authorising the banker to pay the balance to the survivor. *See also* DISPENSING NOTICE..

joint and several liability. A banker dealing with joint account holders should be careful to establish joint and several liability by a suitable clause in the mandate. Then the account holders will be individually as well as jointly liable for the repayment of any accommodation taken, and the bank will have as many rights of action as there are account holders. Formerly the rule was that joint liability among debtors gave only one right of action, so that a bank had to be careful to include all the names of the debtors in its writ. In 1978, however, the Civil Liability (Contribution) Act established a right for the creditor to sue one joint debtor after another. The banks will not make any changes in their procedures, as the establishment of joint and several liability gives important advantages to the bank in other directions. In the bankruptcy of a partnership, for example, the bank gains a right of double proof: against the firm on an equal footing with the firm's creditors, and against each partner on an equal footing with that partner's private creditors. Any security held can be allocated to whichever estate will show the banker an optimum return.

joint and several liability of directors. It is a common practice of bankers to supplement security offered by a company by the joint and several guarantees of the directors. The guarantees themselves may or may not be worth much, but the intention is to bring it home to the directors that they are personally responsible. This will make them more careful in their actions, and more prudent in the use they make of the accommodation granted. As they are asking the bank to express its confidence in the future of the company (by lending it money), they can hardly refuse to show a similar confidence themselves.

joint and several promissory note. *See* PROMISSORY NOTE.

joint annuity. An annuity payable throughout the lifetime of two people (often husband and wife) and continuing until the death of the survivor.

joint consultation. Dialogue between management and workers on matters affecting them both; discussion between government and representatives of capital and labour.

Joint Credit Card Company. The company that promotes the credit card ACCESS. The company is jointly owned and promoted by Lloyds Bank, Midland Bank, National Westminster Bank and Royal Bank of Scotland. *See* ACCESS.

joint heir. One who shares an inheritance with another.

joint liability. Joint holders are regarded by the law as together making up 'the owner', and before 1978 an action against joint debtors had to be brought against all of them together.

Since that year, however, it has been possible to sue joint debtors one after another. *See* JOINT AND SEVERAL LIABILITY.

joint lives policy. A life assurance policy which is payable on the death of the first of joint policy owners.

joint promissory note. *See* PROMISSORY NOTE.

joint stock bank. A bank which has issued shares to shareholders who hold them jointly, as opposed, to a partnership. The term was originally meant to distinguish banks which were public limited companies from private partnership banks, but it is not so much used nowadays, when all the big banks are joint stock banks.

joint stock company. A mercantile, banking or operative association with capital made up of transferable shares.

joint tenancy. A tenure of land, property, etc., by more than one person. On the death of one joint tenant the property passes to the survivor to the exclusion of the personal representative of the deceased joint tenant.

jointure. Property settled on a woman at marriage, to be hers on the death of her husband.

joint venture. A partnership of a temporary nature usually for the purpose of carrying out one particular trading objective. On completion of the venture the partnership is dissolved.

journal. The ledger containing details of the daily transactions of a business; a diary, a daily newspaper, a periodical publication.

judge. A civil officer invested with power to hear and determine causes in a court of justice; one authorised to decide a dispute or contest; to hear and try (a case), to decide (a question), to sentence.

judge-made. Based on legal interpretations of the law as made by judges.

judgment. The act of judging; a legal decision arrived at by a judge in a court of law; an order or decree made by any court.

judgment by default. A decision given in favour of the plaintiff when the defendant fails to appear.

judgment creditor. A creditor who has obtained judgment against a debtor for the payment of a debt. The creditor may enforce this in a number of ways, such as by a writ of *fieri facias,* by a garnishee order, by the issuance of a bankruptcy notice, by a charging order, etc.

judgment debt. A debt secured by a judge's order, under which an execution can be levied at any time.

judgment seat. A judge's bench, a tribunal, a court.

judgment summons. A legal summons for failure to settle a judgment debt.

junk bonds. A US term for tradable financial instruments of below the normal investment grade.

jurat. A person under oath, a person who performs some duty on oath; a municipal officer, especially of the Cinque Ports, corresponding to an alderman; a magistrate in the Channel Islands; a memorandum at the end of an affidavit stating where, when and before whom the affidavit is sworn and bearing the signature and description of the person before whom it was sworn; in France, a municipal magistrate in certain towns, e.g. Bordeaux, or a member of a company or corporation, sworn to see that nothing is done in contravention of its statutes.

jurisdiction. The legal power or right of administering justice, making and enforcing laws, or exercising other authority; the district or extent within which such power may be exercised.

K

keeping house. Under the Bankruptcy Act, 1914, the fact that a debtor kept to his or her house to delay or defeat creditors, was an act of bankruptcy. The inability to pay is now defined in the Insolvency Act, 1986, s.268.

Kennedy Round. An agreement made in 1967, and subsequently carried out, by which the signatory countries to the General Agreement on Tariffs and Trade made a general reduction of tariffs. The conference was the result of a suggestion by President Kennedy of the USA, and the 'round' of tariff reductions was accordingly designated with his name.

key man insurance. The insurance by a firm or company of a partner, director or employee who is particularly valuable to them, such as a top salesman, a technical person working on a new product, or a travelling representative with many years' experience of the trade in foreign countries. The loss of such a man could be a heavy blow to the organisation concerned and can be guarded against by a straightforward term or convertible term insurance cover.

king. *See* SOVEREIGN.

kite. An accommodation bill; a representation of fictitious credit.

kite-flying. Raising money by the use of accommodation bills; a procedure to discover how the public at large will react to some proposal, seeing 'how the wind blows'.

krugerrand. A South African gold coin, popular with the private investor because it contains exactly one ounce of pure gold, is easily transportable, and internationally accepted as a transferable hedge against currency depreciation. From September 1980 there are available $\frac{1}{2}$, $\frac{1}{4}$ and $\frac{1}{10}$ oz. coins. Profits made on the sale of Krugerrands are subject to capital gains tax.

L

labour. Toil, work demanding patience
and endurance; manual workers, col-
lectively or politically; one of the
factors of production. In economics
the term includes all forms of labour
whether manual or clerical, excepting
management. As a factor of production it is similar to the other factors,
land and capital, as being one of a
number of productive resources to be
utilised by entrepreneurs.

laches. Negligence, neglect to do something. The equitable doctrine of laches
may prevent a suitor who has been
remiss or idle in pursuing a claim from
obtaining a judgment from the court.

Lady Day. a quarter day – 25th March.

lag. *See* LEADS AND LAGS.

laissez faire. The principle of non-
interference, especially by government in industrial and commercial
affairs.

land. Land has ben defined in terms
which include anything on the land
(whether natural, e.g. a tree, or
artificial, e.g. house), anything in the
air over the land, and anything in the
ground underneath, right down to the
centre of the earth. It is an old
definition, but then land is a very old
type of security, probably the oldest.
The law was active on the rights of
landowners long before the concept of
a law of contract had taken form. For
lenders, land has a great attraction as a
security because it is always there.
You cannot pick it up and carry it
away. There is no risk of losing control
over the security; all that is necessary
is to make certain that the borrower
has a good title to offer. A statutory
definition is 'Land includes land of
any tenure, and mines and minerals,
whether or not held apart from the
surface, buildings or parts of buildings
(whether the division is horizontal,
vertical, or made in any other way),

and other corporeal hereditaments;
also a manor, an advowson, and a rent
or other incorporeal hereditament,
and an easement, right, or privilege,
or benefit in, over, or derived from
land'. Land includes an interest in
land and, in relation to Scotland,
includes heritable subjects of whatever
description.

land agent. A person employed by an
estate owner to collect rents, let farms,
etc.

land bank. A bank whose function is to
lend to farmers for the purchase of
land or for its development.

land certificate. A document issued
under the seal of the Land Registry to
the registered owner of freehold or
leasehold land. The certificate is a
copy of the entry at the Land Registry
in respect of the particular piece of
land. The entry is in three parts; 1. the
Property Register gives the index
letters and title number accorded to
the land, a short description of the
property, whether freehold or leasehold, and a reference to the Land
Registry General Map for purposes of
identification; 2. the Proprietorship
Register gives the name, address and
description of the proprietor, the date
of the registration, and the type of
freehold or leasehold title and (if the
registered proprietor has made a specific request) the consideration paid; 3.
the Charges Register gives details of
charges affecting the land, such as
restrictive covenants or mortgages.
The registered land certificate is *prima
facie* evidence of ownership, in the
same way as the deeds are in the case
of unregistered land.

land charges. Charges against unregistered land which must be registered at
the Land Charges Department by the
holder of the charge to give notice of it
to anyone else who is, or may become,

interested in the land. There are five main registers at the department, dealing with pending actions, annuities, writs and orders, deeds of arrangement and land charges. *See also* LAND CHARGES REGISTER; LOCAL LAND CHARGES.

land charges register. A register dealing with unregistered land, maintained at the Land Charges Department. Under the Land Charges Act, 1925, five main registers, dealing with pending actions, annuities, writs and orders, deeds of arrangement, and land charges, are kept. The land charges register is sub-divided into six classes, letters A-F. Class A consists of charges on land as the result of an application by some person under the provisions of some statute. Class B consists of similar charges on land imposed by a statute, without the need for any application. Class C is sub-divided into (i) puisne mortgages, (ii) limited owners charges, (iii) general equitable charges, and (iv) estate contracts. Class D is sub-divided into (i) Inland Revenue charges for capital transfer tax. (ii) restrictive convenants, and (iii) equitable easements. Class E is for annuities charged upon land created before 1926, but not registered until after 1925. Flass F is for charges on land registered by spouses under the Matrimonial Homes Act, 1967.

Land Improvements Company. An institution formed more than a century ago and still in operation. It makes loans for up to twenty years to farmers for land purchase, including bridging advances; improvements to farms and estates, including buildings, houses, cottages, fencing, drainage, tree planting, roads, etc., repayment of other borrowings; purchase of machinery and equipment; taxation, including capital transfer tax; and any item eligible for a grant under the Farm and Horticulture Development scheme and the Farm Capital Grant

scheme. Specialist intensive livestock and horticultural proposals will not normally be approved unless supported by a reasonable amount of ordinary agricultural land. Loans are for a minimum of £25,000 and are normally limited to a maximum of two-thirds of the value of the security offered. Variable rate loans carry an interest charge related to the company's base rate. Fixed rate loans may also be negotiated. Repayment is in full at the end of the term, or by annual or half-yearly instalments. The Land Improvement group may also buy on leaseback farms requiring improvement.

landing account. A document issued by a warehouse, giving details of goods and charges incurred.

landlord. One who has tenants holding land under him or her, the lord of the manor; the master of an inn or of a lodging house.

Land Register. The records at the Land Registry dealing with the registration of land. The Land Register is in three parts: 1. the Property Register; 2. the Proprietorship Register; 3. the Charges Register. *See also* LAND CERTIFICATE. The Land Register can be inspected only by permission of the registered proprietor: the customer's written authority must therefore be taken in appropriate cases. The registered land certificate is a copy of those entries in the Land Register which affect the land in question, with the addition of a copy of a Land Registry General Ordnance Map, with the property marked thereon, for purposes of identification. *See also* SASINE.

land registration. A system of registration of title to land, based on the system of registration of title and transfer of stock and shares, arising out of the disadvantages of the system of deeds as evidence of title. A comprehensive system of land registration was set up in 1925, since when the two systems have been running side by side. It is intended that compulsory registration should be extended to the whole of the country, and this process is now nearly complete. A registered land certificate is issued to the title holder, and the Land Register is kept up to date with changes as and when they occur. The accuracy of the certificates is guaranteed by the State. *See also* LAND REGISTER.

land tax. Formerly a tax on land and houses, based on valuation of estates. Land tax was abolished by the Finance Act, 1963.

lapse. To slip or fall; to pass from one proprietor to another because of negligence; to pass slowly by degrees; an error of omission; failure to do one's duty; the termination of legal possession through negligence; the failure of a gift under a will because the donee dies before the testator.

lapsed policy. A policy of insurance which has become worthless to the insured because of failure to maintain payments of the premium.

larceny. Theft, the unlawful taking away of the personal goods of another with intent to convert them for one's own use, that is, to permanently deprive that other of them. Since 1969 the Larceny Act of 1916 has been abolished, the Theft Act, 1968 coming into force in that year. Instead of larceny, a person becomes guilty of theft if he or she dishonestly appropriates property belonging to another, with the intention of permanently depriving that other of it.

last in first out. Commonly known as LIFO. It is an accounting term used for the purpose of valuing stock. The pricing is based on the fact that any issue of stock is withdrawn from the latest delivery. With stocks that move out of the organisation rapidly, this method of stock valuation is more in line with current market values. Although it may appear that only stock from the 'top of the pile' is issued, in fact, the *physical* issue of the stock pays

little attention to the *accountancy* method of valuation.

last time seller. A phrase used to denominate a person who is selling a house and buying a smaller one, or not buying another one at all. Such people are likely to be retired couples who have disposed of their freeholds to a company for cash plus a guarantee that the house can continue in their occupation until the death of the surviving spouse; widows or widowers moving into homes for elderly people; landlords selling property previously rented; and people coming into property under the terms of a will. In all these cases there is a reflux of funds into the building societies either by way of investment or as an existing mortgage is redeemed.

lateral combination. An integration of companies engaged in like stages of industrial production, whether in the same industry or in another.

laundered money. The term refers to funds which are passed through a number of bank accounts in order to conceal the original source. Clearly, such transactions are usually illegal and in the US all banks are bound by laws to advise the local Federal Reserve Board of any large deposits which are made in cash.

LAUTRO. The Life Assurance and Unit Trust Regulatory Organisation. This is a self regulating organisation (SRO), established within the framework of the Financial Services Act, 1986.

law. Rules of conduct imposed by authority or accepted by the community in general as binding; a system of such rules regulating the intercourse of mankind, of individuals within a state, or of states with one another; a condition of order and stability; legal knowledge. *See also* CASE LAW; MARITIME LAW; ROMAN LAW; STATUTE LAW; UNWRITTEN LAW.

law list. A list of barristers, solicitors and other legal practitioners, giving names and addresses and dates of qualification, issued annually by the Law Society.

law merchant. The usages and customs of merchants, adopted by the common law and comprising a body of mercantile regulations for the conduct of commerce.

Law Society. A professional association of solicitors, established in 1825.

lay days. Days allowed for the loading and unloading of a ship's cargo, during which the charterer is not liable to pay for demurrage.

lead manager. The principal house in a syndicate handling a new issue, which co-ordinates and directs the efforts of the syndicate.

leads and lags. The hastening or delaying of payment, by or to residents respectively, of international payments, at a time when the rate of exchange of a country's currency is rising or falling. *Leads* refers to the payment for goods by importers. When, for example, the value of the pound sterling is falling on the exchanges, importers pay as quickly as they can. *Lags* refers to the payment for goods to exporters. In similar circumstances exporters allow their customers longer periods of time than usual to pay for goods. Such actions can have a serious effect in the short-run on the country's balance of payments. Of course, both leads and lags apply only where goods are invoiced in currency.

lease. To grant or to take or hold land on lease; a letting of land or tenements, usually for a fixed rent, for a specified period; the written contract for or the term of such letting.

leaseback. The sale of a property or asset to a leasing company and immediately the vendor becomes the lessee of the same property.

leasehold estate. A right to enjoy the possession of land for a term of years as stated in the lease granting the right. To be a legal estate a lease must either

be created by deed or be one which takes effect in possession for a term not exceeding three years at the best rent obtainable. Any kind of informal lease other than the latter gives rise to an equitable interest only.

leasing. Renting houses, lands, etc., for a specified period of time; the hiring of an asset for the duration of its economic life. The asset is initially purchased by a finance company and then leased to the user who has no option to purchase. The system is suitable for large and costly assets such as computers, aircraft, containers and container ships, and specialised plant and equipment. Leasing is an alternative to purchase of an asset by instalment credit or through the aid of a mortgage or term loan. It has the advantages that it involves no capital outlay, requires no down payment, and may have tax benefits for the user. It does not count as borrowing for the purpose of a company's memorandum and articles of association. *See also* BIG TICKET LEASE; CROSS-BORDER LEASING; FINANCE LEASE; OPERATING LEASE.

ledger. A book in which a business firm enters all debit and credit items in summary form; a cash book; a book in which is kept a list of customer's accounts and balance.

legacy. A bequest, personal property bequeathed by will. *See also* STATUTORY LEGACY.

legal. Of, pertaining to, or according to law; lawful, legitimate.

legal assignment. *See* EQUITABLE ASSIGNMENT.

legal entity. A person, corporation, company or any other organisation having, in the eyes of the law, the capacity to contract or assume legal obligations. It has the capacity to enter into contracts, own property, sue and be sued.

legal estate. In the case of land, a fee simple absolute in possession, or a term of years absolute. In the case of other property, the right to hold the legal title and sell the property if desired. The holder of a legal estate may be a lender who has taken security by way of a legal mortgage from a borrower, whose only remaining right is the equity of redemption; or he or she may be a trustee holding the property for the benefit of the holder of the equitable estate.

legal fiction. The assumption that something is a fact, in order to avoid technical difficulties, and to secure substantial justice.

legal interest. A right, based in law, to some claim against the property of another person. In relation to land, where the term is commonly found, a legal interest has been defined as an easement, right or privilege in or over land for an interest equivalent to a freehold or leasehold estate; a rent charge in possession charged on or issuing out of freehold or leasehold land; a charge by way of legal mortgage; certain rights of entry upon land. A claim against another person's land, as described above, must correspond in duration to one of the two legal estates, freehold or leasehold.

legalisation. An official stamp of approval put on a document.

legal lending limits. Banks in the US are subject to many complex restrictions upon the way they operate their loan portfolios; the most important and well known is the ten per cent rule. Statutory law provides that a national bank may not lend more than an amount equal to ten per cent of its unimpaired capital stock and surplus to any person, partnership, association or corporation. This ruling, which was enacted at the beginning of the century, has significant implications for those smaller banks with a limited capital base and explains the proliferation of overlines (*q.v.*) and syndicated credits among domestic banks in the US. Over the years,

various exceptions to the ten per cent rule have been introduced to take into account changing market conditions and developments in financing methods. Such exceptions to the rule include, for example, federal funds sold; repurchase agreements (REPOs); discounts of commercial paper owned by the person or corporation discounting it; trade acceptances; bankers' acceptances of another banks' bills with less than six months to maturity; obligations secured or guaranteed by the US Government or any federal agency etc. *See also* SYNDICATED LOAN.

legal mortgage. The conveyance of a legal estate in real or personal property as security for a debt or for the discharge of an obligation. A legal mortgage of freehold land is accomplished by a charge by deed expressed to be by way of legal mortgage, or by the demise of a term of years absolute.

legal tender. Any means of payment that a creditor is obliged by law to accept in settlement of a debt. Thus while a debt can be settled by cheque, this is at the option of the creditor, for a cheque is not legal tender. The creditor can, however, be compelled in the UK to accept Bank of England notes, for these are legal tender to any amount. As to coinage, £1 and 50p pieces are legal tender up to £10, other cupro-nickel coins up to £5, and bronze coins up to 20p. A debtor must tender the exact amount owing, that is, change cannot be demanded.

legatee. One to whom a legacy is bequeathed. *See also* RESIDUARY LEGATEE.

lender credit. American banks in the UK and finance houses working through the so-called 'money shops' (*q.v.*) have developed an aggressive selling technique in a determined effort to provide the ordinary man with the kind of specialist consumer banking service which they believe is still not available at any of the big clearing banks. Their speciality is the provision of personal loans untied to specific shop or salesroom purchases. It is this type of distanced lending, known as 'lender credit', which distinguishes them from the UK's traditional finance house concerns, most of which specialise in hire-purchase finance and other forms of 'vendor credit', where the loan is made at the point of sale.

lender of last resort. A lender to whom borrowers may go when all other sources have failed, who will be sure to lend, albeit at a higher rate of interest than other possible lenders. Thus, the Bank of England acts as lenders of last resort for the London discount houses, and the Public Works Loan Board acts as lender of last resort for local authorities.

lending ceilings. During a period of quantitative restrictions, banks and other lending institutions are restricted as to the total amount which they may lend. This figure of maximum permitted advances is the lending ceiling.

lending ratio. The ratio found by a comparison of money lent with money lodged.

lesion. A Scots law term for injury or damage to a person.

lessee. The person to whom a lease is granted.

lessor. The grantor of a lease.

letter. A written or printed communication; to print in special lettering; to stamp a title on a book cover. *See also* FACILITY LETTER.

letter of advice. A letter notifying dispatch of goods, drawing of a bill of exchange or draft, receipt of an item for credit of a customer's account, etc.

letter of allotment. *See* ALLOTMENT LETTER.

letter of application. An application for an allotment of a number of shares out of an issue announced and advertised to the public or to existing shareholders. The letter will state the number of shares required and enclose a cheque for the amount required to be paid on application.

letter of comfort. Where a subsidiary company seeks a loan from a bank, and is asked to supply, in default of other security, a guarantee from its parent company (which may be a very large and strong overseas company), it may reply that the parent company dislikes making formal security available, but that it may be willing to supply a letter of comfort. Such a letter recognises that the bank is providing accommodation, acknowledges that it has the beneficial ownership of the whole of the issued capital of the subsidiary company, that it is not its present intention to dispose of any of these shares, and that, while it is not its practice to guarantee the liabilities of any of its subsidiaries, nevertheless it finds it difficult to conceive of any circumstance where, in its own interests, it would be able to give serious consideration to providing a sufficient degree of financial support for its subsidiary. A lending bank receiving such a letter may take the view that it has received a written support by the parent for its subsidiary and that the amount lent, while large by some standards, is comparatively small from the point of view of the parent. It may suppose that the parent will not let its subsidiary go into liquidation without ensuring that the bank has been repaid its money. Before deciding to lend, however, the bank should recognise that this informal undertaking does not have to appear on the balance sheet of the parent company (which it will of course have carefully scrutinised). It is then relevant for it to ask how many other letters of comfort have been issued. A further danger may occur if in fact the subsidiary does go into liquidation, and the parent company does then repay the bank. The liquidator may attack the bank on the grounds that this repayment constitutes a fraudulent preference (*q.v.*).

letter of credit. *See* DOCUMENTARY CREDIT.

letter of deposit. *See* MEMORANDUM OF DEPOSIT.

letter of hypothecation. A trust release, or a trust letter, signed by a customer who has already given a pledge over goods to a lending banker, and who now wishes to obtain the documents of title for the purpose of obtaining the goods, selling them, and repaying the debt out of the proceeds. *See also* TRUST LETTER.

letter of introduction. A letter addressed by banks, business houses or mercantile concerns to their agents or correspondents abroad, formally presenting the bearer of the letter for their favourable consideration. A customer of a bank travelling abroad or emigrating will find such a letter a considerable help and may through its agency obtain assistance with the purpose of one visit (such as identifying markets or learning local conditions).

letter of licence. A letter embodying an agreement by the creditors of a defaulting and insolvent debtor that they will for a certain time permit the debtor to continue business without taking legal steps against him or her.

letter of lien. *See* LIEN LETTER.

letter of regret. A letter sent, by a company which has made an issue of shares, to an unsuccessful applicant for an allotment.

letter of renunciation. A letter by which the allottee of shares gives up entitlement of shares in favour of some other person. Such a form of renunciation is often printed on the back of an allotment letter.

letter of rights. *See* RIGHTS LETTER.

letter of set-off. *See* LIEN LETTER.

letter of trust. *See* LETTER OF HYPOTHECATION.

letter of weakness. A statement issued by an accountant of a business client, whose accounts have been audited by the accountant, detailing the accounting procedures that are weak or lack security and recommending how matters may be improved.

letters of administration. The document issued by a probate registry to a person who will act in administering the estate of a deceased person who has died intestate. The Letters of Administration are the official authority for the administrator to proceed. An administrator will also be appointed if the deceased left a will but named no executor therein, or where the deceased left a will naming an executor but the person named died before the testator, or refused to act, or was unfit to undertake the duty. If a will exists, the estate will be administered in accordance with its terms.

letters patent. A grant from the Crown, under the seal of the State, granting some property privilege or authority, or conferring the exclusive right to use a design or an invention.

letters requisitory, letters rogatory. A document requesting the court of another country to procure evidence on behalf of the country issuing the request.

leverage. An American term for gearing. *See* GEARING.

leveraged buy-out. *See* BUY-OUT.

leverage fund. An investment or unit trust of a particularly speculative nature. For its investments it uses not only its own money but also other capital such as bank overdrafts or loans. As these last, and the interest charges which they attract, are fixed, losses and gains rebound with increased effect on the fortunes of the trust.

levy of execution. An execution against a debtor by seizure of the debtor's goods under process in an action in any court. A judgment creditor may obtain a writ of *fieri facias* under which the debtor's stock or property may be forcibly seized and auctioned off to raise money to pay the debt. The sheriff is the officer of the court responsible for the proper execution of this remedy. If the goods are sold, or have been held by the sheriff for twenty-one days, the levy of execution is an act of bankruptcy.

lex loci. The law of the place.

lex non scripta. The unwritten law, common law.

lex scripta. The written law.

liabilities. The debts of a person, an estate or a company; the total of the liabilities side of a balance sheet. *See also* CURRENT LIABILITIES; LONG TERM LIABILITIES.

liability. The state of being liable; that for which one is liable; a debt, a pecuniary liability. *See also* LIMITED LIABILITY.

liability swap. A swap based on a liability, e.g. a bank loan, a bond issue, etc. It is a method of restructuring an existing debt or to gain access to another market. The borrower can also lock in the gain on a foreign currency borrowing.

libel. A defamatory statement published in a permanent form, usually writing or printing, but including also a recording; inclusion in the sound track of a film, or radio or television broadcasts. *See* DEFAMATION.

libor. *See* INTERNATIONAL STERLING MARKET.

library. An organised collection of information which is available for study and information. A bank computer centre will have a library of disks containing information and balances of customer's accounts, which are amended as necessary. Many banks also maintain cheque book libraries, from which cheque books are issued, as requested by customers.

licence. Authority, leave, permission, consent granted by a constituted authority for the carrying out of some act or trade. Where imports are controlled by a system of quotas, exporters are issued with licences which specify the amounts allotted to them, In the UK all institutions concerned with consumer credit services, including banks and finance houses, require a licence issued by the Director-General of Fair Trading. Such a licence will normally be renewed every three years, but can be varied or cancelled altogether if the licensee does not comply with its conditions.

licence to assign. A landlord may be content to lease land to a lessee but may not be ready to allow the lessee to underlease or sub-let the property, thus bringing on to the lessor's land someone of whom the landlord may not approve. A lease therefore commonly includes a clause that the lessee may not assign, demise, sub-let or otherwise deal with the property without the permission or licence of the lessor. However, it is provided that a licence to sub-demise by way of mortgage shall not be unreasonably refused.

licenced dealer in securities. One who is permitted by a Self-Regulating Organisation (set up within the framework of the Financial Services Act 1986) to purchase and sell securities to clients.

licenced deposit taker. A term brought in by the Banking Act, 1979. It was used to denote those financial institutions that could accept deposits – as defined by the Act, but were not able, unless permission had been granted, to use the word 'bank' 'banker' or 'banking' in its name. Since the introduction of the Banking Act, 1987, the distinction between a licenced deposit taker and a bank has disappeared.

licensee. One who has been granted by

a constituted authority the right to perform some act which would otherwise have been restricted or unlawful, e.g. to produce a play, to marry, to publish a book, to carry on a business (especially that of a licensed victualler selling wines, spirits, beers, etc.); a person let into occupation of land. *See* TENANCY AT WILL.

lien. The right to retain property belonging to another until a debt due from the owner of the property to the possessor of the property is paid. The ownership of the property is left undisturbed – that is, the borrower continues as owner, but the lender has possession. In general the lender has no right to sell the property. *See also* BANKER'S LIEN; GENERAL LIEN; MARITIME LIEN; PARTICULAR LIEN; POSSESSORY LIEN; UNPAID SELLER'S LIEN; WAREHOUSEKEEPER'S LIEN.

lien letter. Where a customer's credit balance is held as security for his or her advance on another account, the customer should sign an agreement to this effect, which is called a lien letter or a *Letter of Set-Off*. The letter agrees that the credit balance shall not be reduced below a certain figure (that of the debt) and that the banker may combine the accounts without notice.

life. Animate existence, the period of such existence, any specified portion of a person's existence; the average period which a person of a given age may expect to live; a person considered as object of a policy of insurance.

life annuity. A sum of money paid yearly during the portion of a person's life from a specified age to death.

life assurance. A contract by which the insurer/assurer undertakes to pay the person for whose benefit the cover is effected, or to the personal representatives of that person, a certain sum of money on the happening of a given event, or on the death of the person whose life is assured. *See* ENDOWMENT POLICY; TERM POLICY; UNIT-LINKED POLICY; WHOLE LIFE POLICY; 'WITH PROFITS' POLICY..

life-belt. Security for a debt.

Lifeboat Committee Support Group. A rescue operation organised by the Bank of England in 1974 when many of the so-called 'secondary' banks were faced with liquidation. The crisis of confidence was so bad that it was thought that it might spread to the clearing banks, accepting houses and discount houses. Accordingly the sum required to support the ailing banks – £1.200 million – was duly advanced and is thought to have been found by the lifeboat banks in these proportions:

Barclays	£300m
National Westminster	£300m
Midland	£225m
Lloyds	£150m
Bank of England	£120m
Williams & Glyn's, Coutts and the Scottish banks	£105m
	£1,200m

The lifeboat operation was originally expected to last for six months, but it has turned out that several years have been required. The bulk of the security was in the depressed property market, which was slow to recover. It was therefore necessary to divide the secondary banks into: those which had some chance of recovery, so meriting continued support; those which might be taken over; and the others which could be abandoned to liquidation. At the time of writing there are still a few companies in the lifeboat. The Lifeboat Committee is technically known as the 'Support Group'.

life certificate. *See* CERTIFICATE OF EXISTENCE.

life insurance. *See* LIFE ASSURANCE.

life interest. Interest in an estate or business which continues during one's life, or sometimes during the life of another, but which cannot be bequeathed by will.

life policy. A document containing the particulars and conditions of the contract by which the assurance company, in return for a premium, undertakes to pay to the assured or the personal representatives or assigns of the assured a certain sum of money on the happening of a specified event or upon the death of the life assured. *See also* POLICY.

life rent. A rent which one is legally entitled to receive during one's lifetime.

life table. A table of statistics, used by assurance companies, which estimate the expectation of life of persons at different ages.

life tenant. One who has a life interest in an estate.

LIFFE. *See* LONDON INTERNATIONAL FINANCIAL FUTURES EXCHANGE.

LIFO. *See* LAST IN FIRST OUT.

lighter aboard ship vessel (LASH). A vessel transporting a number of heavy barges, loaded with goods, which it releases in the estuary of a foreign river so that the barges may make their way in sheltered waters to the port. This advanced conception received a setback when the sophisticated German ship *Müchen* with lighters aboard vanished in the Atlantic during a hurricane in December 1978, giving rise to insurance claims of £40 million; no trace of her was ever discovered.

limit. 1. The figure to which a customer may overdraw; 2. In the *inter-bank market,* the figure which limits the amount of deposits which can be left with any one bank at any time. Such limits are roughly based on the figure of capital and reserves of the borrowing bank. 3. On the *Stock Exchange,* a fixed price quoted to the broker by a client above which the broker is not to buy, or below which to sell.

limitation. The act of restricting, the state of being limited or confined, qualification; a definite statutory time-limit within which an action must be brought; in land law, a form of words

creating an estate and denoting its extent by specifying the event upon which it is to commence and the time for which it is to endure.

limitation of action. To encourage litigants to bring their actions promptly, it is provided that actions founded upon a simple contract must be brought within six years after the accrual of the cause of action; actions founded upon a special contract must be brought within twelve years after the accrual of the cause of action. Any acknowledgment in writing of the debt, or any part payment, will operate to restart the running of the statutory period, but the mere debiting of quarterly or half-yearly interest by the banker will not be sufficient to have this effect. Although an action may become statute-barred it still exists and recourse can still be had against any security held (except in the case of land).

limited by guarantee. The liability of company members for the debts of a company is limited to the amount they guarantee to pay in the event of the company's being wound up. Where such a company has a share capital the Companies Act, 1980 permits it to continue, but lays down that no such companies may be created in future.

limited by shares. The liability of company shareholders for the debts of a company is limited to the amount of their shareholding (provided that the shares are fully paid). If the value of a shareholding drops to nothing, this is the maximum loss which the shareholders can suffer.

limited company. A form of business organisation legally recognised as having an existence separate and apart from its shareholders or directors. The liability of the shareholders for the debts contracted by the company is limited, either to the amount which they have guaranteed, or to the nominal amount of their shareholding. The Companies Act, 1985 defined the

various types of company (*see* COM-
PANY LIMITED BY GUARANTEE, PRI-
VATE COMPANY, PUBLIC COMPANY).
The Act defines public and private
companies, deals with their regulation
and classification, specifies the method
by which newly formed companies
shall be registered, and requires the re-
registration of all existing companies.
It applies to all forms of company
which can be formed in Great Britain,
but the emphasis is on public companies, and private companies must be
regarded as a residual category. Any
company, regardless of type, can now
be formed by any two people who
subscribe to the Memorandum of
Association (*q.v.*). All companies
whose names end merely with the
world 'Limited' will be taken to be
private companies. Public companies
will end with the description 'Public
Limited Company' or its abbreviation
PLC. (In the case of companies registered in Wales the title *Cyfyngedig* is
allowed as an alternative.)

limited garnishee order. *See* GARNIS-
HEE ORDER.

limited liability. The limitation of the
liability of the shareholders of a company for the debts of the company to
the nominal amount of the shares they
hold or to the amount they have
guaranteed.

limited owner. A tenant for life who
pays capital transfer tax in respect of
the estate out of which his or her life
estate is carved.

limited owner's charge. *See* LAND
CHARGES REGISTER.

limited partner. A partner whose liability is limited to the amount of capital
contributed and who does not take
part in the management of the firm.
The limited partner cannot draw cheques on the firm's banking account,
and cannot bind the firm by his or her
actions. The limited partner's rights
are to inspect the books (but not the
firm's bank statement without the
consent of the other partners) and to
give advice to the general partners.

limited partnership. A partnership
consisting of one or more limited
partners, whose liability is limited to
the amount of capital invested in the
firm, and one or more general
partners, who are fully liable for the
firm's debts.

line of credit. A sum of money available for a debtor to draw upon as long
as the creditor uses it to obtain goods
or services from his or her creditor;
bank accommodation available to a
customer as long as it is used for
agreed purposes and as long as the
customer maintains the account with
the lending bank. In the international
trading sense, a line of credit may be
arranged where a buyer wishes to
place a number of contracts which
may not all be related to a single
project and cannot therefore be practically concluded at the outset. In such
cases a line of credit covers multiple
contracts, is operated on a buyer credit
basis, and covers contracts placed over
a twelve-month period.

liner bill of lading. A bill of lading
issued by a shipping line operating
liners following a predetermined route
which has reserved berths, as opposed
to a tramp steamer which picks up
cargoes wherever it can.

linked transaction. A transaction
entered into by a debtor or hirer, or
relative, with another party in relation
to a principal agreement (of which it
does not form part) and 1. the transaction is entered into in compliance with
a term of the principal agreement; or
2. the principal agreement is a debtor-
creditor-supplier agreement; or 3. the
other party is the creditor or owner or
an associate, or a person who is
represented by a credit-broker who is
also connected with the principal
agreement, or a person who knows
that the principal agreement has been
or might be made. Whichever of these

persons it may be, such person must have initiated the transaction by suggesting it to the debtor or hirer or his or her relative, who in turn must be motivated to enter into the transaction either 1. to induce the creditor or owner to enter into the principal agreement or 2. for another purpose related to the principal agreement, or 3. where the principal agreement is a restricted-use credit agreement, for a purpose related to a transaction financed by the principal agreement. (A simplified paraphrase of s. 19 of the Consumer Credit Act, 1974.) An example of a linked transaction would be where a bank has been introduced by a supplier of goods or services to a prospective purchaser, being the bank's customer, and has subsequently financed an arrangement by that customer to purchase goods or services from that supplier.

liquid. Readily convertible in to cash.

liquid assets. Cash and assets easily convertible into cash; e.g. in a manufacturing company – stock, sundry debtors; in a bank – balances with other banks, money at call and short notice with a maximum maturity of seven days. Treasury Bills, certificates of deposit and bills discounted.

liquidated damages. A sum of money agreed as payable in the case of a breach of contract and written into it as a term.

liquidation. A company goes into liquidation at the moment it passes a resolution for voluntary winding up, or when the court makes an order for the winding up under s. 124(5) Insolvency Act, 1986.

liquidator. A person who is an insolvency practitioner appointed by the court or by the creditors of a company, or by the members of a company to get in what is owed to the company, to take charge of the assets and turn them into money, to pay the company's debts, and then, if there is anything

left, to distribute it amongst the members in proportion to their shareholdings. A banker asked to open an account for the liquidator in a compulsory liquidation should ask to see the court order appointing him or her, together with the evidence of the sanction of the Department of Trade for the banker to maintain a banking account at a bank other than the Bank of England. In the other two cases a liquidator may bank wherever he or she pleases. The banker should see, as evidence of the appointment, the creditors' resolution in the first case, or a certified copy of it, and the members' resolution in the second.

liquid capital. Cash balances and other assets easily converted into cash.

liquid deficiency. The excess of current liabilities over current assets.

liquidity. An immediate capacity to meet one's financial commitments. The degree of liquidity depends upon the relationship between a company's cash assets plus those assets which can be quickly turned into cash, and the liabilities awaiting payment; an ability to turn certain assets into the form of cash.

liquidity ratio. The relationship between those assets of the bank which are in money, or can very quickly be turned into money, and the total balances which the customers of the bank have on their banking accounts (e.g. liquid assets to deposits). Before September 1971, banks in the UK maintained a liquidity ratio of 28 per cent as a minimum, but thereafter the place of this ratio was taken by a reserve asset ratio which was fixed at a minimum of $12\frac{1}{2}$ per cent of total eligible liabilities. The requirement that banks should maintain a fixed figure as a liquidity ratio (which had been reduced to 10 per cent in January 1981) was discontinued in August 1981. The banks are since then required to hold prescribed averages of liquid assets. *See* CONTROL OF THE MONEY SUPPLY.

listed company. A company whose shares are listed on the London Stock Exchange: formerly referred to as a quoted company. The name was changed to avoid confusion; 'listed' is what the Stock Exchange allows the shares to be, 'quotation' is the price at which the market makers say they will deal.

listed investments. Formerly known as 'quoted investments', listed investments are the shares of those public companies which have satisfied the exacting requirements of the Stock Exchange Quotations Committee as to the standing and reliability of the company, and have been granted a quotation on the Stock Exchange Official Daily List.

listed stocks. Stocks and shares dealt with on the Stock Exchange.

listing. Quotation on a stock exchange.

list of members. The list of shareholders of a company as at a given date. This is a return that must be submitted to the Registrar of Companies annually.

living trust. A settlement of assets on named beneficiaries in either revocable or irrevocable form by a settlor who still retains the use and benefit of the money and/or property composing the *corpus* of the trust, but subject to the discretion and tolerance of the legal owners, namely the trustees. It is a device which has flourished in the USA, but as yet has little or no counterpart in this country. It offers both flexibility, because the terms of the trust can be varied according to circumstances, and yet certainty, in that the settlor can see the working of the machinery of the trust whilst living, thus being able to settle any ambiguities which may arise as to his or her intentions under the trust.

Lloyd's. An association of London underwriters, first engaged in the marine insurance business at the end of the seventeenth century, and now an international market for almost any type of insurance. The word is also used to refer to a society, incorporated under Act of Parliament in 1871, and known as the Corporation of Lloyd's, which provides the premises, shipping information services, administrative staff and other facilities by which the market is able to carry on its business.

Lloyd's List. A daily newspaper published by Lloyd's containing shipping, insurance, air and general commercial news, together with reports of the latest shipping movements received and casualty reports – ships and cargoes damaged or sunk.

Lloyd's policy. A policy of marine insurance written by Lloyd's underwriters and sealed by the Corporation.

Lloyd's Register of Shipping. An annual alphabetical list of all merchant ships of any nationality of 100 tons and over, published by a society for the purpose of surveying and classifying ships in order to give an independent opinion as to a ship's seaworthiness and reliability for employment or insurance purposes. The Committee of the society grants certificates after periodical examinations of vessels. Those vessels with the highest standard of efficiency are classed. A.1. A publication – *Lloyd's Register of British & Foreign Shipping* – containing particulars of all vessels afloat of 100 tons upwards, is revised and reissued annually.

loading. An element in the premium of an assurance policy to cover the expenses of management; an increase in the charges passed to the debit of a customer's banking account to reflect some exceptional service given or some exceptional difficulty encountered in the maintenance or supervision of the account.

loan. The act of lending (money); a banking account where upon approval a loan account is opened in the customer's name, the sum being made available by transfer from the loan account to the customer's current account, whence the customer may draw sums out. The loan is to be reduced at agreed intervals by an instalment taken from the current account. Loan interest is charged quarterly or half-yearly on the amount of the loan outstanding and debited to the current account. *See also* BACK-TO-BACK LOAN; BUSINESS DEVELOPMENT LOAN; FARM DEVELOPMENT LOAN; LAND IMPROVEMENTS COMPANY; LONG-TERM LOAN; PERSONAL LOAN; SHORT-TERM LOAN; SUBORDINATED LOAN; SYNDICATED LOAN; TRANSACTION LOANS.

loan application form. A form drawn up by a bank for the use of a customer who wishes to make a formal request for a loan. It will incorporate the necessary information required by the bank and will if necessary conform with the requirements of the Consumer Credit Act, 1974. It may, if necessary, show a record of all items given to the bank as security for the loan.

loanback. An arrangement by which self-employed people, or people not in pensionable employment, who are paying into a personal pension plan run by an insurance company, can borrow before retirement some of the money which would normally be payable after retirement. The insurance company hives off part of the policyholder's pension entitlement, which the policyholder has to repay on retirement. Loanback agreements do not call for a direct loan from the pension fund (which would be contrary to law), nor can the pension fund be used as security for the loan. The policyholder is therefore obliged to find some other acceptable security, such as shares or residential property, against the loan. The plan is not universally recommended. The policyholder has to pay management charges and commercial rates of inter-

est, all of which are added to the hived-off fund, and all of which have to be repaid on the retirement of the policyholder. Indeed, if the policyholder does not pay interest on the loan annually, but allows it to accumulate instead he or she may have to face a situation where the original debt, plus the accumulated interest, is greater than the permitted maximum amount of cash that can be withdrawn from the pension at the time of retirement. Then the policyholder will have to find the difference. This might mean selling assets, or even, in extreme cases, the home which was pledged on the loan. Of course, the rest of the policyholder's pension remains intact – other than the part commuted for cash.

loan capital. That part of the capital of a company which has been derived from outside loans and is so described in the balance sheet.

loans guarantee scheme. *See* SMALL FIRMS LOAN GUARANTEE SCHEME.

Loans Bureau of the Chartered Institute of Public Finance & Accountancy. *See under* LOCAL AUTHORITY BONDS.

loan rate. The rate of interest that will be charged on the loan. It is usual to state the percentage above the bank's own base rate that will be charged and the minimum rate. For example '3 per cent above base rate, minimum 10 per cent'.

loan stock. An acknowledgment of long-term borrowing on which interest is paid – it may be redeemed or issued for a specified period; an alternative name for debentures. Loan stock is 1. unsecured; 2. secured by a floating charge on the company's assets; or 3. secured by a fixed charge on certain assets (usually property). The interest rate is fixed to final maturity and the stock usually has a term of at least fifteen years. It is set up by a trust deed under which the rights of the stockholders are protected, and which specifies certain restrictions to which the company has agreed to conform. A trustee is appointed to look after the holder's interests.

loans to directors. Section 330 – 339 of the Companies Act, 1985 lays down stringent rules controlling the loans made by companies to their directors. While s. 330 states in general terms that it is illegal for a company or its holding company to lend money to a director or enter into a guarantee or provide any security in connection with a loan to a director or shadow director, the Act continues to give some exceptions to this section. For example, in s. 332, a loan to a director of up to a total of a maximum of £1,000 (a quasi loan) is permissible, if the sum is to be repaid within two months. Taking the matter further, s. 334 states: 'Without prejudice to any other provisions of ss. 332 to 338, paragraph (a) of s. 330(2) does not prohibit a company from making a loan to a director of the company or of its holding company if the aggregate of the relevant amounts does not exceed £2,500'. Further, s. 335, permits a company to enter into minor transactions if the relevant amounts do not exceed £5,000. In this case it is stated in s. 335(2a) that the transaction entered into by the company must (a) be in the ordinary course of business and (b) the value of the transaction is not greater, and the terms on which it is entered into are no more favourable, than that or those which it is reasonable to expect the company to have offered to, or in respect of, a person of the same financial standing but unconnected with the company. For a director who has to incur expenses in order to perform his or her proper duties, providing the matter has had the approval of a general meeting and the liability is discharged within six months a loan of up to £10,000 may be granted. Section 338(6) does not prevent a company from making a loan to

one of its directors for the purchase of a house which will be the director's main residence, or improving the main residence, or substitution of a loan made by any other person, providing such loans are ordinarily made by the company to its employees on terms no less favourable that those on which the transaction in question is made and the aggregate of the relevant amounts does not exceed £50,000. Finally a prohibition to s. 330 is contained in s. 338 (1) and (2) which permits a 'money lending company' to make loans, quasi loans and give guarantees, providing the loans so granted are no greater or more favourable than those offered to or in respect of a person of the same financial standing but unconnected with the company, on the condition that the loan is less than £50,000 unless the money lending company is a recognised bank.

lobby. The main banking room of a bank. The area where customers will transact their business. It is usual for customers to go to the cashiers for withdrawal and deposits, but it is common these days to see other members of the staff sitting at desks in the customer areas, so that customers and others may have easy access to staff for the provision of other services.

lobby banking. A description of the system, introduced in this country in 1979, whereby a plastic card gives customers access outside banking hours to a lobby area where they may make deposits and withdrawals *via* teller machines, check their balances, and order cheque books.

local acceptance. *See* QUALIFIED ACCEPTANCE.

local authority. A general name for county councils, boards, municipalities or elected representatives, responsible for administration by local government; a decentralisation from central government. The Local Government Act, 1972, which took effect on 1 April 1974, divided Great

Britain (excluding Greater London) into metropolitan counties or districts, or non-metropolitan counties or districts, represented by local authorities in England, Wales and Scotland. Parish and community councils are also covered by the Act and are regarded as local authorities. Bank accounts of county councils must be in the name of the council, or in the name of the treasurer. In the latter case the name of the treasurer must be qualifed by the description 'Treasurer of the _____ County Council'. A resolution of the council must be obtained to the effect that the treasurer is authorised to maintain the account(s) at the particular branch, together with the instructions as to the way in which cheques are to be signed. Bank accounts of district councils are to be maintained in the name of the council. Parish and community council accounts are similarly to be maintained in the name of the council, cheques being signed by two council members. In each case signing instructions must be covered by a resolution of the appropriate council. Local authorities may keep as many separate accounts as they wish. *Borrowing powers.* A county or district council has authority under the Act to borrow in order to on-lend to any authority, such as water or harbour authorities. A local authority has authority (provided that the sanction of the Secretary of State is procured) to borrow for any purpose. No sanction other than that of the Act is required for temporary borrowing by loan or overdraft, where the purpose of the advance is to defray expenses pending the receipt of revenue due in the same period as that in which the expenses have to be met, or to defray expenses to be met out of a loan to be raised to meet those expenses. Long-term borrowings may be secured by a mortgage of the rates, but short-term advances are often made unsecured. In all cases

an appropriate borrowing resolution should be obtained from the council, or from the finance committee, and, where the sanction of the appropriate government department is necessary, this must also be obtained. The borrowing of a county council will be taken on the County Fund account. If any accommodation is required on subsidiary accounts the necessary resolution should be formally passed by the finance committee. The Act provides that a person lending money to a local authority shall not be bound to enquire whether the borrowing of the money is or was legal or regular, or whether the money raised was properly applied, and shall not be prejudiced by an illegality or irregularity in the matters aforesaid, or by the misapplication or non-application of any such money. This should afford protection to the lending banker unless it can be shown that, prior to the lending of the money, the banker had notice that the purpose of the proposed borrowing was illegal. A general account of a local authority is available for all purposes, and a credit balance may therefore be set off against a debit balance on any other account. Revenue accounts may also be set off against each other, but a credit balance on a capital account is earmarked for some particular purpose and cannot be set off. Items for safe custody should be lodged in the name of the authority and the bank should be supplied with a sealed copy of the resolution authorising withdrawals by the treasurer or other named individuals.

local authority bonds, local authority loans. All local authorities constantly need to borrow money and for this purpose make various offers and issue various bonds or loans *(see below)*. This is a very active market, and various authorities will offer different rates, on various amounts each week. Up-to-date information is therefore very important to the would-be investor. A list of what is on offer is published each week and is obtainable from the Loans Bureau of the Chartered Institute of Public Finance and Accountancy, 232 Vauxhall Bridge Road, London SW1V 1AU, on receipt of a fee of £2.50.

local authority escalator loans. These are loans for fixed periods of one year or longer where the rate of interest applied changes from time to time during the life of the loan, e.g. on a five-year loan the rate would normally change (either upwards or downwards) on the anniversary date.

local authority lenders' option loans. Such loans are similar to Mutual Option Loans (below) except that only the lender of funds may give notice for repayment.

local authority mutual loans. Loans to a local authority for a period of one year or more with a normal maximum of five years. Such loans will include a clause whereby either the lender or the borrower has the option to give one month's notice of repayment at any time after a specified date, usually eleven months from the commencement of the loan. Mutual loans are secured by a mortgage on the rates and revenues of the authority.

local authority yearling bonds. Introduced in 1964, these Bonds are issued by local authorities in Great Britain and Northern Ireland, and by various water boards and drainage authorities. They are normally issued for periods of one year ('yearlings') and, occasionally, for up to five years. The issue of Bonds is placed weekly on Tuesdays for settlement the following day. Some Bonds are placed directly with discount houses and other financial Institutions. Other issues are handled by stockbrokers and will be quoted on the London Stock Exchange. Bonds are registered securities and delivery is effected by normal

form of transfer. Interest rates are very competitive and they have the supreme virtue of simplicity. All a saver has to do is to get an application form from a local authority and return it with a cheque. There is no fuss: no dealing costs; and no worry about whether or not repayment will be duly effected. The Bank of England carefully controls the total of yearling bonds issued in any one week, and local authorities are limited on the amount they can raise. The total is linked to the size of their debt. An important feature is that they can be purchased by the higher tax payer when five months old on an *ex div.* basis, minus one month's interest, and subsequently sold *cum div.* when they are just short of eleven months old.

local currency. In international trade this indicates the currency of the overseas country with whom the traders are dealing.

local land charges. Commitments to which land may be subject as a result of town and country planning legislation. Under planning law, local authorities have decided upon development plans for their areas, and the details of these plans are to be found in the registers of district, borough and county councils. Here will be found such information as road charges, town planning schemes, demolition orders, and building preservation orders. *See also* LOCAL LAND CHARGES REGISTER.

Local Land Charges Register. Under the Town and Country Planning Acts, 1947–1970, local planning authorities have decided upon development plans for their areas, and the details of these plans are to be found in the registers of district, borough and county councils. Here will be found such information as road charges, town planning schemes, demolition orders and building preservation orders. Where land is mortgaged as security a search on the local land charges registers is made, against the address of the property. Usually it is necessary to send two search forms in respect of each property, one to the county council office and one to the borough council, urban district council, or rural district council, whichever is applicable.

local searches. *See* LOCAL LAND CHARGES REGISTER.

lock-box. A service offered by US Banks to their corporate customers, lock boxes provide for the collection of receivables by the bank on its customer's behalf so that the account may be credited as soon as possible. The company's mail is usually directed to a specified post office box and the bank then assumes responsibility for sorting and processing the payments. The vast size of the US and the large number of domestic banks means that payments often take much longer to process than is common in Europe, particularly if checks are sent through the mail; a lock-box system helps to reduce these delays.

loco. In that place (the name of the place being next mentioned).

locum tenens. One who acts as a lawful substitute in an office, a deputy.

locus classicus. The authoritative passage in a judgment, the *ratio decidendi,* the principal authority.

Lombard Street. A term almost synonymous in London with the money market. It is the centre of the banks' head offices and discount houses. The name comes from the Lombards, a group of Italian merchants and bankers who came to this country from Lombardy in the Middle Ages, bringing their trade of money exchange with them.

London Association for the Protection of Trade. A credit-assessment organisation for the protection of those considering lending money. A country-wide register is maintained giving a list of unsatisfactory customers of hire-purchase companies. Banks who are members of the association can search against the name of any person to whom they are thinking of lending, particularly by way of personal loan.

London Bankers' Clearing House. Now London and Scottish Bankers' Clearing House (LSBCH). *See* CLEARING HOUSE.

London Chamber of Commerce. An association representing the interests of its members in all branches of commerce, particularly domestic and overseas trade, banking, insurance and transport. There are a number of such chambers, The London chamber being the largest. It is an examining body for students in a wide range of commercial subjects, and in conjunction with the Royal Society of Arts organises examinations in similar subjects and in ordinary national certificate and diploma studies for overseas students in foreign centres.

London Chamber of Commerce and Industry Business Registry. A register of business names set up by the London Chamber of Commerce and Industry. The scheme became operational in March 1982 and covers England, Scotland and Wales, replacing the government's Register of Business Names. The registry is administered from the London Chamber's head office at 69/73 Cannon Street, London EC4N 5A, from where all certification and other documentation is issued. It is expected that certain other chambers of commerce will join the scheme and issue certificates and documents in due course. The operation of the registry is to be carried out for the LCCI by Computer Registry Searching Ltd. The registry is fully computerised and will be constantly updated. The major services available are: registration of existing businesses and registration of new businesses including provision of a certificate complying with the 'notice' requirements of the Companies Act, 1981; searches; renewals and translations of certificates into other languages.

London Commodities Exchange. A market in tea, coffee, cocoa, spices and rubber, centred in Mark Lane, London.

London Discount Market. *See* BILL BROKER; DISCOUNT MARKET.

London Foreign Exchange Market. A market for fixing the rates at which foreign money will be bought and sold, consisting of banks authorised by the Bank of England to deal in foreign currencies, and some firms of foreign exchange brokers who act as intermediaries. The market is conducted over the telephone and by telex and cable; good communication facilities are therefore vital. Contracts in spot and forward currency deals are made by word of mouth and confirmed by written contract notes.

London Gazette. *See* GAZETTE.

London Gold Market. A market for fixing the price of gold in London. It consists of five firms dealing in gold bullion. The members meet twice on each working day for trading, the results of which fix the price at the end of the day. The price is expressed in US dollars per fine ounce troy. The daily meetings of the members are known as 'fixings'.

London Inter-Bank Offered Rate (LIBOR). *See* INTER-BANK STERLING MARKET.

London International Financial Futures Exchange (LIFFE). The first financial futures market was formed in Chicago in 1972 dealing in amalgamations of large selections of individual mortgages guaranteed by the Government National Mortgage Association. The growth of this market was so vigorous that other countries have considered a similar operation, tailored to their own particular financial operations. At present the only finan-

cial futures market outside the USA is that in Sydney, which was started in the autumn of 1979. In December of that year there was published a study commissioned by the International Commodities Clearing House, which in turn led in March 1980 to the appointment of a working party to examine the feasibility of such a market in London. As a result operations commenced (from the City's old Royal Exchange) in September 1982. Contracts will be traded in short-term sterling time deposits and Eurodollar short-term interest rates, and in four currencies (sterling, the deutschmark, the yen and the Swiss franc, all in terms of the US dollar). A further option is a contract in sterling twenty-year rates, linked to a notional gilt-edged stock. This will provide a hedge against current trends in long-dated gilts. The clearing house at the centre of these transactions will not only process and match all trades, but will also be a party to every transaction, thus eliminating all credit risk to the users of the market. It will be financially independent of the futures exchange and will enforce financial discipline on its clearing members. It will be under the supervision of the Bank of England, which has reserved the right to intervene in the futures market, just as it does in the money and gilt-edged markets. The four foreign currency contracts may be thought to be already provided for on the existing forward foreign exchange markets that have grown up between banks and companies, but there a forward contract, once entered into, must always be carried out. LIFFE contracts, on the other hand, can be sold on, and thus offer a greater degree of flexibility. The new market, open for four or five hours a day, will operate for most of that time when the US markets are closed, thus affording operators world-wide an additional opportunity to deal. *See also* INTERNA-

TIONAL COMMODITIES CLEARING HOUSE (ICCH); INTERNATIONAL MONEY MARKET (IMM); CHICAGO MERCANTILE EXCHANGE.

London Money Market. The market in London for very short-term loans. The market members are the clearing and other commercial banks, the discount and accepting houses, the London branches of some foreign banks, and the Bank of England as a lender of last resort. The discount houses borrow at call or short notice from the commercial banks, but if they are unable to satisfy their wants in this way can always rely on assistance from the Bank of England at a minimum lending rate. The system represents a method of regulation by the Bank of England of the money supply, in that the commercial banks, if they need their cash supplies replenishing, will call in their loans to the discount houses, thereby ensuring that the latter must resort to the lender of last resort. *See also* BILL BROKER; DISCOUNT MARKET.

London Option Clearing House (LOCH). A special corporation controlled by the Council of the Stock Exchange. With a traded option the buyer and seller each have a contract with the London Option Clearing House and not with each other. Consequently one can trade his or her rights in the market without the consent of the other.

London Stock Exchange. *See* STOCK EXCHANGE.

long. Of great extent in time, far-reaching; in the foreign exchange market, the position of a dealer when his or her purchases of a particular currency exceed sales in that currency.

long bill. A bill having a usance of three months or more.

long end of the market. That part of the money market which deals in long dated government stocks. *See* LONG-TERM LOAN.

long exchange. On the foreign exchanges, bills with a currency of sixty or ninety days or more.

'long firm' fraud. A fraud essentially based on the obtaining of goods on credit, with subsequent sales on the street. When pressed by the suppliers for payment, the operators disappear. A business for this purpose may be set up by one or two operators, dealing in a small way with suppliers who are prepared to dispatch goods on monthly credit terms without seeking references. In other cases an existing business with a respectable name can be taken over, and trading continued on the strength of the former concern's good reputation for as long as this will last: or a 'long firm' may be set up with a name and address very similar to that of a well-known company, with the object of deceiving suppliers.

long hedge. A term used in the London International Financial Futures Market (*q.v.*) which indicates that an investor has *bought* a financial futures contract to enable him or her to offset an adverse change in interest or exchange rates within a specified future period. *See also* SHORT HEDGE.

long hundred. one hundred and twenty.

long rate. A term used to indicate the price in one country at which a long bill, drawn payable in another country, can be bought.

longs. Government stocks with a life of more than fifteen years to redemption date.

long tap. Tap (*q.v.*) having say, fifteen years or more to maturity.

long term liabilities. Liabilities which are not to be repaid for some years, e.g. mortgages, debentures, a company's loan capital. *See also* JOINT ACCOUNT; JOINT AND SEVERAL LIABILITY.

long-term loan. A loan for ten years or more, government stocks issued for a similar period, or for redemption in a certain stated year 'or after', or in perpetuity; irredeemable stock.

loro accounts. Third-party accounts in domestic or foreign currency.

loss leader. The practice of offering goods or a service at under cost price in order to bring in customers, who may then make other purchases so that in total the seller will show a profit; a device for stimulating consumer interest in a wider range.

lost cheque. The person who loses a cheque should at once notify the drawer so that the latter may request the bank to stop payment. The holder of a bill lost before it becomes overdue may apply to the drawer for a duplicate bill, but must, if required, give the drawer an indemnity to protect him or her if the bill should be found again and come into the hands of a third person.

lost deed. An attested copy of a lost deed may be accepted by a purchaser of land, but if no such copy is available a declaration by a person having knowledge of the purport and effect of the deed may be offered.

lost share certificate. A shareholder who has lost a share certificate may apply to the company to issue a duplicate. The company will send the shareholder a form of application, for completion, which has on it an indemnity to be completed by the shareholder's banker.

lot. A distinct portion, collection, or parcel of things offered for sale, especially at auction; a parcel of land; choice or decision by chance drawings, as in the redemption of some stocks, debentures or bearer bonds over a period of years.

lot money. The auctioneer's fee on each lot of goods sold by him or her at a public auction.

low-geared. See GEARING.

lump sum. A total sum, as in a single payment of an insurance, instead of instalments spread over several years; a sum of money paid on retirement as an alternative to instalments of pension or in reduction of such instalments.

M

MO, M1, M2. £M3, M3c, M4, M5.
These represent the money aggregates
as specified by the Bank of England.
See MONEY SUPPLY.

macro-economics. The branch of economics dealing with large totals on a
world or nationwide scale, e.g. gross
national product, total employment
figure, savings and investment aggregate, the government's annual spending figures, etc., and the relationships
between them.

made bill. A bill drawn, negotiated and
indorsed in this country, but payable
abroad.

**magnetic ink character recognition
(MICR).** The coding of information
on vouchers before they are fed into a
computer, so that magnetic characters
embodying the information are eva-
luated by a reading head. This evaluation determines the appropriate
action taken within the computer. In
the UK, characters are at the bottom
of a cheque, are recognisable by a
computer, and signify the national
number of the branch bank, the
number of the cheque, and the
number of the customer's account. As
soon as the cheque is paid back into the
banking system, the collecting bank
will add a further set of magnetic
characters indicating the amount of
the cheque. The computer can then
debit the right amount to the account
of the right customer at the right
branch. *See also* ELECTRONIC DATA
PROCESSING (EDP).

mail transfer. This is often abbreviated
to MT. It is the transfer of funds by a
remitter in one country to a beneficiary in another, using banks as intermediaries. At the request of the
remitter, the remitting bank will authorise the receiving bank either to 1.
advise and pay; 2. pay against identification; or 3. advise and credit, the
person specified in the instruction at a
stated address. Funds can be in either
local currency, the remitter's currency
or a third currency. Settlement of the
remittance is either by a credit to the
account of the receiving bank in the
books of the remitting bank (vostro).
Authorising the receiving bank to
debit the account of the remitting bank
in its books (nostro) or requesting a
bank in another country to debit its
(remitting bank) account and credit
the receiving bank (loro). To identify
an M.T. the remitting letter should be
properly signed and have a reference
number. In countries that are contri-
butors to the SWIFT system, then it is
likely that M.Ts will be sent by this
method. *See* SOCIETY FOR WORLD-
WIDE INTERBANK FINANCIAL TELE-
COMMUNICATION.

maintenance. Means of support; keeping equipment in working order; helping a party in a law suit illegally.

make a market. The provision of the
opportunities to investors to buy and
sell particular investments or securities. The financial institution is willing
and able to act either as a broker or
adviser or both.

maker of promissory note. The person
who writes out a promissory note is
called the 'maker'. By making it the
maker engages that he or she will pay it
according to its tenor, and is precluded
from denying to a holder in due course
the existence of the payee and his or
her then capacity to indorse.

making-up day. On the Stock
Exchange, the first day of the bi-
monthly settlement. Also called Contango Day.

making-up price. On the Stock
Exchange, the price at which stocks
and shares are closed off for the
settlement.

mala fide. In bad faith.

managed bonds. An insurance linked investment spread over fixed interest securities, equities and property shares, the management having the power to vary the proportions of holdings from time to time as they see fit.

managed currency. A currency where the country's government intervenes from time to time, whether to buy or sell, in order to maintain a desired exchange value.

managed funds. Funds provided by an investor to a financial institution, e.g. unit trust, insurance company, etc. for the purpose of that institution investing those funds in companies of their choice, in order to provide for the investor either growth or income.

management. The act of directing, controlling and carrying out the functions of an organiser, promoter or contractor; the conduct and control of a branch bank or department by its manager.

management accounting. The provision of accounting information to managers of a business entity to allow them to formulate policies, plan, control and supervise activities, influence decision making and the presentation of statements and budgets to those whom it is considered have some interest in these facts.

management buy-out. The restructuring of British industry has traditionally proceeded by means of takeover and merger. But the deep recession which has forced so many companies into liquidation has resulted in groups divesting themselves of subsidiaries as part of a slimming process, and very often the managerial element in the subsidiary has headed a group of investors who have purchased the concern and then continued to run it under the same management. In a kind of reverse process to the takeover or merger, therefore, a buy-out by existing management is sometimes a practical pro-

position. It is necessary for the managers to raise some sort of capital by whatever means they can, without which commitment no other investors will come forward. These are likely to be banks, pension funds, insurance companies or investment trusts, and in practice these bodies have been surprisingly co-operative. This is probably because the project to be financed is an established business with a profits record available for inspection, assets which can be charged, and experienced management. See MERGER; TAKE-OVER BID.

management services commission (MSC). The government's training and unemployment placement agency. The MSC runs job centres, youth opportunities training schemes, training programmes for 16–18 year olds, community programmes – temporary work for the long term unemployed, job training schemes, restart and counselling services for the unemployed over six months.

management shares. Shares apportioned to the managers of a company with the intention of giving them a personal stake in the company and thus ensuring their energy, interest and enthusiasm in the business.

management trust. An investment or unit trust where complete discretion as to the investments to be made is given to the managers of the trust.

manager. One in charge of a business, especially a branch of a bank, a department, a theatre or a cinema; one appointed by the Court of Chancery to manage affairs on behalf of creditors; the bank arranging a syndicate for the purpose of lending large sums, which acts as paying agent for interest and capital repayments and supervises the service of the loan by the borrower. See also CO-MANAGER; LEAD MANAGER.

managers' discretionary limits (MDLs). The limits to which a branch manager may commit the bank to lend without reference to higher authority. There may be two figures, one for secured lending and a lower one for unsecured lending. MDLs are personal to managers and do not attach to the branches which they manage.

managing director. A director of a limited company who has the responsibility of controlling the day-to-day activities of the company.

managing trustee. In a trust, the trustee who buys and sells the property comprising the trust to the best advantage of the beneficiaries. There is a sharp distinction between this type of trustee's duties and those of a custodian trustee, and the same person or company may not discharge both functions at once. *See* CUSTODIAN TRUSTEE.

mandamus. An order of the Crown requiring a person, corporation or inferior court to perform a particular duty.

mandate. An official order, command or charge; a judicial command to an officer or a subordinate court; a contract of bailment by which the mandatory undertakes to perform gratuitously a duty regarding property entrusted to him or her; a direction from electors to a representative to undertake certain legislation; an authority in writingl signed by a bank customer, authorising another to sign cheques or conduct banking business on the customer's behalf; the instructions from a customer to his or her bank as to the method of signing on the account signal from a borrower to a bank to lead-manage on issue of securities. *See also* PRINCIPAL'S MANDATE.

mandatory injunction. *See* INJUNCTION.

manifest. A detailed list of a ship's cargo for the scrutiny of Customs officers.

manufacturing account. This account shows the direct cost of the production of goods, starting with the cost of the raw materials used and their transport into the factory, and then listing the three items of expense – fuel, power and labour – which are essential in the manufacture. Where there is a considerable amount of work which has passed from the raw materials stage but has not, by the date of the account, reached the status of finished stock, a further entry, work-in-progress, will be seen. A trading concern which buys goods for re-sale does not, of course, manufacture them, and will not, therefore, keep a manufacturing account.

manuscript signature. A signature written by hand (as opposed to one affixed by rubber stamp).

Mareva injunction. A remedy which may be given by the courts where a case is awaiting hearing and the plaintiff, fearing that the defendant may dispossess himself or herself of some or all assets before the case comes to trial, with the intention of becoming unable to meet the claim if judgment is given against the defendant, applies for an injunction to restrain him or her from doing this. The Court of Appeal has decided that there is inherent in the power to grant such an injunction a power to order the discovery of such documents 'as are just and convenient to ensure that the exercise of the Mareva jurisdiction is effective to achieve its purpose'. Experience has shown, however, that the increasing rate at which plaintiffs in legal proceedings have obtained Mareva injunctions has thrown a considerable strain on the head offices of the big clearing banks, who have the expense and work of searching for a defendant's account at any of its branches. Several banks, therefore, have complained to the High Court about the difficulties which are caused consequent upon the service of the order. Subsequent case law has laid down that a plaintiff should identify each particular account at each particular branch of a bank, which is to be affected by the order. If a bank is required to search for a defendant's account at any of its branches, the plaintiff should undertake to pay the costs of such a search. The order itself should, wherever possible, identify the account sought to be restrained by number and branch. It should define exactly what the bank is required to do and should not require the bank to exercise discretion.

margin. The difference between the selling price and the buying price of a commodity; a deposit of money to safeguard a broker against loss; an allowance made for contingencies; the difference between a bank overdraft or loan and the security deposited by the customer; the difference between the spot price and the forward price of a currency expressed as a premium or a discount; the difference between the rate charged by a bank for overdrafts and the rate allowed for deposit.

marginal. Only just worth doing.

marginal cost. The extra cost of increasing output by one more unit.

marginal relief. Tax relief for a taxpayer who exceeds only slightly a figure which would entitle him to a greater relief of duty.

marginal risk. The loss that may possibly arise on foreign exchange operations if, through the failure of a contracting party, the bank has to 'undo' a transaction, or series of transactions, by buying in or selling out the foreign currency, and the rate has meantime moved against them. This risk is represented by the difference between the total of 'boughts' and the total of 'solds' in each currency and that difference, or the total of several such differences if more than one currency is involved, is termed the 'straddle'. This risk only becomes of serious consequence if the rates tend to fluctuate sharply.

margin stock. 'Margin stock', in the US, means any stock which is registered on a national securities exchange, stock traded over the counter and designated in a listing published periodically by the Federal Reserve Board, a debt security convertible into one of the above, and any warrants or rights and any security issued by an investment company other than a small business investment company licensed under the Small Business Investment Company Act. Bank loans extended for the purpose of financing the purchase or carrying of equity securities that fall within the definition of 'margin stock' are subject to a margin requirement if collateralised by stock; such loans are commonly referred to as 'purpose loans'.

marine insurance. A contract by which underwriters engage to indemnify the owner of a ship, cargo or freight against losses from certain perils or sea risks to which their ship or cargo may be exposed. A marine insurance policy is subject to the provisions of the Marine Insurance Act, 1906. *See also* FLOATING POLICY; MIXED POLICY; NAMED POLICY; OPEN POLICY; TIME POLICY; VALUED POLICY; VOYAGE POLICY.

marine insurance broker. An agent between a shipper wishing to obtain cover on a ship or cargo and the Lloyd's underwriter.

maritime law. The law pertaining to ships and the sea. Originally based upon international customs, the law is now administered in the UK by the Admiralty Court, which has instance jurisdiction, dealing with collisons at sea, and prize jurisdiction, which originated with the seizure of enemy ships in time of war and dealt with the questions of international law in this respect and the allocation of prize money. This jurisdiction, of course, can only occur in wartime. The court rarely sits, for insurers in shipping cases may settle claims without dispute, or, where there is dispute, the parties usually go to arbitration, as being quicker and cheaper.

maritime lien. A right which attaches to a ship and/or its cargo in respect of a liability connected with a voyage of the ship. It is independent of possession and attaches to the ship whether in port or at sea. It may be enforced by the arrest and sale of the ship after legal process in the Admiralty Court.

mark. A visible sign, a character made by one who cannot write, a cross. A person signing cheques in this way, or signing a receipt, should put a cross in the presence of two witnesses to the act of marking, one of whom should add the name of the marksman and the fact that it is his or her mark. *See also* TRADE MARK.

mark down. To reduce prices or a valuation of securities held.

marked abstract. An abstract of title mentions some documents which are necessary to show a clear chain of title, but which are not usually handed to a purchaser, such as probate, marriage certificates and death certificates. Such documents will not be with the deeds, but the abstract will be 'marked' in the margin to show that they were, at the time, examined and found to be correct. Thereafter every subsequent solicitor checking the title is content to rely on the marking, which has been made by the solicitor making the examination, or the solicitor's clerk. *See also* ABSTRACT OF TITLE.

marked cheque. At one time it was customary for a banker to 'mark' a cheque to indicate that its payment when presented was guaranteed. The practice is disliked by bankers who would prefer to issue a banker's draft for an equivalent amount. The modern use of a cheque card has a similar effect to marking up to any amount covered by the card.

marked transfer. *See* CERTIFIED TRANSFER.

market. A public meeting place for the purchase and sale of commodities, a trading-centre; demand; a country or geographical area regarded as a buyer of goods; price or value at a stated time.

marketability. The ease and rapidity with which a security can be sold in the market. That is, converted into cash. This concept is important to bankers when they take an asset – land, stocks and shares, etc. – as security for a loan.

marketable loan. A loan that can be transferred from person to person with ease. Many such loans are in the form of either a bond, certificate, note, etc. The instrument may be transferred by delivery or endorsement and delivery, or from time to time by change or ownership recorded in the books lending institution.

marketable securities. Securities dealt with on the Stock Exchange, or otherwise readily turned into cash. *See also* CERTIFICATE OF DEPOSIT; PARALLEL MARKET.

market capitalisation. The total value of a company by ascertaining the current market price of its shares in the market, then multiplying this amount by the number of shares issued. Although this will give an academic valuation of the company, it should be remembered that the value of shares on the market can fluctuate considerably and that the number of shares purchased and sold in any given period is usually small in comparison with the total number held by shareholders. The valuation of the company by a predator may be quite different from this valuation.

marketing. The distribution of a product from the place where it was made, or from the port of import, to the people who are going to use or consume it; the identification and satisfaction of the needs of the consumer or producer; the management process which controls this sequence, from the identification of the market to the profitable satisfaction of the consumer's demand.

market maker. A bank or securities house undertaking to make a secondary market for Eurobonds either by taking any bonds offered on to its own books or by finding takers for them among or through other banks active in the secondary market. Since the 'Big Bang' and the elimination of jobbers, member companies of the Stock Exchange undertake to make a market in certain ranges of shares i.e. to buy and sell shares on a continuous basis.

market overt. A public market where goods are on open offer. By custom, shops in the City of London form a market overt for articles which are sold in the normal business of such shops; elsewhere the term applies to markets established by grant or prescription. Stolen goods which find their way on to market overt become the property of the buyer in such a market, save only if the original thief is prosecuted to conviction, in which case the title reverts to the original owner. But the sale in 'market overt' must take place between sunrise and sunset for the buyer to obtain a good title. 'Market overt' does not apply to Scotland or Wales.

market price. The value placed on an article by the owner who wishes to sell it.

market report. An account describing the conditions of a market and listing the prices; a communication from a broker to banks and others who have money to invest, whether on their own behalf or on behalf of customers; a description of the previous day's trading on the Stock Exchange in the financial pages of a newspaper; a summary by a marketing manager of the results of market research carried out.

market research. An investigation into what the consumer wants, so that a firm may know what to supply, whether in goods or services, and how to package it.

marking. A Stock Exchange term to describe the prices recorded for business done in any security during the day.

marking names. In the case of an American-type certificate the registered holder commonly signs the form of transfer printed on the back of the certificate and this allows the certificate to pass from hand to hand like a bearer bond, delivery transferring title. Unlike a bearer bond, however, there are no coupons, and the dividend is sent to the registered holder, from whom the owner must claim it. At one time dividends were 'marked' on the back of the certificate when they were paid, and this has given rise to the description of the registered holder as a 'marked name'. A list of firms recognised by the Stock Exchange as good for the purpose of receiving and transmitting dividends has been made: they consist mostly of bankers or members of the Stock Exchange. These are known as '*good marking names*', and the more active shares registered in such marking names are quoted in the Stock Exchange Daily Official List as separate entries from the shares of the same companies registered in 'other names'. Shares registered in good marking names command an appreciably better price than those in other marking names because it is known that there will be no trouble in obtaining the dividend each time it is due.

mark to market. The value of a swap in the books of a financial institution which is the 'agreed value' in its books. Where the mark to market takes into consideration the value of the swap if the institution wishes to sell or transfer the instrument.

mark up. The difference between the purchase price of an article and the selling price. For example, if the cost of a book is £10 and it is customary to 'mark up' the cost by 50 percent, then the cost of the book will be £15. The profit is expressed as a percentage of the cost price.

marry up. To link together; to identify the original query when the answer becomes available (as with a status report); to link a credit item with a debit, or *vice versa*; to sort an item under an appropriate head.

marshal. To dispose in order, to arrange.

marshalling. The act of arranging in a certain order: the application of the principle that a prescribed order will always be observed whatever the method of distribution.

marshalling of assets. An equitable doctrine governing the rights of beneficiaries under a will amongst themselves *vis-à-vis* the creditors of the estate. Where the estate is solvent but there is not enough left over after all the debts have been paid to satisfy all the beneficiaries, some beneficiaries must lose their rights so that creditors are paid in full. The order in which they lose their rights is set out in the Administration of Estates Act, 1925, s. 34(3), and Part Two of the First Sch. to that Act. A beneficiary who loses property through the application of this order may claim to be indemnified out of undisposed property to which another beneficiary in a better position in the order is entitled.

marshalling of securities. An equitable doctrine regulating the position of creditors amongst themselves *vis-à-vis* the debtor. Thus where X mortgages properties A and B to Y, and later grants a second mortgage on B to Z, Z may demand that the claim of Y shall be satisfied as far as possible from property A.

matching. The recognition that the purchase and sale of foreign currency must agree, that is that the buyer/seller who deliberately goes into a long or short position in any currency. Ensuring that the purchase/sale in any market agrees. The recognition that receipts and expenditure in a business

is earned and expended in the particular financial period. A Bank of England term relating to 'matching' of a bank's assets and liabilities in terms of time.

material alteration. On a bill of exchange material alterations are alterations to the date, the sum payable, the time or place of payment, any alteration of the crossing on a cheque and, where a bill has been accepted generally, the addition of a place of payment without the acceptor's assent. If a bill or acceptance is materially altered without the assent of all parties liable on the bill, the bill is avoided except as against a party who has personally made, authorised or assented to the alteration, and subsequent indorsers. It is furthermore provided that, where an alteration is not apparent, a holder in due course, in whose hands the bill is, may avail himself of the bill as if it had not been altered, and may enforce payment of it according to its original tenor.

mate's receipt. A receipt for goods received on board by a ship's mate. A mate's receipt is not a document of title and is purely temporary. It is later exchanged for a bill of lading.

matrimonial home. The house in which a husband and wife live. In spite of the modern view of the equality of the sexes, it is still the duty of the husband to support, his wife, and she has a personal right against her husband to live in the matrimonial home. To gain precedence over purchasers and mortgagees this right must be registered as a Class F land charge, at the Land Charges Department. A husband has a similar right of registration. *See also* LAND CHARGES.

matrix. The place where anything is generated or developed; the centre of an organisational structure.

matrix organisation. A design to keep human or material resources fully employed by deployment in different places or in different ways. Thus, members of a working party or a project team may be temporarily assigned from branches or departments to work under a project manager, who has need of their specialist abilities, but who cannot employ them full-time. Such a project manager could determine the schedules and demands of the project's activities and, in conjunction with the branch or department managers, would determine how and when the members of the team would work with the project manager, and when with their own managers or departmental heads. Also an organisation in which managers report to different superiors functionally, and act as line managers simultaneously.

maturity. The date on which a bill of exchange or a promissory note falls due or becomes legally payable. A bill is due and payable in all cases on the last day of the time of payment fixed by the bill or, if that is a non-business day, on the succeeding business day. Non-business days in the UK, for the purposes of the Bills of Exchange Act, 1882, are 1. Saturday, Sunday, Good Friday, Christmas Day; 2. a bank holiday under the Banking & Financial Dealings Act, 1971; 3. a day appointed by Royal Proclamation as a public fast or thanksgiving day; 4. a day declared by an order under s. 2 of the Banking and Financial Dealings Act, 1971 to be a non-business day.

maturity factoring. See FACTORING.

maturity ladder. A system for categorising the deposits of a bank on the one hand, and evaluating its ability to turn assets into ready cash on the other. Such a system is proposed by the Bank of England in pursuance of its duty of supervising banks in the UK and will, on the information gained from each bank, establish a 'maturity ladder' where each 'rung' will measure the extent to which the bank is mismatched within a given time span. This picture, however, will be used merely as the starting point for a much wider assessment of the particular bank's liquidity position, and considerable emphasis will be placed on the ability and techniques of individual bank managements in managing their own liquidity. See MISMATCHING.

maturity transformation. The use of short-term deposits to finance longer-term loans. The clearing banks have found over the years that the overdraft, nominally repayable on demand, is in practice anything but that, and that a significant number of these advances amounted in fact to medium-term loans. These 'hard core' overdrafts have in recent years been augmented by contractual term loans, which are still largely matched against short-term deposits and now amount to over 40 per cent of the banks' non-personal lending. Some larger loans are backed by term deposits from the wholesale market, but it is clear that the importance of the old adage. 'if you borrow short, don't lend long,' has been considerably diminished. Perhaps it is fair to say that only institutions like banks and building societies can afford sometimes to disregard the maxim, because they have a stable deposit base, and the credit and standing to be able to borrow on the wholesale sterling market, if required.

Maundy Money. Money distributed annually by the Queen's Almoner to poor people on Maundy Thursday, the day before Good Friday. These silver coins of 1p, 2p, 3p and 4p become collectors' pieces.

maximum interest rates. Rates of interest on deposits and loans of US banks are strictly controlled. Regulation Q of the Federal Reserve Board prescribes rates governing the payments of and limitations on the rate of interest which may be paid on demand, savings and time deposits. No member bank of the Federal Reserve

System can directly or indirectly pay any interest on any deposit which is payable on demand. Maximum rates of interest which may be charged on loans are laid down in usury laws which can vary between different states.

maximum load line. *See* PLIMSOLL MARK; DEAD WEIGHT.

McFadden Act. One of the most important pieces of financial legislation ever passed in the US, the McFadden Act of 1927 effectively precludes banks from branching outside their own state. National banks are subject to the laws of individual states which have the power to control the expansion of any bank established within their borders.

mean price. *See* MIDDLE PRICE.

media. Popularly this refers to the television, radio, the press and any means of communication to the public at large. This term can also refer to the source of inputs and outputs to a computer. For example, a cheque is a medium whereby the computer will amend the balance of the drawer's account. Other forms of media are magnetic tape, punched cards, etc.

mediation. Interposition between two parties in order to reconcile them; a method of settling industrial disputes; the achievement of a compromise settlement. A mediator must be approved by both parties to the dispute.

medium sized company. This is defined by the Companies Act, 1985 as one which: (*a*) has a turnover between M£1.4 and M£5.75; (*b*) a balance sheet total between M£0.7 and M£2.8; (*c*) employees range from 50 to 250. A medium sized company is permitted to submit to the Registrar of Companies an abbreviated form of accounts.

medium of exchange. *See* MONEY.

mediums. Government stocks with a life of between five and fifteen years to redemption date.

medium-term credit. Loans for from three to ten years.

meeting of creditors. The Insolvency Act, 1986, has given creditors a certain amount of authority to ensure that the winding up of a company or the estate of a bankrupt is being dealt with in an efficient manner and in their interests. For the winding up of a company the administrator appointed by the court under an administration order must within 3 months give 14 days notice for a meeting of creditors to advise them of the purpose of the administration order and approve or disapprove of part or all of the administrator's proposals. Any modification to the original proposal must be approved by the administrator. (ss. 23 and 24). Where a meeting has been summoned, the meeting if it thinks fit, may establish a creditors' committee to act on behalf of the creditors as prescribed by the act (s. 26). Where a company is being wound up by a creditors' voluntary winding up, then a meeting of creditors must be called within 14 days of the company resolution for its voluntary winding up. The notice of the creditors meeting must contain (*a*) the name and address of the person qualified to act as the insolvency practitioner and; (*b*) the place where on the two days prior to the meeting the list of company creditors is available for inspection (s. 98). Should the winding up of a company take longer than one year, then by s. 105, the liquidator shall at the end of the first year summon a general meeting of the company and a meeting of creditors. At this meeting the liquidator will account for his or her acts and conduct in the winding up process. This will be done for each successive year during the winding up period. Should the winding up of a company be done by the court, then a meeting of the creditors is called by a liquidator nominated by the creditors. In the case of an insolvent debtor where an interim order has been made by the court, the liquidator will summon a meeting of the creditors to decide whether to approve the voluntary arrangements made (ss. 257/8). Section 294: where in the case of any bankruptcy (*a*) the official receiver has not yet summoned, or has decided not to summon, a general meeting of the bankrupt's creditors for the purpose of appointing the trustee; and (*b*) a certificate for the summary administration of the estate is not, for the time being, in force; any creditor of the bankrupt may request the official receiver to summon such a meeting for that purpose. Section 301: subject to certain rules a creditor's committee may be formed to exercise certain functions unless the trustee in bankruptcy is the official receiver, in which case, the functions of the committee will be exercised by the Secretary of State.

meetings, company. *See* ANNUAL GENERAL MEETING; EXTRAORDINARY GENERAL MEETING; STATUTORY MEETING.

members' voluntary winding-up. *See* VOLUNTARY LIQUIDATION.

memorandum. A note or reminder, a brief record; a summary, outline or draft of an agreement.

memorandum of association. The memorandum of a company is a document drawn up by the founder members of the company. It has six parts: 1. the name of the company, with 'Public Limited Company' or its abbreviation PLC, or in appropriate cases the Welsh language equivalent, if it is a public company; or the word 'Limited' if it is a private company, or in appropriate cases the Welsh language equivalent; 2. whether the registered office of the company is to be situated in England or in Wales or in Scotland; 3. the objects of the company; 4. whether the liability of the members is limited; 5. details of the capital structure of the company –

that is, the amount of the share capital and the way in which it is divided into shares; 6. the association clause. To ensure a personal stake in the company, it is provided that every subscriber to the memorandum shall take at least one share, writing opposite to his or her name the number of shares taken. The memorandum regulates the affairs of the company as against the outside world. The objects clause sets out the purposes for which the company was formed and the ways in which it is intended to do business. For an activity stated specifically therein, the company has legal power. Anything else has in the past been *'ultra vires'* the company (beyond its powers). The European law on this subject, however (to which we must now subscribe) is that a contract entered into in good faith by a person dealing with a company should not be set on one side on the ground that it is beyond the powers of the company. The memorandum may be altered if the alteration is for the better carrying on of the company's business, for the sale of part or all of its undertakings, or for amalgamation with some other concern. A special resolution of the company is required to make this change, which does not have retrospective effect.

memorandum of deposit. A form of bank charge over securities, usually stock exchange securities. It contains a number of provisions which may or may not be required in any particular charging of security. The form is normally executed under hand, and should describe the security and state that it is deposited as security. The bank is to have the right to sell the security at any time after failure to repay on demand made by the bank. The security is to be a continuing security and the customer agrees to accept on re-transfer stocks and shares of the same class and denomination as those charged. The customer undertakes to do anything or sign any document which the bank may request in order to allow the bank to perfect their security or assist them in selling it. He or she undertakes to maintain a specified margin of cover if so requested. The form can represent an equitable or legal mortgage as required. Not the least of its purposes is to act as evidence of intention, e.g. when bearer bonds are offered as security, or when title deeds or a registered land certificate is deposited on an equitable basis.

memorandum of interview. A note completed by a manager after an interview with a customer, recording brief details of the business discussed. Such a memorandum may be circulated around senior staff for information and should also be filed with the customer's papers, where it may later prove useful in showing what the intention of the parties was, e.g. for demonstrating that the bank was exercising pressure on the customer to repay. A memorandum may also be completed by a staff controller after interviewing a member of the staff, to be filed with the staff member's record.

memorandum of satisfaction. A notice addressed to and filed with the Registrar of Companies, to the effect that a mortgage or charge has been wholly (or partly) satisfied. The notice is originated by the creditor.

mental illness of customer. The difficulty for a banker is to decide when a customer's mental health is so disturbed that the customer does not know what he or she is doing. This may be presumed when the customer is compulsorily admitted to a hospital on the certificate of two medical practitioners, or when the customer is placed under the guardianship of a local authority or of a person authorised by a local authority. In either of these cases the customer can be regarded by the banker as mentally

incapable, and the banker should stop the account and regard all authorities and mandates as cancelled. But a further possibility is that a customer may voluntarily enter a hospital for mental treatment. The mere entry into hospital is not of itself therefore sufficient justification to stop the account.

mercantile. Pertaining to commerce, relating to buying and selling.

mercantile agent. One having in the customary course of business as an agent, authority to sell goods, to buy goods, to consign goods for sale, or to raise money on the security of goods. *See also* FACTOR.

mercantile law. That part of the common law which deals with the customs and practices of business and commerce (also known as the *Law Merchant*).

merchandise. Commodities bought and sold in home or foreign markets.

merchandise advances. The banker will make merchandise advances only to customers of undoubted integrity with experience in the trade. The banker will usually be willing to make such advances against goods imported on consignment, goods being built up by the customer in anticipation of seasonal requirements, or goods presold to reputable buyers. A margin of cover should be obtained, depending on the type and marketability of the goods, and the banker's valuation of the security should take into account the length of time the goods can be held without deterioration, and the condition and quality of the goods. Advances should be by way of loan, one separate loan for each consignment of goods. In this way the margin to be maintained can be more effectively controlled. The security is obtained when the documents of title come into the bank's possession, or when goods are warehoused in the bank's name (including the case where the warehousekeeper attorns to the bank). *See also* ATTORNMENT; DELIVERY ORDER; TRUST LETTER; WAREHOUSEKEEPER'S CERTIFICATE; WAREHOUSEKEEPER'S WARRANT..

merchandise marks. Marks on the outside of cases, packets, bales, etc., containing goods, especially those being imported or exported. The marks are used for identification purposes and are specified on the bill of lading and insurance policy.

merchant banks. Banks which have developed from the activities of immigrants to Britain during the eighteenth century. These man were originally merchants trading in particular commodities such as wool or cotton, during the course of which they acquired a comprehensive knowledge of the world markets relevant to their trading. They became well known and were asked to accept bills of exchange, so as to make them more readily saleable. As London developed and became the financial centre of the world it attracted representatives of foreign merchanting and financial houses: they brought with them a detailed knowledge of the trading resources and customs of their native countries, together with initiative and shrewd abilities to develop new financial methods to meet growing demands. In particular, they took the lead in raising long-term loans for foreign governments and for companies engaged in major enterprises. The present-day activities of the merchant banks include acceptance, deposit banking, raising of capital, participation in consortia, underwriting, management of clients' funds, advice to companies, management of mergers and take-over bids, dealings in foreign exchange, the issue and placing of shares and debentures, and marine and other insurance business.

merger. The absorption of a smaller estate in a larger one; the combination of industrial or commercial firms. In the case of a bill of exchange, a merger occurs where the acceptor becomes the holder of a bill at or after its maturity in his own right. *See* MANAGEMENT BUY-OUT.

metric system. A decimal system of weights and measurements based on the French metre, at present in use in most countries of the world. There are seven base units: length (metre); mass (kilogram); time (second); electric current (ampere); temperature (kelvin); luminous intensity (candele); amount or substance (mole). The system is being gradually introduced into the UK at the present time.

Michaelmas Day. A quarter day – 29th September.

MICR. *See* MAGNETIC INK CHARACTER RECOGNITION.

microcomputer. *See* COMPUTER.

micro-economics. The branch of economics dealing with unit productions, e.g. single firms, their raw materials, costs and output; or the wages or salary of one man, or the fashioning and sale of one product, etc.

middle price. The price half-way between the two prices quoted in the Stock Exchange Daily Official List; it is used for making valuations for most purposes except for probate *(q.v.)*. Most newspapers publish their own estimate of the middle prices, but they are usually the latest available and may differ from those shown on the Official List next day. Valuation of Stock Exchange securities of a deceased person's estate for probate is effected by taking a figure one-quarter of the difference between the buying and selling prices, and adding it to the buying price ('one-quarter up').

Midsummer Day. A quarter day – 24th June.

milker. One variety of thief specialising in travel cheques. He takes a book of travel cheques from a wallet, handbag, or hotel room, and tears out half-a-dozen cheques from the middle of the book before replacing it. The victim will probably not find out for a little while that any are missing, so the loss will not be reported quickly.

milling. The indenting or ridging transversely of the edge of a coin, to defeat the practice of clipping or shaving a little metal from the edge of the coin, a practice profitable only when the coin was of intrinsic value. The temptation does not exist in the case of cupro-nickel coins; nevertheless the milled edge, which was introduced into the London Mint in the second half of the seventeenth century, continues to be used, because it is customary.

mini-bond. Mini-bonds are single-premium policies which make use of share-exchange techniques, developed for the taxpayer who has a very high income and therefore pays a top rate of tax. The value of the bond is reflected by the value of the underlying assets. An individual taking out a single-premium mini-bond policy does not have to pay the premium in cash. Instead he or she can hand over investments in listed shares and will be credited with their value, less a small management charge taken by the assurance company. This counts as a disposal for capital gains tax (*q.v.*) purposes. The advantage which makes mini-bonds attractive comes from the fact that life assurance companies pay tax on the income from their investments at a maximum rate of 37.5 per cent – considerably lower than the higher rates and investment income surcharge levied on the individual. Thus the assurance company can pass on the benefit to the client. The usual procedure is to time the policy so that it matures after the policy holder has retired, because then the policyholder's income will be comparatively low and thus liability to higher rate tax and the investment income surcharge will be correspondingly lighter.

minicomputer. *See* COMPUTER.

minimum lending rate. Previously known as Bank Rate. The minimum rate at which the Bank of England, acting as lender of last resort, normally lends to members of the discount market against security of Treasury bills, other approved bills, or government stocks with five years or less to maturity. Minimum Lending Rate was suspended in August 1981, its place being taken by a new system whereby the authorities steer interest rates in accordance with an unpublished interest rate band. The most important aspect of the new system of monetary management is the increased importance given to the bill market and hence to the traditional role of the discount houses. Instead of setting an official rate, the Bank will influence rates through open market operations only, which means by the buying and selling of bills. In this way the Bank will cease to exert a direct influence on interest rates, except at the very short end of the market. Interest rates will be free to find their own level in line with economic and financial conditions in the economy. It is the Bank's stated intention to permit more flexibility, and to respond to market rates, rather than to lead them. The effect will be that the Bank will confine its money-market operations simply to smoothing out the daily flow of funds into and out of the banking system. The weekly Treasury Bill issue will be kept to the level required to soak up any surplus expected during the following week, while the Bank will meet any daily cash shortages through the intermediary of the discount houses. Banks will have to pay much more attention to short-term interest rates in determining their own lending rates. MLR will not disappear altogether. The Bank has decided to keep open the option to use MLR in exceptional circumstances and then for a limited period only. The kind of situation envisaged is when a major economic package is announced where interest rates would be an important element in the changes expected. *See also* CONTROL OF THE MONEY SUPPLY.

ministerial trust. A trust where the will or trust deed gives the trustee (s) no particular discretion to vary the investments in the trust, or in the running of it, but calls merely for the exercise of normal prudence and business judgment in carrying out the express terms of the trust; as opposed to a discretionary trust (*q.v.*).

minor. A person under the age of eighteen, formerly described legally as an infant. Money lent to a minor cannot be recovered, even if security is given. All contracts entered into by a minor for the repayment of money lent shall be absolutely void. In Scotland the term refers to a young person between the age of fourteen and eighteen (if a boy) or twelve and eighteen (if a girl). Such young people have a limited contractual capacity. If the minor has a curator and the curator has given consent to a contract entered into by the minor, then such contract is as binding upon the minor as it would be upon an adult, subject only to a right of challenge during the remaining period of minority and/or within four years thereafter, on the grounds that the minor has suffered a substantial injury to his or her interests. This right of challenge is even more leniently applied in cases where the minor has entered into the contract without having the benefit of a curator for advice.

minor interests index. An index in the Land Registry for the registration of a third class of interest, not in land but in equitable interests therein, additional to 1. those which can be registered on the Land Registry; and 2. overriding interests – namely, minor interests. These interests may in some cases be binding on a purchaser if registered, or are equitable interests created under a trust for sale, which will be over-reached on a sale. Minor interests are protected by no-

tices, restrictions, cautions, or inhibitions. A deed of arrangement affecting the land would be protected by lodging a notice. Land held upon trust for sale should have a restriction to make sure that sale moneys are paid to two trustees, or to a trust corporation. A pending action affecting the land would be the subject of a caution; a receiving order, of an inhibition. Any of these except a notice will appear in the charges section of the Land Certificate.

minority shareholder. A shareholder in a company who is one of those who does not support a resolution of the company which is passed by the majority. Where the resolution concerns the voluntary winding-up of the company so that the whole or part of its property may be transferred or sold to another company, a minority shareholder may express dissent in writing, addressed to the liquidator, and leave it at the registered office of the company within seven days of the passing of the resolution. The liquidator will then be obliged either to abstain from carrying the resolution into effect, or to purchase the interest of the minority shareholder at a price to be determined by agreement or by arbitration.

mint. The place where money is coined under governmental supervision; to make by stamping, as of coins; fresh, unused, new. *See also* ROYAL MINT.

mintage. A charge made by a mint for turning bullion into coins; the process of minting coins.

mint par of exchange. A par of exchange between the coins of two countries both using the same metal, e.g. silver. The weight and fineness of one, compared with that of the other, will give the mint par of exchange by reference to the amount of pure metal in each coin.

mint price. The value of the quantity of coins into which a bar of metal can be made.

mint ratio. Where a bimetallic currency is in circulation, the ratio between the values of the two metals.

minute book. A book for recording the business carried through at company meetings.

minutes. The official record of business transacted at a meeting. Minutes of all company meetings are to be entered in books kept for that purpose. They are signed by the chairman of the meeting. They list the date and place of the meeting, name those present, and record all resolutions proposed. They are read over as the first item of business at the next meeting to check their accuracy.

Miras. *See* MORTGAGE INTEREST RELIEF AT SOURCE.

mirror account file. An exact duplicate of an account held in the books of another company/bank. An account held abroad (Nostro), will have a variety of debits and credits passed through it. In the books of the account holder, there will be an account also recording these entries to ensure speedy reconciliation and management information.

misappropriation. The conversion of funds by an employee or other person for improper or dishonest purposes, e.g. the use of employer's funds to pay the individual's own expenses.

mismatching. Using assets in one currency to finance advances in another currency (leading to a risk of loss flowing from adverse movements of exchange rates), or using short-term deposits to finance longer-term lending. *See* MATURITY TRANSFORMATION.

misrepresentation. A false or incorrect representation; facts reported inaccurately. *See also* FRAUDULENT MISREPRESENTATION; INNOCENT MISREPRESENTATION.

mis-sort. In banking terms this means that an item has been sorted into the wrong compartment/file, so that there could either be a difference in the book-keeping or an error of commission/principle. Should a cheque or credit be mis-sorted for any reason, then that item would be forwarded to the bank/branch concerned after notifying the remitter of the occurrence.

mixed economy. An economic system planned and directed partly by the State, and partly by private enterprise.

mixed policy. A marine policy combining voyage and time insurance, in that a ship is insured from one certain place to another over a certain period of time.

mobile bank. A motorised caravan fitted out as a small bank, which can tour outlying districts on one or more days per week, or go to fairs or agricultural shows.

modifying agreement. A regulated agreement which varies or supplements an earlier agreement. A modifying agreement revokes the earlier agreement, but its provisions reproduce the combined effect of the two agreements.

monetarism. The view that inflation is caused principally by excessive supply of money by the government. Monetarists believe that this extra money results in a rise in prices as the value of money falls because there is more of it about.

monetary. Concerning money or the coinage.

monetary base. The 'cash base' of the banking system. There are a number of definitions. All include the commercial banks/holdings of notes and coin and balances at the Bank of England; some definitions also include notes and coin in circulation with the public and other liabilities of the Bank of England. Sometimes mooted as a possible alternative way of controlling the amount of money in the country, the monetary base refers to the relationship between a bank's cash base (usually defined as the bank's balance at the Bank of England plus notes and coin in the tills) and the level of the bank's deposits. If such a system of control were ever enforced, it would take the form of requiring all banks to maintain a minimum ratio according to their monetary bases. Control over the money supply would then be exercised by controlling the cash base. The essence of this control would be that, at least in theory, the supply of money is controlled more or less directly, rather than by trying to influence the demand for money by manipulating the level of the interest rate.

monetary economy. An economic system in which exchange is effected by means of money, as opposed to barter.

monetary policy. The regulation by the government of a country of the supply and control of money so as to promote the achievement of national ends, such as the maintenance of full employment, a progressive rate of national economic growth, the restraint of inflation, and the stability of the national currency on the foreign exchanges.

monetary reform. The introduction of a new currency after a period of hyperinflation, or the introduction of a new decimal currency unit.

monetary system. The internal and external provisions of a government for managing the media of exchange. Internally it refers to such things as whether notes are convertible, what is legal tender, whether coins are of intrinsic or conventional value. Externally it refers to the type of exchange adopted, such as the floating pound, a managed currency, exchange rates free to fluctuate within certain limits, whether these are discriminatory rates for specialised use such as property or investment currency, etc.

monetary union. An agreement between countries to maintain a fixed exchange rate between their currencies.

monetary unit. The standard unit of a country's currency.

monetary working capital adjustment. See INFLATION ACCOUNTING.

money. Coin or other material used as a medium of exchange; banknotes, bills, promissory notes and other documents representing coin; wealth, property regarded as convertible into coin; coins of a particular country or denomination; receipts or payments. See also NEAR (OR QUASI-) MONEY; PAPER MONEY; READY MONEY.

money at call and short notice. Bank advances to stockbrokers, jobbers and bill brokers, repayable on demand ('at call') or at up to seven or fourteen days ('at short notice'). This item represents the bank's most liquid item, after cash.

money broker. A firm in the City of London whose function it is – in the money markets – to marry borrower to lender, or buyer to seller. For this function they will be paid a commission.

moneylender. A person whose business it is to lend money at interest; a person whose business was governed by the Moneylenders Acts.

money lent and lodged. A comparison between the total advances made by a bank, whether by way of overdrafts, loans, discounts, etc., and the total of money deposited with it, whether by way of current, deposit, or savings accounts, or by borrowing from the inter-bank market. This comparison gives the bank's lending ratio.

money market. A market consisting of financial institutions and dealers in money and credit who either have money to lend, or want to borrow money. In the UK the London Money Market is composed of the Bank of England, the deposit banks, the discount houses and the accepting houses.

money of account. A denomination (e.g. the guinea) not actually coined, but used for convenience in keeping accounts.

money shops. Quasi-banks operated by finance companies and some American banks in offices in the High Streets of many towns, in London and the provinces. They are designed to be comfortable, informal and to appeal to the private individual. The accent is on lending, and home improvement and mortgage loans, life and general insurance facilities and investment advice are provided. Money shops are open from 9–5 or 5.30, six days a week. In some cases current and deposit account facilities are offered together with other retail banking services. It remains to be seen whether the new banks can build up a viable deposit base and a solid clientele.

money supply. Money supply and monetary policy commences with the simple assumption that there is a connection between the rate of growth in the money supply and the rate at which prices rise – inflation. The government in its 1981 Green Paper stated that while the money supply and prices may diverge in the short term, they do not in the longer term. It therefore set itself the responsibility of controlling inflation by controlling the money supply. The relationship between the money supply and inflation has never been straightforward and the various monetary targets and measurements of the money supply have from time to time been called into question. Over recent decades, the monetary targets have been revised upwards several times, so that as recently as March 1987 targets have been set and in May 1987 a new set of money aggregates were introduced, they are: $M0$ = Notes and coin in circulation with the public, in bank tills and in banks' current accounts at the Bank of England; $M1$ = Notes and coin in circulation with the public, plus private sector sterling sight bank deposits, both interest and non interest bearing (includes current account, call money and overnight money held in the UK banking sector); $M3$ = M1 plus private sector sterling time bank deposits and private sector holdings of sterling bank certificates of deposit; $M4$ = M3 plus private sector holdings of building society shares, deposits and sterling certificates of deposits *less* building societies holdings of bank deposits and bank certificates of deposits, notes and coin; $M5$ = M4 plus private sector (excluding building societies) holdings of money market instruments (Bank bills, Treasury Bills, Bank deposits) certificates of tax deposit and national savings instruments (excluding national saving certificates, SAYE and other long term deposits). $M2$ = Non interest bearing component of M1 plus private sector interest bearing retail sterling bank deposits, plus private sector holdings of retail building society shares and deposits and National Savings Bank ordinary accounts. $M3c$ = M3 plus private sector holdings of foreign currency bank deposits. Money consists of a small proportion of notes and coin, the rest being deposits of which some perform all the functions of money, while others only some. This makes it difficult to give an accurate definition of money. Further, some definitions of money refer to 'Narrow Money' – money for immediate spending, e.g. M0, M2, and 'Broad Money' – money for transaction purposes and as a store of value e.g. M3, M5. The definitions of money supply are, therefore, to some degree arbitrary and with possible future developments to change can be invalidated.

money transmission services. The service operated by banks for their customers for the clearing of cheques, bills of exchange, giro credits, bankers orders, direct debits, etc. With the establishment of the Association of Payment Clearing Services in December 1985, for the purposes of transmission of funds and clearing of items presented to banks, three clearing companies were set up *viz;* 1. Cheque and Credit Clearing Co. Ltd – high volume paper clearing; 2. Chaps and Town Clearing Co. Ltd – high value same day clearing; 3. Bankers Automated Clearing Services Ltd – electronic clearing of direct debits, standing orders, etc.; 4. In due course a system to cover EFTPOS (Electronic Funds Transfer Point of Sale) will be set up.

monopoly. An exclusive right secured to one person, group or company to make, supply or sell a certain commodity. A monopoly supplier is therefore one with no competitors, who is able to charge whatever price he or she likes unless restrained by legislation. The Fair Trading Act, 1973, s. 6(1) defined a 'monopolist' as one having a quarter or more of the market; such a company may be examined by the Monopolies and Mergers Commission.

mopping up. When there is a surplus of money in the discount market the Discount Houses, who never refuse money offered to them by the banks, will lower the price for money by quoting a very low rate of interest for such funds. The banks will not wish to avail themselves of this and money which should have been lent out overnight or at call will be very much more difficult to place. In these circumstances the Bank of England will come to the rescue by selling Treasury Bills to the banks, or houses, thus 'mopping-up' the spare funds. *Also called* operating in reverse.

moratorium. An act authorising the suspension of payments or reparations by a bank or debtor state for a certain period of time; the period of suspension of payments; the agreement by creditors with an insolvent debtor that they will not enforce payment for a certain time.

mortgage. The conveyance of a legal or equitable interest in real or personal property as security for a debt or for the discharge of an obligation. In relation to Scotland, the term includes any heritable security. *See also* ENDOWMENT MORTGAGE; EQUITABLE MORTGAGE; FIRST MORTGAGE; LEGAL MORTGAGE; POWERS OF MORTGAGEE; PUISNE MORTGAGE; SECOND MORTGAGE; SECOND MORTGAGE; SUB-MORTGAGE; VARIABLE RATE MORTGAGE.

mortgage annuity scheme. An arrangement whereby a mortgage is taken out against the uncharged capital value of a property. The sum raised in this way is used to buy an annuity which will be paid to the owners of the property, usually a married couple over sixty-five years of age. Both transactions attract tax relief. If the mortgage is taken out on an interest-only repayment basis, no capital is repaid during the joint lifetimes. The amount borrowed has to be repaid in full on the death of the surviving partner and it may well be necessary to sell the property in order to effect this repayment.

mortgage bond. A bond backed by mortgage of real property. Mortgage bonds carry a specified maturity and interest rate. In Italy and West Germany this is the main method of housing finance. Special mortgage banks arrange the issue, and then lend the money so raised to house buyers.

mortgage caution. Formerly a way of protecting a mortgage by deed of registered land, the mortgage caution was abolished by the Administration of Justice Act, 1977.

mortgage debenture. A debenture accompanied by a charge on the assets of the borrowing company.

mortgagee. The person to whom property is mortgaged by a borrower.

Mortgage Interest Relief at Source. Commonly known as MIRAS. This is a method whereby the taxpayer who pays mortgage interest is given immediate relief from income tax. The mortgagor deducts income tax at the basic rate from the interest component of the repayments.

mortgage market. In the US, a government-sponsored secondary market in mortgages, that is, long-term loans for house purchases. No corresponding market of this nature exists in the UK.

mortgage of company assets. *See* REGISTRATION OF CHARGES.

mortgage of equitable interest. Where property is left by will or deed to trustees for the benefit of others, those beneficiaries have an equitable interest on which they can borrow. Such a beneficiary may be a joint tenant, a beneficiary under a trust for sale, or a remainderman. The property in the trust is eventually intended to be sold but the sale is postponed so that the income from the trust property is paid by the trustees to the life tenant. As a security the interest leaves something to be desired. There is no legal estate to be obtained, for that is held by the trustees, so the ownership of the trust property cannot be transferred to the bank. All the banker can do is to take a legal assignment by way of mortgage of an equitable interest. If there is land included in the trust property, the deeds cannot be obtained, for the trustees hold them. The mortgage cannot be protected by registration in the Land Charges Department, for it is a mortgage, not on land, but on the proceeds of sale of the land. (However, if the land is registered land, a mortgage of the equitable interest can be protected by registration on the Minor Interest Index; and stocks and shares can be protected by notices in lieu of distringas to the various registrars.) A mortgage will be drawn up by the bank's solicitors, and notice of the charge given to the trustees concerned. Their acknowledgment must be obtained and they must confirm that no notice of any prior charge has been received. If the borrower's inter-

est is contingent only, the security must be supported by a life policy to repay the loan if the borrower should die before his or her interest becomes vested in him.

mortgage of ship. Registers of British ships are maintained at most ports in Britain, and in some British possessions abroad. A ship is divided into sixty-four parts or shares, and any person may be registered as owner of any number of shares. A ship is a specialised form of security and has the disadvantages that it is difficult to value, difficult to realise, and suffers from a high rate of depreciation. A legal mortgage must be as prescribed in the Merchant Shipping Act, 1894. On production of this instrument the registrar of the ship's port of registry shall record it in the register book. Mortgages are recorded for priority by hour and date of the day. The statutory mortgage is usually supplemented by a supplementary form of mortgage, which will contain many clauses for the banker's protection not available in the statutory form. Before lending, the banker should make a search on the register to see if there is any prior registration outstanding. The banker should ensure that proper insurance cover has been obtained by way of marine and war risks and club or mutual insurance (*q.v.*). The statutory mortgage, if given by a limited company, should also be registered at Companies House. It is desirable that any mortgage should be of thirty-three shares or more, so that the operation of the ship can be controlled.

mortgage term. The period for which land is vested in the mortgagee by the mortgagor.

mortgagor. The person who mortgages personal property in favour of the lender.

mortmain. Formerly possession or tenure of lands or tenements by a corporation, especially an ecclesiastical corporation or monastery which could not alienate the land. Thus it was said to be held by a 'dead hand'. A corporation may now hold land in practically the same way as an individual.

motion. A proposal put before a company meeting for discussion and possible adoption as a resolution; a proposal made in an assembly; an application to a court for a ruling on some particular point in the course of proceedings.

movables. A term embracing all property other than land.

multilateral. Having several participants.

multilateral trade. A state of complete freedom of trade between countries unhampered by tariffs, quotas, or any other restrictions.

multinational companies. Very large trading concerns with interests and organisations in several countries.

multiple agreement. In the Consumer Credit Act, 1974, an agreement whose terms are such as 1. to place a part of it within one category of agreement mentioned in the Act, and another part of it within a different category of agreement so mentioned, or within a category of agreement not so mentioned; or 2. to place it, or part of it, within two or more categories of agreement so mentioned.

multiple exchange rates. Where a restrictive system of exchange control is in operation it is possible for different exchange rates to be available according to the purpose for which the money is required, e.g. tourist rate, investment rate, property rate. These may be at a premium or a discount according to whether it is desired to encourage or to restrict the particular activity.

municipal. Pertaining to a corporation or city, or to local self-government in general.

municipal bond. Similar to local authority bonds in the UK, municipal bonds in the US are issued by any

government, or authority or agency of government, other than the federal government. Typically used by cities, counties and towns to finance local development and individual projects.

municipal corporation. *See* LOCAL AUTHORITY.

muniment. A title-deed, charter or record kept as evidence or defence of a title.

mutatis mutandis. After making the necessary changes.

mutilated Bank of England notes. Such notes must be presented to the Bank of England for replacement. This will not be unhesitatingly done unless the fragment is of more than half a note, contains the whole of the sentence beginning 'I promise to pay', etc, has some portion of the signature, one complete print of the series index and serial number, and for those denominations that bear one, some part of the other series index and serial number.

mutilated cheque or bill. A cheque or bill may be partly or wholly torn and repaired with adhesive tape. If it is apparent that the instrument has not been wholly torn through it may be treated as any other by a paying banker, but if it has been torn right through the paying banker will expect to see indorsed on the instrument an explanation, confirmed by the collecting banker, of the circumstances of the mutilation. If such an explanation is not present the paying banker should return the draft unpaid with the answer 'Mutilated cheque'. If there is an explanation there, but it lack the confirmation of the collecting banker, the answer should be 'Mutilation requires confirmation'.

mutual fund. The American equivalent of the unit trust. *See also* OPEN-ENDED TRUST *under* OPEN ENDED.

mutual insurance. Insurance provided by shipowners throughout the world who have clubbed together in various mutual protection and indemnity associations to cover hazards which are not covered by marine policies, which have standard clauses leaving a number of contingencies unprovided for, or only partially provided for. The liabilities of the mutual insurance company are periodically divided amongst the subscribers in proportion to the tonnage they have entered with the company. Also known as *Club Insurance.*

mutual savings banks. In the US, thrift institutions which have no stock-holders but are owned by the deposit-ors.

N

naked debenture. An acknowledgement of indebtedness, not accompanied by any security.

naked trustee. One who holds property for the absolute benefit of beneficiaries of full age, and who has no personal beneficial interest in the property and no duty except to transfer it to its owners.

name day. The second day of the Stock Exchange semi-monthly settlement. Also called Ticket Day, it is the day when the names of buyers are transmitted to the sellers of securities.

named policy. A marine policy in which the name of the ship carrying the insured goods is particularised.

narrow market. When there is only a small supply of any particular security available on the Stock Exchange.

NASDAQ. National Association of Securities Dealers and Automated Quotations.

NASDIM. National Association of Dealers and Investment Managers.

national banks. National banks are corporations chartered by the United States Comptroller of the Currency for the purpose of carrying on banking business. The incorporators must consist of not less than five members and the total capital stock is set at not less than $50,000 to $200,000 in value, depending upon the size of the cities in which their principal place of business is located. All stock must be paid in full before the bank may commence business and the capital and surplus must at all times be maintained at or above the limits prescribed by the Comptroller of the Currency. In the US, it is not uncommon for banks, for business or other reasons, to change their status from state to national banks or the reverse. However, national banks can merge with or convert to state banks only in those states where state banks may merge without restriction with national banks under the national bank charter.

national capital. The financial value of the total real capital of a country at any particular time.

National Credit Union Administration. The governing body for some 12,500 federally chartered credit unions throughout the US. Credit unions originated around the beginning of the century as community co-operatives for working-class borrowers and savers; they have since expanded rapidly, particularly since the late 1970s, and now offer a wide range of banking services including loans, mortgages and credit cards. *See* CREDIT UNION.

national debt. The borrowings of governments. The government borrows funds by the issue of gilt-edged stock which, in general terms, can be regarded as long term, while the government's short-term borrowing is by the issue of Treasury bills. The national debt is managed by the Bank of England.

National Economic Development Council (NEDC). A national consultative body that brings together senior government ministers, TUC and CBI representatives and some other interests under the chairmanship of the Chancellor of the Exchequer, for the discussion of national economic and industrial issues with the object of improving the nation's economic performance. The NEDC ('Neddy') was established in 1962. A number of smaller committees (Economic Development Committees or 'little Neddies') and sector working parties have also been set up to deal with individual industries or sectors of industry. These bodies, which consist of senior management, trade union leaders and a government representative and are serviced by the NED Office, aim to improve the performance of their industries or sectors. The main functions of the Council are 1. to advise the Treasury; 2. to search for ways to stabilise industrial incomes; 3. to research into the reasons for Great Britain's disappointing economic growth in recent years; and 4. to educate the public in the importance of applying developed new ideas to industry.

National Enterprise Board (NEB). An association founded under the Industry Act, 1975 to invest on behalf of the State in companies in the private sector which are considered to have potential. The Board is prepared to take a long view, on which may be based long-term loans in return for a share in the equity. Interest charges are at strictly commercial rates. New guidelines issued in August 1980 for the guidance of the Board stipulate that an investment role should be pursued which is directed especially to the development or exploitation of advanced technologies, or to the benefit of industrial companies operating in the assisted areas in England, and with loans of up to £50,000 to small firms. The Board has also been instructed to sell all their holdings to private investors as soon as commercially possible. To ensure maximum private sector involvement the NEB is allowed only to lend or invest where the requirements could not be met by other sources of finance.

National Girobank. *See* GIROBANK.

national income. The value in a country's money of the total production of goods and services in that country for one year.

National Institute for Economic and Social Research (NIESR). A nonprofit making research centre set up in 1938, which works closely with the Treasury in making quarterly projections of the economic trends in the country, using a computer-based model of the British economy.

nationalisation. The acquisition and management of industrial and distributing organisations by the State.

national mark. A grading mark placed on foodstuffs and other products, authenticating their British origin.

National Research Development Corporation (NRDC). Established in 1948 and financed by the Government, the corporation exists to provide 'innovation capital' to assist the development of British inventions. An application for assistance, if approved, will be furnished with funds to patent the idea, set up a working model, and eventually market the product. The corporation, which is part of the Department of Trade and Industry, is repaid by a levy on the sales of the successful project. *See also* VENTURE CAPITAL.

National Savings Bank. Established in 1861, under the name of the Post Office Savings Bank, the National Savings Bank offers simple banking facilities for people who have no need for cheques. Anyone over the age of seven can open an account at any Savings Bank post office with a minimum deposit of £1. A bank book is issued in which all transactions are recorded. Ordinary accounts are subject to a condition that no more than £10,000 may be kept on balance. Interest is paid on these accounts at a rate varying from time to time with general money rate levels. The first £70 of interest is exempt from income tax. Withdrawals on demand are limited to £100, but larger sums may be withdrawn at a few days' notice. Ordinary account holders are offered a cumbersome cheque-type facility through crossed warrants, which can be obtained only by sending a completed withdrawal application form, together with the bank book, to Savings Bank headquarters. The Bank also offers investment accounts, paying a better rate of interest, but requiring one months' notice of withdrawal. A limit of £100,000 is placed on these. All interest on these is subject to tax. These accounts are available to any investor, whether or not the investor has an ordinary account.

National Savings Certificates. Certificates are obtainable at banks and post offices. They are designed to encourage savings. From time to time fresh issues are made offering a competitive rate of interest for the money invested. Such interest earned is free of tax. Interest is by way of accruals to the capital value and is paid out only when the Savings Certificates are cashed. The present issue (33rd) has a minimum investment of £25 and a maximum of £1,000, plus any holdings of previous issues. Certificates that are held longer than five years attract a special rate of interest known as an 'extension rate', which is also tax free. An indexed linked saving certificate is also available with a minimum investment of £25 and a maximum of £5,000, not including any holdings of previous issues. No interest is paid, but the value of any certificate is adjusted monthly in accordance with the general index of retail prices. Additionally an annual bonus of 4.04 per cent is added to the value of the certificate. Repayments are free of all tax. The certificate which has a life of five years, may be held for a longer period and will continue to attract the index linked interest and bonuses. The certificates are also available to trustees, registered friendly societies, eligible charities and other bodies and are especially attractive to the high rate tax payer.

National Savings Deposit Bonds. These are funds deposited by persons with the Department of National Savings who have a lump sum to invest. The minimum amount is £100 and the maximum £50,000. Interest is calculated on a daily basis and added to the amount of the investment on the anniversary of the purchase. The interest rates will vary, but the authorities will advertise any changes in the daily press and in post offices. Any interest earned is subject to income tax. Individuals, companies and trustees may purchase these bonds. Three months notice must be given for any withdrawals.

'Natural' Deposit. A deposit obtained from an industrial or commercial company, or from a private individual, as opposed to those obtained through the interbank sterling market as a result of bidding, in order to finance a particular asset.

natural rights of property. Those rights which supplement the direct rights, for example the right of ownership, by imposing duties on other persons. Examples are the right of a landowner to such support from a neighbour's land as will maintain his or her own land at its natural level; the right of a riparian owner that other similar owners shall not divert the course of the stream. Such a right is distinguished from an easement in that it is not initially created by a grant.

near (or quasi-) money. A term sometimes applied to bills, cheques, promissory notes, postal orders, or anything which is not banknotes, coin or bank deposits.

necessaries. Goods that are required by a person in accordance with his/her standard of life. A minor may bind himself/herself in a contract for such food, drink, apparel and other necessaries (employment, study) (Nash *v* Inman, 1908). A man is not generally liable for the debts of his wife, except if they are necessaries for domestic purposes.

negative. Containing, declaring or implying negation; denying, contradicting, prohibiting, refusing.

negative certificate of origin. A certificate frequently requested by an Arab company, to the effect that no element in any product was imported from or produced by an Israeli firm or associate. These are certified before a notary public and the counter-signed by the Foreign Office.

negative dealing. Eurocurrency market operations not always viewed with approval by the authorities, e.g. US dollars are borrowed for one year fixed, swapped into sterling on a three-month swap (fully covered), and the sterling proceeds lent out for three months, at the end of which period (depending on rate movements) a further three-month swap can take place as before, or the dollars can be lent out for nine months.

negative income tax. Payments from the State to people with incomes below subsistence level.

negative interest. When a country has a strong currency everyone wants to buy its currency. As a result this country finds itself with large foreign deposits on which it would normally pay interest. If, however, there are no profitable outlets for the use of this money, such deposits must be discouraged. Negative interest is a charge for keeping deposits.

negative pledge. A clause in an agreement whereby a borrowing company customer undertakes not to pledge its assets elsewhere without the bank's consent.

negligence. Breach of a duty to take care. As a tort in its own right, there must exist for proof of negligence: 1. a duty of care owed to the plaintiff; 2. breach of that duty by the defendant; 3. consequent loss or damage to the plaintiff. The plaintiff must show all three. The duty may be independent of any contract. In banking, however, negligence is more likely to appear in connection with the banking contract with the customer. If a banker is careless in dealing with the affairs of a customer, the banker will be liable, because being negligent is a breach of his or her contractual duty to take care

of the customer's interest (when sending back a cheque unpaid, for example, the banker must mark it with that answer which, while correct, will harm the customer's reputation least). The majority of actions against a banker alleging negligence, however, are to be found where the banker has collected a cheque for the account of someone not entitled to the proceeds. In this context negligence may be defined as the failure to make inquiry in cases when a reasonably competent banker would make an inquiry; or, when such an inquiry has been duly made, the failure to appreciate that the answer obtained is an unsatisfactory one. Negotiated cheques require special care, especially when they are for large amounts. The conduct of the account for which the cheque is being collected is a relevant factor; where the account has been giving trouble the banker is expected to look more carefully at the transaction. The contributory negligence of the plaintiff has, since 1971, been recognised as a possibility in such cases. *See also* CONTRIBUTORY NEGLIGENCE OF PLAINTIFF.

negotiable instrument. Any instrument which satisfies the three tests of negotiability. These are 1. the property in the instrument passes by mere delivery or by indorsement and delivery; 2. a transferee taking the instrument in good faith and for value with no notice of any defect in the title of the transferor obtains an indefeasible title against all the world, and may sue on the instrument in his or her own name; 3. no notice of the transfer need be given to the person liable on the instrument. Negotiable instruments are banknotes, bearer bonds, Treasury bills, certificates of deposit, bills of exchange, promissory notes, cheques, share warrants and share certificates to bearer, and debentures payable to bearer. Where a bill is negotiable in its origin it continues to be negotiable until it becomes overdue or has been 1. restrictively indorsed; 2. discharged by payment or otherwise; or 3. (if a cheque) crossed 'Not Negotiable'.

negotiable order of withdrawal accounts (NOW accounts). An American term for a current account on which interest is paid. In some cases a minimum balance has been stipulated, below which service charges have been imposed; in others, no service charges have been assessed, whatever the balance. In other cases money is transferred from a time deposit (*q.v.*) to a demand deposit (*q.v.*) automatically as and when needed. These accounts were formerly prohibited by federal law, but this situation changed as from 31 December 1980, although NOW accounts are limited to accounts in which the entire beneficial interest is held by one or more individuals; or a partnership, corporation or association operated primarily for religious, philanthropic, charitable or educational purposes and not operated for profit.

negotiation. 1. The discussion or bargaining over a possible contract or its terms and conditions. 2. One method of financing an outward movement of goods or services to an overseas country, where the exporter's bank buys (discounts) a bill drawn by the exporter on the importer, or on a bank for him or her. Where the negotiated bill is received from an exporter – a customer who has sent goods to a buyer abroad – and has drawn a bill on that person at a term it is usually because the customer is not willing to wait for the proceeds to reach his account under the collection procedure. If the bank agrees to buy the bill it will pay its customer the face value of the bill, less discount. This part of the transaction is exactly the same as if the bank were discounting a bill, but as far as foreign bills are concerned the practice is termed 'negotiation'. In many cases, of course, the bill may be drawn in a foreign currency. A sight bill, or merely documents with no bill attached, may also be negotiated. The banker is naturally concerned to safeguard his position should the bill be dishonoured on presentation, and therefore negotiates 'with recourse'. This means that the customer will be obliged to pay the banker if for any reason payment is not forthcoming within a reasonable time. The banker may ask for security to be deposited to back up the customer's undertaking, and if the bill is a documentary bill the banker will certainly regard the documents as part of his security. Once the banker has bought the bill collection of the proceeds is on the banker's own behalf. 3. The transfer of a bill or note for value received. A bill is negotiated when it is transferred from one person to another in such a manner as to constitute the transferee the holder of the bill. A bill payable to bearer is negotiated by delivery. A bill payable to order is negotiated by the indorsement of the holder, completed by delivery.

negotiation credit. One where an importer opens a credit in favour of the exporter, not in the exporter's country, but in a third country. However, the exporter's bills on the bank which opened the credit are negotiated in the exporter's country. Thus a French buyer from Singapore might pay by means of an irrevocable credit in sterling opened with a London bank. The exporter's bills drawn on the London bank are purchased with recourse by a bank in Singapore.

negotiation fee. The fee charged by anyone for arranging a loan or a service – particularly by the bank arranging a syndicate of lending institutions.

negotiator. For the purposes of the

Consumer Credit Act, 1974, the person by whom negotiations are conducted with the debtor or hirer.

net, nett. Left after all deductions.

net asset value (net worth). Net asset value expresses the net worth of a company or a trust in pence per ordinary share. It is arrived at by adding up the company's assets (in the case of a trust the trust's listed investments valued at mid-market prices, its unlisted investments at directors' valuation, its cash on deposit and current accounts), and subtracting the value of any prior charges and current liabilities. The result is divided by the number of shares issued to give the net asset value per share. This is one possible way of arriving at a figure for the net worth of a company without a Stock Exchange quotation. It is a difficult exercise, requiring the current balance sheet, updated to the valuation day, and adjusted for inflationary factors. Other possibilities are to ask the company secretary for his or her certified value figure, or, if shares have recently changed hands, to rely on the figure then obtained.

net cash flow. Retained profits for the year, plus depreciation as charged (i.e. gross cash flow less dividends paid).

net income. The annual amount received after payment of tax; the annual income from a business after the expenses of running it have been deducted.

net investment. The amount of investment made in a given period after having made allowance for the depreciation of capital in that time.

net price. Cash price without discount.

net profit. Gross profit less expenses listed on the debit side of a Profit and Loss account.

net rate of tax. Where interest payments are taxed at source, the amount which can be reclaimed from the Inland Revenue by a taxpayer who does not pay the full rate of income tax.

Net Relevant Earnings (NRE). Net profit from all employment often deducting business charges and capital allowances – or if employed could be salaries plus bonuses and overtime.

net rental. The rent of a property after payment of all sums for repairs, taxes and expenses.

net saving. Total savings less adjustments for depreciation and stock appreciation.

nett. Left after all deductions.

netting. An arrangement whereby it is not necessary to re-exchange currencies when a swap agreement is terminated. For example, companies X and Y each in different countries sell each others' currencies against their own local currency and during the period of the swap agreement, one currency has moved up and the other down, then the agreement could provide for a 'netting' whereby neither party will gain or lose by the transaction.

net weight. The weight of goods without their packaging.

network. A communications system for speedy transmission of information throughout an organisation. A computer system where there are a number of terminals at some distance away from each other and connected by a telecommunications system.

net worth. The net worth of a business is calculated by subtracting the current liabilities from the total assets, after deducting fictitious assets. The surplus will vary with the nature of the business, but it should be adequate for the company's trading requirements.

net yield. A yield which is assessed after deduction of tax.

new issue. An issue of stocks, etc., to the public by a company in need of capital. Such capital issues are sponsored by an issuing house which makes itself responsible for taking up any of the issue which has not been taken up by others. New issues may be for public companies already having a quotation on the Stock Exchange, or they may be for private companies 'going public'. Securities may be made available to the public either by means of an offer for sale by the issuing house, or by an issue by the company. In the case of an offer for sale the issuing house buys the whole of the issue for cash from the company and itself offers it to the public. In the case of an issue by the company the issuing house undertakes to find subscribers in full for the whole issue. New issues may also be 'placed', that is, sold privately to a limited number of investors, usually the big institutions, but in these cases a proportion of the securities is allocated to the market to be available for the general public. Still another alternative is for the new issues to be made available by the company to existing shareholders only, by rights issue or by open offer. *See also* ISSUE.

next friend. One who acts on behalf of another who is unable, from infirmity or legal incapacity, to act for themselves.

next-of-kin. Nearest blood relative.

NIFS. *See* NOTE ISSUING FACILITIES.

night safe. A bank safe connected by a chute with an aperture in the outer wall of the bank. Customers wishing to pay in cash or cheques after hours may obtain a wallet from the bank, put their money in it, and drop it down the chute. The entrance to the chute has a locked cover to which the customer is given a key. In the morning the bank staff clear all the wallets out of the safe and list them in the night safe record book. Wallets are of two kinds, one to be opened by the bank staff and the proceeds credited to the customer's account; the other to be handed back to the customer, or the customer's agent, during banking hours, because the customer prefers to open the wallet and then pay in personally.

Nikkei Average. The Tokyo Stock Exchange Index which indicates the overall movement of transactions each day.

nisi prius **(unless before).** A name given to trials by jury in civil cases, the words *nisi prius* being the first in the old Latin form of the writ commanding the parties to appear at Westminster 'unless before' this the case had been dealt with on circuit.

node. A substation, housing a computer, on a packet switching network. Each node will determine the route for the next step which the message will take.

nominal. Existing only in name, formal, ostensible.

nominal capital. An alternative name for Authorised Capital (*q.v.*).

nominal consideration. A consideration which is less than a real consideration, but which is inserted in a contract so that its validity may be maintained. Consideration to support a contract need not be adequate, but it must be real, that is, it must consist of some measure of value. Where shares are transferred for other than a monetary consideration a nominal consideration is entered in the instrument of transfer, so as to attract a reduced rate of stamp duty.

nominal damages. Damages awarded when the plaintiff has proved that his legal rights have been infringed, but has been unable to prove that any actual damage was done.

nominal partner. A person with no financial interest in a firm, but who allows his or her name to be used in the firm's title for the sake of preserving goodwill. *See also* QUASI-PARTNER.

nominal price. The face price of stocks and shares, as opposed to the price for which they can be bought or sold on the Stock Exchange.

nominal rate. A rate founded on an estimation, but one at which no transactions have taken place.

nominal value. The face value on a certificate or bond, as compared with the market value.

nominal wages. Wages in money terms, as distinct from the true value of wages in terms of what they will buy in goods and services.

nominee. One named or proposed for office: a person on whose life an annuity or lease depends. One who holds shares in a company on behalf of another, e.g. banks will act as nominee for a customer who for some reason does not wish to be personally registered as a shareholder. However, it should be made known that any person who has more than 5 per cent holding in a company must declare this fact even if the shareholder is shielding behind a nominee: the person nominated to act as an insolvency practitioner – as a trustee or otherwise – having regard for the requirements of s.390 Insolvency Act, 1986.

nominee company. A company formed by a bank to hold the legal title of stocks and shares transferred to the bank as security by borrowing customers, or for the convenience of customers who may be living abroad, in which the execution of transfers, etc., is facilitated.

non-. A prefix in the formation of compound terms signifying absence or omission.

non-assented bonds. Bonds for which a plan of financial re-organisation has not been approved by the bondholder.

non assumpsit. A general legal plea by which a defendant refutes entirely the allegations of his or her opponent.

non-business day. A day which is not counted as one on which normal business is transacted. For the purposes of the Bills of Exchange Act, 1882, 'non-business days are 1. Saturday, Sunday, Good Friday, Christmas Day; 2. a bank holiday under the Banking and Financial Dealings Act, 1971; 3. a day appointed by Royal Proclamation as a public fast or thanksgiving day; 4. a day declared by an order under s. 2 of the Banking and Financial Dealings Act, 1971 to be a non-business day. Any other day is a business day. Where, by the Bills of Exchange Act, 1882, the time limited for doing any act or thing is less than three days, in reckoning time non-business days are excluded. Where a bill is due and payable on a non-business day it is payable on the succeeding business day. *See also* MATURITY.

non-claim. A failure or omission to make a claim within the prescribed limits of time.

non-commercial agreement. A consumer credit agreement or a consumer hire agreement not made by the creditor or owner in the course of business.

non compos mentis. Not of sound mind.

non-contributory pension. A pension awarded on the grounds of age and not on contributions paid during a working life; an old-age pension.

non-cumulative preference shares. Those shares where interest lost one year is lost for ever.

non-depository agency. A form of banking office permitted in California to foreign (i.e. non-US) banks operating in this particular state; Senate Bill 285, which became law in June, 1981, brought the California Financial Code into line with the International Banking Act, 1978. Agencies and branches are unincorporated offices of a foreign bank licensed to engage in banking business in California. A non-depository agency is the most restrictive form of representation and is not allowed to accept any deposits, although it can maintain credit balances as collateral in connection with a letter of credit and/or acceptance financing, provided that such balances are under the complete control of the agency and are not subject to check facilities or withdrawal by the customer until the underlying transaction has been completed.

non-essentials. In foreign trade, a designation for goods which are not judged to be of primary importance for the economy of the country.

non est factum. 'I did not make it'. A plea which can be put forward by a person seeking to avoid a legal obligation, originally applicable to cases where the defendant sought to avoid liability on the grounds that a signature on a document was not the defendant's. Later the plea referred to cases where the signature was genuine, but has been obtained through a mistake, often as the result of a misrepresentation. It was granted sparingly, but blind or illiterate signatories were often favoured. In modern times the doctrine has been more narrowly circumscribed and a high standard of care is required from signatories, however handicapped they may be. As the plea is in direct conflict with the cardinal principle that a person is bound by his or her signature, it is only in exceptional cases that the plea is successful, but it remains a possible threat to the banker who is relying upon a guarantor's signature.

non-feasance. Failure to perform an act that is legally incumbent upon one.

non-intervention. Not intervening or interfering in the affairs or policies of another, especially in international affairs.

non-joinder. Failure to join with another as party in a suit.

non-marketable securities. Securities which are not dealt with on the Stock Exchange.

non-participating policy. A 'without-profits' policy where a fixed sum is to be paid, irrespective of whether the company does well or badly in the currency of the policy.

non-payment of a bill/cheque. Dishonour of a bill by the acceptor or the non-payment of a cheque by the drawee bankers. Whereas the dishonour of a bill may be noted or protested by the holder, a cheque need not go through this procedure as evidence of presentation by the collecting banker's crossing and the reason for non-payment by the drawee bank are written on the face of the cheque.

non-recourse finance. This is finance given by a bank to a borrower, and which the borrower has no liability to repay. Repayment will come from other sources, e.g. the purchaser of the borrowers services or goods. Non-recourse finance is available by various methods: *(a)* an exporter may obtain non recourse finance by making available to a lending banker an ECGD guarantee; *(b)* export finance departments of the major banks will offer similar facilities to those of ECGD, to customers that conform to the conditions that they lay down; *(c)* factoring – the sale of book debts, with the agreement of the factor, cover for the client's bad debts is given, so that invoices presented to the factor that are presented in accordance with the agreement between the parties will be paid without recourse; *(d)* with the confirmation of a documentary credit, the confirming bank will pay the beneficiary, providing the terms and conditions of the credit have been complied with, payment will be without recourse; *(e)* by the forfaiting of a bill of exchange or similar instrument, a bank may agree to forfaiting, that is, should the instrument be dishonoured for any reason, then there will be no recourse to the drawer. With time and the expansion of financial services, there is no reason why other methods of non-recourse finance are made available to borrowers.

non-residents. Persons, firms, or companies who are resident outside the United Kingdom (including the Channel Isles, Gibraltar and the Isle of Man) and Eire; for tax purposes, people who are not residing in the UK and are therefore entitled to UK tax exemption on income from foreign and colonial investments and from some British Government stocks. In the latter case visits to this country amounting to no more than an annual average of three months are permitted, but if this figure is exceeded a review of the non-resident status will be made. The distinction formerly made between resident and non-resident accounts in the books of a bank was due to the then exchange control requirements. Money on a non-resident account was free to be transferred abroad (thus affecting the sterling exchange rate adversely): money on a resident account was not so free. Since the lifting of the restrictions in October 1979 this distinction has disappeared.

non sequitur. 'It does not follow': an illogical inference, an irrelevant conclusion.

non-suit. The withdrawal of a law suit, whether by mutual agreement or by the judgment of the court.

non-trading partnership. A partnership such as that of doctors or solicitors, which does not depend on the buying and selling of goods, but is concerned with the provision of services of a professional nature. In such a case a partner's authority is limited to the drawing of cheques. This distinction will not affect the banker as long as the usual mandate has been taken, by the terms of which any partner makes the firm liable for anything he or she does in the ordinary course of the firm's business.

non-transferable. A crossing placed on a cheque to ensure that the cheque is paid to the named payee only. An alternative would be to make the cheque out to the payee and then to add the word 'only'. To make the drawer's intention quite clear, the words 'order' or 'bearer' should be struck out and the alteration initialled by the drawer.

non-user. Neglect to use a right, by which it may become void.

non-voting shares. Usually called 'A' Ordinary shares, these securities stand on an equal footing with Ordinary shares as far as dividend and capital return rights are concerned, but give to their owners no right to vote at the annual company meeting. Non-voting shares were originally invented to allow the founder of a family concern to be able to bring in outside capital without losing control of the company. In modern times they are not favourably regarded and the Stock Exchange will allow only companies already possessing them to create more. The companies themselves are gradually converting them into Ordinary shares, often on the death of the founder.

no par value. Shares issued with no stated nominal value, but valued according to the current stock exchange assessment.

nostro account. Accounts maintained by home banks with banks abroad. *See also* VOSTRO ACCOUNT.

notarial act of honour. If, after a bill of exchange has been protested, a third party intervenes to pay the bill for the honour of the party on whom it is drawn, such a payment must be attested by a notary public and is known as a notarial act of honour.

notary public. A person, usually a solicitor, authorised to record statements, to certify deeds, to take affidavits, etc., on oath, especially for use in legal proceedings abroad. When a dishonoured bill is 'noted' it is presented again by a notary public and 'noted' for non-acceptance or non-payment. If necessary, the noting can be extended into a protest. It is very common in the US for documents to be notarised or authenticised by a public officer who is known as a notary public. The notary is called to acknowledge, attest and certify deeds as well as official forms, usually under his or her official seal, for a small charge.

Notaries public are licensed by the state in which they operate after passing an examination.

note issue. The total amount of bank notes in circulation in the country at any particular moment. In England and Wales the Bank of England has a monopoly of the issue of notes, but certain Irish and Scottish banks still issue their own notes. The 'note issue' of one of these banks means the total amount of its own notes which it is legally authorised to issue.

note issuing facilities. Popularly known as NIFS. A bank or financial institution pledges to lend money to a borrower if his note issue falls flat.

note of hand. A promissory note, a written promise to pay a certain sum by a stipulated time.

note reserve. The difference between the amount of banknotes in circulation and the highest permitted legal limit.

notice. Information, warning, a written or printed paper giving information or directions, a formal intimation, a communication indicating pending loss of employment; in the law of registered land, a notification to the Land Registrar to protect a minor interest, such as a deed of arrangement affecting land. For the purposes of the Consumer Credit Act, 1974, notice means notice in writing. *See also* DEFAULT NOTICE; DISPENSING NOTICE.

notice deposit. A deposit repayable only after the specified period of notice has been given (e.g. seven days' notice), which may be given by either the borrower or lender. If repayment is requested, and made at less than the prescribed notice, interest is deducted in respect of the days of short notice. The interest rate applicable may also be varied, subject to the appropriate period of notice.

notice in lieu of *distringas*. *See* DISTRINGAS.

notice loan. A loan repayable only after the specified period of notice has been given (i.e. seven days' notice), which may be given either by the borrower or the lender. The interest rate applicable may also be varied, subject to the appropriate period of notice.

notice of assignment. *See* ASSIGNMENT OF DEBTS; ASSIGNMENT OF LIFE POLICY.

notice of cancellation. For the purposes of the Consumer Credit Act, 1974, a notice served within a specified period by the debtor or hirer under a cancellable agreement on 1. the creditor or owner; or 2. the person specified in the notice; or 3. a person who is the agent of the creditor or owner. If the notice, however expressed, indicates the intention of the debtor or hirer to withdraw from the agreement, it shall operate to cancel the agreement and any linked transaction, and to withdraw any offer by the debtor or hirer, or his or her relative, to enter into a linked transaction.

notice of deposit. A Land Registry form which is completed by a banker who has received from a borrowing customer the land certificate which is to serve as security by way of an equitable mortgage. The notice of deposit is addressed to the Land Registrar and informs the Land Registrar that the land certificate has been deposited with the bank as security. The registrar enters the mortgage on the charges register, thus giving notice to any possible purchaser or mortgagee. Also, if the proprietor attempts to sell the land or to deal with it in any way other than by legal mortgage the registrar would notify the banker.

notice of dishonour. Where a bill has been dishonoured by non-acceptance or non-payment, notice of dishonour must be given to the drawer and each indorser, and any drawer or indorser to whom notice is not given is discharged. The notice must be given by or on behalf of the holder, or by or on behalf of an indorser who, at the time of giving it, is liable on the bill. The notice may be given in writing or by personal communication, and may be given in any terms which sufficiently indentify the bill, and intimate that the bill has been dishonoured by non-acceptance or non-payment. The return of a dishonoured bill to the drawer or an indorser, is deemed a sufficient notice of dishonour.

notice of second charge. A banker, being the first lender against deed security, who receives notice of a second charge on the deeds, must rule off the customer's overdrawn account to avoid the operation of the Rule in Clayton's case to the banker's detriment, and must thereafter hold the deeds in trust for the second mortgagee. If the land is registered land, the procedure is the same except that, although notice will almost certainly come direct from the second mortgagee in any case if the second mortgagee makes application to register his or her charge and the bank's prior charge is a registered charge, the Registrar will advise the bank. If the bank's interest is equitable, and protected by notice of deposit, the second mortgagee will be unable to have his mortgage registered until the bank's interest is re-registered as a legal interest. In the case of a company, registration of the second charge at Companies House will constitute notice and must be watched for in *Stubbs Gazette*. If the bank *takes* a second charge it must give notice to the first lender. *See also* SECOND MORTGAGE.

notice to suspend payment. An advice from a debtor to creditors that the debtor is unable to pay debts. Such a notice is an act of bankruptcy. The notice must be a definite statement that payment is suspended. There must be some statement by the debtor from which any reasonable person would infer that it was the debtor's intention to suspend payment. Anything short of this is not notice and therefore not an act of bankruptcy. A meeting of creditors is not of itself an act of bankruptcy, but in the course of the meeting some such statement as above may be made.

noting a bill. *See* NOTARY PUBLIC.

notional amount. A term used by the International Swap Dealers Association to indicate the amount calculated in any period in a rate swap.

notional income. Where an investment is assumed to bring in a yield to the owner of property, which may be taxable, although in reality the owner receives only a non-financial benefit.

not negotiable. Where a person takes a crossed cheque which bears on it the words 'Not negotiable', that person shall not have and shall not be capable of giving a better title to the cheque than that which the person from whom he or she took it had.

notour bankruptcy. *(Sc. Law)* A state of insolvency which has been likened to the insolvency in England or Wales of a debtor who has committed an act of bankruptcy *(q.v.)*. It is similarly arrived at in a number of ways: 1. where the debtor has been adjudicated bankrupt in England, or where a receiving order has been made; 2. by insolvency reinforced by non-payment of a debt after the expiry of the days of charge *(q.v.)*; E3. where no charge is required, by non-payment after the number of days specified in a decree *(q.v.)* before poinding *(q.v.)* can be effected; 4. where the sheriff has executed a warrant for the seizures of any of the debtor's movables for non-payment of rates and taxes; 5. with a decree of adjudication in respect of any part of the debtor's heritable estate as security or for discharge of a debt, or with the sale under a sequestration order *(see* WRIT OF SEQUESTRATION) of any goods or property of the debtor by a landlord in respect of unpaid rent. ('Notour' is an old term meaning 'notorious').

novation. The substitution of a new

obligation or debt for an old one, by mutual agreement. The word may refer to a new arrangement between the same parties, or to the substitution of a new debtor for the old one.

null and void. A phrase to indicate that a contract, agreement, or document has no legal effect as for some reason it is inoperative.

nursery finance. Equity participation lending as carried out by merchant and investment banks in the UK. The lending bank takes a large (but minority) stake in a company and usually puts a director on the company's board. This 'locks-in' the bank on a commitment to provide further capital when and if required, and ensures that the company receives the best available advice.

O

obiter dictum. A casual remark, a remark by the way; a statement by a judge on a point of law which is not essential for the judgment (plural: *obiter dicta,* words by the way). Such an opinion is not binding on other judges, but is 'persuasive'. The higher the standing of the judge, the more persuasive the *obiter dicta.*

objects clause. The clause in the memorandum of association of a company which lists the business objectives which the company will pursue. *See* MEMORANDUM OF ASSOCIATION.

obligation. A debt, most often at a fixed interest, represented by a bond or certificate.

obsolescence. The process of becoming obsolete. In accounting terms the assets has lost most or all of its value due to the fact it is no longer useful as a factor or production or utility. Its value must be written down considerably.

obtaining credit by an undischarged bankrupt. Under the Insolvency Act, 1986, s. 360, a bankrupt is guilty of an offence if alone or jointly with another person the bankrupt obtains credit without notifying the person that he or she is an undischarged bankrupt.

off-balance sheet. A description used to mean a form of borrowing which will not need to be shown on a company's balance sheet. Thus the leasing of a capital asset involves no capital outlay and does not count as borrowing for the purpose of the company's Memorandum and Articles of Association. Another example would be a concession contract where a contractor builds for, say, an oil company a transmission line to the point of outlet, then operating the system for the benefit of the oil company, whose accounts record neither a loan nor an asset but merely a revenue obligation

to pay for the oil transmitted.

offer. To put forward, to tender for acceptance or refusal; to bid (as a price); to show for sale; a price or sum bid. *See also* OPEN OFFER.

offered price. A price quoted by a market maker on the Stock Exchange at which the jobber will sell stocks or shares enquired for. *See also* BID PRICE.

offer for sale. An invitation to the public to buy the shares of a new issue from an Issuing House which has bought the issue from the company concerned. *See also* INTRODUCTION; PLACING.

offer price. A price quoted by the management company of a unit trust at which they will sell sub-units of the trust. *See also* BID PRICE.

Office of Fair Trading (OFT). A government agency set up in 1973 to protect both consumers and traders against unfair practices. Its function is to notify the public of its rights and responsibilities, promote fair competition, recommend changes in law governing trade practices, credit facilities and consumer protection. It will pursue traders whom it suspects of having broken the law. It is controlled by the director-general of fair trading.

official. Pertaining to an office; vouched for by one holding office, authorised; one who holds a public office.

official list. The list of prices ruling on the Stock Exchange, published daily.

official quotations. The prices quoted in the Stock Exchange Daily List.

official rate. The rate at which the authorities of a country are prepared to deal in the foreign exchanges or, between 1968 and 1973 in the UK, in the gold market. There may be 'two-tier' rates, as for example in currency between the official rate on the one hand and a tourist, property or investment rate on the other.

official receiver. Under the Insolvency Act, 1986, the Official Receiver must be a qualified insolvency practitioner who will be appointed by the court so that the bankrupt may submit his statement of affairs within 21 days (s. 288). It is the duty of the Official Receiver to investigate the affairs of the bankrupt and report to the court. At all times the Official Receiver is the trustee of the estate of the bankrupt, but the bankrupt may apply to the Secretary of State for the appointment of a person to act as trustee instead of the official receiver.

official referee. A judicial officer of the High Court to whom is remitted for trial cases which involve prolonged examination of documents or accounts.

official search. The search by the registrar at the request of a bank, solicitor, etc., to find any encumbrance on a piece of land that a prospective purchaser is intending to buy. The certificate issued is evidence that he or she is free from any liability that has not been disclosed by the search.

off market purchase. A purchase of any goods not made in the recognised market for those goods. In the UK an off-market purchase by a company of its own shares is so defined if either 1. the shares are purchased other than on a recognised stock exchange; or 2. the shares were purchased on a recognised stock exchange but were not subject to a marketing arrangement on that stock exchange (Companies Act, 1985).

offshore funds. Unitised investment funds operating in countries with comparatively low taxes. Many of the original funds were set up in the Bahamas or in Bermuda. They were designed to appeal to investors resident in different parts of the world: the assets of a fund are also invested to a very large degree outside its nominal place of residence. There is a clear difference between an offshore fund and the unit funds which attract money in the country where they are located. The tax havens in which most offshore funds are located normally allow them greater freedom of action, and some abuses have occurred. Offshore funds are not now able to offer any great advantage to private persons resident in the UK. The situation is different for those living elsewhere and most of the funds have been set up accordingly. Offshore funds are restricted in advertising or promoting sales in the UK unless they obtain a London stock market quotation. Most unit trust groups with offshore gilts funds have preferred to set up UK-based unit trusts, rather than applying for a London quotation.

oil deficit. The foreign exchange cost of importing oil to any country. The term is also used, however, to mean the money owed by the oil-importing countries to the oil-exporting countries which has not been offset by spending by the exporting countries on imports of goods and services provided by the oil-importing countries.

old-age pension. The weekly allowance paid by a government to persons who have attained a certain age and fulfil certain conditions, usually known as the *retirement pension*.

Old Lady. The popular name given to the Bank of England. Often called *The Old Lady of Threadneedle Street*.

on demand guarantee. This type of guarantee can be found in a Performance Bond, whereby the buyer, in whose favour the guarantee is made out, may on demand and without any proof, demand payment of the amount stated.

ombudsman. A Commissioner appointed by the government to investigate any complaints against the body concerned. e.g. Local Government, Insurance, Banking. *See also* BANKING OMBUDSMAN.

omnibus resolution. *See* RESOLUTION TO BORROW.

omnium. On the Stock Exchange, the value of the aggregate stocks in a funded loan.

on account. A payment made in partial settlement of an amount outstanding. Often when a loan of a bank customer has not been reduced in accordance with the loan agreement, a reminder from the bank will often induce a payment on account, to assure the bank of the good faith of the borrower.

on-board bill of lading. A bill of lading issued in respect of goods which have actually been put on the vessel and will go when the vessel goes, as opposed to being left on the quay for the next vessel, or where no passage has been arranged. A documentary credit should wherever possible stipulate for on-board bills of lading in respect of the goods which are to be paid for.

on consignment. Goods sent to an agent who will sell them at the best terms obtainable.

oncost. Overhead costs, the total charges borne by any commercial or industrial concern, exclusive of salaries and wages.

on demand. At call whenever required; of a bill of exchange, payable on presentation.

one-man company. One in which practically all the shares are held by one person, the remainder being allotted merely to make up the statutory number of persons required to form a company.

one-off. The production of a specialised article or service to suit the needs of one particular customer; a single print from a script; an achievement that can never be repeated.

onerous. Burdensome, oppressive.

onerous covenants. Promises and obligations concerning land which will be expensive for the estate owner to fulfil, as where a leasehold in its last stages requires the repair of the property before it is handed back to the freeholder. A trustee in bankruptcy may, with the leave of the court, refuse to accept any land possessed by the bankrupt if, because of onerous covenants, it is likely to prove a liability rather than an asset.

one-stop banking. The conception of a complete range of banking services, all available in one place. This would consist of an amalgam of the range of services offered by most merchant banks (corporate advice, acceptance credits, fund management, project finance and the Eurobond market) plus the facilities of the clearing banks offered through their network of branches (a range of overdrafts and loans, including house mortgage and savings schemes).

on-line. The descriptive term applied to a certain type of computer-based system. In the British clearing banks, the word 'Branch' is added as a prefix; Branch on-line systems link individual branches to computer centres. Branch customer account records are held and processed centrally, and details of 'counter' transactions are transmitted for action from branch terminals. Additionally the *terminal* can be used for inquiry purposes, with responses being either printed or displayed on visual display units (*q.v.*). There is considerable variation in the capacity and characteristics of the Branch on-line systems used by different banks.

OPEC funds. *See* PETRODOLLARS.

open. Without restrictions; to establish or set going.

open account. 1. In foreign trade, the sending by the seller of the *documents of title to goods* to the buyer without making any condition that the documents are to be given up only against payment or acceptance of a bill of exchange; a method of business whereby the seller allows the buyer, whom he trusts, to have *control over the goods*. 2. An account which is still running or one on which final clearance on, or agreement to, all entries has not yet been secured between the parties; an account on which the final balance is yet to be paid.

open cheque. A cheque not bearing a crossing and therefore payable across the counter of a bank.

open contract. A simple agreement to sell real property, signed by the vendor indentifying the property and naming the price, and by the purchaser as evidence of agreement to purchase.

open ended. A description applied to an agreement by a banker to lend against security although what the security is has not been decided; an agreement to lend a certain sum with an understanding that further sums will later be required; any trust where the trustees have discretion to vary the investments constituting the trust, and, as with an investment trust, sales and purchases do not have to match.

opening a crossing. Where the drawer cancels the crossing on a crossed cheque by writing across it 'Pay Cash' and adding his or her signature. Initials should not be accepted by the banker as they are more easily forged than a full signature.

opening an account. A current account may be opened provided that all necessary formalities are duly completed. The new customer usually pays something in to open the account, and gives the bank a specimen of his or her signature and the name of either one or two referees according to the practice of the bank. When these referees have replied satisfactorily, and in their turn have been favourably reported on by their bankers, a cheque book may be issued to the new customer. In the case of a joint account or a partnership account the appropriate *mandate* must be signed indicating how cheques and correspondence are to be signed, and

establishing joint and several liability. In the case of a limited company the bank must see a certified copy of the *Memorandum and Articles of Association,* the *certificate of incorporation* and, in the case of a public company, the *trading certificate*. A resolution should be provided giving the names of the officials who will act for the company, the way in which cheques and authorities will be signed, and appropriate specimen signatures.

open market. A market where prices are decided solely by supply and demand.

open market operations. The purchase or sale of bills of exchange on the money market by the Bank of England for the purpose of expanding or contracting the money supply. *See* CONTROL OF THE MONEY SUPPLY.

open offer. An offer to a shareholder by a company to take up any amount which is already held. *See also* RIGHTS ISSUE.

open order. An order to a stockbroker which has not been executed. Such orders may instruct the broker to buy/sell securities at a stated price, but this particular price has not yet been reached in the market.

open outcry. Dealing in the Chicago Mercantile Exchange (home of the Commodity Exchange and Financial Futures Market) where dealers fix the contracts by shouting at each other in the various trading pits. The same system is found in the London International Financial Futures Exchange (LIFFE) and in the Traded Options Market of the Stock Exchange.

open policy. A type of marine policy covering goods, the value of which is not stated, but has to be proved in the event of a loss occurring.

open position. A situation in a money market, whereby any purchase or sale, whether spot or forward, has not been covered by the institution.

operating in reverse. *See* MOPPING UP.

operating lease. *See* FINANCE LEASE.

operation. The act or process of operating; working, action, mode of working; activity, performance of function; effect.

operational. In production, working, effective.

operational research. The consideration in business of all possible ways of doing something, the evaluation of different methods possible, the estimated cost of each, etc., in order to arrive at the best, most effective and cheapest solution. *See also* SYSTEMS ANALYSIS.

operative clause. The words in a deed of conveyance which actually have the effect of transferring the property from one party to another.

opportunity cost. The theory that the real cost of a product is the amount of profit on other goods which could have been produced if the factors of production had been used otherwise.

option. The right of choosing, a choice. On the Stock Exchange a method of speculation by which a purchaser obtains, for an agreed sum (the *'Striking Price'*), the right to buy or sell a certain number of shares or amount of stock at a fixed rate on a specified date, usually within three months. A *'Put' Option* is taken out on shares which are thought to be likely to fall, a *'Call' Option* on shares thought likely to rise. If the shares do not perform as expected, the option is allowed to lapse. A *'Put and Call'* is a double option to buy or sell: a double option is not worth-while unless there is a very big swing in the share price. *'Call of More'* is the right to call at a certain date for an amount of stock equal to that already bought; the option to double a purchase. *'Put of More'* is the sale of a certain stock with the option to sell a similar amount on a specified date at a certain price: the option to double a sale. In the foreign exchange market the option is not whether to buy or sell currency on the forward date, but as to the precise date within a

given period on which the transaction will be effected. For tax purposes an option is chargeable asset for capital gains tax purposes. Where there is an option to sell, the cost of the option is added to the proceeds of sale. In the case of an option to buy the cost of option is deducted from the cost of the purchase. There are now option facilities on shares, currencies and debt securities. *See also* SHARE OPTION SCHEME; TRADED OPTIONS.

option forward rate. The rate at which foreign currency can be bought or sold for delivery between two future dates at the option of the buyer or seller. The option is as to the precise day of completion.

option mortgage scheme. A system in the UK having a number of features not found in conventional mortgage loans. Mortgage interest on one's own house is usually allowed as an off-set against personal taxation, but this is no advantage to people who *do not pay tax*. It is for these people that the Option Mortgage Scheme is intended. A borrower who 'opts' agrees to forgo tax relief in return for a lower mortgage rate. For tax payers paying *above the basic rate,* the tax relief system is the more attractive; that is, it is wiser to have a tax relief mortgage if one's taxable income is in excess of a full year's mortgage interest, at the full rate. For borrowers paying tax at the *current basic rate* there is not much in it, but the scheme is likely to be of interest to those starting out on home ownership with lower incomes. An option mortgage is subject to the condition that the home being bought is intended as a main residence. The loan must not be in excess of £25,000. The difference between the option rate and the mortgage rate of interest is paid by the Government. A facility allowing home buyers to switch between an option mortgage and an ordinary tax relief mortgage was introduced in November 1980. For the first time a borrower with an ordinary mortgage has the right to switch to an option mortgage. Secondly, a borrower with an option mortgage can now switch to an ordinary one after only one year instead of four as under the old arrangements. Switching into the option mortgage scheme on hardship grounds is also easier. Borrowers can normally exercise their right to switch only once during the lifetime of their mortgage. It is only possible to switch in one direction and then back again if one switch is to an option mortgage on hardship grounds.

option pit. The area where the dealers for the commodity fix their deals in open outcry.

option premium. The price paid for an option.

option spread. The margin between the buying and selling prices.

oracle. *See* VIEWDATA.

order bill. A bill payable to a specified person or to his or her order.

order cheque. A cheque payable to a named person or to his or her order.

order for foreclosure. *See* FORE-CLOSURE ORDER.

order in council. An order issued by a British Sovereign with the advice of the Privy Council.

order of payment of debts in bankruptcy. When a bankrupt's trustee has converted the estate into cash, as far as possible, by the sale of the bankrupt's assets, he or she has the task of paying the creditors whose proofs the trustee has passed for payment. The trustee is obliged to pay creditors in a certain order of priority, set out in Sch. 6, Insolvency Act, 1986. Where the bankrupt has sufficient funds, then the order of payment of debts from the estate of the bankrupt will be as follows: (*a*) the fees and expenses of the insolvency practitioner; (*b*) secured creditors, but any deficiency in the value of their security will mean that they will prove for the balance as unsecured creditors (*c*)

preferential creditors (*d*) other creditors.

ordinary partner. *See* PARTNER.

ordinary resolution. One which may be passed by a simple majority.

ordinary shares. The usual type of shares issued by a company, which carry the main risk of the business and are rewarded accordingly. Ordinary shares rank for dividend after preference shares, and are paid only if profits permit. In bad years ordinary shareholders may receive nothing in dividend, but in good years there is theoretically no limit to the amount they may receive, often called *equities*. (There may be a limit imposed by the government for political or financial reasons).

organisation development. A plan to implement ways of developing and changing an organisation as a whole in order that it can meet its objectives more effectively, both at the present time and in the future.

Organisation for Economic Co-operation and Development (OECD). An organisation set up under a convention signed in Paris in December 1960 by the United States and Canada together with the member countries of the Organisation for European Economic Co-operation. This convention provided that the OECD should promote policies designed 1. to achieve the highest sustainable economic growth and employment and a rising standard of living in member countries, while maintaining financial stability, and thus to contribute to the development of the world economy; 2. to contribute to sound economic expansion in member as well as non-member countries in the process of economic development; 3. to contribute to the expansion of world trade on a multilateral, non-discriminatory basis in accordance with international obligations. The organisation examines and co-ordinates statistics provided by member countries and publishes economic studies and booklets on a wide range of subjects. The member countries are Australia, Austria, Belgium, Canada, Denmark, Finland, France, West Germany, Greece, Iceland, Ireland, Italy, Japan, Luxembourg, Netherlands, New Zealand, Norway, Portugal, Spain, Sweden, Switzerland, Turkey, the United Kingdom and the United States.

Organisation of Petroleum Exporting Countries (OPEC). *See* PETRODOLLARS.

original bill. A bill drawn and discounted before it has attracted any indorsement.

or-papier. *See* SPECIAL DRAWING RIGHTS.

ostensible authority. An implied authority of an agent in a particular trade or business.

other names. *See* MARKING NAMES.

out clearing. *See* CLEARING.

outgoing partner. A partner who is leaving the firm, whether for retirement or for a change of occupation. The partner is responsible for the firm's debts as at the date of leaving the firm, and should then give notice of retirement to all those with whom the firm deals. This may be done by individual letter or, in the case of a large firm, by advertisement in the *London Gazette* and in a local newspaper. If this is not done the outgoing partner will continue to be liable for the firm's debts contracted after retirement. An overdrawn partnership banking account should be ruled off if reliance is placed on the retiring partner.

out-of-date cheque. *See* ANTEDATED CHEQUE.

out of the money. *See* TRADED OPTIONS.

output. Production, the amount of goods produced in a given time, the produce of a factory, mine, etc.

output media. Reports, print-outs, documents, punched cards, tape, are examples of output media. In fact, they are any methods (or media) of transferring data from the memory of the computer to some external source.

outside broker. A broker not belonging to the Stock Exchange.

over and short account. An account in a branch where any differences in the tills of cashiers are placed and recorded. By this procedure, any claims and refunds can be linked and any continuous shortages or surpluses can be isolated.

overcapitalised. Said of a company whose assets are worth less than its issued capital, or when its earning capacity is insufficient to pay interest on the capital.

overdraft. A borrowing from a bank on current account, up to a maximum agreed with the bank, interest being calculated on a daily basis. The borrower pays only for what he or she uses, and therefore the overdraft is usually described as the cheapest form of bank accommodation. From the point of view of those in the Bank of England and in the Treasury who are charged with the duty of controlling the country's money supply, the overdraft can be criticised for making their task more difficult. For the fact is that once a banker has agreed to an overdraft facility for a customer, he or she has no control over the use which is made of it. Within the agreed limit the level of borrowing can fluctuate quite wildly. Moreover, as British industry is using at any one time only about half the aggregate overdraft facilities which have been agreed, the scope for increased borrowing is both significant, from the point of view of the control of the money supply, and unpredictable. Also, in times when lending rates are lower than money market rates, large companies with an unused margin of overdraft can make money by borrowing to the limit and relending on the money market (*see* HARD ARBITRAGE). In other countries the nearest equivalent is a 'line of credit' for which banks charge a fee to make available. Even then money must be borrowed in distinct and separate instalments, which are not necessarily always the amount required at that moment by the borrower.

overdue bill. A bill of exchange is overdue the day after it is due for payment. A bill payable on demand is deemed to be overdue when it appears on the face of it to have been in circulation for an unreasonable length of time. What is an unreasonable length of time is, is a question of fact. For purposes of negotiation this appears to be *ten to twelve days,* for purposes of payment *six months. See also* ANTEDATED CHEQUE.

overfunding. In the UK, the technical term to describe the action of the central bank which, when in the course of its duty to control the money supply, sells more gilts (*q.v.*) than it really needs to, so creating a liquidity shortage. This shortage it then relieves by buying bills from the discount houses. This has officially ceased to be part of monetary policy.

overhead costs. The cost of services, material and labour which are incurred whether or not any production is achieved, thus the costs of indirect labour, material and expenses.

overheating. This refers to an economic situation where factors are becoming out of control, so that there is an increase in bank borrowing, prices and wages are beginning to increase, and imports exceed exports widening any balance of payment deficit.

overlines. Overlines are credits made available to borrowers of correspondent banks whose legal limit has been or is about to be reached. US banks are constrained by law from lending more than a specific proportion of the value of their capital and reserves to a single customer and, because of the

proliferation of regional and local banks, many of which are very small compared with their European counterparts, the legal lending limit can be very quickly reached. In this situation, the bank with the limit constraint will look for a larger correspondent bank to take over a portion of the commitment; this is referred to as an overline.

overnight loan. Lending by bankers at call to the discount market against the security of bills of exchange from one day to another. Although the loan is initially repayable on the following day, it may be renewed.

overriding interest. Certain interests may affect registered land without being disclosed in the certificate. The two most important are short leases (not more than twenty-one years) and easements, such as rights of way, light, drainage, etc. A purchaser of registered land should visit the property and inspect it for rights of way or light, etc., and should enquire of the occupier the terms on which the land is presently held. A note to this effect will be found on the back page of the registered land certificate. Overriding interests can also exist in respect of unregistered land and may be revealed by search of the Land Charges Register (class D(iii)) or Local Land Charges Register.

overseas trading corporation. A British trading company which does all its trading with overseas countries and none with the home market. To encourage this (for the trend is in favour of the country's balance of trade) tax concessions are given to such a company.

oversubscribed. Where in a new issue the number of applications for shares is in excess of the number of shares available, the issue is said to be 'oversubscribed'.

over the counter. A way of purchasing or selling securities that are not available from the Stock Exchange, but are traded through a firm that is prepared to make a market in such securities. With the introduction by the Stock Exchange of the *Third Market,* more business is inclined to move to this latter market than to the OTC market.

overtrading. A situation which arises when a company engages in too-rapid expansion so that its financial resources become progressively less able to support the increased scale of operations. The only cure is the provision of further capital from one source or another. The signs of over-trading in the bank account are the rising of an existing *overdraft* until it is checked by the return of cheques unpaid. The account ceases to swing and develops a hard core of *debt.* Cheques to suppliers may be in round amounts – something *on account* to keep creditors quiet for the time being. There is a chronic shortage of cash, and difficulty over finding cover for the weekly *wages cheque.*

owner. A lawful proprietor, a rightful possessor. For the purposes of the Consumer Credit Act, 1974, an owner is a person who bails or (in Scotland) hires out goods under a consumer hire agreement, or the person to whom his

or her rights and duties under the agreement have passed by assignment or operation of law. In relation to a prospective consumer hire agreement this includes the prospective bailor or person from whom the goods are to be hired.

owner's equity. That part of a business that belongs to the owner/s. In simplis-tic terms, it is the total assets less the liabilities i.e. the creditors and lenders to the business.

ownership. The legal title to property vested in a person, as opposed to the possession of it which may very well not amount to ownership (e.g. where something has been borrowed). The owner has the right to do anything he or she wants with a property (subject to social laws and the public health) including the right to destroy it, if he or she so wishes.

owner's risk. Where goods are trans-ported from one place to another, particularly by rail or road, it is not infrequent to have the document of movement claused 'owner's risk'. This means that the responsibility of the carrier would be due to either the negligence or dishonesty of an employee.

P

PA. *See* PER ANNUM.

packing list. A list, often requested by Customs, showing what each parcel or packet contains.

paid cheques. Once a cheque is cancelled at the paying bank its purpose as a medium of transmission of money is concluded; indeed, it can no longer be described as a cheque since it no longer satisfies the definition of a bill of exchange (it is no longer 'payable on demand'). A paid cheque is the property of the drawer, although the banker is entitled to keep it as a voucher until the account becomes a settled account. However, the custom was to send the paid cheques with the statement, so that the customer might verify the entries. Increasing postal charges caused some re-thinking on this point, and most banks now retain paid cheques for six years and then destroy them, and never send them to their customers. An unindorsed cheque which appears to have been paid by the banker on whom it is drawn is evidence of the receipt by the payee of the sum payable by the cheque. If therefore the paid cheque is required as evidence in a court of law, the banker must supply it.

paid-up capital. Money received from shareholders in exchange for issued shares.

paid-up policy. A life assurance policy in respect of which no further premiums are payable.

paid-up shares. *See* FULLY-PAID SHARES; PARTLY-PAID SHARES.

panel on take-overs and mergers. A panel set up in the late 1960s, as a result of the City's anxiety about the way in which certain take-overs had been conducted. There is a full-time professional executive which deals with day-to-day problems and enquiries and a panel consisting of leading City representatives who meet to consider any matter of particular interest and to adjudicate upon any cases where a decision of the executive has been disputed by a company. The rules formulated by the panel are published in a City Code.

paper. A newspaper, a document, bills of exchange, promissory notes, a set of examination questions.

paper bid. An offer of its own shares by a company making a take-over bid.

paper currency. Banknotes representing money made legal tender by government, which circulate as an accepted medium of exchange.

paper-gold. *See* SPECIAL DRAWING RIGHTS.

paper money. Documents representing money, such as banknotes, promissory notes, bills of exchange, or postal orders.

paper profit. An increase in the value of an investment which has been retained and not, as yet, sold to realise the profit.

par. Equality of value; the nominal amount of securities. *above par.* At a price above the face value, at a premium. *below par.* At a discount. *on a par with.* Of equal value, degree, etc.

parallel. Precisely corresponding, similar; a thing exactly like another, a counterpart, a comparison.

parallel market. Side by side with the traditional short-term money markets in which the discount houses are prominent, secondary or parallel money markets have developed in short-term funds. These markets are mainly in the foreign currency deposits of non-residents, the sterling deposits of non-residents, or the surplus sterling funds held by domestic banks. They comprise the *Eurocurrency market,* the *sterling and dollar certificate of deposit markets,* the *inter-bank sterling* *market,* and *the local authority market.* The merchant banks, the discount houses, and the British overseas and foreign banks are prominent in each of these markets.

parallel rate of exchange. Where two tier rates of exchange are in operation, the unofficial rate.

parallels of latitude. Imaginary circles whose planes are parallel to that of the equator, the latitude of every point upon each circle being the same.

paraph. The flourish beneath a signature, originally intended as a precaution against forgery; to initial or sign.

parcel. A bundle or package; a number of things forming a group or lot; a piece of land; a number of bills of exchange assembled by a bank which have the same due date, or a similar parcel providing a series of bills which fall due for approximately the same amount each day for a period of days, or each month for a period of months.

parcener. A joint heir. *See* CO-PAR-CENERS.

parent company. A holding or operational company controlling a number of subsidiaries.

pari. Par.

pari passu. At the same rate or pace, with equal step, in the same degree or proportion, likewise, enjoying the same rights.

parities. Rates of exchange – the value of one currency in terms of another. Parities are fixed by supply and demand and therefore reflect confidence in a country's general economic situation. *See also* MULTIPLE EXCHANGE RATES; PURCHASING POWER PARITY.

parol. Word of mouth. All interests in land created by parol and not put in writing and signed by the persons so creating the same have, notwithstanding any consideration having been given for the same, the force and effect of interests at will only.

par rate of exchange. Par values for currencies related to the gold content

of coinage.

partial. Affecting a part only, incomplete, not total, biased in favour of one party, unfair, having a preference for.

partial acceptance. *See* QUALIFIED ACCEPTANCE.

partial intestacy. The case where a testator has left instructions in a will for the disposition of some, but not all, of his or her assets.

partial loss. The damage, short of total loss, suffered by a ship or her cargo from any risks against which insurance has been taken out.

partial payment. An amount paid to a creditor which is in partial settlement of the outstanding debt. Partial payment of a bill of exchange should not be considered as settlement of the bill but can be protested for dishonour.

participating loan. A loan granted to a borrower, where more than one bank or financial institution has participated in granting the full amount. Known more popularly as a syndicated loan. *See* SYNDICATED LOAN.

participating policy. *See* 'WITH PROFITS' POLICY.

participating preference shares. Those entitling the holders to a preferential payment of a fixed dividend before other classes of shareholders and, in addition, to a share in any surplus profits of the company provided that the ordinary shareholders have received a specified maximum rate of dividend.

particular. Pertaining to a single person or thing, special, peculiar, characteristic, single, separate, individual, private, minute; precise, exact; remarkable, noteworthy; specially attentive; an item, detail, an instance.

particular average. An accidental loss involving part of the cargo on a ship, such as damage by fire or sea water, or even by being washed overboard, in circumstances where the safety of the ship itself is not endangered. Such a loss is borne wholly by the owners of the cargo concerned.

particular lien. The right of a dealer, warehousekeeper, etc., to retain goods in possession until the debt in respect of those particular goods is paid.

partly-paid shares. Shares on which there is a percentage of uncalled capital. They are comparatively rare, and are not popular with shareholders because of the liability to further calls. However, the offer of partly-paid shares in recent privatisations has, with the exception of British Petroleum, proved successful. Although the value of the shares may increase as the calls are paid, and in the long-term the shareholder should suffer no loss, nevertheless in the short-term the investor has to find the money at a time which may be inconvenient.

partner. A partaker, a sharer, an associate in business, a member of a partnership. *See also* DECEASED PARTNER; DORMANT PARTNER; INCOMING PARTNER; LIMITED PARTNER; NOMINAL PARTNER; ORDINARY PARTNER; OUTGOING PARTNER; QUASI-PARTNER; SALARIED PARTNER; SURVIVING PARTNER.

partner by estoppel. *See* QUASI-PARTNER.

partnership. The relation which subsists between persons carrying on a business in common with a view of profit. No written agreement or deed between the partners is legally necessary, though it often exists. All that is necessary is a written, verbal or implied agreement between the partners. A partnership can consist of from two to twenty people; qualified persons practising as solicitors or accountants, and persons carrying on business as members of a recognised stock exchange, may number more. *See also* DEED OF PARTNERSHIP.

part payment. A payment of less than the full amount owing, a payment on account. If an acceptor of an inland bill makes part payment only on the due date it may be accepted, but the other parties to the bill should be notified to retain their liability for the balance, and the bill should be noted for the unpaid balance. A record should be indorsed on the bill, which is retained by the holder, that the sum paid has been received in part payment without prejudice to the rights of other parties. In the case of a foreign bill, it must be protested. In England a cheque is either paid in full or not at all, but in Scotland if a cheque is presented and there are funds on the account, but insufficient to meet the bill, they are attached. *See also* CHEQUE AS AN ASSIGNMENT OF FUNDS.

par value. Nominal value.

pasigraphy. A universal system of writing, using signs representing ideas, not words. Although this is a very old and primitive system, modern advertising has come back to it to illustrate and to supplement figures; *viz.,* in the presentation of balance sheets or the asset and liability position of a bank.

passbook. A book in which debit and credit entries on a banking or deposit account are entered. Formerly common on bank current accounts, the passbook has been superseded by the computerised statement which also shows a balance. Passbooks for deposit and savings accounts are also being replaced. The passbook is still found, however, in savings banks and building societies.

passbook savings account. Approximates closely to the typical seven-day deposit account operated by UK commercial banks and is the traditional way for private individuals to save in the US. Interest is compounded continuously and paid quarterly, and the rate is limited by Federal Reserve Regulation Q. Such accounts are offered by commercial banks, savings and loan associations and credit unions, but in recent years have represented an ever decreasing proportion of such institutions' total deposits as other savings mediums, such as money market funds, have provided a more attractive alternative for the small investor.

passing the dividend. Making no dividend payment at the end of the year's trading because insufficient profits, or no profits, have been earned.

passport. A document issued by the Foreign Office of a country to its own citizens and intended to ensure their safe passage through a foreign country. In practical terms it is often used as a means of identification and for the purposes of encashment of cheques, travel cheques while abroad, opening accounts for non-residents and payment of funds in favour of non-customers of the bank.

past due. The Federal Reserve defines delinquency as follows: 1. On single payment notes, the principal amounts shall be considered past due fifteen days following maturity. 2. On demand notes, the principal amount will be considered past due when interest is due and unpaid for fifteen days. However, individual state laws will override this rule where an earlier time for payment may be specified. 3. Consumer, mortgage or term business loans are considered past due in whole after one instalment is thirty days delinquent. 4. For other types of credit, including unpaid outstandings under cancelled advance facilities; discounted outgoing foreign bills matured and unpaid, and overdrafts resulting from a customer not paying the bank for acceptances or drafts paid, delinquency usually begins on the first day following maturity.

pawn. Something deposited as security for money borrowed, a pledge.

pawnbroker. One who lends money on something deposited with him. The borrower may redeem the pledged property within six months, in default of which it can be sold.

pawnee. One who accepts goods as security for a loan. For the purposes of the Consumer Credit Act, 1974, the term includes any person to whom the rights and duties of the original pawnee have passed by assignment or operation of law.

pawner, pawnor. One who pledges goods. For the purposes of the Consumer Credit Act, 1974, the term includes any person to whom the rights and duties of the original pawner have passed by assignment or operation of law.

pawn-receipt. A term used in Consumer Credit Act, 1974 to describe a receipt in a prescribed form given by a person who takes any article in pawn, under a regulated agreement, to the person from whom he receives it at the time of receipt. A person who takes any article in pawn from an individual who he or she knows to be (or who appears to be and is) a *minor,* commits an offence. The above has no application to a pledge of documents of title or a non-commercial agreement (s. 114 of the Act). *See also* NON-COMMERCIAL AGREEMENT; REGULATED AGREEMENT.

pay. To discharge one's obligations; to give money for goods received or a service rendered; to compensate, to discharge a debt; *reward,* wages, salary, compensation.

pay as you earn (PAYE). A system of tax collection whereby the tax owing is deducted from weekly or monthly wage or salary earners by employers who are made responsible for the collection of the tax. Each employee is given a code number dependent upon personal allowances. The employer uses coding tables which give the correct weekly or monthly deductions.

pay day. The last day of the settlement on the Stock Exchange. Also called account day or settling day. *See* PAYMENT.

payee. The person named on a bill to whom, or to whose order, payment is to be made. Where a bill is not payable to bearer, the payee must be named or otherwise indicated therein with reasonable certainty. *See also* FICTITIOUS PAYEE; IMPERSONAL PAYEE.

paying banker. Without a customer's authority the banker has no right to pay away his or her money. The authority is the customer's signature. The first duty of the cancelling clerk is, therefore, to be sure that a signature corresponds to the specimen signature supplied. A banker paying a cheque with a forged signature has no defence unless he or she can plead estoppel. The banker will also check the following points: 1. the cheque must not be 'stale' or postdated; 2. words and figures must agree; 3. the cheque must not be stopped; 4. the cheque must be drawn on the branch; 5. there must be an acceptable payee's name specified; 6. if the cheque is marked to show that a receipt is required, the receipt must have been duly completed; 7. the cheque must not be crossed by two bankers (unless one is acting as agent for the other); 8. the cheque must be complete and regular, i.e. no alterations without the drawer's confirmation; 9. no legal bars; 10. a final practical point is to check that the customer has got the money. Statutory protection is available to the banker paying an *open cheque* bearing a forged indorsement if it is paid in good faith and in the ordinary course of business; to one paying a crossed *cheque* if it is in good faith and without negligence; and to one paying a cheque, whether *crossed or open,* which is not indorsed or is irregularly indorsed. No protection is available to the banker who pays a bill of exchange (other than a cheque) bearing a *forged indorsement.* Indorsements are found only where a bill or cheque has been negotiated; in such cases the paying banker must see that the indorsement(s) purport(s) to be correct. Across the counter cheques payable to 'wages' or 'cash' should be paid only to the drawer or a known agent. In the case of *order cheques* paid across the counter it is the practice to require the signature of the payee by way of indorsement. *See* PAYMENT OF CHEQUES.

paying-in slip. *See* CREDIT SLIP.

Paymaster General. The officer appointed to make payments on behalf of the various Departments of the British Government.

payment. Settlement, discharge of a debt or obligation. For the purpose of the Consumer Credit Act, 1974, 'payment' includes 'tender'. A bill of exchange is discharged by payment in due course by, or on behalf of, the drawee or acceptor. Payment for stocks and shares purchased on the Stock Exchange is 'for cash', that is immediately, in the case of Government stocks and part payments called for under the terms of a new issue. Ordinary stocks or shares are traded 'for the account'. The 'account' runs from Monday to the following Friday week unless a bank holiday comes in the fortnight, in which case the account runs for three weeks. Payment is made on Settlement Day which is ten days after the ending of the account (six working days). *See also* CONTANGO; STOCK EXCHANGE.

payment by mistake. Money paid away under a mistake of law is usually presumed irrecoverable. Where the mistake is one of fact, recovery may be possible. The subject falls under three broad headings: *1. Money credited in error to a customer's bank account.* Here two considerations have seemed important; *(a)* the length of time over which the banker has been making the incorrect entries, and *(b)* the state of awareness of the customer. In the first case the banker has been held by continuous wrong entries to be making representations and to be, thereby, inducing the customer to draw money to which he or she was not entitled; and the longer the period of overcrediting, the more serious the representations. In the second case the courts will not allow a customer to 'snap' at an advantage, but the onus is on the bank to show that *the customer knew,* or ought to have known of the error. In this context the sex, position and character of the customer has been important; e.g. an elderly lady with no business training is more readily accepted as likely to be ignorant of the bank's mistake(s) than, say, an accountant or a solicitor. The customer held to be *understandably ignorant* of the error, who has *bona fide* changed his or her position in reliance on the misrepresentations of the bank, *cannot be made to repay. 2. Money paid away in error across the counter.* Where the mistake of fact lies between the bank and the drawer, an innocent holder will not be made to make restitution. Thus a cashier who has just paid a cheque, then discovers that the drawer has not the funds to meet it, cannot recover the money even though the recipient is still in the bank. But where a cashier pays away too much in error, the amount is recoverable if this can be proved. *3. Payment in error of a 'stopped' cheque.* In such a case the account of the customer cannot be debited, but the sum so paid is recoverable from the payee provided that he or she has not changed his or her position. Here the negligence of the paying banker has been held to be immaterial.

payment for honour *supra* protest. *See* NOTARIAL ACT OF HONOUR.

payment in due course. Payment made at (or after) the maturity of a bill, to the holder thereof in good faith and without notice that his or her title to the bill is defective if such be the case.

payment of cheques. Cheques are normally paid by the paying banker who has protection by ss. 60 and 80 of the Bills of Exchange Act, 1882. Before final payment is made and the customer's account is debited, the banker must ascertain that the cheque is complete and regular on the face of it, i.e. it is correctly dated; there is a

payee; words and figures agree; the signature is in accordance with the mandate; there are no unauthorised alterations; the cheque is not mutilated and any endorsements are correct; there are funds on the account or proper arrangements have been made and there has been no countermand of payment; there is no legal bar; lastly, the cheque is not crossed by two clearing banks.

payment on account. The partial payment of a debt due, a deposit. The intention is that when the work has been completed, the balance will be paid.

payroll credit. A list of weekly or monthly wage or salary payments prepared by a customer for his or her workforce and passed, together with a single debit, through the banking system so that individual credits will reach the accounts of individual employees on a given day, a single total being debited to the account of the employer. Customers who have their own computer may prepare payroll tapes which are passed through the Bankers' Automated Clearing Service. Banks operating a payroll service will prepare periodic payments from information supplied by the employer and continue to pass entries until advised of any change.

payroll tax. A tax on a business according to the number in the workforce employed.

peer review. The practice, mostly in America, of having the work of the firm of auditors who examine a company's accounts vetted by another accounting firm, who will come in to inspect the methods, working papers and auditing procedures of the first firm, to ensure that no mistakes or sloppy procedures have crept into their work. The purpose is to provide an additional safeguard for standards of work.

peg. To fix or mark with a peg; on the *Stock Exchange,* to keep the price of shares steady at a given price by buying (or selling); on the *foreign exchanges,* to maintain a country's currency at a fixed rate of exchange by the intervention of the central authority; of *prices generally,* to control by governmental decree. *See also* CRAWLING PEG.

penalty. A punishment for an offence, a sum to be forfeited for breach of a rule or contract. *See also* STAMPING UNDER PENALTY.

penalty clause. A clause in a contract fixing a sum of money to be paid by the party in default of any of the contractual conditions.

pence rates. Rates of exchange quoted in pence per foreign unit.

pending action. Any law-suit which is to be heard at a future time, but which may well affect the title to property, whether real or personal, in the present. Thus an action pending as to the ownership of land must, in the case of unregistered land, be registered on the Pending Actions Register at the Land Charges Department; or, in the case of registered land, be protected by a caution on the Land Register. In both cases the object is to *warn* intending purchasers of the fact that the title is less than perfect. An action pending as to the validity of a will may lead to the appointment of an administrator *pendente lite.*

penny. The bronze penny was introduced in 1860, superseding the earlier copper coin of the same value. The present penny, orignally called a new penny, was introduced in 1971. It was worth 2.4 old pence. There is a silver penny in the Maundy Money set.

penny bank. A savings bank of the late nineteenth century, so called because it would accept a sum as small as one penny on deposit.

penny stocks. Shares that are quoted at very low prices, usually 50p or less each. Many are regarded as speculative.

pension. A periodical allowance for past services paid by a government or an employer; an annuity paid to retired officers, soldiers, etc. *See also* CONTRIBUTORY PENSION; NON-CONTRIBUTORY PENSION; OLD-AGE PENSION.

pension funds. Investments maintained by companies and other employers to pay the annual sum required under the business organisation's pension scheme. Large pension funds operate quite heavily on the Stock Exchange and in the capital markets. Insurance companies managing private pension schemes also buy and sell stocks, shares, etc., as they endeavour to obtain the highest returns. Many pension funds have power to make wide investments; loans on long-term mortgages are sometimes made available and some pension funds have even taken equity stakes in unquoted companies. Others have gone in for works of art: an example is the British Rail Pension Fund which has one of the biggest art collections formed in this country since the second world war. It covers a huge range: Egyptian antiquities, Ming and other Chinese porcelain, medieval objects, Renaissance jewels, African tribal art, and pictures by Picasso, Renoir and many other masters.

PEP. *See* PERSONAL EQUITY PLAN.

peppercorn rent. A nominal rent.

per annum. By the year, yearly.

per capita. Individually, each, per head.

per cent. per centum. By the hundred.

per contra. On the other side (of the account), to balance it, on the other hand.

per diem. By the day, daily.

performance bond. A customer engaged in the building or construction industry may tender for a contract and be asked to supply a performance bond or tender guarantee. Such a requirement is often found in contracts for work overseas. The authority inviting tenders is really asking to be reassured that the builder or contractor who gets the job will be able to finish it, and will not go bankrupt or into liquidation half way through. The bank, if satisfied that its customer is technically capable of handling the job, and financially strong enough to see it through, will issue a bond for due performance, in which there will be dates and standards for completing the work and provision for penalties in the event of non-compliance. This will enable the customer's tender to get to the stage where it will be considered. The bank takes a counter-indemnity from the customer to cover its own position. *See also* STANDBY LETTER OF CREDIT; SURETY BOND.

performance fund. An investment or unit trust where the investment policy is intended to yield higher than the average.

peripheral. All calculations performed by computer central processing units (*q.v.*) ultimately come down to an ability to 'sense' the presence of an electrical impulse. All data on which we require a computer to work must therefore be presented to it in the form of electrical impulses. The function of peripheral equipment is: 1. to translate words and figures into 'computer-recognisable' impulses, e.g. terminals (*see under* ELECTRONIC DATA PROCESSING); 2. to store data for presentation to CPUs when needed, e.g. magnetic tape and disk units; 3. to present results of computer operations in humanly understandable form, e.g. visual display units (*q.v.*).

per mensem. By the month, monthly.

permissive waste. Allowing the buildings on an estate to fall into a state of decay, thus a wrong of omission.

perpetual. Unending, eternal, persistent, continual, constant.

perpetual annual rent charge. *See* FEE FARM RENT.

perpetual annuity. An annuity payable for ever.

perpetual debenture. A debenture with no date for repayment, intended to be a permanent debt.

perpetual injunction. *See* INJUNCTION.

perpetuity. The number of years purchase to be given for an annuity; a perpetual annuity. *In Perpetuity.* For ever.

per procurationem (per pro). By the agency of, by proxy. A form of words used by an agent when signing for a principal, i.e. '*per pro* John Jones, S. Smith', where Jones is the principal and Smith the agent. '*Per Pro*' is also shortened still further to '*p.p.*'.

per se. By itself, or itself.

personal. Peculiar to a person as a private individual; directed against a person; of possessions, belonging to a person.

personal account. The account of a person, persons or any legal entity held in the account of a business.

personal bar. The Scots law equivalent of the doctrine of estoppel (*q.v.*).

personal cheque. A service for bank customers who wish to issue cheques from time to time but do not wish to have, or to pay for, a full banking service. The personal cheque service is therefore made available to them on a basis of payment per cheque.

personal credit agreement. An agreement between a debtor and a creditor by which the creditor provides the debtor with credit of any amount.

personal equity plan. A method of savings brought in by the Chancellor of the Exchequer which allows the ordinary person to invest between £20 and £250 per month in equities through the agency of a bank, insurance company or unit trust company. Capital profits earned from these investments are not subject to the normal capital gains and income tax. A major criticism of personal equity plans is the lack of spread of funds.

personal estate. Any property other than freehold land is personal estate.

personal identification number. This

is commonly known as PIN. This number issued by a bank to its customer, so that the customer either by using an EFTPOS card, credit card, etc. may obtain funds, transfer funds, or pay debts, by specifying the number during the process of instructing the bank (via a computer terminal) to take a stated action. In a home banking situation, a number of controls and checks are inserted before instructions regarding movement of funds or obtaining balances are complied with.

personalisation of cheques. The printing on each cheque of the name of the customer, to assist in the recognition of signatures and in sorting.

personal liability. A person is jointly and severally liable for the debts of a company if he or she, as a director or shadow director, contravenes s. 216 Insolvency Act, 1986. A person who is a party to a joint account or a partner in a trading concern, is also normally jointly and severally liable for the debts owed.

personal loan. A bank loan where the interest is added to the amount borrowed and the total is then repaid by regular monthly repayments over an agreed period, usually six months to three years, (in some cases, longer). Each repayment consists partly of capital and partly of interest. If any instalment is not paid on time, the whole of the debt becomes repayable immediately. This gives the bank a right to bring an action for the money. Unlike a hire purchase contract (to which the personal loan is intended to be a cheaper alternative) the bank has no rights over the object purchased with the money lent.

personal poinding. (*Sc. Law*) *See* POINDING.

personal property. Movable property, goods, money, etc., leasehold estates.

personal representative. An executor or an administrator, whose duty is to stand in the place of the deceased for the purpose of winding up his or her estate, paying debts and legacies, and distributing any residue according to the will, or to the rules for succession on intestacy. The personal representatives for the period of the executorship of a deceased person are deemed in law his or her heirs and assigns within the meaning of all trusts and powers.

personal security. Security for an advance which consists of a guarantee by a third person.

personal tax. A tax on an individual, such as income tax, in contradistinction to general taxes such as customs duty and value added tax.

personalty. Personal effects, movable property, e.g. furniture, jewels, as distinguished from realty.

petition. An earnest request or prayer, especially one presented to a sovereign or to Parliament; a written supplication, an entreaty; a *formal written application* to a court, as by an unpaid creditor that a debtor be made bankrupt, or that a company be put into liquidation. *See also* BANKRUPTCY; COMPULSORY LIQUIDATION.

petition for bankruptcy. By s. 264, Insolvency Act, 1986, a petition in bankruptcy may be presented to the court as follows: (*a*) by the individual himself; (*b*) by the supervisor or other person bound by the voluntary arrangement; (*c*) in the case of criminal bankruptcy, by an official with powers under the Powers of Criminal Courts Act, 1973. A bankruptcy petition should not be presented to the court unless the debtor is: (*a*) domiciled in England or Wales; (*b*) personally present in England or Wales on the day on which the petition is presented; (*c*) has, at any time in the period of three years, been ordinarily *resident* or has had a place of *residence* in England or Wales or has carried on *business* in England or Wales (s. 265).

petrodollars. Surplus cash gained by the oil exporters (the Arab countries, Nigeria, Venezuela, Indonesia) which they have not spent on imports, but have invested at interest in other countries in varying proportions, mostly on short call. As the oil was at one time mainly invoiced and quoted in dollars, the term 'petrodollars' was invented. These sums were so vast that considerable uneasiness was felt at one stage as to whether the world's existing financial systems could cope with them. It was also thought that so much cash taken out of world trade was one cause of the world recession experienced in 1974. Most of these petrodollars were invested in New York and in London, and there sometimes referred to as 'OPEC funds'. As things turned out, the oil producers' spare revenues declined considerably, so that in the UK the anxiety became that there would not be enough for London to attract the funds necessary for the UK to finance its vastly increased fuel bills, support sterling, live with inflation, and stave off the onset of serious unemployment.

petty cash. Small items of expenditure, especially in an office.

piece goods. Textile fabrics, e.g. shirtings, sold by recognised lengths of the material.

piecemeal distribution. A procedure whereby a business in the process of liquidation, sells its assets and settles the debts due, then distributes funds to the owners' of the business. Any funds due to them are on a pro rata basis.

piece rates. Payment by results. The worker's wages depend upon the volume of production he or she attains.

pig driving. A phrase to indicate a deprecated method of writing up an account by hand vertically rather than horizontally. The normal method of writing up debits to a customer's account would be, first, the *date;* then the *name* of the payee; and finally the *amount.* If a whole series of payees' names is inserted vertically, and then the clerk goes back and fills in all the

amounts, this is 'pig driving'. If the clerk makes an error while doing this, the result will be a whole series of inaccurate postings. In banking the term was frequently used in the days of handwritten ledgers and passbooks.

piggy bank. A china model pig with a slot for money; a symbol of Victorian thrift – the forerunner of the home safe.

pig on pork. Bills drawn by one branch of a firm or company on another, or by one person or firm on another intimately connected, the implication being that the bills are not truly two-name bills.

pin. *See* PERSONAL IDENTIFICATION NUMBER.

pip. A digit after the whole number and decimal point in an amount which specifies the rate of exchange.

pit. The area on the 'floor' of LIFFE where dealers deal by open outcry.

P & L a/c. The abbreviation for profit and loss account.

placing. A private sale of a new issue to a limited number of investors, usually the big institutions, a proportion of the issue being allocated to the market to be available to the general public. *See also* INTRODUCTION; OFFER FOR SALE.

placing broker. An insurance broker who places various percentages of a risk he or she is employed by a client to cover with various syndicates at Lloyd's.

plaint. An accusation, a charge, a statement in writing of the complaint, etc.

plaintiff. The one who sues in a court of law.

plant. Fixed machinery, tools, etc., used in an industrial undertaking.

plc. The abbreviation for public limited company.

plead. To allege in proof or vindication, to offer as an excuse, to argue at the bar, to carry on a law suit, to present any answer to the declarations of the plaintiff.

pleader. One who pleads, especially a

lawyer who makes a plea in a court of justice, an advocate.

pleading. The art of conducting a case, as an advocate. *See also* SPECIAL PLEADING.

pleadings. Written statements of plaintiff and defendant in support of their claims.

pledge. A delivery of goods, or the documents of title to goods, by a debtor to his creditors as security for a debt, or for any other obligation. It is understood that the subject of the pledge will be returned to the pledgor when the debt has been paid or the obligation fulfilled. For the purposes of the Consumer Credit Act, 1974, 'pledge' means the pawnee's rights over an article taken in pawn. *See also* NEGATIVE PLEDGE.

pledgee. A person to whom goods are pledged.

plimsoll mark. A line required to be placed on every British ship, marking the level to which the authorised weight of cargo sinks her.

plus value. Appreciation in price.

poinding. *(Sc. Law) personal poinding* is the seizure of personal property of a debtor in settlement of the debt. As a preliminary there must first be an order of the court, called a *decree* (*q.v.*) leading to a formal requisition, served personally on the debtor if he or she can be found, or by *edict* (*q.v.*) if he cannot, by a sheriff officer. This requisition, or schedule of charge, will specify the days of charge – usually seven days – within which payment must be made. If payment has not been made at the end of this time, the creditor may then proceed to poind. It is the sheriff officer who actually seizes the property (all corporeal movables belonging to the debtor and in possession), which is then valued, listed, and offered for sale. *Real poinding,* or *poinding of the ground,* is a diligence (*q.v.*) which can be called into service where a debt, or the interest on it, in respect of an obligation incurred on

the *security of land,* is in arrears. The person entitled can poind the movables on the ground, i.e. he or she can, after obtaining a decree, seize any movable chattels or movable fixtures on the property. In the case of tenants the right extends only to the amount of rent due but unpaid. *See also* NOTOUR BANKRUPTCY.

point. A unit of measure of a rate or an index number; thus if a rate goes from 60 to 80, (whether per cent or in monetary terms), the increase in the rate is 20 points.

Point of Sale Terminals. *See* ELECTRONIC FUNDS TRANSFER AT POINT OF SALE (EFTPOS).

polarisation. Under the Financial Services Act, banks must choose between selling their own life assurance and financial products or, acting as an independent intermediary and selling the products of other companies. At the time of writing, Barclays, Lloyds and Midland Bank decided to sell their own products, while National Westminster Bank will still act as brokers and sell the products of other financial institutions.

policy. A document issued by an insurance company containing the terms and conditions of an insurance contract and which is legal evidence of the agreement to insure. *See also* COMPREHENSIVE POLICY; ECGD POLICY; ENDOWMENT POLICY; FAMILY PROTECTION POLICY; FLOATING POLICY; GENERAL POLICY; INDUSTRIAL LIFE POLICY; JOINT LIVES POLICY; LIFE POLICY; LLOYD'S POLICY; MIXED POLICY; NAMED POLICY; NON-PARTICIPATING POLICY; OPEN POLICY; PAID-UP POLICY; SHORT-TERM POLICY; SINGLE PREMIUM POLICY; SURVIVORSHIP POLICY; TIME POLICY; TONTINE POLICY; UNIT-LINKED POLICY; VALUED POLICY; VOYAGE POLICY; WHOLE LIFE POLICY; 'WITH PROFITS' POLICY.

policy holder. The person who has a

policy in his or her possession or under his or her control, usually the insured.

policy underwriter. One who writes his or her name under a policy of marine insurance, thus undertaking to indemnify the insured against the risks specified in the policy; a member of an underwriting syndicate at Lloyd's.

port bill of lading. A bill of lading bearing an authorised signature indicating that the goods covered have been received by the signatory at the port of shipment.

portfolio. The securities held by, or on behalf of, an investor; the list of such securities; the holdings of bills of exchange by banks or discount houses.

portfolio management service. The management by a bank or financial institution of the quoted securities of a customer. This includes the safe-keeping of securities, dealing with scrip and rights issues, the collection of dividends, the preparation of valuations, periodic review, and re-allocation of the available funds where this is thought necessary.

portion. A part, a share, an allotment, a dowry, the part of an estate descending to an heir.

port register. See REGISTER OF SHIPS.

position. State, situation; the balance on a running account, etc.

possession. The act or state of possessing, holding or occupying as owner; the exercise of such control as attaches to ownership, actual detention or occupancy; property, goods, wealth. Contrasted with ownership (having the legal right to) in cases where an equitable title is taken by way of security for a loan, the *lender taking possession* of the document of title to the security, while the *owner retains its ownership. See also* WRIT OF POSSESSION. *in possession.* In actual occupancy, holding. *to give possession.* To put another in possession. *to take possession.* To enter on, to seize.

possessory lien. The right to keep possession of the property of another

until a debt due from the latter is paid. There is at common law no right of sale, thus the lien has nuisance value only. In some cases, however, a right of sale is given by some statute.

possessory title. The title acquired by a person who has been in the undisputed possession of real property for a period of twelve or more years, not having paid any rent in that time nor acknowledged the right or claim of any other to that land. In registered land, the title granted by the Registrar in cases where the deeds when examined showed no more than that the applicant was in possession of the land. A purchaser or a mortgagee must therefore investigate the title prior to registration as thoroughly as if it were an unregistered title, for the State guarantee only refers to the period after issue of the certificate and not before. The Registrar has power to convert a *possessory freehold title* into an *absolute freehold title* after fifteen years, and to convert a possessory leasehold title into a *good leasehold title* after ten years.

post. To advertise, to make known, to pass entries to an account; a postal letter-box, a dispatch of mails; a duty; a place of employment.

postal giro. A system of transferring money through the post offices of a country as an alternative to other systems of money transmission provided by either post offices or banks. Many European countries operate a postal giro. The British system was introduced in 1968. See GIROBANK.

postal order. An order for a sum of money, specified on the face of the instrument, issued to a customer at one post office for payment at another. This is not a negotiable instrument. It may be paid into the credit of a customer's account at a bank. At the end of the day the bank will list all the postal orders received, total them, and claim the amount from a local post office.

postdate. To date after the day of issue. On cheques, postdating may be the intention of the drawer in isolated cases, but if it happens frequently it is a sign of financial weakness on the customer's part. Banks are bound to respect the drawer's instruction not to pay a postdated cheque until the due date, but they strongly discourage the practice of postdating because it holds many risks for the banker. If the banker pays the cheque, without noticing the postdating, he or she runs the following risks; the customer may stop payment before the due date, or notice of the customer's death or mental illness may be received. There are a number of possibilities connected with *bankruptcy*. Notice of an *act of bankruptcy* committed by the customer would restrict the banker to paying cheques only to the *customer* himself; notice of a *petition or receiving order* against the customer would stop *all payments*. If the customer is a limited company, the corresponding notice would be *notice of a resolution to wind up,* or a winding-up order. There may be notice that the customer is an *undischarged bankrupt,* when again the account would have to be stopped. There may be service of a *garnishee order or summons.* But most of these, though real risks, are unlikely ones; in practice the most likely danger is that of a *stop* being received, the next most likely, that payment of a post-dated cheque may result in another cheque which ought to have been paid being *returned* for lack of funds, resulting in a possible action by the customer against the bank for breach of contract, or libel, or both. Legally, however, a bill is not invalid by reason only that it is postdated.

posting. The act of recording an entry in a ledger account.

Post Office Register. *See* DIRECTOR OF SAVINGS.

pound. The British money of account consisting of one hundred pence, a sovereign, written £.

poundage. Commission, allowance or charge of so much in the pound.

pound cost averaging. Where stock or shares are bought in instalments over a period at varying prices, an harmonic mean will be established (as with unit-trust linked life assurance policies). The lower this average price, the higher the ultimate profit is likely to be when the securities are sold.

pound sterling. The British standard pound of one hundred pence as a gold coin or a paper note.

power of attorney. A legal document empowering one person to act for another, either generally or for some specific transaction. The power is usually under seal, and must describe precisely the extent of the authority of the agent. It may be for a fixed period of time. A trustee may, by power of attorney, delegate for a period not exceeding twelve months the execution or exercise of all or any of the trusts, powers and discretions vested in him or her either alone or jointly with another or others. Such delegation may not be made to his or her only other co-trustee (unles a trust corporation). The instrument of delegation must be witnessed. The donor of the power is liable for the acts or defaults of the donee. An *irrevocable power of attorney* is one so expressed to be, and which is given to secure a proprietary interest of the donee of the power, or the performance of an obligation owed to the donee. So long as the donee has that interest, or the obligation remains undischarged, the power cannot be revoked by the donor without the consent of the donee; nor by the death, incapacity or bankruptcy of the donor nor, if the donor is a body corporate, by its winding-up or dissolution. In the US, a power of attorney is also a document which authorises a third person to act as agent for the person signing the document; such person is known as the *attorney in fact.* It is common for major US banks involved in syndicated loans to employ in-house counsels to act for other banks involved in the credit but for whom the expense of sending a representative to sign the loan document, in a distant location, would be prohibitive. A general power of attorney authorises the attorney in fact to act for the principal in all matters; a *special power of attorney* is more restrictive in scope.

power of attorney clause. A clause in an equitable mortgage of land by means of which the lending banker can obtain a legal title as a preliminary to sale of the security, in cases where the customer has failed to repay and has also failed to keep a promise to sign any documents which the bank may require him or her to sign (where such a clause has also been incorporated in the form of mortgage). The power of attorney clause may run as follows: 'I hereby irrevocably appoint any one of the Controllers of the Bank to be my attorney, and in my name and on my behalf to sign, seal, or otherwise perfect any deed for conveying the freehold estate in the mortgage property to any purchaser thereof. A suitable conveyance to the bank as mortgagee (a term included in 'purchaser') by the attorney will pass the title to the bank, after which the property can be sold and the indebtedness repaid. Because land must be conveyed under seal, any attorney expected to convey land must be appointed under seal. The Deed of Appointment in this case is the bank's form of equitable mortgage, which must, therefore, be under seal for this reason.

power of sale. A bank, if it is to realise its security should the necessity arise, must be able to sell it. Where the legal interest has been transferred into the name of the bank's nominee company, no difficulty exists, for the bank is the owner, and an owner can sell. Where an equitable mortgage only has been taken, the customer retains the owner-ship. Because of this, the equitable mortgage form contains a clause by which the customer is obliged to promise to sign any papers as desired by the bank in order to realise the security. If the customer will not keep this promise the remedy must be sought in the courts. The bank will usually ask for an order to sell or an order for transfer and foreclosure and, if this is granted, the bank will be able to deal with the security. An alternative to the recourse to the court is to take a blank undated signed form of transfer before the money is lent. This can be filled in later, if required, and does not need the co-operation of the customer. However, because the date of a deed is the day on which it was delivered, this method cannot be used where the transfer has to be executed under seal. In the case of land, the legal mortgagee has a statutory or express power of sale on default. If the mortgage is equitable only, application to the court for an order for sale is again necessary.

powers of mortgagee. The legal mortgagee may, on default by the borrower, enter into possession of the property, apply to the court for an order of foreclosure, sell the property, appoint a receiver of rents, or sue the debtor on his or her personal covenant to repay. (The last of these remedies is appropriate where the lender is only partly secured and wishes to obtain judgement so as to issue a bankruptcy order or levy execution.) The banker seeking to exercise his or her rights will, in practice, either sell the property or appoint a receiver. An *equitable mortgagee* has only the right to sue on the covenant to repay, or to apply to the court for an order of foreclosure.

powers of the liquidator in a winding-up. By Sch. 4 of the Insolvency Act, 1986, the powers exercisable by the liquidator *with sanction* are: 1. pay any class of creditor in full; 2. make any arrangement with creditors or others who have a claim against the company; 3. have power to compromise, on such terms as may be agreed, on all calls and liabilities resulting in debts to the company; 4. take any security for the discharge of any debt or liability and give a good discharge for it. The powers granted *without sanction in voluntary liquidation* but *with sanction* in winding-up by the court are: 1. bring or defend any action or other legal proceedings in the name of, and on behalf of, the company; 2. carry on business if it is deemed necessary for its beneficial winding-up. The powers available *without sanction in any winding-up* are: 1. sell the company's property by public auction or private contract, either in whole or part; 2. execute deeds, if necessary under company seal; 3. prove and claim in any bankruptcy for any balance against the estate; 4. draw, accept, make and indorse bills of exchange or promissory notes on behalf of the company; 5. raise money by securing the assets of the company; 6. take out letters of administration for any deceased contributory and obtain payment of any money due from the contributory or his or her estate which cannot, conveniently, be done by the company; 7. power to appoint an agent to do any business which the liquidator cannot do himself or herself; 8. power to do all such things as may be necessary for the winding-up of the company and distributing its assets.

powers of the liquidator in bankruptcy. By Sch. 5 of the Insolvency Act, 1986 the powers exercisable with sanction are as follows: 1. carry on any business of the bankrupt it it is beneficial for the winding-up; 2. bring, institute, or defend any action relating to the property of the bankrupt's estate; 3. accept payment for the sale of the property of the bankrupt's estate, subject to certain stipulations; 4. mortgage or pledge any property to raise money to pay debts;

5. make payments or incur liabilities for the benefit of creditors; 6. refer to arbitration, any claims by third parties on the property of the bankrupt; 7. make such arrangements as are thought expedient with respect to claims out of the bankrupt's estate.

practical insolvency. *See* INSOLVENCY.

pre-authorised payments. Equivalent to the bank standing orders and direct debits in the UK, pre-authorised payments in the US permit a customer to pay a bill to a company without writing a check. The customer gives the company a standing authorisation to debit his or her bank account for a regular bill payment, and the company uses this authority to generate paperless debits which are sent to the customer's bank.

precatory trust. A trust which arises from a construction of words of supplication or entreaty, which are interpreted to show that the donor intended to impose a trust.

precept. A command, an injunction respecting conduct, a mandate, a writ or warrant, an order directing a payment to be made.

pre-emption. A right to buy, or the act of buying, before others; the right of a vendor in certain cases to buy back land which he or she has had to sell under the terms of some statute, e.g. where the land has been forcibly purchased in the national interest, and is subsequently found not to be required.

pre-emptive bid. A very high bid, as for the shares of another company in an attempted take-over bid, to shut out opposition; or similarly at a public auction.

preference. The act of favouring one person or thing before another or others. *See also* FRAUDULENT PREFERENCE.

preference shares. Those shares carrying a fixed rate of interest, provided for in the company's Articles of Association. Such shares are to receive their interest before any other payments out are made. If, therefore, in any one year the profits made are only just enough to pay the preference shareholders, no other class of shareholder will receive anything.

preferential creditor. One, who in a winding-up or a bankruptcy, is entitled to settlement of his or her debts before ordinary creditors receive anything.

preferential debts. In the event of bankruptcy or winding-up, it is those persons who are entitled to receive settlement of debts before the distribution of the assets to others. By sch. 6, Insolvency Act, 1986, the preferential debtors are: 1. Inland Revenue; 2. Customs and Excise; 3. Social Security Contributions; 4. Contributions to occupational pension schemes; 5. Remuneration to employees.

preferential wages account. See WAGES AND SALARIES ACCOUNT.

pre-finance bill. A bill drawn under a pre-finance credit. See DOCUMENTARY CREDIT.

pre-finance credit. A credit which provides for finance to be made available on certain conditions to the exporter before the goods are actually shipped. Such a credit may also be known as an *anticipatory credit* or a *pre-shipment credit.* It is used in the case of some primary commodities from certain countries. In the UK, special facilities are available if certain conditions are observed. The goods must be of the *capital or project type,* the contract must be *insured* with the Export Credits Guarantee Department (ECGD) (*q.v.*), the exporter must show that he is *unable* to obtain the *necessary finance* through normal channels, and the contract must be for £1m or more. See also RED CLAUSE.

preliminary expenses. Often known as formation expenses. Expenses which are incurred in the formation of a company.

premium. A recompense, a prize, a bounty; a fee paid to learn a profession or trade; the amount exceeding the par value of shares or stock; the periodical instalment paid for insurance. *at a premium.* Above par, in great demand. *to put a premium on.* To act as an incentive to.

premium bond. An acknowledgment by a foreign state of a debt on which interest may not be paid, but which offers a chance to the investor to get a large prize by maintaining regular drawings.

premium bonus. A term applied to any system whereby a worker is paid according to his or her output in a given time, but receives an additional payment if this output exceeds a certain standard.

Premium Savings Bonds. Bonds issued in £1 units in the UK which offer no interest but carry the chance for the investor of winning a large prize free of tax. The maximum holding for any one individual is £10,000: they are sold in multiples of 5 × £1 units. A bond must be held for three months before it qualifies for the draw. Draws are held weekly and monthly.

premium stripping. Formerly, making an illegal profit by breaking the exchange control regulations relating to the payment of the dollar premium on the remittance from abroad of the proceeds from the sale of assets, such as shares or property. The dollar premium was the extra money one had to pay for currency to buy shares or property abroad. (Whatever the actual currency required might be, the premium was payable in dollars. It was a deterrent to discourage buyers). If and when these assets were resold, only 75 per cent of the premium was repaid, the authorities keeping the other 25 per cent. If stock, etc., was bought abroad without 'going through the premium' and was then sold, the money coming into this country being converted at the current rate of exchange did not attract the return of the 75 per cent premium. If, however, the stock were wrongly represented as having been purchased with investment currency (i.e. as being 'premium stock') such a return was made. 'Premium stripping', therefore, was representing foreign currency securities as eligible for the investment currency premium when in fact they did not so qualify. The offence disappeared in October 1979 when the dollar premium ceased to exist as a consequence of the lifting of the exchange control restrictions.

prepay. To pay in advance.

prerogative. An exclusive right or privilege vested in a particular person or body of persons, especially a sovereign, by virtue of his or her position or relationship; any peculiar right, option, privilege, natural advantage, etc.

prerogative orders. Orders, formerly writs based upon the principles of natural justice, devised to protect the rights of the subject against abuse of excess of power by public authorities, government departments, tribunals, courts or individuals. All are discretionary. *See also CERTIORARI; MANDAMUS; PROHIBITION.*

present. Here or at hand; writings or documents; the offer of a bill for acceptance or payment.

presenting bank. When dealing with clean or documentary collections, it is the collecting bank which requests the presenting bank to present the financial document, with or without commercial documents attached, to receive acceptance/payment of the instrument or documents.

presentment. The act or state of presenting, representation, delineation, the laying of a formal statement before a court or an authority; notice taken by a grand jury of an offence from their own knowledge or observation.

presentment for acceptance. It is usual to leave a bill with the drawee for twenty-four hours for acceptance, which should be obtained as soon after the drawing of the bill as possible. If the bill is payable after sight, presentment for acceptance is necessary in order to fix the date of payment. If the bill stipulates it be presented for acceptance, or where a bill is drawn payable elsewhere than at the residence or place of business of the drawee, it must be presented for acceptance before it can be presented for payment. The presentment must be made by or on behalf of the holder to the drawee or someone authorised to accept or refuse payment on his or her behalf, at a reasonable hour on a business day and before the bill is overdue.

presentment for payment. If a bill is not duly presented for payment on the date if falls due, the drawer and indorsers are relieved from their responsibilities on the bill. A bill if *on demand* is 'duly presented' if presented within a reasonable time after its issue (to keep the drawer liable) and, if it has been indorsed, within a reasonable time after its indorsement (to keep the indorser liable). Presentment must be made by the *holder* or by some person authorised to receive payment on his or her behalf at a *reasonable hour* on a *business day,* at the *proper place,* to some *person* authorised to deal with it. If a place of payment is specified in the bill, that is the 'proper place'; if not, but if the address of the drawee or acceptor is given in the bill, then that *address* is the proper place; if neither, then the bill should be presented at the drawee's or acceptor's *place of business,* if known, or otherwise at his or her *ordinary address.* A cheque must be presented for payment within a reasonable time. Where a *promissory note* is made payable at a particular place, it must be presented for payment at that place in order to render the maker liable. In any other case, presentment for payment is not necessary to render the maker liable. However, present-ment for payment *is* necessary to render the *indorser* liable (Bills of Exchange Act, 1882 s. 87(1/2)). *See also* ANTEDATED CHEQUE; OVERDUE BILL.

present value. 1. The sum which will be paid now by a discounting bank for a bill of exchange at a term. This is found by deducting discount rate for the term from the face value of the bill. 2. One method of finding the value now of a series of payments, such as annuity or pension payments, due to be made at regular intervals. 3. The calculation of the value now of a deferred payment taking compound interest on the sum to be paid.

pre-shipment credit. *See* PRE-FINANCE CREDIT.

Prestel. A public viewdata service launched by the British Post Office (now British Telecom) available to the public to obtain information and data by using a 'keying in machine' and a normal television set. Prestel gives up-to-date facts on a variety of topics. It is also possible by a 'home banking' system, to obtain *information* on a number of banking services, *transmit funds,* and *order goods/services* by quoting a credit card number or personal identification number (PIN).

presumption. The act of, or grounds for, taking something for granted; a stong probability.

presumption of fact. An inference as to a fact from facts already known.

presumption of law. Assumption of the truth of a proposition until the contrary is proved; an inference established by law as universally applicable to particular circumstances.

presumption of value. Every party whose signature appears on a bill of exchange is *prima facie* deemed to have become a party thereto for value.

presumptive evidence. Evidence derived from circumstances which necessarily or usually attend a fact.

price. The amount at which a thing is valued, bought or sold; value, cost.

price consumption curve. A graph showing the changes in the consumption of a commodity with price changes, assuming that consumer income remains constant.

price control (price fixing). A limit, usually an upper limit, set on prices by government or a price ring. Price control by government is usually a prominent political factor where trade unions are in negotiation with government, the latter desiring to restrain wage increases, the former demanding price control. A maximum price fixed by the state is to protect consumers against high prices and must be fixed below a 'free' price level, or equilibrium.

price discrimination. The charging of different prices to different groups of customers for the same product or service, e.g. a bank charges companies full rate on the conduct of their current accounts, but charges nominal rates only to a staff group of a very large customer – this is price discrimination. In the past this has been described as 'charging what the traffic will bear'; a similar but more recent pronouncement has been that charges are *'subject to negotiation'*. Other examples are railway cheap day fares, electricity offpeak rates, summer coal prices, etc.

prices earnings ratio. A method of arriving at the relative price of shares. Net earnings per share are found by dividing the profit after taxation by the number of issued shares. This figure is then divided into the current market price of the shares (usually the middle price) and gives the price/earnings ratio. Thus a share with earnings of 5p per share available for distribution to ordinary shareholders, after deduction of corporation tax and prior charges, priced in the market at 60p has a P/E of 12.

price fixing. *See* PRICE CONTROL.

prima facie. On the first view, on the first impression, at first sight.

prima facie **check of deeds.** 1. Check the deeds and documents against the schedule that accompanies them, to make sure that they are all there; 2. check that there is a good root of title, at least fifteen years old; 3. check that there is a good chain of title from the good root to the holding deed; 4. check that the holding deed is in the name of the borrowing customer.

primage. A percentage on the freight, originally paid to the master of the ship, now retained by the ship owners, for care in looking after goods and in loading and unloading them.

primary period. *See* FINANCE LEASE.

primary risks. In some EEC countries banking risks are graded into *Primary* (high risk lending or investment), *Secondary* (average risk) and *Tertiary* (low risk).

prime. Original, foremost, first in degree or importance.

prime bank bill. *See* FINE BANK BILL.

prime costs. Those direct items of cost which enter into and form part of the product; those costs which are primarily and directly connected with it, e.g. materials, wages, expenses, and long-term administrative costs. Also known as direct costs, or first costs.

prime entry. An entry made from particulars given on another document, such as a bill of lading or invoice; a first entry made from a source of information.

prime rate. In the UK prime rate refers to the rate of discount on prime bank bills. Prime rates in the US can be compared to the UK clearing bank base rates, i.e. a level or standard rate around which actual bank lending takes place, dependent upon the type of advance and credit rating of the borrower concerned. Although the larger and more credit-worthy borrowers are now (as in the UK) more commonly charged on the basis of money market rates, or 'cost of funds', the posted prime rate still has a psychological importance for economic policy in general, and the stock and foreign exchange markets in particular.

primogeniture. Seniority by birth amongst children of the same parents; the right, system or rule by which the eldest son succeeded to the real estate of his father or mother where there was no will. Heirship· was abolished in 1925.

principal. Chief, leading, main; constituting the capital sum invested, as distinguished from income; the chief actor for whom another is an agent.

principal's mandate. The document embodying the duties of an agent. Each power delegated must be clearly described. A third party should, for his or her own protection, ascertain the extent of the agent's powers by studying the mandate carefully – the principal will not be bound where the agent has exceeded his or her powers. *See also* UNDISCLOSED PRINCIPAL.

prior charges. Any claims against a security which will prejudice the rights of the present lender. Thus before advancing against the security of a life policy the banker must enquire of the assurance company whether there are any prior charges. Such charges are regulated by the date order of receipt by the company. Priority of mortgages, whether legal or equitable, not protected by deposit of the title deeds is determined by the date of registration in the Land Charges Department. With registered land, charges rank for priority according to the order in which they are entered on the register. Mortgages other than registered charges made under seal may be protected by a caution in the register, and rank for priority according to the order in which the caution is entered in the register. A mortgage on a ship takes priority from the hour and the day on which the statutory form of mortgage is registered at the port of registry.

priority of debts. *See* PREFERENTIAL DEBTS.

priority notice. A puisne mortgage or a general equitable charge, (neither being supported by the deeds) require, therefore, protection by registration in the Land Charges Department. Such a mortgage or charge was, by s. 13 of the Land Charges Act, 1925, to be void against a purchaser of the land, unless it was registered before the completion of the purchase. 'The completion' means the signing and delivery of the deed and until this is done the banker will not lend. If the search certificate, giving a clear title, was dated *before* the date of the mortgage deed, there was, therefore, a danger that after the search of the Register another mortgage of the same land might have been registered in favour of someone else, the effect of which would have been to render his or her mortgage at the moment of its completion void against that other person. When this was appreciated corrective legislation in 1926 (Law of Property Amendment Act, 1926, s. 4. again amended by the Land Charge Rules, 1940) removed the difficulty by providing that any person intending to apply for the registration of any contemplated charge might register notice of his or her intention at the Land Charges Department. This notice is called a priority notice. It must be given at least fourteen days before the registration is to take effect. When the contemplated charge is actually created and later registered, then, as long as it is lodged within fourteen days and registered within twenty-eight days after the priority notice, it takes effect as if registration had been contemporaneous with its creation. If the land is registered land, the priority notice is sent to the Land Registry together with the relevant land certificate, and if the charge is sent for registration within the next fourteen days it will have priority over any other instrument which may have been received at the Land Registry in the meanwhile. In addition to the registers already mentioned, local registers are maintained by the various district and borough councils and county councils in which local land charges may be registered. On these registers also a priority notice may be registered where a local land charge is contemplated. Similar time limits are applicable.

private. Not public, belonging to or concerning an individual, secret, not publicly known; not holding public office, confidential.

private act, private bill. One affecting a private person or persons and not the general public.

private bank. A banking firm in which the number of partners must not exceed twenty. An Act of 1708 limited the number of partners in a banking business to six, the purpose then being to protect the newly formed Bank of England from competition. The Companies Act, 1948 raised the limit to ten, and the Companies Act, 1967 allowed the number to be increased to twenty, on conditions. It was not until 1979 that the distinction between banking partnerships and other associations, companies and partnerships was dropped. In that year the Banking Act so amended the Companies Act, 1948 as to leave it that no group of more than twenty persons shall be formed for the purpose of carrying on any business having as its object the acquisition of gain for the group, unless registered as a limited company. By that time all the original private banks had disappeared. Some famous names live on – Hoare, Drummond, Coutts – but only as part of one of the giant joint stock clearing banks.

There is, of course, nothing to stop any new partnership setting up in business as a private bank if they can satisfy the Bank of England that they are entitled to call themselves a bank – an eventuality which can only be described as highly unlikely.

private bill. *See* PRIVATE ACT.

private company. Any company which is not a public company. A company whose name is followed by the word 'Limited' is taken to be a private company. The minimum number of persons who may form a private company is two. There is now no specific legal definition of a private company.

private company shares. The shares of private companies were not considered good banking security before 1981 because there was no quotation and the shares were virtually unrealisable, transfer of them being restricted by the articles of the company to virtually a few other people, usually the other directors. However, there is now an Unlisted Securities Market (*q.v.*) which may lead to a valuation for some of these shares; also the Companies Act, 1981 provided for all companies to be able to buy back their own shares, thus widening the market for possible realisation of the shares. Investors will now have the knowledge that they are likely to be able to sell such shares, once purchased – in other words, they will not find themselves locked into the company – and banks will be able to take a more serious view of such shares as security. Small companies also will be able to buy out family holders who want to sell without fear of a drastic change in control.

private enterprise. A system of economics whereby private individuals can own property, run businesses and seek to make profits. Such productive enterprises are, however, subject to State control by way of laws of general application, and business profits of private enterprise are subject to tax.

private placing. *See* NEW ISSUE; PLACING.

private sector liquidity (PSL). *See* MONEY SUPPLY.

private treaty. A method of sale whereby the price of the thing to be sold is decided by bargaining between seller and buyer, as in the case of house property.

private trust. A trust which is enforced at the instance of beneficiaries, as opposed to a 'public' or charitable trust which is generally enforced at the suit of the Attorney General acting on behalf of the Crown.

privatisation. It has been the policy of the Conservative Government to sell i.e. return to the private sector, public companies, which have been owned by the State. Among the compaies which have been sold to the public or 'privatised' are: British Gas, British Petroleum, British Telecom, TSB England and Wales. The sale of other companies whose capital is totally or partially owned by government, is likely to continue during the life of the present Government.

privity of contract. The relationship between parties to a contract. Only such people who are 'privy' to a contract can normally be affected by it. Such a contract can bind only the parties to it; it cannot impose obligations on other people, nor confer rights upon them. In the law of leaseholds, privity of contract refers to that relationship which exists between lessor and lessee by virtue of the covenants contained in the lease. This relationship, springing from the contract itself, continues to exist despite any assignment of the respective interests. In banking there is privity of contract between banker and customer, but not, e.g., between the banker and the person who sends a status enquiry (unless that person also happens to be a customer). There is no duty of care, as with the banking contract, although there is a duty to reply carefully, truly and faithfully where such an enquiry is made in reliance on the banker's special knowledge of his or her customer. Liability may be disclaimed by a suitable clause in the reply, but *see* here EXEMPTION CLAUSE.

privity of estate. The relationship between two parties who respectively hold the same estates as those created by a lease, e.g. lessor and lessee, lessor and assignee from the lessee, lessee and assignee of the reversion of the freehold estate. *See also* PRIVITY OF CONTRACT.

pro. For, before, in front of, on behalf of.

probate. The process by which a last will and testament is legally authenticated after the testator's death; an official copy of a will.

probation. The act of proving, proof; a trial or test of a person's character, conduct, ability, etc.; the testing of a candidate before admission to full membership of a body, etc.

proceeds. The sum realised by a sale; produce, yield; the credit resulting from a foreign collection or negotiation.

process costing. A method of costing applied to manufacturers according to the characteristics of the manufacturing process, i.e. that different, though related products are produced simultaneously.

procuration. Management of another's affairs; the instrument empowering a person to transact the affairs of another. *See also PER PROCURATIONEM.*

procuration fee. The money paid for an agent who negotiates a loan.

procuration signature. *See* PER PROCURATIONEM.

procurator. One who acts for another, especially in legal affairs, an agent.

produce advances. *See* MERCHANDISE ADVANCES.

produce broker. An agent engaged in buying or selling on a produce exchange.

production. The manufacture of commodities and the provision of services; the changing of raw material into finished goods together with the distributory services or the training of staff to give good service to customers.

pro et con. For and against.

profit. That portion of the gains of an industry received by the capitalist or the investors; the excess of returns over expenditure; pecuniary gain in any transaction or occupation; emolument.

profit and loss. Gains credited and losses debited to an account so as to show the net profit or loss for the period concerned. The item is also used to describe interest-free banking accounts (PLS accounts), in accordance with strict Islamic law, in Pakistan, Egypt, Jordan, Saudi Arabia, Dubai, Bahrain and the Sudan. Deposits in such accounts earn no interest but share in the profit made by the bank. On loans made by the bank no interest is charged, but the bank takes a share in the profit or loss which the loan generates in the business of the borrower.

profit and loss account. This account shows the gross profit made by a business together with unusual items of gain from sources other than normal trading – for example, a profit on the sale of land. On the debit side will occur the overhead and administrative charges incurred during the year. The balance on the account is the net profit, on which tax is charged. The profit and loss account is concerned with the distribution of goods.

profit and loss appropriation account. An account disclosing the allocation of the balance of the profit and loss account among dividends, transfers to reserves, etc.

profit sharing. A system of remuneration by which the workers in a business or an industrial concern are apportioned a percentage of the profits in order to give them an interest in the business.

pro-forma. As a matter of form.

pro-forma invoice. In foreign trade, both exporters and importers may use a sample specimen invoice of the goods to be consigned, the seller estimating a price from current rates and adding charges, commission and freight, thus informing himself or herself of the total cost; the buyer using it to find out the current market price of the goods, cost of packing, discount, etc., thus arriving at the approximate cost of the proposed order.

progressive tax. A system of taxation which follows the principle that the rate of taxation shall increase as income increases.

prohibition. The act of forbidding; interdict; a prerogative order to prevent excess of jurisdiction by an inferior court, or by any public body or person exercising a public duty or exercising judicial or quasi-judicial powers. It will lie against the Crown, but not against domestic or private tribunals.

prohibitory injunction. *See* INJUNCTION.

project finance. The arrangement from a variety of sources of the finance which will be required to appraise, set up, and begin to operate a large capital project. Such loans would normally be made by a syndicate of lending banks. The financial security for the loans made to the borrowing concern is often considered to be represented by future assured cash flows and is independent of third party guarantees.

project planning. A process whereby management, confronted by a number of possible solutions to a specific problem, considers each in turn before arriving at a decision.

project team. A team formed by temporary attachment from a variety of departments or specialisations, linked together by the need to meet a new statutory requirement (e.g. decimalisation) or to sell a new product or service. Such a team or working party may be required to make recommendations as to the best way in which to achieve the desired end, or may be given the authority and resources to carry the work through in all its stages.

promissory note. An unconditional promise in writing made by one person to another, signed by the maker, engaging to pay, on demand or at a fixed or determinable future time, a sum certain in money to, or to the order of, a specified person, or to bearer. A note payable to the maker's order must be indorsed by the maker. The note is inchoate and incomplete until completed by delivery to the payee or bearer. It is often used in the finance of foreign trade. A promissory note may be made by two or more makers, and they may be liable thereon jointly and severally, according to its tenor.

promoter. One who, or that which, promotes, a supporter, an initiator, one who organises a new business venture; one who undertakes to form a new company and who does the necessary preliminary work to form or float it.

promotion. Advancement, preferment, a higher rank; the advancement of a business interest by advertisement or exhortation.

promotion money. Money paid to the first board of directors of a new limited company for their efforts in floating the company. The money is found from the subscriptions of shareholders, and the sum involved must be disclosed in the prospectus.

proof. A test or trial; any process to ascertain correctness, truth or facts; demonstration; a trial impression of a printed work; trial before a judge alone instead of a jury; designating a certain standard or quality; the balancing of a day's work. In bankruptcy, affidavits by creditors of the claims they are making against the bankrupt's estate. (The Insolvency

Act, 1976 has done away with the need for affidavits unless the Official Receiver or the Trustee insists.)

proofing machine. A machine which lists and details all debits and credits in a day's work in a branch bank and at the same time provides detailed lists of the cheques to be remitted for payment under the headings of the other banks and branches concerned, thus saving a separate machining of these items at the end of the day's work.

proof of death. Production of a death or burial certificate, or of probate or letters of administration.

property. Peculiar or inherent character, nature; that which is owned; a possession, an estate, ownership; anything yielding an income to the owner. *See also* PERSONAL PROPERTY; REAL PROPERTY.

property premium. The excess payment required over the market rate for currency used in purchasing property abroad. Such transactions had to be authorised by the Bank of England and paid for in investment currency. The arrangement lapsed with the abolition of exchange controls in October 1979.

property register. *See* LAND CERTIFICATE.

proportion. Relative size, number or degree; comparison, relation, equal or just share; in the Bank of England Return, the relationship of notes and coins to the total assets of the Banking Department.

proposal. An approach to a life assurance company by a person who wishes to take out life assurance cover, an offer which may be accepted or rejected by the company on the basis of the information set out on the proposal form.

proprietary. Belonging or pertaining to an owner; made and sold by a firm or individual having the *exclusive rights* of manufacture and sale.

proprietary company. A parent company owning a quantity of land suitable for mining, etc., which it lets out to other interested companies on a joint proprietorship basis, all profits to be equally divided.

proprietor. One who is the owner of property; the owner of registered land.

proprietorship register. *See* LAND CERTIFICATE.

proprietor's stake. The fixed capital of a business, including the paid-up capital, the reserves, and the balance of the profit and loss account. The total of all these sums is the proprietor's stake in the business. All this money must be lost before the sums due to creditors become endangered. A comparison between the proprietor's stake and the remaining liabilities should therefore disclose a reasonable position which will ensure a kind of 'buffer' for the creditors.

pro rata. In proportion.

prospectus. A circular or pamphlet outlining the main features of a proposed commercial undertaking, especially a new company. In the UK the prospectus for a new limited company is regulated closely by the Companies Act, 1985, which details the information to be included in a prospectus which offers shares in the company to the public. The prospectus must also comply with the requirements of the Stock Exchange.

pro tanto. For so much, to that extent.

protected goods. Under the Consumer Credit Act, 1974, s. 90, goods which are subject to a regulated agreement in which the debtor has paid one third or more of the total price, cannot be recovered except by court order, or by voluntary surrender by the debtor.

protected shorthold. *See* SHORTHOLD LETTING.

protection of depositors. *See* DEPOSIT INSURANCE.

protective trust. A provision in a trust instrument that the beneficiary shall no longer receive the income if, for any reason, he or she would be deprived of the right to receive it. In a settlement on marriage, for example, where the wife has provided the trust property, the wife may be indicated as the first beneficiary during her life, after which the income may pass to the husband for his life, if he survives her. To guard against his possible extravagance or misfortune, a protective trust may be attached by which the husband is given, not a life interest, but an interest which would cease if he became bankrupt. In such a case the income would be held by the trustees for others, probably the children of the marriage, if any. Without such a protective trust the income would pass to the creditors of the husband. A similar clause may operate if he attempts to alienate or charge the income.

protest. To make a solemn affirmation; to make a *formal declaration* against some act or próposition; to make a formal declaration, usually by a notary public, that acceptance or *payment of a bill* of exchange has been demanded and *refused (see* CERTIFICATE OF PROTEST); a written declaration by the *master of a ship,* usually before a magistrate, assessor or consul, stating the circumstances attending an injury or loss of a ship or its cargo. *See also* FORMAL PROTEST, HOUSEHOLDER'S PROTEST.

proving a debt. Establishing a debt due from the estate of a bankrupt person. Since the Insolvency Act, 1986, it is no longer necessary to swear an affidavit as to the correctness of the creditors' claims unless the trustee insists. Now it can be an unsworn claim. The proof verifies the debt, specifies any vouchers substantiating the debt, and states whether the creditor is a secured creditor or not. The trustee examines every proof, and those admitted will rank for any dividend. A statute-barred debt cannot be proved.

provision. A measure taken beforehand; an amount retained to provide for depreciation; a sum retained to offset against a bad or doubtful debt; a sum of money set on one side to meet a known payment which has to be made, e.g. payment of pensions to retired staff.

provisional certificate. A certificate issued for new shares to evidence ownership until the definitive certificate is ready; a *scrip certificate* issued to a bond purchaser during the payment of instalments of purchase money.

provisions. The articles of an instrument or statute.

proviso. A condition or stipulation in a deed or contract; a special enactment in a statute; a clause in a covenant or other document rendering its operation conditional, e.g. a proviso in a lease for re-entry and forfeiture in case of a breach of a covenant, or a proviso for forfeiture in case of bankruptcy.

proximate damage. Damage which arises naturally from a breach of contract, or damage of an extraordinary nature where it is shown that the parties did in fact contemplate its possibility. In either case compension may be awarded.

proxy. The agency of a substitute for a principal; one deputed to act for another, especially in voting; a document authorising one person to act or vote for another; *a vote* given under this authority.

prudential ratios. The ratios by which the banks ensure that their business is conducted cautiously and judiciously: in particular, the ratio between a bank's capital resources and its total deposit liabilities (the *solvency ratio*); the various ratios of capital adequacy and liquidity. The onset of inflation, by increasing the figure of deposits, has lowered the solvency ratio. This can be restored by raising new equity capital through a rights issue, which has to be carefully timed, or by borrowing on the Euromarket, or by increasing charges and widening the difference between their lending and deposit interest rates. (This last device does not have any direct effect but it has the effect of increasing profits and, therefore, the amount that can be retained in the business.) Following the ending of exchange control in the UK in October 1979 and the consequent nullification of the corset (q.v.) controls, it was mooted that the Bank of England could instead control the money supply by controlling the *cash base*. This would be analogous to using the present system of reserve ratios for monetary control rather than prudential purposes. The difficulty would be that banks overseas could not be controlled in the same way as banks in the UK.

public. Pertaining to the people as a whole, open to general use; the community or its members.

public act, public bill. One involving the interests of the community.

public company. A company 1. which is limited by shares, or limited by guarantee and has a share capital (in either case the share capital must meet the minimum requirements); 2. whose memorandum states that it is public; and 3. which has been correctly registered or re-registered as a public company. Public companies must have a minimum authorised *share capital* of £50,000, all of which must be issued but need only be one quarter paid up; any *share premium* must be fully paid up. The name of a public limited company must in all cases end with either the words *'Public Limited Company'* or the abbreviation *'PLC'*, neither of which may be preceded by the word *'Limited'*. A company whose registered office is in Wales may use the Welsh language equivalent. Any public company can be formed by any two people who subscribe to the Memorandum. The subscriber's shares must be paid for in cash.

public enterprise. Economic activity undertaken by the central government, e.g. nationalised industries, or by local authorities, e.g. provision of a water supply.

public examination. This refers to the examination of a bankrupt in a court. The official receiver may, at any time before the discharge of the bankrupt, apply to the court for public examination. If the court so directs that the public examination should be carried out, then the bankrupt must attend the court to be publicly examined about his or her affairs, dealings, and property.

public funds. Debts owing by the government; government stock and public securities; the National Debt.

public issue. An issue of shares publicly offered to investors.

public law. International Law.

public relations. The relations of an organisation or authority with the general public.

public relations officer. One who is employed in the distribution of information to the public, whose duty is to represent the aims, policies and achievements of the organisation by whom he or she is employed, in the most favourable light possible.

public sector. In the UK, the term includes the Civil Service, Local Authorities, and nationalised industries.

public sector borrowing requirement (PSBR). A term used in the UK to denote the need for the government to finance the gap between receipts and expected expenditure by borrowing, mostly by the issue of Treasury Bills and gilt-edged securities. PSBR includes the borrowing of local authorities and public corporations as well as central government. *See also* GILTS; TREASURY BILLS.

public trust. *See* CHARITABLE TRUST.

public trustee. A trust corporation set up by the Public Trustee Act, 1906, with the object of providing for members of the public stability, continuity and responsibility. Since that date many more banks and insurance companies also established trust corporations, so that the Public Trustee no longer enjoys a monopoly of such services. The Public Trustee may act as an executor or administrator of estates, as a trustee, and as an administrator of small estates of negligible value. The Public Trustee may decline to accept a trust, but not on the sole ground of its being of little value. *See also* CUSTODIAN TRUSTEE; TRUST CORPORATION.

public utilities. Enterprises ensuring certain public services such as gas, water, electricity, telephone, telegraph; on the Stock Exchange, the shares of such concerns.

Public Works Loan Board. A governmental body set up for the purpose of making loans to local authorities, particularly the smaller authorities which might experience difficulties in raising the money required on the capital market. The lender of last resort for local authorities.

puisne mortgage. A legal mortgage not protected by deposit of the title deeds. It should be registered at the Land Charges Department as a land charge, Class C (i). *See also* LAND CHARGES REGISTER.

punitive damages. *See* EXEMPLARY DAMAGES.

pupil. A Scots law term for a child under fourteen (if a boy) or under twelve (if a girl). When the child attains whichever of these ages is applicable he or she becomes a minor. A pupil has no legal power to enter into contracts, sue or be sued, or make a will. Contracts on behalf of a pupil must be made by his or her tutor (*q.v.*) and are then valid unless it can be shown that any particular contract was to his/her disadvantage and caused him/her substantial lesion (*q.v.*).

purchase. To buy, to obtain by any outlay of labour, time, sacrifice, etc., to obtain by any means other than inheritance; value or worth.

purchaser. The one who buys. In land law, a purchaser of real or leasehold property in good faith and for valuable consideration. The term includes a lessee, mortgagee or other person who for valuable consideration acquires an interest in property such as a lending banker.

purchasing power parity. The theory that when exchange rates are free to fluctuate they will be determined by the relative purchasing power of the currencies in their home markets.

pursuer. Scots law term for *Plaintiff.*

put option. *See* OPTION.

put and call option. *See* OPTION.

put of more option. *See* OPTION.

Q

qualified. Invested with the requisite qualities; modified, limited.

qualified acceptance. One which in express terms varies the effect of the bill as drawn. A qualified acceptance is one which is conditional, partial, local, qualified as to time or is the acceptance of some one or more of drawees, but not of all. A *Conditional Acceptance* makes payment by the acceptor dependent on the fulfilment of a condition therein stated. A *Partial Acceptance* is one to pay part only of the amount for which the bill is drawn. A *Local Acceptance* is one to pay only at a particular specified place. It must expressly state that the bill is to be paid there and there only.

qualified audit report. A report by the auditors who have examined the vouchers, papers and accounts of a company and are unable to say for a reason mentioned in their report, that the statements give a true and fair view of the business.

qualified indorsement. An indorsement where an indorser has added after his signature an express stipulation 1. negativing or limiting his or her own liability to the holder (e.g. '*Sans recours*'); 2. waiving as regards himself or herself some or all of the holder's duties.

qualified title. A type of title met with in registered land, given by the Land Registrar in cases where title can be established only for a limited period, or subject to certain reservations. It is very rare.

qualitative directives. Directives from the Bank of England to the lending banks and financial institutions as to classes of customers who may be allowed to borrow. *See also* COMPETITION AND CREDIT CONTROL.

quality certificate. A certificate that goods are of a required standard,

issued by a third party after an inspection.

quality control. Periodic checks at various intervals to ensure that the quality of a product is maintained, as where bank inspectors visit branches at regular intervals to check that the branch is properly run and that the customers are getting proper service.

quantitative directives. Directives from the Bank of England to the lending banks and financial institutions as to the total amount of money which they may lend. *See also* COMPETITION AND CREDIT CONTROL.

quantity rebate. A discount or reduction of price on the purchase of a large number of quantity of a product.

quantity theory of money. Basically, the economic theory that the more money printed, the less its value in terms of goods and services (i.e. prices go up). This basic theory is modified by taking into consideration the factors of velocity of circulation and the volume of production. The theory is expressed as $MV = PT$, where M is the quantity of money, V is the velocity of its circulation, P the general level of prices, and T the tital of all transactions financed by money.

quantum meruit. An amount earned. The name of an action brought under the terms of a contract which has been broken. The aggrieved party may sue upon a *quantum meruit* for the amount earned by the services he or she has performed, as an alternative to claiming damages. It is also a way of recovering a reasonable return where one party has performed his or her duties, or some of them, under a contract for which no specific remuneration has been agreed.

quarter days. *In England:* Lady Day, March 25th; Midsummer Day, June 24th; Michaelmas, September 29th;

Christmas Day, December 25th.

In Scotland: Candlemas, February 2nd; Whitsunday, May 15th; Lammas, August 1st; Martinmas, November 11th.

Quarterly Bulletin. A publication of the Bank of England available in March, June, September and December of each year, which gives economic commentaries, financial reviews, information about credit control, savings, foreign exchange markets, policy decisions, and various tables of statistics.

quasi-. Apparent, seeming, not real.

quasi-loan. A loan which in form differs in some way from the usual act of lending money, whether the subject of the loan is something of value but not money, or whether certain conditions of repayment are imposed or understood which would not be found in a cash loan. In the Companies Act, 1985 the term is used in connection with a loan or quasi-loan made by a public or private company which seeks to confer a monetary or other advantage on one of its directors or on a person connected with him or her. Here the term refers to an occasion when the company pays, or promises to pay, a sum to a third party on behalf of a director or a person connected with the director, as where a company has a credit card which it allows the director to use for his or her own personal purchases. Quasi-loans must not exceed £1,000 in total over two months, by which time the director must have reimbursed the company. *See also* LOANS TO DIRECTORS.

quasi-money. *See* NEAR MONEY.

quasi-negotiable instrument. A document which contains some but not all of the characteristics of a negotiable instrument. Thus a bill of lading can transfer title by indorsement and delivery, the transferee acquiring the right to one in his or her own name. But it cannot transcend any lack or defect of title in the transferor, so that in such a case the transferee, although for value

and in good faith, does not obtain a good and indefeasible title.

quasi-partner. One who is not a partner, but has acted in such a way as to make people think he or she is. Under the doctrine of 'holding out' the quasi-partner may be estopped by conduct from denying that he or she is a partner, and may consequently be held responsible for some or all of the firm's debts.

quasi-rent. A term used for the rent of any property other than land, e.g. as in the case of the leasing of a capital asset to a manufacturing company by a finance company.

quayage. A charge for the use of a berth alongside a quay.

Queen. *See* SOVEREIGN.

quick assets. Assets which can be converted into cash quickly and easily. *See* LIQUID ASSETS.

quid pro quo. Something for something, a mutual consideration, an equivalent.

quit rent. A rent formerly paid to the lord of the manor in lieu of service. It was abolished in 1925.

quittance. Discharge from a debt or obligation, acquittance, receipt, requital, repayment.

quorum. The minimum number of persons that must be present at a meeting to make the meeting valid. The minimum number in a club, society or association will be found in the constitution of that organisation, while the articles of association of a limited company will express the minimum number required for a quorum.

quota. A proportionate share or part: an allowance which must not be exceeded. In an economic context, used to refer to a restriction on imports. A quota is imposed to protect a particular home industry or, if imposed generally, to protect scarce supplies of foreign currency and to influence the balance of trade in favour of the importing country. If every country imposed protective quotas world trade would be damaged severely. Quotas are not, therefore, generally approved.

quotation. A stated price at which a person is prepared to do some work or provide a service; a *price of shares* on the London Stock Exchange as reported in the financial press. For the purposes of the Consumer Credit Act, 1974, any document issued by a person who carries on a consumer credit business or a consumer hire business, which gives prospective customers information about the *terms* on which he is prepared to do business.

quotations committee. The committee appointed by the Stock Exchange to decide the conditions on which an official price quotation can be granted to a company, and to consider such applications and to decide upon them.

quote. *(Ger.) See* QUOTA.

quoted company. *See* LISTED COMPANY.

quotes. Prices, being selling and buying rates of exchange, or bid and offered rates of interst given by brokers or dealers, to customers or other enquiring parties in the market.

R

rack rent. A rent, once considered exorbitant, which is equal to the full annual value of the property; a rent which has been stretched until it is the most that is obtainable.

railway consignment note. *See* CONSIGNMENT NOTE.

rally. To recover, a recovery, as in the price of a commodity, or of stocks and shares on the market.

rate. Degree, standard, proportion, value, price; to estimate, to assess, to calculate, to appraise. *See also* CHEQUE RATE; INTERVENTION RATE; LONG RATE; SHORT RATE.

rateable value. Assessment of local rates is on property-occupiers. Each house, shop, etc., is assessed for its value in relation to the rent which it can command, the rating figure being fixed at so many pence in the pound, with some proportion of the rateable value being payable in two six-monthly instalments.

rate of exchange. *See* PARITIES.

rate of interest. Payment for the use of borrowed money, the rate charged varying with the degree of risk run by the lender. Interest rates in large British banks are fixed by reference to a base rate, which varies as the bank thinks fit. Interest is allowed on the deposit accounts, savings accounts and by some banks on current accounts. Interest at a notional rate is allowed on credit balances against charges on current account. Building societies allow interest on deposits made with them and charge interest on mortgages granted by them, the difference between the rates giving a 'turn' in favour of the institution.

rate of return. A means of calculation of the profit expected from an item of capital investment, based on the relationship of its likely profit figure with its original cost.

rate of turnover. The number of times the value of an average stock figure is sold in a given trading period.

ratification. Confirmation, making valid; official approval of an action taken unofficially, as when a branch manager in an emergency grants a loan in excess of his or her discretionary limits, and later has it approved or ratified by higher authority. In *agency*, an agent who has concluded a contract with a third party, acting in excess of his or her powers in so doing, may have the contract ratified by his or her principal, who thereupon becomes liable upon it. The ratification dates back to the contract. A contract may be ratified only under the following conditions: 1. that the agent contracts as agent; 2. that the whole of the contract is ratified; 3. that the principal was in existence at the time of the contract (if the principal is a limited company not yet incorporated the agent contracting for it is personally liable); 4. that the principal could validly contract at that time.

ratio. Relationship between one value and another.

ratio decidendi. The main legal principle which forms the core of a case.

rationalisation. The unification of control in business, industry and commerce for buying, producing, and distributing goods or services, to secure greater efficiency and profits.

ratios. *See* BALANCE SHEET RATIOS; PRUDENTIAL RATIOS.

raw materials. Primary products forming the basis of industrial manufacture, e.g. cotton, timber, etc., which are made into clothes and furniture.

R.D. Can be extended to RDPR. *See* REFER TO DRAWER.

ready money. Cash; money paid, or ready to be paid, for a purchase, etc.

real. True, genuine; consisting of fixed

and permanent things, e.g. lands or houses, as opposed to personal things.

real cost. As factors of production are limited, they can only be employed in one direction at one time. The real cost of production, therefore, is whatever these factors of production could have produced had they been employed in another direction.

real estate. Immovable property covering freehold land and buildings and proprietary rights in or over lands, e.g. mineral rights.

real income. Money income in terms of the goods and services which it will buy.

real investment. Sinking money into a capital asset, e.g. plant, rather than investing it in the purchase of stocks and shares.

realisable value. On looking upon a business as a 'Gone Concern', any assets would be valued at an amount that would probably be received if they were sold. The basis of this valuation could give a more precise value of the resources employed than the current book value.

realisation account. An account maintained when a business is being wound up or sold, or on the dissolution of a partnership.

realised profit. An investment which has appreciated since it was bought is showing a paper profit until such time as it is actually sold, when the paper profit becomes a realised profit.

real personal disposable income (RPDI). The total income available to private individuals after tax, National Insurance and other contributions, and adjusted for the rise in prices. It describes income in terms of what it will buy.

real property. Freehold land and buildings, as opposed to personal property. Real property can itself be recovered if the owner is dispossessed; the remedy is not an award of damages, but the restoration of the land itself, the real remedy.

real time. A computer term indicating that an account in the computer is updated instantaneously with information fed in at a terminal, as opposed to a system whereby all such information is stored on tape until a daily computer up-dating is undertaken.

real wages. *See* REAL INCOME.

rebate. A deduction, a drawback, a discount; in the case of a bill paid before maturity, the allowance of interest at an agreed rate for the days still to run, deducted from the amount of the bill; an adjustment of discount so that only interest relating to the period covered by accounts is treated as earnings.

recap or recapitulation. The word recapitulation is often abbreviated as recap. Often used in banking to show the grouping of totals from batch sheets or proofing machines and to transfer amounts to a clearing department, cost centre, or control centre.

receipt. An acknowledgment in writing that money or other property has been received. An unindorsed cheque which appears to have been paid by the banker on whom it is drawn is evidence of the receipt by the payee of the sum payable by the cheque (Cheques Act, 1957, s. 3). Some cheques have a form of receipt on the back which has been incorporated into the printing of the cheque because the drawer, not relying on s. 3, *(above)* wishes to obtain the signature of the payee by way of receipt. To draw the attention of the payee to this requirement, a large letter 'R' is printed on the face of the cheque. This also serves to alert the cancelling clerk that it is necessary to turn the cheque over to confirm that the form of receipt has been duly completed. Cheques are not now found expressing the need to sign the receipt as a condition of payment and such a cheque is therefore a true cheque and not a *conditional document:* the banker, who will send the cheque back unpaid with the answer 'receipt required' if the form of receipt is not completed (thus demonstrating that the cheque is conditional in practice although not in law), takes this action merely as a *service* to the customer.

receivables financing. *See* FACTORING.

received for shipment bill of lading. A bill of lading which has been issued in respect of goods which have been received for transporting, but have not been actually loaded on to the ship. This may indicate that the goods are to await the next ship. This raises the question of whether they are *left on the quayside* at the mercy of the weather and pilferers, or whether they are *in a warehouse;* whether they are *insured* for such period, etc. Such a bill is not a good tender under a CIF contract, but it can be converted into a 'shipped' bill by indorsement with the name of the *ship* and *shipment date.*

receiver. An officer appointed by the court to collect debts or rents from property which is in dispute in a suit in that court. Under the Insolvency Act, 1986, s. 29, it is an officer appointed by the court as either a receiver, manager or administrative receiver to a company. While under s. 287, the official receiver may act either as a receiver or special manager of the estate of a bankrupt.

receiver for debenture holders. A debenture deed will specify the acts or omissions of the company (such as failure to repay capital or interest within a specified period) which will entitle the creditor(s) to appoint a receiver. On appointment, any floating charge contained in the debenture will crystallise and fix upon the assets available on the day of the receiver's appointment. The receiver will take charge of the company and administer its assets so as to apply them towards the repayment of the debenture holder's advance. The debenture deed may have appointed the receiver as agent of the company so as to make it

responsible for his or her acts, and remuneration.

receiver for partnership. The Partnership Act, 1890 contains provision for application to the court for dissolution of a partnership, and where this happens the court will appoint a receiver to wind up the firm. The receiver's duty is to complete existing commitments of the firm, realise the assets, pay the debts, and pay any surplus to the partners in the proportions in which they shared the profits. On the appointment of the receiver the partners no longer have power to bind the firm and their signatures should not be accepted.

receiver of rents. One of the remedies open to a mortgagee, upon default by the mortgagor, is to appoint a receiver to collect the rents and manage the estate; this is particularly appropriate for property which is let, e.g. a block of flats. On appointment, the receiver takes possession of the property and therefore collects rents and profits, applying them in reduction of the mortgagor's debt. The receiver is regarded as agent of the mortgagor, who is therefore responsible for his or her defaults. *See also* OFFICIAL RECEIVER.

recession. A falling off in the economic progress of a country, which if it persists will lead to a depression and then to a slump. A recession may be only a temporary check and will not necessarily impair confidence sufficiently to reduce or stop the longer-term investments.

reciprocal business. Banks engaged in international trade use correspondent banks abroad to represent them in various transactions, and usually have a choice of several such correspondent banks with whom to place their business. The selection of the actual bank to be used may well depend upon how much business is placed in the reverse direction, by the correspondent bank with the home bank. Most banks keep records of such reciprocal business and are influenced by them.

reciprocity. Tariff concessions in international trade made by one country to another in return for similar concessions; in banking, business put in the way of a correspondent bank abroad in return for similar favours.

recognised bank. In the UK a bank which has been granted statutory recognition by the Bank of England under the provisions of the Banking Act, 1979. *See* SUPERVISION OF BANKS.

recognised investment exchange. A body declared by the Secretary of State as being recognised as an Investment Exchange for the purposes of the Financial Services Act, 1986, s. 207.

recognised marking names. *See* MARKING NAMES.

reconciliation statement. A check between a firm's cash book and its bank statement, by which the two are brought into agreement by allowances for cheques issued but not yet presented, and credits paid in but not yet credited.

reconstruction of a company. The reorganisation of a company structure in order to obtain new capital, or following an arrangement with creditors of the company, or to give effect to an agreement to merge with another company. Where a compromise or arrangement is proposed between a company and its creditors, the court may order a meeting of creditors. The arrangement, if approved by a majority in number representing three-fourths in value of the creditors shall, if sanctioned by the court, be binding on all the creditors and on the company. In the case of a merger or amalgamation with another company, the approval of the shareholders to the extent of nine-tenths in value of share holdings is required within four months of the making of the offer. *See also* MINORITY SHAREHOLDER.

reconvention. A counter-action in a suit brought by the defendant against the plaintiff.

reconveyance. Transfer of a title to lands back to their original owner. Since 1925, the legal estate in mortgaged property remains with the mortgagor, consequently no reconveyance is necessary, a statutory receipt being enough. A reconveyance is, however, still necessary in cases where part only of the mortgaged land is being released from the charge, because the *statutory receipt is not applicable* to such a case.

recorded delivery. A Post Office service providing, for the sender, proof that the packet, etc., has been received by the addressee. The sender fills in a recorded delivery form giving the name and address of the addressee, pays a small charge and gets a receipt. The delivery postman obtains the signature of the recipient. Recorded Delivery letters must not contain coin, banknotes, or certain other forms of money, nor jewellery.

recourse. A source of help, that which is resorted to. If a bill of exchange is dishonoured at maturity, the holder has the right of recourse against any of the other parties to the bill, unless any such party has expressly negatived this recourse *with recourse*. Where a bank discounts or negotiates a bill of exchange for a customer it does so 'with recourse', that is, if the bill is dishonoured at maturity, the bank is able to claim the amount of the bill from the customer *without recourse*. A party to a bill of exchange may negate liability on the bill by adding these words (or the words *sans recours*) after his or her signature on the bill. Such a clause will make the bill less easily negotiable.

recourse factoring. This is similar to *maturity factoring* with the exception that there is no credit protection extended to the supplier; the factor has full recourse against the supplier in the event of the insolvency of a customer. Recourse factoring is always disclosed. *See also* FACTORING.

recovery stock. A company which has fallen on hard times will have its shares at a rock bottom quotation. If it can see and grasp the various problems and win through, then the fortunes of the investor will improve. On the other hand, the risks involved should be appreciated.

rectification. The act of rectifying or setting right; an equitable remedy applicable where it is sought to correct or rectify a document purporting to contain the terms of a contract, which does not properly reproduce the agreement between the parties.

red clause. A clause in a documentary letter of credit designed to enable the beneficiary to draw up to 100 per cent of the credit amount before shipping documents are presented and even before shipment. The clause is so called because it is typed in red in the letter of credit. It is used principally in the Australian wool trade, where the beneficiaries (reputable wool shippers) require the pre-shipment finance to be able to pay the up-country shearing station from which the wool originates, and to finance its despatch to the port where it is made ready for loading on board an ocean vessel.

redeemable. That which may be regained; money which is capable of repayment; a mortgage of property which may be discharged by the payment of the principal, interest and costs of the mortgage.

redeemable bonds or stock. Government securities and other stocks which are repayable at par on a certain date, at any time between two given dates, or after a certain date.

redeemable debenture. A debenture where the issuing company agrees to repay the money lent at a stipulated time or after a certain period of notice, or by drawings and/or purchase. A company may redeem all or some of its debentures and may either cancel, hold or re-issue its redeemed debentures. Re-issued debentures give the new holder all the priorities which attached to the original issue. The lending banker should, therefore, insist that any such redeemed debentures be cancelled, re-issued to the bank, or placed in safe custody with the bank (so that they cannot be re-issued to anyone else).

redeemable preference shares. Preference shares which the company has stated are liable to be redeemed. Redemption must be out of profits or from the proceeds of a fresh issue of shares made for the purpose; the shares must be fully paid; any premium payable on redemption must be found from company profits before the shares are redeemed.

redemption dates. The dates between which redeemable stock is repayable.

redemption period. For the purposes of the Consumer Credit Act, 1974, a pawn is redeemable at any time within six months after it was taken. Subject to this, the period within which a pawn is redeemable shall be the same as the period fixed by the parties for the duration of the credit secured by the pledge, or such longer period as they may agree.

redemption yield. A return calculated on the total profit obtainable on a fixed interest stock redeemable at a predetermined price. It is composed of 1. the flat yield, and 2. the present value of the future capital profit which will be obtained on redemption. Where redemption is to be at a point in a range of years, it is usual to base the calculation on the latest possible redemption date. Although redemption yield is worked out by reference to a term of years, it is expressed in annual terms for comparison purposes.

re-discount. The act of a person who has discounted a bill of exchange in subsequently selling to another person; for example, a bank discounts a bill for a customer and then has it re-discounted by the central bank.

reducing balance method of depreciation. A method of depreciation where a given percentage is calculated on the closing balance of the asset at the end of the financial period and charged to the profit and loss account.

reduction of share capital. A company may wish to adjust its share capital either because the share value has risen far above the nominal value, with an accompanying difficulty in trading in the shares, or because the share value has fallen so far below the nominal value that it is apparent that the capital has been irretrievably lost. In such cases the company may by special resolution reduce its share capital and alter its memorandum accordingly. It may then apply by way of petition to the court for an order confirming the reduction. The court must be satisfied that creditors of the company have consented or have been secured, and will then issue a confirming order, which may direct that the words *'and Reduced'* shall be added after the word *'Limited'* in the name of the company.

re-entry. The resumption of possession of land; in leasehold land, the re-entry of the lessor into possession of land as a consequence of the failure of the lessee to observe the covenants of the lease.

re-exchange. In the case of a bill of exchange which has been dishonoured abroad, the holder may recover from the drawer or an indorser, and the drawer or an indorser who has been compelled to pay the bill may recover from any party liable, the amount of the re-exchange, with interest thereon, until the time of payment. The *re-exchange* is calculated to produce a sum *equal* to the amount of the dishonoured bill, *plus* costs of dishonour and incidental expenses, at the place where it was dishonoured. This is done by finding out how much would be required to purchase a sight bill at the existing rate of exchange drawn at the time and place of dishonour on the place of residence of the drawer or indorser.

re-export. A commodity re-exported; to export after having been imported. Re-export trade is carried on by a country which has a good location for redistributing goods to other countries and good air and shipping facilities to carry the goods. Also known as *entrepôt trade.*

referee. One to whom a question is referred for settlement, an arbitrator; one whose name is given by a person desiring to open a current account with a banker; one who is named by a candidate for a post as willing to give testimony of good character. *See also* OFFICIAL REFEREE.

referee in case of need. *See* CASE IN NEED.

reference. A declaration as to a person's integrity. A banker opening a new current account must either obtain a personal introduction for the new customer, from someone already known to the banker, or take up either one or two references. The referee should be vouched for in this capacity by his or her own banker. Failure to complete this procedure will leave the banker at risk for negligence with regard to any cheques which he or she handles for the new customer, to which the customer has no title or a defective title.

referential settlement. *See* SETTLED LAND.

refer to drawer. Often abbreviated as RD. This is an answer on a cheque which indicates that the drawee bank refuses to pay due to lack of funds. Rather than state the answer 'lack of funds', or some other answer which may breach secrecy, 'refer to drawer' means precisely what it says – ask the drawer for the reason for non payment. Should the drawee banker be so disposed, he may often add the words 'please represent' or the initials RDPR, which indicates that the payee or holder should represent the cheque with the possibility that payment may take place on the second presentation.

re-finance bill. A bill drawn under a re-finance credit (*q.v.*).

re-finance credit. A credit with a clause to meet the case where the exporter wants to be paid immediately, but the importer needs, for instance, three months' credit. Under such an arrangement, the bank granting and opening the credit will accept the importer's bill at three months, as soon as the exporter's sight bill has been paid by the correspondent bank. The accepted bill is then discounted by the opening bank and the proceeds sent to the correspondent bank, who are thus reimbursed for the payment to the exporter.

reflation. An attempt to inject a sluggish economy with a fresh supply of money with the object of increasing consumer demand. If this is successful, production should increase and if this increased production is sustained, manufacturers will be encouraged to increase their investment in capital equipment and to increase production yet more in the confidence that they can sell the goods they are producing. These measures decrease unemployment and lead to a healthy upswing of trade. Reflation may start by a series of government measures which show that money is easier, e.g. restrictions may be lifted from the banks in the matter of their lending (*monetary methods*) or income tax can be cut or the rate of VAT reduced (*fiscal methods*). If reflation results in increasing demand so much that home manufacturers cannot satisfy the demand, then prices will rise and imports will increase. Inflation and an adverse balance of payments will oblige the government to bring back the various methods of control. Reflation is thus a two-edged tool which must be used very carefully.

regeneration. The act of giving fresh life or vigour to; re-organisation; a word used to describe efforts to bring back companies and firms to London, which have de-centralised to other areas to such an extent that the process of inner city decay was considerably hastened in the capital.

regional trade. Trade between countries with common borders or situated in the same region, as the result of an agreement between them to pursue a common trade policy, e.g. the European Common Market.

register. An official written record; a book, roll or other document in which such a record is kept; an official or authoritative list of names, facts, etc., as of shipping or charges against land; to enter in a register. For the purposes of the Consumer Credit Act, 1974, the Director-General of Fair Trading shall establish and maintain a register giving particulars of 1. applications not yet determined for the issue, variation, or renewal of licences under the Act, or for ending the suspension of a licence; 2. licences which are in force, or have at any time been suspended or revoked, with details of any variation of the terms of a licence; 3. decisions given by the Director-General under the Act, and any appeal from those decisions; and 4. such other matters (if any) as the Director-General thinks fit. Any person shall be entitled on payment of the specified fee to inspect the register during ordinary office hours and take copies of any entry, or to obtain from the Director a copy, certified by the director to be correct, of any entry in the register. *See also* LAND CERTIFICATE; LAND CHARGES REGISTER; LAND REGISTER; LLOYD'S REGISTER OF SHIPPING; LOCAL LAND CHARGES REGISTER.

registered capital. *See* SHARE CAPITAL.

registered charge. A legal mortgage over registered land. The banker lending against this security should take the land certificate from the customer, get the customer to sign a form of legal mortgage, make a search on the Register, and prepare an office copy of the signed mortgage. The banker then sends to the Land Registrar the land certificate and both copies of the mortgage. The appropriate fee for registration of the charge must accompany the application. The Registrar will keep the land certificate and the copy mortgage. He or she will make the appropriate entry in the Register and then issue a charge certificate to the banker as evidence of his or her interest. This will have the original form of mortgage stitched inside it.

registered land certificate. *See* LAND CERTIFICATE.

registered office. The memorandum of every company must state whether the registered office of the company is to be situate in England, Wales or Scotland. The registered office is the official headquarters of the company to which communications are to be addressed, and at which various registers required by law, such as registers of directors, secretaries, members, charges and debentures given by the company, etc., are to be maintained.

registered post. A method of postal delivery by which letters are insured against loss or damage in transit.

registered provident societies. A group of varied institutions registered under the Friendly Societies Acts and other legislation which give them certain privileges, such as limited liability, and impose upon them various limitations and obligations. Friendly societies are mutual insurance societies in which the members subscribe for provident benefits, in particular sickness, death, endowment and old age benefits, and provisions for widows and orphans. Although the National Health Service now meets most of the needs for which the original friendly societies were set up, they still continue to operate and have

diversified to include industrial insurance; industrial, provident and building societies; trade unions; certified loan societies; and some superannuation and pension schemes. All are closely controlled by various Acts.

register of charges. A record maintained by the Registrar of Companies of all charges made by limited companies and requiring registration under s. 396 of the Companies Act 1985. The register may be inspected by any person on payment of a small fee. Additionally, each company is required to keep at its registered office a register of all property charged by the company including all floating charges on the undertaking of the company. The register is available for inspection by any member of the company without fee and by any other person on payment of a small fee. *See also* LAND CHARGES REGISTER.

register of companies. The list of approved limited companies in Great Britain which have complied with the formalities of registration and have been given a certificate of incorporation by the Registrar of Companies. Such a certificate issued by the Registrar is conclusive evidence that all the requirements in respect of the registration of the company have been complied with. A register of company mortgages is maintained by the Registrar, open to inspection by any person on payment of a small charge. If the Registrar gives a certificate of the registration of any mortgage or charge, this is conclusive evidence that the requirements of the Companies Act 1985 have been complied with.

register of debenture holders. A register of holders of debentures issued by a company shall be kept at the registered office of the company and shall be open for at least two hours in each day to the inspection of the registered holder of any such debentures, or any shareholder in the company, without charge; and to the inspection of any other person at a small charge.

register of directors and secretaries.
Every company shall keep at its registered office a register of its directors and secretaries. With respect to each director, the register shall state the full name, address, nationality and business occupation together with particulars of any other directorships held, and, where the company is a public company, date of birth. If the director is a corporation, its corporate name and registered office must be given. With respect to each secretary, the register shall state the full name and address. If the secretary is a corporation or a Scottish firm, its corporate or firm name and registered office must be given.

register of members. Every company shall keep a register of its members, entering therein the following particulars: 1. the names and addresses of the members, and in the case of a company having a share capital, a statement of the shares held by each member, distinguishing each share by its number (so long as the share has a number) and of the amount paid or agreed to be considered as paid on the shares of each member; 2. the date on which each person was entered in the register as a member; 3. the date at which any person ceased to be a member. The register of members shall be kept at the registered office of the company. It must be open for not less than two hours each day to the inspection of any member *gratis* and to the inspection of any other person for a small charge.

register of ships. Every British ship, unless not exceeding fifteen tons burthen and employed solely in navigation on the rivers or coasts of the UK, shall be registered under the Merchant Shipping Act, 1894. The chief officer of customs is the Registrar of British ships and is responsible for the maintenance of registers at any port in the UK approved by the Commissioner of Customs for the registry of ships. The Registrar issues a certificate of registry to the owner of the ship on registration. Mortgages of ships, or parts of a ship, are recorded on the register of the port in which the ship is registered, priority being calculated according to the hour and date of registration. *See* MORTGAGE OF SHIP. Most ships are also registered with Lloyd's Register of Shipping (*q. v.*).

register of transfers. On the application by the transferee of shares, together with the completed Stock Transfer Form, the company will make the transfer in its register of transfers of shares or debentures, recording the date of registration, the number of shares transferred with their descriptive numbers, the names and addresses of the transferor and transferee and the numbers of the old certificate returned and the new one issued. Any alterations to the Members' Register necessitated by the transfer will also be made. The record in the Register of Transfers may also be made at the request of the transferor of the shares. If the company refuses to register the transfer of any shares or debentures it shall send the transferee notice of the refusal within two months after the date on which the transfer was lodged with the company.

registrar. An official whose duty it is to keep a register or record of transactions.

Registrar-General. A public officer who superintends the registration of births, deaths and marriages.

Registrar of Companies. A public officer appointed by the Department of Trade to supervise the registration of companies and limited partnerships, to issue certificates of incorporation and registration of company mortgages, and to maintain facilities for the public inspection of company records.

registration. Act of registering, entry or record, e.g. of births, etc.; a form of insurance on postal packages; the insertion of a company's name on the Register of Companies.

registration fee. The fee payable at a post office for the registration of a letter or packet; the charge made by a company for the registration of shares in the name of a new shareholder.

registration of charges. As to unregistered land, *see* LAND CHARGES. As to registered land, in the case of a deposit of the land certificate with the lender, the latter will make a search on the Register by sending the registered land certificate back to the Registry to be written up to date. At the same time he will lodge Land Registry Form 85A, which operates to give the Registrar notice of his or her interest. The Registrar will enter this on the Charge Register, thus giving notice to any possible purchaser or mortgagee. Also, if the proprietor attempts to dispose of the land or deal with it in any way other than by legal mortgage, the Registrar will notify the lender accordingly. The latter will then have fourteen days (or such other period as is indicated in the notification) in which to take action to protect his or her interest. In the case of a registered charge, the borrower signs a form of legal mortgage and deposits the land certificate with the lender, who makes a search on the Register, using Land Register Form 94. The search form must be accompanied by the authorisation of the mortgagor or the mortgagor's solicitor. The duplicate of Form 94 is returned with the result of the search, and is then known as 'the official certificate of search'. If the certificate shows the title to be clear, the Land Registration (Official Searches) Rules, 1969 give the lender priority for fifteen days after the date of the search, during which time the lender should complete and register his or her charge. The lender should take the form of mortgage, prepare an office copy of it, and send to the

registrar the land certificate, the signed, sealed form of legal mortgage, and the copy mortgage. The Registrar will keep the land certificate and the copy mortgage. The Registrar will make an appropriate entry in the Register and will then issue to the lender, as evidence of his title, a document called a charge certificate. This will have the original form of mortgage stitched inside. As to *companies,* any one of nine charges specified in s. 396 of the Companies Act, 1985 must be registered within twenty-one days of its creation and, if not so registered, becomes void against the liquidator and any creditors of the company. The charges specified are: 1. a charge for securing any issue of debentures; 2. a charge on uncalled share capital of the company; 3. a charge which in the case of an individual would need registration as a bill of sale; 4. a charge on land; 5. a charge on book debts of the company; 6. a floating charge on the undertaking of the property; 7. a charge on calls made but not paid; 8. a charge on a ship or a share of a ship; 9. a charge on goodwill, patent, licence, trademark or copyright. The company is primarily responsible for the registration of the charge but provision is made for registration to be effected by the lender. *See also* AGRICULTURAL CHARGES; LAND CERTIFICATE; REGISTER OF SHIPS.

registration of share transfers. *See* REGISTER OF TRANSFERS.

regressive tax. A tax falling more heavily upon people with low incomes than on those with high incomes; thus as the income falls the proportion of tax increases.

regulated agreement. Under the Consumer Credit Act, 1984, a consumer credit agreement other than an exempt agreement.

regulator. The name given to the power of the Chancellor of the Exchequer to vary the rates of indirect taxation to meet the economic and monetary needs of the time.

reimbursement credit. A credit created when a bank in the country of an importer requests a correspondent bank in the country of an exporter to authorise the exporter to draw bills on the correspondent bank, the opening bank undertaking to re-imburse the correspondent bank as and when such bills have to be honoured by the correspondent bank. Where the trade is between other countries but is to be financed through London (because the banks concerned hold sterling balances in London which can be utilised), the correspondent bank will be authorised to draw in sterling on a London bank in re-imbursement. The opening bank would then have to notify the London bank of any such reimbursements which it had authorised.

re-insurance. Where a risk is considerable an insurance company will insure the risk up to a certain amount themselves, and put the excess risk out to a re-insurance company, or to more than one, on the principle of diversifying the risk.

re-intermediation. The bringing back into the banking system after the end of the corset control of credit formerly arranged through bills accepted by the banks and financed outside the system (*see* ACCEPTANCE CREDIT). It is business coming back through the banks or 'intermediaries', and also possible adjustments within bank balance sheets which may affect the monetary numbers.

re-issue. To issue again, to republish, to make again available; a reprint.

re-issue of bill of exchange. Where a bill is negotiated back to the drawer, or to a prior indorser or the acceptor, such party may re-issue and further negotiate the bill, but may not enforce payment of the bill against any intervening party to whom he or she was previously liable.

re-issue of debenture. *See* REDEEMABLE DEBENTURE.

related company. By s. 92, Sch. 4, of the Companies Act, 1985, a related company is any company that holds a long term qualifying interest for the purpose of securing a contribution to that company's own activities, by the exercise of any control or influence arising from that interest.

release. To set free from restraint or confinement, to loosen, to exempt from an obligation; to remit a claim; exemption, a discharge of a right.

remainder. An interest in property under a will or settlement, whereby trustees hold the property for the benefit of the life tenant until his or her death, whereupon it passes to the remaindermen, e.g. a will may leave property in trust for a widow (the life tenant) subject to the stipulation that on her death the property is to pass absolutely to the children of the marriage, if of full age (the remaindermen).

remedies of mortgages. *See* POWERS OF MORTGAGEE.

remise. Putting back, remittance, delivery, rebate; a surrender, a release, as of a claim; to resign property by deed.

remission. The act of remitting an accused person or a case to another court.

remittance. Act of transferring money or bills to a distant place; the money sent; a parcel of cheques or bills received at a branch or dispatched by it.

remittance basis. UK tax to be paid is worked out either on the income received during the year (earnings, UK pensions, etc.), or received in the previous year (business profits, etc.). Money coming from abroad is liable to tax only on the amount which is actually remitted to the UK, either during the previous year or within the actual year. This is known as the remittance basis. Previous year remittances are applicable to those resident in the UK but not domiciled there. The sources of income concerned are investment income from abroad, pensions from abroad, and income from trades controlled abroad. Actual year remittances apply in any case to UK residents not domiciled in this country in respect of capital gains from assets sold abroad. Where the taxpayer, apart from being resident there for the particular year, is also ordinarily resident in the UK, actual year remittances also apply to emoluments from an employer not resident in the UK or Eire where the duties are performed wholly abroad. Finally, the remittances of the actual year also apply to those who are not ordinarily resident in the UK on emoluments from duties performed wholly abroad.

remittance letter. A letter sent by a bank to its correspondent or branch, which encloses cheques and other negotiable instruments for collection and payment. The remitting bank will request the collecting bank to credit its account under reserve, or after payment. The collecting bank will sort the cheques and other instruments into particular order and make a presentation either, through a clearing system or direct. The remitting letter should instruct the collecting banker on how to deal with any items which have been dishonoured.

remote damage. Damage which arises as a result of a breach of contract, but does not flow naturally from it. Where a loss is too remote from the breach, compensation will not be awarded.

remote parties. The parties to a bill of exchange who are not in immediate relationship with each other.

remuneration. The consideration given for a service. This can be in the form of either a fee, wage, or salary.

remuneration of trustees. This is not usually permitted, except where authorised by the Trust Instrument, or the court, or by statute. Where a bank acts as trustees, then it would be usual to have this fact recorded in the trust instrument.

renewal. Restoration, replacement; a reloan on a new note given in place of a former note; with the consent of all parties, the acceptance of a new bill of exchange for an old one, thus postponing the date when payment has to be made.

renewal bill. The name given to a bill which is drawn to be discounted so as to provide funds to meet another bill maturing; a method of extending borrowing at maturity on a short-term basis.

rent. A periodical payment at an agreed rate for the use and enjoyment of something, such as land, houses, machines, films, etc.; rental hiring charge. In economics, a surplus accruing to a factor of production, the reward gained by any productive agency which is in short supply and cannot easily or quickly be increased. *See also* CHIEF RENT; FEE FARM RENT; GROUND RENT; QUASI-RENT.

rental. A rent-roll, the annual amount of rent payable.

rental contract. *See* FINANCE LEASE.

rentcharge. Any rent expressly made payable out of land, other than rent payable by a tenant, to a reversioner; a charge on land payable to one who is no longer its owner. Rentcharges, created in perpetuity, are payable on freehold properties in the UK, principally in the NW and in the West Country. A freeholder technically pays them forever, unlike a ground rent in connection with a lease which is granted for a fixed number of years. Since 1977, however, the Rentcharge Act has limited the length of all rentcharges in existence to sixty years, and has also prevented the establishment of new ones. Rentcharges can now be bought out by a lump sum payment. The sum required to redeem a sixty-year rentcharge would be about nine times the annual rentcharge figure. *See also* GROUND RENT.

rent-roll. A schedule of rents, a list of those who pay rents.

rent-service. The annual payment by a tenant of land, whether by money, labour or provisions, in return for the right to live on the land. *See also* FEE FARM RENT.

renunciation. The surrender of one's claim or interest, abandonment, disavowal, formal repudiation; the *document* expressing this; the giving up by a shareholder of new shares allocated to him by the completion of the form of renunciation on the back of the allotment letter. When the holder of a bill of exchange, at or after its maturity, absolutely and unconditionally renounces his or her rights against the acceptor, the bill is discharged. The renunciation must be in *writing,* unless the bill is delivered up to the acceptor.

replacement cost. The company purchasing an asset should set on foot a depreciation programme, transferring yearly instalments to an investment fund so that at the end of the period estimated as the useful working life of the asset, there is money to renew the asset. However, the effect of inflation in the period may have considerably raised the replacement cost, so that an additional sum must be provided to offset the inflationary increase. The asset may be written up yearly before depreciation is applied, or the additional sum may be allocated from some other source.

report on title. The borrower who offers title deeds as security must deposit them with the lending bank. The banker will make a *prima facie* check of the deeds and then send them to a solicitor who will check and report on the title of the customer, and state, in writing, any points which are relevant to the title which is about to be acquired by the bank. However, the particular form of words which must appear in this solicitor's report is that, after the title has been mortgaged, the bank will be in possession of a 'good

and marketable title' to the land. It is, of course, essential that the banker should be able to sell the security if so obliged.

represent. To make out to be, to pretend to be, to pretend, to allege; to bring forward for payment a bill or cheque which has already been dishonoured.

representation. Standing in the place of a deceased person, as an executor, etc.; a statement of facts; a protest; a statement made in the preliminary stages of the negotiation of a contract. In the latter sense, it is made by one of the parties to the contract to the other one, with the intention usually of persuading that other to enter into the contract. For the purposes of the Consumer Credit Act, 1974, 'representation' includes any *condition or warranty,* and any other statement or undertaking whether oral or in writing. *See also* CHAIN OF REPRESENTATION.

representative. Fitting or qualified to represent, typical; an agent, deputy, delegate or substitute; one who stands in the place of another as heir, etc. *See also* PERSONAL REPRESENTATIVE.

repurchase agreements (repos). Repurchase agreements ('repos') represent one of the most important financial markets in the United States and are used by banks, large corporations and non-bank financial institutions, as well as state and local governments, for trading large amounts of liquid funds with each other on a daily basis. Repos and reverse repos have also become an important element in the day-to-day workings of the US government's monetary policy as implemented by the Federal Reserve. A repurchase agreement is an acquisition of *immediately available funds* through the sale of securities, together with a simultaneous agreement to *repurchase* them at a later date. The securities involved are almost always obligations of the US government and other federal agencies, so that *risk* of default can be regarded as *minimal*. At the same time, transactions are usually arranged only among institutions with a high degree of confidence in each other. There is no physical market for repurchase agreements and transactions are arranged by telephone, often directly between the parties supplying and acquiring funds, as well as through specialist money brokers. For corporations other than banks, repurchase agreements are an important tool of *cash management;* they generate income for the 'investor' and are generally regarded as secure. Because repos can be arranged for periods as short as one day they have the great advantage of flexibility. For the government, repos and reverse repos are an essential part of the open market operations of the Federal Reserve and are used to influence the reserve position of the whole banking sector either permanently, as a deliberate aspect of current monetary policy, or more commonly, to smooth out day-to-day shortages and excesses of funds in the US domestic money markets resulting from seasonal influences as well as changes in currency in circulation and in the Treasury's balance at the Federal Reserve (*see* INTER-BANK STERLING MARKET).

reputed owner. A person who is in possession of property with the consent of the true owner, in circumstances which lead third parties to conclude that he or she is the owner of the property although in fact this is not the case. In bankruptcy law, the property of the bankrupt passing into the hands of the trustee includes such goods as are at the commencement of the bankruptcy in the possession, order or disposition of the bankrupt, in the bankrupt's trade or business, by the consent of the true owner, in such circumstances that he or she is the reputed owner thereof.

requisition. A written order for materials or supplies, a formal demand; to seize.

requisitions on title. Questions framed by the solicitor to an intending purchaser and addressed to the vendor's solicitor, referring to points in the chain of title of the property to be passed, on which he or she desires further enlightenment.

requisitor. An official empowered by a court to investigate facts.

re-registration of companies. The Companies Act, 1985 ss. 43 – 55, defines the terms whereby (*a*) a private company can become public; (*b*) a limited company can become unlimited; (*c*) an unlimited company can become limited; (*d*) a public company can become private.

resale price maintenance. The upholding of a fixed price for a product by a manufacturer or a group of manufacturers acting together. Concerted action of this kind by manufacturers was made illegal in 1964, unless they could show that it was in the public interest, but the right of an individual manufacturer to cut off supplies to a retailer selling at less than the fixed price has been upheld.

rescheduling of debts. This may mean the spreading out, over a longer period than the term originally agreed, of a debt; or it may refer, as in the international field, to the rearrangement of interest payments. International lending has probably reached an *unrepayable total,* but as long as interest payments are duly made on time the lender will, perforce, be satisfied. Unfortunately, this is not now the case with a growing number of countries in the Eastern bloc or in South America, most of whom have been forced to ask their lending bankers to rearrange even the *payment of interest.* Where conferences between the country concerned and the consortium of lending bankers have resulted in the deferment of interest payment dates on to a new and more lenient schedule, then the bankers have been satisfied and the country is given more time to haul itself out of the state of near-bankruptcy in which it finds itself.

rescind. To annul, e.g. a law or decision; to cancel, to revoke, to repeal, to reverse, to abrogate.

rescission. The act of annulling or abrogating. An *equitable remedy* for the relief of a party to a contract where *mistake* has been a vital factor.

rescissory action. An action whereby deeds, etc., are declared void.

reservation. A clause or proviso in a conveyance or lease by which some right or easement is retained by the vendor or lessee.

reserve. Funds set aside for possible contingencies *(see also* PROVISION); the minimum price acceptable to a vendor at an auction; the total of notes and coins shown on the assets side of the Bank of England return for the Banking Department. *See also* HIDDEN RESERVE; REVENUE RESERVE; SPECIFIC RESERVE.

reserve assets. Formerly a list of short-term assets prescribed by the Bank of England at the time of Competition and Credit Control, to be kept by banks and other financial institutions, which were convertible into cash either directly or through the discount market. These assets made it possible for the Bank to lay down a reserve assets ratio *(q.v.)* to which banks and financial institutions had to adhere. The *change in the policy* of control at the Bank of England, which came into force on 18 August 1981, switched the fulcrum of monetary control from the reserve asset ratio to the bill market, so that reserve assets were no longer important in this context. But banks were asked not to change their policies on the holdings of reserve assets until discussions as to the appropriate prudential level of holdings of such assets had been completed. In the US reserve assets are non-interest bearing de-

posits with the Federal Reserve System (the US central bank). *See* COMPETITION AND CREDIT CONTROL; CONTROL OF THE MONEY SUPPLY; RESERVE ASSETS RATIO.

reserve assets ratio. The ratio between a bank's eligible liabilities and its reserve assets, fixed since 1971 at $12\frac{1}{2}$ per cent, but altered in January 1981 to 10 per cent. Reserve assets ratio was abandoned as a formal measure on 20 August 1981. Its place is taken by requirements for the banks to hold prescribed averages of liquid assets. *See* CONTROL OF THE MONEY SUPPLY; RESERVE ASSETS.

reserve currency. Currencies of other countries held by a country as part of its central monetary reserves *(see* RESERVES); a currency which is widely accepted as a means of settlement and finance of trade. The US $ and sterling are the world's major reserve currencies.

reserved power. A reservation made in deeds, settlements, etc. The most common example is perhaps the clause in a lease whereby the lessor reserves the right to re-enter upon the property if the rent is not punctually paid.

reserve fund. An allocation from profit in any business, to be set aside to meet unforeseen or unexpected expenses. The reserve fund should be invested outside the business.

reserve liability. That part of a company's share capital which it has resolved cannot be called up except in the case of the liquidation of the company.

reserve price. A price below which no offer will be accepted.

reserves. The UKs reserves of gold and convertible currencies are held at the Bank of England and consist of varying amounts of gold bars, special drawing rights, convertible currencies of other countries and credits at the International Monetary Fund. These reserves are affected by *deposits in London* by overseas depositors; *invest-*

ments in British property or paper such as Treasury Bills; *overseas borrowing* by the Government and public enterprises; the *balance of trade*; and *transfers* made by the Bank of England in the course of *stabilising* the exchange rate of sterling.

resettlement. *See* SETTLED LAND.

re-shipment. The re-export of imported goods.

residence. The act of dwelling in a place, the place where one resides; the basis in the UK for tax assessment of a British citizen; under the name of 'domicile' (*q.v.*) the basis for succession duty.

resident. In so far as this refers to the UK, a resident is a person who has decided to live and have a settled life in the UK. For tax purposes, providing a person is resident for 183 days in any year, he/she is considered a resident and is subject to UK tax for that year.

residual value. Often referred to as scrap value. The value of an asset at the end of its useful life.

residuary devisee. The person who takes, under the terms of a will, all the real property remaining after the specific devises have been satisfied.

residuary legatee. The person to whom the residue of personal estate is bequeathed after all other claims are discharged.

residue. That which remains after a part is taken; that which remains of an estate after payment of all charges, debts and particular bequests; the balance or remainder of a debt or account.

residuum. The part of the estate of a testator which remains after payment of debts and legacies; the balance remaining of a bankrupt or trust estate after payment of preferred debts and claims; as a term in economics, the poorest stratum of a community.

res ipsa loquitur. The thing speaks for itself, e.g. where in an accident the negligence of the defendant is so obvious that proof is hardly required.

resolution. The decision of a court or the vote of an assembly; motion, declaration; a proposition put before a meeting of company shareholders for discussion, passed by a majority. *See also* EXTRAORDINARY RESOLUTION; ORDINARY RESOLUTION; SPECIAL RESOLUTION.

resolution to borrow. Any application to borrow by a limited company should be supported by a copy of the resolution passed authorising such an application. The resolution should be certified by the secretary of the company as a true copy of the entry in the minute book. Whether this resolution is properly a resolution of the directors or whether it is one passed by the company in general or special meeting, is a point to be checked by the bank with reference to the articles and memorandum of the company *(See* BORROWING POWERS). The form of resolution should be satisfactory to the bank, and usually the bank will supply its own printed form for completion and return. Ideally the company should complete a *resolution* on each borrowing occasion to cover the sum required, for this ensures that all the members of the board know of the arrangements, and rules out a possible *fraud* by one director having power to sign alone on behalf of the company. However, a company requiring a series of overdrafts or loans is apt to resent having to complete a borrowing resolution each time accommodation is required, and therefore it is common practice to take an *'omnibus resolution'* for 'such sums as the Company may require from time to time and the Bank be willing to lend'. It should cover an overdraft, a loan, or both together. A resolution in support of the giving of a guarantee by the company should name the officials who will sign the guarantee on behalf of the company, authorise them to do so, and identify the guarantee. (One way to do this is to have the resolution typed out and signed on the back of the guarantee itself.)

resolution to wind up. A company wishing to wind-up voluntarily must pass a resolution to that effect. The type of resolution, whether ordinary, special or extraordinary, depends on the reason for winding-up – which may be unconnected with any financial difficulty (as, for example, if it wishes to amalgamate with another concern), or, on the other hand, on whether it cannot by reason of its liabilities continue in business, and that it is advisable to wind-up. The commencement of the winding-up is the passing of the *resolution* for voluntary winding-up. The company must give notice of the resolution within fourteen days, by advertising it in the *Gazette. See also* VOLUNTARY LIQUIDATION.

respondent. One who answers in certain proceedings, especially, in a chancery or divorce suit, the defendant.

respondentia. A loan raised by the master of a ship upon its cargo, for which he is personally responsible; the instrument of hypothecation by which such a loan is raised. The money is repayable only if the ship safely reaches its port of destination, and the loan is for the purpose of paying for repairs to the ship urgently needed if it is to continue its voyage.

restraint of trade. A contract in restraint of trade, as between the buyer and seller of a business, is one which is intended to protect trade secrets and special proprietary rights or processes, or to maintain the goodwill of a business. Such a contract will be enforced only if it is no wider than is reasonably necessary to protect the party in whose interests it is imposed, is *reasonable* with reference to the party against whom it is made, and is reasonable from the point of the public at large. Contracts in restraint of trade are also found in the form of agreements between employers and

employees. Such a contract will be enforced if it is necessary to protect the employer against the *improper use* by the employee of knowledge gained in the employer's service, but will not be upheld merely to stifle ordinary business competition or to prevent the employee using the personal skill and knowledge acquired through employment.

restricted circulation. An instruction to accompany any order, memorandum, or circular which is to be kept confidential among the more senior representatives of an organisation, e.g. the system of dealing with staff frauds, or the staffing policy of a large company, or the measures to be taken in the event of a strike of the work force.

restricted-use credit agreement. A regulated consumer credit agreement 1. to finance a transaction between the debtor and the creditor, whether forming part of that agreement or not; or 2. to finance a transaction between the debtor and a person (the 'supplier') other than the creditor; or 3. to refinance any existing indebtedness of the debtor's, whether to the creditor or another person.

restriction. A limitation, a confinement, a restraint; in the law of registered land, a notification to the Land Registrar to protect a minor interest, such as the necessity to pay the sale monies for land held upon trust for sale to two trustees. (*Fr.*) A limitation, for example, in the granting of credit or in the flow of international payments.

restrictive covenant. A covenant by which the use of the covenantor's land is restricted for the benefit of the covenantee's land which adjoins it.

restrictive indorsement. One which prohibits any further negotiation of a bill of exchange; one which gives the indorsee authority to deal with the bill only as directed in the indorsement. A restrictive indorsement usually destroys the transferability of the bill (e.g. 'pay John Smith only').

resulting trust. A trust which is not expressly created, but arises as a result of certain conduct of the donor from which it is concluded that the donor intended to create a trust. The more common case is where the settlor fails, intentionally or unintentionally, to provide for a gap in the beneficial interests, e.g. a settlement upon children at twenty-one, with nothing said as to what is to happen if they all die under twenty-one, in which case there is a resulting trust in favour of the settlor. *See also* PROTECTIVE TRUST.

retail. To sell in small quantities.

retail banking. The traditional course of business between a banker and domestic customers, as opposed to 'wholesale' banking. One of its principal distinguishing features is that it is conducted through a network of branches.

retail cost. The price of an article in the shop where it is sold.

retail price index. *See* GENERAL INDEX OF RETAIL PRICES.

retail trade. The final stage of distribution, where goods are sold in shops to the people who are going to use or consume the goods.

retaining fee. A preliminary fee paid to a barrister or other professional engaging his or her services.

retention money. Money held back for a certain time (often six months) after a contract has been completed, while the work done proves itself. If in that time repairs are required, they are defrayed out of the retention moneys.

retiring a bill. Payment of a bill of exchange at or before its maturity date, whether by an indorser who takes the bill up by paying the amount of it to a transferee, or by the drawer or acceptor who redeems it from the holder before maturity. Where the acceptor retires a bill at maturity it is in effect paid, and all the remedies on it are extinguished.

retiring partner. *See* OUTGOING PARTNER.

return. To report officially; to yield a profit; the rendering back of a writ to the proper officer or court.

return day. The day on which a defendant is instructed to appear in court.

returned item/cheque. A cheque or some other negotiable instrument which has been sent by the collecting banker to the paying banker either directly or through a clearing system, which has, for some reason, not been paid. It is usual that any items presented by one bank to another will have the answer either written on the instrument or have an alonge attached given the reason for dishonour.

revaluation. To put a fresh value on; the raising in value of a country's currency in terms of the currencies of other countries.

revenue. Income derived from any source, especially the annual income of a state or institution; proceeds, receipts, profits. *See also* INLAND REVENUE.

revenue account. An account showing the income of a company and the expenditure chargeable against it.

revenue officer. An officer employed in the collection of excise or customs duties levied by the state.

revenue reserve. A sum which has been built up out of favourable profit and loss balances in previous years.

reverse. To turn the other way round, to give a contrary decision; to repeal, to revoke.

reverse annuity. A loophole in the tax laws of the UK which appeared in 1970/71, under which insurance companies and other financial institutions could grant a 'reverse annuity' to a high taxpayer and he or she would repay by instalments in the form of an annuity spread over a period of years. The 'annuity payments' were fully allowable against income tax and so the real cost to the taxpayer was very much reduced. The device was attractive to those paying tax at above 60 per cent of income: the scope was therefore limited to the very wealthy. It was announced by the Chancellor of the Exchequer in March 1977 that he was proposing to introduce provisions to annul this system, such provisions to apply immediately.

reverse arbitrage. Borrowing from the market to clear off a bank overdraft when rates permit this.

reverse income tax. *See* NEGATIVE INCOME TAX.

reverse takeover. A takeover of a larger company by a smaller one.

reverse yield gap. When it became felt – at the end of the 1950s – that the future held nothing but steady progress, and that recessions were things of the past, it seemed evident that dividends on equities would to on rising, whereas fixed interest yields gave no protection against inflation. Consequently the yield on equities became less than that on fixed-interest securities and a 'reverse yield gap' arose. In more recent years, however, the relationship between inflation, dividends and earnings appears to have broken down.

reversion. Land granted under a lease to a tenant for a number of years reverts to the lessor at the end of the time. A reversion is an interest arising by operation of law, as distinct from act of parties, whenever the owner of an estate grants a particular estate without disposing of the whole of his or her interest.

reversionary bonus. A bonus added to the value of a 'with-profits' life policy on a periodic valuation of the profits made by the assurance company in the preceding period.

reversionary interest. *See* REMAINDER.

revocable credit. A credit which can be revoked or cancelled by the bank which opened it at any time during the period it is stated to remain in force.

All credits are revocable, unless it is specifically stated that they are irrevocable. This type of credit offers no security to the exporter and is comparatively rare nowadays.

revocation of will. The annulment of a will by the testator, whether expressly or by implication. An express revocation has to be effected by an instrument which is executed with the same formality as a will requires. An implied revocation is effected: 1. by the making of a subsequent inconsistent formal testamentary document which disposes of the whole property mentioned in the original will; 2. by burning, tearing or otherwise destroying the will. There must be both physical destruction and the *intention* to destroy. The destruction must be carried out either by the testator or by someone in his or her presence acting with the testator's authority; 3. by marriage. Subsequent marriage will revoke an existing will, whether made by a man or a woman, unless the will was expressed to be made in contemplation of marriage, and the marriage does take place as contemplated.

revoke. To annul, to repeal, to reverse a decision.

revolving credit. A credit containing a clause for an automatic renewal of the credit on a roll-over basis. Thus any part of the credit used by the borrower (through the beneficiary utilising the power of availment) and reimbursed to the banker within the term of the credit becomes again available, automatically, upon such re-imbursement. There is therefore no limit to the total of turnover, although there is a stated limit to the amount of drafts which may be outstanding at any one time.

rider. An addition to a manuscript or other document; an additional clause, as to a bill; a supplement tacked on to the original motion or verdict.

riding. One of the three territorial divisions of the old county of Yorkshire. It is now divided into two

Metropolitan Counties and three counties. Though no longer relevant for local government administrative purposes, the term still has some significance in Land Law.

right. A just claim, a legal title.

right in personam. A right which can be enforced only against a limited number of persons.

right in rem. A right enforceable against the whole world.

right of action. A right to commence an action in court.

right of survivorship. The right of a surviving joint-tenant to own and enjoy the property, formerly held jointly, as against the personal representative of the deceased joint tenant.

right of way. A right, established by custom, to use a path over or through private property; such a path.

rights issue. The offer by a company of new shares direct to its existing members. The price is usually set below the market price of the existing shares, in order to make the offer attractive. The rights to subscribe, therefore, have themselves a market value, and can be sold. *See also* OPEN OFFER.

rights letter. The document informing an existing shareholder of a company of the right to take up on favourable terms a number of newly-issued shares in the company. If the shareholder does not wish to exercise this right he or she may sell the letter of rights.

rights of holder of bill. The holder may sue on the bill in his or her own name. Where the holder is a *holder in due course* the bill is held free from any defect of title of prior parties and payment may be enforced against all parties liable on the bill.

rights of unpaid seller. The unpaid seller has by implication of law, and notwithstanding that the property in the goods may have passed to the buyer, 1. a lien on the goods or right to retain them for the price while in possession of them; 2. where the buyer

is insolvent, a right of stopping the goods *in transitu* after he or she has parted with the possession of them; 3. a right of resale.

ring. A combination of persons to control prices within a trade; a term used to describe trading in various commodity markets, e.g. the Metal Exchange. (*Fr.*) In the *Bourse,* the circular bar round which the brokers are to be found transacting business when the *Bourse* is in session.

risk. Danger, peril, hazard, chance of loss; amount covered by insurance; person or object insured.

risk-asset ratio. The Bank of England's system for controlling the banks and deposit-taking institutions under its supervision has obliged it to make certain definitions. *Risk-asset* ratio is defined as the free capital plus a figure for premises relative to all assets; substantially, the bank's loan portfolio; and its investments. *See also* CAPITAL BASE; CONTROL OF THE MONEY SUPPLY.

risk capital. The ordinary shares of a company, dividends on which are poor or good according to the fortunes of the company. The term is also applied to a situation where a bank has lent money and can as yet recover neither capital instalment nor even an interest repayment. In such a case both capital and interest are 'rolled over', i.e. capital repayments are postponed until such a time as the borrower can afford them, interest due is placed to a suspense account. There will be some special reason why this treatment is thought to be the appropriate one; normally the obvious solution would be to put the borrower in liquidation or make the borrower bankrupt.

rolling targets. A system of monetary control operated in the US. A target range for monetary growth over the next twelve months for three separate monetary aggregates is fixed every quarter by the Federal Reserve. This enables the central bank to adjust both the target and the trajectory of the 'missile' every month. The chief drawback of the system is its very flexibility. Because money supply is always aiming at a target which moves before it gets there the disciplinary constraints or those in charge of the guidance are not particularly effective. For a system of rolling targets to work successfully the government's resolve has go to be firm and public analysis well informed.

roll-over. A term indicating a continuance of existing credit. A limit on a 'roll-over' basis is renewed once it has been exhausted. If an interest rate is expressed to be on a roll-over basis it means that it will be re-negotiated at intervals, perhaps every three months. (In a time of rising interest rates a lender may not wish to be committed for too long to a specific rate, when the chances are that a better rate may be available later on.)

roll-over loan. A loan for a fixed period but where the interest rate is reviewed at intervals throughout the term of the loan, based on a formula agreed at the time the loan is made (e.g. 1 per cent over three months Inter Bank Offer Rate, usually abbreviated to IBOR).

Romalpa case. A stipulation in a contract that the ownership in the goods shall not pass to the buyer until payment has been made. This is an important case to bankers, who having given an advance to customers against a floating charge, need to know that creditors to the borrowing company have not inserted retention clauses in their contracts so that they have prior rights to the bank. *Aluminium Industrie Vaasen B.V.* v *Romalpa Aluminium Ltd.*

Roman law. The code of laws developed by the Romans, regarded as the basis of jurisprudence by the majority of European countries.

root of title. *See* GOOD ROOT OF TITLE.

round lot. The minimum number of

shares acceptable for sale or purchase on the *Bourse.*

round tripping. *See* HARD ARBITRAGE.

royal charter. A document originating from the sovereign creating a legal entity. A century or two ago, royal charter was granted to trading companies, these days it is now given to universities, charitable institutions, professional associations, e.g. Chartered Institute of Bankers.

Royal Mint. A government department responsible for the provision of coinage for circulation in the United Kingdom, and for the striking of coins for other Commonwealth and some foreign countries. Gold sovereigns are struck for use particularly in the Middle East, where the coin commands a universal respect. The Royal Mint also strikes medals and decorations, and seals for ministerial use. It is situated at Llantrisant, near Cardiff.

royalty. Payment to an owner of land for the right to work minerals, or to an inventor for the use of his or her invention; payment to an author dependent upon the sales of a book.

RUFS. Revolving underwriting facilities.

rule against accumulations. When a settlor desires that the income from property shall be accumulated and given to his or her descendants at some remote future date, some limit must be applied to the time in question, or at compound interest enormous sums will pile up. The modern rule was formulated in 1925, and refined in 1964. Any settlor with such an intention must choose one only of the following periods for the duration of the accumulation: 1. the life or lives of the settlor(s); 2. a term of twenty-one years from the death of the settlor; 3. the minority or respective minorities of any persons living or *en ventre sa mère* at the death of the settlor; 4. the minority or respective minorities only of any person(s) who, under the limitations of the settlement, would, if of full age, be entitled to the income directed to be accumulated; 5. a term of twenty-one years from the date of the settlement; 6. the duration of the minority or respective minorities of any person(s) in being at the date of the settlement.

rule against perpetuities. In English law, the rule that is not permissible to suspend the vesting of interest in property (usually land, but not necessarily so) for longer than a life in being plus twenty-one years. From 1964, a settlor may instead specify a fixed period of time not exceeding eighty years. The rule came to be used to defeat the unbarrable entails by which families sought to keep their estates in perpetuity. Unbarrable entails were first defeated by the introduction of the devices of fines and recoveries. The objection to the remoteness of interests emerged later with the recognition of the trust. A *fine* was no more than a judicial proceeding used for conveying land. For this it was necessary to institute a fictitious suit which was compromised with the consent of the court, an agreement being entered into by the parties concerned as to the disposal of the land in question. A *recovery* was a judgment in a collusive suit brought by a plaintiff against the tenant in tail. The subsequent procedure was rather complicated, and of historical interest now as both fines and recoveries were abolished in 1833 and replaced by a simple disentailing assurance.

rule in Clayton's case. *See* CLAYTON'S CASE.

run. To flee, to flow; to continue in operation; to continue without falling

due, as a promissory note or bill; to have legal force; to manage (a business); a frantic rush on the part of depositors to withdraw their money from a bank believed to be in difficulties.

running. Successive (Numbers); continuous (e.g. an order of account).

running account credit. For the purposes of the Consumer Credit Act, 1974, a facility whereby the debtor may continually obtain cash, goods or services up to an agreed limit, on a revolving basis, after allowing for payments made by or to the credit of the debtor, any limit agreed being at no time exceeded.

running broker. A bill broker who originally took bills from the merchant banks and financial institutions in the City of London, and disposed of them on a commission basis to banks and discount houses. The last two firms of running brokers were admitted to the London Discount Market Association at the end of 1980, since when there have been no running brokers. The difference was that a running broker had no claim on the Bank of England's lender-of-last-resort help, but neither was the broker expected to take a share in the underwriting of the weekly Treasury Bill tender.

running days. Consecutive days, including Saturdays and Sundays, as opposed to business days.

running margin. A man who borrows money to invest it at interest both pays and earns interest. The difference between the interest paid for the loan and the interest derived from the investment, is the running margin.

running yield. *See* FLAT YIELD.

S

safe custody. Articles of value, locked boxes, wills, and many other things are left by customers in bank strongrooms for safety. Boxes should be locked and parcels sealed by the customer before handing them in to the bank. The banker will issue a receipt if so required. The banker must be careful to hand them back only against a signature by the customer or a properly-appointed agent who is known to the bank, Such a safe-keeping is a contract of bailment. If the bank makes a specific charge for the service it is a *paid bailee*. If not, it is gratuitous bailee. The paid bailee has to show a higher standard of care in dealing with the safe custody of articles than does a gratuitous bailee.

safe deposit. Some banks maintain a safe deposit service where the customer is taken into a strong room and personally puts documents or articles of value into a box, or compartment, to which he or she alone has the key (or takes them out). The bank keeps duplicate keys in case of emergency, but does not use them except in the presence of the customer or by express authority.

salaried partner. One whose status within the partnership is defined in the Partnership Deed. As far as the outside world is concerned, a salaried partner is deemed to be held as a partner and therefore to be fully liable with the other partners for the debts of the partnership. Whether or not his or her authority can be taken for instructions concerning the running of the banking account depends again on how it is defined in the terms of the Partnership Deed.

salaries and wages accounts. *See* WAGES AND SALARIES ACCOUNT.

sale and lease back. The raising of immediate finance by a company by selling a capital asset, whether property or capital equipment, to a finance company or insurance company, and then leasing it back and continuing to use it as before. The ownership of the asset passes to the lessee, the finance company or insurance company. The leasing rental will contain an element of the cost of the asset purchased from the lessor company plus an interest charge to cover administrative and service charges. Sale and lease back arrangements are usually found only where the asset to be purchased is worth £25,000, or more. However, smaller figures may be found where a scheme exists for the purchase of houses from retired couples, widows or widowers, subject to an agreement allowing them to continue to live in the house for the rest of their lives at a nominal rental.

sale by auction. *See* AUCTION.

sale by candle. A method of auctioning off goods popular in the eighteenth century. For example, a coffee house known from 1744 onwards as the 'Virginia and Baltic' was so named because the varied merchandise dealt with there came mostly from the plantations of the American colonies or from the countries of the Baltic seaboard. There was a saleroom on the premises in which ships'cargoes were auctioned. Sale was 'by the candle', bids continuing until the inch of the candle burnt itself out. *See also* AUCTION; DUTCH AUCTION.

sale of description. Where there is a contract for the sale of goods by description, there is an implied condition that the goods shall correspond with the description.

sale by sample. In the case of a contract for sale by sample there is an implied condition: 1. that the bulk shall correspond with the sample in quality; 2.

that the buyer shall have a reasonable opportunity of comparing the bulk with the sample; 3. that the goods shall be free from any defect, rendering them unmerchantable, which would not be apparent on reasonable examination of the sample.

sales ledger. A book of accounts of those persons to whom a firm sells goods on credit.

salvage. The act of saving (a ship, goods, etc.) from shipwreck, capture, fire, etc.; compensation allowed for such saving; property so saved.

same day funds. *See also* VALUE DATE.

sample. A specimen of merchandise taken from the bulk for inspection, usually that of a prospective buyer, particularly important in the sales of tea and grains, etc., before an auction; a method of *estimating public demand* or reaction by postal enquiry of, or personal interview with, a representative number; a method of *assessing the efficiency* of a branch bank used by inspectors who select at random a number of administrative details for close checking – if these are satisfactory it is assumed that the generality of that particular activity is also satisfactorily carried out.

sanction. Permission of the bank for an overdraft or loan; the amount of such sanction; ratification by a superior authority.

sandwich debenture. A common arrangement between banks and the Industrial & Commercial Finance Corporation, whereby the ICFC has first call on the fixed assets of a company to which both are lending, and the banks have first call on the floating assets, ranking second to the ICFC on the fixed assets. The arrangement also applies to insurance companies and some merchant banks.

sans recours. An addition to the signature of a drawer or an indorser of a bill, meaning that the signatory will not accept any liability on the bill; literally, 'without recourse'.

sasine, *(Sc. Law)* The act of putting a person into possession of land, by completing an appropriate conveyance and registering it in the General Register of Sasines.

save. To keep from being spent, to keep untouched, to reserve, to lay by.

savings account. *See* HOME SAFE.

savings and loan institutions. Savings and loan institutions in the US are similar to the British building societies, and, like them, have assumed some of the banking functions. They now offer checking accounts (bank current accounts), consumer finance and high yield investments.

savings bank. A term that used to cover a variety of banks whose function it was to encourage small savers. The major services were the deposit and withdrawal of cash, with interest paid on balances. With the changes that have taken place in the banking systems, such banks as TSB and the Yorkshire Bank can no longer be regarded as purely savings banks. The only bank which is covered by this term is the National Savings Bank, whose outlets are the Post Offices and sub-post offices in the country. *See* NATIONAL SAVINGS BANK.

savings bonds. *See* NATIONAL SAVINGS DEPOSIT BOND; INCOME BOND.

savings certificates. *See* NATIONAL SAVINGS CERTIFICATES.

scalar principle. The principle of hierarchy or grading according to a scale, whereby members of an enterprise have their duties graded according to degrees of responsibility and authority. In applying this principle to the business of banking, a superior higher in the 'scalar chain' confers the right to exercise a lower degree of authority on a subordinate, to whom he or she assigns clearly specified and defined targets and duties. The subordinate (e.g. branch manager) then becomes responsible to the superior (e.g. area manager) for executing those duties and meeting those targets, and may indeed delegate some of the duties to further subordinates.

scarcity value. The high price of a commodity in short supply.

schedule. A smaller document forming part of the principal document, deed, bill, etc.; an appendix to an Act of Parliament; an official tabulated list of goods and chattels; an inventory, a list of deeds; a timetable; in tax law, a heading under which is prescribed how a particular source of income is to be dealt with for the purpose of taxing that source.

scheduled territories. Formerly a list of countries whose currencies were linked to the £ sterling – since 1972 consisting only of the UK, including the Channel Islands and the Isle of Man and Gibraltar.

scrip. The document or provisional certificate which is given to a person who has agreed to take up bonds in connection with a government loan and has paid the first instalment. Scrip is principally associated with the issue of bonds or debentures.

scrip issue. A capitalisation of reserves by issuing fully paid-up shares free to present shareholders in proportion to their current holding. No cash changes hands. It is really a book-keeping transaction, designed primarily to bring the share capital more into line with the assets employed in the business. After a scrip issue, a shareholder owns more shares, but as the market price is adjusted accordingly the shareholder is no better off. A scrip issue brings a high share price back to a more manageable sum and thus increases a share's marketability. *See* BONUS ISSUE.

scrivener. One who draws up contracts or other documents; one who places money at interest on behalf of clients; a public writer, a notary.

scrutineer. One who examines votes cast at an election; one who computes the votes of members at a company meeting.

seal. A die or stamp having a device for making an impression on wax or other plastic substance; a piece of wax, lead, or other material stamped with this and attached to a document as a mark of authenticity, etc., or to an envelope, package or box to prevent its being opened without detection; the impressions made thus on wax, lead, etc.; a stamped wafer or other mark affixed to a document *in lieu* of this. As deeds now require the signatures of the parties thereto, the seal has become a formality, and often an adhesive wafer is used. A company may use its seal to authenticate documents, but such documents are usually also signed by two directors and the company secretary to certify that the seal has been affixed in their presence. A contract under seal is valid because of the formality and does not require to be supported by consideration.

SEAQ. Stock Exchange Automated Quotations. A method of displaying share trading information anywhere in the UK. The system is capable of showing the buying and selling prices of shares within minutes of the deal.

searches. Enquiries made by an interested party, usually prior to concluding some contract. In Bankruptcy, a register of undischarged bankrupts is maintained in London at the Thomas More Buildings, Royal Courts of Justice, Strand, London WC2, for personal searches only. The information given consists of the number of the case, the name, occupation and last known address, together with the dates of various stages of past and present bankruptcy proceedings and their advertisement. Searches against a *limited company* are made personally at the *Companies Registry* on payment of a small fee, when the file of the company in which the searcher is interested will be produced for inspection. The administration and registration of limited companies, which used to be in City Road, EC1, moved to Cardiff in 1976. In that year microfilm reading was introduced; in return for the standard search fee, copies of the original documents are supplied on microfilm, which can be taken away. Full-sized copies of the filmed documents are available from microfilm printers which the searcher can operate. A reading room is provided at Companies House in City Road and facilities are available there and at Cardiff. Searches which are against *unregistered land titles* are usually carried out by the bank's solicitor, who will search against the customer's name on the Land Charges Register, using form K15, stamped with the appropriate value in Land Registry stamps. The form is in duplicate and the Registrar will return one copy to the solicitor indicating on it the result of the search. Searches against *registered land titles* are carried out by (in the case of an equitable charge) the sending of the land certificate by the lender to the Land Registry in order that it may be written up to date, or (in the case of a registered charge) the completion and dispatch of Land Registry Form 94. This search form must be accompanied by the authorisation of the mortgagor or his or her solicitor. In the first case the lender can see when the land certificate is returned, whether his or her title is clear, by looking at the copy of the Charges Register in the certificate. The lender's own notice of deposit should be entered therein, and this should be the only charge outstanding. In the second case, the duplicate of Form 94 is returned to the lender with the result of the search marked upon it. It is then known as the 'official certificate of search'. For searches on local land charges registers, *See* LOCAL LAND CHARGES REGISTER. For searches on port registries, *See* MORTGAGE OF SHIP.

seasonal. Occurring or done at the proper time, suitable to the season, opportune. A seasonal advance is one occurring regularly every year – such as to a farmer at the beginning of the season, repayment to be made from the produce of crops. There is a seasonal demand for cash in advance of Christmas each year to cover the heavy expenses of customers at this time; there is a seasonal demand on banks in the spring of each year for advances to pay taxes.

secondary market. The primary market in stocks and shares is the original issue by the government or the company. The secondary market is the purchase and sale of these stocks and shares after the first issue, i.e. second hand stocks/shares.

secondary offering. The placing of parcels of shares held by individuals or by groups.

secondary risk. *See* PRIMARY RISKS.

second mortgage. A mortgage on a property which is already mortgaged to a first mortgagee. A second mortgage should be in legal form, and will comprise the grant of a term of years longer by one day than the term enjoyed by the first mortgagee. Notice should be given to the first mortgagee, who should be asked to confirm the amount due whether he or she claims any right of consolidation, and whether there is any obligation to make further advances. The second mortagage, if of unregistered land, should be registered with the Land Charges Department as a class C (i) charge. In the case of registered land, a second charge can be registered at the Land Registry, who will issue a certificate of second charge to the lender. *See also* LAND CHARGES; NOTICE OF SECOND CHARGE.

second of exchange. *See* BILL IN A SET.

secrecy. Concealment, the maintenance of confidentiality, the exercise of discretion. The duty of the banker to keep customer's affairs secret is one of the terms of the banking contract. This confidential relationship is being progressively eroded by state measures, principally for checking tax evasion. Case law has authorised disclosure of information 1. under compulsion of law; 2. in pursuit of a public duty; 3. where the bank's interest requires disclosure; 4. where disclosure is made with the express or implied consent of the customer. All bank staff are required to sign an oath of secrecy on joining the bank. Banks and others are affected by powers given to officers of the Board of the Inland Revenue by the Finance Act, 1976, to enter any premises and to search for and seize documents and other articles which they believe may be needed as evidence for proceedings in respect of an offence involving a tax fraud. Such a search can only be carried out if a warrant is issued by a judge, and is unlikely to be used against banks.

secretary. Under the Companies Act, 1985, every company must have a secretary. He or she is an official of the company, having specific statutory duties.

secret commission. No agent may take any consideration, whether by way of money, goods, services or favours, as inducement to act in a way prejudicial to the best interests of his or her principal, or to confer favour or preference to the third party offering the bribe or inducement. If this should happen, the secret commission or profit is the property of the principal, and the person offering the inducement, and the person accepting it, are both guilty of offences under the Prevention of Corruption Act, 1906.

secret reserve. *See* HIDDEN RESERVE.

secured creditor. A person holding a mortgage, charge or lien on the property of the debtor, or any part thereof, as a security for a debt, due to him or her by the debtor Insolvency Act, 1986 s. 248.

secured debenture. A debenture providing a fixed charge on specified company assets.

securities. In a wider and less precise sense a word meaning investments generally, e.g. 'Stock Exchange securities'.

Securities and Exchange Commission (SEC). The SEC was created in the US by the Securities Exchange Act of 1934 as a direct result of the stock market crash of 1929; its basic purpose is to protect investors in US securities, which include equities or common stock in a limited partnership, as well as debt instruments such as bonds and debentures. The SEC is responsible for the control and supervision of security trading practices in the US and is a governmental agency created by Congress. It has five commissioners appointed directly by the President of the United States, who serve five-year terms; no more than three commissioners may be members of the same political party. The Commission has very wide powers including the right to carry on legal proceedings, to formulate laws and to initiate judicial actions, and its reporting requirements are probably much more extensive and frequent than is the norm for registered companies operating in countries outside the US.

Securities Association. The securities association was set up to become a self regulating organisation for investment businesses dealing in the domestic and international securities markets. Providing a firm has the necessary criteria, it will approve its application to do business in the investment market. As a relatively new organisation, its rule book has not yet been completed and it is producing its regulations rather slowly so that they will stand the test of close scrutiny.

Securities Investment Board. Under the Financial Services Act, 1986 it is responsible for enforcing codes of conduct in their appropriate area of investment.

Securities Management Trust Ltd. ('SMT Money'). A wholly-owned subsidiary company of the Bank of

England. It is used by the Bank as a nominee company for the placement of funds at market rates in the security and money markets on behalf of, and at the request of, Bank of England customers.

security. The keeping of unauthorised persons out of bank premises, the supervision of cash in an office or strongroom, the guarding of a bank and its cash by day and by night; the valuable paper deposited at a bank by a borrowing customer, such as bearer bonds, stock exchange securities, life policies, guarantees or debentures, as an insurance against the possibility of default in repayment. For the purposes of the Consumer Credit Act, 1974, 'security', in relation to an actual or prospective consumer credit agreement or consumer hire agreement or any linked transaction, means a mortgage, charge, pledge, bond, debenture, indemnity, guarantee, bill, note or other right provided by the debtor or hirer, or at his or her request (express or implied), to secure the carrying out of the obligations of the debtor or hirer under the agreement.

seigniorage. Anything claimed by a sovereign or feudal superior as a prerogative; a charge made by mints for coining ingots of gold or silver into currency; the difference between the bullion value of silver, copper, bronze and cupro-nickel coins and their face value; a share of the profits; a mining royalty.

seisin. Possession of land under a freehold; the act of taking possession; the thing possessed.

self-liquidity. A characteristic of a loan which carries with it the seeds of its own repayment, e.g. a loan to a manufacturing company for the purchase of raw materials. These are worked up into the finished product, sold, and the loan repaid out of the proceeds of sale, sometimes know as self-liquidating advances.

self regulating organisation. For the purposes of s. 8(1), Financial Services Act, 1986, a body which regulates the carrying on of an investment business of any kind by enforcing rules which are binding on persons carrying on business of that kind, either because they are members of that body or because they are subject to its control.

self-service. A response by management to the increasing cost of labour, whereby consumers help or serve themselves, whether or not with the aid of a machine of some kind installed by management, either initiating in the process a system which will eventually debit the consumer's account, or leading to a payment in cash at a check point. In banking the trend is observed in the installation of cash dispensers and developments such as 'Cashpoint', 'Servicetill' etc.

seller. A person who sells, or agrees to sell, goods or services. *See also* UNPAID SELLER'S LIEN.

seller's interest. A supplementary insurance policy which may be taken out by an exporter selling on a C & F (*q.v.*) or FOB (*q.v.*) basis. This may occur where the exporter is not completely happy in selling products to some of the less sophisticated countries and suspects that possible claims on the foreign insurance may not be honoured. The seller's interest policy can be taken out without the knowledge of the importer, to be used only where claims on insurance companies abroad are dishonoured.

seller's market. A condition of markets in which goods are scarce, and there is a great demand for them, so that the seller can make his or her own terms.

selling group. A group formed for the purpose of selling a new issue of stocks, shares or bonds to the investing public. It may or may not be identical with the group of underwriters who are acting for the issue. There is sometimes a smaller inner group which both manages the issue and organises the formation of a larger outer group to handle the disposal of the issue.

selling group terms. The issue price minus the discount (usually $1\frac{1}{4}$–$1\frac{1}{2}$ per cent) allowed to the selling group. Out of this the selling group allows a commission or 're-allowance' of (usually) $\frac{1}{2}$ per cent, to authorised dealers.

selling out. Action taken by a seller on the Stock Exchange when the buyer fails to complete. This consists of an instruction to the Stock Exchange official broker to sell the securities in question, any loss arising being charged to the defaulting purchaser.

send direct. *See* SPECIAL CLEARANCE.

sequestration. Confiscation, appropriation; the taking of some property from parties in dispute over it until some case is decided or some claim paid; a term used in relation to the benefice of a clergyman; under Scots law, a stage in bankruptcy proceedings. *See also* WRIT OF SEQUESTRATION.

SERPS. State Earnings Related Pensions.

service. The act of serving; work done for an employer or for another; a benefit or advantage conferred on someone; willingness to work or act; use, assistance; formal legal delivery, posting up, or publication (e.g. a writ, summons, etc.).

Servicetill. The name of a computerised cash dispenser which can also tell customers what their balances are, and take requests for new cheque books and statements. This machine operates from a Servicecard which bears a magnetised strip. This is returned to the customer at the time of operation. The service is controlled by a personal credit limit incorporated in the strip, arranged with the customer at the time of operation. Up to £100 can be issued in any one day in varying denominations of notes.

set off. The combining of debit and credit accounts so as to arrive at a partial or full repayment of a debt. A banker has the right to set off different accounts in the name of the same customer provided that he or she has not agreed to keep them separate and provided that the accounts are in the same right. It is not entirely certain that a banker has the right to set off balances *without notice* to the customer, especially where they are still on active running accounts. Therefore, it is common practice to take a letter of set-off from the customer giving such a right. A letter of set-off given by a limited company should be registered at Companies House as a measure of prudence.

settled land. Land which is subject to the terms of a settlement; land held under certain conditions by a tenant for life. A strict settlement was a device to preserve land in a family for as long as possible. This was done by the device of a conveyance of the land to trustees upon trust to hold it for the settlor for life, with remainder to the eldest son in tail and successive remainders, in the event of the death of this son without issue, to the younger sons in tail. On the attainment of majority by the son, a re-settlement was made, whereby the land was reconveyed to the trustees on trust to hold it for the settlor for the remainder of his life, subject to an annual sum of money charged on the land in favour of the son, with remainder to the son for life and then to *his* eldest son in tail. A similar re-settlement was made every generation. The re-settlement, read together with the original settlement, was known as a *Compound Settlement*. A settlement taking effect by reference to another settlement was called a *Referential Settlement*. In this way land could be kept in the family, but it was so tied up that it could never be sold. In 1925, in pursuit of the principle of free alienation, it was provided by the Settled Land Act, 1925 that after that year settlements must be made by two deeds. The trust instrument declares the trusts upon which the land is to be held. The vesting deed declares that the legal estate in the land is vested in the person who is, for the time being, entitled to the enjoyment of it as tenant for life. The latter is thus made the 'estate owner' and entitled to sell the land. A purchaser is only permitted to examine the vesting deed and deals with the estate owner therein named. He or she has to pay the money, however, to the trustees, who must hold the money in place of the land, invest it, and apply the income according to the trusts of the settlement.

settlement day. A specified day in the Stock Exchange calendar which occurs every two weeks. Occasionally there is a three week period, when the accounts for the previous accounting period are settled.

sever. To part or divide by violence, to sunder, to cut or break off; to make a separation, to act independently of others in a joint law suit. *See also* WORDS OF SEVERANCE.

several liability. *See* JOINT AND SEVERAL LIABILITY.

severalty. A freehold estate held solely by a tenant in his or her own right.

severance payment. An amount paid to an official or an employee as compensation for either termination of his or her employment contract, or having been dismissed.

shadow director. By the Companies Act, 1985, s. 741, a shadow director means any person in accordance with whose directions or instructions the directors of the company are accustomed to act. This will not include advice given by a person acting in a professional capacity. The position of a bank manager, who advises, requests or directs the company to act in a certain way, is not clear, but it could be construed by his or her conduct that the bank manager could be in the position of a 'shadow director'.

share. The proportion of interest in the capital of a company which a shareholder has. *See also* DEFERRED SHARES; FULLY-PAID SHARES; GROWTH SHARE; INCENTIVE SHARES; NON-VOTING SHARES; ORDINARY SHARES; PARTLY-PAID SHARES; PREFERENCE SHARES; REDEEMABLE PREFERENCE SHARES; SUBSCRIPTION SHARES; UNQUOTED SHARES.

share capital. The *authorised or nominal* or *registered* capital is the amount of capital authorised in the Memorandum of Association of the company. The *issued* capital is that part of the authorised capital which has in fact been issued. Money received from shareholders in exchange for issued shares is called the *paid-up* capital and where the shares are fully paid-up the issued capital and the paid-up capital are the same. But shares may be partly paid, leaving a call perhaps to be made at some future time. This reservoir of capital is known as the *uncalled* capital.

share certificate. A document issued by the company to its shareholders showing the numbers of shares held and the amount paid up.

share drafts. Issued by credit unions in the US, share drafts are equivalent to checks issued by commercial banks, and, when presented for payment, are handled in the normal way through the check clearing system. *See* CREDIT UNION.

shareholder. One who has an interest in a joint property, particularly a member of a limited company.

share option scheme. A system to benefit employees of a company in that they may choose to buy shares of the company on a certain date at a price fixed in advance. Assessment for tax is on the excess of the market value of the shares at the time when the option was granted over the total cost of the option and the shares.

share premium. The amount by which the issue price of a share exceeds the nominal value. This normally occurs when a fresh issue of shares is made some time after the first issue. Under the Companies Act, 1985, the value of the share premium must be credited to a share premium account.

share pushing. The operations of fraudulent dealers who sell worthless stock, acting outside the recognised stock exchanges. *See also* BUCKET SHOP.

share register (or register of members). A book which a limited company is obliged to keep by law, containing the names and addresses of the members of the company. It must specify the numbers of shares held by each member, the date of purchase, the distinctive numbers of the shares, the amount per share and total amount of capital paid, and the date of sale. The register must be kept at the registered office of the company and be open for the inspection of members without fee and to any other person on payment of a fee.

shares of no par value. *See* NO PAR VALUE.

share transfer (or stock transfer) form. The instrument used when the holder of registered shares or stock transfers them to another person.

share warrant. Certificates issued by a limited company certifying that the bearer is entitled to the shares specified therein.

Sheriff. The chief officer of the Crown in every county, appointed annually and nominally entrusted with the execution of the laws and the maintenance of order. *See also* UNDER-SHERIFF.

shilling. The old name for a 5p piece.

ship. Any vessel used for the carriage of goods and passengers by sea. A ship is divided into sixty-four parts for purposes of ownership and any person may own some or all of these shares. Individual shares may be jointly owned by up to five persons. A British ship is registered at any port in the UK where a register is maintained. A certificate of registry is issued to the ship to be used in the lawful navigation of the ship. Most ships are also registered at Lloyd's Register of Shipping.

ship bill of sale. A bill of sale in the form prescribed by the Merchant Shipping Act, 1894, evidencing the transfer to a purchaser of a ship or a share in a ship.

ship-broker. An agent for a shipping company who transacts business for a vessel lying in port; one who transacts marine insurance deals.

shipment. The process of shipping; that which is shipped; a cargo. *See also* GROUPAGE SHIPMENT.

ship mortgage. *See* MORTGAGE OF SHIP.

shipped bill of lading. A consignment of goods for which an on-board bill of lading cannot be issued may be held on the quay for shipment in a specified vessel or next following vessel. A 'received for shipment' bill of lading is issued for these goods. When the shipowners have reserved space in a specified vessel (thus avoiding delay) and are later able to actually load the goods on to the vessel, they are obliged by law to issue, on request, a 'shipped' bill of lading in exchange for the 'received for shipment' bill of lading.

shipping agent. One who arranges the shipment of goods or passengers.

shipping bill. An invoice of goods shipped; customs documents used where drawback is claimed.

shipping note. A document prepared by exporters and used to accompany goods to the dock, setting out the details of the ship, dock and the goods themselves.

ship's certificate of registry. *See* REGISTER OF SHIPS.

ship's husband. The managing owner of a ship, or a manager or agent appointed by the owner(s), who sees to the necessary maintenance and repairs of a ship, provides stores for her when in port, and attends generally to her welfare. His powers include the borrowing of money necessary for the ship; but except in case of necessity the borrowing must not be made on the credit of the shipowner(s). The name of this person must be entered on the register at the ship's port of registry.

shopping list credit. An Export Credits Guarantee Department-backed loan to a government or a foreign bank, often the central bank, which allocates portions of the loan on the same terms to buyers of British goods, within their country; a type of transferable credit where the first beneficiary is the agent of, or principal supplier to, the applicant, for goods stated in the credit. These are usually issued for very large amounts and are sometimes known as 'shopping bag' or 'shopping list' credits. The first beneficiary will be responsible for distributing the portions of the credit to various suppliers, via the advising bank. Depending on the contractual relationship between the applicant and first beneficiary, the first beneficiary may be the commercial attaché of the applicant's country, or the principal supplier, or the applicant's representative agent or subsidiary company.

short. Not long in space; not extended in time; wanting, deficient in cash, hard-up; the position of a foreign exchange dealer when sales of currency exceed the purchases of that currency.

short bill. One which has only a few days to run to maturity, irrespective of the original tenor of the bill. It is also a term applied to any bill left at the branch for collection, irrespective of its maturity date.

short-dated paper. Bills of exchange drawn at not more than three months.

short end of the market. That part of the money market which deals in short-dated government stocks. *See also* SHORT-TERM LOAN.

short exchange. On the foreign exchanges, bills payable within ten days.

short form bill of lading. A bill of lading which does not contain all the conditions of carriage.

short gilt. Government stock which has a five years' security or less.

short hedge. A term used in the London international financial futures exchange (*q.v.*) which indicates that an investor has *sold* a financial futures contract to enable him or her to offset an adverse change in interest or exchange rates within a specified future period. *See also* LONG HEDGE.

shorthold letting. A new concept introduced by the Housing Act, 1980. It is a letting for a fixed term of one to five years, with the landlord having the power to regain possession under the Rent Acts at the end of the tenancy. The rent tribunal no longer has jurisdiction to defer notices to quit in any letting which begins after the Act came into force, although the County Court has an extended jurisdiction to order a delay of up to three months before an order for possession can be put into effect. The aim was to encourage landlords to make available property which they might otherwise be reluctant to let because they could not regain possession under the Rent Acts, and in the first year following the passing of the Act about 3,500 tenancies were created under the shorthold system of tenure. Originally landlords had the duty of registering compulsorily with the local Rent Offices a rent at the start of a shorthold, but in late 1981 this rule was abolished for all areas outside London and it was left open for the tenant to register the rent if he or she so desired. It was thought in some quarters that this gave a landlord an advantage in that he will be able to say to the tenant, 'Register the rent and you will be evicted at the end of the term. Pay what I ask and you may be able to stay on'. In any case, an Opposition pledge to repeal the shorthold provisions may mean that many tenancies will not be renewed.

short lease. A lease for not more than twenty-one years.

short position. The sale of shares by a market maker or an investor, who is not in possession or ownership of those shares and therefore needs to buy them to square his books. A situation where the sale of shares in any particular exceeds purchases.

short rate. The price in one country at which a short-dated draft drawn on another country can be bought.

shorts. Short-dated stocks, repayable inside five years.

short tap. Tap (*q.v.*) having, say, five years or less to maturity.

short-term liabilities. *See* CURRENT LIABILITIES.

short-term loan. A loan for up to three years; Government stocks issued for a similar period.

short-term money market. A well-developed London money market providing for instant borrowing or instant placing of money. The short-term funds range from over-night borrowing to borrowing for periods of weeks or months up to one year. Anybody wishing to borrow for longer than this usually has to negotiate a term of say six or twelve months with an agreement, or further option, to re-negotiate the loan for a period (rolling the loan over). The rate of interest payable when the re-negotiation takes place will be at the going rate at that time.

short-term policy. An insurance policy which covers risks for a short period only, as where a businessman is taking a trip abroad.

short-term rate of interest. The rate of interest for loans of up to three months.

short ton. A unit of weight equal to 2,000 lb.

shutting the window. *See* WINDOW.

SIB. *See* SECURITIES INVESTMENT BOARD.

sight. A term used in connection with a bill of exchange, which may be payable 'at sight' or on demand, i.e.

immediately on presentation to the drawee. If a bill is payable after sight, i.e. at so many days/months after sight, it is a term bill, and in order to fix the maturity it is necessary to know when the drawee 'sighted' it. For this purpose therefore, the drawee will add after signature of acceptance the word 'sighted' and the date of sighting. The term of the bill will then run from that date.

sight bill. A bill payable as soon as the drawee sees it.

sight clause. *See* EXCHANGE CLAUSE.

sight credit. A credit where the beneficiary is to obtain payment immediately, either against a sight draft accompanied by documents of title, or against the documents only.

sight deposits. Current accounts, money deposited overnight, and money at call.

signatory. One who is bound, by his or her signature, to the terms of an agreement; one who signs the Memorandum of Association of a limited company. A limited company may be bound by one or more of its officers signing in their official capacities for and on behalf of the company, or the seal of the company may be used. Any provision of the Consumer Credit Act, 1974 requiring a document to be signed is complied with by a body corporate if the document is sealed by that body (but this does not apply in Scotland).

signature. A sign, stamp or mark impressed, a person's name written by that person, or the act of writing it. The signature of a customer on an instruction to his or her banker is the banker's authority to comply with the instruction and to debit the customer's account with the cost, e.g. a cheque. *See also* FORGED SIGNATURE.

simple Single, not complex, entire, mere.

simple arbitrage. *See* DIRECT ARBITRAGE.

simple contract. One evidenced in

writing, or formed orally.

simple debenture. Debentures which are unsecured.

simple interest. Money paid on the principal borrowed, but not on the accrued interest as in compound interest.

sine. Without.

sine die. Without a day being set, indefinitely.

sine qua non. An indispensable condition, an essential.

single costing. A system of quantifying cost where one commodity only is in question.

single entry. A system of book-keeping in which each item is entered once only in the ledger, etc.

single premium policy. An insurance policy where one premium only, usually for a large sum, is payable at the time when the policy is taken out.

sinking fund. A fund created by sums set aside at regular intervals and invested outside the business in order to provide for the replacement of an asset or the repayment of a particular liability at a known future date.

sixpence. The name of a coin no longer in circulation worth $2\frac{1}{2}$p.

slander. The publication of defamatory matter in an ephemeral form, normally by means of an oral statement.

sleeping partner. *See* DORMANT PARTNER.

slump. A long-term economic decline which manifests itself in high unemployment, increased bankruptcies and liquidations, falling production and low consumption. Slump conditions are usually world-wide, and are aggravated if countries in balance of payments difficulties impose restrictive actions on imports. This tends to decrease world trade even more and makes the existing conditions still worse.

small agreement. A regulated consumer credit agreement for credit not exceeding £30, other than a hire-purchase or conditional sale agreement; or a regulated consumer hire agreement which does not require the hirer to make payments exceeding £30, being an agreement which is either unsecured or secured by a guarantee or indemnity only (whether or not the guarantee or indemnity is itself secured).

Small Estates Payout Procedure. *See* DEATH OF CUSTOMER.

Small Firms Loan Guarantee Scheme. A loan guarantee scheme which was set up in 1981, offering the opportunity to small firms to obtain finance that would otherwise not be provided. By providing a guarantee against default the government enables banks and other financial institutions to lend money that would otherwise be considered too risky. The borrowers must be either sole traders, partnerships, co-operatives and limited companies, who are already trading or intend to start trading within a reasonable time. Normally the Department of Employment will only accept those businesses which have 200 employees or less. The normal activities that are acceptable for such loans include manufacturers, retailers, wholesalers, construction firms and most service industries. However, such activities as banking and associated services, education, house and estate agents, insurance and associated services, sporting organisations, travel agents and others are not eligible under the scheme. The conditions of the scheme are: 1. Loans must not be for more than £75,000; 2. Guarantees are available on medium term loans with a term between 2–7 years. Overdraft facilities will not be guaranteed; 3. The Department guarantees 70 per cent of the outstanding amount due to the lender; 4. Borrowers are required to pay the Department a premium of $2\frac{1}{2}$ per cent per annum on 70 per cent of the outstanding balance of the loan; 5. The loans under the scheme will usually be drawn down in one amount but where appropriate the lender may be willing to arrange for the loan to be drawn down in stages. In these cases the full loan must be drawn down within two years of the initial draw down in a maximum of four stages. Each stage must be a minimum of 25 per cent of the total and the dates must be specified at the date of application. The borrower may be required to pledge the *business assets* as security for the guaranteed loans. In such cases, the lender will take a fixed/floating charge over such assets and in case of default utilise the security to reduce the outstanding debt or reimburse the department for payments made under the guarantee. It will be normal for such security to cover the whole of the loan and not just the 30 per cent not covered by the scheme. To ensure that the business is properly *monitored*, the lender will require cash flow and profit and loss figures at quarterly intervals. The borrower must ensure that he or she has acceptable accounting standards and must be prepared to meet the bank for regular discussions.

Smithsonian agreement. In December 1971, a meeting of the Group of Ten (the world's leading central bankers) at Washington resulted in an agreed realignment of currency parities. The Smithsonian agreement widened the limits of permissible fluctuations of one currency against another. The US dollar was given the role of providing the 'middle rates' around which the system revolved. *See also* SNAKE IN THE TUNNEL.

snake in the tunnel. The restricted exchange rate fluctuations came about as a result of an agreement in December 1971 at the Smithsonian Institute, now called the 'Smithsonian agreement', in which the countries of the EEC formed a monetary union whereby all members – except the UK – agreed that the fluctuation of their exchange rates shall be restricted. The basis of the agreement rested on the European Currency Unit (ECU), whereby each member country contributed an amount of its own currency, which reflected the trade between the members of the Community. The basic details of the agreement are: 1. the ECU will be the denominator of the exchange rate mechanism; 2. the exchange rate fluctuation margins will be 2.25 per cent either side of parity, with the exception of Italy, which will have a fluctuation margin of 6 per cent either side of parity; 3. any further diversions beyond these points will result in the appropriate authorities taking corrective measures; 4. the contribution to the currency weightings will be revised every five years in the light of economic conditions.

social accounting. The reporting of the cost incurred in complying with anti-pollution, safety and health and other socially beneficial requirements, and, more generally, the impact of the business entity on, and its endeavours to protect, society, its amenities and the environment.

social responsibility. The philosophy that a big organisation has duties not only to its shareholders and staff but also to society generally, which provides the environment in which the organisation flourishes, and which is affected by its actions. In recognition of this view big banks may associate themselves with sporting events by donations or give grants to encourage good citizenship in young people, etc. These activities also tend to improve the *public image* of the bank, which is an important factor in an increasingly critical and politically conscious society.

society. A number of persons unified by agreement, or incorporated by law, for some specific purpose; a company, an association, a club. The rules of a society may empower it to borrow and to provide securities held by trustees on its behalf. In the absence of security duly charged by properly-appointed trustees, however, a society has no power to borrow and, not being incorporated, has no separate entity to be made responsible for any borrowing. Any accommodation granted should be against the indemnity of a person interested in the society, who will be personally liable.

Society for Worldwide Interbank Financial Telecommunication (SWIFT). A co-operative society created under Belgian law and registered in Brussels. It is used by all major banks throughout the developed world and is linked with the domestic inter-banking networks in all participating countries. The aims of SWIFT are to enable members to transmit between themselves international payments, statements and other messages connected with international banking. The SWIFT system has enabled the money transmission services of banks – whether mail, cable or telex transfers – to be sent faster, more efficiently and safely, With the continuous improvement in computers and telecommunications, the system is continuously improving and expanding.

Society of Investment Analysts. A society formed by persons whose work is concerned with portfolio management and investment analysis. The members are usually employed in investment companies and fund management companies. An associate of the society obtains his/her diploma by examination or has received exemption from it.

soft arbitrage. Switching between market and bank facilities to take advantage of interest rate differentials, or borrowing from banks while retaining readily realisable money market investments.

soft currency. The currency of any country which is in plentiful supply on the foreign exchanges, i.e. it is not hard to get.

software. The suites of programs needed by a computer installation in order that it can be activated. Software program development has become almost an industry in its own right, and the UK is pre-eminent in the field. Hence the term 'software house', denoting an organisation specialising in the development and marketing of software.

sola bill. A bill consisting of one document only, as contrasted with a bill in a set.

sold note. The contract note supplied by a stockbroker to a client, detailing the particulars of a sale made on the client's behalf.

sole. Single, only, alone in its kind; unmarried.

sole proprietor. The owner of a one-man business.

sole trader. One who works in a wholesale or retail trade for himself or herself only.

solicitor. A person legally qualified to represent another in a court of law, a lawyer, a law agent; a legal practitioner authorised to advise clients and prepare causes for barristers, but not to appear as an advocate in the higher courts.

Solicitor-General. A law officer of the Crown, ranking in England below the Attorney-General and in Scotland below the Lord Advocate.

solicitors' accounts. Because solicitors continually handle the money of their clients, it has been necessary to legislate as to the manner in which this money shall be dealt with. The conduct of the solicitors in this regard is governed by a set of rules known as the *solicitors' accounts rules.* These provide that a solicitor holding money on behalf of a client shall pay such money into a current or deposit account in his or her own name with the word 'client' included in the title. A solicitor will also need an 'office' account for the running of the business, so that any solicitor will normally maintain at least two accounts. Solicitors are often appointed trustees for the funds and settlements of clients, or trustees under clients' wills, and a separate set of rules, called the *solicitors' trust accounts rules,* provides for these. A solicitor-trustee must open a trust bank account in which the description 'executor' or 'trustee' must appear. No overdraft should appear on any 'client' account.

solicitor's undertaking. A written promise, signed by a solicitor, to the effect that securities or deeds temporarily lent to him or her by the banker (against the written instruction of a customer) for inspection will be returned to the bank in the same state as that in which they were received. A similar promise made is that when funds are available, e.g. in the case of a customer's house which is in process of sale, they will be forwarded by the solicitor to the banker for credit to the customer's account. A solicitor's undertaking is an essential factor in a *bridging advance.* The solicitor must be either known to the lending bank as reliable, or be favourably reported on by another bank. The terms of his or her undertaking must be unequivocal.

solicitor-trustee. A solicitor who is a sole trustee, or who is co-trustee only with a partner or employee.

solvency. The state of being able to pay all one's debts.

solvency ratio. The conventional relationship obtaining between a bank's own capital resources and its total deposit liabilities. Inflation has the effect of reducing this percentage, as the advances increase (because the borrowers need more just to stay in the same place in real terms) and the total capital remains at the same figure. The total of the capital is the proprietor's stake in the business, and forms a buffer in the sense that it must all be lost before the creditors need to start worrying. But when creditors see from a balance sheet that a bank's capital is shrinking in real terms and in its relationship with total deposit liabili-

ties, then there comes a time when they will start worrying. Hence the rash of bond issues on the Euromarket, and the raising of capital in foreign currencies, in the last few years. Even so, the position is still very much less happy than it was in, for instance, 1967.

sorter/reader. A computer that can read the encoding on a document, e.g. a cheque, and sort these documents into a given order.

sorting. Arranging in kinds of classes, classifying, putting in order; the arrangement of customers' cheques into alphabetical or numerical order preparatory to posting them to the accounts or to filing them away; the *division* of cheques paid in during the day under the heads of various banks on which they are drawn, preparatory to machining them and dispatching them for collection; filing of customer's letters.

sorting code number. A number placed on the face of a cheque to identify numerically the bank on which the cheque will be drawn. In the UK this consists of three groups of two figures each, the first group referring to the bank and the other two groups indicating the branch. It is also used in connection with credits, particularly dividends and all items distributed through the *bankers' automated clearing services.*

sources and application of funds statement. A statement usually prepared when the final account and balance sheets of a company are produced. This statement would normally show how funds are received i.e. from profits, sale of assets, increased capital, etc. It will also show how these funds have been used, i.e. payment of dividends, purchase of fixed assets, repayment of loans, etc. The date on this statement is usually the same as that on the final accounts and balance sheet.

South Sea Bubble. The name given in

the UK to an early example of widespread and reckless speculation. The South Sea Company was incorporated in 1710, and was given a monopoly of trade in the Pacific Ocean. The company was also engaged in various financial dealings at home: in particular the directors had worked out a scheme for taking over most of the National Debt from the government. Parliament was persuaded to agree to this, although there was strong opposition. The price of South Sea stock rose dramatically and people rushed to buy shares, recklessly investing all their life savings. When the share value reached ten times the nominal value people began to realise that the shares were not worth nearly as much as their quoted value, and confidence suddenly evaporated. There was a rush to sell and prices dropped catastrophically. Thousands of people were ruined.

sovereign. The standard unit of the British coinage, a gold coin representing one pound sterling. Sovereigns are now minted only for export, particularly to the Middle and Far East. Internally the pound sterling is worth 100p. In some countries abroad sovereigns are named Kings or Queens according to the head of the sovereign portrayed. *See also* LEGAL TENDER.

'sovereign' lending. Lending by banks and consortia in the Euromarkets to national governments. In recent times these banks and consortia have become rather more chary about 'sovereign' lending, because of repayment difficulties caused by the balance of payments problems of such countries as Poland, Turkey, and some African and South American nations.

sovereign risk. It used to be thought that loans made to foreign governments abroad were certain to be repaid. Recent experience with such countries as Poland, Rumania, Bulgaria and some Latin American countries such as Mexico and Argentina

has demonstrated that this view is over-optimistic. *See* RESCHEDULING OF DEBTS.

special agent. One authorised to act only on a particular occasion or for a specific service, e.g. to bid at an auction on his or her principal's behalf.

special attorney. *See* POWER OF ATTORNEY.

special buyer. The Bank of England agent in the Discount Market.

special category company. For the purposes of the Companies Act, 1985, s. 257, a special category company can be either a banking company, shipping company or an insurance company. A banking company is defined as a company recognised as a bank under the Banking Act, 1987.

special clearance, special collection. The accelerated clearance of a cheque for a customer, by posting the cheque direct to the branch on which it is drawn with a subsequent telephone call to ascertain its fate.

special crossing. *See* CROSSED CHEQUE.

special deposits. At the request of the Bank of England, following agreement with the Treasury, banks may be asked to place Special Deposits with the Bank of England. The amount to be deposited by each bank will be a specified percentage of some or all of its eligible liabilities as reported to the Bank of England at the latest mid monthly reporting date, the amount being rounded up to the nearest £5,000, The amount of each bank's special deposit will be adjusted as necessary to take account of changes in its eligible liabilities as subsequently reported, such adjustment normally taking place on the third Monday following the reporting date. Special Deposits bear interest at the average Treasury Bill Tender Rate rounded up or down to the nearest $\frac{1}{16}$ per cent. This rate is determined by the Treasury Bill Tender each Friday and is operative from the Monday following.

Interest is paid weekly on a Monday. The principle behind this system is that money so deposited is withdrawn from the pool of funds which determines how much money may be lent. More special deposits means less loans.

special drawing rights. Often abbreviated as SDR. It is a type of international money – a unit of account of the International Monetary Fund. Its value is calculated against the US dollar, while contribution to IMF funds consists of a basket of currencies weighted according to the international trading importance of each contributing country. Drawing rights are available to all member countries and are used particularly as a type of bridging loan when a country has payment difficulties.

special indorsement. One which specifies the person to whom, or to whose order a bill or cheque is to be payable (e.g. 'pay John Smith or order, Thomas Brown').

Special Investment Department. A department in the Trustee Savings Banks where customers maintain accounts which are subject to one month's notice of withdrawal, but which earn a rather higher rate of interest than deposits in the Ordinary Department.

special manager. A qualified insolvency practitioner appointed by the court under s.370, Insolvency Act, 1986, to deal *(a)* with the bankrupt's estate; *(b)* the business of the undischarged bankrupt; *(c)* the property or business of a debtor in whose case the official receiver has been appointed interim receiver under s. 286.

special pleading. Unfair argument; bending the rules to suit one's case.

special resolution. One passed by a majority of not less than three-fourths of such members as vote in person or by proxy, at a general meeting of which not less than twenty-one days' notice specifying the intention to propose the resolution as a special resolution has been duly given.

speciality contract. One executed under seal.

speciality debt. A debt which is acknowledged in a document under seal.

special verdict. A verdict stating the facts, but leaving the decision to be determined by the court.

specie. Gold and silver coins, and bullion.

specie points. Where in currencies there is a fixed relationship to gold, fixed parities exist, and any movement of the rate away from the par of exchange would make it profitable to buy gold in one centre, send it to another, and sell it there. The cost of shipping and insurance sets margins on either side of the par of exchange to which the rate of exchange can vary before it becomes profitable to ship gold. These are the specie points.

specification. A detailed statement of particulars, especially of materials, work to be undertaken or supplied by an architect, builder, manufacturer, etc.; the production of a new commodity out of materials belonging to another person.

specific performance. An equitable remedy sought where damages are not a satisfactory remedy, e.g. in cases of broken contracts concerning land or objects of art. Specific performance may be granted where the parties are on an equal footing, provided always that it is impossible for a money award to provide an agreeable solution.

specific reserve. A provision for specific or contingent liability, such as tax or dividends shortly to be paid. Such provisions may be described as 're-serves', but they should appear under the heading of a current liability and cannot be included in the fixed capital. Provisions linked directly with an asset, such as a provision for bad and doubtful debts or for depreciation of a fixed asset, should be shown as a deduction from the value of the asset.

speculation. The purchase or sale of shares on an estimate of whether the share value will rise or fall, with the intention of making a quick profit, or avoiding a loss; a gamble on future price movements, whether in shares, land, commodities or money. A speculator in stocks and shares buys a security without intending to pay for it on settling day, in the hope that it can be sold again at a higher price, in the same account. If this can be done successfully, the speculator will never have to pay for the security, but will receive the difference between the buying and selling prices as profit. On the foreign exchanges speculation against a currency may be purely in the hope of making a profit, but it is equally likely that it is the cautious placing of a company's money where it will be safest. If sterling is being sold on a large scale the reason is that the economy backing it is weak. International companies offset potential threats to their trading profits by hedging their currency commitments.

split capital trust, split level trust. A description of the device of dividing the ordinary capital of a trust company into income shares and capital shares. Holders of the income shares receive most of the income accruing to the trust's investments for the duration of the life of the trust, plus a predetermined capital value on liquidation. Holders of the capital shares are entitled to all the remaining assets of the trust on its break-up, which is usually at a predetermined future date, say fifteen to twenty years in all. When the company is liquidated the income shares are repaid at par and the balance of funds is then distributed to the capital shareholders. If there has been good capital growth, the capital shareholders should be repaid at a substantially increased value. This this type of trust, also called a *dual purpose trust,* is able to appeal to shareholders who require either maxi-

mum capital appreciation or maximum interest.

splitting. The division of shares in companies into units of smaller denomination in order to increase their marketability, or the division of stock units represented by an *allotment letter* or a *letter of acceptance.* In the last case splitting of the allotment letter is necessary where the holder wishes to dispose of some only of the stock units, or to dispose of all the stock units to more than one person. In such a case the holder completes the Form of Renunciation and forwards the Letter to the company by the appropriate time and date set out (varying as to whether the stock is partly or fully paid), specifying the number of stock units to be comprised in each split letter, whereupon the company will issue split letters as requested, which will be endorsed 'original duly renounced'.

spot, spot price. Cash price for immediate delivery.

spot against forward. *See* SWAP.

spot check. To check the correctness of accounts, stocks, or routine tasks by sample. If the sample is satisfactory no further checks may be undertaken. Inspectors of banking branches in the UK will normally work through each advance to satisfy themselves that the lending is reasonable in the circumstances, but the routine work of the office as laid down by standing instructions will be subjected to spot checks. The cashiers' tills, however, are checked in detail, as is the reserve cash of the branch.

spot rate. The normal rate of exchange quoted in the foreign exchange markets, i.e. the rate for transactions in which the funds are to be paid over in each centre two working days later.

spread. Extended in length and breadth. Thus sundry debtors of a company should show a good spread, as opposed to having three or four big debtors, the failure of any one of whom would have a serious effect on the company. In the same way a bank seeks a good spread of its loans across a wide spectrum of borrowers, and a good spread for its investments over many different fields, in the case of government stocks having repayment staggered over a number of years. In the case of the secondary market for Eurobonds, the difference between a seller's asked and buyer's bid price, normally split between banks acting as market makers. Also used to describe the total of *fees and commissions* earned from the borrower by banks making a *new issue;* on the Stock Exchange, the *difference* between the higher and lower prices at which market makers are prepared to deal. The higher price is the price at which the market maker will sell stock to the broker; the lower is the market makers buying price.

SRO. *See* SELF REGULATING ORGANISATION.

SSAPS. *See* STATEMENT OF ACCOUNTING PRACTICE.

stag. A Stock Exchange expression for a person who applies for shares in any new company, or any new issue, with the sole object of selling any allocation he or she may get as soon as a premium is obtainable, and never intending to hold or even fully subscribe for the shares.

stagflation. A word coined to express the co-existence over many years of high rates of unemployment and a high rate of inflation.

stale cheque. *See* ANTEDATED CHEQUE.

stamping under penalty. Stamping a legal document at an increased rate because the stamping has not been carried out in the time allowed by law.

standard contract. Where the contract is of a type which is constantly occurring, a standard contract will emerge, which will have generally accepted terms which are normal and usual. Either or any of the parties to the contract may stipulate a variation to

the standard form, but if they do not, they are bound by its terms.

standard costing. A technique which calls for a forecast of what sum a product should cost in a particular set of circumstances. This is called the 'standard cost'. When the product is later available the actual cost of producing it will be known, and a comparison of the actual and the standard costs will reveal in most cases an amount, to which the name 'variance' is given. Investigations into the reasons for the emergence of a variance should lead to remedial action, which in turn will make the business more efficient and hence more profitable.

standard liner waybill. A document which is offered by some shipping lines as an alternative to a bill of lading. It is similar to the air waybill in that it is not a document of title and is not required by the consignee to collect the goods at the port of destination. It does not give the shipper control of the goods unless they are consigned to his or her agent, or by prior arrangement to the order of a bank abroad. It cannot therefore be acceptable under the terms of a documentary credit unless so specifically stated. The waybill may state that the goods have been 'received for shipment' or are 'on board'. If the waybill is issued only on a 'received for shipment' basis, and the export has ECGD backing, a Certificate of Shipment will be required.

standard security. *(Sc. Law)* Since 1970 the 'standard security' is the only means whereby a security over heritable property can be created. It is a deed in a form laid down by the Conveyancing and Feudal Reform (Scotland) Act, 1970, which had as one of its aims the simplification of the then existing land law, which in turn has led to a simplification for lenders taking security deeds. The deed is very short and simple, and refers to standard conditions which formerly had to be incorporated by the lender in the form of charge, but now are listed in Sch. 3 of the Act. It has thus been made possible for much repetitive matter to be eliminated.

Standards and Poor. A USA debt rating agency.

standby letter of credit. An agreement to provide funds given by one bank to another or by a bank to its customer, for which a commitment fee is usually taken in respect of undrawn funds. There are various types of such agreement but all are either conditional or unconditional – 90 per cent of those requested are the unconditional variety. Conditional standby credits are normally issued by surety companies rather than banks, but banks issue them as well. The credit is an adaptation of that flexible instrument, the *documentary credit,* but in this instance no goods are involved: however, the documentary credit can be made to cover almost any case provided that the procedure can be reduced to a statement of the documents which will be required before payment is made. A common example is where a parent company which is prevented by the law of its own country from giving a guarantee supporting the borrowing of its own subsidiary company overseas, applies to its own bank to issue a standby credit in favour of an overseas bank from which its own subsidiary is borrowing (or is proposing to borrow). The document to be called for from the lending bank taking advantage of the credit might be no more than a certificate by that lending bank that repayment has been demanded from the subsidiary company but has not been received. The parent company has given a guarantee in all but name. *See also* PERFORMANCE BOND; SURETY BOND; LETTER OF COMFORT.

standing. Fixed, established, permanent.

standing credit. *See* CREDIT ADVICE.

standing order. An order by a customer to his banker to make a regular payment to a named payee to the debit of his account.

standing orders. The statutory rules of any organisation, society, etc., governing the conduct of business at a meeting; orders made by a deliberative assembly as to the manner in which its business shall be conducted.

statement. A formal account, recital or narration; a declaration of fact or circumstance.

statement clerk. A statement clerk in a bank is frequently a junior clerk whose responsibility is either *(a)* to post the various debits and credits to the appropriate accounts, or, with computerised accountancy systems, he or she may have the responsibility *(b)* to verify the entries and vouchers before despatching a statement to a customer.

statement *in lieu* of prospectus. A company having a share capital which does not issue a prospectus, or which has issued a prospectus but has not allotted any shares to the public, must deliver to the Registrar of Companies for registration a statement *in lieu* of prospectus, signed by all directors, three days before proceeding to allot.

statement of account. A document sent to a customer or a client on which is entered the financial transactions between that customer/client and the business. It will also indicate the balance owed to or by the remitting entity. *See also* BANK STATEMENT.

Statement of Standard Accounting Practice (SSAP). A statement made by the accountancy bodies which proposes rules which should be followed when preparing final accounts. It is recommended that a 'true and fair view' of the business will not be presented unless the financial statements comply with the SSAP publications.

statement of affairs. The schedule of assets and liabilities provided by an insolvent person in bankruptcy proceedings, or by a company in compulsory winding-up proceedings.

statistics. Numerical facts or data collected systematically, summarised and tabulated; the science of collecting, studying and interpreting such information.

status enquiry. A bank in the UK will answer status enquiries on its customer and will make similar enquiries about other people's financial position on his or her behalf. For exporters it will obtain reports on traders abroad. To preserve the secrecy about the customer's affairs which banks must maintain, certain rules have been laid down. The bank will only answer enquiries which are put to it by other banks or reputable trade protection organisations. It will not answer private enquiries, nor disclose addresses. It seems likely that banker's confidential reports on customers supplied for the benefit of trade protection organisations will in future be expressed in very general terms. The reason is that legislation for the protection of consumers has given the latter the right of access to these files. Replies to all enquiries must be carefully considered and tactfully phrased. If a favourable reply cannot be given, a form of words should be used which conveys the right impression, without harming the customer's credit. The bank has a duty of care to the enquirer who is relying on the banker's special knowledge of a customer, and must make a true and faithful reply. The banker should always include in his opinion a clause disclaiming responsibility. Since the passing of the Unfair Contract Terms Act, 1977 these disclaimer clauses will be effective only if they are reasonable in the circumstances. *See also* CREDIT RATING.

Statute. An Act of Parliament.

statute-barred. A debt which cannot be recovered at law, because more than six years have elapsed since the cause of action arose. *See* LIMITATION OF ACTIONS.

Statute Book. The complete record of legal enactments.

Statute Law. The law which originates in Acts passed by Parliament (also known as *Written Law*).

statutory books. Those books which companies must keep if they are registered under the Companies Acts. They are: a minute book, and registers of the members, directors and secretaries of the company.

statutory company. A company authorised by special Act of Parliament, e.g. a nationalised industry.

statutory declaration. A declaration by some person before a justice of the peace, notary public, or commissioner for oaths, as to some circumstance or fact of which he or she has knowledge; a declaration made by directors of a company in voluntary liquidation to the effect that they have made a full inquiry into the affairs of the company, and are of the opinion that the company will be able to pay its debts in full in a period not longer than twelve months from the commencement of the winding-up. This declaration must be made within the five weeks immediately preceding the date of the resolution for winding-up, or on that date but before the passing of the resolution, and it must be delivered to the registrar for registration before the expiry of fifteen days from the date on which the resolution was passed. The declaration must include an up-to-date statement of the company's assets and liabilities. Where such a declaration has been made and delivered, the winding-up is known as a members' voluntary winding-up; where it is not made, the winding-up is known as a creditor's voluntary winding-up. This is called a *Declaration of Solvency,* but there are other cases where a formal declaration is called for, to limit the chance of fraud or mistake. In the Companies Act, 1985 for instance, s. 156, dealing with the cases in which a private company may give financial assistance to any person so that he or she may acquire shares of the company, calls for a statutory delcaration by the directors that describes the particulars of the *assistance* to be given and of the business of the company of which they are directors and to *name* the person to whom assistance is to be given; this is required to be coupled with an *assurance* that whatever may happen the company will be able to pay its debts. Again this Act also enables a company to purchase its own shares, but if the company's capital is to be used for this the purchase will not be lawful unless a number of requirements are met. One of these is that the directors should sign a statutory declaration specifying the amount of the *permissible capital payment* for the shares in question, and immediately following the date of the purchase there will be no ground on which the company could then be found unable to pay its debts; moreover, this reassurance is required to be renewed separately for the year following the date of the purchase. It is evident from these examples that in company and liquidation law the statutory declaration is used as a weapon to protect the creditors of the company in question, but of course this is not always so. A person may be called upon to make a statutory declaration that he or she is who he or she claims and is entitled to the particular benefit being claimed.

statutory legacy. The absolute right of the surviving spouse of a deceased intestate to receive a capital sum from the estate, as from time to time fixed by law, plus the personal chattels of the deceased.

statutory meeting. Every company limited by shares or by guarantee and having a share capital shall hold a general meeting of the members of the company between one and three months from the date from which the company is authorised to commence business. This is known as the statutory meeting.

statutory mortgage. As a special form of charge by way of legal mortgage, a mortgage of freehold or leasehold land may be made by a deed expressed to be made by way of statutory mortgage, being in one of the forms set out in the Fourth Schedule to the Law of Property Act, 1925, with such variations and additions as the circumstances may require.

statutory owner. The trustees who take the legal fee simple in settled land when there is no person entitled to take it as tenant for life.

statutory receipt. A receipt indorsed on a mortgage deed, when the mortgage has been satisfied, which acts as a reconveyance. The receipt must be indorsed on, written at the foot of, or annexed to, a mortgage for all money secured. It must state the name of the person who pays the money and must be executed by the chargee by way of legal mortgage.

statutory report. The directors of a limited company shall, at least fourteen days before the date on which the statutory meeting is held, forward a report, referred to as the 'statutory report', to every member of the company. The statutory report shall be certified by at least *two directors* of the company and shall state the total number of *shares* allotted; an abstract of the receipts and payments made up to seven days before the date of the report; and the names, addresses and descriptions of the directors, auditors, managers and secretary of the company. The report shall be *certified as correct* by the auditors of the company, and a copy shall be delivered to the registrar of companies for registration.

statutory restrictions on company loans. In the UK a company may not give direct or indirect financial assistance, whether by loan, guarantee, the provision of security, or in any other way, to any party for the purchase of, or subscription to, its own shares, or the shares of any holding company which it may have. Exceptions are allowed where lending money is part of the company's ordinary business, or where with the approval of the company in general meeting a loan is made to an officer of the company to be used in the furtherance of duties. Similarly, a company may not make a loan to one of its directors, or to a director of its holding company, or provide a guarantee or any other form of security to another person on the terms that he or she will make the loan. *See* QUASI-LOAN.

statutory trust for sale. *See* TRUST FOR SALE.

sterling. Pertaining to standard value, weight or purity, of solid worth; pure, genuine; British currency, generally used of the 'pound sterling'.

sterling area. *See* SCHEDULED TERRITORIES.

Sterling bonds. Bonds of a foreign country payable in British currency.

Sterling Certificate of Deposit. 1. *Prime Issues.* A document evidencing receipt of a deposit by a bank for a fixed period at a fixed rate of interest. Certificates are issued in minimum denominations of £50,000 and thereafter in multiples of £10,000 to a maximum of £500,000 per certificate. The period of issue is from three months up to five years. Interest is paid gross on maturity for Certificates up to one year and thereafter on the anniversary of the issue date and on final maturity. Certificates are in bearer form Additionally, payments of interest and final repayment may only be made on presentation of the certificate by an Authorised Bank. Certificates of deposit are fully negotiable and may be sold before maturity through the Secondary Market (*see below*). 2. *Secondary Sterling Certificate of*

Deposit. Certificates of deposit may be disposed of before maturity through the Secondary Market operated by banks and discount houses. A certificate is sold at a yield to maturity irrespective of the coupon rate at issue, the proceeds being calculated on the basis of the following formula:

$$Proceeds = \text{Principal} \times \frac{36{,}500 \text{ plus}}{(\text{issued rate} \times \text{tenor in days})}$$
$$\frac{36{,}500 \text{ plus}}{(\text{quoted yield} \times \text{days to run})}$$

See also 'STRAIGHT' DEPOSIT.

sterling M3. *See* MONEY SUPPLY.

sterling securities. Any securities on which dividends are payable, and capital repayable, in sterling.

steward. A person employed to manage the property or affairs of another, especially the paid manager of a large estate; one of the officials superintending the conduct of a public meeting.

stipend. Money paid for a person's services, an annual salary, the provision made for the support of a parish minister.

stipendiary magistrate. A paid magistrate.

stipulation. A definite arrangement, a contract, a specified condition.

stock. Capital, the money or goods invested in trade, manufacture, banking, etc., the supply of goods a trader has on hand; government securities; a share or shares in a national, municipal or other debt; the capital of a company.

stock appreciation right. A stock appreciation right is a provision attached to a traditional stock option that allows the holder, in lieu of exercising the option, to receive in cash, shares or a combination of both, an amount equal to the appreciated value of the option. Payment is received directly from the company and the related stock right is then cancelled.

stockbroker/jobber. With the 'Big Bang' the distinction between a jobber and a broker has disappeared. The stockbroker or stockbroking firm is still in evidence and will buy or sell stocks and shares on behalf of a client, but the role of the jobber is now in the hands of very large market makers who will act both in the capacity of a broker and a jobber. There are now broker/dealers and market makers.

stock certificate, share certificate. The document issued by a company to a share or stockholder specifying the number of shares or the amount of stock held by him. A registered certificate is evidence of the title of the person named therein and on a sale of the stock or shares the certificate must be sent with a completed stock transfer form to the company, which will then effect the necessary change of ownership on the register and issue a new certificate to the buyer.

stock dividends. Dividends paid by companies in further stock, instead of in cash. The purpose of stock dividends was partly to reduce tax payable by the recipients, and partly to retain cash within the company, thus raising, or at least maintaining, the level of working and investment capital. Since 5th April 1975, stock dividends are, in the UK, treated as income on which basic tax has been paid, so the notional gross amount now becomes liable for higher rate tax where appropriate. The effect has been the virtual cessation of dividend payments in the form of stock.

Stock Exchange. A market situated in London for the purchase and sale of stocks and shares. All deals from the public must be passed through a firm of brokers who will act on their behalf. The Stock Exchange will provide a daily list of all companies that have a full listing, those on the USM (Unlisted Securities Market) and the Third Market. The daily list will show the movement for the preceeding day.

Stock Exchange daily official list. The list of officially quoted prices of those securities which are considered sufficiently active to merit a daily listing. A monthly supplement contains prices of securities for which markings are not frequently recorded. See OFFICIAL LIST.

Stock Exchange indices. Figures calculated for a number of key share prices in order to give a general view of the movement of such prices and thus of the buoyancy of the market as a whole, e.g. the Financial Times Industrial Ordinary Share Index.

stock-in-trade. Goods and materials in stock, machinery, tools, fittings, etc., necessary to carry on a trade or business; the goods which a merchant, shopkeeper, etc., has on hand for supply to the public; resources, capabilities.

stockpiling. The accumulation of reserves of essential raw materials for an emergency.

stock receipt. A receipt given by the seller of inscribed stocks to the purchaser. It has no value, and is no evidence of title. All inscribed stocks have now been converted into registered stocks.

stock relief. Born in November 1974, out of the need to ease the burden on the corporate sector of excessive inflation, stock relief was a device to mitigate the effects on company liquidity of taxation levied on profits which had been inflated by artificial appreciation in stock values. At first companies in the UK were allowed, for tax purposes, to reduce stock values by the amount by which the increase in book value of stocks exceeded 10 per cent of trading profits, but in April 1976 this level was raised to 15 per cent. The sums of money so saved were to be set aside as 'deferred taxation', but the Chancellor said in March 1977 that 'for the normal continuing business there is little or no risk that any substantial part of the deferred liability

306

will arise'. This encouraged the belief that companies will never have to pay these huge sums of money set aside. However, the deferred tax will become payable if the level of the individual company's activity is reduced, or if the value of stocks falls because commodity prices fall. In the March 1979 Budget it was announced that stock relief can be written off after six years. The result of this legislation is that maintaining high year-end stocks has become an accepted factor in British business in order that full advantage may be taken of stock relief against tax. But in January and February of 1980 there were difficulties arising out of a long drawn out dispute in the steel industry, and for many companies there was little chance for building up their stocks as their year-end approached. There was some apprehension, not only that more tax would have to be paid, but that the clawback provisions, which still extend for five years in retrospect, could bite into cash flow before that time. Representations were therefore made to the Chancellor to ease the clawback provisions in the 1980 Budget. As a result it was laid down that the tax arising on reduced stocks because of the steel strike and high interest rates could be postponed for one year. But this was a temporary panacea only. Industry has been pressing the government for some time about the potential tax bills faced by some companies which had been running down stocks in the second half of 1980 to adjust to lower levels of demand and to reduce borrowings. Proposals were set out in a consultative paper issued by the Inland Revenue in the middle of November 1980. These set out a permanent system of stock relief based on a single index of stock prices prepared by the government, but which is limited by the extent to which stocks are financed by suppliers or borrowings. It is intended, therefore, to help manufac-

turers. After study, the Consultative Committee of Accountancy Bodies, criticised the proposals on the ground that they did not use the current cost accounting standard which, it was thought, ought to be the starting point for tax. The Green Paper is, however, reluctantly accepted as an 'interim measure', but it is hoped that the much-promised reform of the whole of corporate taxation will follow quickly.

stock-taking. The act of preparing an inventory or valuation of the goods on hand in a manufacturing, commercial or trading establishment. It is usual to value stock at the lower of cost or market price.

stock transfer form. The form accompanying the certificate when shares are sold, both being sent to the company issuing the shares for registration and issue of a new certificate to the buyer. The form is in nearly all cases signed by the transferor only and includes the description of the security, the name of the undertaking, the consideration price, the number of shares or amount of stock sold, the names of the registered holder and the buyer and their addresses, and a request that such entries be made in the register as are necessary to give effect to the transfer. The stock transfer form is executed under hand, except in the rare cases where the articles of the company concerned require them to be under seal. Case law has established that a banker forwarding a stock transfer form to a company for registration is deemed to guarantee to the company the genuineness of the signature(s) on the stock transfer form.

stop. To bring to a halt, to obstruct, to check, to suspend.

stop-go. A term for a period of opposing and contradictory monetary policies of government, whereby credit is alternately expanded and contracted, in the interests of containing inflation and yet maintaining full employment. The effect is that industry is encouraged to expand by borrowing, and then restricted by a drying-up of credit.

stop loss order. To limit an eventual loss, an order to sell stock at the best rate obtainable when the price attains or exceeds a given level.

stop order. A notice by the customer to the bank that he or she wishes payment stopped on a cheque which has been drawn and issued. The customer should, ideally, state the number, date, and the amount of the cheque, and give the name of the payee. These details may be telephoned in the first instance, but should be confirmed in writing without delay. The banker's first action on receipt of the notice to stop should be to consult the customer's ledger (where this still exists), the day's vouchers, and the customer's paid vouchers to ensure that the cheque has not already been paid. Next the cashiers must be given the details so that the cheque is not paid if it should be presented over the counter. Finally, the ledger and statement must be marked with a warning note of some kind, or the computer programmed accordingly.

stoppage *in transitu*. An unpaid seller's right to stop the goods in transit and resume possession of them, after he or she has parted with them, in the event of the buyer becoming insolvent.

stopped account. *See* CLAYTON'S CASE.

stopped cheque. A cheque in respect of which the drawer has instructed the bank to refuse payment.

storage. A charge for warehousing goods; the space occupied by them.

straddle. On the Stock Exchange, a contract in which a buyer of stock has the privilege of calling for or delivering it, at a pre-determined price. *See also* MARGINAL RISK.

straight. Passing from one point to another by the most direct route; direct, honest.

straight bill of lading. One purporting to consign goods to a specified person.

straight bonds. Bonds having no right or option of conversion into any other form of shares, stock or bonds.

straight debt. A security without rights of conversion into a borrower's common stock.

'straight' deposit. A deposit accepted by a bank without the issue of a Sterling Certificate of Deposit.

straight line method of depreciation. *See* DEPRECIATION.

street market. A continuation of Stock Exchange business in the street after the London Stock Exchange is closed for the day.

street prices. The prices established on the street market (*q.v.*).

striking price. *See* OPTION.

stripping the premium. *See* PREMIUM STRIPPING.

Stubbs Weekly Gazette. (incorporating the *Edinburgh Gazette and Perry's Gazette*). A weekly trade paper which collects and publishes details as to the bankruptcy proceedings of individuals and as to the liquidations of companies, together with other various matters connected with limited company mortgages and county court judgments. The paper has sections containing extracts from the Bills of Sale Registry, the Registry of Deeds of Arrangement, and the Registry of County Court judgments. In connection with bankruptcy there are notices to creditors as to the holding of meetings, petitions presented with the date of presentation in each case, details of receiving and adjudication orders, lists of principals creditors and, in some cases, details as to the appointment and discharge of trustees. Details are also given of orders made by the court on application for discharge from bankruptcy. In connection with *liquidation*, details are given of winding-up orders and dates, voluntary windings-up and the date of the appropriate resolutions, notices of the appointment of liquidators, notices to creditors relating to statutory meetings of company creditors, the appointments of *receivers* and their dates, details of *receivers ceasing* to act, and a list of declarations of solvency filed. Under the heading *Dissolution of Partnerships* details are given of such dissolutions together with the appropriate dates, and under the heading *Mortgages and Charges by Limited Companies* are given details of such charges, taken from the registry at Companies House. From the same source there is a list of *satisfactions* of such mortgages and charges. Some *banks* take *Stubbs Weekly Gazette* in each of the branches and some only at Area Offices. It is the duty of a particular bank officer to go through the newspaper looking for the names of *customers* affected by county court judgments, bankruptcies or liquidations so that appropriate steps may be taken in connection with the customer's bank account.

sub. Under, below, inferior.

sub-agent. One under the orders of an agent, a deputy agent, an agent's representative.

sub-branch. Small agencies or offices operated by a branch, known as the parent branch. Sub-branches may be open only for specified hours on certain weekdays. There may be a clerk travelling from the parent branch, or there may be a clerk-in-charge. If the business increases, the sub-branch may acquire a separate account at Head Office and be in time up-graded to the status of a full branch.

sub-charge. A charge on a charge certificate, that is, the owner of a charge on a piece of registered land has offered it as security to a lender. A banker deciding to accept the security may take an equitable sub-mortgage or a legal one. In the first case the banker will keep the charge certificate and give notice of its deposit to the registrar on Form 85A. The charge certificate must be written up to date to include the notice of deposit. The

form of sub-mortgage to be signed by the sub-mortgagor may be drafted by the bank's solicitor, or an existing form of bank charge may be adapted. In the second case a search must be made, using Form 94A, and an official certificate of search obtained. An office copy of the form of sub-mortgage is prepared, and the charge certificate is then sent to the Registrar with the signed, sealed form of sub-mortgage, the office copy and the appropriate fee. The Registrar will keep the charge certificate and the copy form of sub-mortgage, and will issue to the banker as evidence of title a certificate of sub-charge with the original form of sub-mortgage stitched inside it. This certificate will contain a reference to the head mortgage. *See* SUB-MORTGAGE.

subject to contract. A phrase used by bargaining parties, especially where land is sold by private treaty, to indicate a general agreement on terms and conditions, but to prevent the actual formation of a contract, upon which action may be taken, until the parties' respective solicitors have drawn up a formal contract which has been agreed, signed and exchanged.

sub judice. Under legal consideration.

sub-lease. The assignment by a tenant to a third person of his or her whole interest for part of the term, or the assignment by a tenant of a part of his or her interest for part or the whole of the term. Landlords usually exact a covenant against assigning or underletting, usually without consent, such consent not to be unreasonably withheld. A sub-lease deposited as security should be accompanied by a certified copy of the head lease.

sub-mortgage. A mortgage of a mortgage. For example. *A* mortgages a property with *B* for £12,000. Later *B* needs to borrow, sat £2,000. *B* could get it by calling in the mortgage, but instead goes to bank *C,* and borrows the money from the bank against the security of the mortgage. The original mortgage then becomes the head mortgage and the newly created mortgage is a sub-mortgage, *B* being the sub-mortgagor and Bank *C* the sub-mortgagee. A legal sub-mortgage takes the form of a grant by the mortgagee (the sub-mortgagor), of a term of years a few days shorter than the term which he or she has. Alternatively, it may be done by a charge by way of legal mortgage. The form of charge may be drawn up by the bank's solicitor, or an existing form of charge by way of legal mortgage may be used. The bank's solicitor should examine the deeds and in a report on title should confirm that a good security is being obtained, bearing in mind the terms of the original mortgage. A search should be made at the Land Charges Registry against the sub-mortgagor. A valuation of the security should be obtained and the insurance position checked. Notice must be given to the mortgagor and acknowledgment received; the mortgagor should confirm the amount of the debt. If *A* is making regular payments of principal he or she should now send these direct to the bank in reduction of the submortgagor's debt. The equivalent of a sub-mortgage of unregistered land is a charge on a charge certificate. If a banker is offered a charge certificate as proposed security, the same general inquiries and acknowledgement must be made and obtained as in the case of a sub-mortgage of unregistered land. If the banker decides to accept the security he or she may take an equitable sub-mortgage or a legal one. In the first case the banker will keep the charge certificate and give notice of its deposit to the Registrar on Land Registry form 85A. The charge certificate must be written up to date to include the notice of deposit. If it is desired to take a legal sub-mortgage a search must be made, using land Registry Form 94A, and an official certificate of search obtained. An office copy of the form of sub-mortgage is prepared, and the following documents are sent to the Registrar: 1. the charge certificate; 2. the signed sealed form of sub-mortgage, with office copy. The Registrar will keep the charge certificate and the copy form of sub-mortgage, and will issue to the banker as evidence of his or her interest a certificate of sub-charge with the original form of sub-mortgage stitched inside. This certificate will contain a reference to the head mortgage.

subordinated loan. A loan which, in the case of the liquidation of a company, is postponed behind the claims of ordinary creditors, and ranks only in front of the interests of the shareholders. Such a loan might be a bank loan, which is specially designed to give reassurance to trade creditors of a company which has only just started business and has not had much time to establish itself. As a result the company's suppliers may allow it more generous credit terms, which will help in cash flow management and, generally, make trading easier.

subpoena. A writ commanding a person's attendance in a court of law under a penalty; to serve with such a writ.

subrogation. The substitution of one person for another, with succession to rights and claims; the standing in the shoes of another.

subscribed capital. That part of the authorised capital which has been issued and taken up.

subscriber. A person or entity who has agreed – usually in writing – to purchase a stated number of shares in a named company at a stated price.

subscription shares. Shares in a building society, where an investor is allowed to purchase shares by instalments in return for an undertaking to subscribe a fixed sum regularly.

subsidiary company. A company

which has another company, which controls the composition of its board of directors, as a member; or a company in which another company holds more than half in nominal value of its equity share capital.

subsidy. Financial aid, a government grant for some purpose such as keeping the cost of living down.

substantial damages. Damages awarded to compensate for actual loss, whether large or small.

sub-underwriter. An issuing house which is to under-write the whole of a new issue may share out the liability among a number of sub-underwriters, each taking a fraction of the liability.

subvention. *See* SUBSIDY.

sue. To seek justice by taking legal proceedings; to prosecute, to make application, to petition.

suicide clause. A clause in a life assurance policy providing that the policy would be void if the assured died by his or her own hand within a certain period, usually six or twelve months, of the date of the policy. 'Suicide' was divided into 'sane suicide' or 'insane suicide'. In the latter case the personal representatives had a right to the policy money except as modified by the clause. In the former case, where the life in question was thought to be fully in possession of all his or her faculties at the time of death, and died as a deliberate act of policy (possibly so that the policy monies would repay debts), a question of public policy intervened. Suicide was, in the UK before 1961, a crime, and no criminal is allowed to benefit from the crime. Therefore in these cases policies were always void. Since 1961, when the law was changed so that suicide is no longer a crime, it depends entirely on the terms of the policy whether or not policy monies are paid out after the suicide of the life assured.

summary administration. In the case of a debtor who presents a petition to the court on the grounds of being unable to pay debts, the court, if it thinks fit, may not make a bankruptcy order if the value of debts is small, or if assets are equal to liabilities. However, where the court makes a bankruptcy order, it will issue a certificate for the summary administration of the bankrupt's estate. The appointment of an insolvency practitioner will, as required under s. 273, Insolvency Act, inquire into the affairs of the person and report to the court within the period specified.

summary diligence. *(Sc. Law)* A form of diligence available to holders of bonds, bills of exchange, promissory notes and certain other documents, which contain a special clause called 'Consent to registration for preservation and execution'. In these cases the creditor can proceed to use any of the normal forms of diligence without prior application to the court. Bills of exchange have to be dishonoured by non-acceptance or non-payment and must then be protested (*see* PROTEST). The protest is then registered in the books of the Sheriff Court of the county in which the debtor is domiciled. A copy of this registration is extracted for the benefit of the creditor, who can then proceed to the arrest or poinding (*q.v.*) of the debtor's effects. *See* DILIGENCE.

summons. The act of summoning; an authoritative call or citation, especially to appear before a court or a judge.

sum payable. The sum payable by a bill of exchange is a sum certain within the meaning of the Bills of Exchange Act, 1882, although it is required to be paid 1. with interest; 2. by stated instalments, with or without a provision that upon default in payment of any instalment the whole shall become due; 3. according to an indicated rate of exchange to be ascertained as directed by the bill.

sumptuary. The regulation of expenditure, one appointed to be responsible for expenditure.

sundry creditors. A heading on the liabilities side of a balance sheet to indicate money owned by the business on any particular day to trade and other creditors; the appellation of a bank account through which may be put isolated transactions not specifically referable to any particular customer's account.

sundry debtors. A heading on the assets side of a balance sheet to indicate the money owing to the business at a particular date by trade and other debtors; the appellation of a bank account through which may be put isolated transactions not specifically referable to any particular customer's account.

sunset law. *See* ZERO BUDGETING.

superannuation. The pensioning off of an employee on the grounds of age or ill-health.

superannuation payment. A deduction from wages or salary towards a contributory pensions scheme; a regular contribution made by an employee towards his or her pension.

supervision of banks. The failures of the fringe banks in the UK and the resulting rescue operation by the Bank of England and the clearing banks, which came to be known as the 'Lifeboat', raised from 1972 onwards the question of a stricter supervision of banks in a much more acute form. It was thought that the Bank of England, not the Department of Trade, should regulate and supervise the banking system. There was also the question of bringing the UK into line with the system in the other countries of the EEC, who have suggested that banks should be defined by law, licensed, and ought to be made to secure official approval for management and for existing and future plans. A White Paper published in August 1976 des-cribed the institutional framework proposed and this was followed by the Banking Act, 1979, which divided deposit-taking institutions into two groups which are licensed deposit takers and recognised banks. Although the system worked well, proposals set out in a government White Paper in December 1985, took into account the modifications needed to improve the banking supervision in the treatment of off balance sheet risks, international supervision and the need for regular dialogue with the Bank. The Banking Act, 1987 became law on 15 May 1987 and replaces the 1979 Act. The supervision of banks is carried out by a Board of Banking Supervision which meets monthly and consists of the Governor, the Deputy Governor, the Executive Director responsible for banking supervision and six other members. The main objectives of the Act are: 1. to restrict the taking of deposits to those institutions that are authorised by the Bank to take deposits (it abolished the two tier system); 2. to prohibit unauthorised institutions from using a name which indicates that they are banks; 3. to continue the Depositors' Protection Fund as a statutory body; 4. to increase the information that a bank must give to the Bank of England; 5. to regulate those who control the authorised institutions; and 6. to control advertisements inviting the public to make deposits. The Act lays down four criteria for the authorisation of an institution: 1. every director, controller and manager must be a fit and proper person to hold the position; 2. the business must be conducted in a prudent manner – this covers, *inter alia*, adequate capital, liquidity, provisions for bad debts, accounting and other records and internal controls; 3. the business must be carried on with integrity and appropriate professional skills; 4. the minimum paid up capital and reserves must be £1 million (£5 million if called a 'bank'). The Bank must be notified of changes in directors, controllers and managers. Any person who can be classified as a significant shareholder i.e. holding between five and 15 per cent of the voting rights, must notify the Bank. Any person who is proposing to hold more than 15 per cent of the voting rights of an authorised institution must give advanced notice to the Bank. Failure to do so is a criminal offence. It is also considered a criminal offence if an institution provides false or misleading information to the Board of Banking Supervision. No institution is permitted to withhold information and, in any case, the Bank has powers under the Act to obtain such information/documents. While information provided is treated as confidential, the Bank may, if necessary, convey such information as it considers necessary to other regulatory bodies and government departments. Any changes in auditors must be notified to the Bank and should any bank auditor wish to qualify the accounts of an institution, it must give notice to the Bank of its intention. Additionally, the Bank may ask auditors to disclose information obtained during the course of an audit, providing that this information is necessary to the Bank for supervision. The Depositors' Protection Scheme now covers 75 per cent of the first £20,000 of sterling deposits. *See* BANKING ACT.

supplement. Something added to fill up or supply a deficiency; an appendix, an extra charge.

supplemental instrument. An instrument containing provisions additional to those in a previous instrument, e.g. a codicil to a will. Any instrument expressed to be supplemental to a previous instrument shall be read and have effect as if the supplemental instrument contained a full recital of the previous instrument.

supplementary costs. Those costs of production which are fixed and do not vary with the output, including short-term administrative costs, as opposed to prime costs.

supplementary special deposit. *See* CORSET.

supplier credit. An arrangement whereby an exporter supplies goods to an overseas customer against a cash sum of up to 20 per cent of the contract price, with promissory notes or sterling bills of exchange payable over a period, which are guaranteed by the Export Credits Guarantee Department for the balance. The exporter then sells the instruments without recourse to his or her bank, the latter obtaining a separate guarantee from ECGD. This arrangement is generally found in the case of contracts up to £2 million, the credit period being restricted to five years.

supply. A sufficiency of things required, necessary stores; the amount of a product or commodity which will come on the market.

support. Used frequently in varying contexts. A bank supporting its customer is lending money to the customer. A 'support operation' signifies financial backing by a strong lender to a weak borrower (*see* LIFEBOAT COMMITTEE). A central bank supports its own currency by spending its holdings of gold and foreign currencies (*see* RESERVE) in buying the currency of its own country in an attempt through the laws of supply and demand to raise the value of the home currency. If the support required is heavy the central bank may find that the country's reserves are in danger of being drained away: the alternative is devaluation or, in the case of a floating rate, the further depreciation of the currency of the country in terms of the currencies of other countries.

support group. *See* LIFEBOAT COMMITTEE.

***supra* protest.** After a bill of exchange

has been protested for dishonour, in the case of dishonour by non-acceptance (provided the bill is not overdue) any person, not being a party already liable thereon, may, with the consent of the holder, intervene and accept the bill *supra* protest, for the honour of any party liable thereon, or for the honour of the person for whose account the bill is drawn. In the case of dishonour by non-payment, any person may intervene and pay it *supra* protest for the honour of any party liable thereon, or for the honour of the person for whose account the bill was drawn.

surcharge. To make an additional charge; to impose extra words or figures; an excessive charge, load or burden; an item which an auditor will not allow to stand among a firm's liabilities, and must therefore be made good by the person responsible.

surety. A guarantor (*q.v.*). 'Surety' has also been held by case law to include a third party who has deposited security as opposed to giving a guarantee. For the purposes of the Consumer Credit Act, 1974, a person by whom any security is provided, or the person to whom his or her rights and duties in relation to the security have passed by assignment or operation of law.

surety bond. An undertaking in writing by an insurance company or other financial institution to fulfil certain conditions, particularly in connection with the completion of constructors' projects in Europe, Africa and the Middle East, and in relation to the international supply industries. The beneficiary under the surety bond wants to ensure that the project will be duly completed, or, if not, that he or she will suffer no financial loss when the contractor defaults. The bond is a promise by the company giving that it will, if necessary, stand in the shoes of the contractor and cover any damage or loss suffered by the beneficiary, sometimes by finding another contractor to step in and take over the

job and by supervising the work until completion, sometimes by making a cash payment. The bond is negotiable against evidence of default. *See* STANDBY LETTER OF CREDIT.

surplus. Excess beyond what is wanted; excess of income over expenditure; the balance in hand after all liabilities; the balance in hand after all liabilities are paid; the residuum of an estate after all debts and liabilities are paid; matter not relevant to a legal case which may, therefore, be rejected.

surrender. To yield or hand over to the power of another, to deliver up possession of anything upon compulsion, to resign; to appear in court in discharge of bail; the giving up of a lease before the end of its term by a lessee to a lessor by mutual consent.

surrender value. The amount which an assurance company will pay on a life assurance policy if the policy-holder surrenders the policy to the company. There is usually no surrender value until two or three years' premiums have been paid. The surrender value is the basic security for an advance made against the security of a life policy. An assurance company will advise a lender on request of the surrender value of a policy, or there may be a table of surrender values incorporated in the policy.

surviving partner. A partner remaining to wind up the business. In doing this the partner has power to mortgage any of the partnership property to secure a debt in the name of the firm, as long as it is necessary for the winding-up of the firm, and not intended for further trading.

survivorship. *See* JOINT ACCOUNT; PRESUMPTION OF SURVIVORSHIP.

survivorship policy. A life assurance policy which is payable on the death of the last survivor of joint policy owners.

suspense account. An account to be used temporarily for items which for lack of detail or information at the time of posting cannot be placed to their regular accounts in the books. A review of such items should be made periodically to ensure that they are not overlooked. The term is also used for an account opened to receive details of unpaid overdue interest or capital from customers of a bank, both as a reminder that the sums are still due, and also to prevent the amounts being taken into bank profits for the year, where they would be liable to tax. *See also* INTEREST IN SUSPENSE.

suspension of payment. The cessation of payments to creditors because of shortage of cash. If a debtor gives notice to any creditors that he or she has suspended, or is about to suspend payment of debts, that is an act of bankruptcy.

swap. To exchange, to barter; an exchange. In foreign exchange operations, 'swap' means a spot sale against a forward purchase, or a spot purchase against a forward sale. 'Swap agreements' or 'swap arrangements' are devices to increase international liquidity. One central bank agrees to lend its currency to another central bank in exchange for a loan from that bank of an equivalent sum in its country's currency. Each country thereby strengthens the backing for its own currency and improves its resources against speculative attacks. It is also a process enabling issues of debts to be swapped between consenting companies, not necessarily in the same country.

SWIFT. *See* SOCIETY FOR WORLDWIDE INTERBANK FINANCIAL TELECOMMUNICATION.

swing. The free movement of an account from one figure to another, or from credit to debit or *vice versa*, as opposed to a gradual and progressive reliance on a bank overdraft where the account becomes 'solid', i.e. settles down at the maximum permitted level of debt. A good swing in an account is a healthy sign showing an active business. When applied to bilateral trade agreements, the limit for reciprocal credit.

switching. Changing from one form of investment to another, or from one foreign currency to another, according to the requirements of the time; raising money by issuing certificates of deposit and then on-lending these funds to borrowers on fixed deposits in order to make a turn.

symbolic delivery. Symbolic or constructive delivery may be made when documents of title to goods (e.g. bills of lading, insurance policies, etc.) are delivered to the person who has just bought the goods, or contracted to buy them; or to a banker who has financed the transaction. Constructive delivery by attornment is made where a warehouse-keeper holding goods under care by order of *A* agrees to hold them henceforth to the order of *B*. *See also* ATTORNMENT.

syndic. A legal representative chosen to act as agent for a corporation or company.

syndicate. A number of persons associated to carry out some enterprise; an association of industrialists or financiers formed to carry out some industrial project, or to acquire a monopoly in certain goods; a group of Lloyd's underwriters; a banking consortium; a meeting of discount houses to decide on the bid to be offered each week for Treasury bills.

syndicated loan. A very large loan ($1 billion or more) for a single borrower to finance a major project, arranged by a consortium (*q.v.*) *See also* LEAD MANAGER.

synergy. An occasion when a whole has greater power or value than the sum of its parts. Synergy is frequently the *raison d'etre* for the formation of groups of companies by take overs and mergers.

systems analysis. An enquiry into the cost of providing a particular service, or group of services. The enquiry should begin with a precise definition of the objective and should then evaluate the different possible ways of achieving it, estimating the cost of each. Any existing systems should be scrutinised for the information which they may yield, and conflicting priorities should be reviewed in connection with supplies (e.g. of labour) available and their cost and estimated future cost. *See also* OPERATIONAL RESEARCH.

T

TA. *See* TRADING AS.

Table A. The first of a number of tables in the First Schedule to the Companies Act, 1948. It sets out a series of model articles for a limited company. Some companies adopt Table A, but amend or re-write some of the articles, while keeping others in the form set out in the Act. A public company limited by shares need not write out its own special articles: it has three options. It may have its own special articles, or it may adopt Table A in its entirety, or it may have a combination of the two. Previous Companies Acts will also have their versions of Table A, but the Companies Act 1985, s. 8, states that companies formed after 1st July 1985, will be able to use regulations as prescribed by the Secretary of State. These may be found in Statutory Regulation 1985 No. 805.

tacking. The right of a mortgagee to priority of a subsequent mortgage over an intermediate one of which he or she had no notice. Tacking, except by a first mortgagee, was abolished in 1925. since then a prospective mortgagee can ascertain if any prior charges not protected by deposit of the deeds are in existence. A first mortgagee can still tack if, by the term of the mortgage, he or she is obliged to make further advances, or if he or she has arranged to do so with the agreement of subsequent mortgagees, or if the mortgagee had no notice of any subsequent mortgage at the time of making a further advance. The right to tack is usually excluded under the conditions of a bank form of mortgage.

takeover bid. An offer by one company to purchase the shares of another, with a view to merging the two businesses so as to make for fuller and more economical use of assets and managerial skills. The offer will always be made to the shareholders of the company sought to be taken over, but in the case of agreement between the boards of two companies, the directors of the company which is being taken over will recommend the bid. Consideration offered may be *cash, shares* in the bidding company, or a *combination* of both of these. As inside knowledge of a takeover can make a fortune for those unscrupulous enough to deal in the shares in advance of information being made public, a code has been devised to control such situations. It is known as the *'City Code on Takeovers and Mergers'* and it lays down general principles of conduct to be followed. (*See* PANEL ON TAKEOVERS and MERGERS). Compliance with these terms is voluntary, but offences against the Code may be followed by suspension of a quotation on the Stock Exchange and/or withdrawal of a dealer's licence by the Department of Trade. Merchant banks are prominent in advising and participating in takeover bids. *See also* MANAGEMENT BUYOUT; REVERSE TAKE-OVER; INSIDER; CHINESE WALL.

talisman. *See under* TRANSFER.

tally. A stick in which notches are cut as a means of keeping account; such a notch or mark, a score, a reckoning, an account; anything made to correspond with something else, a counterpart, a duplicate; a label or tag for identification.

tallyroll. A roll of paper attached to the back of a computer terminal, calculating machine, specialised typewriter, telex machine, etc. which gives the operator a continuous record or printout of data. The paper on which the data is recorded can very easily be neatly torn off the roll, to allow the printing process to continue.

tally system. The system of giving and

receiving goods on credit, to be paid for by regular instalments; the system in some African banks whereby the holder of a cheque desiring encashment is given a numbered token while the cheque is compared with the ledger and the stop list before payment is authorised; a similar system in *Companies House* where those desirous of making a search against a company are allocated a number while the company's records are being fetched.

tally trade. A business arrangement, usually in the drapery trade, whereby customers are allowed to take articles on credit by agreement on a series of instalments to meet the price.

talon. A slip issued along with the coupons attached to a bearer bond, to be used when further coupons are required.

'tandem' account. A banking account on which there is a standing arrangement allowing for the accountholder to take accommodation up to a prearranged limit as and when required (on which interest is paid at commercial rates), but where at other times, when the account is in credit, the bank pays interest on the balance (at a very much lower rate) to the accountholder.

tangible movable assets. Assets capable of realisation. If such an asset is disposed of for £3,000 or less, any gain made is not taxable. There is no liability on any gain made on the sale of a motor vehicle commonly used for private passenger travel, or on the sale of the owner's private dwelling house. *See also* CAPITAL GAINS TAX; FICTITIOUS ASSET.

tap. Government securities which are issued in unlimited quantities available direct from the issuing authority at any time. Bonds are offered for sale at a fixed price and yield, and the government hopes they will all be bought on the day of issue; if not, the government has to hold on to them, selling them as and when it can (i.e. turning the 'tap' on and off). This method involves the need for an accurate judgment on the part of the central bank as to what interest rate will appeal to the market. An underestimate will result in very few sales, while an over-estimate will result in an unnecessarily costly exercise. The tap method has another failing. If investors think the interest rate is going to rise, they have no reason to buy a fixed rate stock, and every interest in holding on to see what happens. This behaviour is in the aggregate anything but conducive to smooth monetary control, for if the investors are right, the government will eventually have to raise interest rates in order to impel them to buy. *See also* LONG TAP; SHORT TAP.

tap bills. The government broker borrows for the government by handling regular issues of gilt edged (*q.v.*) government stock in the market, and some of these issues are referred to as 'tap bills' or 'tap stock', because the government broker can adjust the price at which stock is sold, turning sales on by dropping the price rather like getting more water by turning the tap – hence the expression. *See also* TREASURY BILLS.

tare. An allowance for the weight of boxes, wrapping, etc. in which goods are packed; an allowance for the weight of a container, such as a cask, crate, etc., in reckoning the price of dutiable goods; the weight of a vehicle when empty.

tare weight. The weight of an aircraft minus crew and cargo.

target. A mark to aim at; a maximum sum of money aimed at in public subscription, e.g. 'savings target'; the minimum consumption of fuel aimed at in an economy drive, e.g. 'fuel target'.

target company. The name given to a company which is the subject of some kind of take-over bid by another company or a number of persons acting together (*see* CONCERT PARTY).

It is used (but not defined in ss. 67 and 68 of the Companies Act, 1981, which impose legal requirements on persons acting together to acquire a sufficient number of shares in the target company for its control to ensure that all individual interests are aggregated and notified to the target company.

target population. A term used to describe any section of the population intended to be reached by any method of communication, such as an advertising campaign. It is also a term used in the programmed learning method of instruction to describe the students for whom any particular teaching programme is devised.

target price. The fixing of farming prices in the EEC which might be obtained in the open market. Imports may then be subjected to levies if they are below the target price. In particular areas where it is desirable to encourage production, a higher regional target may be set.

tariff. A list of imported and exported goods on which duty is payable.

tariff company. An insurance company having a standard range of premiums.

tax. A compulsory contribution levied on persons, property or businesses to meet the expenses of government or other public services; to impose tax on; to fix the amounts of costs, etc., in a legal action. *See also* CORPORATION TAX; INCOME TAX; WITHHOLDING TAX.

taxable income. The amount which is left after deducting personal and other allowances from total income (but not payments under deed of covenant, or life assurance relief). When taxable income exceeds a certain figure, the rate of tax mounts on an ascending scale in accordance with the amount of the taxable income, up to the maximum rate (which varies from time to time) on any taxable income in excess of a figure currently in force.

tax and price index (TPI). A monthly indicator for which it is claimed that it fills a gap in official statistics, particularly the widely used retail price index. The latter reflects only changes in prices while the TPI covers both direct taxes and prices. The thinking behind the TPI is that most families face two elements of household costs – one is income tax and national insurance contributions and the other is the price of the things they buy. The RPI covers only price changes but the TPI covers both direct taxes and prices. It provides a broad measure in the purchasing power of incomes before tax and so measures the increase in gross income needed to maintain net income or 'take-home pay' in real terms. Those households paying no tax, and those on high incomes, are excluded and the index represents those paying tax at standard rate.

tax avoidance. The act of claiming every allowance and relief which is available under the tax laws. Such avoidance, being allowable by law, is quite legal; failure to pay tax which is legally due is *tax evasion*.

tax certificate. A certificate by an issuing authority that tax on an interest payment has been deducted at source. A certificate of tax credit is issued in respect of dividends.

tax credit scheme. *See* NEGATIVE INCOME TAX.

tax exile. The description of a person who would, if he or she lived in his or her own country, be subject to a high rate of tax. For this reason he or she is permanently domiciled in a foreign country, where the tax rate is lower.

tax free. Any income received free of tax is regarded by the Inland Revenue as such a sum which, taxed at the basic rate, will leave the amount actually received. The recipient of the sum will also obtain from the payer a certificate in respect of the tax deducted to be submitted with his or her annual return to the Tax Inspector. Calculations of higher rate tax or investment income surcharge on the recipient will be based on the higher sum. *See also* FRANCO.

tax havens. *See* OFFSHORE FUNDS.

taxman. The common name for the Inland Revenue.

tax planning. To prepare the financial operations of a business so as to take advantage of any tax concessions and minimise the total tax liability in a legal way.

tax return. A legal obligation on all persons to make an annual return to the Inland Revenue, stating all taxable earned and unearned income, capital gains and any tax allowances that the individual is permitted. Often customers of banks that have complex returns, or for any reason are unable to perform this function themselves, will request the bank's tax department to act on their behalf and regularly submit the annual tax return.

tax-sheltered account. Any account on which the interest is tax-free.

tax year. Often called the 'fiscal year'. It commences on 6 April of one year and ends on 5 April the next year. It is over this period that the amount of tax an individual is likely to pay is calculated.

Technical Development Capital, Ltd. (TDC). *See* VENTURE CAPITAL..

teeming and lading. A fraudulent method of converting the money paid to a bank or creditor to a dishonest employee. Basically, money received from a customer/debtor will be misappropriated by an employee, but before a statement is sent out to that person, funds, misappropriated from another customer, are placed on the first customer's account. As this is a progressive activity, the danger multiplies. The accounts of customers and the handling of cash or cheques, should be maintained by different persons.

telegraphic transfer. A payment made in international commerce by a transfer of money by cable or tele-graph from a bank account in one country to a beneficiary in another (also called *cable transfer*). The cost of the cable is charged to the customer who authorises the payment, unless stated that all charges are for the account of the payee. As with mail transfers, payment may be made in sterling or in currency, to the payee under advice, or on application and identification, or for credit to his or her account. The rate for the telegraphic transfer exceeds the rate for the mail transfer only by the cost for the cable, which may be at urgent, ordinary or deferred rate. *See* SOCIETY FOR WORLDWIDE INTERBANK FINANCIAL COMMUNICATION.

teletext. A service offered particularly by the broadcasting authorities which can provide information on either a VDU or television screen. This method of transmission is the forerunner of home banking.

telex. A system whereby a message sent by teleprinter is reproduced simultaneously at a distant point as it is typed.

teller. A member of the House of Commons who counts votes; an officer at an election who performs a similar function; any person who counts votes at any voting meeting. Also, the US equivalent of a UK bank cashier, responsible for control of the tills, cashing checks and physically handling transactions with the bank's customers. The teller's main function is to receive deposits and to pay out funds. The emphasis on customer service, as well as increasing competition between US banks in the 1980s, has seen the introduction of the Automated Teller Machine (ATM) (*q.v.*).

teller terminal. A substitute for a human cashier. A teller terminal is an electronic machine connected on-line (*q.v.*) with a computer, which can put out predetermined accounts, accept requests for statements or new cheque books, or give the balance of a customer's account. In some cases a visual display unit (*q.v.*) may be incorporated. In a wider sense the phrase could include a credit-taking facility or a cash dispenser such as 'Cashpoint' or 'Servicetill'.

tel quel rate. An exchange rate calculated when buying a currency bill drawn on a foreign centre where the bill still has some time to run before maturity; a rate not taking interest into account: a flat rate.

temporary annuity. An annual payment for a fixed number of years, starting immediately.

tenancy at will. A tenancy terminable at the option either of the landlord or of the tenant. It is rarely expressly created, but usually arises when someone is given exclusive possession of premises for an indefinite period without there being any exact description of the interest held, nor any reason specified as to why this person has been allowed into occupation. In such cases there is a presumption that he or she holds as a tenant at will, but his position is basically dependent upon the true intention of the parties, and it may be that the tenant is really only a licensee, that is, a person having a merely personal privilege of occupation (as between himself and the landlord) but no definite interest in the land itself.

tenancy in common. Two or more tenants having equal shares in the property of which they are tenants, usually land. On the death of one tenant, his or her share passes to a personal representative and not to co-tenant(s). Tenancy in common is found in the case of partnership land (unless one partner is made sole owner as trustee for his co-partners), or under the terms of a will, e.g. where land is left to children equally. The tenancy in common has the disadvantage that on a sale of the whole land it is necessary to prove a separate title to each separate share. *See also* JOINT TENANCY.

tenant. One who has legal possession of real estate; one who pays rent for property which he or she occupies.

tenant at sufferance. A tenant of land whose original entry upon the land was lawful, but who wrongly continues in possession after his or her estate in the land has ended.

tenant by the curtesy. A widower entitled to a life interest in the land of which his wife dies seised in fee simple or in tail. Curtesy was abolished in 1925 with regard to all interests except an entailed interest and therefore now such a tenancy applies only when a female tenant in tail dies intestate.

tenant-farmer. One who occupies a farm on payment of rent to a landlord.

tenant for life. A person of full age who is for the time being beneficially entitled under a settlement to possession of settled land for his or her lifetime. If two or more persons are jointly entitled to possession, they together constitute the tenant for life.

tenant right. The legal right of a tenant to occupy property on regular payment of reasonable rent and to receive compensation if the contract is broken by the landlord; any right of the tenant of property, whether expressly stated or implied, such as a right to remove fixtures at the end of the tenancy, or to receive an allowance for seeds or fertiliser put on the land.

tender. To offer in payment or for acceptance, to make an estimate; money proffered in payment of a debt; an offer to purchase Treasury bills. As far as these are concerned (and gilts generally) the Bank of England now has a partial tender system in operation. The Bank announces the minimum price it is prepared to accept. In the case of an over-subscription the highest bidders will succeed, but otherwise bidders are met at the minimum price and the rest of the issue is sold by tap. *See also* LEGAL TENDER.

tender bills. *See* TREASURY BILLS.

tender bond, tender guarantee. A

guarantee given by a banker or an insurance company in support of a contractor tendering for a public works contract abroad. The guarantee is against the risk that the contractor, having gained the contract, will then fail to go on with the work. It is usually for 5 per cent of the value of the contract. *See also* PERFORMANCE BOND; STANDBY LETTER OF CREDIT; SURETY BOND.

tenement. A dwelling-house; a building divided into separate flats and let to different tenants; any property which is permanently held by a tenant.

tenor. The exact purport or meaning.Applied to a bill of exchange it means the purpose and intent of the bill on construction of the words and figures used in it.

tenure. The act, manner or right of holding an office or property, especially real estate; the manner or conditions of holding; the period or term of holding.

term. A boundary, a limit, especially of time; a period during which the law courts are sitting; a fixed day when rent is due to be paid.

term bill. A bill incorporating a period of credit and payable at the end of the term of credit.

term (or acceptance) credit. A credit where the beneficiary is to obtain payment upon the maturity of a bill of exchange drawn in compliance with the terms of the credit and accompanied by the relevant documents. Such a bill will usually be drawn upon the correspondent bank for the stipulated period of time and accepted by it. The drawer then has a credit instrument which can be discounted or held to maturity.

term days. The days on which rent falls due.

term deposits. Deposits which are repayable after a pre-determined time and not on demand; deposits in a Savings Bank for which a long period of notice for withdrawal is required.

terminable annuity. An annuity which will stop on a fixed date, or after a certain time, or on the beneficiary's death.

terminal. A machine or device in a office/bank linked to a computer whereby input data is transmitted, output data is received for the various operations of the bank or business.

terminal bonus. A bonus paid when a life assurance policy matures. It is usually in addition to any other bonus stated in the policy.

term loan. A loan given to a borrower for a specific period.

term of a bill. The period of time for which a bill of exchange is drawn.

term of years. A period of years for which it is intended that an estate shall endure. Unless it satisfies the definition of a term of years absolute it is an equitable interest. A term of years absolute is a term which is to last for a certain fixed period, even though for one reason or another it may be liable to come to an end before the expiration of that period (e.g. by re-entry of the landlord, operation of law, etc.)

termor. One who has an estate for a term of years, or for life.

term policy. A policy of life assurance which assures a person's life over a certain period. Thus anyone wishing to cover the risk of loss of life through an aircraft crash when about to fly on holiday would take out a term policy for a few weeks. Term policies can, however, last for thirty years or more – all depends on the length of time stipulated by the policyholder. If the policyholder dies during the term his or her heirs get the benefit. If the policyholder survives the term there is no benefit. These are purely protective policies, with no investment element.

terms, to come to. To reach a compromise agreement.

terms, cash. Payment at time of purchase.

terms control. Hire purchase business in the UK is subject to directives issued from time to time by the government. These lay down a minimum down payment on goods which are being sold, which the purchaser has to find at once, and a maximum period for the contract during which time the debt must be cleared.

term shares. Money deposited with a building society on the basis that it cannot be withdrawn for a fixed period, normally from two to four years. In return the investor receives a higher rate of interest than on a normal share account.

terms of delivery. Indications as to whether sender or consignee shall pay delivery charges on a consignment of goods or whether the charges are to be divided between them, e.g. CIF, C & F, FOB.

terms of payment. The conditions of payment associated with any particular sale of goods, e.g. cash with order, hire-purchase terms, credit card, monthly account, etc.

terms of reference. Points for discussion and settlement.

terms of trade. The comparison of the country's imports and exports by price. If the general price of imports rises faster than the price of exports, the terms of trade are becoming less favourable. In the UK the indicator is calculated by dividing the index of export prices by the index of import prices and multiplying by 100. Thus a fall in the final index indicates an adverse movement.

term transfer. The introduction of an indebtedness at a term into a market dealing with debts at shorter or longer terms, e.g. the introduction by banks of interbank deposits into the local authority market for a longer term. *See also* MATURITY TRANSFORMATION.

testament. *See* WILL.

testator. A person who makes a will.

testimonium. The clause at the end of a deed or will which begins 'In witness, etc.' and goes on to certify that the

parties have signed the document in witness of what it contains.

theft. The act of dishonestly appropriating property belonging to another with the intention of permanently depriving that other of it.

theory of comparative costs. The theory that even if one country has an absolute advantage in costs of producing all things, the world will still benefit if each country specialises in producing those goods in which it has the greatest relative cost advantage or least disadvantage.

things in possession. *See* CHOSE IN POSSESSION.

Third Market. A market established by the Stock Exchange in 1986 for the purchase and sale of shares in public limited companies that are not big enough or do not reach the criteria necessary to have a full listing, or a listing on the Unlisted Securities Market.

third of exchange. *See* BILL IN A SET.

third party. A person involved in some arrangement with a bank, who is neither the banker nor a customer (*see* COLLATERAL), an insurance term for some person other than the insurance company and the person insured.

thrift institution. Common name for those institutions in the US whose primary function is the acceptance of time deposits. Savings and loans associations, which are the US equivalent of the British building societies, and mutual savings banks are typical thrift institutions.

through bill of lading. A bill of lading which covers shipment on more than one vessel or more than one type of transport.

transport agreement. These agreements are used in, and associated with, the financing of oil and natural gas pipelines. A pipeline is constructed with the proceeds of a loan and the lender recognises that a high utilisation and continuous operation at a high capacity level is required to generate sufficient cash flow to service the debt and to make a profit. Including the lender, four parties are concerned. The other three are the pipeline owners, the owners of the source to which it is to be connected, and the purchasers of the output. The pipeline can link the primary producer to a utility company, a refiner, or a large industrial user. The lender must be satisfied that input to the line is insured by adequate oil or natural gas reserves to which the pipeline will be linked (the producer agrees to deliver a quantity which will be sufficient to service and repay the loan), that at the other end the purchaser has the financial ability to perform his or her obligations under the purchase agreement, and that the period required for the pipeline to maximise its profit potential (which may be up to twenty years) is satisfactory. Further protection may be afforded to the lender by obtaining a mortgage on the pipeline and an assignment of the payments due under the contract with the consumer.

ticket day. *See* NAME DAY.

tick up. The last resort procedure for finding an error in the day's work in a bank. In the case of an error in the debit side of the control it is necessary to call every debit item in the control list against the corresponding entry in the out-clearing sheets; in the case of an error in a ledger it is necessary to call back every item of the check ledger sheets day by day back to the day when the ledger was last known to be correct. (Procedures are somewhat different where computer accounting is in force.)

till. A drawer or tray under the supervision of a cashier from which he/she will place funds received and withdraw funds to pay customers. It is usual for tills to have separate compartments for the various coin denominations and note values.

till float. The minimum/maximum that a cashier should start the day with. Should the agreed amount fall below the minimum required, this is replenished from the float under the control of the chief cashier. Should the amount exceed the permitted amount, then a transfer is made to the chief cashier.

time and motion study. A check on the time taken by an employee to do any particular task in order to see whether it can be done more efficiently.

time bargain. An agreement to contract business at a given time; a term applied to dealings on the Stock Exchange by 'bulls' or 'bears'.

time charter. A charter party whereby the ship is chartered for a specific period.

time deposits. Deposits at a term (including certificates of deposit). *See also* SPECIAL DEPOSITS.

time draft. A bill of exchange which is payable at a stated number of days (30, 60, 90 days) after date, or after acceptance.

time order. An order of the court defined in the Consumer Credit Act, 1974 as follows: 1. If it appears to the court just to do so *(a)* on an application for an enforcement order, or *(b)* on an application made by a debtor or hirer under this paragraph after service on him or her of a default notice, or *(c)* in an action brought by a creditor or owner to enforce a regulated agreement or any security, or recover possession of any goods or land to which a regulated agreement relates, the court may make an order under this section (a 'time order'). 2. A time order shall provide for one or both of the following, as the court considers just – *(a)* the payment by the debtor or hirer or any surety of any sum owed under a regulated agreement or a security by such instalments, payable at such times as the court, having regard to the means of the debtor or hirer and any surety, considers reasonable; *(b)* the remedying by the debtor or hirer of any breach of a regulated agreement (other than non-payment of money) within such period as the court may specify.

time policy. A marine policy extending cover for a fixed time only.

time sharing options (TSO). A system which allows centralised computer capacity to be available to many users with differing needs. Used in banks by specialist departments, e.g. premises, engineers, chief accountants. Availability is through terminals connected to central processing units (*q.v.*) by land lines, and users develop their own programs. These are stored centrally, then called into use when needed.

tithe. A tenth part; originally the tenth part of the produce of land and cattle allotted to the upkeep of the church and the clergy, later paid in the form of a tax.

tithe rentcharge. Tithes (*q.v.*) were usually commuted for a rentcharge, but the Tithe Act, 1936 replaced tithe rentcharges by redemption annuities, payable for sixty years to the Crown. The owners were compensated by an issue of government stock. Provision for the compulsory redemption of such annuities on the sale of land was made in the Finance Act, 1962, and their payment was finally ended under the Finance Act, 1977. The term is therefore now of historical importance only.

title. An inscription serving as a name or designation; the distinguishing formula at the head of a legal document, statute etc., including caption and text, as arranged for reference; the right to ownership of property, the legal evidence of this; an acknowledged claim, the grounds of this; fineness, especially of gold, expressed in carats.

title deed. A legal instrument giving the evidence of a person's right to property.

title insurance. Very common to real estate transactions in the US, title insurance covers financial loss from claims arising out of defects in the title to real property which may come to light subsequent to purchase. Title insurance companies issue policies which protect purchasers, mortgagees, etc., as well as guaranteeing title to the property being purchased.

token. A sign, a symbol; a coin or disc issued by a firm or company to be used by employees, e.g. in a canteen; a card issued with a stamp of a certain value and exchangeable for goods in a shop, e.g. book token, record token.

token money. Coins where the value of the metal in them is less than the value attached to them by law, such as the cupro-nickel and bronze coins of the UK.

token payment. A deposit paid as token of later payment of full debt; earnest money.

toll. A tax or duty charged for some privilege or service, especially for the use of road, bridge, or tunnel.

tombstone. The list of underwriters advertised as acting in connection with a new issue. These names are placed one after another vertically and as there are usually enough of them to form a more or less solid block of print there can be said to be a reference to a 'tombstone', a reference perhaps strengthened by the resemblance between the words 'underwriter' and 'undertaker'. 'Tombstone' is, therefore, a short way of alluding to the members of the underwriting group.

tontine. A form of joint assurance whereby the sum received by the subscribers increases as their number decreases, until with the death of the last survivor, the tontine completely lapses.

tontine annuity. A form of joint annuity whereby the sum received by the subscribers increases as their number decreases, until with the death of the last survivor the tontine completely lapses. *See also* REVERSE ANNUITY.

tontine policy. A life assurance policy under the terms of which no bonus is payable if the death of the policy holder occurs before the end of a specified period, usually about twenty years. During that time the policy has no surrender value. At the end of the period the bonus vests in the maturing policy. The barren period is called the tontine period. The word originated in the eighteenth century with an Italian banker named Lorenzo Tonti, who had the idea that a number of persons should subscribe to a fund which is invested and eventually becomes the property of the last survivor. In France and Great Britain at that time the state raised money by tontines. *See also* TONTINE ANNUITY.

topic. The Stock Exchange view data system which is available to all subscribers. The system carries all current share prices, announcements, analytical details, foreign exchange rates, etc.

topping-up clause. Where, in a form of charge, a borrowing customer agrees to maintain a margin of security at all times, a clause recording his or her agreement to deposit further security if the lending bank asks for it. The lender might decide to make this request if the security which the customer already has falls in value to the point where it no longer covers the amount of the loan. If the borrower is then unable to meet this request the 'topping-up clause' provides that the whole of the accommodation becomes instantly repayable, so giving the lender an immediate right of action.

top slicing. In the case of unit-linked single-premium bonds a tax liability will arise payable by the bondholder when a bond is converted, either by surrender, or maturity, or assignment, or in other ways, into cash. The tax payable is calculated by a process known as 'top slicing', whereby the gain arising is divided by the number of years for which the policy, taken out

as life cover, has run. This amount is then taxed as though it were the top slice of the investor's income in the year of encashment. The resultant figure is then multiplied by the number of years for which the policy has run, to arrive at the total liability.

tort. A private or civil wrong, an injury to person or property for which damages may be claimed in a court of law. It has been said that in tort the banker is on the defensive. He or she is not likely to be bringing an action, but will be looking for a good defence to an action being brought against him or her by someone else. The most likely grounds are for conversion or negligence.

total price. For the purposes of the Consumer Credit Act, 1974, total price means the total sum payable by the debtor under a hire-purchase agreement or a conditional sale agreement, including any sum payable on the exercise of an option to purchase, but excluding any sum payable as a penalty or as compensation or damages for a breach of the agreement.

touch screen. A VDU or screen which is sensitive to the touch of the user which gives a command to the computer or complies with a command given. Used very extensively in the foreign exchange departments of banks, other areas linked to financial markets, and where there is need for speedy communications.

touch signature. A euphemism for fingerprinting a customer who wishes to cash travellers' cheques in USA. It is not applicable to a customer who produces a passport as proof of identity, but is intended as a deterrent to fraud. The reasoning is that a dishonest person attempting to pass fraudulent paper is hardly likely to want to give fingerprints to the bank. In African countries, where many customers cannot write, it is commonplace for fingerprints to be taken on withdrawal slips. These may if necessary be compared with a record card which contains a specimen fingerprint and a photograph.

town and country planning. For the checking of haphazard and ribbon development, the government imposed, in a series of Acts from 1947 onwards, rules for planning the future way in which the country's land is to be used, and decreed that consent must be obtained for any development. 'Development' was defined as 'the carrying out of building, engineering, mining or other operations in, on, over and under land, or the making of any material change in the use of buildings or land'. Under planning law, local planning authorities have decided upon development plans for their areas, and the details of these plans are to be found in the register of districts, borough and county councils. Here will be found such information as road charges, town planning schemes, demolition orders and building-preservation orders. *See also* LOCAL LAND CHARGES REGISTER.

Town Clearing. Deals with articles of £10,000 and over drawn on and paid into the banks and branches in the 'Town Clearing', all within the City of London and therefore within easy walking distance of the Clearing House. By using this clearing large cheques can be paid in up to the close of business each day and still be cleared, or returned unpaid, the same day. All other cheques drawn on branches of the clearing banks, are passed through the General Clearing. The Town Clearing was substantially replaced in 1983 by the Clearing House Automated Payments System (CHAPS) (*q.v.*).

trade. The business of buying and selling, commerce, barter, shopkeeping; occupation (in industry); the purchase or sale of goods or services at home (*domestic trade*) or abroad (*foreign trade*).

trade balance. *See* BALANCE OF TRADE.

trade bill. A bill drawn by one trader on another against an actual trade transaction, but not bearing a bank indorsement.

trade board. A board of representatives of employers and employees, nominated by the Department of Trade to settle trade disputes, etc.

trade credit. Credit granted by one trader to another who has bought goods from him or her.

trade cycle. The alternately recurring periods of prosperity and depression affecting world commerce; the tendency of business activity to fluctuate regularly between periods of boom and depression.

trade discount. An allowance made by wholesalers to traders who buy goods for the purpose of re-sale; an allowance on a quantity or number of articles.

traded options. Options to buy or sell certain shares on the Stock Exchange have a life of three, six or nine months, the cost of the options varying with their life. The value of an option to buy increases if the price of the shares concerned rises in the months of the option, and an active market can develop, not so much in the shares themselves, as in the options to buy the shares. Conversely, the value of an option to sell increases if the price of the shares concerned falls in the early months of the option. There is no limit to the number of options that dealers in an option can write. The system of traded options allows the investor to sell his or her option or purchase other options on the traded option market in the same way as stocks and shares are dealt in. This market consists of 57 equities, plus two currency option markets (dollar/deutschmark, dollar/sterling) and for the moment one gilt (11¾ per cent treasury 1991) but this is likely to increase in the near future. Six have just call options available. Prices are at pre-set levels, one below the market price of the shares ('in the money') and one above ('out of the money'). The investor has a choice of expiry dates, each three months from the next. The premiums payable on the shorter-dated options are less than those on the longer-dated options. Unlike a conventional option, a traded option has a market price and can be valued from day to day. There is also a European Options Market in Amsterdam. Other countries interested are the UK, France, West Germany, Belgium, Luxembourg, Austria, Switzerland, Spain and Italy. *See also* CABINET BID; OPEN OUTCRY.

trade gap. The excess of visible imports over visible exports.

trade investments. In a balance sheet, the sum representing the total of the company's investments in affiliated companies or associated organisations.

trade mark. A registered name or device marked on goods to show that they have been produced by a certain manufacturer.

trade name. A registered name given by a manufacturer to a proprietary article; a name used among traders and manufacturers for a certain commodity; a name under which an individual or company trades.

trade protection society. An organisation which supplies information as to the credit standing of companies, firms and individuals, primarily those engaged in trade.

traders' credit. A system of settlement for traders offered by banks, whereby the trader hands the bank a list of amounts to be paid with names, bank, branch and sorting code number of each bank keeping each of the accounts, with a separate bank giro credit slip for each one. The bank supplies the printed blank credit forms and a book with the sorting code numbers of all the banks. The trader gives the bank one cheque for the total and the bank distributes the credits. This system is now part of the credit clearing.

trade union. A legally recognised association of clerks, workmen, etc. for the purpose of securing their rights, safeguarding wage scales, and preventing exploitation by employers. Any property of the union should be vested in trustees, to whom a banker must make any advance. Any borrowing must be covered by the rules of the union.

trading account. The account of a business concern which shows how the gross profit has been arrived at.

trading as. Often abbreviated as t/a. This phrase is used when a business entity is known for business purposes in another name. e.g. A & E Jones t/a Super Launderettes. This designation will be printed on cheques, invoices and other business documents.

trading certificate. A certificate issued by the Registrar of Companies to public companies, on receipt of which they are entitled to commence business. The Companies Act, 1985 lays down a new procedure for obtaining a trading certificate. Section 117 of the Act provides that a trading certificate will be issued if a statutory declaration, to be made by a director or secretary of the company, certifies that the nominal amount of the issued capital is at least £50,000, and states: 1. the amount paid up on the share capital at the time of the application; 2. any actual or estimated preliminary expenses, and by whom paid or payable; 3. details of any promotion expenses. It is an offence for any public company to trade or exercise its borrowing powers in contravention of s. 117 (above), and the penalty for so doing is a fine on the company and on any officer of the company who is in default. However, any transaction entered into by the company before issue of a trading certificate will not be invalid. Instead, if the company fails to meet its obligations under such a transaction within twenty-one days of being asked in writing to do so, the directors of the company will be personally liable for any loss suffered by the other party to the transaction.

trading cheques. Vouchers issued by clothing clubs which can be exchanged at designated local shops for articles of clothing, members repaying the club by instalments over a period, usually about twenty weeks.

trading company. A company formed for the purpose of carrying on trade and making a profit.

trading down, trading up. Trading down is to sell something of value and buy something of less value, e.g. to sell a £30,000 house and buy one for £25,000. Trading up is to follow the reverse procedure.

trading partnership. A partnership in which any partner has authority to bind the firm in drawing, accepting or indorsing bills of exchange, in making agreements, and generally in contracting debts on the firm's behalf.

trading profit. Gross profit.

trading stamps. Stamps given by retailers to their customers in proportion to their purchases, which can be exchanged with the company supplying the stamps for a range of attractive goods.

tranche. A slice, an instalment. A phrase used where wholesale finance is concerned and where the sums in question are substantial, to indicate the taking or 'drawing down' of an instalment or tranche of the sum agreed. Also often used to indicate a borrowing by a country from the IMF, which consists of a part of an agreed sum.

transaction. The act of carrying through or negotiating a piece of business; an affair, a proceeding; the

adjustment of a dispute by mutual concessions.

transaction reporting. *See* CASH MANAGEMENT SERVICE.

transaction loans. The term used in US banking for loans for a specified period and purpose. They may be extended on either a secured or an unsecured basis but rarely exceed 180 days, although renewals or partial renewals are typical. Repayment may be a *balloon* at maturity or on an instalment basis over a longer time period.

transactions at undervalue. By s. 339, Insolvency Act, 1986, a transaction of undervalue has occurred when a person who, before a petition has been presented, carried out a transaction by way of: 1. A gift; or 2. a gift in consideration of marriage; or 3. where no consideration passed or the consideration was significantly less than the value of the transaction. For the trustee to be able to claw back the value of the transaction for the benefit of the creditors, it must be proved that: 1. the transaction at undervalue took place within five years before the presentation of the petition; and 2. the person making the transaction at undervalue was insolvent or become insolvent in consequence of the transaction.

transactions to defraud creditors. These sections of the Insolvency Act (423-425) are similar to the Bankruptcy Acts relating to fraudulent conveyance. Should the court be satisfied that the transaction: *(a)* put the asset/s beyond the reach of person/s making a claim against a debtor; or *(b)* otherwise prejudiced the interests of such a person (creditor) in relation to his or her claim, the court, may *(a)* restore the position to what it would have been; and *(b)* protect the interests of persons who were victims of the transaction.

transfer. To move from one place to

another; to convey property to another; the document authorising this. *See also* TERM TRANSFER.

transferability of cheque. A cheque is transferable when it circulates quite freely. It may or may not be negotiable also. A transferable cheque gives each successive transferee a good title, provided that the title is good in the first place and that it does not become defective while in the course of passing from hand to hand. *See also* NON TRANSFERABLE.

transferable account. Formerly an account maintained in this country by a non-resident on which sterling was freely convertible into any other currency. Transferable accounts disappeared with the ending of exchange control restrictions in the autumn of 1979. It could now be said that all accounts are transferable accounts.

transferable credit. A credit where the benefit of a credit opened in favour of a middle-man by the importer is transferred to the exporter of the goods. This is a convenient way for the middle-man to pay the actual supplier of the goods without having to find temporary finance or arrange a credit. The credit opened by the negotiating bank in favour of the exporter will be for a lesser sum that that shown on the original transferable credit (the difference being the middle-man's profit) and will show the middle-man as the buyer. It may stipulate for an earlier shipment date. The name of the exporter should not be divulged to the importer (and *vice versa*), nor should the importer be able to find out what the original price of the goods was. When the exporter's documents are to hand, the middle-man's invoices are substituted for the exporters' and sent with the other documents of title to the importer, whose bank will re-imburse the exporter's bank. The procedure is similar to that in a back-to-back credit, the main difference being that in that

case the second credit is opened only on the strength of the first one, whereas with a transferable credit the benefit of the original credit is transferred to the exporter; there must therefore be a provision in the credit for the transfer.

transfer accounting lodgment for investors, stock management for jobbers (Talisman). Talisman is a recognised clearing house (RCH) for the Stock Exchange. It is a central pooling system for the purchase and sale of listed securities, incorporating a computerised settlement system for all UK and Irish registered stocks. Stock is delivered by the vendor in advance of settlement and held temporarily by the Stock Exchange nominee company, SEPON (Stock Exchange Pool Nominees), until it is transferred to the new owner.

transfer agent. The office (very often a bank department) which handles transfers of registered shares and delivers the certificates in the names of new purchasers.

transfer certificate. Where, exceptionally, a company does not issue a new share certificate to a new shareholder, it may issue a transfer certificate authenticating the transfer, which should be held by the buyer together with the old certificate(s).

transfer days. Days set aside by companies for registering the transfers of registered stock; the official days at the Bank of England for the transfer of Government stocks.

transfer deed. The instrument transferring the ownership of securities from one person to another, a stock transfer form.

transfer fee. A fee charged by a company upon registration of a change of ownership of shares.

transfer of mortgage. The conveyance of mortgaged property from one owner to another. This may happen where a banker takes over such a security from another bank which has been lending, against repayment by the banker. Such a new lending must be by way of loan with permanent reductions to defeat the operation of the 'rule in Clayton's case'. Normally a banker will take a new form of mortgage in such a case. A transfer of a mortgage may also occur where the customer requests the lending banker, who is about to be repaid, to reconvey the property, not to the customer but to a third party. The method of transfer is by a deed which declares that the mortgagee transfers the benefit of the mortgage. Such a deed vests in the transferee all the rights under the mortgage formerly enjoyed by the transferor. The mortgagor should join in the deed of transfer. Alternatively, a statutory receipt may be prepared for the moneys due under the mortgage, indorsed on or annexed to it, stating the name of the person paying the money and executed by the chargee by way of legal mortgage.

transfer of shares. *See* REGISTER OF TRANSFERS; SHARE TRANSFER FORM.

transferor by delivery. The holder of a bill payable to bearer who negotiates it by delivery without indorsing it. The transferor is not liable on the instrument (because he or she has not indorsed it) but warrants to his or her immediate transferee being a holder for value, that the bill is what it purports to be, that he or she has a right to transfer it, and that at the time of transfer is not aware of any fact which renders it valueless.

transfer order. An order addressed by a bank holding a warehouse keeper's certificate or receipt in its own name, to the warehouse keeper, requesting transfer of the goods into the name of another, usually a customer.

transfer receipt. The receipt given by a company when a document for the transfer of stocks and shares is presented for registration.

transfer register. *See* REGISTER OF TRANSFERS.

transfer risk. A risk encountered in lending abroad, where although the borrower can repay a loan, his or her country has imposed restrictions because it lacks sufficient foreign exchange for meeting the debt.

transit number. Because of the vast number of banks within the US (over 14,000 in 1982) the ABA National Numerical System provides each institution with a unique identifying number known as the transit number. This number appears on all US bank checks and identifies the city, state or territory in which the issuing bank is located as well as the bank itself, and is an essential element in the check clearing mechanism in North America. *See* MAGNETIC INK CHARACTER RECOGNITION (MICR).

transit trade. *See* RE-EXPORT.

travel agent. An agent who arranges tickets and reservations for road, sea, rail or air transport for persons desirous of travelling from one place to another, whether within a country or overseas, on business or holiday. The agent acts on behalf of his or her principal, the carrier company.

travel cheques (traveller's cheques). Cheques issued in sterling or in certain other currencies by banks to their customers wishing to travel abroad. Each cheque has a space for the customer to sign immediately on receipt of the cheques, and another space to sign in the presence of the paying agent at the time of cashing the cheque. The customer pays for the cheques in full (plus the bank's commission) when they are issued, and must then keep them in a safe place. If they are lost or stolen through no fault of the traveller, the bank when notified will usually replace them free.

travel department. A department in a bank which deals with the issue of travel cheques, obtaining passports and other services related to travel required by customers.

treasurer. A person who is responsible for the safety and deployment of funds. For clubs and other non-profit making organisations the treasurer holds an honorary position, is responsible for the receipt and payment of funds and is accountable to the members for his or her stewardship. In a banking situation a treasurer is responsible for placing funds in various markets and ensuring that borrowing and lending, buying and selling of funds, within his or her own portfolio, are matched.

treasure trove. Any money, plate or bullion of unknown ownership found buried in the ground. It becomes the property of the Crown.

Treasury Bills. In the UK, obligations of the British government representing floating debt used to finance the short-term gaps between government receipts and expenditure. Treasury Bills are documents representing short-term loans to the government which are repayable ninety days after issue. Issue is effected by 'tap' (*q.v.*) or by 'tender' (*q.v.*). The tap issue is intended for the official holdings of certain overseas governments and for government departments at home and abroad. The rate of discount at which the tap issue is put out is not known. The 'tender' issue is offered to London bankers (including foreign banks), discount houses and brokers on a weekly basis each Friday by the Bank of England. The issue is in denominations of £5,000, £10,000, £25,000, £50,000, £100,000, £250,000 and £1,000,000. Treasury Bills are in bearer form. If the issue is oversubscribed allotment is made at the highest tender rate and downwards, until the whole issue has been allotted (but *see* TENDER). Each tender must be for an amount not less than £50,000. The clearing banks have an understanding

with the Bank of England and with the discount houses that they do not bid for Treasury Bills on their own account (but may do so on behalf of clients) but obtain any they need from the discount market. It is the London Discount Market Association which puts in a syndicated bid at the weekly tender, making an offer for each £100 which the Bank of England will repay to them three months later. The offer of Treasury bills is subject to strong seasonal variation. It is fairly low in the peak revenue-gathering months January to March, and increases again in the April of each year in order to finance the public sector borrowing requirement for the new financial year, in so far as the tax received has fallen short of the required figure. Treasury Bills were an important instrument of government monetary policy. They qualified as reserve assets for UK banks and were thus an instrument for controlling bank liquidity. In August 1981, however, a new system was adopted for control of the money supply (*q.v.*) and the market in Treasury Bills and commercial bills was widened to allow interest rates to be influenced there by the buying and selling of eligible bills, rather than by announcements about minimum lending rate. Consequently the concept of reserve assets as a measure of control is no longer appropriate, and in that context Treasury Bills no longer have any influence. As the Bank of England no longer influences interest rates via its dealing with Treasury Bills, it does so with eligible bank bills.

treasury directive. When the Bank of England was nationalised in 1946 by the Bank of England Act, s. 4 of that Act gave powers to the Treasury to give from time to time such directions to the Bank as, after consultation with the Governor of the Bank, they think necessary in the public interest. The bank, in turn, is empowered to make requests of, and issue directives to, the clearing bankers and other financial institutions. In the past these directives have been concerned with the purpose for which loans were being granted (qualitative) or with the volume of lending (quantitative). When Competition and Credit Control was adopted, quantitative directives were supposed to end, but the system of non-interest-bearing special deposits related to increases in the banks' interest-bearing eligible liabilities, introduced in December 1973, was a quantitative control in all but name.

Treaty of Rome (1957). The treaty which established the European Common Market. *See* COMMON MARKET.

trial balance. In double-entry bookkeeping, the extraction of debit and credit balances from a ledger, the totals of which should agree.

triptique. A document for Customs inspection in connection with cars touring abroad.

trover. The acquisition or appropriation of any goods; an action for the recovery of personal property wrongfully converted by another to his or her own use. The term is also applied to an action for conversion.

truck system. A former practice where unscrupulous employers took advantage of their workforce by paying wages in goods or tokens rather than in money. Very often the tokens or vouchers supplied were redeemable only in shops owned by the employer, where inferior goods were sometimes supplied at high prices. This practice was terminated by the Truck Acts 1831-1940, by which Acts the full amount of a workman's wages must actually be paid to him in cash, without any unauthorised deductions, and any clause in a contract of employment which seeks to specify the manner in which any part of the wages is to be expended is illegal. In time this led to an increase in robbery with

violence, as the vehicles taking the weekly wages to the companies were held up by criminals. It also meant that banks had to organise at great expense the transmission up and down the country of huge sums of money to put their branches in funds to meet the weekly wage cheques. This was one reason why it seemed desirable to alter the law so that wages and salaries could legally be paid into employee's bank accounts, and the Payment of Wages Act, 1960 provided that it may be agreed between employer and employee that his or her wage should be paid into his or her bank account, or by cheque, postal or money order.

true and fair view. The auditor's report of a limited company is required to express an opinion on the truth of the final accounts and balance sheet of the business as at a given date. The directors of a company must, in compliance with the Companies Act, 1985 s.227, prepare such statements and accounts for distribution to its members.

true owner. The true owner of a bill of exchange is the person rightfully in possession of it; first the drawer who draws it, then the payee, then the indorsee, if any. When theft or fraud enters into such a series of operations, however, the true owner becomes someone different from the person in possession of it, and may sue either the possessor, or the banker collecting the bill, for conversion. The true owner is the person rightfully entitled at any particular time to the proceeds of the bill.

truncation. A cutting short; in the UK applied to the decision not to send a cheque paid in for collection at Bank A to the paying bank, Bank B, but to rely instead on a sophisticated system based on the record of the credit and cheque at the collecting Bank A where a computer transmits electronically to the paying Bank B all information, including either the number of the cheque or the payee's name, or both, so that the account of the drawer may be debited. This would be an important cost reduction factor, but difficulties arise under the Bills of Exchange Act, 1882 where the paying banker's statutory protection may be lost. The cheque has recently been described as a convenient but archaic instrument, surrounded by legalities. Its constituents of negotiability (related to its status as a bill) are mostly no longer needed, and what seems to be required is to find some way of excluding it from the definition of the bill of exchange and relating it more closely to the concept of debit transfer authority with some built-in protection for handlers against fraudulent signatures. So far, therefore, the use of truncation has been limited, but banks are going to have to change the nature of the cheque (or take a commercial risk on loss of statutory protection) if they want to economise drastically in the movement of paper, which now threatens to 'drown' the clearing system. Some solution will also have to be found to the problem of the customer's common law right to have paid cheques returned if so desired. In the US the word has a simpler meaning: there it refers merely to the cessation of the practice whereby paid checks were formerly sent to the customer with his or her statement of account. Now they are retained at the branch and filed away.

trust. Confidence, reliance, implicit faith; property used for the benefit of another; a combine of business companies in which the shareholders turn over their holdings to a board of trustees; a business combine to restrict competition and establish a monopoly. In regard to land, a trust arises where any person who is the legal owner of property is bound to hold and administer that property on behalf of another. *See also* BREACH OF TRUST; CHARITABLE TRUST; CONSTRUCTIVE TRUST; EXPRESS TRUST; FLEXIBLE TRUST; IMPLIED TRUST; INVESTMENT TRUST; MANAGEMENT TRUST; MINISTERIAL TRUST; OPEN-ENDED; PRECATORY TRUST; PRIVATE TRUST; PROTECTIVE TRUST; RESULTING TRUST; SPLIT-LEVEL TRUST.

trust certificate. *See* TRUST LETTER.

trust corporation. The Public Trustee or a corporation either appointed by the court to be a trustee or entitled by rules made under the Public Trustee Act, 1906 to act as custodian trustee. A trust corporation is an alternative in many statutes to 'not less than two trustees'. Thus money arising from the sale of land formerly subject to a trust for sale must be paid over to at least two trustees, or to a trust corporation. A trustee delegating powers, where entitled to do so, may delegate to any person except to his or her only other co-trustee, unless a trust corporation. The banks' executor and trustee corporations come under his or her head.

trust deed. An instrument commonly used in many states in the US in place of a mortgage, by which the legal title to property is placed in one or more trustees to secure the repayment of money.

trustee. One to whom property is committed for the benefit of others; one of a body of men and women, often elective, managing the affairs of an institution. *See also* CUSTODIAN TRUSTEE; NAKED TRUSTEE; PUBLIC TRUSTEE.

trustee clause. A clause in an equitable mortgage of land by means of which the lending banker can obtain a legal title as a preliminary to the sale of the security, in cases where the customer has failed to repay, and has also failed to keep a promise to sign any documents which the bank may require (where such a clause has also been incorporated in the form of mortgage). The Trustee clause may run as follows: 'I will hold the mortgaged property in trust for the bank as mortgagee and the bank may at any time remove me and appoint another person to be trustee, and the mortgaged property shall vest in the person so appointed'. If the customer will not sign, the bank can appoint someone else who will.

trustee for sale. The person, including a personal representative, holding land on trust for sale.

trustee in bankruptcy. A person, in compliance with the Insolvency Act, 1986, must be a qualified insolvency practitioner and have been appointed either by (a) general meeting of creditors; (b) by the Secretary of State under ss. 295(2), 296(2), or 300(6); or (c) by the court under s. 297. Where two or more persons hold the position of trustee, provision must be made for circumstances when they act together and when one may act for the others. The appointment of the trustee takes effect from the date specified on his or her certificate of appointment. The official receiver can, in certain circumstances, be appointed as the trustee to the estate.

trustee securities. Securities delcared by law to be suitable and authorised for the investment of money held on trust.

trust estate. An estate managed by trustees.

trust for sale. Property established in a trust for the beneficiaries, with the intention that the property shall be sold, whether immediately or eventually. In relation to land, 'trust for sale' means an immediate binding trust for sale, whether or not exercisable at the request or with the consent of any person, and with or without a power of discretion to postpone the sale.

trust instrument. An instrument, whether a will or deed, setting up a trust, naming trustees, specifying the objects of the trust, and indicating the

trust property. With regard to settled land, the trust instrument shall declare the trusts affecting the land, appoint trustees of the settlement, contain any power to appoint new trustees, set out any powers intended to be conveyed by the settlement over and above those conferred by the Settled Land Act, 1925, and bear the appropriate stamp duty. Under this Act, every settlement of a legal estate in land *inter vivos* must be effected by two deeds, a 'vesting deed' and a 'trust instrument'. The first operates to vest the land in the tenant for life, and the second declares the trusts on which the settled land is to be held.

trust letter, trust receipt. A document signed by a customer of a banker where goods have been pledged as security for an advance. To repay the advance it is necessary for the customer to get the goods and sell them, but the documents of title which would enable the customer to get them, are in the possession of the bank. The bank therefore releases the documents of title to the customer against signature on a trust receipt, by the terms of which the customer undertakes to deal with the goods as an agent for the banker for the purpose of getting delivery of the goods and then selling or warehousing them. The customer undertakes to effect any necessary insurance and to hold the proceeds of sale on behalf of the banker until the loan is repaid. The trust letter protects the rights of the banker as pledgee, which would otherwise be lost when the banker gave up the documents of title, and protects the banker in the case of the customer's bankruptcy, by taking the relative goods out of the operation of the reputed ownership clause. The bank's books must show that the documents of title actually came into the hands of the bank before the trust receipt relating to those same goods was signed. This shows that the pledge was created by the deposit of the documents, and was extended by the terms of the trust receipt.

trust officer. An officer of a bank or a subsiduary of a bank who administers the estates, trusts and accounts of customers.

Truth in Lending. The Truth in Lending Act is implemented by Regulation Z of the US Federal Reserve Board. The regulation is meant to ensure that every customer who has need for consumer credit is given full information as to the 'true' cost of that credit. Creditors must respond to any oral enquiry concerning the cost of credit and the annual rate of the total finance charges must be quoted only in terms of the 'annual percentage rate'. In the case of credit in which a security interest will be retained in any real property which is used as the customer's principal residence, the borrower has the right to rescind the transaction for the next three business days following disclosure of the lien over the property. *See* CONSUMER CREDIT ACT, 1974 *under* CONSUMER CREDIT.

turn. A difference between buying and selling prices or the bid and offered prices, as quoted by foreign exchange dealers, or by market makers on the London Stock Exchange. Often called a *spread*.

turn-key contract. Where a large or complex building or industrial plant is being erected, the phrase signifies that when everything is finished and work can begin, the contractor will so inform the client (by analogy, he hands the 'key' over and says 'Turn it and begin'), from which moment production should proceed without trouble. The trial period before 'the key is handed over' will include tests of machinery in action and may include training the client's work force.

turnover. The total sales of a business in a trading period. *See also* RATE OF TURNOVER.

tutor. In Scotland, the guardian of a pupil, having control of the person and the estates of his or her ward (usually the father, or if there is no father, the mother alone or with tutors appointed by the father during his lifetime, or by the court).

two-tier systems. Differentials in price costings to various classes of consumers or users, e.g. first and second class mail, tourist and par exchange rates, investment and par exchange rate, interest rates for loans intended for differing purposes (e.g. farm investment and property speculations), gold prices where transfers of officially held gold between monetary authorities are made at an official price, while other transfers are made at prices determined entirely by supply and demand.

types of life policy. *See* POLICY.

U

uberrimae fidei. Of the utmost good faith. A description of a type of contract where one party has in the nature of things information which only he or she can know, but which is vital to the contract. In such a case there is a duty to supply this information truthfully and to make a full disclosure. If this is not done the contract may be voided at the option of the other party. The prime example of this type of contract is the contract of life assurance, where the previous medical history of the assured, and that of his or her family, is clearly of great importance to the question of whether a contract shall be entertained and, if it is, what the premium shall be.

ullage certificate. One showing the measurement of the liquid or semi-liquid removed from a tanker.

ultimate balance. A phrase used in a form of guarantee to describe the sum owing to the bank on the last day of notice given by the guarantor, or on the day the bank calls upon the guarantor. On that day the overdrawn account of the principal debtor should be ruled off and subsequent credits may be posted to another account, newly opened if necessary, where they will have no effect on the final debt. The ultimate balance is arrived at by combining all accounts.

ultimo. The last day of the commercial or *Bourse* month.

ultra vires. Beyond the (legal) powers of. The phrase is applied in particular to limited companies, whose legal powers are defined in the objects clause of the memorandum of association. Any act not covered in the objects clause is said to be *ultra vires* the company, and any debt thus incurred is irrecoverable at law. In Europe a different view has been taken. There it is enacted that a contract entered into in good faith by a person dealing with a company should not be set on one side because it is *ultra vires* the company. The phrase is also used in connection with the powers, particularly the borrowing powers, of *company directors*. The usual provision in the Articles of Association is that the directors may exercise the company's powers. Often, however, the company imposes a top limit beyond which the directors may not commit the company without the prior sanction of members or a special meeting. Where Table A has been adopted, the directors' powers will be set out in the Table A clause appropriate to the company.

unable to pay debts. For the purposes of the Insolvency Act, 1986, s. 123, a company is deemed unable to pay its debts (*a*) if a creditor to whom the company is indebted in a sum exceeding £750 then due, has served on the company (by leaving it at the company's registered office) a written demand, requiring the company to pay the sum so due, and the company has for 3 weeks thereafter neglected to pay the sum or to secure or compound for it to the reasonable satisfaction of the creditor; or (*b*) if in England and Wales, execution or other process issued on a judgment, decree or order of any court in favour of a creditor of the company is returned unsatisfied (in whole or in part); or (*c*) in Scotland, the *induciae* of a charge for payment on an extract decree, or an extract registered bond, or an extract registered protest, have expired without payment being made; or (*d*) if in Northern Ireland, a certificate of unenforceability has been granted in respect of a judgment against the company; or (*e*) if it is proved to the satisfaction of the court that the company is unable to pay its debts as they fall due. By s. 268 of the Act an individual appears unable to pay debts if (a) the petitioning creditor has served a demand in the prescribed form requiring payment of the debt and at least three weeks have elapsed since the demand was served and the demand has not been complied with; or (b) execution or other process in respect of the debt on a judgment of any court has not been satisfied.

unauthorised signature. See FORGED SIGNATURE.

unbanked. Not having a bank account.

uncalled capital. See SHARE CAPITAL.

unclaimed balance. See DORMANT ACCOUNT.

uncleared effects. The total of cheques collected for a customer, which is credited to his or her account on the day they are paid in. The proceeds remain uncleared for three days, or five if a week-end intervenes. During this time the bank is presenting the cheques to the paying banks through the clearing house. If they are unpaid they should be received back through the post on the morning of the fourth (or sixth) day. (Town clearing cheques are cleared more quickly.) Whether or not the customer is allowed to draw against the proceeds of these cheques before they are cleared is a question of fact in each case, but the banker is not obliged to pay against uncleared effects. If the banker does do so, however, he or she may encourage the customer to think that similar concessions may be made on future occasions, and an implied permission may be construed.

unconnected depositor. A depositor in a deposit-taking institution whose only business connection with the institution is that he or she has invested money in it. The relationship may become important in the event of the liquidation of the deposit-taking institution, in which case the liquidator may look upon an unconnected depositor with more favour than a depositor who has other business interests with the liquidated company, some of which may have gained an interest other than the mere payment of interest on deposit.

undated stock. Gilt-edged security issued by the government on a perpetual basis and having therefore no date by which it will be redeemed.

under bond. Imported goods stored in a Customs bonded warehouse until such time as the duty is paid or they are re-exported.

under-lease. The granting by a lessee of a part of his or her interest in a lease to another person, whether part of the property for any or all of the term, or all the property for part of the term.

under-sheriff. An English sheriff's deputy who performs the execution of writs.

undertaking. A business enterprise; a stipulation, promise or guarantee, given to or by a bank in various connections, e.g. an undertaking to review conditions of service. See DEED OF POSTPONEMENT; SOLICITOR'S UNDERTAKING.

under the counter. See COUNTER.

underwriter. A person who in the seventeenth century wrote his name under the wording on an insurance policy, which provided cover on a limited and personal basis for merchants' undertakings. These were almost wholly concerned with ship voyages and cargoes. In modern times an underwriter may be concerned with marine insurance policies, issued by Lloyd's, where the underwriting members are formed into syndicates which are represented at Lloyd's by underwriting agents, or on the Stock Exchange with the taking up of capital issues, where the underwriters engage to buy and pay for any shares issued by a company which are not taken up by the public; or in connection with a loan in currency to a large company where a group of banks is assembled of which one is that bank arranging the issue (the lead bank) and the others come from the remainder of the group making the loan and 'underwriting' the issue. In this last sense the word means more that the respectability and resources of the named banks guarantee the success of the operation. Where the issue is of government securities and, therefore, of some considerable size a difficulty may arise if the underwriting institution is required to fulfil its obligations – such institutions must not be within the definition of banks. An example would be the 1987 British Petroleum flotation. Sales of government stock must be to the non-bank private sector to prevent a rise in the money supply. The difficulty lies in the fact that there are not many non-bank institutions with the financial resources to meet such a situation. *See also* INSURANCE; ISSUING HOUSE; SELLING GROUP.

undischarged bankrupt. Under the Insolvency Act, 1986, provision has been made for the automatic discharge of a bankrupt providing certain obligations have been carried out. The legal state of a bankrupt person commences from the date the bankruptcy order is made and continues until discharge which, under a summary administration, may be after two years. Under a criminal bankruptcy, authority of the court is necessary only after a period of five years has elapsed. Should a person be bankrupt for a second time within a period of fifteen years, then an application for discharge may be made to the court after a period of five years has elapsed. In all other cases automatic discharge is given after three years has elapsed. During the period a person is an undischarged bankrupt he or she may not 1. maintain a bank account without the knowledge of trustees or the Department of Trade; 2. either alone or jointly with another obtain credit to the value of £50 or more without

disclosing his or her disability; 3. engage in any trade or business under a name different from the one under which he or she was adjudicated bankrupt, without disclosing that name to all with whom business is carried out; 4. act as a company director or take part in the management of any company except by leave of the court. The bankrupt is entitled to a number of *assets* which are as follows: 1. property held by the bankrupt as a trustee; 2. tools, vehicles and other items of business; 3. wearing apparel or furniture, household goods and bedding for himself or herself, spouse or children; 4. personal earnings which are considered necessary for support of himself/herself and family; 5. rights of action for damages for injury to personal credit. Under the Matrimonial Homes Act, 1983, the spouse of a bankrupt acquires a right to the occupation of that house which cannot be overriden without a court order. Where the family home is jointly owned by the bankrupt and the spouse, the court will take various factors into consideration before arriving at its decision.

undisclosed principal. Where an agent contracts on behalf of his or her principal without disclosing the fact that there is a principal, but nevertheless contracting within the powers given by the principal, the third party may think that he or she is contracting with another principal. If the third party wishes to sue on the contract, and has in the meantime discovered the true state of affairs, he or she has the choice of suing either the principal or the agent.

under influence. An influence which excludes free consent to a contract. Where no special relationship exists between the parties, the party seeking to avoid the contract must prove the undue influence as a fact. But where a fiduciary relationship exists between the parties, undue influence will be presumed and must be disproved by the party sued.

unearned income. For the purposes of tax, income derived from investment.

unearned increment. An increase in the value of an asset due to increased demand rather than to any improvement in the asset carried out by the owner; increased bank profits due to an increase in the minimum lending rate.

unemployment. Lack of paid work. In Britain, the estimate of unemployed persons is based on the number drawing unemployment benefit. As this figure includes to varying extents those retired early, those disabled, students on holiday, and the unemployable, some inaccuracy is inevitable. In the USA unemployment is measured by surveys which determine the number of people who are looking for employment.

unencumbered. An asset which is free from any claims, covenants and rights granted to another person or persons.

unexecuted agreement. This means a document embodying the terms of a prospective regulated agreement, or such of them as it is intended to reduce to writing.

unfunded debt. Short-term government debt.

uniform customs and practice for documentary credits. A set of rules drawn up by the International Chamber of Commerce and accepted as a standard of practice and conduct by trading nations. These rules cover (a) the definition of a documentary credit; (b) the responsibilities of the parties; (c) the various forms of credits; (d) the documents that are acceptable; (e) the terms that can be used and their accepted meaning.

uniform rules for collection. Issued by the International Chamber of Commerce in order to lay down the standards, provisions and definitions in dealing with clean collections and documentary collections. It specifies (a) the definitions of words used; (b) the responsibilities of the parties to the collection; (c) the method of presentation; (d) payment and acceptance of the bill and/or documents; (e) matters arising due to non payment and/or non acceptance; (f) expenses and interest.

unilateral. One-sided.

unilateral contract. One which is binding on one of the parties only.

unilateral relief. Where income arises from an overseas country to a taxpayer resident in the UK, unilateral relief is the credit which will be given against UK tax liabilities for any overseas tax suffered on such income. In the majority of cases there is a reciprocal agreement between the countries concerned.

unincorporated association. An association of persons grouped together for a non-commercial purpose, such as a social, sports, or literary and dramatic club. Such groups are managed by officers and committees elected from their own number. The banking account is usually opened in the name of the society and operated by the treasurer and one or more members of the committee. There is no legal entity which can be sued for repayment of any borrowing where accommodation is requested, therefore there must be a firm undertaking by an individual or individuals to be personally responsible for any debt.

unit. A single person, thing or group, regarded as one for the purposes of calculation.

unit assurance. *See* UNIT-LINKED POLICY.

unit bank. A unit bank conducts all of its business at one location and has no branches; such a bank is often independently owned and managed. There are probably around ten thousand unit banks in the US, and they are common even in those states, such as California, New York and Oregon, which permit branch banking. In a number of states, including Colorado, Utah and Texas, unit banking is the only form of banking allowed and helps to explain the very great importance of the correspondent network among domestic banks in the US.

unit costing. A method of costing used where manufacture is continuous and units are identical.

United Association for the Protection of Trade. *See* CREDIT RATING.

United States rule method. A method of calculating the annual percentage rate which is necessary for compliance with Federal Reserve Regulation Z, Truth in Lending. It is defined as follows. At the end of each payment period, the unpaid balance of the amount financed shall be increased by the finance charge accrued during such payment period and shall be decreased by the payment made at the end of such payment period. If the payment is less than the finance charge accrued, the adjustment of the unpaid balance of the amount financed shall be postponed until the end of the next payment period. If at that time the sum of the two payments is still less than the total accrued finance charge for the two payment periods, the adjustment of the unpaid balance of the amount financed shall be postponed for still another payment period and so forth. In all cases the time interval between the date of consummation and the first addition of accrued finance charge to the unpaid balance of the amount financed, or between successive additions of accrued finance charge to the unpaid balance of the amount financed, shall not exceed one year.

unitisation. The conversion of an investment trust company into a unit trust.

unit-linked policy. A type of life assurance policy where a part of the premium is invested on behalf of the assured in a unit trust. There are two basically different types of unit-linked

policy. Where the emphasis is placed on the life assurance aspects, a small part of the premiums only is invested in units, the remainder being kept by the assurance company in order to provide assurance benefits. The income earned by the policy-holder's units is retained by the company and paid out in the form of regular bonuses. Where the emphasis is placed on the investment aspect, the major part of the premiums is invested in units. The company keeps a small proportion to meet the cost of the life assurance cover. The income earned on the units is re-invested in more units on the policy-holder's behalf.

unit of account. A unit used by the EEC as a kind of international currency. Its value has been fixed at 0.88867088 grains of fine gold, which was the value of the gold-pegged dollar in the Bretton Woods system. Because the Common Market is unlikely to have a common currency for some considerable time the unit has persisted, although it is now said to have up to sixteen different definitions. The unit of account is the 'currency' for all EEC transactions such as the calculations for the common agricultural policy, loans to Britain and so on.

unit trust. A unit trust is a method of investment whereby money subscribed by many people is pooled in a fund, the investment and management of which is subject to the legal provisions of a trust deed. The fund is invested in securities on behalf of the subscribers by a management company. The management company and the trustee must be quite independent of each other. They are parties to the trust deed which defines their collective responsibilities towards the subscribers to the trust fund and sets out the rules for the operation of the trust. A fixed trust spreads the risk over a period of ten to twenty years with severe restrictions on the management's ability to vary the investments.

In later companies the trust deed empowered managers to substitute securities at their discretion, although restricting their choice to a given list. Thus the unit trust idea moved nearer to the investment trust idea, where there is free discretion for the management company to buy and sell securities as it thinks best. The advantages claimed for the unit trust idea of investment are a good yield, security, regular income distribution, and, above all, spread of risk. The units are not normally listed on the Stock Exchange, but are bought and sold by the management company, which works out purchase and sale prices ('bid' and 'offer') based on the market value of the underlying securities. The management company undertakes to purchase all sub-units offered to it, thus there is an assured market for those wishing to realise their investment. Before the units are offered for sale to the public a unit trust must be authorised by the Department of Trade. The department will not issue a certificate of authorisation unless it is satisfied that the trust deed is drawn up in a way to satisfy the Department's requirements. The conception of linking unit trust holdings with life assurance was introduced during the 1970s and insurance-linked business now accounts for nearly half the sales, and is expanding rapidly. *See* INVESTMENT TRUST.

unlimited company. A company where there is no limitation to the liability of the shareholders for the debts of the company.

unlimited liability. The liability of an individual to pay the debts of a business entity. Unlimited liability is incurred when a person either acting alone (sole trader) or in partnership is carrying on a business or profession and is, therefore, personally liable for all the debts.

Unlisted Securities Market (USM). The Stock Exchange introduced a new securities market on 10 November 1980, for unlisted securities, formerly called 'unquoted securities'. It was hoped that the market would make a positive contribution in helping small, but growing, companies to obtain the finance they need, and so play an effective part in generating extra growth and more jobs in the economy. The expenses of obtaining a quotation are much less than for the listed securities market, and the requirements less onerous. Normally, however, a good track record over the last three years, with demonstrably competent management, is usually a *sine qua non,* although brand new companies without a track record are sometimes accepted. Trading in the companies' securities is subject to the normal dealing rules, and investors are protected through the Stock Exchange Compensation Fund on the same terms as for investors in listed securities. The new market has proved an undoubted success. It started life with a mere handful of companies, and is still growing. Although there have been some poor performances by individual companies where results have fallen short of issue forecasts or indications, the market as a whole has fared no worse than the main share market.

unpaid seller. One to whom the whole of the price has not been paid or tendered, or one who has taken a bill of exchange or other negotiable instrument as conditional payment, and the condition on which it was received has not been fulfilled by reason of the dishonour of the instrument or otherwise.

unpaid seller's lien. The unpaid seller of goods who is in possesion of them is entitled to retain possession of them until payment or tender of the price if 1. the goods have been sold without any stipulation as to credit; 2. the goods have been sold on credit, but the term of credit has expired; 3. the buyer becomes insolvent.

unquoted shares. Shares of a public limited company which has not applied, or has not yet applied, for a quotation on the Stock Exchange; and shares of a private limited company. *See also* PRIVATE COMPANY SHARES; UNLISTED SECURITIES MARKET.

unregistered company. A company not registered in any part of the UK under the Companies Acts. Any Trustee Savings Bank certified under the Trustee Savings Banks Acts of 1863, 1954 and 1969.

unregistered land. That system of land ownership where title is evidenced by a set of deeds and documents, as opposed to *Registered Land,* where title is evidenced by a registered land certificate.

unsecured creditor. A creditor whose only claim is against the general assets of the debtor; one who has no specific security. Such a creditor may, however, be a preferential creditor if he or she falls into one of the statutory classes.

unwritten law. Any law not originating in Parliament; the common law. *See also* COMMON LAW; EQUITY; GRESHAM'S LAW; INTERNATIONAL LAW.

update. The process whereby the records on a computer file are amended or changed.

upper chamber. In a bicameral legislature, the House that is the more restricted in terms of membership, e.g. the House of Lords, the Senate of the United States of America and some others.

upset price. The lowest fixed price at an auction sale at which, by agreement of the vendor, the property will be in the first instance offered, and at which it will be sold if no better offers are forthcoming.

usance. The usual time allowed for payment of bills of exchange, particularly in connection with foreign trade. Thus bills are drawn upon differing centres at different terms, according to the customer in that trade and between those centres.

usance bill. A bill drawn at a term governed by the custom in the trade, for example three months' date for bills on Paris, thirty days' sight for bills on Bombay, or ninety days' date for bills on Lisbon. *See also* PIG ON PORK; TREASURY BILL; BILL BROKER; BILL FOR COLLECTION; BILL FOR NEGOTIATION.

US Money Supply. Controlling the growth of the Money Supply is the responsibility of the Federal Reserve and is an important tool of US economic policy, probably even more so than in the European economies. There are three basic measures of money supply in the US which are defined as follows: M1 equals currency *plus* demand deposits *plus* travellers' checks *plus* other checkable deposits at banks and thrift institutions (until 1982, M1 was referred to as M1B). M2 equals M1 *plus* overnight repurchase agreements (Repos) and Eurodollars, money-market fund shares, and savings and short-time deposits at commercial banks and thrift institutions. M3 equals M2 *plus* longer-time deposits and term Repos at commercial banks and thrift institutions. *See also* MONEY SUPPLY.

usufruct. The right of using and enjoying the produce, benefit or profits of another's property provided that the property remains undamaged.

usury. Lending at an exorbitant rate of interest. From the time of Henry VIII onwards many statutes were passed to regulate the rate of interest. The Usury Laws were repealed in 1854 to provide a greater flow of capital to industry, and a new Moneylenders Act was passed which enacted that a rate of anything over 48 per cent per annum was *prima facie* unreasonable and would be set aside unless the lender could satisfy the burden of proof that in the circumstances the rate charged was justifiable. The Moneylenders Act was repealed by the Consumer Credit Act, 1974, by which the courts are given wide powers to adjust or re-open transactions where a borrower who considers the terms of an agreement are extortionate has obtained a court ruling. On the continent *'usure'* is also a civil contract

instancing an evident disproportion between the position of the parties, in that the dominant party has exploited the need, weakness or lack of experience of the other.

utter. To put into circulation, e.g. to utter a false cheque, to put forged notes, base coins, etc. into circulation.

V

vacant possession. Property available for purchase with no tenant in possession, and, therefore, able to command a higher price, is said to be 'for sale with vacant possession'.

valid. Well-grounded, cogent, logical; legally sound, sufficient, effective, binding.

validate. To make valid, to ratify.

validity. Legal force; soundness; power to convince.

valuable consideration. 'Some right, interest, profit or benefit accruing to one party, or some forbearance, detriment, loss, or responsibility given, suffered or undertaken by the other.' Any contract not under seal must be supported by valuable consideration if it is to be enforceable at law. Valuable consideration for a bill may be constituted by 1. any consideration sufficient to support a simple contract; 2. an antecedent debt or liability. Such a debt or liability is deemed valuable consideration whether the bill is payable on demand or at a future time.

valuation. The act of valuing or appraising; in banking, the value placed upon security offered by a borrowing customer. In the case of real property, valuation is effected by a branch manager who physically inspects the property or a professional valuer depending on the type of property involved; in the case of Stock Exchange security, valuation is taken from the daily Stock Exchange list of quotations; in the case of unquoted or private company shares, valuation is estimated from the company balance sheet or by application to the secretary of the company; in the case of a life assurance policy, valuation is obtained from the assurance company who, upon request, will state the surrender value of a policy. Valuation of a company's stock for balance sheet purposes will be made by the company directors. Valuation of Stock Exchange securities of a deceased person's estate for probate is effected by taking a figure one-quarter of the difference between the buying and selling prices, and adding it to the buying price (one quarter up).

value. Worth; the desirability of anything; the qualities that are the basis of this; worth estimated in money or other equivalent; the market price, estimation, appreciation of worth; to place a value upon, to estimate the worth of. *See also* PRESUMPTION OF VALUE.

value added tax (VAT). A form of turnover or sales tax; introduced in the UK in 1973. It is a tax on final consumer expenditure in the domestic economy. VAT is collected in instalments: liability to tax arises at each stage in the chain, whenever taxable transactions are carried out by taxable persons, on all goods and services except those which are specifically exempted or zero rated. VAT replaced SET and purchase tax. It falls on imports and exports of goods, in the latter case VAT is not only charged directly but also provides machinery for rebating tax entering indirectly into export costs.

value date. The date on which funds are actually available for use by a bank in foreign currency accounts maintained by the bank abroad. Value dates are important for transactions in foreign exchange or eurocurrency deposits where the dealing date (when rates are determined) may be one or two days ahead of the actual date when monies are officially transferred. Funds which are dealt and transferred during one business day are referred to as *same day funds* or *immediately available funds*.

valued policy. A marine policy having the value of the ship or freight insured stated in the policy.

value in account. A term used in bills of exchange to indicate that there remains a balance in the drawer's favour.

value received. A term used in bills of exchange to indicate that the drawee has received either money or goods from the drawer of the bill. It is not legally necessary in the UK to include these words, for every party whose signature appears on a bill is *prima facie* deemed to have become a party thereto for value, but the law is different on the continent of Europe.

variable costs. Costs which vary directly though not necessarily proportionately, with the volume of production. The most important variable costs are power, wages and raw materials.

variable rate mortgage. A relatively new form of residential property mortgage in the US which allows for periodic adjustments of the mortgage rate in line with other market interest rates and the prevailing cost of money to the lender. Unlike the UK, for example, until the late 1970s almost all residential mortgages provided by banks and Savings and Loan Associations in the US were typically for thirty years at fixed rates of interest. However, the rising cost of consumer deposits and the collapse of many savings and loan associations in the US in the early 1980s effectively ended the supply of fixed rate mortgages except at very high rates. Another important difference with the UK system is the ability to assume an existing mortgage by a subsequent buyer of a residential property, on the same rate and conditions as were originally granted to the seller. This practice was also beginning to disappear in the 1980s and is still the subject of argument between the federal and certain state governments.

variable rate stock. Variable interest stock, etc. The Treasury as an innovation introduced £400 million to the market in May 1977, where the interest on the stock varies in line with the rate on three months' Treasury Bills, and is payable at a rate half a percentage point above Treasury Bill rate, calculated weekly. The stock thus provides much the same characteristic as a money market deposit renewable every seven days. However, the issue has not been successful.

variance. An accounting term for the difference between a budget, or an estimate and actual performance. *See also* FAVOURABLE VARIANCE.

vault. A large well protected room or rooms often situated in the basement of a bank where cash, valuables and securities are kept. The vault is built to withstand any damage by flood, fire and theft.

velocity of circulation. The average number of times each unit of money is used in a given time.

vend. To sell, to dispose of by sale.

vendee. The person to whom anything is sold.

vendor. The seller.

venture capital. Capital provided by a financial institution to a business enterprise, particularly at its start or in its early development. This capital is often considered as risk capital which has a chance of failure, but also has a significant chance of providing a higher than average profit.

vested. Placed in possession of; that which cannot be transferred to another, or taken away.

vested interest. An interest which passes unreservedly to the beneficiary, so that if he or she dies before receiving it, it will, when it is due, pass to his or her estate.

vested remainder. An interest which passes eventually to a remainderman if alive; if dead, it passes to his or her estate.

vesting assent. *See* ASSENT.

vesting deed. *See* TRUST INSTRUMENT.

Veterans Administration (VA). Established by the federal government in 1944, the VA is an independent agency responsible for the administration of benefit programs for veterans including, for example, veterans administration loans which are loans guaranteed by the VA, and are usually for housing or educational purposes.

veterinary certificate. A certificate required to indicate live stock as free from specified diseases.

via. By way of.

viable. Capable of maintaining independent existence. Applied to a company which is insolvent, but whose work staff have formed a co-operative with government support.

viewdata. A term signifying the visual presentation of information held centrally at a number of remote locations, which could include bank branches and already include homes and offices. A visual display unit (*q.v.*) is provided with a key pad which allows users to consult records held centrally. At present the three main systems in use are Ceefax (by the BBC), Oracle (by ITA), and Prestel (*q.v.*) (by British Telecom). Research being undertaken into this method of communication may well link bank branches with head office, so that much of the information now to be found in books of instruction and circulars can be made available on a screen in the branch. Customers who may wish to be included in the system will be able to key for information on details of their accounts, ask for details of the bank's services, and make payments from their own homes.

vindictive damages. *See* EXEMPLARY DAMAGES.

virement. Payment by means of a book entry.

Visa. An official endorsement, as on a passport, to show that the document has been examined and found correct; an international credit card scheme.

vi-sà-vis. Opposite, over against, towards, in relation to.

visible exports. Goods and commodities exported from one country to another, as opposed to services rendered by one country to another. *See also* INVISIBLE EXPORTS.

visual display unit (VDU). A type of Terminal (*see under* ELECTRONIC DATA PROCESSING) which, when linked to a computer, can display information on a television type screen as required. In branch banks, VDUs are much less common than the normal 'back office' branch accounting terminals associated with On-Line (*q.v.*) customer accounting systems. Usually VDUs are restricted to branches with high-volume counter inquiry needs, where the machine room – and therefore the accounting terminals – are remote from the counter. In these circumstances much time and effort is saved if balance enquiries and the like can be satisfied by reference to VDUs sited on the cashier's side of the counter. Much use of VDUs is made in banks by computer systems not directly related to branch operations. Share registration systems, staff records and programming are all examples.

void. Destitute of all legal effect.

void *ab initio.* Of no binding importance at any time from the beginning (of the supposed contract).

voidable. Legal and binding, but capable of being set on one side by one party to the contract at his or her option.

voluntary. Proceeding from choice or free will, unrestrained, spontaneous.

voluntary arrangement. A court may be approached by the debtor who, being in financial difficulties, requests that someone supervise his or her estate. Section 253, Insolvency Act. However, if the debtor is an undischarged bankrupt, then a request to the court may additionally be made by the trustee or official receiver for an arrangement or composition (e.g. 80p in the £) for the benefit of creditors. The aim of the court in granting an interim order is to protect the debtor's estate from any bankruptcy that may be presented. Thus the debtor is given time to submit to the court, via the supervisor *(a)* the terms of the voluntary arrangement; and *(b)* the assets, liabilities and other items of information that may be required. For a *limited company*, it is a proposal under which the directors of a company and its creditors have agreed to a composition in satisfaction of its debts or a scheme of arrangement of its affairs. Section 1.

voluntary conveyance. A conveyance of property against no valuable consideration; a deed of gift. A voluntary settlement by a debtor subsequently becoming bankrupt is an act of bankruptcy. If the settlor becomes bankrupt within two years of the date of the settlement, it is void as against the trustee in bankruptcy; if subsequently but within ten years from the date of the settlement, it is void as against the trustee unless the parties claiming under the settlement can prove that the settlor was, at the time of making the settlement, able to pay all his or her debts without the aid of the property comprised in the settlement. *See also* FRAUDULENT CONVEYANCE.

voluntary liquidation, voluntary winding-up. The winding-up of a company following a resolution to that effect. The winding-up may be because of difficulty in paying its debts, or it may be for quite a different reason, such as an amalgamation with another company, or because the company's existence may have served the purpose for which it was formed. In the UK a company may be wound up voluntarily 1. when the period, if any, fixed for the duration of the company by the articles expires, or the event, if any, occurs, on the occurrence of which the articles provide that

the company is to be dissolved, and the company in general meeting has passed a resolution requiring the company to be wound up voluntarily; 2. if the company resolves by special resolution that the company be wound up voluntarily; 3. if the company resolves by extraordinary resolution to the effect that it cannot by reason of its liabilities continue its business, and that it is advisable to wind up. Where a statutory declaration has been made, the winding-up is a members' voluntary winding-up; otherwise it is a creditors' voluntary winding-up. *See also* WINDING-UP OF A COMPANY.

voluntary patient. *See* MENTAL ILLNESS OF CUSTOMER.

voluntary waste. A wrong of commission amounting to a positive act of injury to the inheritance, such as pulling down or altering houses, digging for gravel, clay etc., converting wood or pasture into arable land or cutting timber. *See also* EQUITABLE WASTE.

voluntary winding-up. *See* VOLUNTARY LIQUIDATION.

vostro **account.** Banks that maintain accounts, in local currency, for banks abroad – literally, 'your account with us.' *See also* NOSTRO ACCOUNT.

voucher. A paper or document that serves to vouch for the correctness of accounts, or to establish facts; a receipt; a cheque; a paying-in slip; office debit or credit.

vowel index. An index whereby items are sorted first under the letter of the alphabet with which the title of the item begins, and then under the vowel which first occurs in the spelling of the title of the item.

voyage charter. A charter party whereby the ship is chartered for a single voyage.

voyage policy. A marine policy for a particular voyage only.

W

wage drift. The term used to describe the tendency for employers who are short of labour to bid against each other, thus forcing wages higher than the normal rates.

wage freeze. An attempt to restrain inflationary wage increases by holding them at their existing levels by force of law, for a period of time. A small increase in actual or percentage terms may be allowed. Such attempts, which have to be made against the interests of the trade unions, give a temporary relief only and are liable, when control is relaxed, to give way to a 'wages explosion'. (Also known as a *Pay Pause.*)

wages and salaries account. Special accounts opened by companies at the request of lending banks where the company is in danger of liquidation. The purpose is to segregate the amount of money lent by banks for the purpose of paying wages, in order to acquire a preferential claim in the event of liquidation. In such a case the bank can take over the claim which the clerk, workman, servant or labourer would have had, had he or she not been paid out of money advanced by the bank for that purpose. The claim is limited to £800 per person in the four months preceding the liquidation. A separate account simplifies claims but is not essential for the establishment of a preferential claim.

waiter. An attendant at the London Stock Exchange, or one in the Room of Lloyd's of London.

waiver. A forgoing, a renunciation. The term is applied to bills of exchange to signify the case where the holder of a bill at or after is maturity absolutely and unconditionally renounces his or her rights against the acceptor.

waiver clause. A clause in a contract which enables an obligation to be avoided in certain circumstances.

walks department. Cheques drawn on non-clearing banks, mostly in London, are presented by clerks or messengers from the clearing banks, which maintain a 'Walks Department' for this purpose.

Wall Street. The place where the New York Stock Exchange is situated. Any changes that take place in this exchange are popularly referred to as changes on Wall Street.

ward. Guardianship, control; a pupil, minor or person under guardianship.

ward in chancery. A minor under the protection of the court.

wardship. The office of a guardian; the state of being under a guardian.

warehousekeeper's certificate, warehousekeeper's receipt. An acknowledgement by a warehousekeeper that certain goods have been received which are stored in the warehouse. Such an instrument is not a document of title, nor is it transferable. The goods are not deliverable against its production. If bank is asked to lend against goods already held in an independent warehouse the customer will be in possession of such a receipt. Because it is only a receipt, its deposit with a bank will not create a pledge in the bank's favour.

warehousekeeper's lien. The right of a warehousekeeper to retain possession of property left for storage until payment for the service is made. Such a lien may be particular or general. *(See* GENERAL LIEN; PARTICULAR LIEN.*)* A warehousekeeper's lien may be of special importance to a banker who has taken a charge over his or her customer's goods in warehouse. It may be necessary for the banker to try to get the warehousekeeper to release a general lien so as to allow the particular goods to be made available for sale. Naturally the particular charge will have to be paid first.

warehousekeeper's receipt. See WAREHOUSEKEEPER'S CERTIFICATE.

warehousekeeper's warrant. A document of title transferable by indorsement, if it is issued by a recognised warehousekeeper having power under an Act of Parliament to issue transferable warrants. Warrants issued by other warehousekeepers not having statutory powers are not transferable, and a pledge can only be obtained by returning the warrant to the warehousekeeper together with a delivery, or transfer order signed by the customer, which will result in the issue of a new warrant in favour of the bank.

warehouse to warehouse clause. A clause in an insurance policy taken out to protect goods in transit, indicating that the goods are covered from the seller's warehouse up to arrival in the buyer's warehouse.

warehousing. The use of money invested in an insurance company or in a unit trust to buy and hold shares which would otherwise have fallen sharply in price; the use of such money to build up a concealed takeover stake; the building up of a significant stake by spreading purchases of shares over a group of people acting in concert and sometimes as nominees for one person. See also CONCERT PARTY.

warrandice. Chiefly in Scots law, a clause in a deed binding the grantor to make good to the grantee any loss arising out of obligations antecedent to the date of the conveyance; the right conveyed; warranty.

warrant. An instrument which justifies an act which otherwise would not be permissible nor legal; a negotiable writing, which authorises a person to receive money, as a warrant in repayment of Saving Bank balances issued in favour of a beneficiary by the Director of Savings and cashable at a Post Office. A crossed warrant may be passed through a bank account, but it is not a negotiable instrument . See also DOCK WARRANT; WAREHOUSEKEEPER'S WARRANT.

warrant for goods. Any document or writing evidencing the title of any person named therein, or his or her assignees, or the holder thereof, to the property in any goods, wares or merchandise lying in any warehouse or dock, or upon any wharf, and signed or certified by or on behalf of the person having the custody of the goods, etc.

warranty. An assurance that a thing is as represented, security; a term for a guarantee that an article is free from defective workmanship; an agreement with reference to goods which are the subject of a contract of sale, but collateral to the main purpose of such contract, the breach of which gives rise to a claim for damages, but not to a right to reject the goods and treat the contract as repudiatd. As regards Scotland, a breach of warranty is deemed to be a failure to perform a material part of the contract.

war risks insurance. Ship insurance is in three parts; marine, war risks, and club or mutual insurance. A marine policy protects the insured against loss by perils of the sea. The policy has standard clauses, but leaves a number of contingencies unprovided for, or only partially provided for. Among these contingencies is that of war risks cover. The risk of war is sometimes covered, subject to an additional premium. Some discrepancies may be expected as to what war risks are. A policy may cover damage as a result of an outbreak of war while the ship is at sea, but may not cover damage by collision with an old mine left over from the last war. Such remote contingencies remain to be covered by club insurance.

waste. Such damage to houses or lands as tends to the permanent and lasting loss of the person entitled to the inheritance.

wasting assets. Assets which become used up in the course of time as they are worked, e.g. mines or quarries. This progressive depreciation should be provided for any an annual allocation out of profits.

waybill. A list of passengers or articles carried by a vehicle. *See also* AIR WAYBILL.

wayleave. A right of way granted by a landowner for some specific purpose in consideration of payment.

ways and means advances. Advances made by the Bank of England to the Treasury to pay for the annual supply services.

weak. A term applied to a currency which has become worth less in terms of another currency.

weekly return. The weekly balance sheet of the Bank of England.

weighting. An adjustment on a banking charge in recognition of an exceptional service given to a customer; the giving of a greater importance to certain items in the construction of an index number.

weight note. In trade, a note issued by an independent third party evidencing gross and net weights of goods.

white goods. Refrigerators; cookers; chest, upright and two-door freezers; automatic washing machines; tumble and spin driers; kitchen equipment generally: so called because most of these articles are finished in white to suggest hygiene in the kitchen.

white knight. The bidder who has received agreement to take over a company to prevent another predator from taking possession of that company.

White Paper. An official statement of government policy on an issue of the day.

whole life policy. A life assurance policy under the terms of which a fixed sum is payable on the death of the life assured, passing into his or her estate for the benefit of the heirs.

wholesale. Sale of goods in bulk to retailers; selling or buying in large quantities; extensive; indiscriminate.

wholesale banking. Borrowing or lending, usually in large sums, by big banks amongst themselves through the medium of the interbank market; dealing with other financial institutions, as opposed to retail banking, which consists of the traditional course of business between a bank and its customers.

wholesale cost. The cost to the retailer of buying goods in bulk from the producer or wholesaler.

will. A declaration made in writing by a person of full age, showing how he or she wishes property to be disposed of after death. The person making the will is called a testator. The testator's signature must be witnessed by two persons, both present at the same time, who attest that in the testator's presence and at his or her request and in the presence of each other they have signed as witnesses.

windbill. An accommodation bill accepted by the drawee to oblige the drawer, without consideration for so doing; a 'kite'.

windfall. An unexpected receipt or gain of funds. Sometimes it can refer to an unexpected loss of funds. A sudden increase in demand for goods; an increase in the valuation of stock. A surprise win in a lottery or receipt of funds as a beneficiary.

winding-up of a company. The winding-up of a company can be either compulsory – by order of the court – or voluntary by order of the creditors, or by order of the shareholders of the company. The court will order the winding-up of a company if: (*a*) the company has passed a special resolution to that effect; (*b*) the company does not commence business within a year of its incorporation; *(c)* the number of members is reduced to below two; *(d)* the court considers it just and equitable that the company should be wound up; *(e)* the company is unable to pay its debts, (i.e. a debt of £750 or more after due demand remains unsettled for a period exceeding three weeks); *(f)* a company registered as a public company has not been issued with its certificate. By s. 84, Insolvency Act, 1986, a company will wind up voluntarily when: *(a)* the period for its duration has been reached, or an event has occurred which was specified in the Articles of Association as an event that would herald the winding-up of the company; *(b)* a special resolution of the company; *(c)* the company by extraordinary resolution cannot continue to trade and wishes to wind up. Where claims of creditors are unlikely to be met, they may appoint a liquidator (under s. 100) to supervise the winding-up.

window. A money market term for the supply of cash by a central bank to the banking system by a method other than the usual one, which can be made available or terminated at any time ('opening' or 'closing' the window). In the UK, for example, the 'discount window' is the supply by the Bank of England of cash to the banking system by buying back Treasury Bills, deliberately issued in excess of funding requirements, from the banks and discount houses. In *Germany* the word refers to the suspension by the Bundesbank of its usual Lombard facility, at which it is normally prepared to lend to commercial banks, and the substitution of a 'special Lombard' or window which can be opened or closed daily at whatever interest rate it chooses. 'Shutting the window' means raising the interest rate. *See also* FEDERAL DISCOUNT WINDOW.

window dressing. Specious manipulation of accounts of a company or one's assets to produce a more favourable impression than the circumstances actually warrant. In the case of banks it has lately (1981) been a question of borrowing from the inter-bank market prior to the mid-monthly return to the Bank of England, so as to show a reserve asset holding of 10 per cent of eligible liabilities *(q.v.)* as then required. The consequent run on funds available on the inter-bank market sent the overnight interest rate up to very high levels indeed, and attracted the attention of the Bank of England, which later gave the banks to understand that the reserve asset figure was to be maintained at all times and not just on return days.

wiping. The passing of a plastic card through a card reader to record the information/card details to process the transaction. It is currently used in ATMs for the withdrawal of cash and is also likely to be used on EFTPOS systems when available.

wire fate. *See* SPECIAL CLEARANCE.

withdrawal. The act of taking money out of an account at a bank, building society or other financial institution. This may be done by taking cash out of an account, or by the transfer of funds to another person.

withholding tax. A tax imposed by some countries on interest and/or dividends remitted abroad to residents outside that country. If a double taxation agreement exists between the UK and a country which levies a withholding tax, it is possible for the tax on the interest payable on a loan from the UK to the country imposing the tax to be largely deductible against the UK lender's tax liability, e.g. a part of the interest receivable by an UK firm is 'withheld' abroad as a 'tax', and part of this sum may be offset against UK tax liabilities. More generally, a tax deduction at source.

Banks lending to non-residents, and able to offset any withholding tax payable abroad in this way, could pass on the benefits of this saving in the form of lower interest rates at the expense of their liability for corporation tax. The Finance Act, 1982 limited the double taxation relief on all banks' overseas loans to a maximum of 15 per cent of the gross interest. *See* DOUBLE TAXATION RELIEF.

without engagement. A term used when quoting prices of articles liable to fluctuate suddenly; the price quoted is the market price at the moment, but the quotation is not binding on the one who gives it.

without prejudice. Without abandoning a claim or right; without impairing any pre-existing right.

without recourse. A party to a bill of exchange may negate his or her liability on the bill by adding these words (or the words *sans recours*) after signature on the bill. Such a clause will make the bill less easily negotiable.

without reserve. At an auction, an indication of complete freedom as to bidding and a guarantee that goods will be sold at whatever price is bid.

with particular average (WPA). A clause in an insurance policy taken out to protect goods in transit, which covers the loss of single parcels or partial quantities. *See* FREE OF PARTICULAR AVERAGE.

'with profits' policy. A life assurance policy, whether endowment or whole life, which provides that in return for an increased premium the policy holder will share in the profits made by the assurance company. Bonuses are declared usually at three-year revaluations. (Also known as a *Participating Policy).*

with recourse. Where a bank discounts or negotiates a bill of exchange for a customer it does so 'with recourse', that is, if the bill is dishonoured at maturity the bank is able to claim the amount of the bill from the customer.

witness. Attestation of a fact, testimony, evidence; a thing that serves as evidence or proof; one who gives evidence in a law court or for judicial purposes, especially on oath; one who affixes his or her name to a document to testify to the genuineness of the signature; to sign as a witness, to attest, to state in evidence.

words of severance. When land is conveyed or devised to two or more persons in such a way as to show that they are to take distinct and separate shares, they take as tenants in common and not as joint tenants. Words of severance show that the beneficiaries are to take 'equally', in equal shares, etc.

work. Labour, toil, an undertaking, a task, employment as a means of livelihood, occupation, deed, performance, achievement.

working capital. What is left out of the paid-up capital after all the fixed and fictitious assets have been paid for. It should be sufficient to provide all the circulating capital and to cover the day-to-day running of the business. Another way of arriving at the working capital is to subtract the current liabilities from the floating assets.

working day. For the purposes of the Consumer Credit Act, 1974, any day other than 1. Saturday or Sunday; 2. Christmas Day or Good Friday; 3. a bank holiday within the meaning given by s. 1 of the Banking and Financial Dealings Act, 1971.

working expenses. All expenses necessarily incurred in the running of a business (e.g. rent, rates, wages, etc.) and entered in the profit and loss account.

working party. A group appointed in an advisory capacity, to study methods of obtaining maximum efficiency in industry; a group appointed to undertake an enquiry and report their findings.

work-in-progress. The state of raw materials, to which some work has been done in the manufacturing stage, but which have not yet been completed to the point of being regarded as stock.

works oncost. Production overheads: the cost of the expenses of production.

work study. *See* TIME AND MOTION STUDY.

World Bank. *See* INTERNATIONAL BANK FOR RECONSTRUCTION AND DEVELOPMENT.

writ. A written command or precept issued by a court, e.g. one requiring the attendance of a defendant in a civil or criminal action; an order to a person commanding him or her to do or refrain from doing some particular act therein specified.

writ of attachment. *See* ATTACHMENT.

writ of *capias*. A judicial order directing an officer of the court to arrest and imprison a judgment debtor. It is very rarely used nowadays.

writ of delivery. A writ which authorises the return of property other than land or money by the defendant to the plaintiff. It orders the sheriff to cause the return of the property or to levy against the defendant its judgment value.

writ of *distringas*. *See* DISTRINGAS.

writ of *elegit*. A writ by means of which a judgment creditor sought to obtain satisfaction of his or her debt out of the proceeds of land belonging to the debtor. Its place is now taken by a charging order.

writ of execution. A writ directed to the sheriff, commanding him to take certain compulsory proceedings for the purpose of carrying into effect a judgment of the court.

writ of *fieri facias*. *See also* FIERI FACIAS.

writ of possession. An order directing a sheriff to put a person in possession. The appropriate writ for the recovery of possession of land. It issues against the person in possession and if this person is the tenant he or she is bound to give notice of the writ to the landlord, who may then apply for leave to enter an appearance and defend the action.

writ of sequestration. A process available against a person who is in contempt for disobedience of the court. Following the issue of the writ, those on whose behalf it was issued (the sequestrators) may demand information and transfer of property from the third party. Once a bank knows that a writ has been issued against a customer, the account should be conducted normally until demand for payment is made. The bank must act upon this, and must also give up any articles held on safe custody if demanded by the sequestrators. The fullest information must be given on request – the bank's normal duty of secrecy is over-ridden – and this would even extend to giving information of any attempts by the customer to avoid sequestration, such as transferring sums out of the account.

writ of summons. The formal document by which a High Court action is commenced.

write down. To reduce the book value of an asset.

write off. To remove entirely from the asset book values, as with a bad debt which it has proved impossible to recover; to cancel; to dismiss from consideration.

write-up. The making of an entry or entries to an account, or the completion of entries onto a statement prior to despatch to a customer.

written law. *See* STATUTE LAW.

wrongful trading. Wrongful trading must be distinguished from fraudulent trading as it is subject to civil proceedings. Wrongful trading is applied to a person if: *(a)* the company has gone into insolvent liquidation; *(b)* at some time before the commencement of the winding-up of the company, that person knew or ought to have concluded that there was no reasonable prospect that the company would avoid going into insolvent liquidation; and (c) that person was a director of the company at that time (Section 214, Insolvency Act). The court will not make a declaration if it is satisfied that the person took every step to minimise the potential loss. For the purposes of this Act, the facts which the person ought to have known, or ascertained and the conclusions that ought to have been reached, or the steps which ought to have been taken will be considered in the light of the general knowledge, skill and experience that may be expected of a person carrying out the functions of a director of that company, and the actual general knowledge, skill and experience the director in question has. This section also includes a shadow director. *See* SHADOW DIRECTOR. Should a director be found guilty of wrongful trading, he or she may be ordered to contribute to the assets of the company by way of compensation, the sum being as the court thinks fit.

wrongly delivered. Cheques which by mitake are presented for payment to branches different from the ones on which they are drawn. Such a cheque must be presented to the correct paying bank branch on the same day, if possible; if not, it must be sent direct to the paying branch by post, and an adjustment made in the Clearing House total. Articles wrongly delivered at the Clearing House itself are to be returned to the presenting bank at the Clearing House on the following day. The bank will then present it again, correctly. The totals of all articles wrongly delivered in this way are agreed by representatives of all the clearing banks meeting at the Clearing House on the next day; adjustments between the banks in respect of them are then made.

wrong post. The placing of a debit or a credit amount to a wrong account.

Y

yearling bond. *See* LOCAL AUTHORITY BONDS.

yearly tenancy. A tenancy from year to year. Notice to terminate, whether from landlord or tenant, must be given to expire just before an anniversary of the commencing date of the tenancy. The notice must be in unmistakable terms. Not less than half a year's notice is necessary, unless a different agreement has been made by the parties.

years' purchase. A method of expressing the value of real property as equal to the rent over a certain number of years.

yield. That which is produced to give a return or profit; a measure of the income which an investor gets from holding a repayable loan stock expressed as a percentage; the percentage return on capital invested. *See also* DIVIDEND YIELD; EARNINGS YIELD; FLAT (OR RUNNING) YIELD; GROSSED-UP REDEMPTION YIELD; GROSS YIELD; NET YIELD; REDEMPTION YIELD.

yield gap. In the past the dividend yield on equities has been higher than the gross yield on long-dated Government stocks because the income from equities has been considered less assured. The difference between them – the yield graph – has usually been taken to be the difference between the return on $2\frac{1}{2}$ per cent Consols (which have no redemption date) and the yield on the shares making up the Financial Times Ordinary Share Index. *See also* REVERSE YIELD GAP.

yours. A phrase used by foreign exchange dealers to indicate that they are sellers of the currency in question.

Z

zero budgeting. Considering a period of expenditure, and how it is to be financed, on the basis that no present commitments exist, and no balance is carried forward (used in public expenditure in the USA where it is known as the 'sunset law'), as opposed to the conception, as is done with the annual review of public expenditure in this country, of examination of new programmes and the increases in current programmes. Zero budgeting aims at starting each annual spending budget from nought, and looking at the whole range of public spending. It puts a definite term to each spending programme with the onus on the spenders to justify continuation.

zero coupon bonds. This concept has been developed in the US as a result of the sustained high cost of raising money. Zero coupon bonds are bonds issued by a company in need of capital on the terms that the company will pay no interest at all during the life of the bonds (anything from five to fifteen years), during which time the investor earns no income. When the bond matures, however, the company will pay out to the holder anything up to six times the amount originally borrowed, so that the investor secures a proportionate capital gain. Borrowers claim tax relief each year on the implied interest liability which they have incurred but not actually paid out. The idea has spread internationally and zero coupon bonds are finding a market wherever tax rates on income are higher than tax on capital gains. They do not appeal as yet in the UK because the Inland Revenue takes the view that the gain should be treated as income whether the bonds are sold or held to maturity.

zero rating. For the purposes of Value Added Tax (VAT), there will be no tax charged on listed goods and services.

zone sterling. *See* SCHEDULED TERRITORIES.

zoning. Enclosing, dividing into belts or sub-divisions; the divisions of a country into regional areas, e.g. for the distribution of commodities, for the control of bank branches by a regional manager, etc.; the allocation of use for a particular area under Town and Country Planning regulations.

zoological certificate. Also known as a health certificate. A certificate required to indicate hides and certain foodstuffs as free from contamination.